TEXT TOOL FLYOUT

17   18

17. **Text** is used to enter text strings in the figure.

18. **Symbols** switches to a symbols set to use in the figure.

OUTLINE PEN TOOL FLYOUT

19   20   21   22

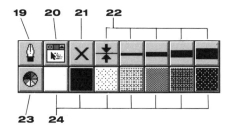

23   24

19. **Custom Outline** is used to specify the characteristics used by the Outline Pen Tool.

20. The **Pen Roll-Up Window** is a quick-access dialog for changing the attributes of the Outline Pen Tool.

21. **None** indicates that there should be no outlines in the current object.

22. **Line Widths** is used to set the line width of an outline in ¼ (hairline), 2, 8, 16, or 24 points.

23. **Custom Outline Color** displays the Outline dialog box for controlling the color attributes of the outline.

24. **Black, White, Gray** sets the outline to black, white, or one of five shades of gray.

FILL TOOL FLYOUT

25   26   27   28   29   30   31

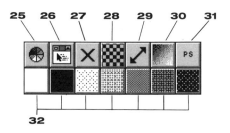

32

25. **Uniform Fill Color** displays the Uniform Fill dialog box for defining the color attributes for filling the currently selected object.

26. **Fill Roll-Up Window** is a quick-access dialog for setting color attributes for the Fill Tool.

27. **None** indicates that no fill should be used in the currently selected object.

28. **Two-Color Pattern** displays the Two-Color Pattern dialog box for creating or editing patterns with only two colors.

29. **Full-Color Pattern** displays the Full-Color Pattern dialog box for creating or editing patterns with more than two colors.

30. **Fountain Fill** displays the Full-Color Pattern dialog box for creating or editing fountain fills.

31. **PostScript Textures** is used to define PostScript-specific textures, which can be used only if the figure is printed on a PostScript printer.

32. **Black, White, Gray** sets the fill to black, white, or one of five shades of gray.

Computer users are not all alike.
Neither are SYBEX books.

We know our customers have a variety of needs. They've told us so. And because we've listened, we've developed several distinct types of books to meet the needs of each of our customers. What are you looking for in computer help?

If you're looking for the basics, try the **ABC's** series. You'll find short, unintimidating tutorials and helpful illustrations. For a more visual approach, select **Teach Yourself,** featuring screen-by-screen illustrations of how to use your latest software purchase.

Running Start books are really two books in one—a tutorial to get you off to a fast start and a reference to answer your questions when you're ready to tackle advanced tasks.

Mastering and **Understanding** titles offer you a step-by-step introduction, plus an in-depth examination of intermediate-level features, to use as you progress.

Our **Up & Running** series is designed for computer-literate consumers who want a no-nonsense overview of new programs. Just 20 basic lessons, and you're on your way.

We also publish two types of reference books. Our **Instant References** provide quick access to each of a program's commands and functions. SYBEX **Encyclopedias** and **Desktop References** provide a *comprehensive reference* and explanation of all of the commands, features, and functions of the subject software.

Our **Programming** books are specifically written for a technically sophisticated audience and provide a no-nonsense value-added approach to each topic covered, with plenty of tips, tricks, and time-saving hints.

Sometimes a subject requires a special treatment that our standard series don't provide. So you'll find we have titles like **Advanced Techniques, Handbooks, Tips & Tricks,** and others that are specifically tailored to satisfy a unique need.

We carefully select our authors for their in-depth understanding of the software they're writing about, as well as their ability to write clearly and communicate effectively. Each manuscript is thoroughly reviewed by our technical staff to ensure its complete accuracy. Our production department makes sure it's easy to use. All of this adds up to the highest quality books available, consistently appearing on best-seller charts worldwide.

You'll find SYBEX publishes a variety of books on every popular software package. Looking for computer help? Help Yourself to SYBEX.

For a brochure of our best-selling publications:

SYBEX Inc. 2021 Challenger Drive, Alameda, CA 94501
Tel: (510) 523-8233/(800) 227-2346 Telex: 336311
Fax: (510) 523-2373

SYBEX®

SYBEX is committed to using natural resources wisely to preserve and improve our environment. As a leader in the computer book publishing industry, we are aware that over 40% of America's solid waste is paper. This is why we have been printing the text of books like this one on recycled paper since 1982.

This year our use of recycled paper will result in the saving of more than 15,300 trees. We will lower air pollution effluents by 54,000 pounds, save 6,300,000 gallons of water, and reduce landfill by 2,700 cubic yards.

In choosing a SYBEX book you are not only making a choice for the best in skills and information, you are also choosing to enhance the quality of life for all of us.

MASTERING CORELDRAW 3

MASTERING CORELDRAW 3

Steve Rimmer

SYBEX ®

San Francisco • Paris • Düsseldorf • Soest

Acquisitions Editor: David Clark
Developmental Editor: Kenyon Brown
Editor: Savitha Varadan
Technical Editors: Rebecca Lyles, Sheldon M. Dunn, Richard Anderson
Additional Technical Writing: Sheldon M. Dunn
Word Processors: Chris Meredith, Ann Dunn
Book Designer: Amparo del Rio
Chapter Art and Layout: Lisa Jaffe
Screen Graphics: Cuong Le, Aldo Bermudez, John Corrigan
Typesetters: Len Gilbert, Thomas Goudie
Production Assistant: Lisa Haden
Indexer: Matthew Spence
Cover Designer: Ingalls + Associates
Cover Photographer: Mark Johann

Cover CorelDRAW graphics by Bill Frymire and Chris Purcell reproduced courtesy of Corel Systems.

Screen reproductions produced with Collage Plus.
Collage Plus is a trademark of Inner Media Inc.

SYBEX is a registered trademark of SYBEX Inc.

TRADEMARKS: SYBEX has attempted throughout this book to distinguish proprietary trademarks from descriptive terms by following the capitalization style used by the manufacturer.

SYBEX is not affiliated with any manufacturer.

Library of Congress Card Number: 92-82602

ISBN: 0-7821-1154-8

Manufactured in the United States of America

10 9 8 7 6 5 4 3 2 1

For Sarah Jane Newman, who discovered through experimentation that publishers really do bleed non-repro blue.

Acknowledgments

My thanks to Vivi Nichol, tech support provider extraordinaire at Corel Systems, who answered all sorts of obscure questions; and to Fiona Rochester, who sent the betas along so quickly the disks hardly stopped spinning.

The six superb illustrations used in the color insert of this book are the work of some of the winners in the CorelDRAW World Design Contest—Bill Frymire created *Rex,* which also appears on the cover of the book; Matti Kaarala created *Laiva*; Ceri Lines created *Lifetime*; Peter McCormick created *Venice*; Lea Tjeng Kian created *Magic*; and Guy Terrier created *Techdraw.* These drawings are reprinted here courtesy of Corel Systems.

Some of the details of the history of Helvetica in Chapter 14 came from Ed Cleary's excellent column on typography appearing in the May/June issue of *Studio* magazine.

Some of the ideas on logo design set forth in Chapter 12 are indebted to Tony Leighton's feature entitled "The Art and Science of Corporate Iconography" in the Summer 1986 issue of *Applied Arts Quarterly.*

Jones the Dog improved several of the figures and diagrams in this book by consuming the early—and altogether inferior—drafts.

Delia Brown of SYBEX created the cow logo in Chapter 12.

And finally, acknowledgment should be given to John, King of England, Lord of Ireland, Duke of Normandy and Aquitaine, and Count of Anjou, whose great charter provided the civilization upon which this book is founded and, perhaps more importantly, several tens of kilobytes of wholly copyright-free text to use in some of the examples.

CONTENTS AT A GLANCE

TABLE OF
CONTENTS

Chapter 3
MANIPULATING TYPE AND TEXT

Chapter 4

USING FILLS

Chapter 5
IMPORTING AND EXPORTING

Chapter 6

PRINTING

Chapter 7

SPECIAL EFFECTS AND TECHNIQUES

Chapter 8

USING COLOR

Chapter 9

USING CORELPHOTO-PAINT

Chapter 14
DESIGNING WITH TYPE

APPENDICES

Introduction

The thickness of this book probably disguises one of the fundamental qualities of CorelDRAW—namely, that it is easy to use. The actual mechanical processes of drawing lines, placing text, and printing files, among other things, can be mastered in a few hours. With an intuitive user interface, a well-designed structure that is very forgiving of mistakes, and a toolbox that does pretty much what you'd think it should do, the package lets new users produce gratifying results without even cracking the manual.

In a sense, CorelDRAW is a digital analog to pencils, rulers, rule tape, Rapidographs, French curves, Zip-a-Tone, and the other paraphernalia of drawing and design. With the possible exception of Rapidographs, which seem to require lengthy dissertations on their cleaning and maintenance, none of the afore-mentioned design tools requires detailed instructions for use. The mechanics of operating a pencil, for example, are pretty self-evident.

Similarly, once you get over the initial problems of installing and becoming familiar with CorelDRAW, you'll find that you can start using it with relatively little instruction.

So you're probably wondering why this book is so thick. Getting truly satisfying results from your design tools is more than a matter of learning how to hold them, move them, or otherwise make them go. Getting worthwhile results from your design software, likewise, is not just a matter of learning what all the menus and dialog boxes do. Aside from the task of mastering all the parts of CorelDRAW, you should also learn the benefits of using a personal computer in working with the elements of drawing, design, typography, and other aspects of producing commercial art.

This book will teach you what a computer and various output machines can and cannot do when it comes to creating art. It tells you what to expect and what to avoid, and it offers advice in the area of design aesthetics. Now, this is a rather tricky undertaking. This book certainly won't make you into the equivalent of a designer with four years of study at an art college. It also won't teach you how to draw if you can't do so now. That is because original design—whether you're designing individual graphics, publication pages, or soup-can labels— is an art, and art is something you can't learn from a book. Creating professional-looking, well-executed, and functional designs, on the other hand, is often a mechanical process, especially when you have access to libraries of previously drawn, professionally produced clip art (provided with CorelDRAW). There are guidelines you can apply to a design project, traditions to be aware of, rules to follow, and so on. *Mastering CorelDRAW 3* will help you to learn them.

HARDWARE AND SOFTWARE REQUIREMENTS

If you have not yet acquired CorelDRAW and are looking at this book just to get an idea of whether you ought to, you should know that CorelDRAW is definitely the "mother" of all illustration programs! The program takes up almost 30 megabytes of hard disk space. For practical purposes, you'll need at least an 80386 machine and 4 megabytes of RAM, plus a mouse. You should also be aware that CorelDRAW was created to operate on a PC under the Microsoft Windows operating environment. CorelDRAW 3, the version covered in this book, requires at least version 3.0 of Windows, preferably version 3.1. If you are not yet acquainted with Windows, you'll find a succinct guide to running Windows in the second half of Appendix A of this book. Appendix A also discusses memory and hardware and software considerations for using CorelDRAW and Windows to their optimum capacities. If you already have an idea of what you want to get out of CorelDRAW, Appendix A can guide you to the best way to accomplish it.

In discussions of integrating CorelDRAW with desktop publishing programs, the other programs and hardware referred to in this book are those currently available or in common use. For example, discussions of Ventura Publisher refer to version 3 of the GEM implementation and to version 4.01 of Ventura Publisher for Windows; discussions of PageMaker refer to PageMaker 4.

WHAT'S NEW IN CORELDRAW 3

CorelDRAW 3 offers some significant improvements over version 2. The program's intuitive interface has been enhanced with features such as movable roll-up menus, streamlined menus and dialog boxes, and direct visual manipulation of options. CorelDRAW's text-handling capabilities now permit on-screen text entry and support Adobe Type Manager and TrueType fonts. You'll also find context-sensitive help; the ability to *layer* your drawings for better control over objects; "snap-to" options, such as the Snap-to-Grid feature; a powerful Spelling Checker and Thesaurus; and an editable preview mode. In addition, the new version of CorelDRAW comes with a bonus CD for users with a CD-ROM drive; this CD offers extensive libraries of clip art and fonts, and you can even set up the program to run from the CD.

The CorelDRAW package now includes five modules in addition to the CorelDRAW program:

◆ The new *CorelCHART* module gives you the ability to create a wide variety of chart types, including bar, pie, three-dimensional, and pictograph. In addition, you have a variety of options for inputting your data, and context-sensitive popup menus to make your charting tasks easier.

◆ With the new *CorelPHOTO-PAINT* module, you can create bit-mapped objects and retouch scanned bitmapped photos. This module also supports the new Kodak Photo CDs, giving you the opportunity to edit photos in the CD format.

◆ *CorelSHOW,* another new product, uses Windows OLE technology to allow you to assemble your own electronic slide shows.

◆ The CorelDRAW package still provides the *CorelMOSAIC* (visual file management) and *CorelTRACE* (tracing utility) modules as well.

HOW THIS BOOK IS ORGANIZED

This book has been written to help you make CorelDRAW into a workable extension of your fingers, to help you use it to accomplish your designs. It has also been written to help you apply CorelDRAW to the reality of commercial art—getting things out under time pressures, having your graphics integrate with your page designs (or somebody else's), coming up with quick art to fill holes in a publication, and so on.

Part 1 presents the various features and applications of CorelDRAW. Chapters 1–4 contain a series of hands-on exercises that you might want to work through to get a feel for the package and become familiar with how things are done. Chapters 5–8 get into the special considerations that crop up when you're trying to reconcile what your project ought to look like with the images your monitor and printer are capable of showing you. Chapters 9–11 teach you the use of the package's three new modules. The three chapters in Part 2 offer a general guide to design, in the context of real-world design issues. The four appendices offer a beginner's guide to Windows, customization techniques, and instruction on using CorelMOSAIC and CorelTRACE.

The book also contains an eight-page, four-color insert that illustrates some of CorelDRAW's drawing and output capabilities. Of special interest are reproductions of six of the prize-winning drawings from the Corel-DRAW World Design Contest.

These drawings plus several utilities can also be found on the two companion disks to this book. Turn to the inside back cover of the book to see a full description of the disks and instructions for their use.

PART 1

Features

and

Applications

he chapters in this section of *Mastering CorelDRAW 3* will walk you through the operation of the package and through the ancillary applications that accompany the CorelDRAW bundle. It will demonstrate the creation of different drawings to help you master the mechanics of using CorelDRAW. When you've completed it, you'll have the skills necessary to put CorelDRAW to work on your ideas.

FAST TRACK

CHAPTER

1

Learning

the

Basics

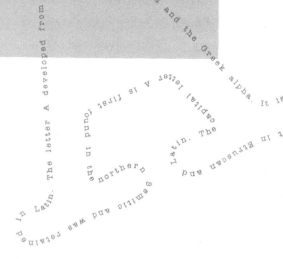

Before you can work with CorelDRAW, it's important to understand what it's intended to do. This entails understanding how the program approaches the fundamental elements of illustration and design, and it entails becoming familiar with the tools CorelDRAW provides.

This chapter will deal with these things. How much of this chapter pertains to you will be a function of how much you already know about computers and drawing packages, and about Microsoft Windows, the environment in which CorelDRAW lives. The Windows package, necessary to running CorelDRAW, is very easy to work with, and is actually rather intuitive once you have been introduced to its essentials. If you are unfamiliar with Windows, the essentials are presented in Appendix A of this book.

As you read this chapter, bear in mind that its purpose is not to serve as a tutorial on using CorelDRAW. The remaining chapters will do that. This chapter should serve to introduce the concepts, tools, and vocabulary of CorelDRAW so that you can learn the techniques presented throughout the rest of the book more quickly.

It's probably worth noting that since its introduction, CorelDRAW has grown from being simply a drawing package into a large suite of applications. This includes separate applications which will perform the following tasks:

In order to keep up with its competition, Corel Systems has added a lot of extra features to the CorelDRAW package. Some of these may be features you'll never need. It's quite permissible to skip portions of this book—and to ignore portions of the CorelDRAW package—which don't pertain to you. The software has been designed to let you do this with a minimum of confusion.

◆ Drawing

◆ Bitmapped graphic manipulation

◆ Charting

◆ Presentation

There are all sorts of ancillary functions available as well.

The important thing to keep in mind about all this, however, is that the basic CorelDRAW drawing application—the program which appears when you double click on the CorelDRAW icon—has really gotten simpler and more intuitive to use. Successive generations of users have helped wear down its rough edges and less understandable aspects. The current CorelDRAW package is exceedingly easy to get into, despite its enormous power.

The other functions provided with the CorelDRAW package are handled as separate applications. Consequently, you can avoid having to deal with them when you first start using CorelDRAW by simply not clicking them into existence for a while. They'll be dealt with in detail later in this book, after you've mastered CorelDRAW itself.

THE BASIS OF DRAWING

The simplicity of CorelDRAW is deceptive. Its toolbox includes fewer tools than most paint programs, and far fewer than comparable drawing packages. This is something you'll probably come to appreciate, because CorelDRAW is a great deal less complex to use as a result of its small set of basic functions.

Before you can understand how to use CorelDRAW, you should understand what it does when it draws pictures. Most computer users are at least somewhat familiar with paint programs, such as PC Paintbrush, and it often takes a bit of effort not to treat CorelDRAW as a peculiar sort of paint program. In fact, it's a very different application entirely, and therein lies its power. CorelDRAW works with *objects*. It's essential to understand the concept of objects in order to really make the program perform for you.

OBJECTS AND PATHS

The fundamental entity from which pictures are created under CorelDRAW is called a *path*. For the moment, a path may be thought of as a line—the distinction will become clear shortly. If you draw a line across the work space of CorelDRAW, that line represents a path. A circle also represents a path. The letter A represents a path as well, or, perhaps more correctly, a number of paths joined together. Figure 1.1 illustrates some paths.

A path has rather intangible properties. For example, paths themselves are not actually visible. If you were to create a multitude of paths in the drawing area of CorelDRAW and print the page, the sheet that would come out of your printer would be blank.

You can make a path into a visible part of your drawing in two ways. If you want to have it appear as a line, you can *stroke* the path. This is analogous to tracing the path with a pen, although under CorelDRAW you can accomplish this simply by picking a path and telling CorelDraw that it's

FIGURE 1.1:

An example of paths under CorelDRAW

to be stroked. If the path represents a closed figure, such as a rectangle or the letter A, you can *fill* the path, to make it solid.

In order to be filled, a path must be *closed*; that is, it must enclose an area with no leaks to the outside. If you have used a paint program and experimented with its fill functions, the idea of an enclosed area without leaks will be familiar. Under Windows Paint, for example, attempting to fill an area which is not closed results in the paint spilling out over the rest of your drawing. Under CorelDRAW, you would simply not be able to fill such an object.

When you consider one or more paths as constituting a complete entity, such as the letter A or a logical element of a drawing, that entity is called an *object*. Admittedly, this term is a bit vague, because you can make any number of paths into an object to suit yourself. However, it is in dealing with collections of paths as objects that CorelDRAW really gets up and dances.

MANAGING OBJECTS

If you load a drawing file into CorelDRAW, the picture will appear on your screen one object at a time, irrespective of the locations of the objects on the page. This is because of the way CorelDRAW handles drawings. A drawing is really a list of objects arranged in a file.

If you draw a rectangle under CorelDRAW, the software adds the definition of that rectangle to its current object list. All this means is that somewhere in memory there's a note to CorelDRAW which says, in effect, "Place a one-by-two-inch rectangle three inches from the top of the page and two inches in from the left, stroke it with a thin line, and fill it with 50 percent gray."

If you modify an object—for example, by moving it—CorelDRAW looks through its object list until it finds the object you're working with and changes the appropriate parts of its notes to itself. When it needs to redraw the screen, it does so according to the revised object list.

The two drawings in Figure 1.2 both started life as the same object. The only difference is that the second one appears to be flattened, or perhaps it's a reflection in a fun-house mirror. The fact that CorelDRAW can make this transformation illustrates a very important aspect of objects: Objects are scalable.

Look closely at Figure 1.2. While the second drawing has been flattened, its lines are still smooth and there's no evidence of the sort of crunching that happens to paint-program images when you try something like this.

A simple modification of an object

 Paths are said to be "device independent," which really means that they can be drawn on anything. This means that if a drawing made up of paths is drawn on your monitor, it will be handled as well as monitors can display things—which isn't usually very impressive. If it's drawn on a laser printer's page, it will be drawn with considerably tighter resolution. An important rule in using CorelDRAW is that what you see is what you get, but only to the extent that your monitor can show it to you. A lot more will be said about this in the later chapters of this book.

The original picture in Figure 1.2 might be thought of as a number of points with paths between them, and to make the discussion easy, let's allow that all the points are positioned relative to the bottom of the page. In order to turn the original object into the squashed object, we might divide the vertical dimensions of all the points by a constant number—let's say three—and then have CorelDRAW erase the screen and redraw the object.

In fact, I didn't have to do any of these calculations. All I really did was grab the top of the object and drag it down until it looked suitably squashed. CorelDRAW did all the figuring internally.

Because CorelDRAW's objects are just paths between points, you can change the overall size of an object relative to the rest of a drawing, or you can adjust its dimensions anamorphically; that is, you can stretch it in one dimension more than in the other. As soon as you're finished adjusting an object, CorelDRAW will redraw it with clean lines.

It's not always easy to keep an eye on how paths are used in a complex drawing, but knowing how CorelDRAW deals with its paths is fundamental in understanding the package and, thus, in making it do what you want it to do. The example in Figure 1.3 serves to illustrate an important concept about the structure of objects. It is an elementary use of fitting text to paths.

This drawing began as the letter A in the American Typewriter typeface—what CorelDRAW calls Memorandum—one of the many fonts which Corel supplies with its basic drawing package. Figure 1.4 illustrates

The outside paths of the letter A traced with still more letters

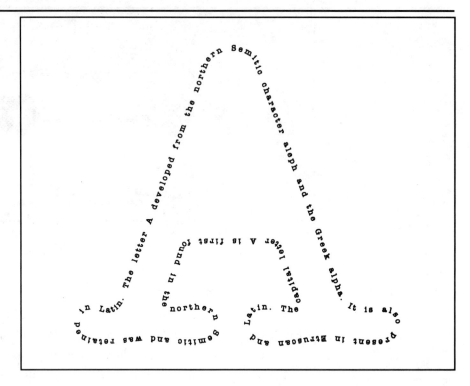

the CorelDRAW screen with just the exterior paths of the letter A, expanded a bit. Each line between boxes represents one of the paths which make up the shape of this character in this font. For the purposes of this exercise, I have chosen not to work with the enclosed interior paths of the character, that is, the interior triangle in the upper half of the A.

When you place text on a CorelDRAW page, it's drawn by default in relation to an invisible baseline. If you pick up the text and drag it to another location on the page, what you're really doing is moving the baseline. The text, having been tied to the baseline, moves as well.

The baseline of the text is itself a path of sorts, although it isn't treated as such under CorelDRAW. It needn't be a straight path, nor must it be a single path. For the text in Figure 1.3 the baseline is, in fact, the series of paths constituting the exterior of a letter A.

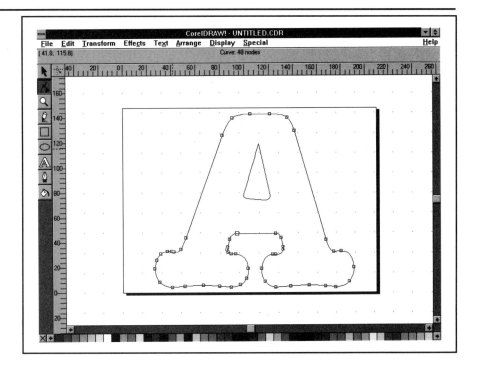

While the math involved in drawing Figure 1.3 was pretty involved for CorelDRAW itself, the principle is easy to understand if you have a good grip on the concept of paths. Drawing text in this way need be no more involved than typing it along a straight baseline and issuing a few simple commands.

OBJECT CHARACTERISTICS

When you add an object to a drawing, CorelDRAW records all of its pertinent characteristics in its internal object list. Every one of these characteristics is available for later modification. Different sorts of objects have different characteristics.

◆ *An open path,* that is, a path that doesn't form an enclosed area, will have characteristics such as stroke thickness and color, location on the page, and the style of its ends. This latter characteristic allows you to specify lines which end in arrows, have rounded ends, and so on.

◆ *A closed path,* that is, a path that encloses an area with no leaks to the outside, will have some of the characteristics of an open path. It will also have a fill characteristic. You can fill a closed path with a particular color or pattern. Note that a closed path can have both a stroke characteristic and a fill characteristic. For example, consider a red rectangle with a black line around it.

◆ *Text* will have the characteristics just discussed, plus a whole list of others. The characteristics of a text object determine its typeface, the size of the text, whether it's normal, bold, or italicized, the spacing between lines, and so on. CorelDRAW has an unusually rich assortment of text effects.

Under CorelDRAW you can alter any of the characteristics of an object, even after it has been added to a drawing. These alterations are called *transformations.* These usually involve changing the objects' dimensions, but the category includes a number of specialized functions, such as editing previously drawn text.

Bézier Curves

Figure 1.5 is notable in that much of it cannot be drawn with simple lines, circles, or rectangles. This picture represents a special sort of drawing element, that of Bézier complex curves.

Complex curved lines are difficult to manage in a drawing program. The math involved internally in having the computer draw such a curve is

FIGURE 1.5:

A drawing involving complex curves

not too fierce, but there remains the problem of devising a way for users of the drawing application to manipulate the curves. CorelDRAW has settled on a handle system, which works reasonably intuitively.

We'll discuss the manipulation of curved lines in much greater detail later in this book, but for now you should be aware that CorelDRAW allows for them. They have the same stroke characteristics as lines, but they have the additional characteristic of being able to be bent and shaped over complex outlines.

In addition to drawing single curves, you can also create several sorts of objects which are made up of multiple curved segments. The segments are combined automatically by CorelDRAW when you draw with the freehand mode of the pencil tool and when you trace *bitmapped images,* which will be discussed in detail later in this book.

Fill Patterns

Another subject which will be treated in greater detail later in this book is that of fill patterns. CorelDRAW features a rather generous assortment of ways to fill areas in a drawing, from simple gray shades through fountains and special PostScript fills.

The simplest of fill patterns are shades of gray. Gray shades are expressed in terms of the amount of black in an area versus the amount of white. A 50 percent gray area has equal amounts of black and white. A 10 percent gray fill is almost white, while a 90 percent gray fill is nearly black. Gray shades actually pose some interesting problems for CorelDRAW, as they don't behave as predictably as you might like. For example, in cartoons you might encounter a gray car with a perfectly uniform gray surface, but in real life the contours of the metal and variations of light on the surface of the car will make the surface appear to be a gradation of various gray tones. This is one of those things our eyes do not bother telling us about unless we consciously make ourselves aware of it.

Figure 1.6 illustrates a solid object which has simply been filled with gray on the left and has had something rather more involved done to it on the right. The pop can on the left doesn't look very three-dimensional. In fact, it doesn't even look very interesting. The pop can on the right exhibits a reasonable simulation of natural light and depth. If you consider a real pop can for a moment, you'll notice that it has similar variations in light intensity, as the sides of a cylinder don't reflect as much light to your eyes.

The right pop can was filled with a variable gray fill called a *fountain*. In its simplest sense, a fountain is just a fill pattern in which the gray starts at some arbitrary percentage and changes smoothly to some other percentage over a defined distance. Fountains can also be *radial*. A radial fountain starts with a particular gray percentage in the center of an area and changes outward in all directions. Figure 1.7 illustrates a radial fountain being used to make a circle look spherical.

If you have a means of outputting your CorelDRAW pictures to a color printer or other color device, areas of solid gray can be augmented with areas of solid color. CorelDRAW has some first-class color facilities.

Additionally, CorelDRAW provides you with a large assortment of PostScript fills. However, to use these fills you must output your drawing to a PostScript printer. A great deal more needs to be said about this before it will be completely clear, but suffice it to say here that in using PostScript fills you can fill an area with all sorts of predefined patterns, including bricks, broken glass, and so on. Figure 1.8 illustrates some PostScript fills.

FIGURE 1.7:

A radial fountain

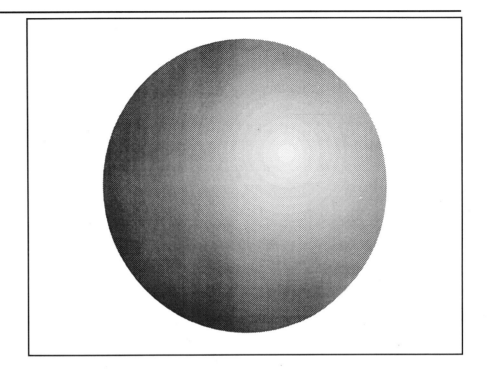

FIGURE 1.8:

A few of the many PostScript pattern fills provided with CorelDRAW

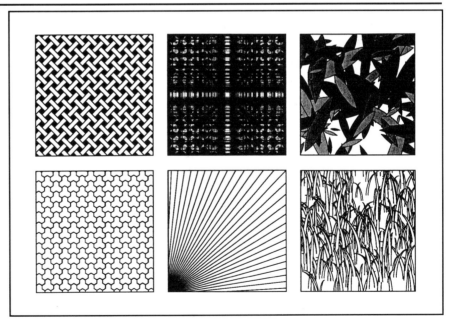

CorelDRAW has a number of ways you can create your own patterns and textures. You can, for example, create tiles out of objects or out of fragments of bitmaps—scanned photographs, for example—and have CorelDRAW fill things with these. There are numerous tools in CorelDRAW for creating these sorts of custom fill patterns, and Windows' Paintbrush program for working with bitmaps might also prove useful.

Figure 1.9 illustrates an object filled with tiles created from a bitmap.

Transformations

CorelDRAW allows you to transform an object or group of objects. A transformation changes the relationship of the points which define the paths of an object. In the example shown in Figure 1.2, flattening the Volkswagen was

FIGURE 1.9:
An object filled with bitmap tiles

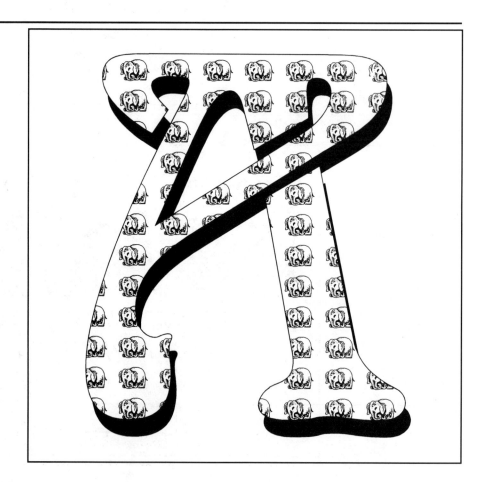

really a simple transformation. In fact, this procedure is considered to be so basic to the capabilities of CorelDRAW that it's hardly regarded as a transformation. More involved transformations require special menu commands.

Most of the more interesting transformations involve having CorelDRAW do some internal mathematics with the points of an object. For example, you can flip an object horizontally and vertically. You can skew it. Objects can be bent, stretched, and otherwise distorted. All transformations can be repeated multiple times. Figure 1.10 illustrates the results of some transformations on a simple object.

Part of the usefulness of transformations is in the way they mimic how the real world transforms our perception of what things look like. If you close this book for a moment and hold it before you, you'll see a rectangle. If the angle is just right that's all you'll see—the sides of the book will be invisible. You can do this with all six faces of the book. All of them are rectangular.

When you hold the book so that it becomes visible as a three-dimensional solid, however, none of the faces of the book will appear as rectangles. They all will have been apparently transformed by the effect of moving some of the corners farther from your eye than others. In order to create a drawing of a three-dimensional book using a two-dimensional sheet

FIGURE 1.10:

Some of the object transformations CorelDRAW can do

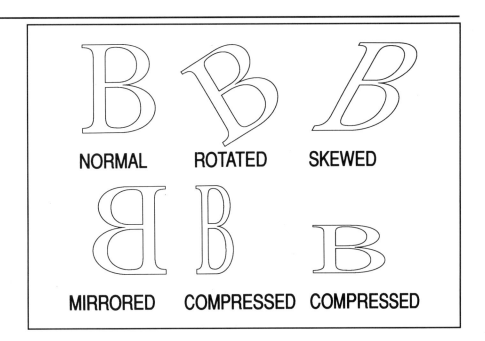

NORMAL   ROTATED   SKEWED

MIRRORED   COMPRESSED   COMPRESSED

of laser printer paper, CorelDRAW must be able to effect the digital equivalent of these optical transformations. Once you get used to working with the transformations which CorelDRAW offers you, you'll find that they can do just that.

Text As Objects

If you use CorelDRAW to place the word *Aardvark* on a page, the letter A will automatically be combined with seven other letters to form a single object. If you wanted to move the word down the page, you could simply grab the whole thing as one entity with your mouse and drag it.

Words and letters are a special case of objects under CorelDRAW, inasmuch as they're text. Because you ordinarily would not want to get at the individual paths of text characters, text comes with its paths precombined.

The distinction between CorelDRAW and a true desktop publishing package is essentially in how it deals with text internally. This, in turn, defines how quickly it can deal with pages that include lots of text. Confronted with several paragraphs of text, CorelDRAW will slow down pretty noticeably. If you're designing pages which are rich with text, you might find that having CorelDRAW handle the graphics and using a desktop publishing package like Ventura or Page-Maker to assemble the complete pages is a bit more workable.

There are times, however, when you *will* want to deal with text as individual paths. Figure 1.3, the letter A with text wrapped around it, is an example of one of those times. Obviously, then, CorelDRAW doesn't prohibit you from dealing with text at the path level, as, for example, Adobe Illustrator does. It does, however, insulate you from doing so when you don't really want to.

As will be discussed later in this book, CorelDRAW is frequently employed to provide graphics for sophisticated text-handling programs such as desktop publishing and high-end word processing software. However, CorelDRAW can manipulate text in ways which are very much like what a desktop publishing package can do. While its text-handling facilities are limited as compared to, say, Ventura Publisher, CorelDRAW now allows you to create complex pages involving significant amounts of text.

It would be unrealistic to attempt to create a magazine or an annual report using CorelDRAW as a substitute for a desktop publishing package. However, you will probably find that for things like advertisements and fliers—single, stand-alone pages—CorelDRAW is much more flexible than a true desktop publishing program. With its ability to work with large amounts of text, the current version of CorelDRAW represents a significant advancement over previous versions.

Figure 1.11 illustrates a page created using nothing but CorelDRAW.

In addition to merely letting you enter text, CorelDRAW includes an online spell checker, thesaurus, and hyphenation dictionary to help you enter

FIGURE 1.11:

Using CorelDraw to do complex page layout

EXISTENTIAL STONECARVING

A FREQUENTLY IGNORED AREA OF CITY PLANNING, STONE CUT IN FOUR DIMENSIONS CAN ADD A NEW SENSE OF PLACE AND PURPOSE TO OTHERWISE DRAB BUILDINGS. THIS ARTICLE DISCUSSES THE TRENDS IN IMPOSSIBLE MASONRY

Know that in the presence of God, and for the health of Our soul, and the souls of Our ancestors and heirs to the honor of God, and the exaltation of the Holy Church, and amendments of Our kingdom, by the advice of Our reverend fathers Stephen, Archbishop of Canterbury, Primate of all England and Cardinal of the Holy Roman Church; Henry Archbishop of Dublin; William of London, Peter of Winchester, Jocelin of Bath and Glostonbury, Hugh of Lincoln, Walter of Worcester, William of Coventry, and Benedict of Rochester, Master Pandulf, the

AUGUSTUS P. ROBES

really superb text. Few things are worse than outputting a glorious poster-size four-color graphic with almost three hundred hours of work behind it only to find that the largest word on the page has been spelled incorrectly.

WHERE OBJECTS COME FROM

The main reason for buying CorelDRAW, for most of its potential users, is to turn out finished graphics. CorelDRAW is a very flexible package, one that can be adapted to a surprising variety of requirements. It can be used to conjure up illustrations at a moment's notice, and it can be used to render stunning, visually exciting graphics with depth and meaning and all the other stuff they talk about at art college. Regrettably, the difference is more often a factor of the proximity of one's deadlines than of the skill in one's fingers.

Drawing

The most obvious way in which objects can get into a drawing is for someone to draw them. This seems so simple as to scarcely need mentioning, but in fact there are several other ways to get an illustration together under CorelDRAW. The basic drawing tools which are part of the package, however, are among its more shining features.

We've discussed CorelDRAW's basic approach to drawing, and in a large sense this defines its drawing tools. However, there are all sorts of enhancements to these. Some of the more important ones include:

◆ *Cut, Copy, Paste,* and *Duplicate.* Objects can be cut or copied to the Clipboard, then pasted back into a drawing or replicated to produce extra copies of them.

◆ *Snap To Grid.* This allows you to force the end points of a path onto the nearest point of a grid. You can define the grid size. Grid snap can be toggled on and off.

◆ *Object alignment.* You can select several objects and have them aligned or centered, vertically, horizontally, or on a line of your choosing.

◆ *Node editing.* Having created a path, you can modify it—by moving its points, splitting and joining paths, modifying curves, transforming straight lines into curves, and so on.

As you will probably appreciate by now, just about anything can be drawn in CorelDRAW. To be sure, drawing still takes time and a reasonable degree of talent. Fortunately, there are other ways to get a drawing together under CorelDRAW besides actually drawing it.

Tracing

Among the more sophisticated abilities of CorelDRAW are its *autotrace* feature and its still more powerful CorelTRACE application, which is a separate program included in the CorelDRAW package. Under certain circumstances you can import a bitmapped drawing—such as a picture from a paint program or a file from a scanner—into CorelDRAW and have CorelDRAW or CorelTRACE automatically generate a line drawing based on the bitmapped picture. In theory, if all goes well, you will wind up with a very nice-looking piece of line art and without having done much work. In practice, even under ideal circumstances, traced bitmapped drawings can require a bit of hand polishing after the fact.

The tracing facilities of CorelDRAW and CorelTRACE enable Corel-DRAW to accept pictures which have been scanned, downloaded from public domain file collections, or cooked up in PC Paintbrush and other art packages that can produce bitmaps. This means that images ranging from Victorian etchings to architectural blueprints can be imported into Corel-DRAW and given all the characteristics of object-oriented art.

This sounds almost too good to be true—and, of course, it is. CorelDRAW does include tracing facilities for bitmapped images and they do work. In fact, they work better than any other bitmapped-image tracing function currently available for the PC. However, this does not mean that just any bitmapped image can be traced.

When you hand CorelDRAW or CorelTRACE an image to be traced, they attempt to create paths around the dark areas of the picture, ultimately to form objects. This will work well if the picture has well-defined dark areas and dreadfully if it does not. Images which are complex will confuse the tracing algorithms into outlining the wrong areas.

Figure 1.12 illustrates a bitmapped image and the CorelDRAW drawing which resulted from using the autotrace function. This is the sort of bitmapped image which traces rather well, and the results shown are quite acceptable. There is no illustration here of a bitmapped image which didn't trace well, because the results of a bad tracing are rarely even recognizable. There's very little middle ground between a good autotrace and a bad one. The results are either breathtaking or they're spaghetti.

If you're in a hurry to generate some art, tracing a scanned image of some existing paper art may be a very good way indeed to get some quick

FIGURE 1.12:

A bitmapped image (left) and CorelDRAW's autotraced copy of it (right)

Traced and partially filled bitmap

results. The result of autotracing is a drawing formed of objects, and it's fairly easy to modify such a drawing once CorelDRAW or CorelTRACE has finished tracing it. You can easily customize pictures obtained from another source.

As you play with them, you will get a better feel for how the CorelDRAW tracing facilities work and what sort of original makes for good tracings, but a few basic guidelines will help save you from frustration.

- Pictures which have clean, defined edges tend to trace well.

- There is a limit to the number of points in a path that a drawing can have and still print properly. Even though the limit is pretty high, the CorelDRAW tracing tools are capable of causing problems by exceeding it.

- While it's possible to trace gray-scale or color pictures, such images offer a lot more potential for confusing the tracing software.

The techniques for successful tracing will be discussed later in this book.

Using Clip Art

It's amazing that small local newspapers, low-budget magazines, and junk-mail fliers often have professional-looking graphics. Sometimes they can't even get the type straight on their pages, but they'll have drawings that look like a professional artist has labored over them for hours.

In fact, a professional artist often does labor over these graphics, although usually not at the offices of the publishing company which produced the documents in question. Recognizing that pages often look a lot nicer with professional graphics on them—even if they're not quite appropriate graphics—many small publishers use clip art. Originally, clip art was just what its name implies: professionally drawn pictures you could cut out and stick to a page, quickly and with little fuss.

Clip art has made the transition to computers. When you're in a hurry to generate a graphic, it's often a lot easier to pull one ready-made out of a file than to create your own from scratch. An additional attraction of this electronic form of clip art is CorelDRAW's ability to modify it somewhat to suit your needs.

There is a growing industry of electronic clip art supply companies, some of which are the same companies that supply paper clip art to conventional publishers. The quality of electronic clip art has seen dramatic improvements over the past couple of years.

CorelDRAW comes with a clip art sampler which offers something on the order of ten megabytes of clip art files all ready to try out. Most of these are examples drawn from the libraries of a number of the better clip art suppliers—they've been bundled with CorelDRAW with the blessings of their owners in the hope that if you like the samples you'll buy more of the clip art. Figure 1.13 illustrates some of the many sample images which come with CorelDRAW.

One of the features which makes CorelDRAW so powerful is its ability to import files from many other applications; it's able to use clip art files from practically everywhere. A great deal more about importing and exporting foreign file formats will appear in Chapter 5.

The clip art which comes with CorelDRAW is compressed into clip art libraries. Another separate CorelDRAW accessory included with the package makes working with these libraries quick and painless. The CorelMOSAIC program allows you to peek inside a library to see what's available in it and extract any clip art you want to work with.

Compressing the clip art into libraries means that the ten megabytes of clip art included with CorelDRAW only occupies about five megabytes of disk space. Figure 1.14 illustrates CorelMOSAIC at work. All you have to do to get at an image in this library is click on it and select a menu function.

FIGURE 1.13:

A tiny fraction of the sample clip art library provided with CorelDRAW

Clip Art and the Law If you haven't been involved in publishing, you might be wondering about the legal status of clip art. The drawings in some of the example files which come with CorelDRAW look pretty sophisticated, and it might seem a bit questionable to find them thrown in for free. In fact, there are some restrictions on the use of clip art.

As a rule, you can use clip art for any purpose except to repackage it as clip art. For example, you can do anything you like with the electronic clip art samples which came with CorelDRAW so long as the eventual audience

CorelMOSAIC looking at part of one of the CorelDRAW clip art libraries

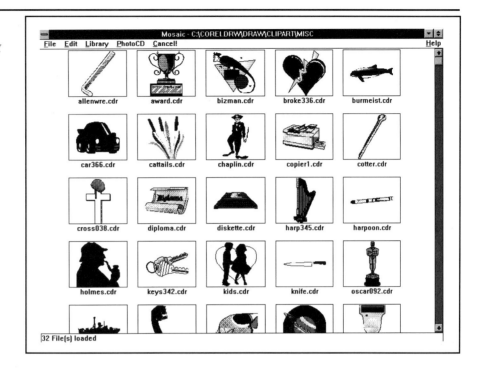

of your pictures or publications can't use the art in an electronic form. Thus, you can print the pictures out and use them as part of a newsletter or magazine, but you can't give the original files—or any variations on them—to someone else as files.

There is a large body of paper clip art in the public domain. The existing copyright laws only date back to the turn of the century, and all sorts of commercial art predates them. There are books of Victorian line art, French advertising art, Baroque engravings, and so on which are all available with no strings attached. The most notable of these are the voluminous Dover books and the now rather rare Hart picture archives. If you have a scanner and a bit of time, many of these images make first-rate input for Corel-DRAW's tracing facilities.

With the exception of those pictures which predate the copyright laws or whose copyright has expired, pretty well all pictures are owned by someone. These include magazine advertisements and graphics, apparently anonymous image and drawing files found on computer bulletin boards and in public-domain software collections, and so on. Images are just as much the property of the artists who created them as books are the property of their authors. The difference is that usually images don't carry written copyright notices.

CorelDRAW's powerful tracing and manipulation tools make it fairly easy to abuse the copyrights of artists. Before you use a graphic as clip art, make sure you know you have the right to do so. Aside from being a conscientious and decent thing to do, it can keep you out of court.

THE PROGRAM AND ITS TOOLS

The rest of this chapter will be devoted to a quick look at the basic features and tools of CorelDRAW itself. Once again, this is not intended to make you a master of the package in this short space, but rather to give you an overview of the geography of the program and the capabilities of the various tools and menus. A great deal more will be said throughout the rest of the book about the particular uses of these things.

Figure 1.15 illustrates CorelDRAW at rest. It has had a drawing loaded into it. This is the default magnification for a drawing which has just been

FIGURE 1.15:

CorelDRAW just after booting up and loading a drawing

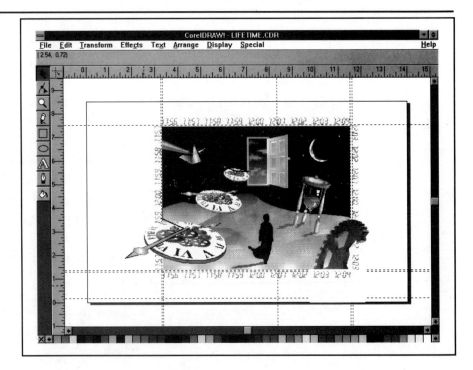

CorelDRAW will work with whatever size drawing page you tell it to use, up to 30 inches on a side. You can draw full size posters if you like. If you don't have a laser printer that will work with paper 30 inches across—they are a bit uncommon— you can have CorelDRAW "tile" your picture onto multiple smaller sheets. This will be discussed in detail later in this book.

If you have installed a Windows driver that provides you with a large screen—1024 by 768 pixels or better— you might find that the toolbox icons seem a bit small compared to the rest of the CorelDRAW workspace. If you find them hard to work with in this condition, you can tell CorelDRAW to provide you with double-size icons. This is discussed in detail in Appendix B.

loaded—you can zoom in and out, as we'll see. The rectangle with a drop shadow behind it in the center of the screen is the drawing page. You can draw anywhere on the screen you like, but only the drawing page will get printed.

It's very often useful to work in the space outside of the drawing page. For instance, you can work on something too big to fit on a page and then reduce it later, or work on a complex object all by itself and pull it into your drawing when it's done. The layout of CorelDRAW's screen is very flexible in this respect.

You can also work with complex drawings in multiple layers, something else that will be discussed in detail later in this book.

If you've used a Windows-based application before, you will recognize the Windows-related elements of the CorelDRAW screen: the menu bar, the minimize and maximize controls, and so on. You will also recognize the scroll bars along the right and bottom edges of the CorelDRAW window, although their functions in this application might not be immediately apparent. In fact, the scroll bars serve to move around the drawing space when you've zoomed in to get a more detailed view of a section of your drawing. Should you be unfamiliar with these terms, Appendix A contains an introduction to Windows.

Figure 1.16 illustrates the most important part of the CorelDRAW application window—the toolbox. If you've used a paint program, such as Windows Paintbrush, the idea of a drawing toolbox may be familiar to you. The functions of the individual tools probably will not. Understanding CorelDRAW is partially a matter of understanding its tools and what affects their use.

To select a particular tool, all you need do is move your mouse cursor to the appropriate tool icon and click on it. The newly selected tool will change color to remind you which tool you're currently using. In some cases, your cursor will also change.

Although you might not recognize them, the tool names used here do actually correspond to the documentation accompanying CorelDRAW. It's just that usually whenever the name of a tool is required in the text of the CorelDRAW manual, its authors have used a character which resembles the tool icon shown on the screen. While it is a clever application of technology, this approach makes it a bit hard to write or speak about CorelDRAW. One finds oneself speaking of the up-arrow tool, for example, or the wavy-line-with-box-in-the-middle tool, which is clumsy at best. For the purposes of

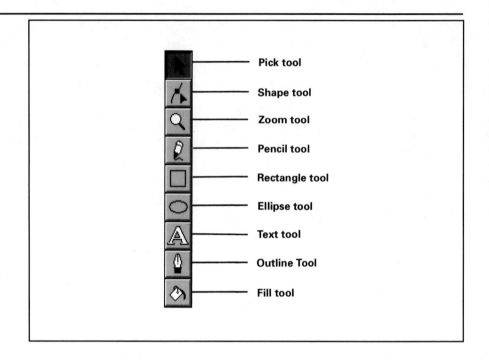

this book, I'll use the names CorelDRAW has assigned but rarely uses. If you don't like these, of course, you can make up your own.

Over the next few pages, we'll have a quick look at each of the CorelDRAW tools. Don't worry if their functions still seem a bit vague at the end of this section—you'll be getting hands-on experience with them and more detailed explanations throughout the course of the book.

FLYOUT MENUS AND ROLL-UPS

Some of the tools in CorelDRAW support *flyout menus,* and some of these in turn support *roll-ups.* Both of these are phenomena more or less unique to CorelDRAW. They help to simplify the use of CorelDRAW's pretty extensive selection of tools without forcing you to dig through multiple nested menus every time you want to do something different.

A flyout menu is a horizontal row of icons which will spring from several of the toolbox icons. If you select one of the bottom two tools, a large flyout menu will appear. This will allow you to select specific characteristics for these two functions. The meaning of each of these icons will be discussed in detail over the next few chapters.

Some flyout menus are much smaller, and serve to change the modes in which tools operate. For example, if you select the text tool—the icon with the letter A in it—and hold down your mouse button for a moment, a short flyout menu will appear, offering you a second A icon and one with a star in it. The A icon represents the normal text mode of CorelDRAW, allowing you to enter words into your drawings. The star icon represents the symbol mode, which will allow you to place non-alphabetic symbol characters in your drawings one at a time.

Selecting one of the icons from this sort of flyout menu will put CorelDRAW in the mode you choose until you next call for the menu and choose a different mode. For example, if you select the text tool's star icon, the text tool will become the symbol tool, and the actions you would normally use to place text in a drawing would subsequently serve to place symbols.

Roll-up menus allow you to customize your workspace in CorelDRAW for whatever you're busy with at the moment. Because it would be impractical to have, for example, all the line controls and fill controls available on your screen all the time—at least, it would be if you anticipated having any room left over to draw things—roll-up menus allow you to open small windows which contain just those controls you need. The windows can be moved around your screen, such that you can push them out of the way when you don't need them. They can be closed when they're no longer needed.

The most confusing thing about roll-up menus, if you come upon them unprepared, is that they duplicate controls which are available in other sorts of dialog boxes and menus under CorelDRAW. For example, you can set the fill characteristics of an object under CorelDRAW either through the fill tool flyout menu or with the fill characteristic roll-up menu. Both offer the same facilities, and the one you choose will be determined by which approach you find the most convenient.

 The use of flyout menus in CorelDRAW allows you to have access to its quite respectable library of tools without being knee deep in icons. While finding the right tool and flyout menu may seem a bit daunting at first, you'll find that as you become familiar with the way CorelDRAW works, their locations will prove to have been logically chosen.

THE PICK TOOL

The first tool in the toolbox is used to pick, or select, objects or groups of objects in your drawing. You might think it should be called the arrow tool, but there are enough arrows in CorelDRAW that to call just one of them the arrow tool would be to invite confusion.

After using the pick tool to select objects, you can select menu commands to duplicate them, delete them, cut and paste them, and drag them to a new location on the screen. You can also transform them—for example, you can rotate them, stretch them, mirror them, and so on.

Objects can be selected either explicitly or by area:

♦   *Selecting explicitly.* If you select the pick tool and then place the point of the arrow cursor over some path of an object on your screen and click, that object will be selected. When an object is selected, little black squares, or *selection marks,* appear at the corners and midpoints of the otherwise invisible sides of the smallest rectangle with which CorelDRAW can enclose the object. Figure 1.17 shows these selection marks around the back wheel of a bicycle.

♦   *Selecting by area.* If you select the pick tool and place the cursor at the upper left of a collection of objects, then hold the mouse

FIGURE 1.17:

A selected object

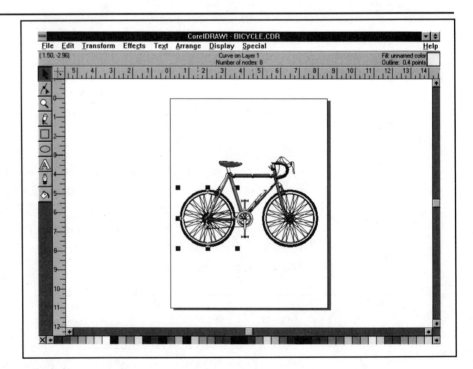

button down and drag the cursor toward the lower-right corner of the window on your screen, you will create a broken-line rectangle, with your cursor serving as the lower-right corner. All the objects within the rectangular area so defined will be selected when you release the mouse button. Figure 1.18 shows the area that will be selected when the mouse button is released.

When you select objects by area, the entire object must reside in the rectangular area defined by the mouse. The broken-line box indicating the area being selected is called a *marquee* in CorelDRAW. The Macintosh has a more descriptive term for it: a *rubber band box*. The former is the term I will use in the course of this book.

Having selected one or more objects, you can unselect them by simply clicking in an open space somewhere in the drawing area. The selection marks will vanish.

The pick tool is one of the most frequently used of the CorelDRAW tools, especially when you're modifying a drawing.

FIGURE 1.18:

An area being selected

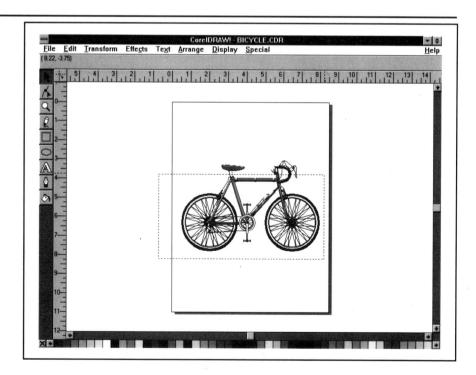

THE SHAPE TOOL

The function of the shape tool will be a lot less obvious than that of the pick tool, and this section will not help all that much. In order to understand it, you will have to know a lot more about how CorelDRAW manages its objects.

All paths in a CorelDRAW picture are defined as being *nodes* with something connecting them. For now, a node can be thought of as a point along a path which has something to do with its position relative to the rest of the drawing. A straight line has two nodes, one at each end. A complex curve may have many nodes. If you move the nodes, you'll move the path or change its shape.

The shape tool allows you to do all sorts of things with nodes. For example, you can change the location of individual nodes, rather than whole objects. Figure 1.19 illustrates the effects of simply moving a few nodes around.

FIGURE 1.19:

Using the shape tool

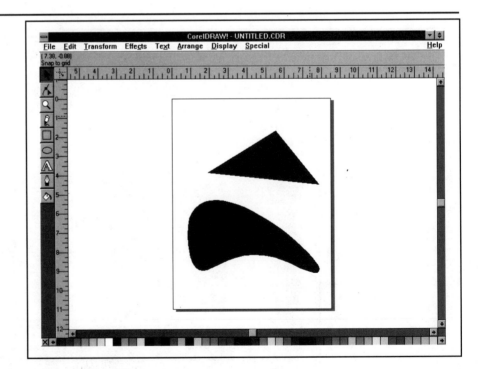

The shape tool also allows you to change the characteristics of the path attached to a node. For example, you can convert a straight path to a curved path and then manipulate the resulting curve to shape it the way you want it.

The shape tool can break a path, inserting nodes where there previously were none. Figure 1.20 illustrates the result of converting a circle to a pie chart—or to a PacMan character, if you prefer—by means of the shape tool.

A lot remains to be said about the shape tool.

THE ZOOM TOOL

The function of the zoom tool is simple. It allows you to magnify sections of a drawing, so that you can work with details on a manageable scale. If you select the zoom tool, the flyout menu shown in Figure 1.21 will appear, allowing you to decide how you want the magnification to work. The two most commonly used forms of magnification are zooming in, indicated by the magnifying glass with a plus sign in it, and zooming out, which predictably uses a magnifying glass with a minus sign in it.

FIGURE 1.20:

A pie chart created with the shape tool

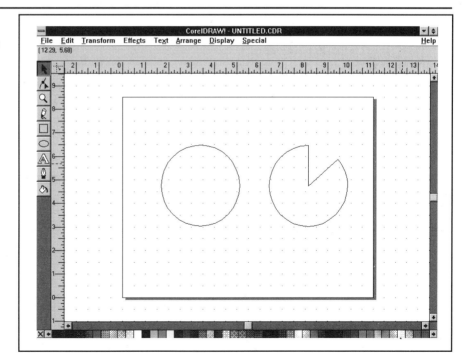

FIGURE 1.21:

The zoom tool menu

In zooming in, the cursor will change to a magnifying glass. To zoom in on a particular area of a drawing, you would do the following:

1. Select the zoom in tool.

2. Place the cursor in the drawing page, in the upper-left corner of the area you wish to magnify.

3. Click and hold the left mouse button.

4. Drag the mouse down and to the right so that the area you wish to zoom in on is enclosed.

5. Release the mouse button. The area you have defined with the zoom tool will replace the previous view.

You can use the zoom in tool repeatedly to zoom in on sections within sections you have already zoomed in on.

Each time you zoom in, CorelDRAW makes a note of what the view looked like before you clicked on the zoom tool. It keeps a stack of these notes, adding one note to the stack each time you zoom in. When you select the zoom out tool, it takes the most recent note off the stack and restores the view it describes. As such, you can step backwards through successive zoomings-in by using the zoom out function.

Having completed a zoom in either direction, CorelDRAW will automatically reselect whichever tool you were using before you selected the zoom tool.

The other zoom tool options will be discussed later as appropriate.

Should you discover that you've selected the zoom tool in error, clicking outside the zoom flyout menu unselects the tool and dismisses the menu without changing anything.

 Users of Aldus applications will find the CorelDRAW zoom tool a bit confusing at first. While it looks like the zoom tool in PageMaker or PhotoStyler, for example, it doesn't work the same way. In an Aldus application, you would zoom in by clicking the zoom tool in the center of the area you'd like to expand. Under CorelDRAW, you would draw a marquee around the area. The Aldus approach is faster, while the Corel-DRAW zoom tool gives you better control over how much you zoom in and what you'll see in the zoomed view.

THE PENCIL TOOL

The pencil tool is used to draw lines. It can be used to draw straight lines, complex curves, or freehand curves, which are in fact assemblages of complex curves.

Complex curves, also called Bézier curves, are curved line segments in which you can control the curve characteristics precisely. In mechanical drawings, these would be referred to as "spline" curves. The body of a car is a good example of complex curves in use.

The pencil tool is always capable of drawing straight lines. You must select whether you wish to have it draw freehand curves or complex curves. To do this, select the pencil icon and continue to hold the mouse button. A flyout menu will appear. The leftmost icon selects the freehand mode. The rightmost one selects the complex Bézier curve mode. Once selected, one of these modes will remain in effect until you explicitly select a new mode.

Most things about CorelDRAW will be reset to the application's defaults when you load a new drawing. This is not true of the toolbox settings. If you select the complex Bézier curve mode from the pencil tool flyout menu, the pencil tool will remain in this mode until you explicitly change it or until you exit CorelDRAW.

Drawing a Straight Line

1. Select the pencil tool.

2. Click the mouse at the point you want the line to start.

3. Move the mouse to the point where you want the line to end. As you move the mouse, a straight line extends from the mouse to your starting point.

4. Click the mouse to anchor the free end of the line.

Drawing Freehand Curves

1. Select the pencil tool. Make sure it's in the freehand mode.

2. Place the mouse at the point where you want the line to start.

3. Click *and hold* the left mouse button.

4. Move the mouse to form the line you want to draw. It's extremely difficult to get this to work out properly most of the time.

5. Release the mouse button to anchor the free end of the line and to stop drawing.

Drawing Complex Bézier Curves

1. Select the pencil tool. Make sure it's in the Bézier curve mode.

2. Place the mouse at the point where you want the line to start.

3. Click *and hold* the left mouse button and drag it from the place where you started the line. Blue handles will sprout from the point where you started the line.

4. Click the left mouse button where you want the line to end, and drag it from the place where you clicked. Blue handles will sprout from the point where you ended the line. The line itself will appear, probably as a C- or S-shaped curve.

5. Grab the ends of the curve handles and manipulate the curve to the shape you're after. Note that manipulating Bézier curve handles takes some practice.

Freehand lines, once drawn, can be edited with the shape tool to clean them up and fix mistakes. Bézier curves can be split up into smaller Bézier curves to produce more complex lines, something that will be dealt with in more detail in the next chapter.

Until you go to draw or select something else, any line you have just drawn will be automatically selected. As such, it need not be explicitly selected again in order to change any of its characteristics, such as its line width. This is true using any of the tools which actually draw objects.

THE RECTANGLE AND ELLIPSE TOOLS

The rectangle and ellipse tools draw rectangles and ellipses, respectively. (You probably guessed that from their names.) In fact, it's more correct to say that they draw rectangular and elliptical objects. Once drawn, these objects can have their attributes changed. You can meddle with their line weights, fill patterns, and so on.

To draw a rectangle, simply select the rectangle tool and click and hold the mouse where you want the upper-left corner of your rectangle to be. Drag the mouse to where you want the lower-right corner to be, and release it.

The ellipse tool works the same way. The rectangular area defined by dragging the mouse identifies the area in which the ellipse is being drawn.

THE TEXT TOOL

The text tool—referred to by many as the big A tool—is used for placing text in a drawing. CorelDRAW has good text-manipulation facilities, far more sophisticated than can be dealt with in this simple introduction. We'll cover the basic features here, with extensive elaboration to follow in Chapter 3 and elsewhere.

When you select the text tool, the cursor will change to a cross. If you click it somewhere in the drawing area of the CorelDRAW window, a blinking text insertion mark will appear. You can type text into your drawing when this cursor is visible. It will appear in the currently selected font and with the currently selected font attributes. If you have not selected any font characteristics, CorelDRAW will use whatever it has chosen as its defaults.

Having entered some text into a drawing, you can select it with the pick tool and change both the text itself and its typographic characteristics by selecting Edit Text from the Edit menu. A dialog box will appear, as shown in Figure 1.22.

The Artistic Text dialog box allows you to enter new text and to edit text which you have previously created. If you click in the window at the top

You can get to this box quickly by selecting the text you want to edit and then hitting Ctrl-T.

FIGURE 1.22:
The Artistic Text dialog box

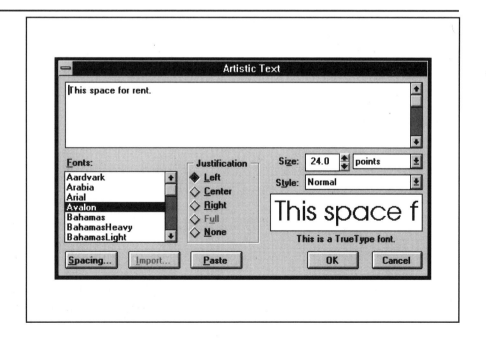

of the dialog box, a flashing cursor will appear on the first line, allowing you to type in some text.

The other items in this dialog box are used to change the appearance of the text. The typeface can be changed to one of those listed in the Fonts scroll box on the left side of the dialog box. The Justification options box includes a series of five radio buttons: Left, Center, Right, Full, and None. They are used to set the justification of the selected text. On the right side of the dialog box are several option boxes that are used to change the size and style of the text. As you change the Font, Size, or Style settings of the text, you can see the modifications that you've made in the window below the Style list box. Across the bottom of the dialog box are three pushbuttons for Spacing, Import, and Paste options.

The Artistic Text dialog box is also used to deal with large blocks of type. You can now import large text files from an external word processor.

There are also several other typographic controls available in CorelDRAW.

If you're already well versed in the lore of type and typography, you might have glanced at the typeface window in Figure 1.22 with a moment of concern. Typefaces like Avalon and Bangkok may not sound like anything you've heard of before. The reason for this is that CorelDRAW cannot use the common names of the typefaces it includes. Those names themselves are registered trademarks. It uses contrived names instead. For example, the Helvetica typeface under CorelDRAW is referred to as Switzerland. In fact, all of the typefaces included with CorelDRAW have other, more commonly used names.

You will need the Artistic Text dialog box to set the complex typographic characteristics of text under CorelDRAW. It's worth noting that while you can use it merely to edit text, you don't have to. If you select the text tool and click on some existing text, a text editing cursor will appear between the two characters nearest to where you clicked, allowing you to add or delete text right in your drawing.

THE OUTLINE PEN TOOL

The outline pen tool—also called the pen tool, the nib tool, and the clogged Rapidograph tool by experienced draftspeople—is one of the two tools used to modify the graphic attributes of selected objects. If you select an object in your drawing and then select this tool, a menu like the one in Figure 1.23 will appear at the bottom of your screen. This will allow you to specify the line weight and the line pattern or color for the object or objects you have selected. If you have selected multiple objects, all of them will be given the line characteristics you select.

The line widths and line shades shown in this menu represent a handy selection of commonly used values. Note that the line with arrows above and below it—a hairline—is set by default to a quarter of a point, which is roughly equivalent to one dot on a 300 dot-per-inch printer.

If you need more control of widths and shades, you can click on the outline tool icon or the color wheel at the left edge of this menu. These two tools will pop up precise-adjustment dialog boxes, as shown in Figure 1.24.

The precise-adjustment controls are referred to by software designers as being "modal." This means that if you select a line and then select the outline tool's precise-adjustment box, you must make the changes you want and then select OK or Cancel before you go back to working on your drawing. CorelDRAW will beep otherwise. Roll-up menus are not modal. You can have one open on your screen and work on your drawing at the same time. If you select an object to which a roll-up pertains, you will be able to edit the object's characteristics using the roll-up control. At all other times, the roll-up will effectively be asleep.

The roll-up icon to the right of the outline pen icon will activate the appropriate roll-up menu. As noted earlier, you can control essentially the same characteristics using these two sets of controls. You should choose the one which you find more appropriate.

The outline pen dialog box and roll-up allow you to specify more line characteristics than you might have thought even existed, and widths in increments so precise that you'll never be able to afford an output device capable of making them that exact. The Outline Color dialog box—invoked by selecting the color wheel from the outline tool menu—allows you to

FIGURE 1.23:

The outline pen tool menu

FIGURE 1.24:

The Outline Pen and Outline Color dialog boxes for making precise adjustments

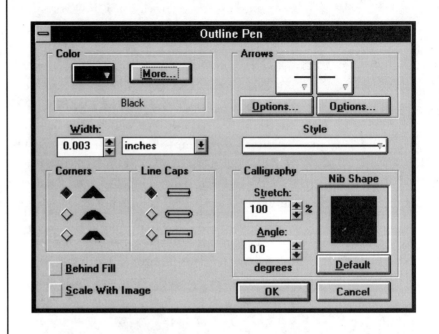

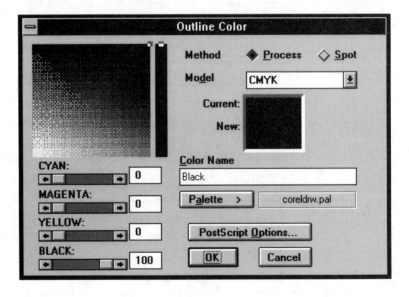

define the shade or color of a line with impressive accuracy using your choice of several color models. A lot more will be said about this later in this book.

THE FILL TOOL

The fill tool is used to set the fill color or pattern of selected objects. Obviously, these would have to be objects which lend themselves to filling. You can't fill a line, for example. Specifically, for objects to be filled they must be defined with closed paths.

Figure 1.25 illustrates the flyout menu which pops up when you select the fill tool. The rectangles in this menu represent the available fill types. As with the outline tool menu, the leftmost icon in the fill tool menu will pop up a precise-adjustment dialog box.

The next icon over will enable the fill roll-up menu.

There are several specialized ways of filling objects represented in the fill tool's menu. The checkerboard represents bitmap fills, which I have mentioned earlier. The two-headed diagonal arrow represents what are called vector fills, which involve using tiles of drawn objects, something we'll get to later in this book.

The icon with a fuzzy white area in its lower-right corner is the fountain-fill icon. We've discussed fountains briefly earlier in this chapter. This icon pops up a fountain selection dialog box.

The PS icon is used to select among the incredible library of PostScript patterns which comes with CorelDRAW. However, this icon will be useful only if you output your drawings to a PostScript printer.

NOTE NOTE *The fill tool's icon dates back to the early days of paint programs. Under a paint program, filling an area with a color or pattern is accomplished by the digital equivalent of pouring paint into it. A paint program literally starts with a point inside the area and paints all the pixels adjacent to it until it encounters a line. While the process is different under CorelDRAW, the icon has remained.*

FIGURE 1.25:
The fill tool menu

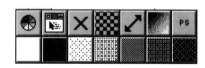

COLOR AND CORELDRAW

While color will be dealt with in detail later in this book, it deserves mention here as one of CorelDRAW's more outstanding features.

CorelDRAW supports drawing with an almost unlimited palette of colors. The representation of colored objects on your screen, however, will be handled by a best guess approximation of the colors you've selected, in keeping with the color facilities of your display card as well as what Windows will let CorelDRAW get away with.

Having created a color drawing with CorelDRAW, you can output it to a color printer. Unfortunately, it takes a color PostScript printer to accurately reproduce the colors which CorelDRAW can define, and these are very expensive. However, there's a more useful purpose to which color drawings can be put under CorelDRAW, that of generating color separations.

The CorelDRAW package is capable of outputting spot-color and four-color separations. What this means is that you can use CorelDRAW to sidestep one of the more expensive parts of color printing.

Color under CorelDRAW can be specified in any of several systems—you can choose a color model which suits the way you think of color, and which is in keeping with the way your CorelDRAW art will be printed. There are two systems particular to commercial printing. The first of these is called process color and the second Pantone color. In defining a particular color as a *process color,* one specifies the percentages of cyan, magenta, yellow, and black inks required to represent the color in question. *Pantone colors* are specific colors of ink which are numbered in a color-matching system widely accepted by the graphics industry. Thus, for example, one can specify the fill color of a certain area as being Pantone 525 and know precisely what color the area will wind up when it's printed.

WRAPPING UP

You can read about CorelDRAW for hours and learn less about it than twenty minutes in front of a computer will teach you. It's a package of sufficient complexity as to really require a hands-on approach to using it. To this end, the rest of this book should properly be read not by the light of an incandescent lamp, but rather by the glow emitted by your monitor.

In learning CorelDRAW, you should bear in mind that you're actually learning how to make it do the things you are particularly interested in. It's quite forgivable to ignore those of its features which have no application for your needs. It's also well in keeping with the spirit of the software itself to close this book part way through and simply mouse away at the package until you run up against something you don't understand. CorelDRAW is very forgiving of users who make a few mistakes.

The rest of this book will go a long way toward making you into a CorelDRAW artist instead of just a CorelDRAW user. Behind its clever object-manipulation tools, its impressive library of typefaces, and its intuitive user interface is a tool for your imagination.

FAST TRACK

CHAPTER

2

> double click on the object with the pick tool and grab one of
> the bent arrow corner marks. Drag the object around.

> select the ellipse tool and draw an ellipse with the Ctrl
> key held down.

> click and drag in one of the rulers and pull a guideline into the
> CorelDRAW workspace.

> draw a line with the pencil tool which spans the distance you
> wish to measure. The distance it occupies will be displayed in
> the status bar. Hit the Del key to delete the line.

2

Creating

Line

Drawings

The most basic level of CorelDRAW is drawing lines. If you have a good understanding of the line-drawing capabilities of CorelDRAW, you'll find that the rest of the package is pretty easy to master.

As I noted in the introduction to this book, you can go at learning CorelDRAW from the perspective of a designer or the perspective of someone simply following instructions. Both of these will give you a pretty clear understanding of what you're doing, but the latter will take a lot longer, and you will probably wind up with somebody else's idea of what you were trying to create.

This chapter will talk about drawing both simple and complex figures using little more than lines. Complex fills and transformations, involved text manipulations, and other intermediate features and applications will be presented in later chapters.

In the spirit of the designer's approach, we'll be looking at a number of the CorelDRAW tools, but this will be a drawing-oriented tutorial rather than a tool-oriented one. When you finish with this chapter and go for a Coke you should feel confident in your abilities to use the following:

- ◆ The pencil tool for drawing lines
- ◆ The pick tool for selecting them
- ◆ The shape tool for changing them into curves
- ◆ The rectangle and ellipse tools
- ◆ The zoom tool for looking at what you're doing
- ◆ The duplicate function
- ◆ The group function

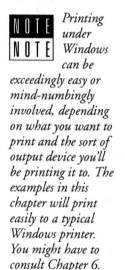

Printing under Windows can be exceedingly easy or mind-numbingly involved, depending on what you want to print and the sort of output device you'll be printing it to. The examples in this chapter will print easily to a typical Windows printer. You might have to consult Chapter 6.

You will also see how to print a simple graphic from CorelDRAW, although this isn't much of an accomplishment. CorelDRAW makes printing at this level almost effortless. More complex printing will be dealt with later in this book.

Despite the apparent complexity of some of the things we'll be drawing in this chapter, you'll find that CorelDRAW makes handling large drawings pretty painless. As with most large tasks—house building, for example—a large drawing under CorelDRAW is really just a lot of small drawings stuck together. CorelDRAW is particularly adept at letting you deal with drawings in this way. You can work on small sections, get them right, and then drag them into your main image. You can also reuse pieces of a drawing if they're applicable elsewhere, saving you the task of drawing the same or similar items over and over again.

DRAWING LINES AND RECTANGLES: A ROOF AND WINDOWS

The first thing we'll be drawing is shown in Figure 2.1. It's a simple representation of the top section of a suburban house. Despite its apparent complexity, this drawing took only twenty minutes to complete. It has a number of elements which will help you to explore the basic line drawing facilities of CorelDRAW. There are no fills and no tricky shading—applications we will discuss later in the book—but there are repetitive elements, mirrored curves (on the rain gutters), and various objects that entail measuring and moving.

FIGURE 2.1:

*The upper story
of a house*

The most complex elements in this picture are the windows. They consist of numerous lines, all of which can be drawn in any of several ways. You may notice that all of the windows are identical. This means you will actually have to draw only one of them, and only selected parts at that.

Another important aspect of this picture is that every line in it occurs at integral points on the page; that is, you could draw a grid such that all the end points of the lines in the picture would fall on points of the grid. This makes the accurate placement of objects in the picture a lot easier.

DRAWING WITH A GRID

The Snap To Grid feature allows you to force CorelDRAW to align all the nodes of the paths you draw to fixed grid points. Depending upon your preferences, the grid points can be visible as faint blue dots or invisible. When the grid is active, your lines and other drawn objects will snap to the nearest grid position.

Using a grid makes accurately positioning objects a lot easier. However, it does make positioning things by eye nearly impossible—you'll want to switch it off in instances which call for visual alignment rather than absolute accuracy.

Note that when you have the Snap To Grid feature active, the position and length values on the status line at the top of the work space also snap to the nearest grid value.

Let's make this grid do some of our work. Start by pulling down the Display menu. The two items of interest at the moment are Snap To Grid

TIP

The unit of measurement you use under CorelDRAW will not affect the accuracy of your drawings. CorelDRAW converts whatever units it displays into its own internal units. You might well find that you favor different units for different things under CorelDRAW. A few conversions may prove helpful. One inch is equivalent to 2.54 centimeters, 25.4 millimeters, about 72 points, and 6 picas.

and Grid Setup. Click on Grid Setup. The dialog box in Figure 2.2 will appear.

The grid setup dialog box allows you to specify the number of squares per unit of measure on the screen. The units of measure are also up to you—we'll use millimeters in this example. For various reasons, millimeters provide a generally useful number of increments across the screen. If your grid size dialog box indicates units other than the ones you want to use, click on the downward pointing arrow to open the selector box and choose the units you're comfortable with. Although CorelDRAW does not explicitly offer centimeters as a grid size, keep in mind that one centimeter equals ten millimeters.

The Grid Origin setting determines where the horizontal and vertical zero points are relative to the upper-left corner of your paper. Assuming that your paper is 8½ by 11 inches—the default size of CorelDRAW's printable work space unless you explicitly change it—you should enter 0 for the horizontal value and 11 inches for the vertical value. This will put the origin of the grid and rulers in the upper left-hand corner.

If you've had an extensive exposure to high-school geometry, you might be more comfortable with the origin of the rulers in the lower-left corner.

FIGURE 2.2:

The grid setup dialog box

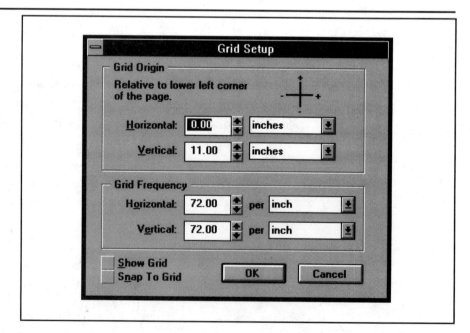

You can put it there by entering 0 into both of the grid origin fields. For this chapter, however, let's leave it in the upper-left corner.

The box with Show Grid beside it will determine whether the grid points will be visible. You might want to start with it enabled. Click in this box so a check mark appears through it.

The visible grid dots are a bit deceptive under CorelDRAW. You will not always see a blue dot at every grid point. If you specify a fine enough grid, there could in theory be a blue dot at every pixel in the workspace of your screen, which would be of little use. CorelDRAW will always thin out the proximity of the visible grid points on your screen for the current level of magnification you're working with. As such, there may be far more grid points to snap to than there are blue dots, especially when your work space is fully zoomed out.

The number of squares per unit of measure is entered by means of a special type of control which appears throughout CorelDRAW whenever the need arises for entering numbers. This number-entry control allows you a choice of methods. You can click on the up or down arrows to the right of the number to increase or decrease the value, or you can click and hold one of the arrows to step through a succession of values. Alternatively, you can click on the number itself and then use the keyboard to enter the value you desire. This would be the method to use when you need a fractional value, a need that will arise more often than you might think. Recall that what you are deciding is not how many millimeters (or inches or whatever) wide your grid squares should be; rather, you are deciding how many grid squares you want to fit into the space of a millimeter (or inch or whatever). Thus, if you enter 4 in the grid size dialog box, you will be getting four boxes per millimeter—far too many grid points to be useful.

In this chapter, a frequency of one grid point every quarter of a *centimeter* will be about right. However, CorelDRAW doesn't support centimeters—only millimeters. Thus, you would enter .4 grid points per millimeter into each of the grid frequency fields.

The Snap To Grid item in the Display menu is what is called a *toggle*. You can change its status between on and off as many times as you need to by repeatedly selecting its menu item. If you select it when it's *off*, you'll toggle it *on*, and a check mark will appear beside it. Selecting it when it is *on* toggles it *off*, and the check mark disappears. Note that you can also toggle the Snap To Grid feature by simply holding down the Ctrl key and pressing

You can find all the keyboard equivalents to the menu items listed in the CorelDRAW menus themselves.

Y on the keyboard. For the purposes of this drawing, toggle the Snap To Grid feature *on.*

When the Snap To Grid feature is toggled on, you'll see the words Snap To Grid toward the leftmost end of the status bar above the workspace.

Drawing a Rectangle: The Window Glass

Figure 2.3 illustrates one of the double windows of the drawing. It's easiest to work from the inside of an object outward, so let's begin by drawing the glass panes of the windows.

The six panes of each window are actually six rectangles, each of which could be drawn separately. However, it's easier to draw one large rectangle and then draw three lines through it. To draw the rectangle, you will be selecting the rectangle tool, which is easy, and drawing a rectangle fifty millimeters across by ninety millimeters deep, which is not all that easy in the default magnification of CorelDRAW. Let's improve things a bit. First of all, use the Show Rulers item of the Display menu to turn on the ruler display if the rulers are not already visible. This will place rulers along the top and left sides of the work space of the CorelDRAW window. Next, select the zoom tool and zoom in on the upper-left corner of the work space—as described in Chapter 1—until the rulers are large enough to give you room to move the cursor within one-centimeter areas. You might have to use the scroll bars to position the work space so that the 0,0 intersection of the rulers becomes visible. If you overdo the magnification on

FIGURE 2.3:
A double window

your first try, select the zoom tool again and use the zoom out function to return to your previous magnification level, then have another shot at it.

In drawing the rectangle, note that the position of your mouse cursor is reflected in the rulers by two faint lines. This makes it easy to line up the corners of the rectangle with the ruler graduations. Keep in mind that you only have to get the position close—with the Snap To Grid feature active, the rectangle will snap to the nearest grid line.

This drawing does not use any fill patterns, but at the moment CorelDRAW doesn't know this. Chances are the rectangle you've just drawn will have a fill associated with it, probably solid black.

CorelDRAW defaults to using its "draw in preview mode," which means that it will show you the fills of your objects as you work with them. If you're running CorelDRAW on a fast 80386- or 80486-based system, this is the ideal way to work. Slower machines may make this mode less desirable—while it helps to see what your fills are up to, the time it takes to frequently redraw filled objects can make CorelDRAW too slow to use on low-end hardware. In this case, toggle the Edit Wireframe mode on the Display menu by holding the shift key down and pressing the F9 key. In this mode, only the paths of your objects will be drawn. You can see a preview of what your picture will look like at any time by selecting the Show Preview item of the Display menu, or by hitting the F9 key.

If you're working in the Edit Wireframe mode of CorelDRAW, keep in mind that while your fills will not be visible as you work, your objects may have fill characteristics nonetheless. Check the preview frequently. Figure 2.4 shows the rectangle with a preview.

There's an alternate form of the preview—the one you eventually adopt, if you use the Edit Wireframe mode at all, will probably be a matter of taste. Hitting F9 without the Shift key will display a full-screen preview. Hitting the Esc key will return you to CorelDRAW.

You'll notice that the fill of a single selected object is also indicated in the *status line* at the top of the CorelDRAW workspace. This is very useful when you're working with single objects; however, the status line cannot show you the fills of multiple grouped objects, the relative position of objects, the result of their fills, and other aspects of your drawing that can best be seen in the preview window if you usually work in Edit Wireframe mode.

If you have a high-end system to run CorelDRAW on, you'll rarely need the Edit Wireframe mode of the software, with its attendant preview modes. You might find that drawings with complex fills, such as those to be discussed in the next chapter, often call for the Edit Wireframe mode even if you have a computer that runs like the wind. It's worth knowing about these options.

FIGURE 2.4:

The preview window

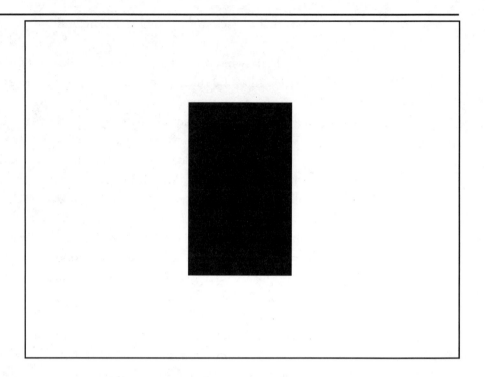

The Fill characteristic shown in Figure 2.4 is not what you need for this drawing. In order to change it, you must select the pick tool and then click on a line of the rectangle you've just drawn. Now select the fill tool. Click on the gray icon with an X in it in the flyout menu. The X is always used to indicate the negation of things under CorelDRAW—in this case, no fill. You might consider that Ctrl-X for Exit is the negation of CorelDRAW itself.

While you're changing things, select the outline pen tool and click on the *hairline* item to select the hairline width. This is the gray icon with a line being squeezed between two arrows; that is, the thinnest possible line.

If you're using the Edit Wireframe mode, you should put the preview window away by hitting Shift-F9 when you're done with it. Because the preview window ties up screen and memory space and slows down your drawing as it updates itself, you should get in the habit of toggling it off when you don't need it.

Note that the preview window, like any other Windows window, can be moved and resized as described in Appendix A of this book.

Drawing Straight Lines: Dividing the Window

To draw the separate lines which divide the window into six window panes, select the pencil tool. Move the pencil cursor so that it rests over the top of your rectangle midway between the two sides. As the rectangle is 50 millimeters across, this should be 25 millimeters along.

In fact, while CorelDRAW defaults to constraining things in 15-degree increments, you can set this value to anything you like. Open the Preferences dialog box from the Special menu and change the number in the Constrain Angle control to select the constrain value you'd like to use.

To enable you to draw straight lines, CorelDRAW offers a Constrain feature. As long as you hold down the Ctrl key while drawing a line, the Constrain feature will cause a line to be drawn straight. Part of the constraining nature of this feature is the fact that CorelDRAW will force the line to lie along a path which is either horizontal or an even multiple of 15 degrees from horizontal (by default). All you have to worry about is keeping your mouse within 15 degrees of the direction you want to go.

The procedure for drawing straight lines, then, is the following:

1. Select the pencil tool and move the pencil cursor to the point where you want to begin drawing the line.

2. Hold down the Ctrl key and click the mouse button once. This will start the line and anchor it.

3. Move the mouse cursor to extend the line in the direction you want.

4. When you've reached the point where you want to end the line (the outside edge of your rectangle), click again. This anchors the other end of the line.

Repeat this procedure to draw the two horizontal lines. As the window is ninety millimeters deep, these conveniently fall at thirty and sixty millimeters from the top. Your work space should now look like Figure 2.5.

FIXING MISTAKES

If you get one of the lines wrong, you'll have several options to correct it. One easy mistake to make in drawing lines under CorelDRAW is to click and hold the mouse to anchor a line, rather than simply clicking and releasing it. This will put you in the freehand drawing mode, which will result in a very drunken-looking window, or in the Bézier curve mode, which will be explained in greater detail later on.

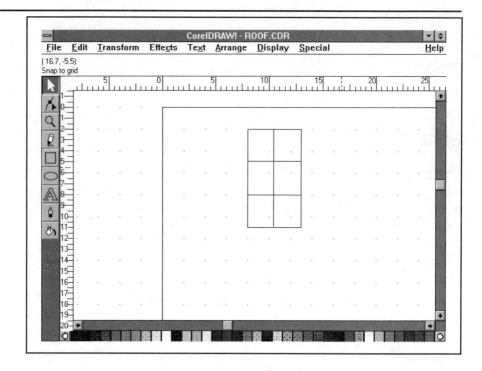

If you wind up with the wrong sort of line, you can delete it. This can be done by using the Clear item of the Edit menu or, even more simply, by pressing the Delete key—Del—on your keyboard. Both of these approaches will get rid of currently selected paths. Recalling that once drawn a path is automatically selected, you can use either of these methods to simply kill the path you have just drawn.

You can also undo your mistake. If you select the Undo item of the Edit menu at any time under CorelDRAW, your most recent action will be reversed and your drawing will immediately revert to the way it was one action ago. Holding down the Alt key while hitting the Backspace key will also undo your most recent change.

If you draw the right sort of line but you discover that it has come out a bit too long or a bit too short, you can simply resize it. Select the pick tool and click on the line. *Handles* like those in Figure 2.6 will appear. Grab the center handle from the group of marks at the end you want to adjust and then pull or push the line until it's the right length.

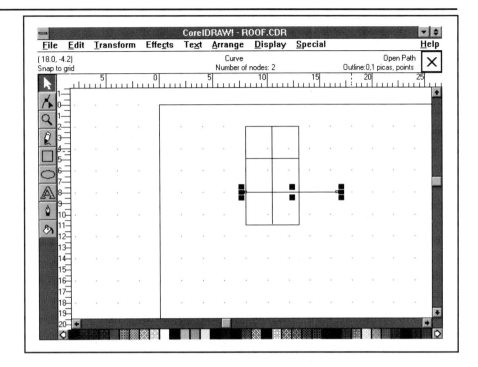

Looking back at the completed window in Figure 2.3, you'll notice that there's a second rectangle around the glass, representing the wooden frame of the window. This is a quarter of a centimeter—2½ millimeters—bigger than your first rectangle. Select the rectangle tool and draw this.

If you don't happen to get this rectangle quite right, you can adjust it just as you did the line above. Use the pick tool to select the offending rectangle by clicking on it. Handles will appear. If you merely want to reposition the rectangle without changing its size, grab a line of the rectangle itself and drag it where you want it. The whole rectangle will move with it. If you have to resize the rectangle, grab a handle and drag that in or out until the rectangle is correctly sized. The handles of a rectangle, ellipse, or complex selected area allow you various automatic constraints depending upon which of the marks you choose to grab. If you grab a handle at one of the corners of the selected area, you'll be able to stretch the selected object in both directions. If you grab one that's in the middle of a side, you'll be able to stretch the object in only one direction.

Resizing an object like this is a simple example of a *transformation*. Any object which is transformed retains its original dimensions and characteristics in the CorelDRAW object list, as well as a record of all the transformations performed upon it. Thus, you can clear all of the transformations of an object and return it to its original state at any time, even three months and four hundred actions later, should you find yourself regretting having transformed the object in the first place.

Transformations and how to work with them will crop up in greater detail throughout the rest of this book.

If you're working in Edit Wireframe mode, having drawn the complete glass part of the window, you might want to have a peek at it with the preview window to make sure that all the fills are correct, and to adjust any that aren't. If you're working in the default drawing mode of CorelDRAW, in which the fills are always visible, you'll be able to see any fill problems as you work.

GROUPING OBJECTS

If everything is correct so far, you should not have to make any further changes to the individual paths that make up the glass part of the window. Because this part of the drawing will be used several times over, it's convenient to group the objects in this part of the drawing into a single object. You can do this by selecting the objects you want in your group and then selecting the Group item from the Arrange menu.

You can select items to be grouped in several ways. The most commonly used approach is to use the pick tool to draw a *selection box* around everything to be grouped. To do this with the window you have drawn thus far,

1. Select the pick tool, then place the point of the arrow cursor slightly above and to the left of the outer rectangle you've drawn.

2. Click and hold the mouse button.

3. Drag the mouse cursor down and to the right. A marquee will reel out behind it.

4. When the marquee encloses your entire drawing, release the mouse button.

Handles will appear around the rectangle. Everything inside the marks is now selected.

If a single marquee cannot include all the objects you want to select at one time, or if it would include objects you don't want selected, simply use the pick tool instead and click on each object you want while holding down the Shift key. This technique will prevent the first object you select from being unselected by the next one, and so on. Thus you can select several irregularly spaced objects—for grouping, transforming, deleting, and so on— by doing so one at a time.

Since the glass part of the window is the only thing you've drawn so far, you could select it with an even easier technique: Simply use the Select All item from the Edit menu. This will select every object in your drawing, which is just the glass and the window frame at the moment.

Once you have selected the items for your group, direct CorelDRAW to group them by clicking on Group from the Arrange menu. With the objects selected and grouped, you can treat the glass part of your window as a single object. Anything which would affect a simple object can now be applied to this complex object. For example, you might want to make sure that all of the lines in this part of your drawing have the same line attribute. Using the pick tool, select the object—either by drawing a marquee around it or simply clicking on any line in the object. Then select the outline pen tool, and click on a line attribute to apply to all the lines in the object.

A complex object *can* contain individual paths with different line widths and color attributes. If you had such an object in a drawing you could preserve the individual path characteristics by simply making sure you didn't do to it what you just did to the window pane object, that is, assign a single line characteristic to the whole object.

As long as they are in a group, paths are not accessible individually. You can't, for example, resize just one of the lines. However, grouped objects can be *ungrouped* at any time. Thus, you can always ungroup a complex object, alter one or more of its paths, and then regroup it.

As you get more familiar with CorelDRAW, you may look back on this example and realize that the objects that make up your window pane should not have been grouped at all. They should have been *combined*. Combining objects is more involved than grouping them, and for this reason we'll leave it for later.

You can group selected objects by hitting Ctrl-G, which will save your mouse a trip to the menu bar.

CorelDRAW allows you to nest groups of objects. Consequently, you can group several groups of grouped objects, and so on. This can be very useful in assembling large drawings with lots of details, such as the one you're working on now. It can also be very, very cumbersome if you find you have to get at an object that's six levels deep in nested groups. Use this facility with forethought.

Saving Your Work

Before you go any further you should save your file. This will prevent you from losing all your work if your cat happens to trip over the power cord of your computer and pull it out of the wall. Another very good reason to save your file is that you can always revert to a previously saved file if you discover that you have mangled your drawing beyond the capabilities of the Undo function to recover it.

Until you save a new drawing, it will be named UNTITLED.CDR. The *first* time you save any drawing you should select the Save or Save As item from the File menu. This will pop up the dialog box shown in Figure 2.7.

With this box, you should not need to change drives or directories when you save a file. Your current path should point to the directory called \CORELDRW\DRAW\SAMPLES, the default place to store CorelDRAW drawing files. If this is the case, all you need do is type in a file name of up to eight letters and then press ↵ or click on the OK control. You will notice that the OK control becomes active only after you have typed in at least one character for the file name.

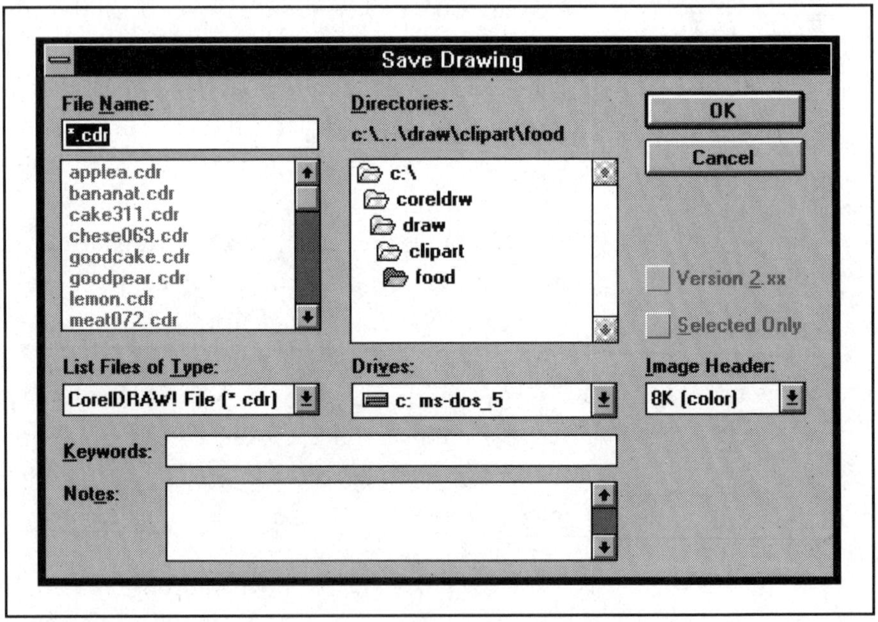

FIGURE 2.7:

The dialog box brought up by selecting Save As

Once you have assigned a file name to your file, the name will appear at the top of the CorelDRAW window. This file will be unaffected by any changes you subsequently make to it on-screen unless you decide to save it again. Then you will have two choices:

◆ You can *update* the original file at any time, so that it includes your changes. Do this by selecting the Save item from the File menu (or by using the keyboard shortcut, Ctrl-S).

◆ You can *preserve* the original file, leaving it unchanged, by saving the changed file under a different name. Do this by using the Save As option from the File menu and entering a new file name.

If, in making changes to a file that has been saved, you do manage to mangle your drawing and decide you don't want to save any changes, preferring instead to revert to the previously saved version, select Open from the File menu. A dialog box will appear, asking if you want to save the changes you've made. Since the changes didn't quite work out, click on *No.* An Open Drawing File dialog box will then pop up. Select your file and click on OK.

When you open a file—whether because you're reverting to a previously saved version or because you just want to work with a drawing previously saved to disk—the name of that file becomes the default name of the drawing you're working with. Subsequently, if you select Save rather than Save As, any changes you have made will change the file. If you want to save your modified drawing but you also want the original to remain untouched, you must use Save As, which gives you the opportunity to choose a different file name for the modified drawing.

By default, CorelDRAW creates BAK files whenever you update a drawing. For example, if you save a drawing called PICTURE.CDR and use the Save item of the File menu or just hit Ctrl-S from time to time to update it, the previous version will be renamed to PICTURE.BAK. This means that there will always be a penultimate version of your work on disk, should you damage your current CDR file somehow. There is a drawback to this, of course—those BAK files accumulate, and can ultimately take up a lot of space. You can periodically go into the directory where your CDR files reside and perform BAK file genocide. You can also inhibit the creation of BAK files altogether, as discussed in Appendix B of this book.

DUPLICATING AND MOVING OBJECTS

Each double window in your drawing consists of two sets of panes. There's no need to go through the work of drawing the second set by hand—you can just duplicate the first one and place it in the correct position.

Whenever you duplicate an object under CorelDRAW, the new object is displaced from the original by a predetermined amount, which is .25 inches by default. This is a very useful feature, as we'll see. The duplicate does not snap to the grid even if the Snap To Grid feature is on, however, which can make it difficult to place the duplicate precisely where you want it, especially if you're trying to keep objects in a straight line.

To avoid this—and to make placing duplicates easier—it's a good idea to change the displacement of duplicates to suit your needs at the moment. To do this,

1. Select the Preferences item from the Special menu. The Preferences dialog box will pop up, as seen in Figure 2.8.

2. Change the Place Duplicate units of measure to coincide with the units of measure your grid is working with.

3. Change the Place Duplicate number values.

Once again, you can open the unit control to select from the available units. The Place Duplicate values control the horizontal and vertical displacement respectively. Since we want the second window to appear to the right of the

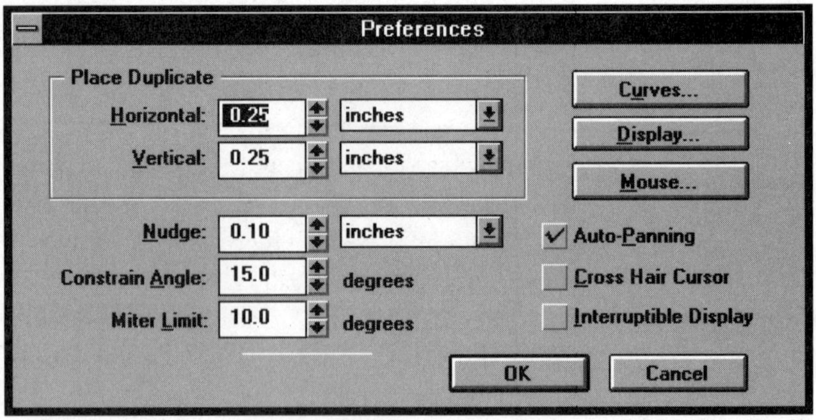

FIGURE 2.8:

The Preferences dialog box from the Special menu

first one, we might as well make the vertical displacement 0. For horizontal displacement, let's choose 10 millimeters—1 centimeter. This might look arbitrary, and it is. There is a good reason for this. If you're methodical, you could figure out how far the second window has to be displaced in order to make it appear in the desired location without any further positioning and enter this for the horizontal displacement value. However, it's usually easier to drag it over once it has been duplicated.

Note that if you change the units of measurement for a dialog such as this one, the numeric values associated with the units will be recalculated in the new units. Thus, if you had one inch of displacement and then changed to millimeters, you'd wind up with 25.4, which is the number of millimeters in an inch. Changing units usually involves entering new numbers as well.

Click on OK to accept the changes.

Now you can go about actually duplicating the window. Select the window pane with the pick tool. You can duplicate it either by using the Duplicate item from the Edit menu or by using the keyboard equivalent, Ctrl-D. This keyboard equivalent is well worth learning—you'll be using it repeatedly in a few minutes.

Once duplicated, the new object will automatically be selected by CorelDRAW. Grab any line on the selected object and drag it to the right until there is half a centimeter—five millimeters—between the windows.

It will be easier to check the exact positioning of the two windows if you zoom in on the space between them. Use the zoom tool to do this. Figure 2.9 illustrates the increased magnification used to align the window panes.

Once you have the windows positioned, you will probably want to set the magnification so as to allow you to see both of them. Select the zoom tool again and then select the white box—the whole printable page—from the flyout menu. This will throw away any intermediate zoom steps and return you to the basic magnification level of CorelDRAW so you can see the whole page. Now select the zoom tool and zoom in on the area which contains your window panes.

You will find that changing the magnification level of CorelDRAW frequently greatly simplifies the execution of complex drawings.

The Duplicate item from the File menu and the Ctrl-D command will both place the duplicate above the object it's duplicated from. If the objects are filled, then the new object will obscure the old one. If you were to press the plus key (+) with an object or group of objects selected, rather than Ctrl-D, a duplicate would also be created, but would be placed behind the original. More will be said about the relative placement of objects later in this book.

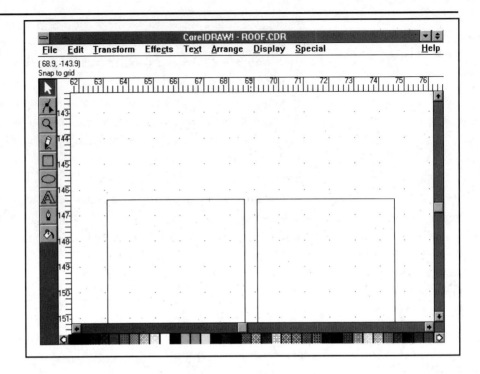

A Different Approach

The foregoing approach to duplicating and moving the window represents what you will probably do when you're working on complex drawings. CorelDRAW offers numerous ways to handle these sorts or procedures, though, and you might find that one of the other approaches is more in keeping with how you like to draw.

You can move things under CorelDRAW numerically, as well as by eye. Here's how you could handle the foregoing task using this facility.

To begin with, open the Preferences dialog box of the Special menu and set both the Place Duplicate displacement values to zero. This will cause any duplicated objects to be placed precisely on top of the objects they're duplicated from. Click on OK to leave the Preferences dialog box.

Now select and duplicate the window, as was discussed previously. Nothing much will happen, save that your CorelDRAW work space will flash momentarily as the new object is drawn. Inasmuch as it will be drawn right where the first window is, you won't see any evidence of a new object. The selection marks, however, will now pertain to the duplicate window.

We would like the new window to move right by the width of the window itself—50 millimeters—plus the five millimeters between them. To have CorelDRAW position the duplicate window, select the Move item from the Transform menu. Change the units in it if necessary, and enter 55 millimeters for the horizontal displacement. Note that positive values will move right and negative values will move left. Leave the vertical displacement at zero. When you click on OK, CorelDRAW will position your duplicate window right where you want it.

Draw Adjoining Rectangles: The Window Frame

The two window panes have a rectangle enclosing them both, again a quarter of a centimeter ($2^{1/2}$ millimeters) bigger than the area it encloses. You should draw this next, using the rectangle tool. Make sure the new rectangle has a hairline width and no fill. Again, you can use the preview to make sure that everything is as it should be. You'll be drawing in Edit Wireframe mode.

Next, add the sill below the windows—it's half a centimeter deep—and the piece of wood below that. This latter rectangle is half a centimeter deep as well but it extends a quarter of a centimeter further out in each direction. Finally, add quarter-centimeter rectangles up each side, these being the boards that the shutters will be attached to.

Your work space should now look like Figure 2.10. Also check the preview to make sure that everything looks right.

Once all of the line widths and positions and such are correct, you should not have to change any of the individual paths in this part of the drawing again. Therefore, let's group everything we've done so far into a single object. As noted previously, CorelDRAW allows you to include previously grouped objects into new groups, so you need not ungroup the individual panes before you create a new group with both of them.

To group everything in your drawing thus far, you can choose the Select All item from the Edit menu or select everything by area using the pick tool. Then go ahead and group them. The Group function is selected from the Arrange menu.

Draw Stacked Lines: The Shutter Slats

The last elements of the window to be installed are the shutters. We'll create them in the same way we did the window panes, that is, by drawing one and

The window with all its woodwork in place

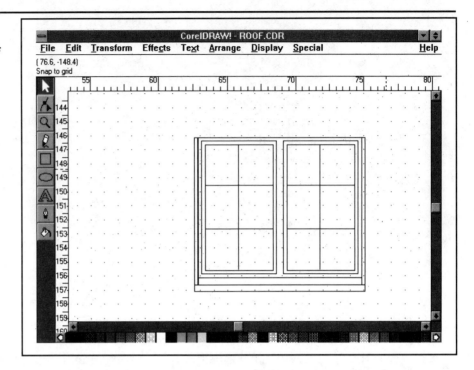

then duplicating it. You might have to use the horizontal scroll bar to move the picture over slightly so you'll have enough room to draw the shutter.

The outer rectangle of the shutter is 4¼ by 10½ centimeters. The inner rectangle is a quarter of a centimeter inside the outer one. Draw both of these using the rectangle tool. Your shutter should look like the one in Figure 2.11.

The slats on the shutter are just lines. However, there are a lot of lines, and it would be inconvenient to have to draw them all. Fortunately, CorelDRAW offers ways around this problem.

If we were using fills and knew that this drawing would be printed on a PostScript printer, we could simply fill the inner rectangle with a horizontal line pattern. For this example, however, we'll use real lines. One way to get all those lines in place is to draw one and then duplicate it many times. The lines will appear in the right locations if you set the displacement values in the Preferences dialog box appropriately before you start. Open the Preferences

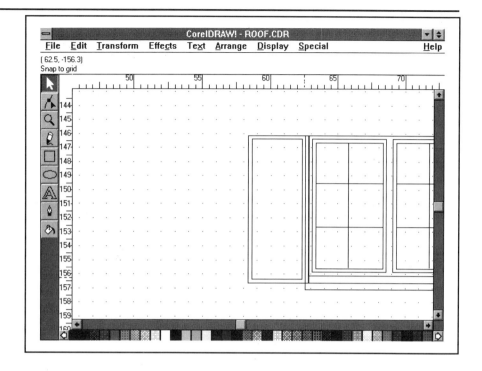

dialog box in the Special menu and set the horizontal displacement to 0 and the vertical displacement to −2.5 millimeters. The latter minus value will cause the duplicate to appear a quarter of a centimeter—or one of our grid units—*below* the original.

Now you're set to draw and duplicate the horizontal lines in the shutter. Start by zooming in so the shutter is fairly large. Then select the pencil tool and draw the top slat one quarter of a centimeter below the top inside line of the shutter frame. Hold down the Ctrl key to constrain the line to be horizontal. Remember that you should click the mouse button—don't hold it—and move the mouse so the line extends straight, then click it again when it touches the right inside line of the shutter frame.

Now hit Ctrl-D. A second line should appear below the first one if you have set up the Preferences dialog box properly. Press Ctrl-D repeatedly until you have created enough slats to fill the shutter. If you accidentally create too many, you can just select them with the pick tool and get rid of them with the Delete key.

Your work space should look like the one in Figure 2.12.

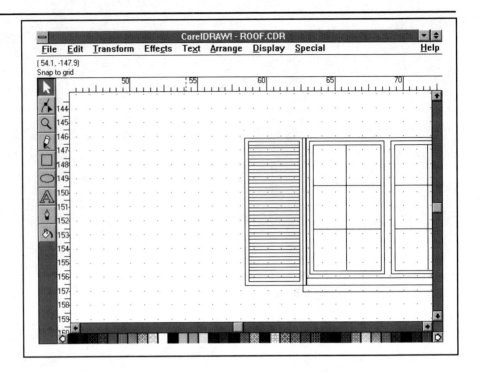

REGROUPING COMPLEX OBJECTS

This double window is almost complete—it's only missing one shutter. You can add it by duplicating the shutter you've just created and dragging it to the other side of the window. To complete the window do the following:

1. Group all the elements of the shutter together. (Select them, then select Group from the Arrange menu.)

2. Set the displacement values (in the Preferences dialog box of the Special menu) for no displacement.

3. Hit Ctrl-D to duplicate the shutter.

4. Drag the duplicate over to the other side of the window and position it. You might need to zoom in on the area where it meets the window to see if it's properly aligned. Alternately, you might prefer to use the Move function of the Transform menu, as discussed previously.

There's yet another alternate way to move the duplicated window, and one which can be very useful in mechanical drawings like this one. In the Preferences item of the Special menu there's a field to enter a Nudge value. Make it 2.5 millimeters—again, one of our grid units. Close this box and select the duplicated window. Each time you hit the → key on your keyboard's numeric keypad, the selected object will move right by one grid unit. You can nudge an object in any direction with the four arrow keys.

Now that you have a complete double window with shutters, you can select all the elements and group them. This will make the whole window behave as a single complex object, which will save some time in duplicating it and moving it around.

This would be a good time to save your work by hitting Ctrl-S.

There are four windows in the drawing, and by now you'll probably appreciate that CorelDRAW will let you reuse all the work you've just done. Simply select the window object, duplicate it, and move the duplicate window to the right until it is positioned like the second window in the complete drawing in Figure 2.13.

In my version of this drawing, there are two groups of two windows, rather than four windows spaced equally. Having placed the second window, I grouped the two windows together and duplicated the resulting group. The space between the right pair of windows is thus the same as the space between the left pair. If you want the windows equally spaced, just duplicate the one you've drawn twice more and move the copies into position.

The wall that the windows are set into is just a rectangle. Since none of the objects in this drawing have any fill patterns associated with them, it

FIGURE 2.13:

What you're aiming at. This is how the drawing should look when it is completed.

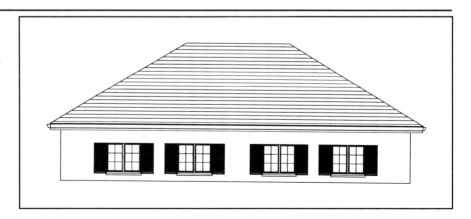

doesn't matter whether the wall is drawn before or after the windows. In a drawing where fill patterns were being used, we would have to make sure the wall was behind the windows as far as CorelDRAW is concerned. Otherwise, the fill of the wall would obscure the windows.

Draw a suitable rectangle around the windows. This will probably extend outside the drawing page—don't worry about this for now. Once again, you should probably use the preview window to check your drawing. If everything looks right, press Ctrl-S to save your work.

<table>
<tr><td>

NOTE
NOTE

</td><td>

Plan on having to practice with the

</td></tr>
</table>

scrolling work space feature of Corel-DRAW a bit. It takes some getting used to. Especially on faster hardware, it may initially scroll so quickly as to leave you wondering where your mouse cursor is in relation to the rest of your drawing. It takes a fair bit of mouse coordination to make this feature behave itself.

SCROLLING THE CORELDRAW WINDOW

Create the eaves by drawing some very shallow, long rectangles. If you look closely at the complete drawing you might be able to discern that there are three rectangles. The lowest one represents the wood of the roof itself. The next one is the rain gutter, and the upper one the lip of the roof. The upper one can be one quarter of a centimeter deep, with the others somewhat deeper. You can see a detail of these rectangles in Figure 2.14.

Because these rectangles will be so shallow relative to their widths, it can be extremely difficult to try to draw them in one easy motion. You will need to start each rectangle in a zoomed-in section of the drawing to position it accurately. You'll find that as you extend the rectangle to the edge of the CorelDRAW work space, the whole drawing will scroll, allowing you to effectively draw over a larger area than you could initially see.

CURVING A STRAIGHT LINE

If you look closely at the extremes of the eaves, you'll notice the curved profiles of the side gutters. Curves are something we have not yet discussed.

In drawing the side gutter, you will draw two straight lines and convert one of them to a curve. You might conceptualize this as starting off with an art-deco rain gutter which is triangular in cross-section and then hammering it out into a more familiar sort of gutter. There are actually two ways to handle these curved elements. We'll present one method here and the other in just a moment.

First, zoom in on the left edge of the eaves. Select the pencil tool, and click on the upper edge of the roof to anchor the first line. Use the Constrain function—the Ctrl key—to get the line perfectly horizontal. Draw the line

FIGURE 2.14:

The eaves, which are too
wide to draw in one sec-
tion of the work space

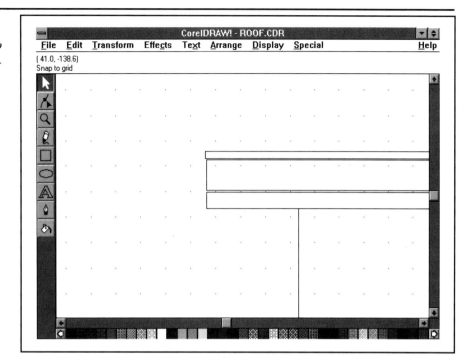

to the left a half of a centimeter or so and click again to anchor it. Click once more on the same place to start a second line, and bring that down to the lower edge of the roof. Do not use the Constrain feature for this line. Your art deco gutter should now look like the one in the first screen of Figure 2.15.

One of the interesting features of the pencil tool is its propensity for combining paths if it thinks this will help you. If you click to start a new line within five screen pixels of the end of your previous line, CorelDRAW will start the new line at the end point of the previous line and combine the paths automatically. In this case, the horizontal line and the diagonal one will wind up as a single object without your having to explicitly tell CorelDRAW to make it so.

We're now going to convert the diagonal line into a curve. Select the shape tool and double click on the end point of the diagonal line, where it meets the roof. The diagonal line will appear thicker, and a menu like the one in the second screen of Figure 2.15 should appear. Select *toCurve* from among the active options. The menu disappears and the line loses its thickness.

FIGURE 2.15:

The steps in drawing a curved gutter

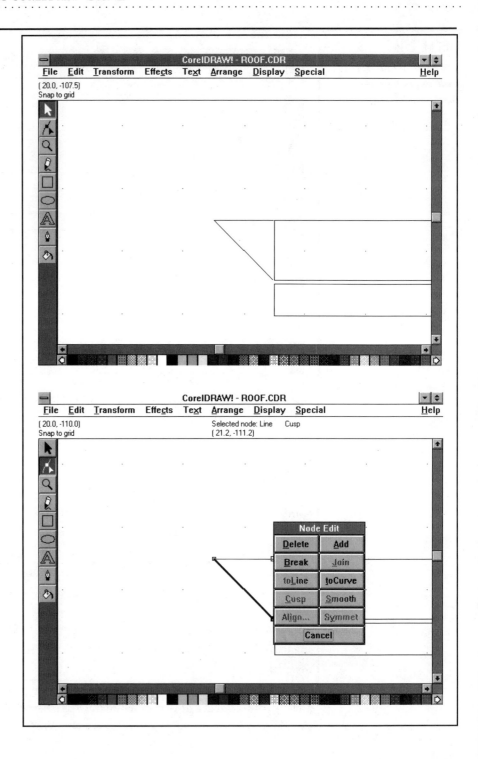

FIGURE 2.15:

*The steps in drawing
a curved gutter
(continued)*

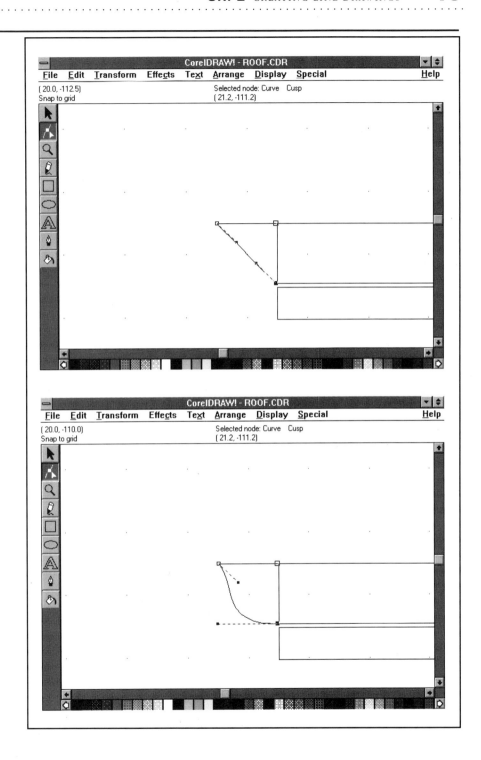

The diagonal line is now a diagonal curve. It happens to have no twist to it yet, but it now has all the properties of a Bézier curve rather than of a line. The most obvious manifestation of this is the appearance of two handles, as shown in third screen of Figure 2.15.

The curve handles are used to bend the curve and make it follow the contours you need. You will find that using them is largely an intuitive process. To begin with, grab one of them with your cursor and move it around to see what the line does.

Moving a curve handle alters the distance between the handle and its origin. You will have to adjust both handles to some extent to get the curve of the gutter to look right. When you're finished, your work space should look something like the one in the final screen of Figure 2.15.

Using the Bézier Curve Drawing Mode

As with all objects under CorelDRAW, you can change the characteristics of a Bézier curve after you have added it to your drawing. There are two things to keep in mind about this. The first is that when you select a curved line element with the pick tool, the selection marks that appear will actually enclose not only the line, but also the extremes of its handles. Secondly, you can manipulate the handles of a previously created curve, but you'll need the shape tool to do so. Click on one of the curve's end points to make its handles visible.

Creating straight lines and then converting them to curves is one way to arrive at complex curves, and in some cases it's the most effective way to do so. However, you can come up with essentially the same results directly by using the Bézier curve drawing mode.

You can select the Bézier curve mode of the pencil tool, rather than the default freehand mode, by clicking and holding on the pencil icon in the CorelDRAW toolbox. When the flyout menu appears, select the rightmost icon. Note that the toolbox icon for the pencil tool will change to remind you of which mode you have selected.

In this mode, you can draw Bézier curves directly. Click on the place where you want the curved line of the rain gutter to begin and drag the mouse cursor away at about a thirty-degree angle. One set of curve handles will appear. Next, do the same thing where you want the end point of the line to be. This will produce a second set of curve handles and a curved line between the start and end points of the line. Manipulate the curve handles to produce the curved element you want.

The Bézier drawing mode is faster to use once you've developed a feel for how to manipulate curve handles, but it will probably seem a bit awkward at first. It's worth practicing with, however, as it will help you enormously if you're working with complex drawings that contain a lot of curves.

CREATING MIRROR IMAGES

Having drawn one gutter, you must arrange to have another one with the same shape at the other end of the roof—or rather, you'll need a mirror image of it. Although you could just move over and draw it again, this would be both wasteful of time and a bit tricky, because drawing Bézier curves to match other Bézier curves is not an easy task. Fortunately, there's no need to attempt this.

CorelDRAW allows you to duplicate the curve you've just drawn, flip it end for end, and move it to the other side of the roof.

1. Select the curve and the top of the gutter. (Because the curve began so close to the end of the top line, CorelDRAW should already have combined these two paths into one object.)

2. Hit Ctrl-D to duplicate this object.

3. Use the Stretch & Mirror item of the Transform menu to flip the duplicated object horizontally. Click on Horz Mirror, then on OK in the Stretch & Mirror dialog box.

4. Grab the duplicated item and drag it right. The CorelDRAW work space will scroll when you reach the extreme edge of the visible part of your drawing.

5. Place the curve at the other end of the rain gutter.

This would be a good point to save your work again.

USING CONSTRAIN TO DRAW ANGLES

The roof itself is a lot easier to draw than it would be to construct. It involves no complex line manipulation and very few objects. You will have to zoom out so as to be able to see the entire roof.

The sloping sides of the roof are 30 degrees from the horizontal. This slope was chosen because it provides the maximum utilization of materials for a climate-related design which is still in keeping with the aesthetics and functionality of the overall architectural criteria of the structure. Well, it was really chosen because CorelDRAW can do 30-degree angles very easily. It's worth noting here that although it's easier to draw angled lines using the Constrain feature's 15-degree increments, CorelDRAW is quite capable of producing lines at any angle you like. Changing the line Constrain Angle using the Preferences dialog box was touched on earlier.

Select the pencil tool to draw the outlines of the roof. Constrain the lines to horizontal (top) and 30 degrees (sides) by using the Ctrl key while drawing. I placed the top line seventy millimeters above the eaves, but you can choose any distance which looks good to you.

If you drew your top line before you drew your angled sides, chances are the horizontal line is the wrong length. Select the pick tool and click on the line. Handles will appear around it. Grab an end handle—the center one from either end's triplet of marks—and adjust the length of the line until it meets the angled lines of the sides. You might want to zoom in to make sure that everything matches perfectly.

The last task in completing the drawing is to fill the roof area with horizontal lines. Once again, except for the fact that we aren't using fills just yet, this could be done with a PostScript fill. In this case, we'll fill it with individual lines.

Using the Constrain feature and the pencil tool, draw a horizontal line a half a centimeter below the top of the roof. Use the Preferences item of the Special menu to set the horizontal displacement for duplicates to 0 and the vertical displacement to −5 millimeters. Now duplicate the line by pressing Ctrl-D as often as is required to fill the roof area.

Your work space should look like the one in Figure 2.16.

Unfortunately, there's no easy way to make the lines expand to meet the edges of the roof. You will have to select each one and drag it until it's long enough. This doesn't take very long—there aren't all that many lines.

Save your work—you're done.

PRINTING LARGE DRAWINGS

The printers that CorelDRAW will drive come in all sorts of sizes. This picture will not print on a single sheet of $8^1/_2$-by-11" paper. It will fit on a larger 11-by-17" sheet, should you have a laser printer capable of handling one. It can also be tiled, spreading it over multiple sheets. All these options—and quite a few more—will be discussed in detail in Chapter 6. For the moment, this example assumes that you'll be using regular letter-size paper in a conventional laser printer.

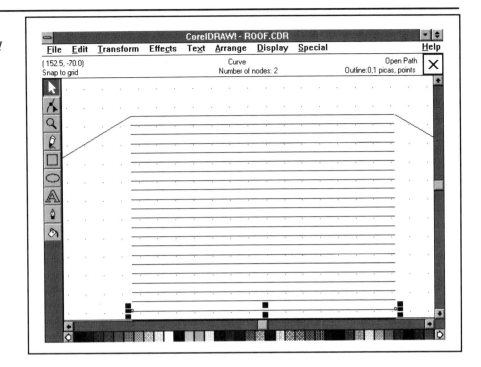

The roof with identical horizontal lines

At this point, the drawing of the roof is probably too large to print. If you zoom to display the entire printable work space, you will probably find that the image is bigger than the printable part of the work area, as shown in Figure 2.17. You will have to scale it down a bit.

Reducing the Picture

The easiest way to scale the picture down is to select the whole thing—either with the pick tool or by using the Select All item of the Edit menu—and group it into a single object. Use the Stretch & Mirror item of the Transform menu to resize this object. If you set both the Stretch Horizontally and Stretch Vertically values to 75, the drawing will be reduced—kind of the opposite of being stretched—to 75 percent of its current size. This box is shown with the controls set up for this scale factor in Figure 2.18.

Now try printing the picture. Printing under CorelDRAW is dead easy—all you have to do is select Print from the File menu. A dialog box with a lot of options will appear. Since you'll be printing exactly what appears in this drawing with no embellishments, you can ignore all of these. Just click

FIGURE 2.17:

*The picture larger
than the page*

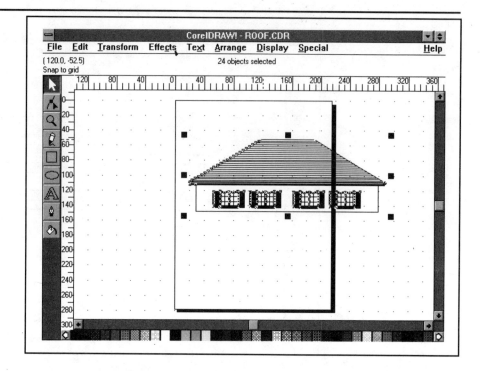

FIGURE 2.18:

*The Stretch & Mirror
dialog box set to scale
the image down to
three quarters of its
original size*

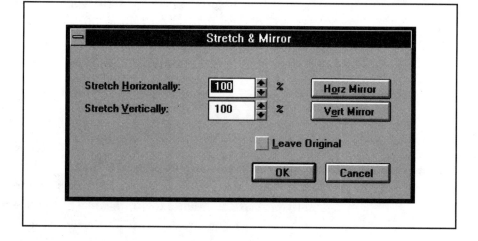

on OK or hit ↵ to accept the defaults. We'll be discussing most of these options later.

Depending on your printer and several other factors, you might not
like the results that you get from your first attempt at printing the completed

drawing. The lines which make up the shutter slats are close enough that they might run together into solid black areas. Some of the other fine detail may also get lost. Remember that if you reduce the size of a drawing under CorelDRAW the details are not lost in the picture itself, but they may get so fine as to be beyond the ability of your printer to manage them.

Another problem is the one illustrated in Figure 2.19. In this print, magnified to show the effect, the shutter slats are distinct lines, but they have become irregularly spaced. This has occurred because the printer has been told to print lines with greater positional accuracy than it could manage. The vertical positions of the lines have been fudged by the printer to the nearest increments of its own internal grid, with the result that they are no longer uniformly spaced.

When you're creating complex drawings under CorelDRAW it's very important to keep in mind the characteristics of the output device which will ultimately reproduce your work. Inasmuch as this chapter started off with a picture of the complete drawing—and inasmuch as that drawing exhibited none of the problems we've just discussed—there's obviously a way around printer difficulties. The solution is actually pretty simple: All of these print aberrations will vanish if the image being printed gets a little bigger.

FIGURE 2.19:

A spacing problem

Rotating and Enlarging the Picture

As things stand, enlarging the drawing would cause it to spill off the paper. That's why we reduced it in the first place. However, since the sheet we're printing on is longer than it is wide, we could expand the image if it were to be printed lengthwise along the paper instead of across it. This is called printing in landscape mode.

The first thing to do in making the drawing use more of the paper is to rotate it. You could do this with the Rotate & Skew item from the Transform menu, but it's probably more interesting at this point to use Corel-DRAW's free-rotation feature.

Using the Rotation and Skew Marks

If you're in a hurry to get to this rotate-and-skew mode you can just double click on an object. Conversely, if you get to this mode by mistake, clicking on the object yet again will get you back to the normal selection mode.

If you select an object, such as a rectangle or a group of paths, the by-now-familiar handles will appear around it. However, if you click again on one of the lines of the object—that is, if you select it while it's already selected—the handles will change to arrows, as shown in Figure 2.20. These arrows are called *rotation marks* for the ones at the corners of the selection rectangle and *skew marks* for those along the sides. You will also notice that a dot with a circle around it has appeared roughly in the center of the object. This is called the *pivot*.

Select the drawing—it should previously have been grouped into a single object. Click on the selected object to change the handles into rotation and skew marks. Move your cursor to one of the rotation marks. Your cursor will turn into a cross when it's correctly positioned. Grab the rotation mark and turn the image until it's aligned with the long edge of the page. Your cursor will turn into a partial circle with upward-pointing arrow heads. If you move slowly enough, you can read the current rotation angle displayed at the top of the window. You should be aiming for exactly 90 degrees.

You might find that it's a bit tricky to get the rotation value to stop at exactly 90 degrees. You can hold down the Ctrl key to enable the angle Constrain feature. As with drawing lines, this forces rotation to move in 15-degree increments.

FIGURE 2.20:

Rotation and skew marks

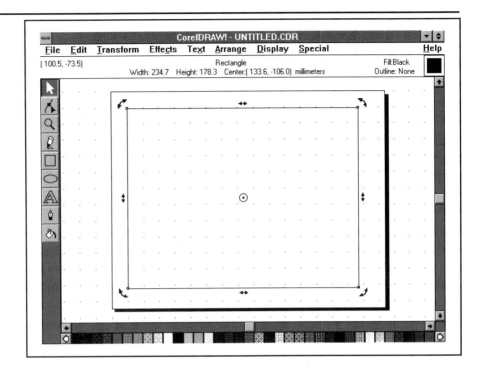

CAUTION *There is a very important consideration in scaling the drawing up for printing. Laser printers do not print right to the edges of their paper. The exact amount of dead space varies from printer to printer, but it's not a bad idea to leave a quarter of an inch between the extremes of your drawing and the edge of the printable area of the CorelDRAW workspace.*

When you stop rotating the image, your cursor will turn into an hourglass. This indicates that CorelDRAW is working on transforming all the paths in the object you've rotated so they will appear as you've positioned them. This may take a few moments.

With the drawing rotated, you'll be able to increase its size to fill a lot more of the page. Click on the drawing to change the rotate and skew marks back to selection marks. Grab one of the corner marks and drag it to increase the size of the object. As long as you use a corner mark, the drawing will expand in both dimensions equally. Adjust the drawing using whichever corner marks you need until it fairly fills the page.

Try printing your drawing again. You should find some pretty respectable hard copy emerging from your printer.

It's worth noting that some of the things you've just done to the drawing to make it print—scaling it and such—can be handled by the printer driver itself without your having to actually change anything in your drawing. However, in doing it the hard way, you've gotten to try out a number of CorelDRAW tools and facilities.

A Digression on Complex Drawings

In drawing the upper story of a house, we did quite a few things in less than ideal ways for the sake of illustrating things about CorelDRAW. These are things you would want to improve upon if you were confronted with really having to produce a complex architectural drawing or other intricate piece of art.

One of the things which seems to limit CorelDRAW's ability to draw things like the upper story—and perhaps the whole house that it would be a part of—is the way the program bogs down when it's confronted with lots of objects. You might have noticed that it got a bit tedious when it was redrawing its screen after zooming out, and even when you were simply adding objects to the drawing toward the end of the session. This is partially the fault of the way we created the picture.

CorelDRAW treats grouped objects as individual paths which just happen to have something to do with each other. Thus, if there are 385 objects in a drawing—this being the actual number of objects in my version of the second story—CorelDRAW will have 385 entries in its object list to paw through every time you ask it to select an object or add something to the list.

Combined paths, however, are treated as single objects. This speeds up CorelDRAW enormously, and also reduces the amount of memory it uses to store its object list. In many situations, you should combine objects rather than group them. We'll discuss those situations in greater detail later.

Another drawback to handling big drawings with lots of paths is that when you work on part of a drawing, all the other parts must regenerate themselves to become visible. If we had drawn the entire house that this second story is part of, the whole house would have been redrawn to the screen each time you zoomed to the full page. This would have involved some intolerable waiting.

CorelDRAW offers an easy way around this. You can draw complex pictures in sections, one section to a file. When all the sections are complete, CorelDRAW lets you import them into a single file and combine them into a finished picture. This, too, will be discussed in greater detail later in this book.

There's a lot that can be done with CorelDRAW when you're confronted with large images to manipulate. Much of what you can get together when you're running at the edges of CorelDRAW's abilities will be determined by your understanding of the package itself and by a little common sense.

NOTE NOTE *The current profusion of high-speed systems with 16 or more megabytes of memory, huge hard drives, and sophisticated display systems is due to interest in using applications like CorelDRAW to handle complex tasks. The amount of juggling you will have to undertake to deal with large CorelDRAW graphics will be determined both by your level of patience and by the power of your computer. See Appendix A for a more complete discussion of the hardware CorelDRAW will run on.*

DRAWING CIRCLES AND SECTIONS: A PIE CHART

The upper story of the house was a complex drawing, but a very simple exercise, as there were really no difficult drawing techniques used to execute it.

CorelDRAW gurus will argue that nothing is really difficult. In a sense this is true—any drawing can be reduced to a series of simple tasks. The drawing in Figure 2.21 may or may not look to you like a series of simple tasks. If you have ever tried to get professional looking business graphics created—or worse, tried to do them yourself with a software package ostensibly designed for the task—you may well be daunted by the prospect of trying to make this pie chart.

This pie chart can be done in five or ten minutes if you're familiar with CorelDRAW. By the time you've got this book under your belt, things like this will spring from your fingertips in less time than it takes most people to get a purchase order written up for a graphics house.

This drawing encompasses a number of elements which are not strictly speaking part of this chapter, most notably fills and text; however, we'll be making only light use of them here. You'll encounter the proper explanations of these facilities over the next two chapters.

There are a number of important things to note about the pie chart. It has sections, of course, each of which is filled with a different gray shade. All of them match up perfectly. There's an exploded section which also looks as if it would match perfectly. There's a drop shadow behind the chart to give it depth. There are smooth, angled lines pointing to the various sections.

The whole work appears professional, and if these guys ever had a chance of getting a color PostScript printer for their art department—which they don't, due to the nature of the exploded segment of the chart—this chart would do it for them.

The reason this chart was so easy to put together is largely tied up in the way the CorelDRAW shape tool behaves when it's applied to ellipses. Because business graphics are very hot now, the authors of the package have gone to some length to make things like this work out easily.

To begin with, you will observe that this drawing lends itself to landscape orientation—it's wider than it is long. For this reason, we'll start by doing something we would have done with the house drawing had it been a real-world project. We'll change the orientation of the page in the work space.

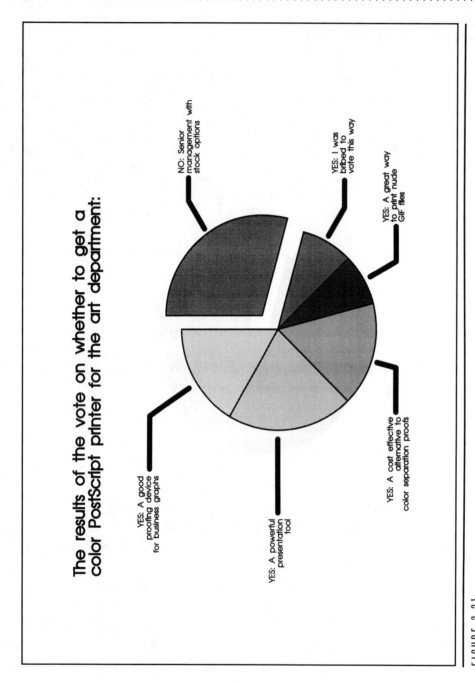

The results of the vote on whether to get a
color PostScript printer for the art department:

NO: Senior
management with
stock options

YES: I was
bribed to
vote this way

YES: A great way
to print nude
GIF files

YES: A good
proofing device
for business graphs

YES: A powerful
presentation
tool

YES: A cost effective
alternative to
color separation proofs

FIGURE 2.21:
A pie chart

Start with a blank work space by selecting New from the File menu. If you have not already exited CorelDRAW since completing the previous drawing, this will wipe out any remnants of the house drawing which might be hanging around.

Select Page Setup from the File menu. A dialog box like the one in Figure 2.22 will appear. Change the Orientation item from portrait to landscape by clicking on the radio button next to Landscape. When you click on OK to accept this change, you will note that the printable part of the CorelDRAW page is now oriented with its long dimension horizontal.

Select the ellipse tool. As with most of the tools that actually do any drawing, the ellipse tool can be constrained with the Ctrl key. If you constrain it, you'll find that it draws perfect circles, rather than ellipses. Use it in this way to draw a circle 12 centimeters (120 millimeters) across. Actually, neither the size nor the units of measurement of the circle matter in this drawing. If you want to revert to inches or explore the as-yet-unexplained world of picas and points, you are free to do so.

Business graphics tend to get modified a lot. In this case, sufficient lobbying or threats by the art department could reduce the relative size of the exploded segment, in which case the chart would have to be redrawn.

FIGURE 2.22:

The Page Setup dialog box from the File menu

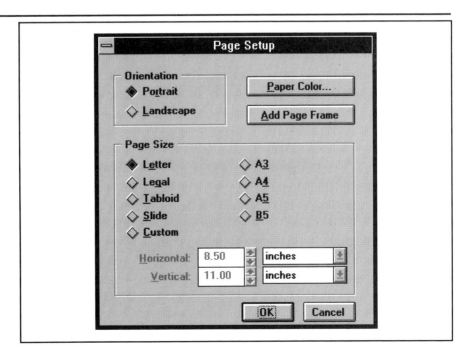

For this reason, it's handy to have the original circle nearby to change or add segments later on.

We are going to make use of the work area outside the printable page in this drawing. Select the circle you've drawn and drag it off the drawing page into the work area. This will be your template for creating the various segments of the pie chart; it will be duplicated many times, but the original object will remain. Having the basic pie outside the printed area allows you to leave it in the drawing file without having it appear in your hard copy.

Your work space should look like the one in Figure 2.23.

CREATING A SEGMENT

Let's create the segment of the chart which represents people who felt that a color PostScript printer would make a good proofing device for business graphs. Select your template circle and duplicate it by hitting Ctrl-D. Drag the duplicate into the printable area. Select the shape tool and select the circle you'll be working with.

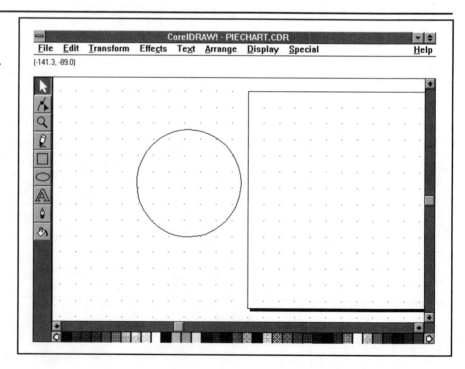

FIGURE 2.23:

CorelDRAW all ready to draw a pie chart. The basic pie is off to the left

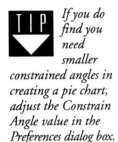

If you do find you need smaller constrained angles in creating a pie chart, adjust the Constrain Angle value in the Preferences dialog box.

If you have a need for an arc without the lines, just move the shape-tool cursor slightly outside the perimeter as you're dragging the node. The connecting lines will vanish.

You'll be splitting the circle into pie slices. If you hold down the Ctrl key, these slices will be constrained to multiples of 15 degrees. You don't have to constrain your segments in this way, but it sure speeds things up a lot as it makes aligning the various segments easy. At least for the sake of this exercise, I recommend that you constrain the angles. When you try to create a real pie chart you'll probably find anyway that very few people can quickly spot the difference between, for example, a 15-degree angle and a 17-degree angle.

When you select a circle or an ellipse with the shape tool, a single node mark will appear either at the top or the bottom of the object. In this case it should be at the top. Using the shape tool cursor, grab the node and drag it counterclockwise around the perimeter. If you keep the cursor just inside the perimeter, the ends of the arc will automatically generate lines to the original center of the circle.

When you began dragging the node around, you may have noticed that you left a second node behind. In splitting the circle into an arc, CorelDRAW had to add a node to the object. Both nodes can be dragged, as we'll see in a moment.

When you have created a wedge which looks to be about right, release the node you've been dragging. Your work space should look like the one in Figure 2.24.

You will be adding the text and other objects of the drawing later once the graph has been completed.

ALIGNING ADDITIONAL SEGMENTS

Let's add the next segment to the graph. This is where CorelDRAW will prove to be very clever at this sort of drawing. As before, select the template circle, duplicate it, and drag the duplicate over to the printable area. Don't worry about positioning it exactly. Select it with the shape tool and start dragging the node around, as before. Make sure you have the Ctrl key down while you're dragging the node.

In this case, you will have to drag both nodes. Once you have moved the first one down to the far end of where the new segment will be, you'll have to release it and go drag the second one—the node CorelDRAW added when you started dragging to form the first arc. This will form the other side of the wedge.

FIGURE 2.24:
One segment of the pie chart in place

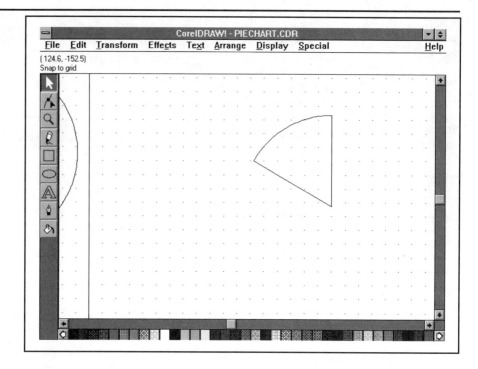

You might have to take several shots at getting the nodes positioned properly. CorelDRAW allows you to go back and move them as often as you need to in order to arrive at the arc you're after.

Your work space should now look something like the one shown in Figure 2.25.

Chances are the second segment will not be positioned properly with respect to the first one. You can have CorelDRAW move it automatically so the alignment is perfect. As far as CorelDRAW is concerned, when you turn a circle into a wedge—a pie chart segment—the whole circle still remains as an object. You can see this if you select one of the segments you've drawn. The rectangle formed by the selection marks will be the size of the original circle even though only a portion of the circle is displayed.

If you click on the selected circle to get the rotation and skew marks, you'll note that the pivot marking the center of the object is at the point of the wedge, that is, at the original center of the circle. In order to make the two segments fit together, you must get the centers of the two original circles to rest on the same point. CorelDRAW will handle this for you. Use the pick

*Adding a second seg-
ment to the pie chart*

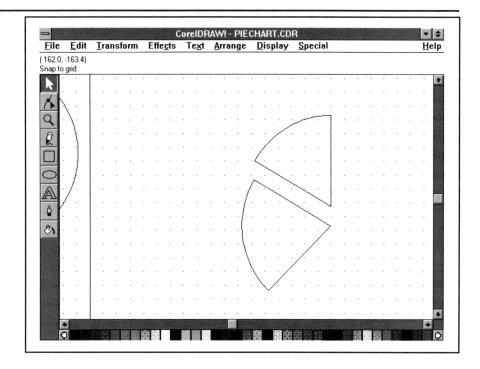

tool to select both segments by drawing a marquee to encompass them both.
You might notice that the status line above the work space informs you that
you have two objects selected. Now select Align from the Arrange menu.
You will see a dialog box like the one in Figure 2.26.

Select the Center option for both the horizontal and vertical directions
and click on OK. The two segments will be redrawn perfectly aligned.

Add the remaining segments to the pie chart by duplicating the
template circle and making each duplicate into another wedge. You can align
them as you go or all at once when you've completed all the Yes sections of
the pie chart.

The No portion of the chart then is obviously just a last segment which
is not positioned to fit perfectly into the gap left in the chart.

If you're working in the Edit Wireframe mode, you might want to use
one of the preview options to look at your work. The segments should have
no fills as yet.

Group together the objects you have created thus far.

The Align dialog box
from the Arrange menu

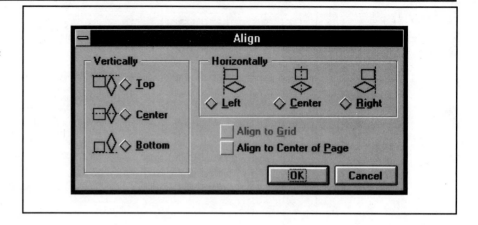

USING FILLS—THE VERY SHORT FORM

In order to make the drop shadow appear as a shadow, you will have to give it a fill. We haven't actually used fills for anything as yet, but at this level they're pretty easy. We will use numerical fill values for this drawing, rather than the basic default fills that the fill tool flyout menu offers us.

Adding a Drop Shadow

The Edit Wireframe mode can be very useful for finding objects with no fill and no outline which seem to have become lost in a complex drawing. In Edit Wireframe mode, all outlines will be shown in your CorelDRAW workspace, even if they wouldn't really print.

The drop shadow behind the pie chart is very easy to manage, and will serve as a useful example of how CorelDRAW deals with overlapping objects. Select the pie chart you have grouped into a single object and duplicate it. Place the duplicate slightly above and to the left of the original. Snap To Grid, Snap To Guidelines, and Snap To Objects all must be off.

Select the duplicate pie chart, which is to become the drop shadow. You will notice in the completed example back in Figure 2.21 that the drop shadow has no rules around it. You should make invisible the rules it inherited from its parent object, the real pie chart.

Select the outline pen tool. Click on the no-line-width icon, the X. If you're working in the default drawing in preview mode of CorelDRAW, the drop shadow will appear to vanish. It's still there—it just has no fill and no outline, and consequently nothing to indicate its presence save for its handles.

With the drop shadow selected, click on the fill tool. When the fly out menu appears, click on the leftmost item to pop up the fill precise-adjustment box. It should look like Figure 2.27, except that the tint value

TIP

If you use the Shift-F9 split-screen preview, you might have to click in the preview window to get it to redraw the pie chart. This is because in some situations the program hesitates to see if you're going to do something further before it decides you want an image redrawn. Clicking in the preview window overrides the hesitation.

will initially be set to 100, that is, fully black. Change it to 10 percent black, as shown in the figure, and click on OK.

You will notice that you have a slight problem—it will be immediately visible in the default CorelDRAW display mode, and in the preview if you've been working in the Edit Wireframe mode. The drop shadow appears to be in front of the pie chart. This has happened because CorelDRAW places objects on the screen in the order they're created unless it's told to do otherwise. With the drop shadow selected, use the To Back item in the Arrange menu to put it behind the pie chart object. CorelDRAW will automatically hide the part of the back object obscured by the front object.

It's worth noting that there are other ways to set fill colors, several of which would be quicker than the one you've just used. They'll be discussed at length in the next chapter of this book.

Shading and Outlining the Segments

There are two major tasks left in drawing the pie chart itself. The first involves setting the line thickness, or weight, of the outlines of the segments. As the segments of the pie chart have been grouped into a single object, it's

FIGURE 2.27:

Setting the fill for the drop shadow

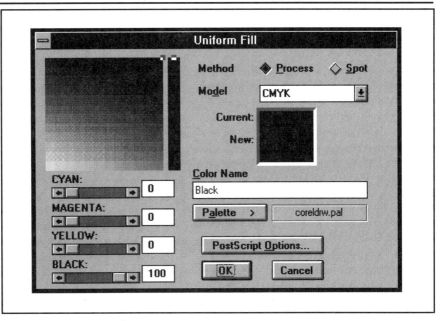

very easy to set all the lines at the same time. Select the pie chart object with the pick tool—making sure you don't get the drop shadow by mistake—and then select the outline pen tool. Click on one of the middle line-thickness icons. This line weight will now be applied to all the lines in the selected object.

Note that the line colors will default to black, so you don't have to set the line color explicitly. The only time you'll need the lower level of icons in the outline pen tool's flyout menu is when a line is to be drawn in color or in gray rather than solid black.

The next step of the drawing involves changing the fill patterns of the individual segments. You can't do this while the segments are grouped into a single object, so select the pie chart if it isn't currently selected and use the Ungroup item of the Arrange menu to return the segments to individual objects.

Select each segment in turn and use the fill tool's flyout menu to select a fill for it. In the case of a drawing like this one, it's probably preferable to use the precise-adjustment box to set the gray levels, just as you did with the drop shadow.

Avoid the extremes of the gray levels. The lightest gray shade you use for a segment shouldn't be much below 20 percent black. The darkest probably shouldn't be above 70 percent black. This helps prevent the tone from getting lost in the outlines. Try to arrange not to have two similar gray levels in adjacent segments.

When you've finished shading each segment, your work space should look like Figure 2.28. This would be a good time to use the Save As item in the File menu to assign a file name to your drawing and save your work to disk.

In real-world business graphics, you would probably use colored fills, rather than gray levels. These will be discussed in detail in the next chapter. It might well be argued that they'd be inappropriate here, in that the creators of this pie chart hope to use it to talk their way into a color printer. If they could reproduce the chart in color, there would be no need for its existence in the first place.

USING TEXT: ADDING LABELS

Adding text to a drawing under CorelDRAW is both one of the most effortless of its capabilities and ultimately one of the most fun when you get into

*The completed pie chart
and drop shadow*

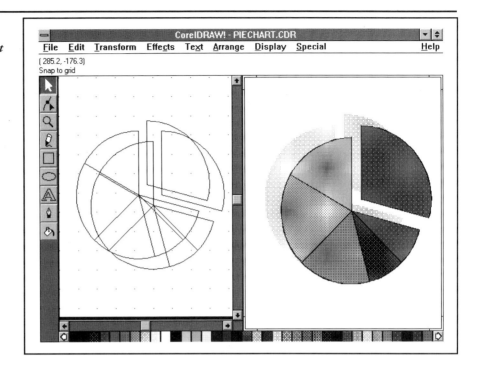

the nuances of it. It will be dealt with in much greater detail later in this book, but we'll have a quick look at it here to see how to polish off the pie chart.

Zoom out as necessary so you can see the whole pie chart.

Select the text tool. Your cursor will change to a cross. This is the CorelDRAW text cursor. Click on your drawing where you think the text for the first segment should go—let's start with the "YES: A good proofing device for business graphs" segment. Don't worry about exactly where the text is to go. You can position it accurately after it has been placed.

A text cursor will appear. Type in your text. Chances are that just about everything about the text will not be as you intended—you'll be changing it in a moment. With your text entered, select the pick tool. This will automatically select your text.

To change the characteristics of a selected block of text, choose Edit Text from the Edit menu, or just hit Ctrl-T. A dialog box like the one in Figure 2.29 will appear with your text in it. The Justification will be Left, and the default Point Size will be 24 points, which is entirely too big. Change this to 12 points. You can edit the text if you like.

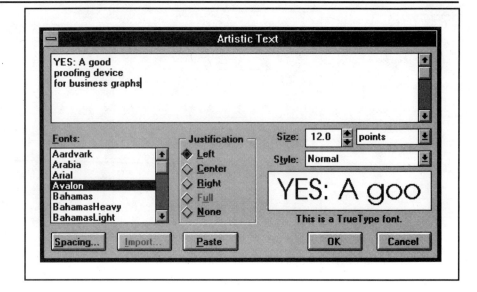

The text for the segments on the left should line up along the right margin of the areas they occupy. They are thus said to be right-aligned. The text on the other side of the chart is left-aligned. The text editing window defaults to left alignment. Select the Right justification radio button located to the right of the Fonts selection window, and click on OK to accept your text.

If you discover after you've left the Artistic Text dialog box that you've committed a few typographical errors in entering the text, or that you forgot to reduce the point size, for example, you'll be happy to know that you can edit any of the parameters of previously entered text. You can edit text under CorelDRAW even after you've transformed it, twisted it, wrapped it into spirals, or pasted it onto the back of a royal ball python and sent it slithering off into the grass. Simply select the offending text with the pick tool and then use the Edit Text item of the Edit menu—or use the Ctrl-T keyboard shortcut—to return to the Artistic Text dialog box for another shot at it.

You can now position the text roughly where you think it should go in relation to the pie chart segment it describes. Simply select it with the pick tool and drag it as you would any other object. The nudge function—using the four cursor-positioning keys of your keyboard—can also be handy for adjusting the location of some text. You might have to fine-tune the location of your text later on.

You can make changes to the actual text in a text object by selecting the text tool and clicking in the text to be altered. A text insertion cursor will appear. Use the Backspace and Delete keys to delete text to the left and the right of the cursor, respectively, and the left and right arrow keys to move the cursor. While you can also edit text using the Text Edit dialog box, as discussed a moment ago, this is a lot quicker and it allows you to see exactly how your edited text fits among the other elements of your drawing.

Add the rest of the text to the drawing in the same way, changing the alignment when you switch from one side of the chart to the other. Note that once you've selected the typographic characteristics for the first text you entered into your drawing, these characteristics will apply to all the subsequent text you create until you again explicitly change some of them with the Artistic Text dialog box.

Now add the title of the chart: "The results of the vote on whether to get a color PostScript printer for the art department:". This is the same font in 24 points rather than in 12. The title text is left-aligned.

Just like the simpler objects we've seen thus far, text under CorelDRAW has outline and fill attributes. These may not have defaulted to the most sensible values for the text you've just placed in your drawing. You can select all the text and set the outline and fill attributes of the whole lot at once.

To select all the text blocks at one time, click on the first one as you would normally do to select it. Having done this, hold down the Shift key while you proceed to click on all the others. As long as Shift is down, you can add objects to the selected group. This will not actually group the objects together as the Group feature under the Arrange menu would; it will only select them long enough for you to change them all.

Use the outline pen tool's flyout menu to select a hairline rule for text— that's the icon with a line and two arrowheads—and then the fill tool's flyout menu to select black fill.

Drawing Connecting Lines for the Labels

The last step in completing the pie chart is adding the heavy lines which run from the text to the segments. Except for the straight line associated with the "YES: A powerful presentation tool" segment, each of these is made up of two line segments handled by CorelDRAW as a single object.

Let's start with the line for the segment which represents the senior management with stock options. It will probably help if you zoom in on this area. To refresh your memory on how to draw this kind of object, the steps are listed here.

1. Select the pencil tool.

2. Place your mouse cursor to the left of the text.

3. Hold down the Ctrl key throughout the rest of these steps to constrain the line.

4. Click to anchor the line.

5. Move the cursor left for about half the distance between the text and the pie chart segment.

6. Click to anchor the end of the line.

7. Click again in the same spot to start the second line. This will add it to the object formed by the first line, rather than starting a new object.

8. Move the cursor further left and down. Because the Ctrl key is down—the Constrain feature is active—the line will jump down by 15 degrees.

9. When you have the line where you want it, click to anchor its free end.

Having drawn the line, you can set the line width and a few other attributes to make it look like the lines back in Figure 2.21. Use the pick tool to select the two-line object you've just created if it's not presently selected. Click on the outline pen tool and select the fattest line width, the one at the far right of the flyout menu. Then click on the outline pen tool again and click on the upper-left icon to pop up the precise-alignment box. Set the Line Caps and Corners as shown in Figure 2.30.

You might want to experiment with this dialog box to see what other sorts of lines you can come up with.

You can add the connecting lines to the rest of the segments in the same way. When you're finished, make sure you save your work.

If you print your pie chart it should look something like the one back in Figure 2.21.

The pie chart you've just created is a very versatile drawing. It can be exported as any of a number of sorts of files, to pour into desktop-published documents under Ventura Publisher and PageMaker or some of the higher-end word processors like Microsoft Word and WordPerfect. Assuming that your side of the argument lost in the discussion about getting a color PostScript printer, you could still change the fill patterns to colors and have the

FIGURE 2.30:

Setting up the line characteristics for a connecting line

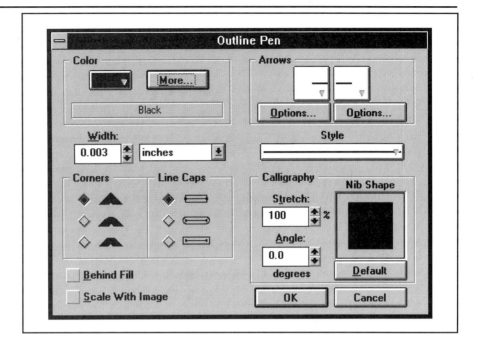

resulting file output by a graphics house that does have a color printer. There are companies which will take your CorelDRAW files and make presentation-quality slides from them. You can even have CorelDRAW generate color separations for use with web or offset printing.

There's a final note about this pie chart. The CorelDRAW package comes with a dedicated charting application, CorelCHART, which will also graph numerical information and produce attractive, sophisticated displays from it. The real purpose of this project was to play with the CorelDRAW shape tool more than to create a real-world drawing; you might find that CorelCHART provides a better way to produce graphics like this one when the need for them really turns up. It will be discussed in detail in Chapter 10 of this book.

If you consider how long it took you to draw this chart—and how much less it will take next time, now that you know what you're doing—you'll probably see why CorelDRAW is such a powerful tool to have around.

DRAWING WITH CURVES AND MIRRORS: THE ART OF THE LUTE

The lute was a medieval instrument which was a precursor to the modern guitar—in much the same way that the Rolls Royce Silver Phantom IV was a precursor to the modern Honda Civic. Lutes were characterized by large, bowl-shaped bodies and short necks having a large number of doubled strings. The exact string count varied from lute to lute.

An aerial view of a typical lute can be seen in Figure 2.31. Actually, this is CorelDRAW's interpretation of a lute. Two very important bits of lute lore are missing from this illustration. The first is any vestige of strings, which have been omitted for the sake of clarity. The other is the rose. The sound hole of a lute is not simply an opening in the top, as is the case with a guitar. It is traditionally inlaid with a complex carved wooden disk, or rose. The rose has been omitted from this drawing because a lute rose is a very involved

FIGURE 2.31:

A lute as seen by CorelDRAW

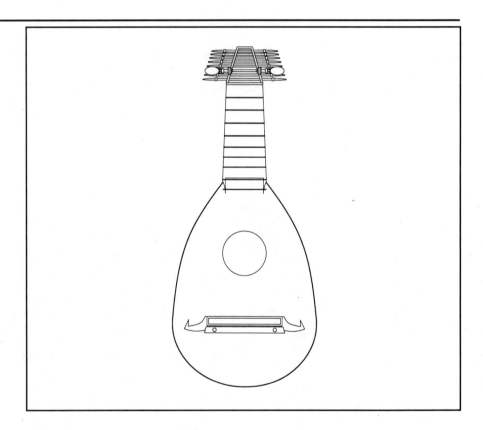

object, and quite the chore to draw. We will return to the topic of lute roses later in this book.

The drawing in Figure 2.31 is of a contemporary lute, from a design by Robert S. Cooper of Savannah, Georgia.

Inasmuch as the title of this book makes little mention of the construction or history of lutes, you might well ask what this one is doing here. In fact, lutes are representative of a large body of objects which get drawn using packages like CorelDRAW. The important aspect of the lute from the point of view of this book is not so much its history as its symmetry: One half of a lute looks very much like the other half of a lute. For purposes of simplicity, we will ignore the fact that the tuning pegs on a real lute are not in fact arranged symmetrically. Figure 2.32 illustrates what you'll actually be drawing. When it's complete, you'll be able to create the whole lute by simply duplicating this collection of objects, mirroring it vertically, and dragging the duplicate so it lines up with the original.

FIGURE 2.32:
Half a lute

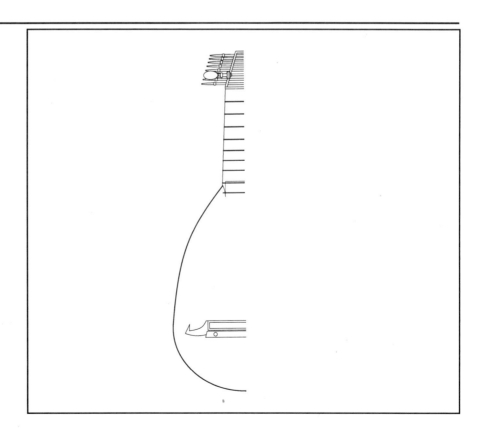

CorelDRAW offers all sorts of ways to deal with complex, symmetrical drawings like this one. Whether you're designing a logo, a carburetor, or a better lute, being able to work with symmetrical drawings will save you at least half the time it would have taken to draw everything from scratch.

Save your work periodically as you go through this drawing. There are a number of areas in which it's fairly easy to trash what you've done beyond easy repair. It's a great deal easier to simply revert to your most recently saved version when this happens than it is to try to pick through a tangle of paths and objects.

If your work space is still in landscape mode from the last drawing, return it to portrait mode with the Page Setup item of the File menu.

DRAWING THE LUTE BODY

In drawing the lute, make sure the Snap To Grid feature, as found in the Display menu, is off. There's too much tiny detail in this drawing to make the grid feature of much use.

You can extract horizontal guides from the ruler at the top of the Corel-DRAW work space as well. You can have multiple guides of each type in a single drawing. If you have the Snap To Grid feature enabled, the guides will snap themselves to grid marks. If you have the Snap To Guidelines feature enabled—also available in the Display menu—other objects will tend to snap to the nearest guide, as they might otherwise have done to the nearest grid mark.

The first thing to place in the drawing of the lute will ultimately not be there when the drawing is finally printed. We're going to use a hitherto undiscovered feature of CorelDRAW—its guidelines. *Guidelines* are lines that appear on your screen, but not in your final drawing.

If the rules in your CorelDRAW work space have not been previously enabled, enable them now using the Show Rulers item of the Display menu. Move your mouse cursor to the vertical ruler at the left side of your work space and click and drag the ruler to the right. Actually, you can't move the rulers—a dotted line will accompany your mouse cursor. This is a guideline—it will let you know where your axis of symmetry lies. Position the guideline in the center of the printed part of the work space.

The outline of the lute body is created with two curves. The upper one is a straight path which has been converted to curves and bent using curve handles. The lower curve is a portion of an ellipse. You may recall using both of these capabilities earlier in this chapter. You will apply these techniques a bit differently in this instance.

There is a certain amount of freehand manipulation inherent in drawing a lute, and your drawing may not come out looking exactly like the one in Figure 2.31. This is quite acceptable—the relative shapes and dimensions of lutes varied a lot. No matter what your lute winds up looking like, chances are there used to be one just like it.

Start by drawing the lower part of the body. Select the ellipse tool and draw a large ellipse which is wider than it is high. You will not want to have the Constrain feature active for this object—in other words, leave the Ctrl key alone—as you'll want an ellipse rather than a true circle. Select and drag the ellipse with the pick tool so it lies across the axis line of the drawing. When you mirror the lute half, the tails of the ellipses that extend across the center guide line can be moved to smooth out the curve.

Unless you plan to output this drawing on a pen plotter, slight overlaps in horizontal lines where the two halves of the lute join will not show on the final drawing. On the other hand, a gap between the two halves most certainly will be visible. Thus, it's better to have the lines which touch the center line of the drawing a bit too long rather than a bit too short.

Using the shape tool, grab the node of the ellipse and turn the ellipse into an arc which runs from about six o'clock until a bit beyond nine o'clock. You may have to adjust the upper end of the arc slightly later on.

Make sure you keep the shape tool's cursor slightly outside the perimeter of the ellipse so you wind up simply with an arc rather than a wedge. When you're finished, zoom in on the lower end of the arc temporarily to make sure that it lies over the center guide.

The upper part of the body involves bending curves, which is still more inexact, but kind of pleasing to do. Select the pencil tool and draw a line from the upper end of the arc you've just created up to where you want the neck of the lute to start. This will be an approximation, of course. Use the shape tool to select the upper node of the line you've just drawn. The line should thicken to indicate that it has been selected. Click on the node again to pop up the node menu. Select *toCurve*. Handles should sprout from the ends of the line.

Grab the handles and manipulate the curve until it flows smoothly into the arc of the ellipse. When you think you have it about right, zoom in on the joint between the upper and lower curves. If the two lines don't quite meet, use the shape tool cursor to pull the end of the upper line to meet the top of the lower one. You might also have to adjust the end of the lower arc a bit.

Your work space should now look like the one in Figure 2.33.

This is another area wherein you could use the Bézier drawing mode of the CorelDRAW pencil tool, rather than draw a straight line and convert it to a curve. I prefer to start with a straight line for an object like this one, as the final line really is a slightly bent segment, rather than a very pronounced curve. You might want to try creating this line segment both ways to see which approach seems more natural to you.

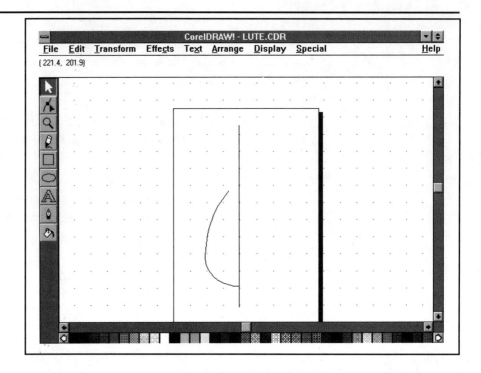

If getting these curves to come out the way you want them seems a bit frustrating, bear in mind that it takes a week and a half to lay up the body of a real lute. You're getting off relatively easily.

DRAWING THE BRIDGE

The bridge of the lute is a fairly involved detail. You might want to zoom in a bit. The various elements can be seen in Figure 2.34.

The center part of the bridge—the functional bit which holds the strings—is made up of lines drawn with the pencil tool. Because you're actually going to draw only half the lute, the center of the bridge must be left open. This is why you can't use the rectangle tool for this task. Use the Constrain feature to make sure your lines come out straight.

Draw the dowel in the lower part of the bridge with the circle tool—the ellipse tool constrained with the Ctrl key.

FIGURE 2.34:

The bridge of the lute

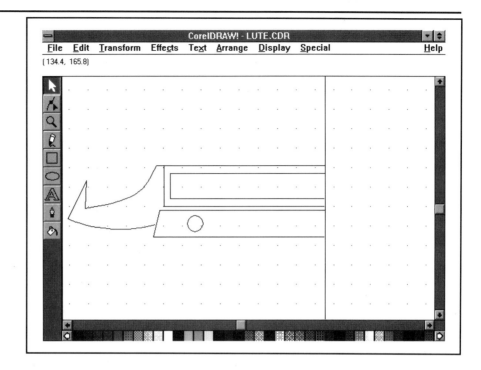

The horn that sticks out to the left of the bridge is somewhat ornamental. Draw it by approximating it with straight lines and then converting some of the lines to curves, or use the Bézier curve drawing mode of the pencil tool.

You could draw the circle for the sound hole of the lute at this time, but it would be very hard to position it accurately. Because it would overlap the center guide of the drawing, there would be two of them when the first half of the lute was duplicated and flipped. It's a lot easier to add the circle when the two halves have been assembled.

DRAWING THE NECK AND MEASURING FRET DISTANCES

The neck of the lute is fairly easy to draw. The hook where it meets the body is formed by drawing straight lines with the pencil tool and then converting the appropriate one to a curve with the shape tool, or by using the Bézier curve mode of the pencil tool. Once again, it's important to zoom in on the place where the horizontal line meets the center guide of the drawing and make sure that it just overlaps the guide.

The frets of a lute consisted of strings made of animal gut tied around the neck at suitable intervals. To create a fret, draw a line anywhere across the neck with the pencil tool, using the Constrain feature. Next, set the vertical duplicate displacement values in the Preferences dialog box to result in duplicates being placed very slightly below the original. Something on the order of −0.50 to −1.00 millimeters was about right for my drawing. Select the line and duplicate it.

The rounded end of the fret is drawn by using the ellipse tool. Zoom in and use the shape tool to make the ellipse into an arc running from six o'clock to twelve o'clock. Then select and grab it with the pick tool, and drag it to the edge of the fret, as shown in Figure 2.35.

The positioning of the frets on the neck of a lute can be handled in one of two ways. You can just stick them down where they look about right, inasmuch as this is only a drawing and not a real lute. Alternatively, you can place them where a proper lutanist would have placed them using the rule of eighteen, to be discussed momentarily. (The rule of eighteen actually

FIGURE 2.35:

Fretting the lute

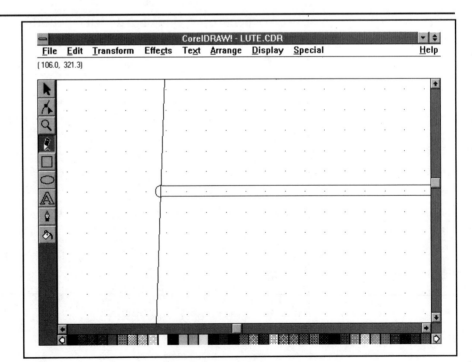

turned out to be the rule of 17.835 when pocket calculators came along, but eighteen will be accurate enough for this drawing.)

If you bought this book with more interest in learning CorelDRAW than in building a lute of your own, you might well wonder about the rationale behind this digression into fret theory. In fact, it points up a very important problem under CorelDRAW and the solution thereof.

If you attempt to locate the frets using the rule of eighteen, you will discover that short of hunting for the plastic ruler that comes with the package and holding it up to your monitor, CorelDRAW offers you no obvious way to measure the distance between two objects in a drawing. Knowing how to position the frets would thus seem to be of very little use.

In fact, there is a fairly convenient way to measure distance under CorelDRAW—it's just not explained anywhere. If you select the pencil tool and draw a line with it, the length of the line will be displayed up on the status line above the work space. In order to measure the distance between two objects, simply draw a line between them and see how long the line is. When you no longer need the line, hit the Delete key to blow it away.

In the case of working out the fret positions, make sure to use the Constrain feature and draw a vertical measurement line, as any other line will be slightly longer than a vertical one covering the same distance.

Figure 2.36 shows the status line illustrating the distance measurement. Note that this will not be visible if you have disabled the status line using the Show Status Line item of the Display menu. If you can't see the measurement values, select this item to toggle the display back on.

To place the first fret on the neck of the lute, measure the distance between the end of the neck and the top of the bridge. Divide this value by eighteen—if you're particularly enamored of Windows, you can use its Calculator application. The resulting value is the distance between the top of the neck and the first fret. Select the fret you have drawn and move it to the desired location.

To locate the next fret, divide the distance between the previous fret and the top of the bridge by eighteen. The resulting value will be the distance between that fret and the next fret. Duplicate the first fret line and move it into place. Repeat this process until you run out of neck. Note that the line just below the point where the neck joins the body is also a fret. It was usually made of hardwood or bone glued to the top of the lute.

*Measuring distance
with the pencil tool*

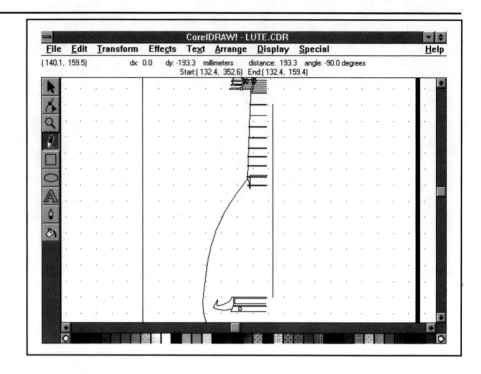

DRAWING THE TUNING PEGS

The peghead is the most involved detail of the lute. By now you will appreciate that it will be nowhere near as hard as it looks, because most of the details are simply objects—the tuning pegs—which have been duplicated several times.

For largely aesthetic reasons, the peghead tapers. Over the course of the development of the lute, the number of strings grew, and it eventually became impractical to contain all the tuning pegs within the peghead. The ones at the far end of the box would have had to be so short as to be unusable. For this reason, toward the latter part of its evolution, the lute began to sprout secondary flying pegs, such as the ones shown in our example. Each extra peg rests in a scroll which sits above the peghead.

You will be drawing the basic peghead peg shown in Figure 2.37 using the pencil tool for the shaft and the handle, and separate lines for the continuation of each shaft through the peghead. The lines of the handle are converted to curves with the shape tool and bent slightly. You will be drawing the knob-like object in the middle with the rectangle tool. You may have

FIGURE 2.37:

Peghead pegs up close

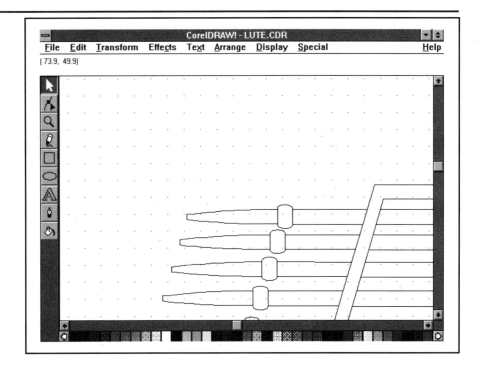

noticed that the middle bit appears to be not a rectangle so much as a lozenge. In fact, it's a rectangle with its corners rounded.

If you draw a rectangle and then grab one of its corners with the shape tool, you'll find that all the corners begin to get round. The further you drag the corner toward the center of the rectangle, the greater the rounding will become. If you drag it far enough, you can turn the rectangle into a circle or a lozenge, depending on how square the rectangle was in the first place.

Once you have drawn one peg, group all its elements together into a single object and duplicate it down the length of the peghead. There is no fixed number of strings on a lute, so you can simply add enough pegs to make the peghead look full.

The flying peg shown in Figure 2.38 is not much more difficult to draw. The handle is an ellipse. The rounded lines joining it to the shaft are straight lines drawn with the pencil tool and bent into shape with the shape tool. In order to make them both look the same, it's best to draw one, bend it to fit, and then duplicate and mirror it to form the other line. The capstan—the thing the string winds on at the right end of the peg—is just a

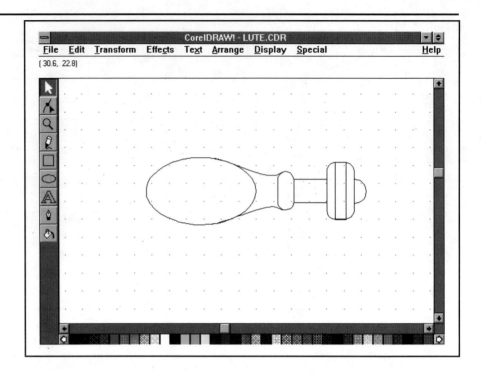

rectangle with rounded corners and two lines drawn through it. There's a half circle stuck on the end of it to represent the end of the peg.

When you've finished drawing this peg, group all its elements into a single object and drag it into position on the peghead.

On a real lute, the flying peg is placed above the other pegs. To simulate this on your drawing, you can just select the flying peg object and give it a white fill. This will have the effect of obscuring the lines below it. This might be thought of as the most primitive form of hidden-line removal. CAD packages such as AutoCAD can take nine hours to remove hidden lines from a complex drawing, although admittedly the process is a lot more involved.

FINISHING THE LUTE

At this point, you should have half a lute in your work space. The rest of the drawing is so easy as to be almost effortless. Select all the objects in the left half of the lute—you can use the Select All item of the Edit menu for this, since there's nothing else in your drawing—and group them together.

When you want to mirror an object, that is, create a copy of it which is flipped along one axis, you could simply use the Stretch & Mirror box from the Transform menu and select Horz or Vert Mirror. However, your real objective here is not simply to mirror what you have drawn, but to align your mirror image with your original drawing. This entails making a mirror-image copy while leaving an original, unflipped image with which to join.

You can handle the process in more than one way. One is to duplicate the object in question using Ctrl-D and then use the Horz Mirror in the Stretch & Mirror box to flip the duplicate. Another is to go straight to the Stretch & Mirror box and click on the Leave Original option before selecting Horz Mirror. The results are no different from what you'd have arrived at had you duplicated the left half of the lute explicitly and then flipped it.

This Leave Original option will crop up again in other contexts. It's often important in creating multiple copies of an object with progressive changes in position or other characteristics.

Align the two halves of the lute by zooming in on a fairly detailed area of the joint—the bridge or the peghead will do—and grab the right half. Drag it toward the left half until the horizontal lines meet.

You might want to zoom in tighter still to make sure that there are no gaps in any of the horizontal lines between the two halves of the lute. If there are, use the shape tool to stretch the lines a bit.

Draw a circle in the middle of the body, using the ellipse tool with the Constrain feature. Your work space should now contain one basically complete lute.

No mention has been made thus far about the line thickness attributes of the objects which make up the lute. Hairlines or lines of one point would suit this sort of drawing, especially if you'll be outputting the lute on a 300 dot-per-inch laser printer. You can quickly give all the lines in the drawing a suitable thickness attribute.

Select all the objects of the lute with the Select All item of the Edit menu. Select the outline pen tool and click on the appropriate thickness item.

In my version of the lute, I gave the outline of the body a slightly thicker line. You might want to do this as well, although it's not really essential.

PRINTING THE LUTE

If you've drawn your lute according to the preceding guidelines, it may be a bit too big to be printed. This happens a lot under CorelDRAW. You could select all the objects and scale the drawing so it would fit within the printable area of the CorelDRAW work space. However, there's an easier way. You can make the printer driver of CorelDRAW handle the scaling for you while it's printing, so that your drawing need not be modified.

Select the Print item of the File menu. The Print Options dialog box will appear, as in Figure 2.39.

The Printing dialog box contains two items which deal with scaling a large drawing to fit a small sheet of paper—Fit To Page and Scale. The latter of these lets you specify the amount by which you want to scale the drawing down. You could also scale it up using this feature if you had a reason to. The former item allows you to have CorelDRAW scale your drawing to fit the available paper. Actually, this feature is a bit erratic on many PostScript printers. PostScript tends to deal with objects at the edge of its printing area somewhat unpredictably. If you use this option you might find that parts of your drawing do not print. When you've selected one of these options, click on OK to begin printing.

WRAPPING UP

This chapter should have given you a pretty good handle on the basic line-drawing facilities of CorelDRAW. If you've succeeded in getting the example drawings to work out, you should not encounter difficulties with any line-based objects, no matter how complex they get.

There is more to be said about drawing lines under CorelDRAW, especially about some of the more involved node and path manipulations. Seeing as it is the basis for just about everything that CorelDRAW can produce, we'll be coming back to line drawing throughout this book.

FIGURE 2.39:

*The Print Options
dialog box from the
File menu*

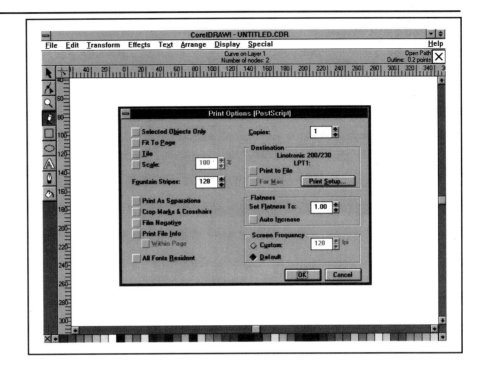

FAST
TRACK

CHAPTER

3

Manipulating

Type and

Text

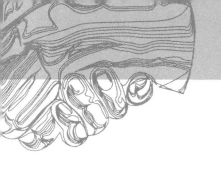

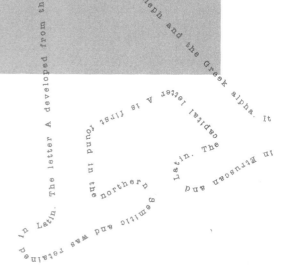

t would probably be presumptuous to suggest that Corel-DRAW's type facilities are its best feature. However, if you work with text you'll probably be staggered by what it can do with type—as well as by all the type it offers you. Users of desktop-publishing software will unquestionably find CorelDRAW to be useful in this respect. You can pop into CorelDRAW and generate headlines in hundreds of typefaces—plus a few symbol faces—and save them into files suitable for importing into desktop-publishing documents. A special mode lets you use symbol faces as individual graphic objects for such applications as drawing maps or typesetting sheet music.

Aside from just setting type, CorelDRAW allows you to manipulate the characters of your text just as you would any other drawing objects. Unless your requirements call for you to thoroughly mangle the objects which make up your text, you can have CorelDRAW deal with them in both ways: as text when it's convenient to do so, and as objects the rest of the time.

One of the things that makes CorelDRAW so interesting is its library of fonts. When you install CorelDRAW, it will add over 150 new typefaces to Windows—aside from being available in CorelDRAW itself, these faces can also be used from within other Windows applications that use fonts, such as Windows Write and Microsoft Word. These are fully hinted True-Type fonts, which means that they'll print as well as the default TrueType fonts that come with Windows. You will need Windows 3.1 or better to use the TrueType fonts.

Text effects are among the most attractive of object-oriented art. People are used to seeing type as being fairly plain. It's easy to catch someone's eye with type that is otherwise. Figure 3.1 illustrates a tiny fraction of the effects CorelDRAW is capable of producing. As with all its other facilities, the full scope of what it can do with text is limited only by your imagination.

FIGURE 3.1:

Some example text effects

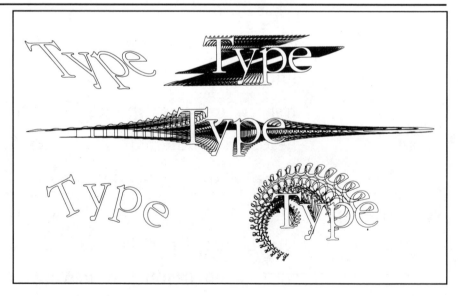

Words are humankind's most successful abstraction, and the expression of printed words perhaps the most refined technology people have ever come up with. Book publishers usually won't agree with this, and frequently regard printed communication as part of a 6000-year beta test, with a working version of the package to be available any day now.

CorelDRAW—which has evolved over a somewhat shorter development cycle—seeks to provide its users with as much flexibility in the way they use words as possible. The text interface of CorelDRAW is very powerful—and a bit complex. This chapter will discuss it in detail. However, it will contain the phrase "to be dealt with later in the chapter" perhaps more frequently than usual. The structure of this chapter will let you get into the text facilities of CorelDRAW gradually, without having huge, writhing coils of type launch themselves from overhead branches and slither across your desk, hissing and punctuating at you.

UNDERSTANDING TYPE AND TYPOGRAPHY

Before you can begin to work with type intelligently, it's important to understand some of the art—and a bit of the tradition—which lurks behind it. Type is very much an art form, if a rather esoteric one. Before the advent of laser printers and the gradual flow of typographic terms and ideas into microcomputer software, type lore was almost exclusively the province of typesetters.

The simplest form of type is the text generated by a typewriter. Typewriter text is very primitive by type standards. It's *monospaced,* for one thing. All the characters on a line occupy the same amount of space, even though some, such as the letter M, are a great deal fatter than others, such as the letter i. Typewriter text is also incapable of changing size, expressing emphasis with italics, and displaying most of the other subtleties we expect to see in typeset text.

Typeset text is generally *proportionally spaced;* that is, each character on a line occupies only as much space as it needs. This makes the text look more attractive, makes it generally easier to read unless you choose a particularly ornate font, and allows a great deal more text to fit on a page. To be sure, monospaced fonts do exist for typesetters, but these tend to be used as special effects or in those rare cases where you want to imitate monospacing, as in computer program listings or spreadsheets.

The earliest typesetting was, of course, done by hand. Late in the nineteenth century, several manufacturers began to create mechanical type-setting machines, of which the Linotype is probably the best known. These machines set type by forming each character from molten lead and assembling the lead slugs into trays of type, or *galleys*. Metal type after it has been used and stored somewhere is referred to as *cold type*.

Metal type was used until quite recently in some circles, and a few Linotype typesetting machines are probably still functioning somewhere. The Linotype company now makes laser typesetters—including several very high-resolution PostScript typesetters suitable for the output of Corel-DRAW files. You can usually see one of their old hot metal machines at printers' trade shows.

Many of the things which make up modern typography are derived from the traditions of hand-set text and hot metal type. For example, the *serifs,* the little points on the corners of the characters of many typefaces (including the one you're reading at the moment) were put there back in the days of hand-set type to keep the corners of the characters from wearing down and getting rounded too quickly.

Many of the typefaces we now use with laser printers and programs like CorelDRAW date back to the heyday of hot metal type. Times Roman and Helvetica, perhaps the most widely used typefaces, were both born around the turn of the century. Among typesetters, printers, and other parties well versed in type lore, certain typefaces are well known, and something set in a particular face should look the same no matter where you get the work done.

The commonly used typefaces are commonly used because back at the beginning of this century the type *foundries*—the companies that employed type designers and produced the dies, and often the machines, for hot metal typesetting—were very aggressive about selling their typefaces. In its own circles, marketing type remains as much a battle as marketing colas or political candidates.

TYPOGRAPHIC TERMS

NOTE *Type purists will take exception to this. There is no precise definition for the size of a point— the value of 72 points to the inch is a convenient approximation. It's worth noting that most applications that deal with type on your screen equate one point with the size of one dot on your monitor, a still looser approximation.*

The fundamental unit of type measurement is the *point*. There are 72 of them in an inch, so type which is one inch high would be referred to as 72-point type. One typically measures the capital letter E in the normal style for that typeface in order to determine the point size for the entire set of fonts and weights available with that typeface.

Space on a line of text is measured in *picas*. A pica is 12 points long, and there are 6 picas to the inch. Under CorelDRAW, as we've seen, you're free to measure things in any units you like, so you need not deal with picas and points if you don't want to—not even in specifying type size. When you do use picas and points, you will find that they're expressed as the number of picas followed by the number of points with a comma between them. If you specify a number higher than 12 in the points part of this value, CorelDRAW will automatically convert it to the correct number of *picas* and points. Thus, entering 6,13 is incorrect, but CorelDRAW will adjust it to 7,1. CorelDRAW comes with a plastic ruler which, among other things, features a pica scale for measuring things and a type gauge for determining how big printed type is.

Leading

The origin of the term for space between lines of type, *leading,* is another bit of obscurity from the days of hot metal: Originally the space was formed by placing strips of lead between the rows of characters. Leading is expressed in points. Most text is set with one or two points of leading beyond the size of the text. Nine-point type would normally be set with ten-point leading, or set nine-on-ten in typesetters' terms. Text which is set nine-on-nine would run the risk of having the *descenders* of one line occasionally touching the *ascenders* of the next.

Traditional capital letters do not have descenders, so it's quite forgivable to set text which is all in capitals with less leading than you could get away with in lowercase type.

Figure 3.2 illustrates the effect of leading using CorelDRAW's interline spacing control.

FIGURE 3.2:

*Different amounts
of leading*

Martin said to his man
"Fie, man, fie."
Martin said to his man
"Who's the fool now?"

80 percent

Martin said to his man
"Fie, man, fie."
Martin said to his man
"Who's the fool now?"

100 percent

Martin said to his man

"Fie, man, fie."

Martin said to his man

"Who's the fool now?"

150 percent

Ems and Ens

On a typewriter, the Spacebar produces something which is of a fixed and predictable width. So does the dash key. Neither of these is true in setting type. As with most typeset material, this book is set in what is called *justified* text, that is, with straight right and left margins. The typesetting system which produced this book managed this by padding out short lines with additional space between the words. CorelDRAW can also automatically justify text.

Often, there are calls for specific sizes of fixed spaces and fixed dashes. These are measured using still more arcane typesetting terminology. Wide dashes—such as the ones you see in this sentence—are defined as being the width of the letter M in whatever typeface you're using at the moment. This space is called one *em,* so the dashes you just saw were *em dashes.* There are also slightly smaller dashes called *en* dashes—originally the width of the letter N, now typically one half the width of an em dash.

Kerning

It is quite common in using proportionally spaced type to find letters which appear to have too much space between them—not because the typeface has been badly designed, but simply because the letters themselves seem as if they should fit together more neatly. For example, the letters A and W often look this way if they're set together.

In some cases, these two letters would be moved close together to overcome this effect. This is called *kerning,* and if these two letters required kerning to make them look right in a particular font, they'd be referred to as a *kerning pair.* Desktop publishing packages such as Ventura Publisher can automatically kern text based on kerning pairs.

Figure 3.3 illustrates the effects of kerning.

CorelDRAW will automatically kern type as well. In fact, this is almost always true. CorelDRAW will use the kerning information in TrueType fonts. There are other, somewhat archaic paths to import fonts which may cause it to ignore any kerning information present in the original fonts. In most cases, you'd use these paths, if you use them at all, for ornate display faces, which can usually get away without automatic kerning. Fonts and their sources will be discussed later in this chapter.

In addition to CorelDRAW's automatic kerning, you can manually kern text. Kerning techniques will be presented toward the end of this chapter.

TIP *You can usually get a pretty good idea of a font's kerning capabilities by looking directly below the font list selector window anywhere it appears in CorelDRAW. The phrase "This is a TrueType font" will appear whenever you have selected a True-Type font, which includes kerning information.*

TYPES OF TYPE

Typefaces can be broadly classified in a number of ways. The first—and perhaps the most important under CorelDRAW—is the distinction between *display* and *body* faces.

FIGURE 3.3:

Kerning some text

Display faces are designed to be used in large point sizes, primarily as headlines. Body faces are designed for use in body text, such as that which you are reading now. Few faces are suited for both. Display faces are usually either too pudgy or too ornate to be easily readable when they're reduced to 9 or 10 points and used to set body copy. Body faces look spindly and anorexic if they're expanded out to 72 points and used to set headlines.

There are exceptions to this. One frequently finds Helvetica—the font CorelDRAW calls Switzerland—used in both cases, although heavy versions of Helvetica exist which are more suited for use as display faces.

Most of the typefaces which come with CorelDRAW are ones which have been designed and fine-tuned for use as display faces.

Typefaces are also often described as being either *serif* or *sans serif.* Serifs are the ornaments and pointy bits at the ends and corners of the characters of typefaces such as Times Roman, what CorelDRAW calls Toronto. Helvetica is a typical sans serif face; that is, it has no serifs. Because they can help to tie letters in a word together and make the baseline easy to distinguish, serif faces are traditionally used for large quantities of tightly spaced text, i.e., body copy.

Type is usually specified in a specific *weight,* that is, how bold it is. The weight of type is a somewhat subjective quantity, and much of what defines particular type as being bold or extra bold dates back into the history of typesetting.

Normal type—such as the text you're reading—is called medium or book weight, and darker text is called bold. Type weights at the extremes of these—light, and extrabold, ultrabold, or heavy—really require slightly different versions of the typefaces in question. For example, Helvetica is available in Helvetica and Helvetica Black, the latter being the extrabold version.

Not all typefaces are available in all weights under CorelDRAW.

Typeface Names

Although the terms typeface and font often appear to be used interchangeably, *typeface* is used most often when referring to a uniquely named type style, such as New Baskerville, which will appear to be the same style even when you are comparing different versions of it, such as italic or boldface. The term *font* is used to refer to the basic styles generally available within a named typeface—for example, most text typefaces come with an italic font.

Font is also used somewhat inclusively to identify any complete collection of a certain style of type; thus, you will often see font where typeface would be equally correct.

It's in dealing with specific typefaces by name that things really start getting confusing. You almost need a program and a score card some of the time.

The name Helvetica, when it's applied to type, is a registered trademark of the International Type Corporation, or ITC. ITC was recently purchased by Letraset, the press-on letters company.

Anyone can produce a typeface which looks pretty much like Helvetica, and similar faces abound. One could not, however, call it Helvetica without the permission of ITC.

For this reason, desktop-publishing software which comes with a typeface compatible with Helvetica usually calls it something else, frequently Swiss or, as in the case of CorelDRAW, Switzerland.

Prior to the advent of laser printers, typesetting companies which sought to compete with ITC faced a similar problem and came up with a similar solution. Thus, you might encounter Compugraphic typefaces called Helios and English Times which look pretty much like ITC Helvetica and Times Roman. Both are available for use with microcomputers and laser printers.

When Adobe, the creator of the PostScript laser-printer language, set out to design its software, it negotiated a license with ITC rather than attempting to knock off copies of ITC typefaces. As a result, they were able to use the ITC names in their language. If you use Ventura Publisher, for example, you may have noticed that Helvetica is specified as Helvetica if you're printing to a PostScript printer and as Swiss if you're not.

In dealing with body text, the distinction between real faces and copies of those faces becomes fairly important. For example, the minute differences in character widths between real Helvetica and a knockoff called Swiss will frequently cause one to occupy a greater amount of space than the other over three or four pages of text.

When Adobe created PostScript with its authentic ITC fonts, it allowed for other, non-ITC fonts to be used as well, but it encrypted the real ITC fonts it sold to prevent other companies from using them in their own products. They also limited PostScript to prevent someone from writing a PostScript program which would unravel their font protection. This has served to cripple several PostScript-related applications from Adobe, such as Adobe Illustrator. One of the reasons CorelDRAW is able to do a lot of things Illustrator cannot is that CorelDRAW can use its own fonts or those provided by Windows, rather than the ones resident in PostScript printers, when doing so will give it more flexibility.

Even though many of its fonts correspond exactly to real commercial fonts, CorelDRAW is not legally permitted to ship its software with the real names for its typefaces. Appendix B of this book will discuss the font name situation.

Figure 3.4 illustrates some of the text typefaces which come with CorelDRAW. I've used the generally accepted names of those faces where

FIGURE 3.4:

Some of the typefaces which come with CorelDRAW, and their special CorelDRAW names (small print)

Avant Garde (Avalon)
Aachen (Aardvark)
American Typewriter (Memorandum)
Arnold Böcklin (Arabia)
Bauhaus (Bahamas)
Bauhaus Heavy (Bahamas Heavy)
Bauhaus Light (Bahamas Light)
Brush Script (Banff)
Benguiat (Bangkok)
Bodoni Poster (Bodnoff)
Bookman (Brooklyn)
Caslon (Casablanca)
Caslon Open Face (Casper OpenFace)
Century Oldstyle (Centurion Old)
COTTONWOOD (Cottage)
Cooper Black (Cupertino)
Dom Casual (Dawn Castle)
Eras (Erie)
Eras Black (Erie Black)
Eras Light (Erie Light)
Friz Quadrata (France)
Fette Fraktur (Frankenstein)
Franklin Gothic (Frankfurt Gothic)
Franklin Gothic Heavy (Frankfurt Gothic Heavy)
Freestyle Script (Freeport)
Futura (Fujiyama)
Futura ExtraBold (Fujiyama ExtraBold)
Futura Light (Fujiyama Light)
Garamond (Gatineau)
Helvetica (Switzerland)
Helvetica-Black (Switzerland Black)
Helvetica-Light (Switzerland Light)
Helvetica-Narrow (Switzerland Narrow)
Helvetica Cond (Switzerland Cond)
Helvetica CondBlk (Switzerland Cond Black)

(Switzerland Cond Light) Helvetica Cond Light
(Switzerland Inserat) Helvetica Inserat
(Homeward Bound) Hobo
(Ireland) IRONWOOD
(Jupiter) JUNIPER
(Koala) Kaufman
(Monospaced) Letter Gothic
(Lincoln) Linotext
(Linus) Linoscript
(Motor) MACHINE
(Mystical) Mistral
(Nebraska) New Baskerville
(New Brunswick) New Century Schoolbook
(Ottawa) Optima
(Palm Springs) Palatino
(Paradise) Park Avenue
(Paragon) Parisian
(Penguin) PEIGNOT
(Penguin Light) PEIGNOT LIGHT
(Posse) ■
(President) Present Script
(Prose Antique) Post Antiqua
(Renfrew) Revue
(Southern) Souvenir
(Stamp) STENCIL
(Technical) Tekton
(Timpani) Tiffany
(Timpany Heavy) Tiffany Heavy
(Toronto) Times Roman
(Umbrella) UMBRA
(Unicorn) University Roman
(USA Black) Univers Black
(USA Light) Univers Light
(Vogue) VAG Rounded
(Zurich Calligraphic) Zapf Chancery

they're applicable, with the names as they're shipped with CorelDRAW in small print beside them. This list excludes the several symbol faces which also come with CorelDRAW.

You can add new fonts to CorelDRAW. There's a discussion of font import paths later on.

A lot more will be said about type names later in this book. You might be interested to know the origins of the more common ones used in computer type, however.

The name Helvetica is derived from *Helvetii,* an ancient Celtic tribe that lived in what is now Switzerland. Switzerland is often referred to as Helvetia on things like its postage stamps. Accordingly, substitutes for Helvetica are often called "Swiss," or, in the case of CorelDRAW, "Switzerland."

Times Roman is a serif type face, as has been discussed. The word "serif" is from the Dutch word "shreef," which means "stroke," as with a pen—from which also comes the more common English word "scribe." The serifs on type suggest the picks left on handwriting done with a quill pen. The Dutch origin of the word serif has led this common serif face to be called "Dutch" in many applications. CorelDRAW has broken with this tradition and called it Toronto, for no easily explained reason.

Symbols and Dingbats

In addition to the text fonts supplied with CorelDRAW, there are several fonts consisting entirely of symbols or ornaments. These fonts are extremely useful, especially for creating unusual graphics in a hurry. The fonts include Greek/Math Symbols, equivalent to the Symbols font in other applications, a music notation font which is similar to the PostScript Sonata font, and Dixieland, which is equivalent to the widely used Zapf Dingbat font. There is also a massive library of dedicated symbols under CorelDRAW.

The basic symbols and Dingbats are installed and stored as fonts in Windows, and you could use them this way if you wished to. However, there's a second way to add them to a drawing, this being through the special symbol entry mode of the text tool. This will allow you to pick the symbol you want from a visual display of symbols, rather than forcing you to look up symbol reference numbers from a printed list. The symbol mode of CorelDRAW will be discussed in detail later in this chapter.

TYPE—TRUE AND OTHERWISE

Typesetting with personal computers is a complex and rather funky example of bad planning and conflicting standards. As a rule, every attempt to deal with it makes it worse, as every attempt seems to involve yet another standard.

The release of Windows 3.1 saw the introduction of TrueType, which was Windows' attempt to deal with the emerging can of worms that type on a PC had become. While it is a well crafted solution to the type problem—and, incidentally, one that does actually work—TrueType as seen by Corel-DRAW is not without its rough edges.

While you need not understand TrueType in its entirety to work with type under CorelDRAW, a brief introduction to it might help you avoid some of its more frustrating side effects.

As will be discussed in the next section of this chapter, a character, such as the letter A in Times Roman, is just a collection of paths that define what the character will look like. This is called a character "outline," for obvious reasons. When CorelDRAW wants to add the letter A to a drawing, it calls for the appropriate outline.

Back in the early days of CorelDRAW, it would call on itself for text outlines, as Windows didn't have a usable way to provide them. Those earlier implementations of CorelDRAW came with a library of typefaces stored in a proprietary font format called WFN. The origin of the N is obscure, F probably stood for font and W stood for Waldo. Prior to its being called CorelDRAW, the earliest versions of the software were affectionately referred to as Waldo.

Windows 3.1 implements TrueType. This is a common font manager with a library of font outlines. Any application that needs a font outline can call the TrueType manager in Windows and have it provided. It need not have its own font format—it doesn't even have to know how the outlines have come to be.

There are numerous advantages to TrueType. It allows that installing one set of fonts in Windows will provide them for all applications; and True-Type fonts have features which the old WFN fonts did not have—most notably "hinting," something to be discussed in greater detail later on.

The current version of CorelDRAW looks to TrueType as its primary source of fonts—installing CorelDRAW also installs its generous assortment

TIP *CorelDRAW used to come with an application called WFNBOSS, which would translate fonts in a variety of other formats into WFN fonts and back again. With the advent of TrueType, Corel ceased including WFNBOSS with the package. If you have an older version of CorelDRAW, you might want to hang onto WFNBOSS. In the absence of a more workable path—one which will translate other font formats into TrueType fonts— WFNBOSS will allow you to make them into WFN fonts, which CorelDRAW will still accept, however reluctantly.*

of fonts into Windows. However, it will also add old WFN fonts to this list if you like for its own use, a procedure that's discussed in Appendix B. This will allow you to use custom fonts created under previous implementations of CorelDRAW.

There are programs which will translate to and from TrueType fonts. There's a coupon for a discounted version of one of them, FontMonger, included with the CorelDRAW package. However, FontMonger is still fairly expensive even with the coupon, and you may not need it if you can use one of the older, "back door" font import paths. Appendix B will discuss these in greater detail.

Type As Objects

Under CorelDRAW, text characters are drawn on the screen just like other objects are. However, text is stored in CorelDRAW's object list differently from, say, the object which defines a rectangle. CorelDRAW's note to itself for a line of text defines its location on the screen; transformations which have been applied to it; the font; the point size and other typographic qualities of the text; and, most important, the text itself.

CorelDRAW always attempts to hold onto the original text as you entered it. It's only forced to abandon the text and deal with the resulting drawing strictly as paths when you explicitly convert the text to objects. Each letter is defined as a path which traces the outline of the character such that if the paths are placed on a CorelDRAW page and filled, the result will be text. Text of this sort can be scaled and stretched any way you like without any loss in the quality of the type.

ENTERING AND EDITING TEXT

Entering text under CorelDRAW is easy—it was touched on in Chapter 2. Select the text tool and click where you want your text to appear. Type in the text you want to appear there. Pat yourself gently on the back—you've just accomplished something that would have required two men and thirty pounds of molten lead a century ago.

Editing the contents of text under CorelDRAW is hardly more difficult. With the text tool selected, place the cross cursor somewhere in the text

If you hold down the Ctrl key when you're resizing text, it will be constrained to integral multiples of its original point size.

The paragraph mode of CorelDRAW allows you to use the package as sort of single-page desktop-publishing package. It's handy for creating advertisements, flyers, and such—situations in which you have to integrate graphics and a respectable amount of text. Note, however, that CorelDRAW is relatively slow at redrawing paragraph-mode text frames, and a page with a lot of text included in this way may become tedious to work with. For example, a stereo shop advertisement—with countless tiny unrecognizable photographs and blocks of three-point fine print covering every square inch of the page—would be a trial to do in CorelDRAW.

you'd like to change and click. A text I-beam will appear where you clicked. You can enter text at the cursor by typing and move the cursor using the cursor movement keys on your keyboard. The Backspace and Delete keys will delete characters to the left and right of the text cursor respectively—a complete discussion of entering and editing in CorelDRAW's text fields will appear later in this chapter.

You can change the size of text interactively with the pick tool. Select the text you'd like to resize and grab one of the corner handles. Note that the current point size is shown in the status line at the top of your CorelDRAW work space. Drag the selection mark until the text is the size you require.

You can use the center selection marks to resize text anamorphically, that is, to stretch it in only one dimension.

In addition to simple "onscreen" editing, you can precisely control all the qualities of text by using the Artistic Text dialog box. To call it up, select some text with the pick tool and then select Edit Text from the CorelDRAW Edit menu, or use the keyboard shortcut Ctrl-T.

Clicking once with the text tool to enter text will put you in CorelDRAW's *string mode*. This is useful for entering a few words at a time—you would use this mode for creating headlines, decorative text, and so on. The string mode has a limit of 256 characters per text object. Note that carriage returns count as characters.

You can enter much larger blocks of text in *paragraph mode*. To use the paragraph mode, select the text tool and click and drag it to form a rectangle. This will create a text entry frame with a cursor in it.

A CorelDRAW text entry box can be thought of as being a tiny word processor. As you type, your text will wrap automatically when it reaches the end of a line. As with more conventional word processors, you can edit previously entered text, change its size and font, and so on.

If you select a text box with the pick tool and resize it, the text within it will "reflow" to fill the new dimensions of the box. It will not change size itself, however, as is the case with text in the string mode.

We'll be discussing more of the details of these two modes in a moment.

You can edit paragraph-mode text pretty much as you would string-mode text. The Paragraph Text dialog box will serve to set the type characteristics. Note that if you use the Artistic Text dialog box to edit string-mode text, the button marked Import will be disabled and the title bar will say Artistic Text. The button will function in working with paragraph-mode text only.

This will allow you to fetch text from text files on disk and place it into a CorelDRAW text frame, something else we'll look at later in this chapter.

Figure 3.5 illustrates the Artistic Text and Paragraph Text dialog boxes in both modes.

FIGURE 3.5:

The Artistic Text and Paragraph Text dialog boxes in the string and paragraph modes, respectively

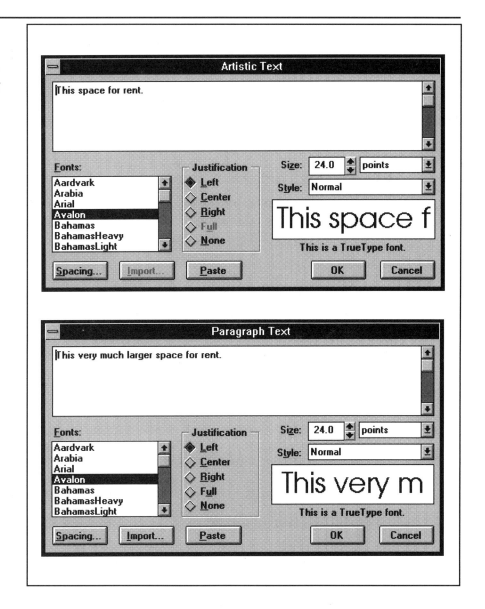

STRING MODE

In the string mode, text will appear beginning at the point where you first clicked with the text tool cursor. If the Snap To Grid feature was on when you called for the dialog box, the text will begin at the nearest grid point. However, because it's an object, you will be able to move the text with the pick tool if it doesn't wind up exactly where you want it.

Text will be drawn using the most recently chosen typeface, point size, text fill and outline color and characteristics, and so on. This includes the justification mode—that is, whether the type will be centered, pushed to the left or right, and so on. If the current justification mode happens to be right, your text will begin where you initially clicked with the text tool, but it will extend to the left of the insertion cursor as you type.

The Artistic Text and Paragraph Text dialog boxes can be used to set all these characteristics.

You can change the text attributes of one or more characters in a string-mode text object. Use the text tool cursor to highlight the text you want to change. Specifically you can:

◆ Use the outline pen tool's various controls—including the palette at the bottom of your screen and the fill tool roll up menu—to change the fill of the selected text.

◆ Use the line tool's controls to change the outline characteristics of the selected text.

◆ Select the Character item from the Text menu to change the font, point size, and other typographic characteristics of the selected text.

You can also perform these changes and several others using the shape tool, something that will be discussed in detail presently.

PARAGRAPH MODE

Creating a paragraph-mode text frame was touched on previously. Entering text into one works just like entering text into a string-mode text object does, except your text will wrap when it reaches the edge of the box. If you enter more text than there is room for in a text frame, the extra text will be hidden below the bottom of the box. If you subsequently make the box longer or the text smaller, it will reappear. CorelDRAW will truncate the text in a paragraph-mode text frame to 4000 characters; if you need more than 4000 characters you should either use multiple text frames or consider buying a desktop-publishing package.

You should consider that paragraph-mode text frames have two sets of type characteristics. Global characteristics affect all the type in the frame. You can set the global characteristics of a text frame's contents by selecting the frame with the pick tool and using the Paragraph Text dialog box. As with string mode, you can also override these global characteristics by selecting some text in a text frame with the text cursor and then using the various controls of CorelDRAW (listed in the previous section) to modify it.

Entering Special Characters

In addition to the keyboard characters which can be entered directly into the text-entry window, most fonts support additional high-order characters. These are so called because they reside in the ASCII character numbers above 128, that is, above the usual range of printable characters.

TrueType fonts have a more or less defined high order character set. There's a small application called Character Map that comes with Windows that will help you use these characters without having to pin lists of obscure numbers to the wall beside your desk.

Figure 3.6 illustrates the Character Map window.

To insert a special character into a text object under CorelDRAW—either in string mode or paragraph mode—do the following:

1. Hold down the Ctrl key and hit the Esc key. This will cause the Windows Task List to appear.

The Character Map application

2. Assuming that you are not currently running the Character Map application, select Program Manager from the task selector and, when the Program Manager appears, boot up Character Map. If you have cause to use Character Map again, its name will be in the Task List window, and you will be able to select it directly.

3. Use the Font selector to select the font from which you want to use a special character. Ideally, this should be the font of the text object into which you'll be inserting the character, unless you plan to explicitly change the font of the inserted character.

4. Click on the small character symbols in the Character Map display. This will call up a slightly larger version of the character, should you be uncertain you're looking at the character you're after. (They're often a bit hard to make out in the character chart.) When you have located the character you want, double click on it. This will cause it to be added to the Characters to Copy field at the top of the Character Map window.

5. If you accidentally add characters to the Characters to Copy field that you'd rather not use, click in the field and edit it appropriately.

6. When the character or characters you need are in the Characters to Copy field, click on the Copy button. This will place them in the Windows Clipboard.

7. Switch back to CorelDRAW—hold down the Ctrl key and hit Esc if you want to use the Task List window to do this.

8. Place your text cursor where you want the special characters to appear.

9. Hold down the Shift key and hit Ins. Your characters will be inserted into the selected text object.

You can insert characters into text through the Paragraph Text dialog box in exactly the same way.

There is another method for entering special characters that might prove to be a shortcut for you. This is the technique that was used prior to the installation of the Character Map application with Windows. Note that when you select a character under Character Map, a number appears in the lower-right corner of the screen. For example, the number for the character *ä* with a diaeresis above it is 0228. If your applications call for you to use this character a lot, write this number down. As a shortcut to inserting this character in a text object under CorelDRAW, hold down the Alt key on your keyboard and type the number 0228 on the numeric keypad. When you release the Alt key, your character will appear. Note that the leading zero is important, and that the number keys at the top of your keyboard will not work.

You might find it useful to insert special characters from another font. For example, the Zapf Dingbats font—what CorelDRAW calls Dixieland—is full of interesting symbols that make good bullets for lists and ornaments for decorative text. To use one in a string or paragraph of otherwise normal text:

1. Enter the character code for the special character you want, using either Character Map or an Alt number code, as discussed previously.

2. Highlight the resulting character using the text tool cursor by clicking and dragging over the character.

3. Select the Character item of the Text menu.

4. Change the font for the character to the one you chose the special symbol from—in this case, Dixieland.

It's important to note that when you paste a character from the Clipboard—that is, one that was placed there by Character Map—the character code will make the trip. The font you originally chose it from will not, and the character will appear in your text object in the font used by the adjacent characters it appears among.

Editing Text

The editing facilities of the text-entry window are actually quite sophisticated for such a tiny amount of text. We've used them informally until now—here's an exhaustive explanation of all the features of text entry and editing. Note that this discussion pertains both to the text-editing window in the Text Edit dialog box and to the on-screen text-editing mode in the CorelDRAW work space.

Most of the text-editing facilities are pretty intuitive and you should not experience any difficulties in learning how to deal with them. If you've used a word processor at all you probably already know how most of them operate.

When you type text it always appears at the current *insertion point,* which would normally be at the end of the string of text you're typing. This is indicated by the bar cursor. However, you can move this around in a number of ways.

If you move your mouse cursor to some place in the existing text and click, the insertion point will appear between the nearest two characters. Anything you type subsequently will appear at this point, pushing the text in front of it along. You can also position the cursor using the cursor-movement arrow keys of your keyboard. These are usually found on the numeric keypad, and as a triangle of arrow keys on some newer keyboards as well.

In addition, the Home and End keys will position the insertion-point cursor at the beginning and end of the text string respectively. The PgUp and PgDn keys will move it up and down by six lines in the Paragraph Text window. The Backspace key will delete the character immediately to the left of the cursor, pulling any text to the right of the cursor back by one space. The Delete key will delete the character to the right of the cursor.

If you place your mouse cursor to the left of some text and click and drag it (or if you use Shift plus the cursor movement keys), the text which it passes over will be selected and highlighted. If you then hold down the Shift key and hit Delete, the selected text will be removed from the text window and placed in the Windows Clipboard, which will be discussed in greater detail in the sections on importing text below. If you hold down the Ctrl key and hit Insert, the text will be copied to the Clipboard but left in the text window. (If you hit the Delete key by itself, the highlighted text will be removed without being placed in the Clipboard.)

If you hold down the Shift key and hit Insert, text previously cut or copied to the Clipboard will be pasted into the text-entry window at the current insertion point as if it had been typed there. By using Cut and Paste, you can move pieces of a string around within the text-entry window.

Importing Text in String Mode

There is a limit to the complexity of a single string-mode text object under CorelDRAW. If you put a lot of text in one—even if it's less than 256 characters—and then set it in a very elaborate font, you might get a message from CorelDRAW telling you that your string's too long and will be truncated. In this case, either use a shorter string—perhaps breaking your text up into two string-mode text objects—or choose a simpler font.

In addition to typing text directly into the text window or a text object in string mode, you can also paste it in from the Windows Clipboard. The Clipboard is the repository of anything which is cut or copied from a document in any Windows application. This can be text, pictures, CorelDRAW objects, and so on. The text-entry window is smart enough to know if it's being fed something other than text and it will refuse to accept inappropriate Clipboard contents.

If you open the Artistic Text dialog box, you can paste the current contents of the Windows Clipboard into the text-entry window by holding down the Shift key and hitting the Insert key. If there is nothing in the Clipboard, if the nature of the current Clipboard contents are indigestible by the text window, or if there are more than 250 characters of text in the CorelDRAW text box and the Clipboard combined, an error message will display and nothing will happen.

This also works if you just place the text cursor in an onscreen string-mode text object.

You might want to try importing some text from Windows Write into CorelDRAW in this way. Write is the small word processor which comes with Microsoft Windows. Bear in mind that Windows Write and CorelDRAW can be running at the same time. Here's how it's done:

1. Select no more than 250 characters of text from a Windows Write document. Spaces count as characters and the end of each line counts as 2 characters.

2. Cut or copy this text into the Windows Clipboard with the appropriate items of Write's Edit menu. You can use the Windows Clipboard application to make sure that your text is really in the Clipboard.

3. Boot up CorelDRAW, or click it into the foreground of your screen if it's already running.

4. Place the text-insertion cursor where you want the imported text to appear.

5. Hold down the Shift key and hit Insert.

The contents of the Clipboard should appear in the text-entry window as if you'd typed them there directly. Figure 3.7 illustrates the steps involved in importing text from Write into CorelDRAW.

FIGURE 3.7:

Importing text from Windows Write into CorelDRAW

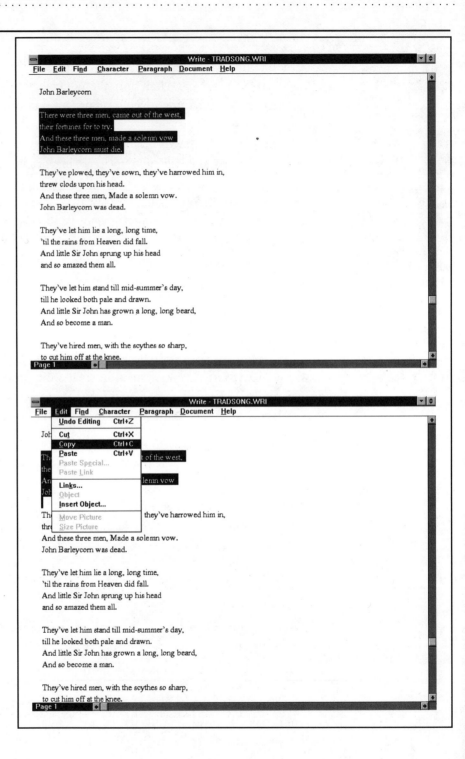

FIGURE 3.7:

Importing text from
Windows Write into
CorelDRAW (continued)

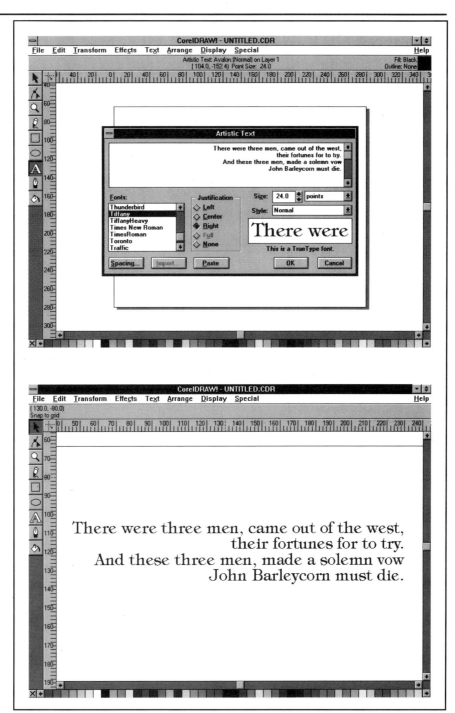

Importing Text in Paragraph Mode

Aside from pasting text from the Clipboard, as discussed in the previous section, you can import text into the paragraph mode from any word processor which can save its files in pure ASCII. This means that the text can contain no special formatting codes and no embedded binary characters unless it has come from another Windows application. Finally, there should be no hard carriage returns in your text except at the ends of paragraphs.

Here's an even easier way to import text. Once again, you will need a pure text file. Select the Import item from the File menu and choose the Text import filter. Open the file you wish to import. CorelDRAW will automatically create a paragraph-mode text frame and place your imported text into it. It will use its default font—see Appendix B for a discussion of changing this. In the meantime, you can change the size of the frame and all the typographic characteristics of one of these text frames just as you would for a text frame you created with the text tool.

You might want to consult your word processor's documentation to figure out how to make it generate such a file. Alternatively, you can create suitable files using the Write word processor application which comes with Microsoft Windows. Make sure you save your files with the Text Only option enabled. You can save yourself a bit of typing by making sure you save files destined for CorelDRAW's text import with the extension .TXT, as this is what CorelDRAW defaults to using.

To import a text file into the Paragraph Text dialog box in paragraph mode, click on the Import button and open the file you want to import. If it has more than four thousand characters in it, you'll see a box telling you that the extra characters have been truncated. This won't change the contents of your file—only the number of characters in the text object you've created in CorelDRAW.

UNDERSTANDING TEXT ATTRIBUTES

You can set the attributes—the weight, the size, and so on—of an entire text object from within the Paragraph and Artistic Text dialog boxes. You can also change the attributes of selected characters of a string by highlighting them and using the Character item of the Text menu, as has been discussed.

Here's a detailed discussion of what these characteristics mean.

Justification or Alignment

Directly below the text-entry window is a series of radio buttons which set the text justification or, more properly, alignment. The effects of left, center, and right alignment are shown in Figure 3.8.

The Full justification setting is only enabled when you're using the Paragraph Text dialog box in paragraph mode. It selects full columnar right and left justification, as is used in setting the body text of this book.

In string mode, the text will initially be drawn in the work space relative to the place where you clicked to pop up the dialog box. If you select Left justification, all the text will be drawn to the right of where you clicked. If you select Right, it will be drawn to the left of where you clicked. Center justification will cause it to be centered horizontally on the point where you clicked. Fall specifies that the text be justified at both left and right margins.

None is the justification you would select to keep CorelDRAW from imposing alignment on text that you have effectively aligned by hand by means of kerning individual characters using the shape tool. Specific instructions for kerning will be presented under the general topic "Manipulating Type within Text Strings" at the end of this chapter.

Fonts

The Fonts list will display the names of all the available typefaces. You can use the scroll bar to the right of the box to scroll through the list. Clicking on one of the names will select it as the current typeface for the text you have entered or are about to enter.

The sample window will show you several characters of the typeface you've selected. This will be the letters AaBbYyZz when there's no text in the editing window, and the first several characters of the text you've entered or

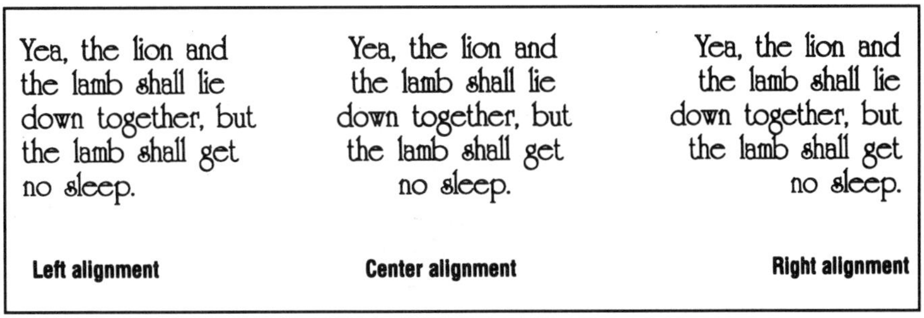

FIGURE 3.8:

Text justification, or alignment

Yea, the lion and the lamb shall lie down together, but the lamb shall get no sleep.	Yea, the lion and the lamb shall lie down together, but the lamb shall get no sleep.	Yea, the lion and the lamb shall lie down together, but the lamb shall get no sleep.
Left alignment	**Center alignment**	**Right alignment**

are editing when there is. These samples are approximations of what your text will look like, and often not terribly good ones. The chart in Figure 3.4 offers a better representation of what your text will look like.

Note that not all typefaces have a complete set of characters. The Machine face, for example—or Motor, as CorelDRAW thinks of it—lacks lowercase letters. Such caps-only fonts will substitute uppercase for lowercase characters, although lowercase characters will still show up in the text-editing window of the Paragraph Text and Artistic Text dialog boxes.

Some special third-party typefaces—especially shareware and public-domain TrueType fonts—may have even less complete character sets.

Point Size

The Size item in the Paragraph Text and Artistic Text dialog boxes works like all the other numeric controls in CorelDRAW dialogs. You can click on the arrowheads to change the point size in unit increments—in this item, in increments of one point. You can also type in the number to specify any point size directly. CorelDRAW allows you to specify point sizes from .7 to 2160 points in increments of one tenth of a point.

If you don't like points, you can work in any of the other units CorelDRAW supports. Fathoms, furlongs, cubits, and angstroms are as yet not provided for.

Type smaller than 6-point is very nearly unreadable on a 300-dot-per-inch laser printer, and you should not hurt people's eyes in this way if you can avoid it.

You should also know that laser-printer typefaces often do not print as nicely at small point sizes as they do at larger ones, because as the characters decrease in size the printer dots start to represent a significant amount of area in relation to the character as a whole. The algorithm which fills the outline for a 6-point font is frequently confronted with the question of how to handle half dots, that is, places where a dot would be half inside the character and half outside it. Because the algorithm isn't smart enough to be able to consider the aesthetics of the characters it's creating, it can be assumed to guess wrong half the time. The results are occasionally crunchy-looking small characters.

One of the improvements in type which TrueType fonts offer CorelDRAW is the inclusion of "hinting." This is a feature which helps

PostScript printers decide how best to resolve the problem of partial dots. It's worth noting that hinting did not exist in the older WFN fonts that Corel-DRAW used to use. If you have carried any over to the current revision of CorelDRAW, they may not print as well as real TrueType fonts at small point sizes for this reason.

Hinting is a cheat to make printing to 300-dot-per-inch laser printers a bit less unattractive than it would otherwise be. It has decreasing usefulness at larger point sizes—type which is set at 10 points or larger won't care if it has been hinted or not. It is also of little importance to higher-resolution output devices. A Linotronic PostScript phototypesetter running at 1200 dots per inch or better will typically ignore all vestiges of hinting, as it can produce fine enough dots as to eliminate the need for dealing with partial ones.

Style

The Style selector below the Size control selects the weight of your type. Not all its options will be available for all typefaces. Many of the more specialized typefaces, such as Zapf Chancery and Machine—known as Zurich Calligraphic and Motor, respectively, in CorelDRAW—come in only one weight.

Note that bold text will usually take up more space horizontally than normal text, all other things being equal.

Spacing

If you click on the button marked Spacing below the typeface selection window, you'll see a new dialog box, as shown in Figure 3.9.

This dialog box allows you to adjust the amount of space between the characters in your text string. There are four sorts of space:

◆ Intercharacter space is the amount of space between characters. CorelDRAW measures this as a percentage.

◆ Interword space is the amount of space between words. CorelDRAW also measures this as a percentage.

◆ Interline space, or leading, is the space between lines of text in the same string. CorelDRAW defines this as being a percentage.

◆ Interparagraph spacing is only enabled if you're using the Text dialog box in paragraph mode. It adjusts the space between paragraphs as a percentage.

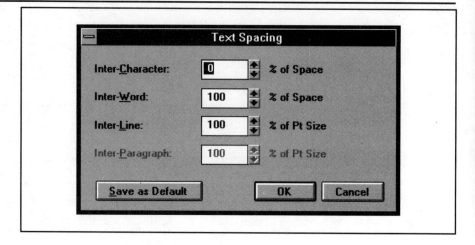

As will be discussed later in this chapter, you can use these controls in creating special effects with text. The simplest changes can improve the aesthetics tremendously. For example, headlines often look better with less than the usual space between their characters. Conversely, you can feather text out to completely fill an area by adjusting the interword and intercharacter spacing to make it fit.

Frame Control

The Frame item of the Text menu allows you to define those characteristics of paragraph-mode text frames which affect the way your text "pours" in the frame. Specifically, this dialog will allow you to define the number of columns in a text frame, how much space should exist between paragraphs of text, and so on.

Figure 3.10 illustrates the Frames dialog box.

The Columns control allows you to specify the number of columns the text in a text frame will pour into. Keep in mind that narrow columns will tend to leave an increasing amount of white space or peculiar justification as you work with larger point sizes. The Gutter Width control specified the amount of space between columns—allowing this to be zero will result in columns which touch each other, a condition considered to be singularly repugnant by professional page designers.

The Spacing controls affect the amount of extra space to add between paragraphs, lines, words, and characters, respectively. Note that the first two

FIGURE 3.10:

The Frames dialog box

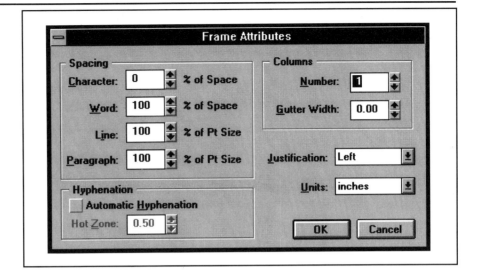

specify extra space as a percentage of the line space. If you increase the point size, this extra space will increase proportionally.

The Hyphenation control allows you to invoke CorelDRAW's automatic hyphenation for paragraph-mode text. The Hot Zone control allows you to specify an area to the left of the right edge of each column in which hyphenation can take place. Specifically, if a word extends into the hot zone, it will attract the attention of the hyphenation function. If the hyphenation algorithm decided that a word extending into the hot zone can be broken within the hot zone, it will hyphenate it. If not, it will move the whole word to the next line. Increasing the size of the hot zone will effectively make it more likely that words will be hyphenated.

GRAPHICS OPERATIONS ON TEXT

Once CorelDRAW has placed a string of text in its drawing space, you're free to manipulate it. CorelDRAW allows you to transform text in much the same way that you can transform other objects. The problem in creating visually interesting text effects is often more a question of what to do than how to do it.

It's quite easy to manipulate text beyond the point of recognizability under CorelDRAW. While this isn't always bad—thoroughly mutated text can produce very interesting abstract graphics—you should make sure that what you produce will not have to be read before you really lay on the special effects. Figure 3.11 illustrates text effects taken, perhaps, to extremes.

Attractive text effects are not merely a matter of clicking on some menu options until your text looks sufficiently strange. You really do have to understand what you're doing. In the process of exploring how to manipulate text, you'll also learn a lot about manipulating objects in general under CorelDRAW.

To set new defaults for the text outline and fill characteristics, make sure there are no objects currently selected in your CorelDRAW workspace. Select the outline pen tool and then one of the line thickness icons. A dialog box will appear to ask if you want the new default to apply to all objects, text objects, or other objects. Select text objects. Repeat this procedure for the line color and fill characteristics.

Using Text as Graphics

As with any object under CorelDRAW, text has basic graphic attributes. It consists of paths which can be stroked, and, because text paths are always closed, filled as well.

You might want to boot up CorelDRAW and follow along with this portion of the book to see if you can reproduce the effects we'll be discussing. Note that if you're printing your results as you go, you'll find that it takes longer to print the more complex examples in this chapter. Down towards the end, you might find that you have to wait for several minutes before some output deigns to emerge from your printer.

When you first place a text string in the work space, it will be stroked with whatever your default text outline thickness and color are. You might want to change this to a black hairline, or even no stroke at all if your text is to be filled with a solid color.

FIGURE 3.11:

Manipulating text to extremes

One of the common uglies that happens on first printing a drawing is having your text stroked with a rule that's thicker than you might have wanted. Figure 3.12 illustrates the effect of varying rule thicknesses on text.

Just about every unwanted effect has its potential uses under CorelDRAW, and fat, pudgy strokes applied accidentally to text do too. For instance, one common problem in complex drawings is arranging to have text stand out from its background. One way to deal with this problem is to stroke a duplicate of the text with a thicker line and a contrasting color and place the duplicate *behind* the original text. This serves to outline the original text, as shown in Figure 3.13.

Outlining text by stacking it on a copy of itself is managed very easily under CorelDRAW. Try it for yourself by writing some text into the work space and then following these steps:

1. First, select and duplicate the text.

2. Stroke the rearward text with a fat rule and make its stroke color white. You might want to set the fill color to white as well.

3. Next, position the second text directly over the first and set its stroke and fill attributes normally. It's a lot easier to position text if you use the Snap to Grid feature.

Quite a number of the more interesting text effects involve using multiple copies of the same bit of type, as we'll see. For example, a drop shadow is particularly easy to do if you use two copies of the same text slightly displaced. A different kind of effect can be created by duplicating the same text multiple times and changing the stroke width and stroke density with each new iteration. The results can be seen in Figure 3.14. The two precise-adjustment boxes of the pen tool control the stroke qualities—we'll discuss them in detail about five paragraphs from now.

The first or backmost object was set with a stroke width of 2 picas—a very fat line—and a stroke density of 10 percent. This object was then duplicated and the duplicate was given a slightly narrower width—1 pica, 10 points—with a slightly denser stroke of 15 percent. This was repeated until the stroke width reached 1 point and the density reached 70 percent.

This whole process is a great deal easier if you set the duplicate displacement values in the Preferences dialog box to zero so that the duplicates are

The reverse of this effect is also interesting—it's called an "inline." Set the lowermost copy of some text with a black outline and no fill. Set the stroke thickness fairly wide. Next, set a copy of the text above the black one with no fill and a thinner white rule. This is an eye-catching way to use text, and one which isn't seen often because it has traditionally been very tricky to handle using photographic techniques. Try combining this effect with a distorted nib shape for one or both of the text objects. Changing the nib shape will be discussed in a moment.

FIGURE 3.12:
Increasing the stroke weight for text

Hairline
One Point
Two Points
Four Points
Eight Points
Sixteen Points

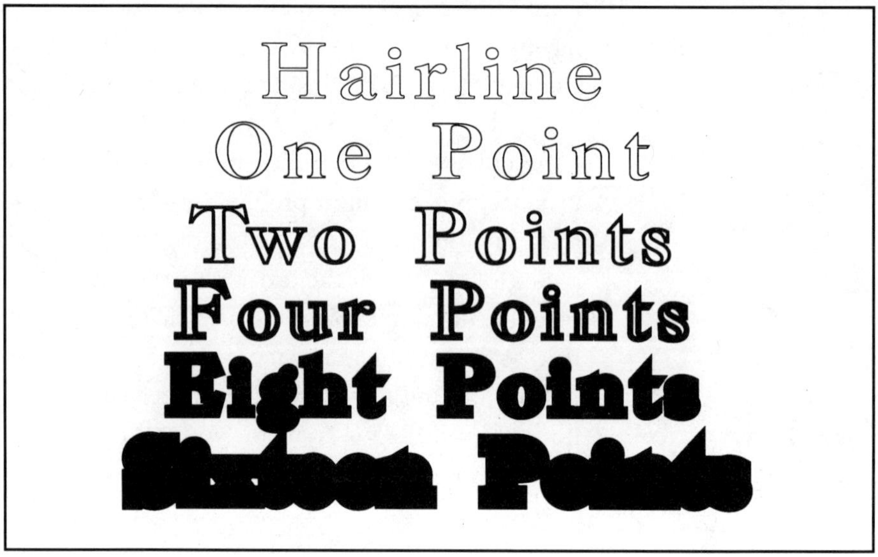

automatically placed directly on the original without the need for any adjustment by hand.

Effects such as the glow added to text in Figure 3.14 can be created much more easily by using the CorelDRAW *blend* effect, which will be discussed in Chapter 7.

If you'll ultimately be printing to a color output device or if you'll be having CorelDRAW create color separations for you, you can do all sorts of interesting things with these basic text attributes.

The fill attributes of text also offer a lot of interesting possibilities—as well as a few pitfalls. We'll discuss fills in greater detail in the next chapter.

Fine-Tuning Outlines

In choosing the stroke weight for your text you can, of course, use the default values displayed in the outline pen tool's flyout menu. However, considerably more control can be had through the use of the precise-adjustment boxes, available through the leftmost icons in this menu. Figure 3.15 illustrates the Outline Pen box with a few as yet undiscussed items.

Keeping text from being engulfed by its background

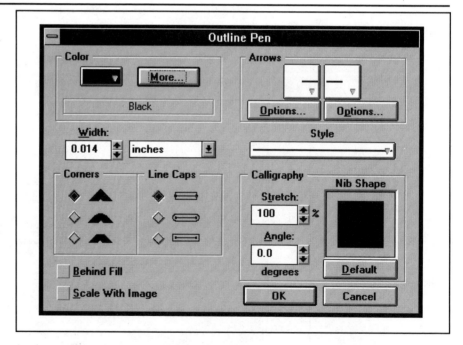

You can set the stroke of the paths that define your text in several ways. The most obvious one is to use a solid line. However, you can also have a path stroked with dashes by clicking on the Style button. This will pop up a selector list of dash options. If you select a dashed line, the example line in the Style window will change to reflect your choice.

The two check boxes at the bottom of the dialog box are particularly applicable to text. The Behind Fill box tells CorelDRAW to stroke your text before filling it. By not selecting this box, the stroke will appear on top of the fill. If this is selected, the stroke weight of text which also has a fill pattern will appear about half as thick as it should, as the inner portion of the line will be obscured by the fill.

The Scale With Image box tells CorelDRAW what to do with the stroke width of your text should you decide to stretch the text. If it's selected, the width of the rule used to stroke your text will expand in the direction you stretch the text. You should use this feature if you plan to change the size of your text by transforming it, especially if the text you have in mind involves a fat rule.

Changing the Corners and Line Caps settings for the stroke of your text will have decided effects on its appearance if you're stroking it with a heavy rule, and you should experiment with these settings to see what happens. Likewise, play with the Nib Shape box as well. Figure 3.16 illustrates the effects of some variations on these values.

The last effect uses the Nib Shape controls of the Outline Pen dialog box.

The Nib Shape window isn't just a display—it's also a control. Click and hold your mouse in it and drag the mouse pointer around. This will adjust the shape and angle of the nib with which your lines will be stroked. It might take you a few moments to get a feel for how this works.

FIGURE 3.16:

Changing the outline pen characteristics for stroking text

Square Corners
Round Corners
Flat Corners
Calligraphic Pen

TRANSFORMING TEXT

The transformations which CorelDRAW can apply to text are particularly effective. They range from simply changing how it lies on your page to modifying it extensively.

If you select a text string with the pick tool, you will find that you can stretch it just as you can other objects. If you grab one of the corner handles, you can stretch it while preserving its aspect ratio. If you grab a center handle you can stretch it more in one direction than in the other.

This sort of transformation does not cause CorelDRAW to stop dealing with the text as text. If after stretching the text you hit Ctrl-T to pop up the Paragraph Text and Artistic Text dialog boxes, you will notice that not only has the point size changed to reflect the new, stretched size of the text, but the text is still editable. You can also still edit transformed text on-screen.

If you select the Clear Transformations item from the Transform menu, the text will return to its original size and aspect ratio, exactly as it was before you started meddling with it.

You can rotate text just as you have rotated simple objects. Select a bit of text, then click on the selected text with the pick tool and grab one of the rotation marks. The text will freely rotate about the pivot. Likewise, if you grab one of the skew marks, you can bend the text along one dimension. Figure 3.17 illustrates these basic transformations.

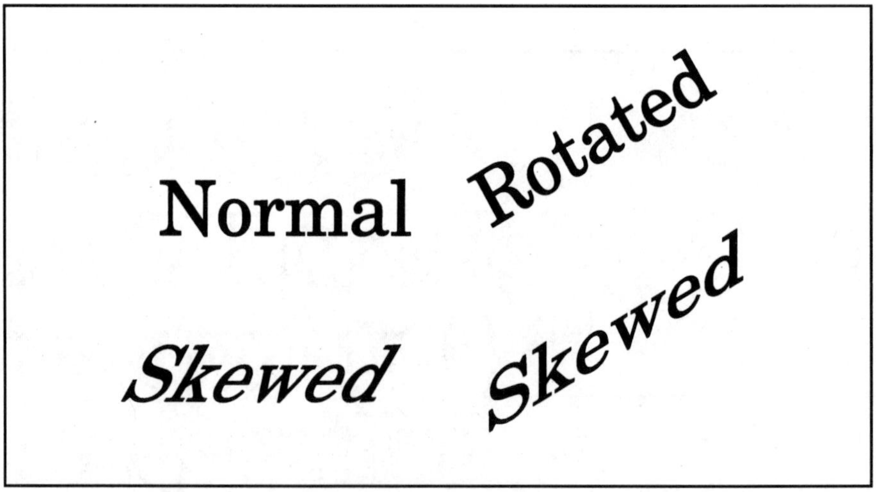

FIGURE 3.17:
Simple transformations

Using the Transform Menu

If you hold down the Ctrl key while skewing text, the skew angle will be constrained to the angle set in the Preferences dialog box of your copy of CorelDRAW.

Rotating and skewing text using the pick tool is great for matching it to the rest of a drawing by eye, but not quite as useful if you want to manipulate it by a specified number of degrees. Fortunately, the same rotation and skew effects can be handled through the Rotate & Skew item of the Transform menu. This dialog box was discussed previously in Chapter 2.

A lot of very interesting text effects can be achieved by using this box along with the Repeat item of the Edit menu (or the Ctrl-R keyboard shortcut). Bearing in mind that the act of applying a transformation, like rotating or skewing a bit of text, automatically selects the *result* of the transformation, you will understand why you need to leave an original in the drawing if you want to create iterations of a progressive transformation by using the Repeat function several times.

For example, if you tell CorelDRAW to skew some text by 10 degrees and repeat this several times, you can wind up with something which looks like Figure 3.18.

Actually, this isn't quite true. There's one more step involved. As you will recall, as objects are added to a drawing they're placed, by default, forward of the existing objects. You might imagine each object to have been drawn on a sheet of clear acetate and placed atop a pile of earlier objects. Thus, the original text in the example of Figure 3.18 was actually behind all the copies, rather than in front of them. This was easy to correct using the following procedure.

1. Select all the objects in this effect with the pick tool by drawing a rubber-band box around them.

2. Select the Reverse Order item from the Arrange menu.

FIGURE 3.18:
Progressive skewing

The progressively darker gray fills of the duplicated text did not happen automatically either. Each one was selected and a particular fill level was applied to it.

The Stretch & Mirror item of the Transform menu offers similar possibilities for special effects. The mirror functions allow you to flip an object either horizontally or vertically. You would have to use this function twice to flip it across both axes. The stretch functions allow you to expand or contract an object in both dimensions by specified amounts.

As with the previous example, you can invoke this function several times using the Repeat function. Figure 3.19 illustrates an effect created using the stretch function. These objects, too, were created in the wrong order and had to be reversed before they appeared like this.

You can probably dream up a number of effects which entail using several transformations on a single object for each stage of the effect. This could get a little tedious because CorelDRAW allows you to repeat only the last thing you did. For example, if you wanted to create a text effect which involved rotating *and* reducing each duplicated object, the repeat function would be of little use.

There is a way around this. It involves the use of the CorelDRAW *blend* effect, which will be discussed in Chapter 7.

CONVERTING TEXT TO CURVES

The most radical text effects available under CorelDRAW involve manipulating the paths which make up the individual characters of your text. At this level, the text ceases to be text as such and reverts to being basic objects.

FIGURE 3.19:

A text effect using progressive stretching

Once you have reduced text to its component parts it can never be turned back into text objects. It will no longer be possible to edit or change the text attributes of such text with the Artistic Text dialog box or the Character Attribute dialog box.

While converting text into paths prohibits you from dealing with it as text any longer, it does open up a whole world of new possibilities in dealing with it as graphics. If you plan ahead and perform all the text-related modifications to your text objects before you convert them to graphic objects, this shouldn't be a problem.

In order to convert a text object into a purely graphic object (with string-mode text only), select the text object or objects with the pick tool and then select the Convert To Curves item from the Arrange menu. The resulting object will display all the Bézier curves used to outline the selected text. The curves will all be combined together. If you plan to manipulate some of the curves, you should subsequently select the Break Apart item from the Arrange menu. You can use the Combine item after you've changed these paths. This will make all the paths into a single object again.

The Bigfoot graphic in Figure 3.20 is an example of text which has been converted to curves and worked over.

FIGURE 3.20:

Text converted to curves

The top line is simply text which has been set normally. This is the New Century Schoolbook font, or what CorelDRAW calls New Brunswick. It's a good choice for this graphic as it has big, chunky serifs at the bottom of its uppercase characters, suitable for expansion into big feet.

If you convert this text into curves, node marks will appear at strategic locations around the text. As you will be working in this example with all the characters at once, there's no need to break them apart. You can select the curves which represent the bottoms of all the characters by using the shape tool to draw a marquee that encompasses just the bottoms of the characters. That way, when you grab just one of the selected nodes and drag it down, all the nodes will follow. Use this technique to expand the bases of the characters to give them feet of any proportions you like.

Some final touching up may be necessary. The lower curves on the B and the G didn't expand all that well initially, and it was necessary to manually pull those nodes down a bit.

You can create some eye-catching graphics by playing with the component parts of text. It's possible to make parts of your characters into other sorts of graphics, to fuse text and other objects, and so on. Figure 3.21 is some text in University Roman and one of the clip art images which comes with CorelDRAW.

In creating graphics which use text converted to curves, bear in mind that there are lots of ways to mangle such a collection of objects. Most of the time, the results of making a mistake are complex at best to untangle. It's a good idea to save your file frequently while you're working on graphics of this sort, so you can revert to your most recently saved version if things go amiss.

FIGURE 3.21:

Brass and horn, fused objects

THE JOY OF DINGBATS

In addition to the text typefaces which came with CorelDRAW, you will have received several symbol sets. These include a music notation typeface, a Greek and math symbol set, and something which CorelDRAW calls Dixieland but which the rest of the world knows as Zapf Dingbats.

Dingbats is a peculiar little typeface. It's intended for use as ornaments, bullets, and other typographic regalia which appear in text from time to time. Figure 3.22 illustrates some of the many denizens of the Dingbats font.

The most obvious use of Dingbats is to set the odd dingbat in your text. Depending on how off the wall you can allow your text to get, you can work in quite a few of them.

It's not hard to use Dingbats—they're just special characters, and can be dealt with using the Character Map application discussed earlier in this chapter.

In some cases, it's desirable to make dingbats slightly larger than the text they're part of. Their natural sizes tend to make them look a bit diminutive.

Dingbats are also useful as graphics which don't have anything much to do with text. If you blow up a dingbat so it looks like a graphic you can use it for all sorts of things. The heart-shaped leaf object in Figure 3.23 is actually a dingbat.

FIGURE 3.22:
Some Dingbats

FIGURE 3.23:

*A dingbat, some clip
art, and two thousand
calories*

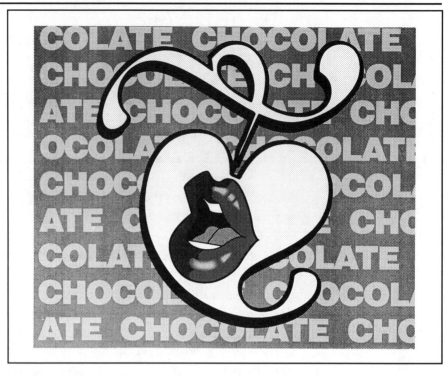

You might also want to have a look at another font that will appear in
the CorelDRAW font selector, WingDings. It's very much like Dingbats—
Dixieland—but has a slightly different assortment of bats.

SYMBOL MODE

There is a very easy way to work with special, non-alphabetic symbol fonts.
CorelDRAW provides a dedicated symbol mode, which is designed to let
you place individual symbols in your drawing without having to call up the
Character Map application or resort to badly printed, third-generation
photocopies of symbol charts.

Symbol mode may be a bit confusing in concept. It actually uses symbols which are stored as fonts. However, it will place graphic objects, not text
objects, in your drawings.

The symbols mode can be accessed by clicking and holding the text
tool in the CorelDRAW toolbox until a flyout menu appears. Select the star

icon and the text tool will become the symbol tool. Repeat this process and select the A icon to restore the text tool to its usual function.

When you click in the CorelDRAW work space with the symbol tool, the symbol selector dialog box will appear, as seen in Figure 3.24.

The Symbols dialog box is pretty easy to understand. To begin with, choose a symbol library from the list at the right side of the box. Having done this, click in the white symbol display window to call up a display of all the symbols in the selected library. Double click on the symbol you want to use. You can change the size of the symbol using the Size control—you can also interactively stretch symbols once they have been placed, of course.

While you will no doubt want to experiment with the symbol libraries to get a feel for what's in them, Table 3.1 offers a quick overview of what they contain.

FIGURE 3.24:
The symbol entry window

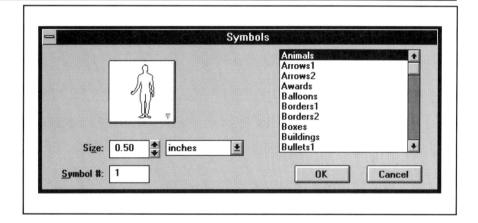

TABLE 3.1:
The CorelDRAW symbol libraries

LIBRARY	DESCRIPTIONS
Animals	Outlines of animals. Note that the first symbol in this library is a human being.
Arrows	Two libraries with enough arrowheads to start your own archaeological dig.
Awards	Crests, trophies, and ribbons.

TABLE 3.1:

The CorelDRAW symbol libraries (continued)

LIBRARY	DESCRIPTIONS
Balloons	Speech bubbles, perfect for creating your own comic strips or political campaign advertisements.
Borders	Two libraries of frames and borders.
Boxes	Dozens of two-section containers.
Buildings	Instant subdivision, just add water. Includes houses, office towers, several castles, and a tepee.
Bullets	Three libraries of decorative symbols to start list items with.
Business and Government	Objects found in offices, and several United States political symbols.
Common Bullets	Commonly used symbols.
Computers	Computers, terminals, networks, hard-drive crashes, and so on.
Electronics	Schematic symbols.
Festive	Icons of holidays, including Christmas, Saint Patrick's Day, Halloween and others, ranked in order of commercial interest. Christmas comes first, of course.
Floorplan	Symbols for laying out architectural floor plans of houses and offices.
Food	Everything from Swiss cheese to pineapples.
Furniture	Chairs, tables, dressers, beds, appliances, and, inexplicably, a set of saloon doors.
Geographic Symbols	Things you might find on road signs.
Household	Common household objects, including an inordinate number of candles.
Hygiene	Bathtubs, towels, and a hair dryer, among other things.
Landmarks	Famous edifices. Oddly, the Statue of Liberty comes immediately after the stone faces on Easter Island.
Medicine	Medical symbols.

TABLE 3.1:
The CorelDRAW symbol libraries (continued)

LIBRARY	DESCRIPTIONS
Military	Fighter jets, tanks, guns, soldiers… and knights on horseback, should the foregoing fall to budget cuts.
Military ID	Insignia.
Music	Instruments. (Sadly, no lutes are among them.)
Musical Symbols	Sheet music notation.
Nautical Flags	Flags for boating enthusiasts.
People	A subclass of the Animals library, above.
Plants	Trees, mushrooms, leaves, berries, and so on.
Science	Scientific symbols, chemistry apparatus, several very simple molecules.
Shapes	Two libraries of simple, closed paths.
Signs	Lots of commonly used symbol signs, including "no smoking," "poison," "picnic area ahead," and the always useful nuclear energy trifoil, which is very handy if you're just putting the finishing touches on a reactor.
Space	Rockets, satellites, and shuttles.
Sports and Hobbies	Various balls, pucks, stones, guns, arrows, and a fire extinguisher£ (Not too sure which sport that last one relates to.)
Sports Figures	Silhouetted people playing games.
Stars	Two libraries worth of them.
Technology	Calculators, CD players, television sets, WalkMans, WatchMans, DiscMans, camcorders, and so on. A crippled Visa card is notably absent.
Tools	Hammers, saws, shovels, and potted plants.
Tracks	Animal, human, and railroad.
Transportation	Cars, trucks, steering wheels, and an assortment of hubcaps.
Weather	A library of the symbols used by television weather forecasters.

In addition to the foregoing list, the symbol library also allows you to apply Dixieland, WingDings, and the Greek/Math symbol set through the Symbols dialog box.

There are countless applications for these symbols. Figure 3.25 is one example of the CorelDRAW symbol facility at work.

Typesetting music is a natural application of the CorelDRAW symbol facilities. It takes a bit of forethought to do it well, however. You should begin by setting the Snap To Grid so that there are two grid points for each staff line. One grid point per millimeter works well, with the staff lines at two-millimeter intervals. You will also want to set the size of the symbols appropriately. If you use one grid point per millimeter, nine-millimeter symbols are about the right size. You should also set the Nudge value to one millimeter, which will allow you to move notes around in one-tone intervals using the arrow keys.

You really need only place the first of any symbol using the Symbols dialog box. After that, it's quicker to just duplicate it.

Note that in this piece of music, grouped eighth-notes are really just quarter-note symbols with a bar running through them. The bar is a rectangle which has been skewed, rather than just a line.

FIGURE 3.25:

Loftus Jones by CorelDRAW

FITTING TEXT TO PATHS

Text is normally drawn with respect to a baseline. When you drag text around, you actually just move the baseline, and the text which is tied to it moves with it. The baseline is, by default, straight. If you change the shape of the baseline the shape of the text string will also be altered.

CorelDRAW does not allow you to manipulate the baseline as you would a true path. However, and instead, it provides a facility for fitting the baseline—and hence the text—to a real path. This Fit Text To Path function (in the Text menu) is the genesis of countless text effects.

Let's start with a simple example. The upper screen in Figure 3.26 illustrates a text string and an ellipse. If you select them both—either with the pick tool or by using the Select All item of the Edit menu—and then select the Fit Text To Path item of the Text menu, the result should look like the lower screen. In fact, there will be a brief encounter with one of CorelDRAW's roll-up menus in the process, which we'll get to in a moment.

When you ask CorelDRAW to fit text to a path, it will display a roll-up menu to let you choose how the text and the path should relate to each other. This menu and its various options are illustrated in Figure 3.27.

The uppermost selector in the Fit Text To Path roll-up menu will tell CorelDRAW how to deal with letters that appear on curved sections of a path. The next one down determines where the text will appear in relation to the path it's fitted to—above, below, or in the center. The third one selects the text justification, that is, whether the text should begin at the start of the path, in the center of the path or at the end of the path and work backward.

The *Place on other side* option of the Fit Text To Path roll-up will cause the text to be drawn in a mirror image if this option is selected. The Edit button will call up a dialog box to let you adjust the distance between the text and the path it's fitted to.

Note that, having made some changes to these values, you must click on the Apply button to make them appear in your drawing. Calculating the positions of characters fitted to a path is time-consuming—be patient.

Once you have fitted text to a path, you can delete the path if you like. However, it's a better idea to retain the path and just prevent it from appearing in your finished drawing. To do this, select the path and give it no fill

Hitting Ctrl-F will call up the Fit Text To Path roll-up menu any time you need it.

FIGURE 3.26:

*Fitting a text string
to a path*

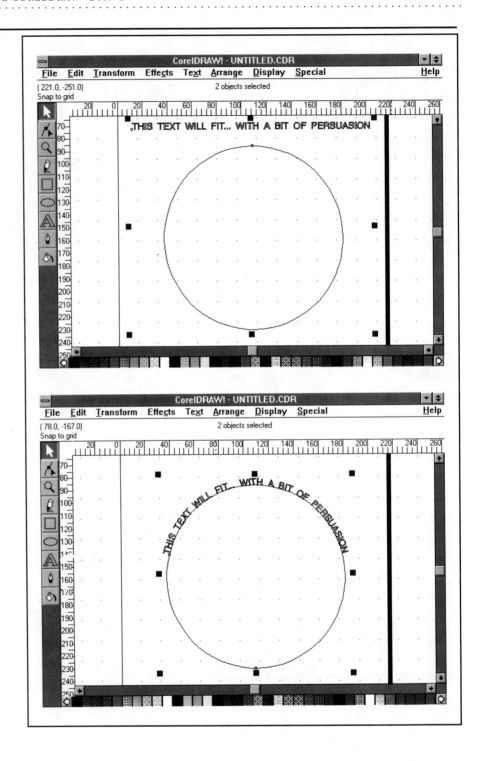

FIGURE 3.27:

Justification and text fitting

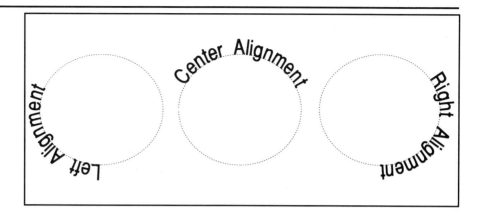

FIGURE 3.27:

Justification and text fitting

and no stroke. It will still appear in the CorelDRAW work space if you use the Edit Wireframe mode, but your final hard copy will not show it.

FITTING TEXT TO COMPLEX PATHS

The idea of fitting text to paths often works better than the reality of it. There are a few important points to keep in mind when you go to fit text around complex paths.

Figure 3.28 is the letter A we first encountered in Chapter 1. You should now know roughly how this drawing was created. The path for the A was formed by setting an immense capital A and converting it to curves. The text which wraps around the A was entered as a straight text string—its length being determined largely by the 250-character maximum for a text string. Finally, the text and the capital A path were selected, and the text was fitted to the path.

In fact, there's a lot more to it than this. To begin with, the choice of the typeface for the big A is very important. Text wrapped around sharp corners doesn't look very good. It was important to select a typeface in which the capital A was composed only of gently rounded paths. American Typewriter—what CorelDRAW refers to as Memorandum—is a good choice for this.

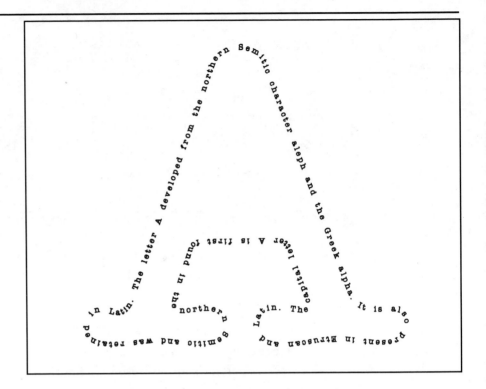

Having been drawn on the page and converted to curves, the A was modified slightly by removing the paths that formed the inside of the character. The stroke of the path was then set to no thickness so the path itself would not appear in the final hard copy.

The next tricky bit was to get the text to encompass the path which comprised the periphery of the big A with neither a gap nor an overlap. Actually, you might not see any overlap using this technique. If you make the text too long, CorelDRAW may leave off the offending part of the string. Fitting the text without losing any of it was done through trial and error. The length of the text string can be adjusted by putting more or less space between characters and words using the Spacing adjustment of the Artistic Text dialog box and then fitting the text to the path again.

Figure 3.29 illustrates the steps in creating the A graphic.

FIGURE 3.29:

*Fitting a text string
to the letter A*

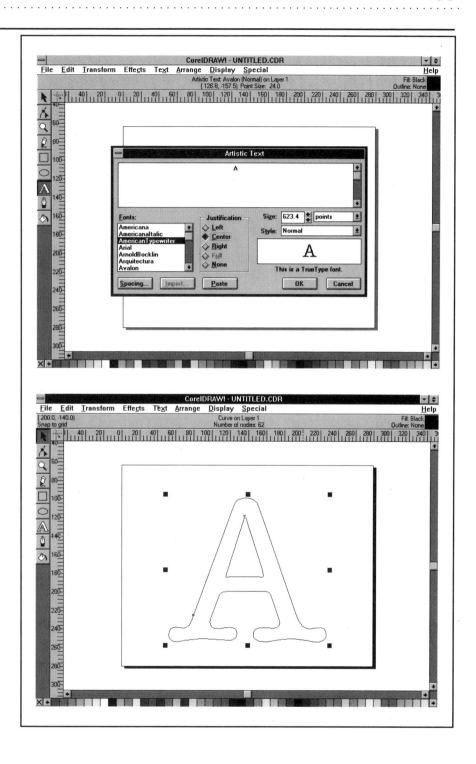

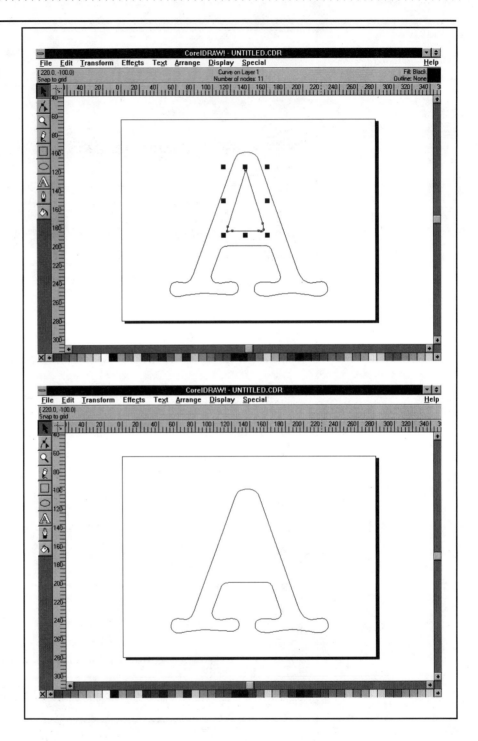

FIGURE 3.29:

*Fitting a text string to
the letter A (continued)*

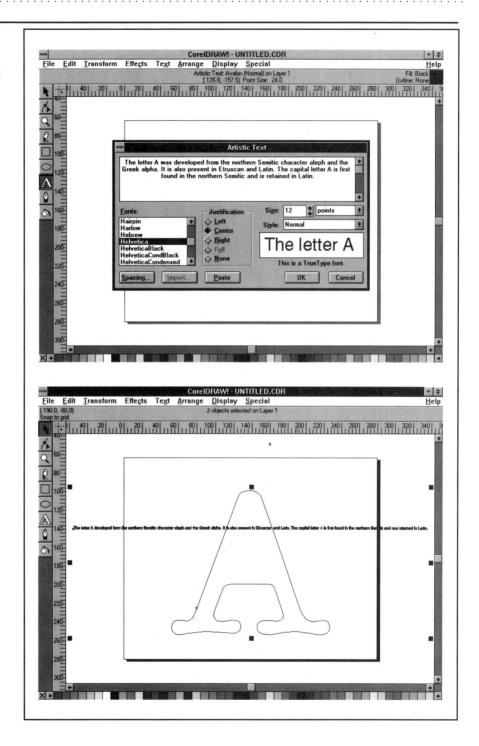

MANIPULATING TYPE WITHIN TEXT STRINGS

CorelDRAW allows you to compress or stretch a text string such that the point size and aspect ratio of the text does not change. Only the space between the characters is affected, and this is adjusted proportionally. Thus, text which is fitted to an area larger than it would otherwise occupy still looks to be set properly—it will just be a bit loose.

You can achieve this result by using the Spacing features in the Artistic Text dialog box, as we discussed in connection with the big A graphic above. However, repeatedly having to pop back into this box in a trial-and-error attempt to fine-tune the spacing is inconvenient. CorelDRAW lets you do the same thing by eye when this is more appropriate.

To adjust the spacing of a text string by eye, select the string with the shape tool. Along with individual node marks for each character, two special text-spacing marks will appear, one at each end of the last line of the string. The left text-spacing mark adjusts interline spacing. The rightmost mark adjusts the space between words and letters.

If you grab the right text-spacing mark and drag it to the right, the spacing between the letters of your text will increase proportionally. If you hold the Ctrl key down while you drag it, the space between the letters will not be affected but the space between the words will.

Figure 3.30 is the cover of the popular *Timewarp Quarterly,* a magazine which is rarely seen these days but was very popular in the Late Middle Ages. As with most magazine covers, this design embodies several examples of text fitting and kerning.

The T and the Q of the main title have been made larger—by a process to be discussed in the next section—and the T was shifted vertically. The text below the main title—The Magazine for Temporal Tourists—was set in Switzerland Narrow and fitted to the appropriate width with the right text-spacing mark. The issue date was handled in the same way.

The current fashion in using fitted text in this way is to have lots of space between the characters. If you like to keep up with such fashions, it's also not a bad idea to use a laterally condensed font like Helvetica—or Switzerland—Narrow. Fitted text is rarely all that readable in quantity, and it is usually used more for decoration than to convey any serious amount

FIGURE 3.30:

*The cover of the July
1643 edition of*
Timewarp Quarterly

of information. However, it's a powerful tool in creating contemporary-looking type.

The cover contents, In This Issue, are all handled as a single block of text which has been expanded vertically using the left text-spacing mark. The text was set in University Roman; then the block as a whole was expanded by increasing the line spacing until the contents filled the cover.

The first line of this text block was then set larger than the rest of the type by the following process.

SETTING INDIVIDUAL CHARACTER ATTRIBUTES

CorelDRAW allows you to select individual characters in any text string and change their size, font, and several other characteristics. You can manipulate the text attributes of every character in a text string. Figure 3.31 is an example of a text string in which each character has been given a different typeface. This serves to illustrate both the flexibility of CorelDRAW and a good reason why you shouldn't overuse this powerful feature.

Let's create a text string in which the first and last characters are bigger than the rest of the text. The graphic is shown in Figure 3.32.

Here's how this graphic is created:

1. Set the word "QUEST" in 96-point Garamond, the face that CorelDRAW calls Gatineau.

2. Select this text with the shape tool.

3. Double click on the node for the letter *Q* (the one to the left of the letter). Alternatively, select Character from the Text menu. The Character Attributes dialog box will appear.

4. Change the Size value in the dialog box to 144 and the Vertical Shift in Preferences to −35 percent. (This latter number was arrived at through trial and error.) The dialog box should look like Figure 3.33.

FIGURE 3.31:

A text string with lots of different typefaces

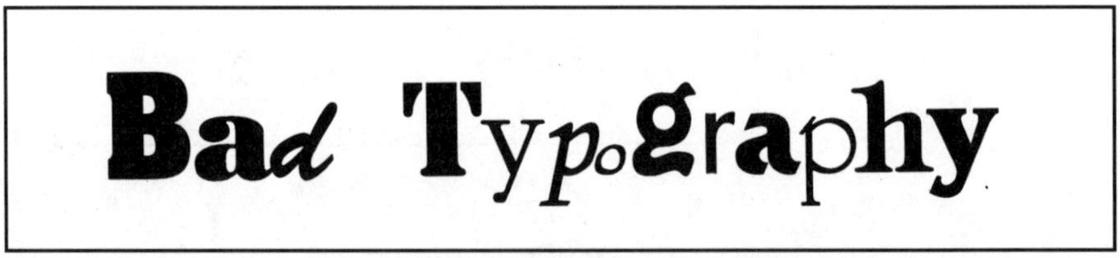

FIGURE 3.32:

Changing the size of individual characters

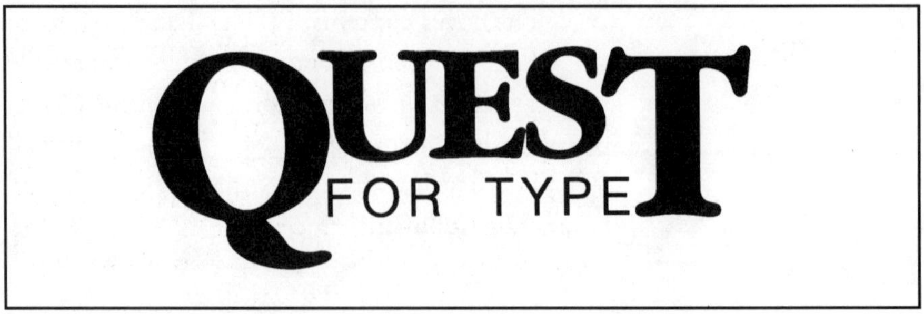

5. Click on OK, then repeat this process for the letter *T.*

6. Set the words "FOR TYPE" in Helvetica—Switzerland—Light and fit it to the space between the *Q* and the *T.*

Any combination of attributes can be set for any number of characters. If you want to change the attributes of more than one character at a time—for example, to boldface one word in a sentence—use the shape tool to select the characters to be changed and click on one of the selected nodes. The dialog box in Figure 3.33 will appear, but this time any changes you make will pertain to all the selected characters.

This can be tricky if you've already changed some attributes in a text string. For example, the string in Figure 3.30 had a different typeface attribute for each character, although all of them were the same size. If you were to select the first two characters and double click on the first node, the typeface displayed in the Character Attributes dialog box would reflect the typeface of the first character, the one you double clicked on.

If you don't touch the typeface selection window, each character's typeface attributes will still remain as they were. However, if you were to change the point size in this box, both characters would change in size. In a situation where you have selected several characters with different attributes, only those attributes you explicitly change will be applied to all the selected characters.

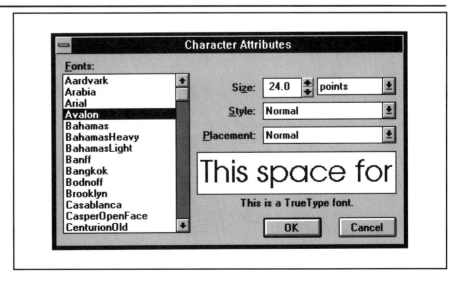

FIGURE 3.33:

The Character Attributes dialog box

The Horizontal and Vertical Shift values in the Preferences dialog box correspond to the horizontal and vertical positioning which you can adjust with the shape tool in kerning text. These controls allow you to adjust these attributes numerically rather than by eye. This is handy for fine-tuning character positions which you've set by eye with the shape tool.

The Character Angle attribute allows you to cause selected characters to be rotated about their individual midpoints. This is not the same as skewing them so they look italicized, nor is it the same as rotating a whole block of text. These three effects are different, and they are illustrated in Figure 3.34.

KERNING AND TEXT FITTING

When you fit text to a path, it's very often the case that the characters tend to bunch up in sharply concave areas and get spread out in convex ones. In some cases you can minimize this problem by using the first of the three selector items in the Fit Text To Path roll-up. In others, you'll have to deal

FIGURE 3.34:

Various ways to change the character angle

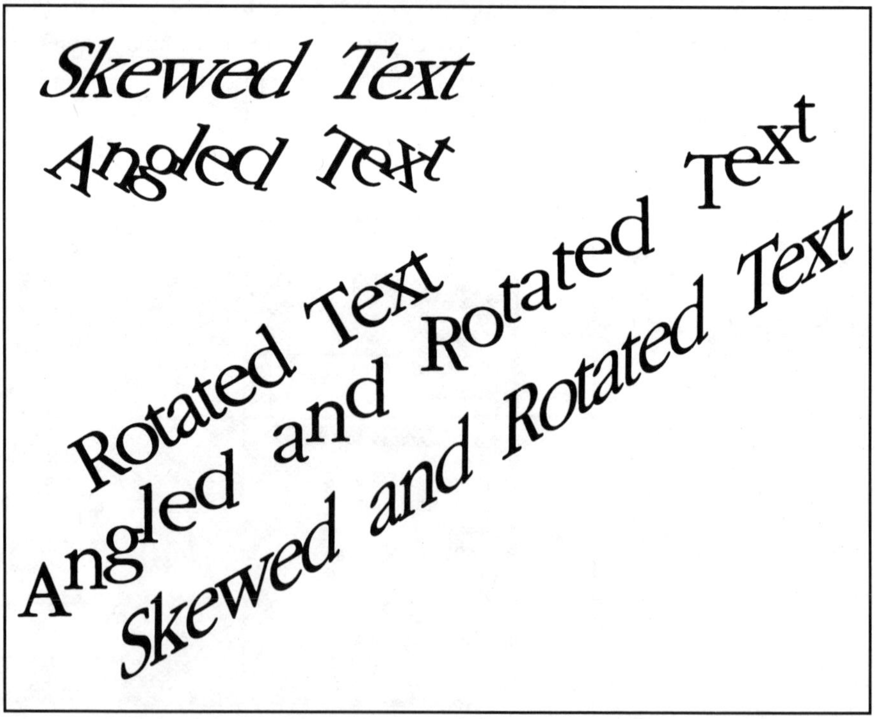

with it by hand. You can fix this problem by manually adjusting the spacing between the characters, a process known as *kerning*.

Figure 3.35 illustrates the effects of kerning text.

Text kerning is another of those operations which does not entail turning your text irretrievably into objects. Even though you will be dealing with the characters from a string individually, CorelDRAW will still treat kerned text objects as text, allowing you to subsequently edit them and change their text attributes, as we've discussed.

It's worth reiterating that CorelDRAW does kern text automatically based on the kerning information which is part of TrueType fonts. You

Kerning text

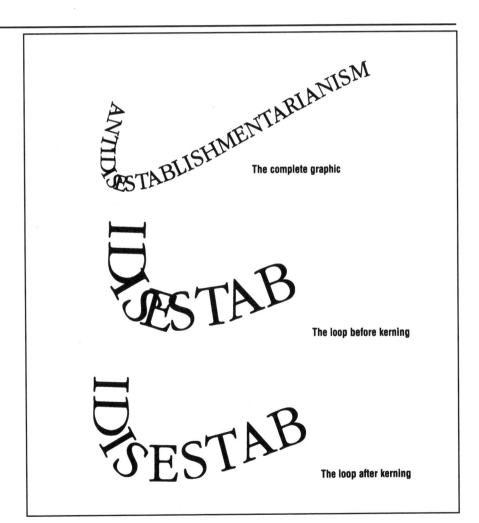

The complete graphic

The loop before kerning

The loop after kerning

might want to manually kern text because you're using a third-party font with no kerning information, because you aren't happy with the kerning CorelDRAW does in a particular case, or because you want to create an unusual type effect.

Simple Kerning

Figure 3.36 illustrates text which could do with some kerning. Note that this is a matter both of personal taste and of the typeface which was used to set this text. Some fonts, because of their design, are more likely to leave large or irregular gaps between certain pairs of characters. As a rule, fonts which are laterally condensed, such as Helvetica Narrow or University Roman— CorelDRAW's Switzerland Narrow and Unicorn fonts respectively—are less likely to encounter these problems.

Having placed this text in the work space, you can kern it by selecting it with the shape tool. This will cause the individual character nodes to be displayed, one to the lower left of each character, as well as the two text-spacing marks, one at each end of the last line of the string.

FIGURE 3.36:

Some text to be kerned

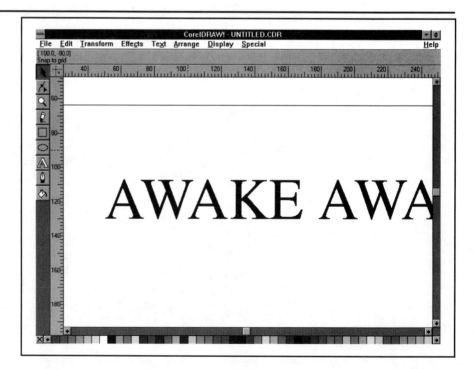

If you click and hold on one of the character nodes, you'll find that you'll be able to drag the character around. This will let you adjust the kerning between any of the characters in the string. Figure 3.37 shows the letter W selected and kerned.

In designing logos and other specialized bits of type, kerning text so that all the characters touch is a very effective technique. This does not make for particularly readable text—you would probably not want to do it to really fat text, for example—but it serves to make the text look solid and more like a single object than a group of characters. In the case of a logo, where you are really designing a symbol rather than a word, this frequently works well.

When you kern text like this, it's extremely difficult to keep from moving the text vertically while you're adjusting it horizontally. You might decide you *want* to put some vertical shift in your text string, but if you don't, there's a way around it. Once you're finished kerning a string of text, just use the Align To Baseline item of the Text menu. This automatically restores the text to the baseline without disturbing your kerning.

FIGURE 3.37:
Kerning a letter

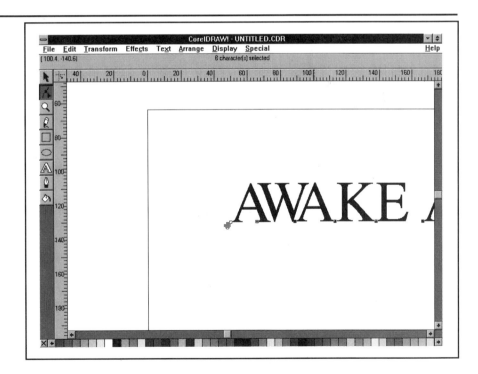

It's usually the case that you will want to kern only the occasional pair of letters in a text string, ones where the gap between adjoining characters is particularly noticeable. If you move the right character of the pair left, however, you will merely transfer the gap over by one character. You could, of course, kern all the other characters by hand, but this is tedious, and fortunately unnecessary. Instead, you can drag all the remaining characters in a text string by using the shape tool cursor to draw a marquee box around the characters you want to drag. The node marks of the selected characters will turn black. Grab one of the selected node marks and drag the block of text into position.

If you use the shape tool to move characters in a string which has already been set with one of the conventional alignment settings (Left, Center, and Right justification), and the moved characters end up beyond the previous beginning or end of the string, CorelDRAW might reposition the other characters in the string when it goes to redraw the text. To avoid this problem, change the string justification to None. This will prevent CorelDRAW from imposing alignment on a string that you have taken pains to align by hand.

In selecting multiple characters with the shape tool, it's not always immediately obvious whether you've selected all the text you think you have. Note that CorelDRAW displays the number of characters which have actually been selected in the status line above the work space.

Creating Ligatures

One of the more extreme uses of kerning under CorelDRAW is in the creation of ligatures. Depending upon the graphic circles you frequent, using ligatures will have you regarded either as erudite and sophisticated or as a type snob.

A ligature is a single character formed by joining two or more characters, or, in the case of CorelDRAW, by kerning two characters so close together that they overlap in places. Ligatures usually involve lowercase characters. One common example is ff, as shown in Figure 3.38.

By using a ligature rather than two separate characters, the second example has allowed the word to occupy a bit less space on the line without looking unnecessarily crowded. In fact, used correctly, ligatures can be very attractive.

One ligature which is still frequently used is fi. In some fonts, the dot of the i will bump into the upper end of the f, which looks peculiar. In the days of metal type, a special fi character was created in which the dot of the i was missing entirely—it was supplanted by the bulge at the top of the f.

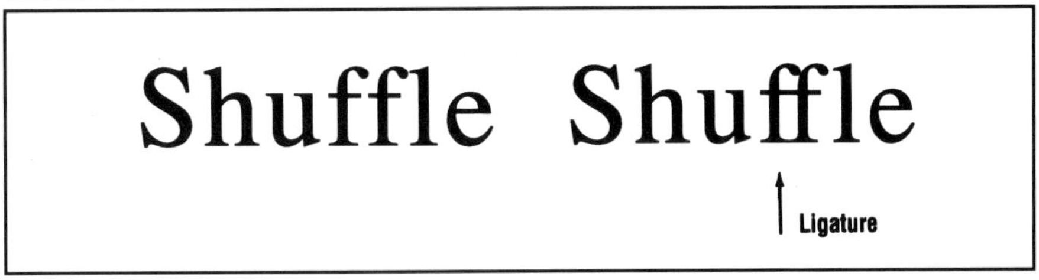

FIGURE 3.38:
A ligature

Shuffle Shuffle

↑ Ligature

The use of ligatures is not at all common anymore, for several reasons. One of these is that it's usually regarded as being too much work to bother with them. Secondly, the broad, flowing typefaces of the turn of the century—which supported ligatures nicely—have given way to type which is laterally condensed, as designers have required typefaces which squeeze more words onto a page. Fairly narrow faces neither lend themselves to ligatures nor really require them, and the minuscule reduction in line width offered by the odd ligature is rarely worth the effort.

In setting type with CorelDRAW, you might want to experiment with making ligatures. None of the faces included with the package suffer from the problem cured by the fi ligature, but several of the more elongated ones—such as Cooper Black, what CorelDRAW ships as Cupertino—look attractive when some adjoining lowercase letters are kerned together into ligatures. Particularly tall characters, such as f and l, lend themselves to forming ligatures.

Spell Checking

Any text in a CorelDRAW drawing which hasn't previously been converted to curves can be checked for misspellings using the online CorelDRAW spelling checker. The spelling checker has a huge dictionary of correctly spelled words, and will check each word in a text object against it. It will bring any words it doesn't recognize to your attention.

The spelling checker has a dictionary of about 116,000 words, compiled by Houghton Mifflin.

To invoke the spelling checker, select a text object for it to check and then select Spell Checker from the text menu. The dialog box in Figure 3.39 will appear.

FIGURE 3.39:

The Spell Checker dialog box

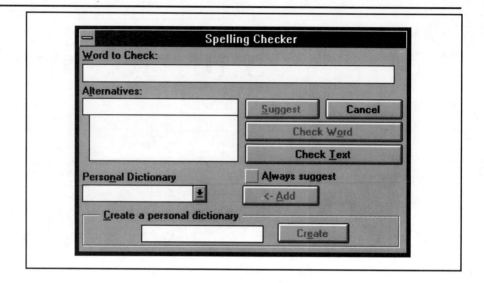

American users may want to take note that CorelDRAW was created in Canada. Its spelling checker's dictionary includes both British and American spellings for many words. As far as it's concerned, the words "color" and "colour," for example, are both spelled correctly.

Note that the spelling checker can only look for words which are genuinely misspelled. It will not protest if you use the word "there" when you should have used "their" or "they're," nor will it catch misspelled words which happen to be other, correctly spelled words, such as "thought" when you meant to use "though."

When the Spelling Checker dialog box appears, click on Check Text to check each word in your selected text object. When a suspect word appears, CorelDRAW will pause and allow you either to correct it or to have the spelling checker suggest possible replacements for it. Click on the Suggest button to have it do the latter, or enable the Always suggest item to have it suggest possible replacements for all the suspect words it encounters.

The Replace All button will cause all the instances of a misspelled word to be corrected without further prompting. The Ignore button will cause the current instance of an unrecognized word to be ignored. The Ignore All button will cause all instances of the current unrecognized word to be ignored in the text being checked.

The Personal Dictionary options of the spelling checker allow you to add words to a secondary dictionary. Whenever a questionable word turns up based on the primary dictionary that the spelling checker uses, it will see if the word appears in your personal dictionary, should you be using one.

Use the spelling checker. There's nothing more embarrassing than a spelling error in 144-point type. There's also nothing less likely to be noticed until it's too late to easily fix.

This will allow you to keep the spelling checker from complaining about words such as your name, specialized acronyms, or specific terminology that you use a lot.

Note that you can also use the spelling checker interactively. If you don't have a text object selected, select Spell Checker from the Text menu and it will let you type in a word and have it check to see if it's properly spelled.

You can also use the spelling checker to check part of a text object. Use the text cursor to highlight the words you'd like to check and then invoke the spelling checker.

THESAURUS

In addition to its online spelling checker, CorelDRAW offers an online thesaurus. This is a function which will ostensibly help you improve your writing by suggesting alternate words to use. For example, if you wanted to use a word like "umbrella" but couldn't think of a good synonym, you could select the Thesaurus item from the Text menu and it could offer you some other choices, as well providing you with a brief definition of the word.

Actually, it could, but it wouldn't. The word "umbrella" is not one of the ones in CorelDRAW's synonym dictionary. Despite its having a pretty good dictionary as thesaurus functions go, the CorelDRAW thesaurus can only deal with a tiny fraction of the words commonly used in colloquial English.

Just because the thesaurus doesn't know of a synonym for a word doesn't mean there isn't one.

You can invoke the thesaurus either interactively or by selecting one word in a text object with the text cursor and then selecting Thesaurus from the Text menu. In this latter approach, you can have the thesaurus replace the selected word with one of its synonyms, assuming it finds one. Click on the synonym you want to use and then on the Replace button of the Thesaurus dialog box.

WRAPPING UP

To use the text facilities of CorelDRAW effectively, you need to go beyond simply learning to work the software. The ostensibly uninvolved task of slapping a few words on a piece of paper is really a rich, fascinating art form all by itself.

A lot more discussion of text will crop up throughout the course of this book. This will be especially true as we start looking at design techniques in Part 2.

A S T
R A C K

H A P T E R

4

divide the dimensions of the bitmap in pixels by the number of dots per inch of your printer. If you need a larger tile, multiply this value by an integral value.

select the checkerboard tile icon from the fill tool flyout menu. Click on the Create button. Use the left mouse button to create black pixels and the right mouse button to create white pixels.

select the PS icon from the fill tool flyout menu. Consult the CorelDRAW reference guide for example values to use with the PostScript Texture dialog box. You must print your drawing to a PostScript printer.

Using

Fills

The letter A developed from the Aleph and the Greek alpha. It is the capital letter A, and is first found in Etruscan and in Latin. The northern Semitic and was retained in Latin.

T

he topic of filling objects under CorelDRAW has been touched on in the previous chapters, but not really discussed. In principle, the subject is pretty simple. The realization of it, however, can become complex, partly because CorelDRAW offers a lot of ways to handle fills, but especially because the capabilities of your printer will greatly affect the way in which you can use CorelDRAW's fill facilities.

NOTE NOTE *Depending on the sort of drawings you will be creating with CorelDRAW, you might need a great deal of the information in this chapter, or almost none. If you will be using some of the more exotic fill styles, you might want to have a quick look through Chapter 6 before you read this one.*

There are a number of fills that CorelDRAW will print on any output device, but there are a lot more which are specific to certain types of output devices, most notably laser printers.

There are also a lot of aesthetic and design considerations in using fills, probably more so than in using the other facilities we have discussed previously. The aesthetically appropriate use of shading and shadow, which can make your two-dimensional objects spring to life, will be discussed in later chapters. This chapter will focus mainly on the technical aspects of what goes on between CorelDRAW, its fills, and the printers it will deal with.

CLOSING PATHS TO ACCEPT FILLS

The statement that an open path cannot be given a fill characteristic is actually not quite true. You can select an open path and give it a fill, but because the path is open, there will be no enclosed area for the fill to appear in, and no fill will show up on your screen. However, the fill will have become part of the object. If you subsequently close the path, the fill will appear.

Any closed path can be given a fill characteristic. This includes text and complex curves as well as simple objects such as rectangles and ellipses. You cannot fill an open path, but open paths can be closed to form fillable objects.

If you create an object out of multiple line segments, the path so defined will probably not be closed initially even if the end nodes of the segments line up. Similarly, if you create a single path which simply overlaps itself, it will still be an open path. You should check the status line above the work space to see if your currently selected path is open or closed. If it is open, you need to join the end nodes. The following steps illustrate how to do this:

1. Select the shape tool.

2. Select the two nodes you want to join, either by drawing a marquee around them or by clicking on one and then the other with the Shift key held down.

3. Double click on one of the selected nodes. A pop-up menu will appear.

4. Select the Join item.

The two nodes will move together and CorelDRAW will join them. The Break item in the Node Edit pop-up menu can unjoin them later if need be. Note that joining any two nodes will not necessarily form a closed path. The two nodes in question must be the ends of an otherwise closed path; if there are unjoined nodes within the course of the path, you'll have to join those too.

If you wish to join two paths into a single path, for the purpose of ultimately creating a closed path, you can do so by using CorelDRAW's Combine feature. Select the two paths in question with the pick tool and then select the Combine item from the Arrange menu. The paths can subsequently be uncombined using the Break Apart feature of the same menu. For as long as they're combined, the two paths will behave as a single path.

BASIC FILL QUALITIES

There are several basic types of fills under CorelDRAW. The simplest, and most widely used, is a solid gray fill. Gray fills are the simplest sort of fill, and you'll probably find that they are the ones you use the most often. They are also the fill patterns which take the least amount of time to print, which is something worth considering. The second type is a solid color fill. The third are fountain fills. Next, there are tiled vector and bitmap fills. Finally, there are PostScript fills, or textures. As the name implies, PostScript fills are available only if you'll be outputting your drawing to a PostScript printer. These will crop up later in this chapter.

It's easiest to think of a fill as being a color, even if the color in question is gray. If you imagine a closed path as being a container, filling it simply involves pouring colored ink into it. In fact, when CorelDRAW draws a filled object on your screen or creates a bitmap of it for output to a printer, it performs a digital process analogous to this.

In addition to the fill patterns to be discussed in this chapter, CorelDRAW also offers you a fill type indicated by the X icon in the fill tool flyout menu. This stands for no fill. No fill should not be confused with a pure white fill. The two are not the same, and in one case in particular the difference is significant. If you create two overlapping objects and fill the front one with pure white, the parts of the rear one which are overlapped will be obscured. However, if you give the front object no fill, it will appear transparent or hollow. Figure 4.1 illustrates the difference.

FIGURE 4.1:

White fill versus no fill

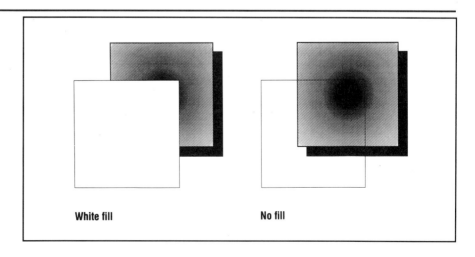

White fill   No fill

In cases where there is no overlap, you won't notice this difference, and it would be easy to get these two apparently similar fills mixed up. If you mix them up when you're doing a complex drawing, parts of your drawing may vanish when they're not supposed to.

UNDERSTANDING FILLS AND SCREENS

NOTE
NOTE
The term "screen" is derived from the way traditional print houses create halftones—areas of gray using alternating black and white spots. To create a halftone of a photograph, for example, the photograph is reproduced through a sheet of glass or plastic having a fine cross hatch on it, very much like a piece of window screen with somewhat more precise characteristics.

Laser printers, and the more affordable print houses as well, do not mix inks to arrive at specific shades of gray. To fill an area of a page with a particular shade of gray, printers utilize what is called a screen to place black spots of a certain size in a certain pattern so that, up close, the area looks like it was printed through a piece of screen or fabric. At a normal viewing distance the spots blend together over the white background to produce the illusion of gray.

There are a lot of variables in handling screens. One way or another, they represent the most complex element of printing, whether you're doing it with a printing press or a laser. In order to work with fills effectively under CorelDRAW, it's important to understand how they behave, and how the characteristics of a screen will affect the way your printed drawings look.

Note that in the following discussions, the word *dot* will be used to refer to one laser printer dot, that is, a black square $1/300$ of an inch across for a typical laser. The word *spot* will be used to refer to an individual element of a screen. A spot may be larger than a single dot on your laser printer or a single pixel on your monitor. A spot may also be smaller than either of these—and therein lie many of the problems which plague CorelDRAW's screens.

Screen Frequencies and Densities

Neither printing presses nor laser printers are perfect devices. Both have problems in resolving fine details. This is true whether the details in question are fine lines or the tiny spots of a screened area.

When using an actual printing press, you will not be able to print details which are smaller than a certain size, because the ink will be too thick to flow into tiny areas of the plate. When using a laser printer, you will not be able to print details smaller than one dot. In practical terms, you won't be able to print even a one-dot detail unless the detail in question lies right where the printer prints its dots.

In dealing with computer images, there are two related factors that can be affected by the resolution of the output device. The first is the screen frequency, that is, the number of spots per inch in the screened area. The second is the screen density, that is, the percentage of black, determined by both the size and the shape of the spots. Depending on the type of printer you will be using, CorelDRAW will allow you to control some or all of these variables.

Figure 4.2 illustrates a number of screened areas having different screen frequencies and densities. This figure may look a bit different than it did when it was first created due to the screen characteristics of the press which printed this book; however, you will notice that as the screens get finer they also begin to get more irregular.

Note also that the finer screens look darker than the coarser ones of the same density.

People who work with screens a lot become attuned to the problem of interference between multiple screens, called moiré patterns. When any two screens are printed one atop the other, a moiré pattern is likely to result. However, moiré patterns can be eliminated if the two screens are perfectly aligned—both of the same frequency, or one an integral multiple of the other, and located such that they do not interfere. They will also not produce visible results if they are of widely differing frequencies. Always remember that your laser printer has a screen frequency of its own, that of the dot size of its engine.

When the number of spots per inch of a screen approaches the number of dots per inch of the output device, aberrations can appear as a result of the algorithm which renders the screen spots as printer dots. The spots of the screen—which ideally are round—will begin to turn out pixellated, in effect, chunky and irregular. If you attempt to print a 150 spot-per-inch screen on a 300 dot-per-inch laser printer, for example, each spot of the screen will be drawn by no more than four dots of the laser. The results will certainly not be round, and they probably won't be arranged uniformly unless the screen of the image being printed just happens to register—or align—perfectly with the dot pattern of the laser, not a likely occurrence.

If you're printing to a PostScript device, CorelDRAW allows you to select the printer's default frequency as the screen for your drawing. This usually results in the best fills, but it doesn't always. We'll discuss this in greater detail shortly.

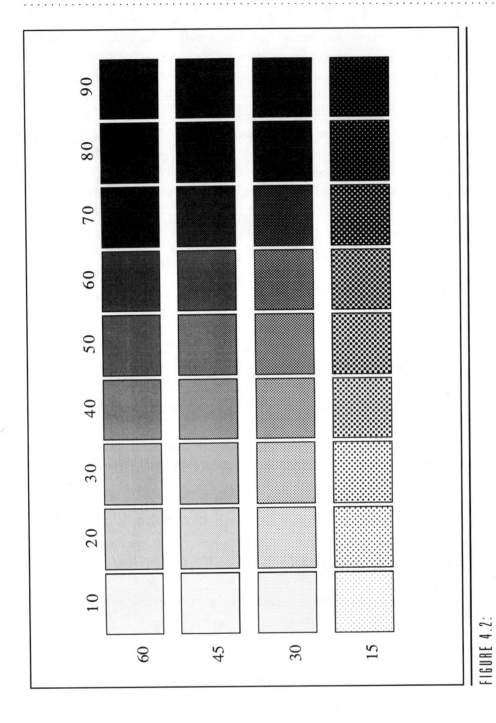

FIGURE 4.2:

Different screen frequencies (up and down) and densities (across)

*In high-end printing circles, printing snobs like to boast of printing presses that can handle increasingly fine screen sizes. Indeed, a press that can **genuinely** reproduce a 160-line screen should be able to print more attractive work than one which can reproduce only a 144-line screen. But a press whose owner managed to print a single decent 160-line proof page once on a Monday morning just after it had been aligned will most likely produce decidedly inferior work at 160 lines under ordinary circumstances.*

For practical purposes, screens with more than about fifty or sixty spots per inch start to fall apart on a 300 dot-per-inch laser printer. You can improve on this if you will be using a higher resolution output device—for example, a Linotronic PostScript phototypesetter. However, this doesn't necessarily mean that you should. If you plan to reproduce your drawing, you need to take into account the screen capabilities of the device doing the reproducing.

Photocopiers—even good ones which have been tuned up recently—can't reproduce screens much above fifty or sixty spots per inch without starting to mangle them, and you'll probably find that you get more attractive results if you use a 45 spot-per-inch screen.

Printing presses have varying screen requirements, and you should consult the printing company you'll be using for the details of their presses. In general, though, web presses which will be printing on uncoated paper—such as newsprint—can't manage much better than 80 spot-per-inch screens (80-line screens, in printer talk). Web presses running on coated paper can handle 120 spot-per-inch screens. Sheet-fed presses running on coated paper can typically deal with 144 spot-per-inch screens, and some of the really high-end ones can do even better than this.

If you can't afford to pay for a trial-and-error approach to getting your screens right, or if you aren't sure that you might not want to reproduce your images later, choose a screen frequency which is coarser than it has to be. For one thing, coarse screens don't necessarily look bad. Furthermore, as you saw in Figure 4.2, screens which are too fine can look muddy and unattractive.

SELECTING SCREENS

CorelDRAW is flexible in how it allows you to specify the frequencies of the screens used for fills. At least, it is if you're using a PostScript printer. LaserJet-compatible printers have only a single resolution as far as CorelDRAW is concerned, and it outputs all screens to LaserJet compatibles at what its designers have considered to be an optimized resolution. In fact, CorelDRAW handles LaserJet compatibles as well as any other drawing package available, and one would be hard pressed to find ways to improve on the arrangement.

PostScript printers offer dozens of screening options under CorelDRAW. Like much of CorelDRAW, these things default to sensible values if you ignore

The default screen in a laser printer's PostScript implementation is a somewhat ambiguous thing. It will have been set up by the designer of the printer to produce optimized screens based on whatever the designer thought screens should look like. Some laser printers which are capable of producing quite acceptable screens have very badly chosen defaults. Allowing CorelDRAW to override the defaults will often have profound results on the quality of your screened fills.

them, and you can use the fills under CorelDRAW without touching any of these items. Once you've mastered the basics of fill characteristics, however, you might want to use these controls to fine-tune the characteristics of your screen patterns.

Figure 4.3 illustrates the CorelDRAW Print Options dialog box from the File menu. Normally, this will print to a PostScript printer with the default screen frequency for the printer in question. This means, for example, that you'll get a different screen if your drawing is output to a Linotronic PostScript phototypesetter than you will if it's printed to a Laser-Writer. However, for the most part it means that you'll never get wildly inappropriate screens, no matter what you print your drawing on.

You can enter a different screen frequency by choosing Custom in the Screen Frequency box within the Print Options dialog box. The default screen frequency for your current output device will appear in the edit field first, allowing you to change it if you want to. The default is usually 60. If you do change the value, it's up to you to make sure you choose a frequency suitable for your output device. CorelDRAW will not complain if you attempt to print your drawing with a 1500 spot-per-inch screen, for example—it'll just output a dreadful picture.

Note that the Screen Frequency control in the Print Options dialog box pertains only to objects which you have not explicitly filled with other sorts of screens in the course of creating your drawing.

FIGURE 4.3:

The Printing dialog box from the File menu

Print Options [PostScript]	
Selected Objects Only	Copies: 1
Fit To Page	**Destination**
Tile	Linotronic 200/230
Scale: 100 %	LPT1:
	Print to File
Fountain Stripes: 64	For Mac Print Setup...
Print As Separations	**Flatness**
Crop Marks & Crosshairs	Set Flatness To: 1.00
Film Negative	Auto Increase
Print File Info	**Screen Frequency**
Within Page	◇ Custom: 128 lpi
All Fonts Resident	◆ Default
	OK Cancel

A PostScript printer allows you to control additional screen characteristics for individual objects in a drawing. In order to do this, however, you must find your way through a few dialog boxes and controls. First, you must select an object suitable for filling. Then select the fill tool, and click on the paint bucket icon to call up the precise-adjustment box for the fill tool. You should see the dialog box illustrated in Figure 4.4. If you don't see this dialog box, this means that CorelDRAW is in one of its other fill modes. Click on the Others button to switch to the dialog box pictured.

Ignoring the items concerning method, color, and tint—all of which will be discussed later in this book—click on the PostScript Options button. This will call up the PostScript Options dialog box shown in Figure 4.5, which will allow you to choose a number of other interesting characteristics, including:

◆ The frequency of the screen.

◆ The angle of the screen, that is, the angle at which the lines between the spots run; and the type, or shape, of the spots.

FIGURE 4.4:

The Uniform Fill dialog box of the fill tool

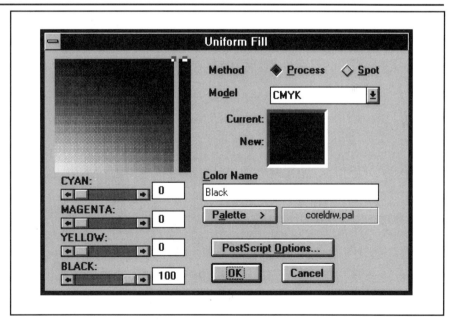

FIGURE 4.5:

*The dialog box called by
selecting the PostScript
button from the fill tool's
Uniform Fill dialog box*

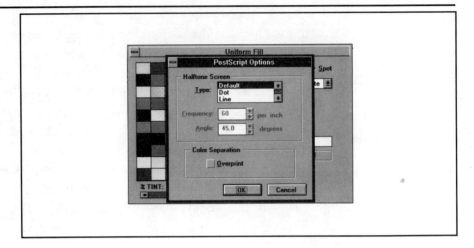

The shape of the spots in a screen is a matter of considerable controversy in some circles. Round spots display aberrational characteristics at certain densities, something we'll touch on in a moment. Oblong spots are better; however, for special effects all sorts of shapes are possible. For example, you can create a fill out of lines or geometric figures. The selector window in the PostScript Options dialog box enables you to choose dot shapes other than the default shape for your printer.

Figure 4.6 illustrates some of the possible effects of varying the Post-Script fill characteristics. You should plan to spend a while experimenting with these facilities to fully appreciate what they can do.

If you change any of the default values in the PostScript Options dialog box, the settings you choose will pertain only to the object you've selected at the moment. These will override whatever default screen frequency you select for the drawing as a whole when you're printing, so your drawing can contain some objects with the global defaults you select when you go to print, and some with the specific fill characteristics you specified earlier with the fill tool.

Note that neither the CorelDRAW preview window nor the edit-in-preview mode screen display will show you the results of any changes you make in the PostScript Options dialog box. You'll have to print your drawing to see what effect they've had.

FIGURE 4.6:

PostScript fill characteristics

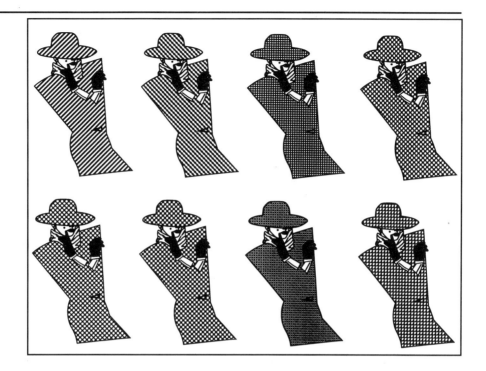

You should also know that CorelDRAW allows for a second set of considerably more radical PostScript fill effects: its textures. We'll be discussing these at the end of this chapter.

UNDERSTANDING GRAY FAILURE AND SPOT PROBLEMS

If you were to fill a rectangle with a varying gray level which went from 0 percent at one end to 100 percent at the other—which you can do with CorelDRAW, though we haven't discussed it as yet—you might expect that the result would show a uniformly varying gray field. In fact, this is one of those cases where the result would probably not live up to your expectations.

There are a number of factors which can cause the actual percentage of black in a fill emerging from your printer to differ from the specified percentage of black which was sent to the printer. The most commonly encountered one is called *spot failure*.

At the extreme ends of the scale—when the percentage of black approaches either zero or one hundred—your printer will find itself increasingly confronted with spots which are too small to print accurately. In the case of, say, a 2 percent gray screen, the spots of the screen may well be smaller than one dot of the laser. This will usually result in the printer simply filling the object in question with pure white.

Likewise, at almost 100 percent black, the white areas between the black areas can get smaller than one printer dot, with the result that the printer will probably fill the entire area with pure black.

Another type of spot failure occurs when the spot size is not significantly larger than the dot size. In this case, the printer will have difficulty in accurately forming some or all of the spots which make up a screened area. This can manifest itself in several sorts of visual effects, depending on how the errors work out. For example, in Figure 4.7, the configuration of dots (shown as squares) used to represent a regular pattern of spots (shown as circles) will exhibit two problems: misrepresentation and interference. The right-hand part of the illustration shows which dots would show as black. None of the arrangements of the dots are very good representations of circular spots—for one thing, the representations are not symmetrical. Furthermore, because each spot aligns differently with the matrix of printer dots, each spot is represented by a different configuration. In a regular pattern, such as a gray fill,

FIGURE 4.7:

Screen spot errors

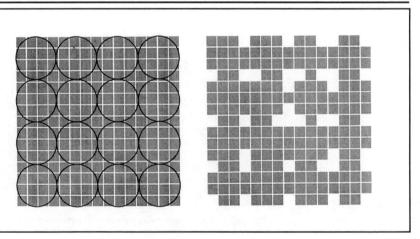

this variation in spots will lead to interference patterns—moirés—as the amount of black or white separating adjacent spots varies across the pattern. An interference pattern will look like light or dark patches or lines within a screened area.

On a 300 dot-per-inch printer, gray levels of more than 50 percent usually print darker than you might expect. This is because the printer usually errs toward using another dot rather than no dot to represent a partial dot along the edge of a screen spot. Higher resolution output devices, which can more accurately represent screen spots, suffer considerably less from this problem. This can create difficulties if you are using the output from one printer to give you an idea of how your final output will look on another printer. Screens printed on a 300 dot-per-inch laser printer will frequently look noticeably darker than the same screens printed on a Linotronic Post-Script Phototypesetter, for example.

The problem of compatibility from printer to printer becomes more noticeable for screens which have more spots per inch. If you anticipate outputting your CorelDRAW art to a higher resolution output device and your drawings call for accurate gray levels, you might want to reduce the screen frequency a bit.

A second facet of this problem involves what is called *dot gain*. A laser printer is effectively a photocopier; that is, it works by a process called xerography. As you may have noticed if you've used a photocopier a lot, black areas on photocopies tend to come out a bit bigger than those of the originals. This is due to the way xerography works and because the particles of toner on a photocopier's drum tend to spread slightly. The problem is shared by laser printers. The extent of the problem varies among different laser printer designs, and it's affected by things like the current humidity and the state of one's toner cartridge.

Dot gain doesn't affect type and lines noticeably, but it does affect the apparent density of screens. It is much less of a problem if your drawing uses relatively coarse screens. Many 300 dot-per-inch laser printers, however, can't print much more than 90 percent gray screens without having them fill in due to dot gain and come up as pure black. Purely photographic processes, such as the raster image processor of a high-end PostScript typesetter, do not suffer from this problem.

A final potential problem is that of *optical jump*. This isn't much of a concern on 300 dot-per-inch laser printers, as it's caused by the interaction of very accurate screen spot shapes. It does crop up quite noticeably when you output certain sorts of CorelDRAW drawings to a PostScript typesetter.

Optical jump is a change in the apparent gray level of a screened area due to the effect of screen spots which touch. For a screen which uses square spots in a checkerboard pattern, at densities of less than 50 percent, the spots would all be isolated from one another. At densities of more than 50 percent, the spots would overlap, and the screen would effectively consist of a black area with white spots. At 50 percent, however, the corners of the spots would just touch, and the effect visually would be a screen which looked darker than 50 percent gray.

CorelDRAW defaults to using round spots for its screens. This spot shape exhibits an optical jump at 25 percent gray. If you're sufficiently interested, you will discover that all spot shapes have optical jump problems at one density or other. Spot shapes which are oblong—elliptical spots, for example—exhibit two optical jumps.

None of the screen problems we've just discussed is crippling, especially if you're aware of them and keep them in mind when you're using CorelDRAW. Many of them will trouble you only if you're planning to develop your artwork on a 300-dot-per-inch laser printer and then use a PostScript typesetter for final output. Even then, a bit of experimentation and some common sense will help you work around them.

Here are a few useful rules of thumb which will help you avoid screen problems.

◆ Experiment with your laser printer to determine the minimum and maximum gray levels it can really reproduce.

◆ Avoid particularly high screen frequencies, especially for extreme gray levels.

◆ Avoid extreme gray levels when you're planning to send your output to a higher resolution PostScript printer, such as a Linotronic PostScript Phototypesetter.

◆ Avoid filling adjacent objects with screens of similar density if you want them to be perceived as being distinct.

◆ If your applications frequently call for gray screens, keep your laser printer well maintained and in an environmentally controlled area.

TIP *If you're using a laser printer with a variable dot size engine—such as a Canon LBP or Hewlett-Packard LaserJet III series printer—the engine will adjust the size of its dots to attempt to minimize some of the problems discussed in this section. Chapter 6 will discuss this in greater detail.*

USING COLOR FILLS

Color is treated in essentially the same way as gray fills under CorelDRAW. However, when you're using color fills, CorelDRAW provides some additional controls to help you work with color in a convenient way.

If you have a color printer which is capable of handling fairly precise color specifications, such as a color PostScript printer or a Hewlett-Packard DeskJet 500C, you will be able to output color CorelDRAW artwork directly to your printer and see what your pictures look like. However, it's often more useful to be able to produce color artwork in a form that print houses like to use. CorelDRAW will do this as well.

It's worth pointing out, before you get deeply into using color under CorelDRAW, that CorelDRAW's monitor graphics reflect the color facilities and limitations of Microsoft Windows. Depending on how you've configured Windows, CorelDRAW may have only 16 unique colors to work with, even if you have a 256-color VGA card installed in your system. CorelDRAW shows color fills and objects by combining these 16 colors, using its best guess at the colors you have selected. However, the results are an approximation at best. This does not affect the final accuracy of the colors you print, of course, except insofar as you cannot always see what you're dealing with before you print them.

A complete discussion of color can be found in Chapter 8. If you are unfamiliar with the details of process colors, spot (Pantone) colors, and so on, you might want to read that chapter before proceeding any further in this one.

 CorelDRAW has enormously sophisticated color specification and matching facilities. We will discuss them all in time, though this initial discussion of color under CorelDRAW will leave a few things out.

SPECIFYING COLOR FILLS

Having selected an object, you can give it a color fill under CorelDRAW by popping up the precise-adjustment box of the fill tool. The color defaults to black (Color #0), the density (% Tint) to 100 percent, and the color specification system (Method) to spot color. All of these things can be changed.

If you click in the large color palette which occupies most of this box, different colors will be selected and their Pantone numbers and names will be displayed in the name field of the box. Bearing in mind that these colors are approximations even if you have a 256-color Windows driver—and especially so if you have a 16-color one—you should consider getting a Pantone color matching book. These are available from most graphics supply houses. They aren't cheap, but they're pretty much essential for accurate color matching.

If you click in the Spot box, you'll be presented with a list of Pantone names and numbers to select from, rather than a palette of color swatches.

If you select Process colors rather than Spot colors, the controls will change, allowing you to specify your fill color as percentages of colored light or ink. A complete description of the color processes available under CorelDRAW can be found in Chapter 8.

Having specified a particular color, you can also specify a screen density for your fill. For example, if you mix up a medium blue ink—whether as a Pantone color or from process colors—you can tell CorelDRAW to fill your drawing with a 50 percent screen of it by adjusting the Tint control, just as you would for a gray fill.

You should think about what colors look like when they're screened. In effect, if you fill an object with a color screen, you will be mixing white with your specified color. For example, if you fill an area with a 30 percent screen of red ink that is made up of 100 percent magenta and 100 percent yellow, the result will be pink, and not even a particularly attractive shade of it. Likewise, a lot of shades of blue that look forceful and interesting at 100 percent look like baby blue at lesser percentages.

A lot of fairly weird—and usually undesirable—effects can be achieved by printing process color fills at very coarse screen settings. If you use a 20 line-per-inch screen, for example—an interesting technique in black-and-white—the result will probably be a lot of colored smudges with bits of process colors peeking out around them.

You might well ask what happens if you choose colored fills under CorelDRAW, and then print them to a black and white printer. In fact, CorelDRAW will represent colors as gray levels in black and white. It attempts to select grays that match the *luminosity*—the overall brightness—of the colors it's replacing. It does so by using a formula to calculate the percentage of gray based on the percentages of the primary colors used to generate the colored fill in question. This can be a bit questionable, as it's possible to have two very different colors—say medium red and medium dark blue—with similar luminosity values, and thus, with the same gray levels. Such colors may contrast on your monitor but print as identical gray levels. This will be discussed in greater detail in Chapter 6.

Using Crop Marks

If you create color artwork to be sent to a printer—even if the color is only a single spot-color overlay—you can assist the printer and eliminate some potential errors by printing crop marks, alignment marks, and color information on your artwork. The Print Options dialog box from the File menu enables you to implement these options. Figure 4.8 illustrates a drawing with its crop marks and other information included.

The only drawback in doing this is that the crop marks for an 8½-by-11-inch page will print beyond the edges of the page. You must either use the Page Setup dialog box to choose a smaller paper size or arrange to output your drawing on a larger laser printer.

USING FOUNTAIN FILLS

Any object which can be filled with a solid gray or colored fill can also be filled with a *fountain*. A fountain is a fill which changes its gray level or its color. Figure 4.9 illustrates the two types of fountains CorelDRAW allows for, linear and radial fountains.

If you hold down the Ctrl key while you're manipulating the example window in the Fountain Fill dialog box, the movement of the angle line or the fountain center will be constrained. The linear fountain angle will be constrained to increments of 15 degrees. The center location will be constrained to increments of 10 percent.

You can fill any object with either kind of fountain—an object need not be circular to be filled with a radial fountain. If you fill an irregular object with a fountain, the fill will be visible only within the object, just as with a solid gray or colored fill.

You can select a fountain fill from the fill tool's flyout menu by choosing the second-to-the-rightmost icon. The Fountain Fill dialog box will then appear. This will allow you to select the minimum and maximum gray level or the two extremes of the color range which the fountain will span. The color specifications can be handled using either spot or process colors, as with normal fills.

The example window in the center of the Fountain Fill dialog box will show you what your fountain looks like, as well as provide you with a control to manipulate it. Initially, it will show you a 90-degree linear fountain. Click inside it and a line will appear. You can adjust the angle of the line by moving your mouse. When you release it, the fountain's angle will change.

FIGURE 4.8:

A drawing showing crop and alignment marks. This is the yellow plate of a four-color drawing.

If you're working with a radial fountain—as selected by the radio buttons to the left of the example window—you'll find you can grab the center of the fountain in the example window and move it.

Radial (left) and linear (right) fountain

Both the linear fill angle and the location of the center of radial fountains relative to the objects they reside in can also be set numerically, using the Angle and Center Offset controls respectively. The easiest way to get a feel for how these controls work is probably to change the characteristics of the fountains you work with using the interactive example window and then see how what you've done has affected the appropriate numbers.

The From and To fields of the Fountain Fill dialog box allow you to set the colors or gray levels which represent the two extremes of a fountain. Click on the colored buttons for quick color selection windows, or on the More buttons for complete color adjustment controls.

When you're selecting the extremes of a gray fill, bear in mind the foregoing discussion about extreme gray levels. Fountains do not look terribly attractive if their dark areas block up and their light areas vanish. In most cases, a fountain ranging from 10 to 90 percent black will look much nicer than one ranging from 0 to 100 percent black.

In creating a fountain which changes color, keep in mind how you plan to print your drawing. If you'll be creating four-color separations or printing directly to a color printer, you can pretty well do as you like. On the other hand, if you plan to create spot-color separations, make sure that your fountain uses only one color, and change the % Tint level of it over the course of the fountain.

The Fountain Fill dialog box also allows you to specify the PostScript fill parameters we discussed earlier in conjunction with normal fills. Fountains which use alternate spot shapes and such can be quite striking, and offer considerable opportunity for experimentation.

Fountains under CorelDRAW are actually handled as a series of stripes or concentric rings. The number of stripes in a fountain fill is an important issue if you want to optimize the quality and print time of complex drawings. If you have too few stripes, the result will be noticeable banding in your final art. If you have too many stripes, your drawings will take longer to print. This is particularly important if you'll be using a PostScript phototypesetter as your final output device. PostScript phototypesetters—Linotronics and related output devices—are discussed in Chapter 6.

Depending upon your output device, you'll probably be able to define the number of stripes used for fountain fills when you go to print. It's worth doing a bit of experimenting to find the optimum value for your laser printer.

When you work with drawings that have fountain fills in them in the default edit-in-preview mode of CorelDRAW, you might find that watching all those fountains redraw themselves over and over again as you zoom in and out gets a little tedious. This is a good time to use the Edit Wireframe mode. You might want to switch into it when you'll be performing complex drawing operations that require a lot of zooming, panning, or redrawing, and then switch back to the usual edit-in-preview mode when you're done. Because the Edit Wireframe mode inhibits the drawing of fills in the CorelDRAW workspace, you won't have to wait for your fountains to regenerate. You can toggle Edit Wireframe on and off using the Display menu or by pressing Shift-F9.

Every object under CorelDRAW— even a complex or very irregular one—has an invisible highlighting box around it. You can see this box if you select the object in question. The highlighting box will be drawn with selection marks at its periphery. When you fill an object with a fountain, what actually happens from CorelDRAW's point of view is that the fountain fills the highlighting box and the object serves as a hole through which part of the fountain can be seen.

The Edge Pad adjustment of the Fountain Fill dialog box (as shown in Figure 4.10) allows you to compensate for irregularly shaped objects. If you select an edge-padding value which is greater than 0 percent, the start of the fountain will move in from the periphery of the highlighting box it's drawn in. The difference is filled by the initial color. This will keep the extreme colors in your fountain fills from getting lost in a small outer detail of an object, such as the serif on a character, for example.

FOUNTAIN OVERLOAD

As discussed earlier in this book, fountain fills can make just about any object look more lifelike because they imitate the way in which our eyes see variations in light intensity. The only potential problem with fountains is in the way CorelDRAW goes to print them on a PostScript printer: A fountain is actually drawn as many small, filled areas, with each area handled as a PostScript path. As mentioned earlier in this book, it's possible to create drawings which are too complex to print on a PostScript printer just by using a lot of fountain fills.

FIGURE 4.10:

Adjusting the edge padding of a radial fountain fill

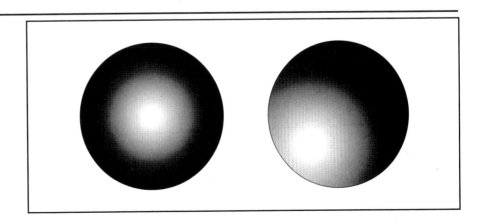

There is no easy way to tell when you've exceeded the bounds of good taste and available PostScript paths merely by looking at the CorelDRAW work space. If nothing comes out of your printer when you have a lot of fountain fills, however, you should suspect them as the cause of it.

It's often possible to simplify your drawing a bit when this happens. If you use the PostScript Options dialog box from the Fountain Fill dialog box to select a coarser screen, the fountain will require fewer paths to print. Alternately, if you're filling text with a fountain, selecting a less ornate typeface might do it. Often, selecting normal weight type rather than bold type will reduce the path count sufficiently. Finally, since the problem is in the absolute number of paths, reducing the size of the filled area—such as by scaling your drawing down—will often let you print an otherwise reluctant picture.

Fountains take a long time to print to a PostScript printer because they make the printer do a lot of calculations. The time is proportional to the amount of area the fountain fills. All other things being equal, a 24-point character filled with a fountain will take four times as long as will a 12-point character.

If you're working on a drawing with fountain fills, consider printing your intermediate versions scaled down to save time.

USING VECTOR FILLS

The fills which have been discussed until now might be considered analogous to paint. They fill objects either with solid colors or with airbrushed transitions from one color to the next.

In filling real-life objects with color, there are alternatives to paint, of course. The most obvious examples are wallpaper and tiles. From CorelDRAW's point of view, wallpaper is just tile with very long vertical dimensions.

CorelDRAW allows you to use tiles to fill objects in the same way that you use a solid color or a fountain. A tiled fill consists of as many small rectangular areas as fit in the larger area of the object you want to fill. You can define the size of the tiles so that the ratio of the tile size to the overall size of the area you want to fill makes sense.

Figure 4.11 illustrates a couple of tiled fills.

Tiles can come from two sources. The most obvious way to generate them is as CorelDRAW objects. The other is to use bitmaps, which we'll get to in the next section.

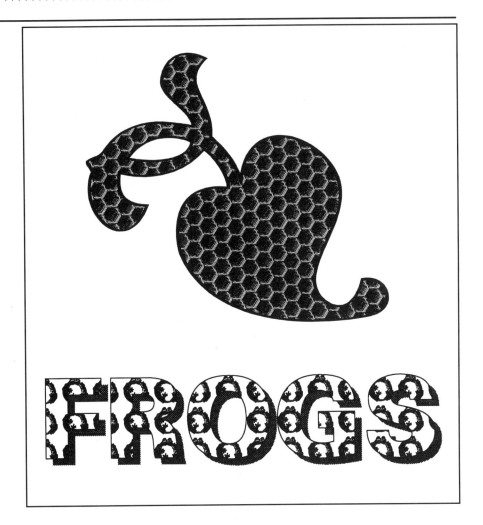

If you select the Create Pattern item from the Special menu, CorelDRAW will let you select an area of your drawing and copy it into a special type of drawing file called a *pattern*. These files are differentiated from normal CorelDRAW files by their extension, which is PAT. As we'll see, this is actually the only thing that differentiates them from normal CDR files. Ultimately, the small drawing in a PAT file will become one tile which will be repeated over and over again to form a fill pattern.

CorelDRAW comes with a number of very interesting default PAT files too.

To create a custom PAT file, do the following:

1. Select the Create Pattern item of the Special menu. A box appears to prompt you for a type and resolution setting. Select the options you want, then click on OK.

2. Use the cross wires to select the area of your workspace which contains the objects to be included in the pattern.

3. Release your mouse button. A dialog box will appear; click on OK.

4. A file selector box will appear. Choose a name for your pattern file.

To fill an object with the tile in a PAT file, select the object and then the vector fill icon from the fill tool flyout menu. This is a diagonal line with an arrowhead at each end. A file selector box will appear to allow you to load a PAT file. After you've selected one, the tile adjustment box will appear, as shown in Figure 4.12.

The Full-Color Pattern dialog box lets you define the size of each tile. Vector tiles will load in with their aspect ratio set properly; if you resize a tile by typing in new dimensions for it, you might want to take care that the ratio between the horizontal and vertical dimensions remains the same unless you deliberately want to distort your tile. To manually enter the sizes, you must first click on the Tiling button.

FIGURE 4.12:

The tile adjustment box

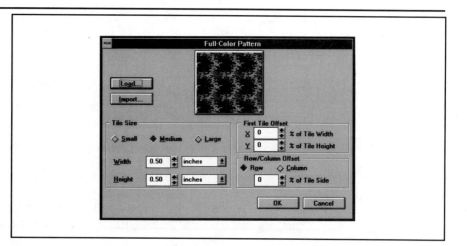

If you open the Load file selector in the Vector Tile dialog box, you can preview each tile using the preview window at the right of the box. There's also an easier way to select a tile. The example window in the center of the Full-Color Pattern dialog box will initially have a cross through it, indicating that no tile has been selected. Click in this window and a new window will open, showing example swatches of all the tiles in your current directory. Double click on one of the swatches to load it.

Normally, tiles are laid out in a grid, just like floor tiles are. However, you might want to try staggering them, so that the rows or columns don't always start on the same boundaries. If you change Offset values in the Two-Color and Full-Color dialog boxes, you can adjust the offsets for one or both directions.

SOME DARK SECRETS OF VECTOR TILES

It's probably worth noting that vector-tile PAT files are actually CDR files. They're given a different extension because it's convenient to keep them distinct from complete drawings, but their internal structure is the same. To edit a pattern, then, simply use the Open command of the CorelDRAW File menu, change the file specification from CDR to PAT, open the pattern file you're interested in, and work with it as you would any other CorelDRAW drawing file.

It is important to bear in mind that individual tiles can't be larger than three inches in either direction. They can, however, contain any colors, fills, effects, and other CorelDRAW regalia you can come up with. Having said this, complex tiles can take ages to print, and you risk creating drawings which are so complex as to overload a PostScript printer with really elaborate tiles. From a design perspective, tiles which are very intricate frequently create fills which are too busy to really be eye-catching.

Something which makes an interesting stand-alone drawing will not automatically make a good tile. The best tiles are ones which repeat along their edges—you might want to look at the example PAT files which come with CorelDRAW to see how this can be done. These tiles are very clever, because they merge together in a seamless carpet of shapes. Some of these tiles are actually drawn from the textures which are available as PostScript textures, which will be discussed at the end of the chapter. Consider the tile and the fill in Figure 4.13.

Finally, tiles are not affected by transformations wrought upon the objects they fill. Thus, if you fill an object with tiles and then skew the object, the tiles themselves, which are rectangular, will remain unskewed.

USING BITMAP FILLS

In addition to creating tiled fills with vector drawings, CorelDRAW also allows you to fill things with small bitmap fragments. Bitmaps are images which come from programs like PC Paintbrush and Windows Paintbrush. Bitmaps have not been discussed yet, and if you're unfamiliar with the term you might want to read Chapter 5 before you proceed to learn how to fill things with them.

Figure 4.14 illustrates an example of using a bitmap fill.

Bitmap tiles can be up to 256 pixels on a side. You can create them using any of a number of programs—Windows Paintbrush is exceedingly easy to work with for this sort of task, and the CorelPHOTO-PAINT application that accompanies CorelDRAW will also manage it, although it represents severe overkill. You can draw anything you like and then save it into a small tile. Alternately, you can start with an existing drawing and crop out a suitable fragment, as we'll do in the following example.

Figure 4.15 illustrates the steps involved in creating the elephant tile from a larger image file. This image actually started life in MacPaint on a Macintosh, but for the sake of this discussion we'll come in on it as a PCX file.

FIGURE 4.14:

*Pouring elephants
into text*

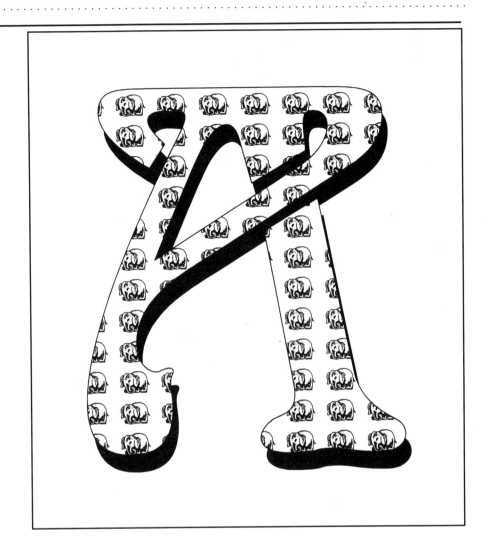

FIGURE 4.14:

*Pouring elephants
into text*

The Graphic Workshop package that's included on the companion disk for this book will allow you to crop small sections from a bitmapped image relatively easily—it will be discussed in greater detail later on. The advantage to using it for this task, rather than Windows Paintbrush, is that it will provide you with the exact dimensions of the fragment you're excising as you crop.

*Separating one elephant
from a herd of graphics*

To create a small bitmap tile of the elephant, do the following:

1. Load the PCX file into Windows Paintbrush.

2. Select an area with the elephant in it.

3. Use the Copy To function of the Edit menu of Windows
Paintbrush to write the selected elephant to a small PCX file
called ELEPHANT.PCX.

4. Select the Open function of Paintbrush's File menu. Select
ELEPHANT.PCX from the file list and click on the Info button.
This will pop up a window which will tell you the dimensions in
pixels of the small PCX file you've created. Write these down. In
this example, the size was 132 by 98 pixels.

5. Quit Windows Paintbrush and return to CorelDRAW.

6. Select the object you wish to fill with elephants in your
CorelDRAW drawing.

7. Select the two-color pattern icon from the fill tool's flyout menu.
This is the box with a checkerboard in it.

8. The two-color pattern selector will appear. It comes with a library of default bitmap fills already loaded, and you can add more of them by loading in PCX or other bitmapped files. Click on the PCX button to bring up a file box. Load ELEPHANT.PCX, changing directories if necessary to locate it. Select it from the library of tiles by clicking in it.

Unlike vector fills, bitmaps have an optimum size at which they'll print with no distortion. Printing them at other sizes will produce bitmaps which look somewhat crunchy. Large bitmaps can survive a lot of crunchiness without looking too dreadful. Small bitmaps, of the sort used for fill tiles, can look quite dreadful unless you take care to have them printed at their optimum size. The optimum size for a bitmap fill is one pixel of the bitmap for each dot of your laser printer. The next best size is some whole-number multiple or submultiple.

The Two-Color Pattern dialog box allows you to define the size (if you have clicked on the Tiling button) of the bitmap tile you've just selected. You can define it as any size you like and CorelDRAW will stretch it to fit. However, you should define it at its optimum size for the best results.

The optimum size of each dimension of the bitmap in inches can be calculated as:

Dimension in pixels ÷ Printer dots per inch

The elephant tile is 132 pixels across, so to have it appear at its best on a 300-dot-per-inch laser printer, you would divide 132 by 300, which would leave you with a horizontal dimension of 0.44 inches. The vertical dimension would be 0.33 inches. Enter these in the dimension fields of the Two-Color Pattern dialog box.

Having done this calculation in inches, you should make sure these fields have their units set to inches.

Among the controls in the Two-Color Pattern dialog box are selector buttons which will allow you to choose the Back and Front colors for the fill you're working with. By default, these will be white and black respectively, but you can change them to any colors you like. You can also use gray levels, which can look very effective. These controls work like the fountain color buttons discussed previously.

If you click on the example window in the Two-Color Pattern dialog box, a selector with all the available bitmap fills will appear. Double click on one to choose it as the current bitmap fill.

TIPS FOR BITMAP FILLS

Bitmap tiles can have only two colors—if you attempt to import one with more than two colors, it will be dithered down to two colors by CorelDRAW. CorelDRAW does not dither color bitmaps to black and white very well, and the results of importing color bitmaps for use as tiles are rarely attractive.

You can import a picture of any size into CorelDRAW's Two-Color Pattern dialog box for use as a tile, but anything larger than 256 pixels on a side will be scaled down to this dimension, usually with a considerable loss of image quality. It's a good idea to check the size of the bitmap fragment you want to use before you go to import it.

The Two-Color Pattern dialog box also has a button called Create, which will call up a simple bitmap editor. This will let you toggle pixels on and off in a bitmap of up to 64 pixels on a side, and use the resulting tile as a bitmap fill.

Figure 4.16 illustrates a bitmap fill being edited and the resulting tiled fill in a CorelDRAW object.

FIGURE 4.16:

The bitmap fill editor

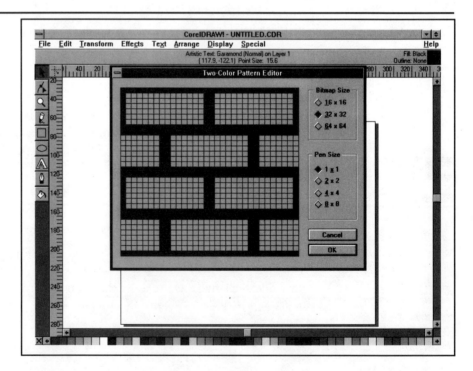

As with vector fills, if you transform an object filled with bitmap tiles, the tiles themselves will not be transformed.

One handy thing about bitmap tiles is that you can use the bitmap fill box of the fill tool to change the colors used in drawing each tile as often as you like. Changing the colors used by a vector fill is a bit more involved, as you must actually edit the PAT file and then reimport it.

USING POSTSCRIPT TEXTURES

Aside from the PostScript screen characteristics we've discussed thus far, there's a whole set of very elaborate PostScript fill patterns, or textures, available through the rightmost item—the PS—in the fill tool's flyout menu. While not without their limitations, these patterns can add some breathtaking effects to your drawings.

You will want to consult the CorelDRAW manual for a complete list of the PostScript fills and some examples of the parameters used with them.

The PostScript fills are, as you might have expected, available only if you will be outputting your drawing to a PostScript printer. What you might not have expected is that they will not appear in the preview window. Instead, any object filled with a PostScript pattern will show up in the preview with the letters PS pasted across it.

Each of the PostScript fills is actually a complex PostScript program. The text of these programs resides in a disk file called USERPROC.TXT in the \CORELDRW\DRAW subdirectory. The programs have a number of variables associated with them which you can set from within CorelDRAW using the PS item of the fill tool's flyout menu.

There are a number of potential problems associated with the PostScript textures. For one thing, they are very complex programs, often creating large numbers of paths. As with fountain fills—in fact, quite a bit more so—it's easy to use the PostScript textures to create a graphic which is too complex for your printer to handle.

Even if you don't exceed this limit, you'll find that objects filled with PostScript textures take ages to print. Figure 4.17 illustrates a few of the many PostScript fills available. It took about seven minutes to print on a fairly fast laser printer.

NOTE
NOTE

The exceedingly adventurous can create their own PostScript textures by adding to the contents of USERPROC-.TXT. This will take some experimentation even if you are a gifted PostScript programmer, however. Though well documented, the contents of USERPROC-.TXT are still pretty inscrutable. However, this might be a useful facility if you want to have your company logo as a PostScript texturee, for example.

FIGURE 4.17:

Some PostScript textures

In using the PostScript textures, there are a few things you should be aware of. First of all, the time and memory a pattern requires increase exponentially with the size of the area you fill with it. A two-inch-square object will contain four times as many paths as a one-inch-square object. Small objects are less likely to exceed the limits of your printer. Secondly, it's not uncommon when using PostScript textures to create a drawing that prints from CorelDRAW but fails to do so when you export and use it in, say, Ventura or PageMaker.

Most of the PostScript textures have variable levels of complexity. They get a lot more interesting as they get more complex. Once again, though, bear in mind that complex textures contain a lot more paths. Each of the examples of the textures in the CorelDRAW manual has at least four possible sets of parameters to produce four variations on the effects. Because the PostScript Texture dialog box allows you to enter any value you like, you can use parameters besides the ones listed in the book. Many of the patterns are based on random numbers, and even slight changes in the parameters or in the size of the object being filled will alter the resulting pattern.

You should also understand the *random-seed* parameter used by some of the textures. Computers can't actually produce random numbers—what they do is generate pseudo-random numbers. These numbers do have a predictable pattern, but it's so complex as to appear random for many useful purposes. The structure of the pattern is dictated by a seed number, which serves as the starting place in the random sequence. If you change the seed, you'll change the nature of the random numbers and hence the appearance of a texture based on some element of randomness. Choose any value you like for the seed. In keeping with its nature, it should be chosen randomly.

In all other respects, the PostScript textures behave just like the simpler fills we've discussed in this chapter. You can use them to fill any sort of object you like, provided you bear in mind that drawings created this way can take forever to print, and some might not print at all. Textures which create intrinsically complex patterns—the CrystalLattice texture is my favorite—are best used to fill fairly small, simple objects.

If you don't have a PostScript printer, you should note that some of the PostScript texture patterns are duplicated in the default PAT files provided for use as vector fills. These fills aren't as flexible as the equivalent PostScript textures, but they're better than nothing.

FILL OPTIONS AND SHORTCUTS

Filling objects in a complex drawing is one of the more common actions in creating CorelDRAW graphics. Therefore, it's probably not surprising that the software offers a number of ways to make selecting the fill characteristics of things easier.

You will no doubt have noticed that there is a band of colored swatches along the bottom of the CorelDRAW workspace. This is the quick fill color palette. If you select an object or objects and then click on one of these swatches with the left button of your mouse, the objects will be filled with the color you have selected.

If you click on a color with the right button of your mouse, your chosen color will be assigned to the lines of the object or objects you have selected. You might also notice that there's an icon with an X in it at the extreme left end of the quick palette selector. Click on this with the left button of your mouse to assign a selected object no fill, and with the right button to assign it no line width or color.

There are arrow buttons at each end of the quick palette selector. Click on these with the left button of your mouse to scroll slowly through the available colors. Click on the arrows with the right button to move quickly.

In working with drawings that will be printed on monochrome devices—laser printers, for example—you'll find the lower row of icons in the fill tool's flyout menu to be particularly helpful. These will assign fills of pure white, pure black, and five intermediate levels of gray to selected objects.

The color wheel icon of the fill tool's flyout menu will call up the Uniform Fill dialog box for solid color fills. This will be discussed in detail in Chapter 8.

Finally, you might want to investigate the fill roll-up menu. It can be activated by selecting the second icon in the upper row of the fill tool's flyout menu. This represents an alternate way to work with fills, and you'll probably find that it's a very handy thing to keep open when you're working on complex drawings. There is nothing the fill roll-up menu offers that can't be managed using other facilities of CorelDRAW—the roll-up just lets you get at some of them more readily.

The fill roll-up will affect the fills of whatever object or objects you have selected. Its icons duplicate those in the fill tool's flyout menu, and behave in the same way. However, note that you must click on the Apply button to cause whatever changes you make with the roll-up menu controls to take effect in your selected object.

The Edit button will call up the Uniform Fill dialog box that appears if you click on the color wheel icon of the fill tool's flyout menu.

If you choose a fill characteristic with any of the controls discussed in this chapter—with the exception of the tiled fills—when no object is selected, you will set the default fill characteristics for CorelDRAW. A dialog box will appear to ask whether you want to set the default fill for text objects, other objects, or all objects.

You can have different default fill characteristics for text and non-text objects, if you like.

This feature can be very handy if you'll be creating a lot of objects with the same fill characteristics, as it will save you having to assign fills to them all explicitly. Note that setting the default fill will not retroactively change the fills of existing objects, so you can change it multiple times as you work through a drawing if necessary.

NOTE
NOTE
It's important to keep in mind that roll-up menus, unlike the other dialog boxes in CorelDRAW, are not modal. They won't cause Windows to beep if you try to do something outside one. In fact, this is the really useful aspect of roll-ups—you can have them open on your screen and use them as they're needed.

WRAPPING UP

As with much of CorelDRAW, fills can be as simple or as complex as you want them to be, once you've mastered the basic skills of using the package. If you've been following the examples in the book so far, you probably picked up enough basic information to use the fill tool under CorelDRAW before you even reached this chapter.

Some of the elements of this chapter may still be a bit unclear; as is the case with many aspects of CorelDRAW, the fill tools involve an understanding of other areas of the software. You'll find that as you work through the following chapters, you'll get a better idea of how the fill functions work as well.

If you'll be using CorelDRAW to create pure graphics, you'll find its mastery of fills to be a profound extension of your own fingers. Accomplished CorelDRAW artists can use fills as digital paint, creating stunning effects. Some of the techniques for doing so will be discussed in Part 2 of this book, when we deal with complex drawings.

FAST
TRACK

CHAPTER

5

is a more critical process than importing. You should read the sections regarding color and the use of CorelDRAW fountain fills before exporting in specific file formats. Also, look at the discussions of the differences in file sizes in the different formats if you are restricted in your hard drive space or anticipate uploading these over a modem.

regarding preview files, image control, and fonts.

Importing

and

Exporting

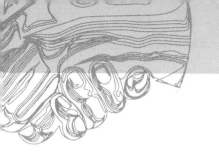

The letter A developed from the aleph and the Greek alpha. It in Etruscan and Latin. The capital letter A is first found in the northern Semitic and was retained in Latin. The

ll by itself, CorelDRAW is a powerful tool for creating drawings. However, one of its additional attributes is that of being able to create and edit files for other applications. You can use it to modify Adobe Illustrator's encapsulated PostScript files, edit an AutoCAD drawing, create graphics for Ventura Publisher and PageMaker, generate pictures for PC Paintbrush, and quite a lot more. Version 3 of CorelDRAW even lets you create your own typefaces and export them for use as text fonts. By virtue of its exceptional import and export facilities, CorelDRAW is compatible with nearly all of the major drawing and painting programs, and with other applications which use their files.

In this chapter, you'll find references to an application called Graphic Workshop. This is provided on the companion Disk 2 for this book.

In learning about importing and exporting, you will encounter what CorelDRAW calls *filters*. A filter is simply a module of CorelDRAW which relates two otherwise incompatible drawing formats. If you ask CorelDRAW to import a file from Adobe Illustrator, for example, CorelDRAW will load the appropriate filter and run the Illustrator file through it. Filters are used both for importing and exporting files under CorelDRAW.

BITMAPS AND OBJECT-ORIENTED FILES

There are really only two sorts of picture files found on a PC. These are bit-mapped pictures and object-oriented pictures. To some extent, CorelDRAW will allow you to work with pictures of either type.

As we have discussed, CorelDRAW files are object-oriented. Object-oriented files are generated by quite a few other PC applications, including AutoCAD, GEM Artline, Adobe Illustrator, and several Windows-based applications, such as Micrografx Designer, which can create Windows Meta-files and others.

You might want to think of your eye as being a bitmapped device and your hand holding a pencil as being an object-oriented drawing device. Your eye sees things pretty much as they are. Your hand holding a pencil can only draw lines— an approximation of reality.

Bitmapped images, or paint files, are pictures which are defined as a matrix of pixels. These are the sorts of images one associates with PC Paintbrush and with image scanners. Photographs which have been digitized are created in one of several bitmapped formats. Some things can be represented a lot better by bitmaps than by object-oriented art. Bitmaps can make photographic art look photographic even after your computer gets hold of it. Because it's a bitmap, however, it cannot be manipulated in the same ways as an object-oriented drawing. For example, if you attempt to resize a bit-mapped drawing you've imported, the result, while certainly scaled to fit the space you've requested, will not look very good. Bitmapped pictures simply don't scale well.

CorelDRAW will allow you to import both object-oriented and bit-map files into a drawing, but it will deal with them differently. The object-oriented formats will be converted into CorelDRAW's internal notation, and once such a file has been imported it will behave just like a normal CorelDRAW drawing. You will be able to manipulate it as if you'd drawn it in CorelDRAW yourself.

Bitmapped images can be imported as well, but only for two specific purposes. The first is to include a bitmap in a CorelDRAW drawing.

Bitmaps so imported can be resized—although not with the most attractive results—cropped, possibly rotated, and placed on a page. CorelDRAW itself does not allow you any facilities for editing them, but one of the ancillary applications that accompanies it, CorelPHOTO-PAINT, does. It will be discussed in detail in Chapter 9.

The other use of bitmapped art under CorelDRAW is for tracing, which will be dealt with in detail in Appendix D.

IMPORT AND EXPORT FILTERS

The following is a list of the most common import and export filters provided by CorelDRAW. We'll discuss the specific uses of most of these later in this chapter.

FORMAT	IMPORT/EXPORT
CorelDRAW CDR	Import
CorelTRACE EPS	Import
CorelPHOTO-PAINT PCX, PCC	Both
PC Paintbrush bitmap PCX	Both
Windows bitmap BMP	Both
Windows Metafile WMF	Both
AutoCAD DXF	Both
CompuServe bitmap GIF	Both
Computer Graphics Metafile CGM	Both
Encapsulated PostScript EPS	Export
GEM metafile GEM	Both
Hewlett Packard HPGL plotter file PLT	Both
IBM PIF	Both
Adobe Illustrator 88, AI 3.0, EPS	Both
Adobe Type 1 Font PFB	Export

FORMAT	IMPORT/EXPORT
Lotus PIC	Import
Macintosh PICT PCT	Both
Truevision TARGA bitmap TGA	Import
Tagged Image File Format 5.0 bitmap TIF	Import
Text TXT	Import
Matrix/Imapro SCODL SCD	Export
WordPerfect Graphics WPG	Export
TrueType Font TTF	Export

In the foregoing list, all of the formats which contain bitmapped images are so indicated; the others are object-oriented drawing formats. All but the last three can be imported and exported by CorelDRAW. The text filter only imports. The SCODL and WordPerfect Graphics filters only export. In addition to the filters on this list, there are filters for exporting Adobe Type 1 and TrueType fonts from CorelDRAW, something that will be discussed in detail later in this book.

Graphic files are most often referred to by the two- or three-letter designations that form their file extensions. In this list, the file extensions are the last thing on each line.

IMPORTING

The most common application of importing drawings into CorelDRAW is to import CorelDRAW's native CDR files. You might well wonder why one would import a CDR file rather than merely open it. When you import something into CorelDRAW's work space, whatever is currently there is not deleted, as is the case when you open a new drawing file. Importing CDR files is useful when you want to merge several smaller drawings into one.

The other importation facilities of CorelDRAW which pertain to art will probably only be of use if you have occasion to edit or convert drawing files from other programs.

You will never have to deal with CorelDRAW's import filters directly. They're installed when you install CorelDRAW and used transparently whenever you ask CorelDRAW to import a file. However, you should keep in mind that when you do go to import something, CorelDRAW must load up one of these little programs and keep it in memory for a while as the importation process is being handled. If you run CorelDRAW on a system that's exceedingly strapped for memory, it might prove unable to use some of its import and export filters.

Figure 5.1 illustrates some files which CorelDRAW has imported from other applications.

All importing is handled through the Import item of the File menu. When you select it, you will see the dialog box in Figure 5.2. Select the type of file you want to import and click on OK.

If you select one of the bitmapped formats, such as PCX or TIFF, the For Tracing option will become active. Leave this alone for the time being—it will be discussed in Appendix D.

FIGURE 5.1:
Some imported files

PCX file from PC Paintbrush

GEM file from GEM Artline

EPS file from Adobe Illustrator

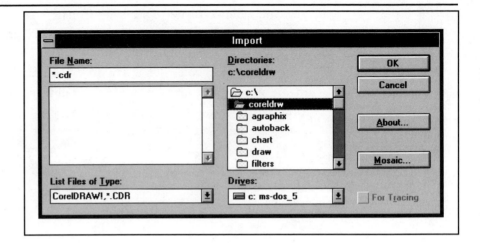

IMPORTING BITMAPPED IMAGES

Normal CorelDRAW objects can be sized to suit your requirements, and they'll always print perfectly. This is not true of bitmapped graphics. A bitmap is a matrix of colored dots, or *pixels*. If you size it such that each pixel will be printed by one dot of your printer, you'll achieve the optimum quality from your imported bitmaps. The next best size is exactly twice as big, such that one pixel is printed as a two by two dot block on your printer. Having an integral relationship between the pixels in a bitmap and the dots of your printer avoids the problem of moiré patterns discussed in Chapter 3.

There's a catch to this, and it's a rather large one.

CorelDRAW regards its printable workspace as having finite dimensions—for example, $8\frac{1}{2}$ by 11 inches for a standard letter-size page. This will represent differing numbers of bitmapped pixels, depending on the resolution of the printer that will ultimately reproduce your CorelDRAW art. For the sake of this discussion, CorelDRAW doesn't know the resolution of the printer you'll be using—after all, you might fool it by changing printers some time in the future.

When you import graphics in most of the bitmapped formats that CorelDRAW supports, it will arbitrarily scale them to fill the horizontal dimension of your current workspace. This, of course, gives no thought to the optimum print size for imported bitmapped pictures, and graphics so imported will frequently exhibit profound scaling aberrations when you go to print them.

Not all TIFF files include resolution information, and some include resolution definitions which have been designed for older or just plain unusual output devices. In this case, you can convert from the TIFF format to the TIFF format with Graphic Workshop to establish the resolution of your TIFF files at 300 dots per inch.

The TIFF bitmapped graphic file format is capable of including information in a graphic that effectively defines its size in inches based on its dimensions in pixels. If you import such a TIFF file into CorelDRAW, it will import at a size which maintains an integral relationship between its pixels and the dots of your laser printer. At least, this will be true if the creator of the TIFF file assumed a resolution that's the same as that of your printer.

Most TIFF files that contain resolution information presuppose a printer that prints at 300 dots per inch, which is a safe guess for most printing applications.

If you want to import bitmapped graphics into CorelDRAW, then, you can achieve the best possible quality by converting them to TIFF files using Graphic Workshop and then importing the TIFF files. You'll find that they'll import as very small images in this case—use the Stretch & Mirror item of the Transform menu to scale them up by an integral value—200 percent, 300 percent, and so on.

Bitmapped Graphics and Color

In computer graphics, a black and white graphic contains only black and white, with no intermediate gray levels. A graphic which includes gray—as does black and white photographic film— is called a "grayscale" image. In reality, gray-scale images are usually just color images in which all the colors are shades of gray.

Unlike one of CorelDRAW's CDR files, a bitmapped graphic will always have an inherent upper limit to the number of distinct colors it can support. There are four common classes of bitmap graphic color depths—two colors, or black and white; 16 colors; 256 colors; and what's called true color, which means that every pixel in the image can be a unique color, drawn from a total range of about sixteen million colors.

You won't need to know this to use CorelDRAW, but the relationship between colors and the number of bits of color in a file is in powers of two. Files with one bit of color have 2^1, or two, colors. Files with four bits have 2^4, or 16, colors. Files with eight bits of color have 2^8, or 256, colors. Files with 24 bits of color have 2^{24}, or 16,777,216, colors. In all cases these values represent the maximum number of distinct colors a file can support.

Bitmapped graphics are also occasionally described by the number of bits of color they represent. Two-color files have one bit of color, 16-color files have four bits of color, 256-color files have eight bits of color, and true-color files have 24 bits of color.

A 256-color bitmapped graphic can represent an essentially photographic image. True-color graphics have still better color control, at the expense of requiring a lot of disk space and memory to store them. A true-color graphic the size of a default VGA screen in the mode Windows likes to run in—that's 640 by 480 pixels—would require 900 megabytes of memory or disk space.

If you import a color bitmap into CorelDRAW, the colors will be preserved. You can thus include scanned color photographs in a drawing.

If you go to print a CorelDRAW drawing with a color bitmap to a black and white laser printer, CorelDRAW will do its best to translate the colored pixels into gray levels. Using a gray-scale bitmap is preferable when you know your drawing will be output to a black and white output device, as you can control the gray-scale characteristics when you create the file.

Figure 5.3 illustrates the result of importing a color TIFF file for output to a black and white PostScript printer as opposed to using a gray-scale TIFF file.

CorelDRAW will import color and gray-scale images from Windows Paintbrush, from DOS paint programs such as PC Paintbrush and Deluxe Paint, and, of course, from its own CorelPHOTO-PAINT application. It

FIGURE 5.3:

Color and gray-scale
TIFF files under
CorelDRAW

will also import public-domain GIF files directly. If you want to use pictures in formats that CorelDRAW will not import directly, you can use an external file conversion package, such as Graphic Workshop.

There's an important rule in working with color. You can't create color where there was none, nor can you make color go away when there's more of it than you can use. If you have a 256-color picture to print on a device that can only print black and white, you will have a considerable surplus of color information looking for trouble.

There are numerous ways to cheat on this problem. The most common one is what CorelDRAW does when it prints color bitmaps on a black and white PostScript printer. It forms halftone spots which look like gray levels. In effect, it finds a gray level that matches the density of each color in the source picture and then fools your printer into handling it as a halftone.

If you attempt to print a color or gray-scale image to a non-PostScript black and white output device—a LaserJet, for example—your graphics probably won't fare as well. When CorelDRAW attempts to print a gray-scale image to one, it will have to do some pretty crude halftoning before the image gets printed. The results often look like bad poster art.

 You might find that importing color graphics without regard for their optimum print size produces acceptable results. This is virtually never true of dithered monochrome files. If you scale one to a non-integral size, its alternating black and white dots will merge together.

This isn't CorelDRAW's fault; as will come up several times in this book, it does the best it can with the printer it's given to use.

You can often improve on the problem of importing color or gray-scale graphics into CorelDRAW for ultimate reproduction on a non-PostScript device by "dithering" the graphics down to monochrome TIFF files and then importing these. Dithering seeks to simulate halftoning through alternating black and white dots. The results don't look much like conventional newspaper halftones, but they're frequently very attractive nonetheless. The Graphic Workshop package will convert color and gray-scale bitmapped graphics to dithered monochrome files.

Figure 5.4 illustrates the same image handled as a gray-scale halftone and as a monochrome dither.

IMPORTING OBJECT-ORIENTED IMAGES

Things are a lot less troublesome when you import object-oriented formats into CorelDRAW. Most drawing formats, such as GEM and AutoCAD DXF, pretty well have a one-to-one correspondence between what they can

Dithered

Halftoned

represent and what CorelDRAW can handle. Importing them should result in no difficulties.

PostScript files are a notable exception to this statement.

Importing EPS, or encapsulated PostScript, files can be frustrating under CorelDRAW, depending on where the EPS files originally came from. PostScript is an extremely complex language—in order to import a PostScript file, CorelDRAW must include the equivalent of a laser-printer PostScript interpreter as part of its operational code. Having gone to these lengths, CorelDRAW expects EPS files to be well behaved, in computer terms.

The complete PostScript language is exceedingly rich, and being able to interpret it all would require that CorelDRAW be about twice its current size and work at the speed of lukewarm tar running up a hill. In fact, CorelDRAW gets around this problem rather elegantly: It only supports those aspects of PostScript that are required to actually draw things. This subset was originally defined by the Adobe Illustrator application.

CorelDRAW imports EPS files from Adobe Illustrator without complaint, and it's quite happy to accept files from other applications that conform to the Illustrator subset of PostScript. Applications which generate EPS files to different standards might not be quite so well received by Corel-DRAW. For example, CorelDRAW can import and export EPS files, but it can't reimport its own exported EPS files unless they have been saved as Illustrator-specific AI files.

You might well ask why all the EPS files exported by CorelDRAW don't use the Illustrator subset of PostScript, so that they'd all be reimportable. The problem in this is that the Illustrator subset is a bit limited. One of the reasons that CorelDRAW is much more popular than Adobe Illustrator is that CorelDRAW can do a lot more with its drawings, and likes to store things that the Illustrator definition of PostScript can't represent. For example, you cannot export proper fountain fills to an Illustrator AI file, as AI files don't support fountains. This sort of restriction would seriously limit the power of CorelDRAW if AI files represented the only way to export Post-Script graphics.

There's a very elaborate trick built into the EPS file format which allows applications that aren't smart enough to actually interpret encapsulated Post-Script files to include them in complex documents anyway. An EPS file created for use with applications like Ventura Publisher and PageMaker actually consists of two versions of the same graphic—the complex one that will be sent to your printer and a much simpler one, called a "preview," that can be displayed on your screen. The preview can't be manipulated, however. This means that Ventura Publisher, for example, may be able to import EPS files that confound CorelDRAW. Ventura may seem to be making sense of them, but it's really just sneaking around the problem.

A great deal more will be said about EPS previews in Part 2 of this book.

SOME IMPORTING CONSIDERATIONS

Despite the substantial range of foreign files CorelDRAW deals with, it rarely complains or mangles a drawing unless you deliberately try to feed it something it doesn't like.

It is possible to overuse CorelDRAW's import facilities. If you attempt to import several fairly complex files into your work space at one time, the resulting drawing may be so complex as to slow CorelDRAW down when it goes to redraw its screen. A two-minute wait every time you want to change magnifications will probably put you off the idea of handling enormous pictures, even if CorelDRAW is prepared to work with them. Large compressed TIFF files and complex GEM files are among the formats which tend to bog CorelDRAW down noticeably.

In all discussions of things that slow CorelDRAW down, note that the degree to which this happens will be a factor of the hardware you attempt to run CorelDRAW on. A 33 megahertz 80486-based system with 16 megabytes of memory will find itself noticeably less bogged down than will an old 80286-based AT-compatible system with four megabytes of memory. Your own level of patience will also affect how much you perceive CorelDRAW slowing down.

Imported bitmaps can be treated like any other objects as far as CorelDRAW is concerned. You can resize them, rotate them, skew them, and so on. However, the results may turn out to be unattractive. Unlike drawn objects, bitmaps are not cleaned up by CorelDRAW after a transformation. If you resize a bitmapped object, for example, the results may look crunchy and unattractive. Rotating one by something other than an even multiple of 90 degrees may also introduce some aberrations into the picture. This is one of those cases in which CorelDRAW allows you to perform an operation which you might do well to avoid.

If you transform a bitmap in some way other than simply resizing it, the rough screen representation of the bitmap which CorelDRAW normally shows you will vanish, to be replaced by a gray rectangle with one corner missing, CorelDRAW's transformed-bitmap indicator. Transformed bitmaps can be printed on PostScript printers only.

Small bitmaps exhibit more pronounced aberrations than do big ones, as bitmaps with large dimensions have more pixels to spread the screening errors over. In addition, you'll probably find that you can get away with doing a lot more to color and gray-scale bitmaps than you can to black and white ones. The process of screening a bitmap tends to average out the individual pixel values, reducing the undesirable effects of rotation and arbitrary scaling.

Imported bitmapped images require a long time to print, and take up lots of memory as well. Both of these concerns grow with the size of your bitmapped objects. If you can keep them small, the performance of CorelDRAW will be improved.

IMPORTING RESTRICTIONS

Considering the huge number of applications that produce files which CorelDRAW will ostensibly import, it's perhaps not surprising that a few files turn up from time to time in the right format, but will not import just the same. File format specifications are frequently not as precise as the authors of software such as CorelDRAW would like them to be.

The people who write import and export filters tend to collect peculiar, pathological files that don't read properly, so as ultimately to be able to produce better filters. If you find files that CorelDRAW won't import, you should probably get in touch with Corel Systems. Assuming they haven't previously encountered the problem and subsequently fixed it, they'll probably be grateful for copies of your problem graphics.

Importing problems in CorelDRAW can be thought of as falling into two classes. Some will arise due to genuine oversights in the CorelDRAW import filters—things the authors of the filters hadn't encountered. This most often happens when the software that initially created your files didn't do so exactly as it should have.

There are also aspects of some of CorelDRAW's import filters which are incomplete by design. There are some things supported by other graphic file formats which CorelDRAW simply has no equivalent for, and which cannot be translated by its import filters.

If you attempt to import a bitmapped graphic which CorelDRAW's import filters can't deal with, the result will either be an error message telling you so or a very plainly mangled graphic, leaving little doubt that something has gone wrong. Imported object-oriented graphics can be a lot more subtle—if CorelDRAW encounters elements in an object-oriented graphic that it can't translate, it might just omit them, or try to approximate them. Until you're familiar with those import filters which pertain to your applications, you might want to scrutinize those object-oriented graphics you do import.

RESTRICTIONS ON IMPORTING INTO CORELDRAW

The following is a list of the CorelDRAW import filters and their limitations. Note that in most cases these are pretty esoteric limitations, and ones that are unlikely to trouble you.

Adobe Illustrator AI and EPS

Everything in an AI file will be imported as a group, which will require ungrouping in CorelDRAW if you wish to modify it. Note that you can use this filter to import EPS files exported from Adobe Illustrator, but not those exported from CorelDRAW using its EPS export filter.

AutoCAD DXF

You can create a DXF file from within AutoCAD by using the DXFOUT command. Note that while DXF files can be three dimensional, CorelDRAW handles everything in two dimensions. Three-dimensional images should be saved in the view in which you want them to appear in CorelDRAW.

There is a limit to the complexity of DXF files that CorelDRAW's DXF import filter can handle. If your drawings exceed this, you can sneak around the problem by setting up AutoCAD to drive a Hewlett Packard 7475A plotter and exporting your DXF files to PLT plot files. These can be imported as HPGL files into CorelDRAW, as discussed later in this section.

A DXF file which contains a drawing larger than eighteen by eighteen inches will be scaled down when it's imported into CorelDRAW.

CorelDRAW will attempt to approximate dashed lines in imported DXF files, although the correspondence isn't always perfect.

AutoCAD polylines—lines of varying width—have no corresponding line type under CorelDRAW. They'll be imported as lines of the minimum width of the original polylines or four inches, whichever is thinnest.

Isolated points are imported as very small ellipses. Points in three-dimensional space are imported as line segments.

Unexploded dimensional entities usually don't import correctly into CorelDRAW. You should explode them prior to exporting your DXF file.

CorelDRAW will not import the following elements if they appear in a DXF file:

◆ Shape entities

◆ Polylines, as discussed

◆ Three-dimensional shapes and extrusions

◆ Invisible lines in three-dimensional face entities

◆ Automatic wire frames

◆ Paper space entities within a modal space

◆ Anything in a binary DXF file

CorelDRAW cannot handle hidden line removal of three-dimensional drawings.

When it imports text from a DXF file, CorelDRAW will convert AutoCAD's text entities to a suitable font. As there is a limit to the size of CorelDRAW's text objects, really enormous text may be scaled down. CorelDRAW will attempt to preserve the justification of the text it imports, but it's not always able to do so. Minor character shifts may occur.

Note that in importing text in a DXF file, CorelDRAW has the following limitations:

◆ It will ignore control characters.

◆ It will ignore underscores and overscores.

◆ Characters represented as numbers will only be correctly interpreted if they have three digits. The first one can be a leading zero for characters with ASCII codes of less than 100.

◆ Special characters that CorelDRAW can't translate will be replaced with question marks.

The following is a list of the fonts CorelDRAW will use to translate text in a DXF file.

DXF FONT	CORELDRAW FONT	COMMERCIAL FONT
Complex	Toronto	Times
Gothic	Frankenstein	Fette Fraktur
Greek	Symbols	Greek/Math Symbols
Italic	Toronto	Times (Italic)
Monotext	Monospaced	Letter Gothic
Roman	Toronto	Times
Script	Banff	Brush Script
Simplex	Toronto	Times
Standard	Toronto	Times
Symap	Geographic	Carta
Symath	Symbols	Greek/Math Symbols
Symusic	Musical	Sonata
All others	Toronto	Times

AutoCAD works with dimensions specified in real numbers, that is, in numbers with decimal points. This is why AutoCAD requires a math coprocessor to handle its floating point calculations, and to a large extent why math coprocessors exist. CorelDRAW handles its dimensions as integers, which are very much faster to work with, but much less precise. Very detailed drawings imported from DXF files might turn out to have their points shifted a bit under CorelDRAW.

BITMAPPED FORMATS—BMP, GIF, PCX, TGA, TIF

Bitmapped formats usually have fewer vagaries to deal with. Here are a few limitations to consider in working with them:

◆ Short of an actual corrupted BMP file, CorelDRAW will read all flavors of this format. Note that the Windows RLE format is also a species of BMP files—it will read these as well.

◆ CorelDRAW will only read the first image in multiple-image GIF files.

◆ CorelDRAW will import most PCX files. It does not correctly handle eight-color PCX files. If you find a PCX file that it will not read, use Graphic Workshop to convert it to the TIFF format and import it as a TIFF file.

◆ CorelDRAW will import most TGA files. If you encounter one it won't read, use Graphic Workshop to convert it to a TIFF file.

◆ CorelDRAW will read many types of TIFF files, but there are quite a few more it will not handle. You might be able to get around this by using Graphic Workshop to convert from TIFF to TIFF— and then again, you might not. The TIFF format is very contentious in this way. You might also find that using Graphic Workshop to convert from the TIFF format to the TIFF format will establish a better choice of resolution values in your TIFF files, as discussed earlier in this chapter.

CDR Files

Perhaps not surprisingly, CorelDRAW can reliably import its own files without problems. It's worth noting that very old CDR files from version 1 of CorelDRAW may exhibit slight character spacing problems when they're imported into the current version of the software.

GEM Files

Files in the GEM format are created by several applications running under Digital Research's GEM windowing environment, GEM Artline being the most notable. The GEM format is fairly primitive in comparison to CDR files, and there are few problems in importing GEM files into CorelDRAW.

Having said this, I should mention that the GEM format is somewhat "extensible," which means that applications which create GEM files are free to add things to the format for their own needs. In most cases, CorelDRAW's import filter will successfully deal with these undefined areas of the format, but occasionally you'll encounter a GEM file that doesn't read correctly.

Here are the limitations of the GEM import filter:

◆ Patterned fills in GEM objects are converted to gray fills under CorelDRAW.

◆ GEM files created by GEM Artline will lose their special line caps and corners. GEM files created by GEM Draw will lose their arrowheads.

◆ Text in GEM files created by GEM Artline will be imported as curves, rather than editable text. Text in GEM files created by GEM Draw will be imported as text, although there may be minor justification differences in it when it appears in CorelDRAW. The GEM Dutch font will be converted to CorelDRAW Toronto, or Times Roman, and the GEM Swiss font will be converted to CorelDRAW Switzerland, or Helvetica.

◆ Special characters in the GEM fonts which have no equivalent in Windows TrueType fonts will be replaced with question marks.

CGM FILES

Files in the CGM format frequently import into CorelDRAW so that they display way too large. You might have to scale them down before they can be used.

Bitmapped-image fragment objects in CGM files will not be imported into CorelDRAW.

Most text in CGM files will be imported as editable text, although the font used by CorelDRAW may not match the one provided by whatever application created the CGM file. If you create CGM files under Harvard Graphics, select the CGM font. Note that applications which use the IBM PC character set in creating CGM files will confuse CorelDRAW a bit, as the upper 128 character symbols won't match those in CorelDRAW. In that CorelDRAW can't know where a CGM file has come from, these symbols will usually appear as meaningless characters when they're imported into CorelDRAW.

Hewlett Packard HPGL Plotter (PLT) Files

HPGL files are actually files of codes which would otherwise be sent to a plotter. When CorelDRAW imports an HPGL file, it pretends it's a plotter and draws whatever a real plotter would have drawn.

The usual file extension for HPGL files is PLT.

The CorelDRAW import filter will handle most of the HPGL instructions. There are a few, specifically in HPGL/2, which it will not correctly interpret. Encountering one may also upset its interpretation of the next few instructions, usually resulting in missing elements in an imported drawing.

Plotters handle color by selecting different pens, and HPGL files indicate a change in color by issuing an instruction for the plotter to fetch a different color pen. There is no defined relationship between pen numbers and pen colors. (On a real plotter, if you put a red pen in the first bay of the pen holder, for example, color number one would be red.)

The CORELDRW.INI file in the \CORELDRW\DRAW\ directory of your hard drive can be used to define the colors to be used for specific pen numbers in HPGL files. Once you have initially used the HPGL import filter once, sections will appear in CORELDRW.INI headed [CorelHPGLPens] and [CorelHPGLColors]. Edit these to redefine the pen characteristics as you require. Note that these tables will also affect the HPGL export filter.

Appendix B of this book includes a detailed discussion of editing CORELDRW.INI.

The HPGL standard defines line types as numbers. These will be interpreted by CorelDRAW as follows:

0	Solid line
1	Dotted line
2	Small dash line
3	Large dash line
4 and 5	Dot-dash line
6	Double dot dash
7 and above	Pen number two

Text will be imported in the Monospaced font. This will look significantly different from the usual stick-figure font of a plotter. It will have the currently defined fill color, based on earlier commands in the file being imported, and no outline color.

Many HPGL files—specifically those created for earlier Hewlett Packard plotters—will have no fills at all.

Lotus PIC Files

Lotus PIC files are used to hold graphs of data from Lotus 1-2-3 spreadsheets. Note that the Lotus PIC format is not the same as the Pictor/Grasp PIC format. To import the latter into CorelDRAW, use Graphic Workshop to translate your PIC files into TIFF files.

Colors in Lotus PIC files will be converted into shades of gray under CorelDRAW. The Title font will be replaced by Toronto, or Times Roman. All other text will appear in the Monospaced font.

Macintosh PICT Files

The PICT format is the default object-oriented format used by Macintosh applications. It can be exported from packages such as MacDraw. Because the structure of the Macintosh is quite different from that of a PC, PICT files offer a wide range of potential compatibility problems for CorelDRAW.

Here are some of the most common ones:

◆ Objects in PICT files which have both fills and outlines will appear in CorelDRAW as two superimposed objects, one with a fill and the other with an outline.

◆ Some PICT fills are actually bitmaps. CorelDRAW will approximate these as bitmap fills as best it can.

◆ Arrowheads and dashed lines are not imported into CorelDRAW. These lines will appear as solid lines with no arrowheads.

◆ Text imported from a PICT file will remain as editable text, but it will be translated by CorelDRAW. Helvetica will become Switzerland, Symbols will become Greek/Math Symbols, and everything else will become Toronto. The alignment of imported text may change slightly due to the font translation. Underlined text is not supported. The Macintosh Cairo font is particularly troublesome, as it's a wholly nonalphabetic graphic font with no correspondence under CorelDRAW.

TEXT

Text can be imported from raw ASCII files directly into CorelDRAW. It will appear in text frames. You can import up to 4000 characters into a single frame—anything beyond this will be ignored. The source files must be raw ASCII, with no formatting. Most word processors, including the Windows Write application, can export text in this format.

WINDOWS METAFILE (WMF) FILES

There are no restrictions on importing WMF files into CorelDRAW. However, note that the import filter may have to translate the fonts used for text in WMF files. Here's how it handles this:

WMF FONT	CORELDRAW FONT	COMMERCIAL FONT
Swiss (default)	Switzerland	Helvetica
Swiss Light	Switzerland Light	Helvetica Light
Swiss Extrabold	Switzerland Black	Helvetica Black
Roman	Toronto	Times Roman
Modern	Memorandum	American
Typewriter		
Script	Banff	Brush Script
Decorative	Lincoln	Linotext

EXPORTING

You can export CorelDRAW drawings in different formats as object-oriented drawing files or as bitmapped-image files. In the former case, the resulting drawing will be as scalable as your original CorelDRAW drawing was. If you export an object-oriented file such as a Windows Metafile or a GEM file from CorelDRAW and import it into Ventura Publisher or Page-Maker, for example, the resulting picture will have all the attributes of line art under Ventura or PageMaker, including the ability to resize it without distortion.

Actually, there are a few catches to this, which will be discussed later in this chapter.

If you output a bitmapped file, such as a PCX or TIFF file, the resulting image will have a fixed resolution. However, you'll be able to use it in applications which require image rather than drawing files. For example, you could output a CorelDRAW drawing as a bitmap and then use the resulting PCX file in PC Paintbrush. Exporting a PCX file from CorelDRAW is also a quick way to generate graphics for inclusion in FAX documents if you have a FAX board in your computer.

You can export all or part of a drawing by means of the Export item from the File menu. Selecting this will pop up the dialog box shown in Figure 5.5.

The less-than-obvious controls in this box will be explained as we get to the various file formats they pertain to. The important one is the file-type selector in the lower-left corner.

FIGURE 5.5:

The Export dialog box

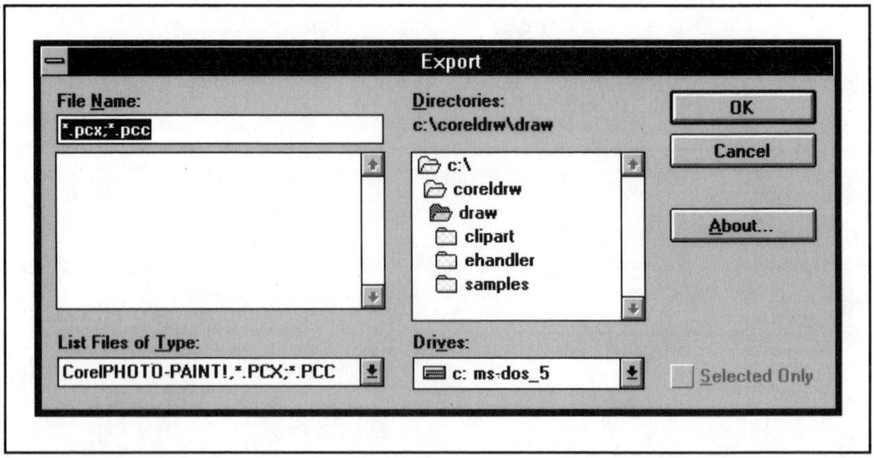

Note the option called Selected Only. If you choose this feature, only those objects of your drawing which were selected when you opened the Export dialog box will be exported. This allows you to export part of a drawing without having to delete the parts of it you don't want to include.

Once you select an export file type using the type selector at the bottom of the box and enter a file name to export to, clicking on OK will take you to the specific export filter dialog box for the format you have selected.

Exporting is a bit more complicated than importing because you have to take into account the applications you'll be using your exported files with, something CorelDRAW can't really do by itself.

Let's look at some common applications of exporting CorelDRAW drawings.

ADOBE ILLUSTRATOR AI AND EPS FILES

The distinction between general EPS files and Adobe Illustrator files has been discussed at length. If you export a CorelDRAW drawing to an EPS file, virtually everything in the original image will make the trip. Exporting to the AI format using the Adobe Illustrator export filter will not be quite as kind to your drawings—the following things will change on their way through the filter:

◆ Fountain fills will be exported as a series of bands, the number being defined by the Preview Fountain Stripes setting in the Display section of the CorelDRAW Preferences box. This will usually look a lot coarser than a proper CorelDRAW fountain.

◆ PostScript textures will not be exported.

◆ Arrowhead line caps will be drawn as discrete objects.

◆ Text fitted to a path will no longer appear as a string, but rather as discrete characters. This will also be true of text strings in which the characters have distinct attributes.

◆ If the CalligraphicClipboard value in your CORELDRW.INI file is set to 1, calligraphic lines will be exported as a series of polygons to simulate their original appearance under CorelDRAW. Otherwise, they'll be exported as lines of fixed width. See appendix B for a discussion of CORELDRW.INI.

Use the EPS export filter, rather than the AI filter, unless you wish to export files specifically for the purpose of subsequently importing them into an application that interprets AI PostScript—such as Adobe Illustrator or CorelDRAW.

◆ Bitmap fragments in your source file will not appear in an exported AI file.

As a rule, only Times Roman, Helvetica, and Courier—Toronto, Switzerland, and Courier in CorelDRAW's terms—should be used in drawings destined for export to AI files. An AI file assumes that the PostScript printer that will ultimately reproduce it will have the fonts it requires on hand, as the file carries none itself. If your printer has more resident fonts—most newer PostScript printers do—or if you will be manually downloading fonts to it prior to printing, you can expand on this somewhat.

AUTOCAD DXF FILES

There are a lot of things that CorelDRAW can do for which AutoCAD has no corresponding drawing primitives to handle. These drawing attributes will vanish if you export a CorelDRAW drawing to the DXF format. Here's a list of them:

◆ No fills of any type will be exported to DXF files. Be particularly careful of this—an object with a fill but no outline will have an arbitrary outline applied to it when it's exported to the DXF format.

◆ Calligraphic and dashed lines will be converted to solid lines 0.003 inches thick.

◆ Bitmapped fragments will not be exported.

◆ Curves will be converted to polylines.

The Standard Colors option of the DXF Export dialog box will match all the colors in your source drawing to the standard seven AutoCAD colors. The Full Colors option will allow for a range of 255 colors, but in many cases the color matching won't be particularly good.

The ExportTextAsCurves line in CORELDRW.INI will determine whether text will be exported as curves—in which case it will look reasonable but will not be editable under AutoCAD—or as text—in which case it will be editable but it will look markedly different from how it appeared in CorelDRAW. See Appendix B for a complete discussion of CORELDRW.INI.

The DXF format has the distinction of using the most file space of any of the object-oriented formats supported by CorelDRAW. A one-hundred kilobyte CDR file can top a megabyte when it's exported to the DXF format—have lots of free disk space on hand.

BITMAP GRAPHIC FILES

You can export a bitmapped version of your drawing as a bitmapped graphic, that is, as a PCX, BMP, GIF, TGA, or TIFF file. In creating a bitmap, CorelDRAW does essentially what your printer would do when it generates the huge bitmap which represents your final output. It chooses a fixed size for all the objects in your drawing and renders them in memory, doing any fills and so on as specified. It then writes the whole works to a file rather than to your printer.

The features in the Export dialog box which concern outputting a bitmapped version of a CorelDRAW drawing are the Resolution options. These will allow you to decide how many dots per inch your exported file will use. None of these formats has any inherent limitations on how big a picture you can create, so you can select whatever resolution is appropriate so long as you have the disk space to accommodate the resulting file.

It's worth noting that BMP files are exported with their image data uncompressed. BMP files containing anything beyond trivial, small drawings will tend towards being huge.

In fact, each of the bitmapped image file formats supported by CorelDRAW has specific compression characteristics. The BMP format uses uncompressed images, which will be quick to load but very, very big. The PCX and TIFF formats use simple compression, which will produce files that are moderately well compressed and moderately quick to load. The GIF format uses a very sophisticated form of compression which will usually provide you with the smallest possible image files, at the cost of their taking longer to unpack. Targa, or TGA files, and TIFF files can be saved either compressed or uncompressed. In their compressed versions, they support compression similar to that of PCX.

The bitmapped output options of CorelDRAW will allow you to select the "resolution" of the files they create. This defines the number of pixels per inch. There are a number of preset choices, and you can select any other resolution you like by choosing Custom from the Resolution selector and typing the resolution you'd like to use into the edit field below it.

Bit-mapped images can get very big. An 8½-by-11 inch drawing exported at 300 dots per inch into an uncompressed format, such as BMP, will occupy about a megabyte for a 2-color image, four megabytes for a 16-color image, eight megabytes for a 256-color image and 24 megabytes for a true-color image.

As a quick rule of thumb, your screen has a resolution of about 75 dots per inch—choosing this sort of resolution will produce an exported bitmap that looks about as well defined as the image on your monitor. A FAX machine has a resolution of 200 dots per inch in its fine mode and 200 dots per inch horizontally by 100 dots per inch vertically in its normal mode. A laser printer has a resolution of 300 dots per inch.

The amount of space a bitmapped graphic occupies on your disk, all other things being equal, will increase as the square of the resolution. Increasing the resolution from 75 dots per inch to 150 dots per inch should create an exported bitmapped graphic about four times as big. This will certainly be true of uncompressed formats, such as BMP.

Keep in mind that the relationship of the dimensions of a bitmapped graphic in pixels and the size it will print in inches depends on the resolution of the printer that will output it. You can work out the actual printed size of a graphic by dividing its dimensions in pixels by the number of dots per inch of your printer. For example, a 640 by 480 pixel picture printed at 300 dots per inch will occupy (640 ÷ 300) by (480 ÷ 300), or 2.13 by 1.60, inches.

In some cases, you will not care about the resolution of an exported bitmap so much as its actual exported dimensions. In this case, ignore the resolution setting in the Export dialog box and look below it, to the Size box. If you use this control, you will be able to define the actual dimensions of the bitmap file CorelDRAW will create, forcing it to work out the resolution required.

If you select Custom in the Size field, you can define any dimensions in pixels that you like.

In addition to specifying the size of an exported bitmapped graphic, CorelDRAW will give you a choice of color depth options, that is, the maximum number of colors the exported graphic can support. In addition to choosing a range of colors, you'll also be able to choose a maximum number of gray levels. The choices will be black and white (two colors), 16 colors or levels of gray, 256 colors or levels of gray, or 16 million colors. The latter choice is not available in exporting GIF files, as the GIF format has an upper limit of 256 colors.

Among other things, black and white exported, bitmapped graphics will allow you to use CorelDRAW art as the header for faxes sent from a FAX board.

Keep in mind when selecting the maximum number of colors in an exported graphic that a file with more colors takes up more space and more memory when you work on it, and may not be compatible with all applications. For example, many desktop publishing packages and word processors which will ostensibly import PCX and TIFF files will not handle these graphics in their 24-bit, or 16-million color, formats. Don't choose more color depth than you really require.

If you'll be printing an exported bitmap on a 300 dot-per-inch laser printer, you'll probably find that 16 colors or gray levels are sufficient. You'll probably only require 16-million colors if you'll be outputting your graphics to a high-end color printer, importing it into another package that will be generating color separations from it, or using it in a photographic retouching or paint package such as CorelPHOTO-PAINT.

You should also think about the maximum number of colors in the drawing you'll be exporting. There's little point in creating a 256-color bitmap from a CorelDRAW drawing that only has four colors in it.

Note that if your CorelDRAW file has fountain fills in it, the fountains will be represented as bands in an exported bitmapped graphic. The number of bands can be set using the Preview Fountain Stripes control in the Display section of the CorelDRAW Preferences box.

If you need bit-mapped graphics in a file format that CorelDRAW won't export directly—such as PIC files to use with Grasp or LBM files to import into Deluxe Paint— export them to the supported bitmap formats and use Graphic Workshop to translate them into the format you require.

EPS OR ENCAPSULATED POSTSCRIPT FILES

If you know that your exported file will ultimately be printed to a PostScript printer, the encapsulated PostScript format isn't a bad choice. It offers the least opportunity for aspects of your drawing to be lost or mangled in the conversion between file formats. The EPS format can support all the features of CorelDRAW faithfully—it's the only format to which you can export PostScript textures.

If you wanted to export a CorelDRAW drawing for use in a Ventura Publisher document, for example, you might consider doing it as a GEM file or a Windows Metafile. However, Ventura would then have to convert it with an internal PostScript program for printing. On the other hand, if you were to output your drawing directly as an EPS file, Ventura would not have to do any conversion. In fact, it would not even really look at your EPS file beyond simply reading it in and shipping it directly to the printer.

Encapsulated PostScript files do have a few possible drawbacks, however. To begin with, they're big—much more so than most of the other object-oriented formats. They're also potentially troublesome. As has been touched on, most applications which use EPS files can't actually interpret them. Instead, they read a short header at the beginning of the file which tells them about the size and general nature of the drawing they're about to use. Everything else is dealt with using a great deal of faith.

As mentioned earlier in this chapter, because an application like Ventura Publisher or PageMaker cannot interpret a PostScript file, it can't show you what an exported CorelDRAW EPS file contains when you include one in a Ventura document—at least not directly. In order to get around this, EPS files can include a preview, a small bitmapped image tacked onto the end of the file, which applications such as Ventura can display. Ideally, the preview will contain enough detail from the original image to allow the EPS file to be positioned and cropped. In fact, because of the limited resolution of an EPS preview, the relationship between what you see and what you get isn't always terribly good. Accurate positioning of an EPS file is difficult in some cases.

If you are exporting EPS files to be used with a Macintosh system, you should export plain EPS files with no previews, because the preview structure differs between PC and Macintosh architectures, even though the file format itself does not.

Finally, PostScript is a bit temperamental and version-dependent. CorelDRAW's exported files assume a fairly recent version. If you print your exported drawing on a really old LaserWriter, for example, odd things may happen: Some objects might not print, lines might not appear where you expect them, or fills might not do what you planned. The PostScript language, like most things having to do with computers, has grown and evolved since its inception.

As long as you appreciate the potential catches in using EPS files, they're a good way to export CorelDRAW art for applications which will use them. They usually produce the best results with the least fuss.

NOTE *NOTE* *Versions of Ventura Publisher prior to 2.0 are unable to display an EPS preview even if one is present.*

Relevant Controls for EPS Export

There are several controls in the EPS Export dialog box to take into account when you're creating EPS files.

Image Header The Image Header options control the generation of the preview image. You should choose something other than None if you plan to use your exported image in a program which does not interpret Post-Script but which will show you the preview, such as Ventura Publisher, PageMaker, WordPerfect, and so on. You can select None to disable it if you'll be using your exported file in the old Ventura 1.1, which can't read EPS previews; if you'll be porting your EPS files to a Macintosh; or if you specifically need a "pure" EPS file with no non-PostScript elements.

Disabling this option when you don't need the preview will reduce the size of the EPS file somewhat.

The three Size options will define the resolution, and thus, the level of detail in the preview image. Low Resolution will create previews which are so coarse as to be all but unintelligible. High Resolution will create 300 dot-per-inch previews—these will usually allow for the most effective preview images, but with a notable speed and memory penalty in most applications. Predictably, Medium Resolution is a good compromise.

All Fonts Resident The All Fonts Resident option tells CorelDRAW to assume that all the fonts you've used in your drawing are available at the printer which will ultimately be printing your exported file. This means that if your drawing contains some straight, untouched text, CorelDRAW would output the text as such with a request for the destination printer to supply the font, rather than providing the font as part of the exported EPS file as usual.

This option is useful if you know that the destination printer will have the fonts you want to use. It also makes for a smaller EPS file.

If you select this option when all fonts are not in fact resident in the destination printer, the affected text will be printed in Courier type if it prints at all.

Convert Color Bitmaps to Gray Scale This is an important control if you will be including color bitmaps in an EPS file that will ultimately be printed to a monochrome printer. Left unselected, it will cause the EPS export filter to create color bitmap elements in your file. These are suitable for printing color bitmaps on a color printer, such as a QMS ColorScript, and for crashing most black and white laser printers, which do not come equipped with a version of PostScript capable of making sense of the color-specific instructions in PostScript.

If you have bitmapped elements in your drawings and your EPS files will ultimately find themselves printed in monochrome or gray scale, select this option.

Windows Metafile, CGM, and GEM

Windows Metafile, CGM, and GEM can be interpreted by any applications which can import them, with one exception. WordPerfect can't read Corel-DRAW's CGM files—you should export to WPG files in this case.

If you import a GEM file into Ventura Publisher, for example, Ventura will draw each object on the screen just as CorelDRAW will do with a CDR file. This being the case, these formats do not require a PostScript printer to output them. They're portable to any output device the application will drive.

These file formats generally give you better position control over your drawings for cropping if you're importing them into a desktop-publishing program. However, there are certain drawbacks to using GEM, CGM, or Windows Metafile drawings rather than encapsulated PostScript files when you know that the final output device will be a PostScript printer.

A small minority of drawings don't handle their fill characteristics as well when they're exported as GEM files, and you will occasionally find the fills bleeding out of the objects which contain them. There's no simple rule as to when this will happen or why.

Most Windows-based applications which can use object-oriented art will accept Windows Metafile drawings.

There are some general things to keep in mind about these formats and the applications they might be imported into. Here are the limitations for GEM files:

◆ GEM objects can contain no more than 128 nodes each. The CorelDRAW export filter frequently has to simplify complex objects being exported to GEM, with the result that they can look a little crunchy.

◆ GEM only supports 16 colors. Objects with color outlines or fills under CorelDRAW will be mapped to the nearest GEM color upon export—don't expect too close a match.

◆ Bitmaps are not supported by GEM.

◆ Fountains don't export to GEM in any useful way.

◆ Objects with fat outlines often exhibit bad joins at irregular corners in GEM files.

◆ Objects which are both filled and outlined will be exported to GEM files as two objects, one for the fill and one for the outline.

◆ Dashed lines and lines with arrowheads will be exported as multiple distinct objects—this will result in very awkward drawings in the case of dashed lines.

◆ Text is always exported as curves to a GEM file.

◆ Bézier curves are represented by multiple straight line segments.

◆ PostScript textures and tile fills can't be exported to GEM files.

There's a complexity limit to the GEM format—if you attempt to export a sufficiently complex CorelDRAW drawing to the GEM format, you might encounter a warning box about this. Such GEM files will usually be found to be missing some elements.

The CGM file format has a much shorter list of limitations. Specifically, these are:

◆ PostScript textures can't be exported to CGM files.

◆ Bitmaps can't be exported to CGM files either.

◆ Fountain fills will be exported as a series of bands, the number being defined by the Preview Fountain Stripes setting in the Display section of the CorelDRAW Preferences box. This will usually look a lot coarser than a proper CorelDRAW fountain.

Note that the CGM format is a bit loosely defined in a few places. While CorelDRAW creates pretty neutral, well formed CGM files, it is possible that some obscure applications which import drawings in this format may object to them.

The WMF file format is another one with a relatively short list of difficulties. In fact, the WMF format is a metafile that defines everything

Windows itself can draw. With a few exceptions, anything that can appear in CorelDRAW's workspace and be passed through the Windows Clipboard can also be saved as a Windows Metafile.

Here's a list of the limitations of the CorelDRAW WMF export filter:

◆ PostScript textures can't be exported to WMF files.

◆ Bitmaps can't be exported to WMF files.

◆ Pattern fills will be converted to solid gray fills.

◆ Fountain fills will be exported as a series of bands, the number being defined by the Preview Fountain Stripes setting in the Display section of the CorelDRAW Preferences box. This will usually look a lot coarser than a proper CorelDRAW fountain.

The Image Header option of the Windows Metafile Export dialog box will add a preview not unlike that of an Encapsulated PostScript file to the WMF file being exported. It will make the file suitable for use with Ventura Publisher and PageMaker, among others. However, it will confuse most other applications that want to read and directly interpret WMF files.

The WMF format is not particularly compact. Complex graphics exported to the WMF format tend toward obesity.

HEWLETT PACKARD HPGL (PLT) PLOTTER FILES

In exporting to an HPGL file, it's important to keep in mind that you're really creating a list of plotter commands. Plotters are fun to watch, but are relatively unadventurous graphic devices. As a rule, if you can't draw it with a pen, it won't export to an HPGL file.

Among the limitations of the CorelDRAW HPGL export filter are these:

◆ No fills will be exported. Exporting a CDR file to the HPGL file and then reimporting it back into CorelDRAW is a quick way to make a wireframe drawing out of it.

◆ No bitmaps will be exported—plotters can't really draw bitmaps, if you think about it.

◆ Calligraphic pen effects will be exported as solid lines.

◆ Dashed and dotted lines will be converted to the standard HPGL dashed lines.

◆ Bézier curves are converted to line segments.

◆ Colors in your CorelDRAW drawing will be remapped to the HPGL pen colors as defined in CORELDRW.INI. See Appendix B for a complete discussion of these.

◆ Objects with no outline thickness or color in your CorelDRAW drawing will be assigned arbitrary outlines by the HPGL export filter. Hitherto hidden objects might appear unexpectedly.

◆ The ExportTextAsCurves line in CORELDRW.INI will determine whether text will be exported as curves, in which case it will look reasonable but will not be editable if it's imported into another application; or as text, in which case it will be editable but will look markedly different from the way it did in CorelDRAW.

MACINTOSH PICT

In exporting a CorelDRAW drawing to a PICT file, it's important to keep in mind that things work differently in Macintosh circles. There are several things that CorelDRAW can do, but which cannot be represented in a PICT file. Here's a list of the prominent ones:

◆ If the CalligraphicClipboard value in your CORELDRW.INI file is set to 1, calligraphic lines and line caps will be exported as a series of polygons to simulate their original appearance under Corel-DRAW. Otherwise, they'll be exported as lines of fixed width. See Appendix B for a discussion of CORELDRW.INI.

◆ Bitmap fragments in your source file will not appear in an exported PICT file.

◆ PostScript textures and pattern fills will be exported as solid gray fills.

◆ Objects which are both filled and outlined will be exported as two objects—one for the fill and one for the outline.

◆ Fountain fills will be exported as a series of bands, the number being defined by the Preview Fountain Stripes setting in the Display section of the CorelDRAW Preferences box. This will usually look a lot coarser than a proper CorelDRAW fountain.

◆ Colors exported to a PICT file may appear with marked color shifts if your PICT files are viewed on a Macintosh with an eight-bit color display.

◆ The ExportTextAsCurves line in CORELDRW.INI will determine whether text will be exported as curves, in which case it will look reasonable but will not be editable under whatever Macintosh applications open your PICT files; or as text, in which case it will be editable but will appear in whatever font is the current default in the application that first opens the file. See Appendix B for a complete discussion of CORELDRW.INI.

WORDPERFECT GRAPHICS

The WPG file format is only useful if you want to export CorelDRAW art into WordPerfect documents, or into another application created by the WordPerfect Corporation, such as DrawPerfect. The WPG format is a bit crude as drawing formats go, and you should keep in mind its limitations.

◆ Large WPG files tend to blow up WordPerfect in ways that only a reboot will solve. There's no absolute definition for the word "large" in this context—be careful in exporting complex Corel-DRAW art to the WPG format. Note that these files will import into WordPerfect correctly—the crash will come if you attempt to preview or print documents which contain overly large graphics.

◆ If the CalligraphicClipboard value in your CORELDRW.INI file is set to 1, calligraphic lines and line caps will be exported as a series of polygons to simulate their original appearance under Corel-DRAW. Otherwise, they'll be exported as lines of fixed width. See Appendix B for a discussion of CORELDRW.INI. Keep in mind the foregoing warning, however—exported calligraphic lines make for larger WPG files.

◆ Bitmap fragments in your source file will not appear in an exported PICT file.

◆ PostScript textures and pattern fills will be exported as solid gray fills.

◆ Fountain fills will be exported as a series of bands, the number being defined by the Preview Fountain Stripes setting in the Display section of the CorelDRAW Preferences box. This will usually look a lot coarser than a proper CorelDRAW fountain.

◆ The ExportTextAsCurves line in CORELDRW.INI will determine whether text will be exported as curves, in which case it will look reasonable but will not be editable under DrawPerfect; or as text; in which case it will be editable but will appear in one of WordPerfect's unattractive internal fonts. See Appendix B for a complete discussion of CORELDRW.INI.

The WPG files exported by CorelDRAW contain vector images. These cannot be read by Graphic Workshop.

You can usually get the best results in exporting CorelDRAW files with colored objects to the WPG format if you use the 16-color export options. This will cause some color shifts in drawings with a lot of colors. The 256-color output option will offer much less opportunity for a color shift in your exported WPG files, but not all WordPerfect screen and printer drivers will get along with 256-color graphics.

CREATING AND SAVING YOUR OWN FONTS

A new feature added to CorelDRAW with Version 3 is the ability to create your own typeface and save it as one of the two most commonly used Windows font types—TrueType or Adobe Type 1.

You create each character of your character set as an individual graphic. Then use the Export option on the File menu to bring up the Export dialog box (see Figure 5.6). Select either Adobe Type 1 or TrueType from the bottom of the file types list and enter the file name.

When you click on OK, you will be taken into the Adobe Type 1 Export or TrueType Export dialog box. At this point, you enter a font family name (or accept an existing one) in Typeface Information. You can set the style of the character and the other typeface attributes in the Typeface Information box.

In the Character Information box, you select which of the 255 characters you want to save this individual graphic as. You can click on the Auto Width check box or manually set the character width.

*The font Export
dialog box*

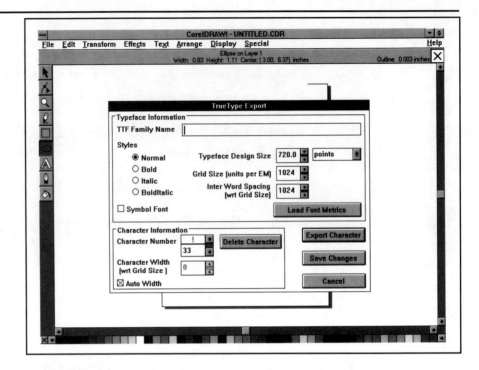

Once you have set all of the information needed, click on Export Character, and the graphic you are currently working on will be saved in the typeface family whose font file name you originally entered in the Export dialog box.

You can use your custom font in any Windows application, instead of having to insert a graphic, scale to the desired size, wait for redraws, and so on, and so on.

IMPORTING AND EXPORTING THROUGH THE CLIPBOARD

There is a very convenient path for importing and exporting modest size drawings between Windows applications, this being the Windows Clipboard. The Clipboard's application to importing text into CorelDRAW was discussed in Chapter 3.

Whenever you use the Cut or Copy functions of the CorelDRAW Edit menu, the objects you've selected will be stashed in the Clipboard. You can subsequently paste them back into CorelDRAW. You can also paste them into another Windows application.

If you're running the Windows version of Ventura, for example, you can paste things directly from CorelDRAW into a Ventura chapter through the Clipboard. We'll have a more detailed look at using the Clipboard in this way in Chapter 11.

WRAPPING UP

You'll probably find that it takes a lot longer to discuss the importing and exporting features of CorelDRAW than it does to actually try them out.

Different applications require differing degrees of involvement with importing and exporting. You may find that little in this chapter is really relevant to you if you create images in CorelDRAW, print them, and never get involved with other software. On the other hand, if you work extensively with other applications in addition to CorelDRAW, you'll probably constantly find new ways to integrate CorelDRAW's omnivorous diet of file formats into your other tasks.

FAST TRACK

HAPTER

6

Printing

P rinting drawings from CorelDRAW is usually pretty pain-less, and if your applications for hard copy are typical, you won't need much of the information in this chap-ter. However, there are a lot of fairly exotic hard-copy devices suitable for use with CorelDRAW, and most of them will require at least some special considerations. In addition, there are some facilities of CorelDRAW which will affect what you print, and how you go about doing it.

In a perfect world, you would not have to know anything about the printer that will reproduce your drawings in order to be able to draw. In the somewhat more realistic world where Windows and its applications must operate, nothing like this is true. To make the most of CorelDRAW, some knowledge of how your printer works will probably be essential.

This chapter will help clarify the often convoluted world of PC printers and CorelDRAW.

UNDERSTANDING PRINTERS

A printer sees the world in a way that's fundamentally different from that of CorelDRAW. Whereas CorelDRAW's graphics are lines and fills for the most part, a printer sees everything as a bitmap. Specifically, it prints pages as a matrix of dots. Conventional "dot-matrix" printers use a fairly coarse matrix of dots, so coarse in fact, that you can see the individual dots if you look closely. Laser printers use much smaller dots, which are more difficult to distinguish. PostScript phototypesetters use exceedingly small dots, so that it's practically impossible to tell that their output is anything other than solid objects.

When CorelDRAW prints something, its objects must be "rasterized." This means that somewhere between CorelDRAW and the output tray of your printer, suitable software must create a bitmap representation of the objects to be printed. In theory, this is relatively simple: Just as CorelDRAW draws things on your screen—itself a bitmapped device—so too can it draw on the bitmapped surface of a sheet of printer paper.

In practice, this isn't really what happens for many types of printers. The theory also ignores a number of salient characteristics of computer printers. There are two that we'll deal with immediately—printers have a much finer resolution than monitors do, and conventional laser and dot-matrix printers can't print in anything other than black and white.

Under Windows, printing is handled by printer drivers. This is a term that gets bandied about a lot, without much explanation. Here's a fairly simple way to look at printer drivers. A printer driver is a "black box" which translates a standard set of instructions to print things into the instructions that are specific to your printer.

Consider the recently released Hypothetical Deluxe IV printer—ignore for a moment the fact that it doesn't exist. The Hypothetical Deluxe IV is a wonderful printer, but it insists on being communicated with in a way that's unique to itself. Because of this, and because it was released after the creation of the current versions of both Windows and CorelDRAW, it would be unreasonable to expect CorelDRAW to be able to print to it.

In fact, CorelDRAW can print to the Hypothetical Deluxe IV and all sorts of other printers because it does so through Windows. For example, if in printing a drawing CorelDRAW wants to print an ellipse, it simply calls

Windows and says, "Print this ellipse." It has no idea what sort of printer it's talking to, and cares not a whit. Driving the printer is Windows' problem.

Windows, for its part, calls the current printer driver. In this case, it will be a driver which has been included with the Hypothetical Deluxe IV printer, and presumably understands how to communicate with this unconventional output device. The driver is responsible for knowing how to translate a standard Windows call to print an ellipse into whatever it takes to perform this task on its particular printer.

This is called "device independence." CorelDRAW can print independent of the sort of printer it's connected to.

There's a problem of sorts in this principle. It assumes that all the printers which might ever be driven by Windows applications have at least a common core of things they can print. For example, it assumes that there's some way to print an ellipse on every printer, whether it's an old Epson you found at a garage sale for ten dollars or a brand new Hypothetical Deluxe IV with its optional uninterruptable nuclear-power supply. This would be very handy if it were the case.

Old Epson printers commonly found at garage sales cannot print ellipses—or much else, for that matter. This is why they're commonly found at garage sales.

The Windows printer driver standard sneaks around some of these problems. When a driver is asked to print things its printer knows nothing about, it hands the problem back to Windows and says, "Draw me a picture of what you want and I'll print the picture instead." In effect, printers that can't handle graphic objects of the sort CorelDRAW likes to print will have Windows generate a bitmapped image of the final printed page, and then print the bitmap.

While this is a useful cheat of sorts, it still makes the upper limit of what can be printed through a Windows printer driver somewhat rudimentary. This problem becomes fairly noticeable when attempting to print things to a PostScript printer. There are all sorts of things which a PostScript printer can print, but which Windows' printer-driver calls are incapable of specifying.

Windows includes a dedicated cheat for this problem. It regards Post-Script printers as a special case, and allows high-end applications like CorelDRAW to negotiate with them directly, essentially bypassing the printer driver, in those circumstances where an application wants to print something beyond the capability of the standard Windows printer calls.

For example, when CorelDRAW wants to print a drawing having objects with PostScript fills, it tells the Windows printer driver to take a break and deals directly with the printer.

There are a number of other areas in which this sort of problem can occur. For example, you might consider what a dot-matrix printer—which can print only in black and white—would make of a gray object. In fact, the answer to this conundrum varies between applications. Left to its own devices, Windows will look at the level of gray and "threshold" it. Anything less than 50 percent gray will be printed as black and anything else will be printed as white. Recognizing that this is a little crude, CorelDRAW handles these sorts of printers by creating gray patterns with alternating black and white pixels, that is, by dithering. Dithering is better than nothing, but it's rarely all that attractive.

PostScript printers have internal halftoning facilities. They can print gray as gray by generating halftones.

Here's another gray issue that confronts printers. When you ask CorelDRAW to print a graphic with colored objects to a monochrome printer, it will select a gray level for PostScript printers or a dither pattern for other printers based on the *luminance,* or brightness, of the objects to be printed. This is worked out using a fairly simple calculation. Allowing that the colors are represented as percentages of red, green, and blue light, the gray level of a color can be found like this:

$$gray = 0.30 * red + 0.59 * green + 0.11 * blue$$

There are various things which might change the actual values at which identical gray levels occur for contrasting colors. The important thing to keep in mind is that it can happen.

You'll never require this calculation yourself—it's performed internally within CorelDRAW. However, it's very important to keep in mind how this works. If you have two colored objects, one of which is 37 percent red and the other is 100 percent blue, they will look noticeably different on your screen. However, both will have a gray level of about 11 percent if they're printed on a black and white printer.

One of the ways to make CorelDRAW really perform for you is to think about the characteristics of your printer when you're creating drawings. You might have to do some experimenting to get a feel for what CorelDRAW can and cannot manage on your particular hardware. Some aspects of this were discussed in Chapter 4 when we dealt with using fills. Here are a few things you should probably think about:

1. Can your printer handle halftones, or must CorelDRAW dither gray levels? PostScript and PCL5 printers can do halftones—most other printers must allow CorelDRAW to create dithered fills. If your printer is of the latter type, experiment to see what gray levels produce attractive fills.

2. What's the smallest point size at which your printer can produce attractive text? As a rule, text printed to a 300 dot-per-inch laser printer will be readable at six points, respectable at nine points and pretty sharp at eleven points. Serif faces worsen these values by about two points. Variable-dot printers, such as the Hewlett Packard LaserJet III machines, improve these values by two or three points at least. Dot-matrix printers will require some experimentation.

3. Are there some line angles that produce jaggies that are more noticeable than others on your printer? This is worth considering if you're using a dot-matrix printer—the dots on these machines aren't always perfectly square, and result in some odd interference patterns along the edges of angled lines.

4. What happens to small details when they hit your printer? Depending on the printer driver, lines or fragments of lines that require less than one dot to represent may be expanded to one dot, or they might vanish or become erratic. This is especially true of dot-matrix printers.

By getting a feel for what your printer can and cannot do, you should be able to better choose the elements you'll include in CorelDRAW artwork. If you know that your printer cannot produce halftones and you don't like CorelDRAW's dither substitutes, you might have to forego gray fills, or you might have to restrict yourself to a limited number of gray levels that produce acceptable results. CorelDRAW's dithering for 50 percent gray is reasonably attractive. Its dithering for, say, 37.62 percent gray can look a bit crunchy.

Obviously, this will become less of an issue if you have a more capable printer. Regrettably, the owners of dot-matrix printers will be confronted by all sorts of these considerations. If you'll be outputting your graphics to a PostScript laser printer, you'll encounter far fewer of them. For the most part,

CorelDRAW has been written with the hope that it will get to output its drawings to a PostScript printer—PostScript devices are the most capable printers available for microcomputers at the moment. In a sense, its abilities to print to all other sorts of printers will be a subset of what it can do with a PostScript device.

Some printers, such as the PCL5-based LaserJet III series machines, offer almost the same functionality as PostScript devices.

POSTSCRIPT—A FIVE-MINUTE TOUR

If you're new to printer technology, PostScript may seem like another one of those terms that one hears people talk about but which is never explained. It's actually quite simple.

A 300 dot-per-inch laser printer will print a matrix of about 7,560,000 dots each time it outputs a page. Any of these dots can be either black or white. When CorelDRAW—or any other application—prints something, it requires a way to tell the printer to turn on the appropriate dots. PostScript is a language by which applications can do this without having to work out the status of every dot on the page.

As a simple example, PostScript allows an application to print the letter A in the Times Roman font by saying, in effect, "Print the letter A in Times Roman, if you would," rather than by figuring out which of those seven and a half million dots must be black to make an A appear.

In a sense, PostScript allows CorelDRAW to worry about drawing and the printer to worry about printing. PostScript is a language specifically written to allow software to express what should appear on a printed page, a "page-description language." Every printer or other device that "speaks" PostScript has a computer on board that can convert PostScript commands into printed pages.

At present, PostScript is the most sophisticated of the popular printer page-description languages. It allows virtually any object to be drawn. Most implementations of PostScript include at least 35 built-in typefaces, which can be printed at any size you like. PostScript can print text at any angle, bent along paths, outlined, skewed—as a rule, if CorelDRAW can draw it, a PostScript printer can print it.

One of the powerful aspects of PostScript is that it's a genuine programming language. This is why it can handle things like CorelDRAW's PostScript textures. These things are not drawings of graphics, in the way that tile fills are, but rather are programs that run in your printer and generate the complex patterns associated with this facility.

Just as with an application running under Windows, a program run on a PostScript printer to create a page will be confronted with a finite amount of memory. Every operation performed by a PostScript printer requires some memory, and a sufficiently complex page may require more memory than your printer has available. PostScript printers aren't as resourceful as Windows in this respect—they can't spill things to disk and such. They usually just don't print anything.

There's no way of knowing how complex a PostScript page can get before it won't print, and different printers have different upper limits of complexity.

There are two very useful aspects to PostScript—and one minor catch. The first one is that PostScript is resolution independent. This means that you can output the same drawing to a 300 dot-per-inch PostScript laser and to a 2540 dot-per-inch PostScript phototypesetter. The latter will, of course, look a lot better.

Many professional users handle page creation in this way. The relatively quick and inexpensive output of a PostScript laser is used as page proofs, and final film is generated by a high-end PostScript typesetter. More will be said about this later in this chapter.

The other handy thing about PostScript is that it can print in color. Color PostScript printers exist—the QMS ColorScript machines are among the most commonly used ones. While breathtakingly expensive as compared to conventional laser printers, these systems can produce really dazzling output.

On the other hand, the same pages can be sent to a conventional monochrome PostScript laser and to a color PostScript printer—with one catch, as we'll discuss in a moment. You can use a monochrome printer for proofs and a color PostScript printer for your final artwork.

The one catch alluded to in the foregoing paragraph involves bitmaps. You cannot print color bitmaps in color to most black and white PostScript printers. While colored lines, fills, and type will simply print as corresponding levels of gray on a black and white printer, color bitmaps will crash printers which have not been specifically designed to handle them. They constitute an extension of the basic PostScript language.

CorelDRAW knows how to handle bitmaps in its pages for each occasion.

PRINTER DRIVERS

When you installed Windows, you probably selected one or more printers to be installed as well. This process installs a driver for each one. If you have several printers installed, you can select one as the current printer through the Control Panel's Printer section. In many Windows applications, including CorelDRAW, you can also select a printer when you actually go to print.

It's not uncommon, for example, to have drivers installed for both Post-Script and LaserJet printers if you have a high-end laser, as most PostScript laser printers can emulate LaserJets. I also have a FAX board installed in my system—I have a driver to make it look like a printer to Windows. If you'll be driving a PostScript phototypesetter or a color printer, you might well have several more drivers installed as well.

You must tell CorelDRAW which of your drivers represent PostScript devices if you subsequently install additional ones. There's a discussion of this in Appendix B.

The list of available printers under Windows 3.0 and later is pretty extensive, and the truth is that some of them are a bit fictional. For example, most of the PostScript printers will be handled by the same printer driver, PSCRIPT.DRV. If you have a conventional PostScript printer that isn't on the list—one made after the release of Windows 3.1, for example—you can handle it by selecting any other PostScript printer. The Apple LaserWriter Plus is a good choice.

The same also holds true for most LaserJet-compatible printers. Unless your printer specifically emulates PCL5—the language of the Hewlett Packard LaserJet III series printers—you should select the LaserJet Plus driver.

Unusual or exotic printers will require dedicated drivers. In many cases, a Windows driver will be provided with your printer if it does not behave like a conventional device.

PRINTING FROM CORELDRAW

You can print a CorelDRAW graphic by selecting Print from the File menu. A dialog box like one of the two in Figure 6.1 will appear.

If you have several printer drivers installed in Windows and a dialog box other than the one you wanted pops up—if you want to print to a PostScript

FIGURE 6.1:

*The Print Options
dialog box for Post-
Script printers (left)
and non-PostScript
printers (right)*

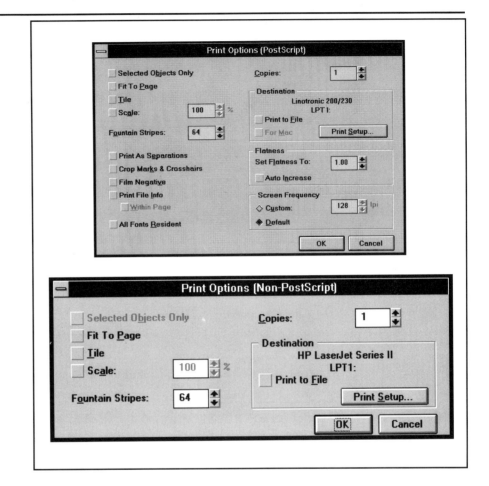

printer but the dialog box for a LaserJet appears, for example—click on the Print Setup button. Another dialog box will appear, as in Figure 6.2.

If you click on the Specific Printer control button, a list will open to allow you to select a different printer driver. Click on OK to return to the Printer dialog box. It will change to suit the currently selected printer driver.

In most cases, you can ignore everything in the Print Options dialog box and go straight for the OK button. Click on it and whatever was in your CorelDRAW workspace should wind up on paper.

FIGURE 6.2:

*The Print Setup
dialog box*

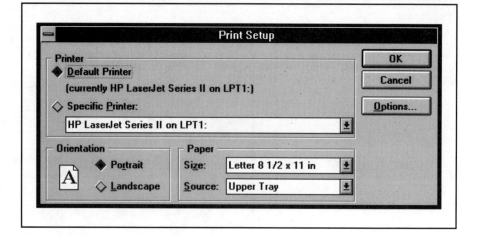

PRINT MANAGER

By default, Windows prints through the Print Manager. The Print Manager has two functions—it queues multiple documents to be printed and it handles "spooling." When an application prints through the Print Manager, the printer in question will seem exceptionally fast. In fact, what really happens is that Print Manager stores whatever is to be printed somewhere—in effect lying to your application about the speed of your printer—and then proceeds to send the data to the printer behind your back. The effect of this is that you can get back to work almost immediately, even if your print job takes several minutes.

You can actually send additional print jobs to the Print Manager while the first one is printing. The Print Manager will stack them up, printing each one in turn.

In most cases, you'll want to use the Print Manager, as it will eliminate almost all of the waiting associated with printing. There are a few printers which don't get along well with it, however. In this case, you can turn it off through the Printers section of the Windows Control Panel.

LASER PRINTER MARGINS

When printing from CorelDRAW, it's important to keep in mind that laser printers have margins. A laser printer that prints on $8\frac{1}{2}$-by-11 inch paper will not print an $8\frac{1}{2}$-by-11 inch area—there'll be a blank area about a quarter of an inch in from each edge in which no print will appear. If you have objects extending into this area, they'll be cropped off.

POSTSCRIPT PRINTING OPTIONS

There are a lot of controls in the PostScript Printing dialog box for Corel-DRAW. As touched on a moment ago, you won't need most of them for normal printing. However, they represent much of the flexibility of Corel-DRAW's output facilities, and you might want to be familiar with them.

SELECTED OBJECTS ONLY

If you select objects in the CorelDRAW work space, enabling this option will cause only those objects to be printed. This facility has numerous conventional uses—it's also very handy for sorting out printing problems. If you encounter a drawing which will not print (a problem to be discussed in greater detail later in this chapter) you can try printing portions of it with this option to narrow down where the problem lies.

FIT TO PAGE

With this option selected, your drawing will be scaled to more or less fill the page it will be printed on. In fact, the scale factor will be adjusted so that the picture fits in its smallest dimension. In using this option, keep in mind the limitations inherent in scaled bitmap objects, should you have any in your graphics. These will be discussed in greater detail in a moment.

This option works with an understanding of how large your printer's margins are. Some printers with wider-than-usual margins may crop your graphics if you use this option.

TILE

This option can be used to print large graphics that span several pages. If it's enabled, your drawing will be reproduced over several pages, which can subsequently be stuck together to form a complete image. You can use it to create posters and banners, for example.

SCALE

If you enable this option, you can enter a scale factor in the control next to it. This will adjust the size at which your drawing prints. Note that it's your responsibility to choose a suitable scale factor—for example, one which will not cause what you want printed to exceed the size of the paper it will be printed on.

If your graphic includes bitmaps, keep in mind that applying arbitrary scale factors to them may cause them to exhibit moiré patterns. If you can, choose an integral scaling factor rather than an arbitrary one. (Refer to Chapter 5 for more information about bitmap scale factors.)

FOUNTAIN STRIPES

NOTE
NOTE

All other things being equal, you will need more fountain stripes to make your fountains look convincing on a PostScript phototypesetter than you will on a 300 dot-per-inch laser printer.

The Fountain Stripes control determines the number of bands that will be used to represent fountain fills. Increasing this value will improve the appearance of objects with fountain fills—at least, to a point—but it will also increase the complexity of your printed graphics. This will, in turn, make them take longer to print. It will also increase the likelihood of a graphic being too complex to print.

If you're working on a graphic with numerous fountain fills in it, it's worth setting this value fairly low when you print intermediate proofs, and cranking it up only when you go for final output.

PRINT AS SEPARATIONS

If you enable the Print As Separations option, your graphic will be separated into four pages—one representing its cyan component, one its magenta component, one its yellow component, and one for its black component. Chapter 8 will discuss this in greater detail.

When you select this option, you will be presented with several others, which you might want to change:

◆ Crop Marks & Crosshairs—prints alignment marks outside your graphic if it's enabled. This is important in creating separations, as it allows a printer to align the four-color plates.

◆ Film Negative—this creates negative images, rather than positive ones, suitable for use in making plates.

◆ Print File Info—this adds file information to the printed graphic.

Figure 4.8, back in Chapter 4, illustrates an example of a page with crop marks, cross hairs, and file information.

Note that the Crop Marks & Crosshairs and the Print File Info options assume that your graphic will be smaller than your printed page, so that there'll be some space outside the graphic in which to print these objects. If you enable these options when you're printing an 8½-by-11 inch graphic to an 8½-by-11 inch page, the crop marks, cross hairs, and file information will be printed beyond the edge of the page, and will not appear.

If you enable the Within Page option, the file information will be printed within the page area, rather than outside it.

ALL FONTS RESIDENT

If you select this option, CorelDRAW will assume that all the fonts used in your drawing are already resident in your printer, or have been previously downloaded, and will not download any font information. This can greatly reduce the time it takes to send a graphic to your printer, but it will make an awful mess of things if all those fonts aren't, in fact, resident. This will be discussed toward the end of this chapter.

COPIES

The Copies option will allow you to print more than one copy of a graphic. Note that when you use this feature to print multiple copies, your graphic will only be downloaded to your printer once. This represents a considerable time saving.

PRINT TO FILE

If you enable the Print to File option, everything that would have been sent to your printer will be sent to a disk file instead—you'll be prompted for the name of the destination file. This facility is handy should you want to have your final output done by an output service. It will be discussed later in this chapter.

FOR MAC

The For Mac option will only be active if you have enabled Print to File. It allows CorelDRAW to create printer files which will be easily manageable by Macintosh systems. This is handy if your output service actually uses Macintosh hardware to drive its PostScript phototypesetters. Once again, we'll come back to this later in this chapter.

SET FLATNESS TO

The Set Flatness To control will allow you to define how accurate CorelDRAW must be when it prints curved objects. If you increase the flatness value, your curves will be represented as increasingly large straight-line segments.

You might want to increase the flatness value if you need quick output and don't care what it looks like. It's more often useful as a way to sneak past drawings that are too complex to print under the default flatness setting—increasing the flatness value effectively simplifies them.

On a 300 dot-per-inch laser you can often get away with a flatness value of at least 2.00 without any visible effects.

If you enable the Auto Increase option of the Set Flatness To control, CorelDRAW will keep increasing the flatness of troublesome drawings until it manages to print them, up to a maximum value of 10.

SCREEN FREQUENCY

The Screen Frequency control allows you to select the number of halftone spots per inch that your printer will use to represent gray levels. If you enable the Default option, the halftone frequency will be whatever the designers of your printer decided was appropriate for its print engine.

The Custom control will allow you to enter a screen frequency of your choice. (There's a complete discussion of halftone screen frequency in Chapter 4.) Note that the setting of this control will only apply to filled objects which have not had their screen characteristics explicitly set using the PostScript option of the Fill dialog box.

NON-POSTSCRIPT PRINTING OPTIONS

The non-PostScript Print Options dialog box, as illustrated back in Figure 6.1, is relatively simple. Many of CorelDRAW's PostScript options actually involve facilities provided by the PostScript language. In the absence of PostScript, there are substantially fewer controls to contend with.

Selected Objects Only

If you select objects in the CorelDRAW work space, enabling this option will cause only those objects to be printed.

Fit To Page

With this option selected, your drawing will be scaled to more or less fill the page it will be printed on. In fact, the scale factor will be adjusted so that the picture fits in its smallest dimension. When using this option, keep in mind the limitations inherent in scaled bitmap objects, in case you have any in your graphics.

This option works with an understanding of how large your printer's margins are. Some printers with wider-than-usual margins may crop your graphics if you use this option.

Tile

This option can be used to print large graphics that span several pages. If it's enabled, your drawing will be reproduced over several pages, which can subsequently be stuck together to form a complete image. You can use it to create posters and banners, for example.

Scale

If you enable this option, you can enter a scale factor in the control next to it. This will adjust the size at which your drawing prints. Note that it's your responsibility to choose a suitable scale factor—for example, one which will not cause what you want printed to exceed the size of the paper it will be printed on.

If your graphic includes bitmaps, keep in mind that applying arbitrary scale factors to them may cause them to exhibit moiré patterns. If you can, choose an integral scaling factor rather than an arbitrary one.

FOUNTAIN STRIPES

The Fountain Stripes control determines the number of bands that will be used to represent fountain fills. Increasing this value will improve the appearance of objects with fountain fills—at least, to a point. It will also increase the time it takes CorelDRAW to print drawings which use fountain fills. Because the halftoning used in non-PostScript graphics is a bit crude, increasing the number of fountain stripes beyond the default value of 64 rarely has much of an effect on your final output.

COPIES

The Copies option will allow you to print more than one copy of a graphic. Note that when you use this feature to print multiple copies, your graphic will only be downloaded to your printer once. This represents a considerable time saving.

PRINT TO FILE

If you enable the Print to File option, everything that would have been sent to your printer will be sent to a disk file instead—you'll be prompted for the name of the destination file.

USING AN OUTPUT SERVICE

The resolution of a conventional 300 dot-per-inch laser printer is good, but not quite good enough to fool your eye into thinking that the printer has reproduced perfectly formed type. You can improve on this in several ways. Printers with variable dot sizes, such as the Hewlett Packard LaserJet III can make 300 dots per inch look pretty respectable. Several of the newer 300 dot-per-inch printers have options which will allow you to drive them at 600 or

800 dots per inch as well. At these resolutions, the output of a laser printer can look about as good as that of a phototypesetter.

By contemporary printer standards, these higher resolution printers are expensive. However, this is a relative thing—the Canon LBP-4 laser printer with its 600 dot-per-inch printer option installed costs less today than my 300 dot-per-inch NEC LC890 laser printer did a few years ago when I bought it.

 Watch the economics of an output service carefully. At $5–$10 a page, you might find that you could buy a high-resolution laser for what you spend at an output service over a few months.

If you require still higher quality output, or if you don't want to drop several thousand dollars into a high-resolution laser at the moment, you might want to look at having your CorelDRAW art printed by an output service. An output service is a company which will send your files to its Post-Script phototypesetter for a fee.

Using an output service is fairly easy. Rather than print your Corel-DRAW art in the usual way, select the Print to File option. When CorelDRAW has finished printing, copy the files it has created to floppy disks and take the disks to your output service.

Output services are usually pretty easy to find—if your local yellow pages don't list any, look under typesetting houses.

Most output services will bill you by the page and by the minute, the latter being the time it takes to render your drawing as output. This works well for simple pages which are mostly text, but it can get costly for complex drawings. As a rule, a PostScript phototypesetter will be slower than a Post-Script laser printer, as it must calculate about 16 times the number of actual points on its final page.

If you anticipate having to output a lot of complex graphics, plan to shop around a bit for an output service. You can occasionally find smaller services which are able to be a lot more accommodating. In rural areas, Post-Script phototypesetters seem to have replaced welding machines as the cottage industry of choice—the output service I use is actually located in a cottage. Its owner deals with files that will take a while to print by leaving them until the end of the day. He runs them just before going to bed, and lets them go all night.

Have a talk with someone working at an output service prior to bringing them your files. Explain what you're doing and which software you'll be using to create your drawings. If your output service uses Macintosh hardware to drive its phototypesetter, make sure you enable the For Mac option in the Print Options (PostScript) dialog box.

Take particular care to discuss your use of fonts. Most output services have all the common fonts on hand, but it's worth making sure of this before you get anything printed. You should let the operator of the phototypesetter know which fonts you've used.

A PostScript phototypesetter can output your graphics in one of four ways—on paper or film, and either normal or reversed black to white. Make sure you tell your output service what you require. If you tell CorelDRAW to output negatives, tell your output service to output your artwork normally, lest they invert them a second time, leaving you with positives.

In commercial printing, plates are usually made by first shooting your positive pages onto large sheets of photographic film. The resulting negatives are then contact-printed onto photosensitive plates. The process of shooting your positive artwork onto negative film involves some cost, and will reduce the quality of your art very slightly. If your CorelDRAW graphics are destined for commercial printing, talk to your print house and see if you can provide them as film negatives, rather than positive art. This will usually save you some money and get you better pages in the process.

 If you're creating pages to be commercially printed, in most cases it's cheaper to pay an output service for phototypesetter output, or film negatives, than it is to use 300 dot-per-inch laser-printer output and pay your printer to shoot negatives from it. Of course, you'll get infinitely better looking pages this way as well.

Keep in mind the discussion of dot gain from Chapter 4 when you're creating drawings for output by a phototypesetter. Things will tend to look somewhat darker on 300 dot-per-inch laser output than they will when they're reproduced by an output service.

A growing number of output services also provide color PostScript services.

If you ask an output service to create color separations from your CorelDRAW art, make sure you enable the Crop Marks & Crosshairs option in the CorelDRAW Print Options dialog box. Also, tell your output service that there will be crop marks beyond the actual printed area of your drawing.

TROUBLESHOOTING PRINTING PROBLEMS

There are a number of fairly subtle things that can go wrong in printing pages from CorelDRAW. While this section won't deal with all the possible problems—a book the size of this one devoted to the subject probably wouldn't be able to either—here are a few of the most common ones.

This section will not discuss problems with your printer itself. It assumes that your printer is plugged in, turned on, loaded with paper and toner, and connected to your computer.

NOTHING PRINTS

This is one of the more troubling problems, especially because it usually takes four or five minutes to happen—or not to happen.

It's rare that this will happen on non-PostScript printers, as all graphics are essentially the same to these devices. If it does happen, try switching the printer off for a minute and then on again, and repeat the print command.

You can make sure a LaserJet printer is functioning properly by doing the following (assuming that your printer is on LPT1).

1. Use the MS-DOS icon of the Windows Program Manager to get to a DOS prompt.

2. Type **copy con lpt1:**.

3. Press Ctrl-L.

4. Press Ctrl-Z.

5. Press Enter.

After a few moments, a page should be ejected from your printer. If this doesn't happen, the printer is hung and should be restarted.

PostScript printers are much more prone to not printing pages. This can happen for a number of reasons. The most likely one for pages generated by CorelDRAW is having too many objects on the page, or having a page that's too complex in some other way.

If you encounter a page that won't print to your PostScript printer, here are a few things to try:

◆ Reduce the number of fountain stripes if there are fountain fills in your drawing.

◆ Increase the flatness value.

◆ Adjust the *PSComplexityThreshold* value in your CORELDRW.INI file, as discussed in Appendix B of this book.

◆ Simplify your drawing, perhaps by using fewer blend steps, solid fills rather than fountains, less ornate typefaces, and so on.

◆ Eliminate PostScript textures.

◆ See if the drawing will print if you scale it down. This effectively reduces the number of paths in complex fills.

◆ Remove some objects from your drawing.

◆ Try printing with the Windows Print Manager disabled.

If you don't find a likely reason for the failure of a drawing to print, you might want to begin by getting a feel for which objects are upsetting your printer. Try printing only selected objects, increasing the amount of your drawing that prints until you again encounter a problem. It's very often the case that only minor simplifying is required to overcome these sorts of problems.

If you often print complex graphics, consider getting a memory upgrade for your printer. A PostScript printer with two megabytes of memory, for example, is well suited to most desktop publishing applications but is a bit thin for CorelDRAW.

If a graphic fails to print, or if you abort printing part way through a job, your printer may be left in a somewhat confused state. It will have received half of a job and will be waiting for the rest of it, unaware that nothing more will be forthcoming. You can reset a PostScript printer using the PBREAK program from companion Disk 2 of this book. Assuming that you have previously copied PBREAK.EXE into your \WINDOWS subdirectory, do the following:

1. Get to a DOS prompt by double clicking on the MS-DOS icon from the Windows Program Manager.

2. Type **pbreak.**

3. Repeat the previous step until the status display of your printer indicates that it has gone idle.

4. Type **exit** to return to Windows.

You can make sure a PostScript printer is functioning by causing it to eject a page. Here's how to do this:

1. Get to a DOS prompt by double clicking on the MS-DOS icon from the Windows Program Manager.

2. Type **copy con lpt1:.**

3. Press Enter.

4. Type **showpage**.

5. Press Enter.

6. Press Ctrl-Z.

7. Type **exit** to return to Windows.

If a page doesn't emerge from your printer after a few moments, the printer is hung and must be restarted. Note that both of the foregoing procedures assume that your printer is connected to LPT1.

MEANINGLESS CHARACTERS PRINT ON A NON-POSTSCRIPT LASER PRINTER

Unlike a PostScript printer, a LaserJet-compatible printer defaults to printing whatever it receives as text. It will only print graphics if it's sent special code sequences. If one of the code sequences is mangled, it will begin to interpret the following data as text.

If you see meaningless characters in your LaserJet output, chances are there's a communication problem between your computer and your printer. Check all the cables. If you have a very low-cost printer, it might not be behaving itself—a few of them don't get along well with huge graphics.

If your LaserJet-compatible printer begins to emit reams of computer code, it's because you're attempting to print to it with a PostScript driver. Check the Windows Control Panel's Printers section.

POSTSCRIPT FONTS PRINT IN COURIER

When a PostScript printer is asked to print in a font that it does not have in its resident font library and that has not been previously downloaded to it, it indicates its displeasure by printing in Courier.

Normally, when CorelDRAW prints a graphic that contains text, it downloads the fonts in question to the printer prior to actually printing with them. In this case, you should never encounter Courier text where it doesn't belong. It will not download the fonts, however, if it's under the impression that the fonts it wants to use are already resident in your printer. This can happen if you enable the All Fonts Resident option of the Print Options dialog box, or if you have set up some of the fonts in CORELDRW.INI as being resident when, in fact, they aren't.

It's important to keep in mind that while most PostScript printers have at least 35 resident fonts, not all of them do. If you'll be outputting your CorelDRAW graphics to a somewhat unusual printer, you might want to ascertain exactly which fonts are resident. You can usually do this by looking at the test page it emits when it first comes online.

FAST
TRACK

CHAPTER

7

select the line. Open the Outline Pen dialog box from the outline pen tool's flyout menu. Click on one of the Arrows boxes in the upper-right corner.

select the Layers Roll-Up item from the Arrange menu. Select the layer you want to work with from the Layers roll-up menu.

Special

Effects

and

Techniques

The letter A developed from the north Semitic and was retained in Latin. The letter A is first found in the northern Etruscan and Latin. The capital letter A and the Greek alpha. It

ne of the two most essential elements of design is the ability to use the visual elements at your disposal in a subtle, artistic way to graphically tease the imagination of someone looking at your pages, to lure them into the images you create and engross them with their content. The second most essential element of design is to be able to create loud, garish pages which shriek at everyone who looks at them, yanking them into the images whether they want to look at them or not. I've not listed these two points in order of importance.

This chapter will deal, for the most part, with tools to implement the second of these elements. I will deal first with the CorelDRAW effects tools—conveniently located in the menu of the same name—and follow with a few drawing techniques which properly qualify under this category as well. Toward the end of chapter, you'll see how to use *masks* and how to do mechanical drawings in which all the arrowheads are 747s. There's nothing at all subtle about a 747.

We'll also look at working with CorelDRAW's layering facility in this chapter.

EFFECTS AND ENVELOPES

Every object you draw under CorelDRAW has an envelope. You've been creating them all along. They haven't been mentioned before because they only pertain to special effects.

An envelope can be thought of as being a box which is the same size as the highlighting box of an object (highlighting boxes were described in Chapter 4). It just encloses the object in question, and when you select an object and see its highlighting box surrounding it, you're also seeing where the envelope would be.

Grouped or combined objects count as single objects in this respect. A group of twenty objects would have a single envelope enclosing the entire group.

Envelopes have peculiar characteristics. Initially rectangular, the edges of an envelope are connected to all the paths of the objects within it. However, the degree of connectedness may vary with the distance between the edge of the envelope and the path in question, depending upon what you choose to do with the envelope.

The important thing about envelopes is that while they start off rectangular, they aren't constrained to remain that way. You might want to think of the sides of an envelope as actually being composed of curves, as you might see if you converted straight lines to curves with CorelDRAW's shape tool. You can bend the sides of an envelope.

You can unbend an envelope quickly by selecting Clear Envelope from the Effects menu.

Once you've bent the edges of an envelope, the objects contained within it will also bend, depending upon the amount of connectedness between them and the envelope. If you begin with an essentially rectangular object within a fresh, rectangular envelope and then bend the sides of the envelope until it is roughly circular, the object within it will also become roughly circular. As you might suspect, envelope manipulation is extremely useful for creating logos and perspectives.

Figure 7.1 illustrates an object with a rectangular envelope and the same object with the envelope bent a bit.

You can manipulate the envelopes of objects to whatever degree you like. As with the simpler transformations of CorelDRAW, what actually gets stored in the CorelDRAW object list is the definition of a simple object and then one or more changes you have applied to the object. Thus, you can

FIGURE 7.1:

Bending an envelope

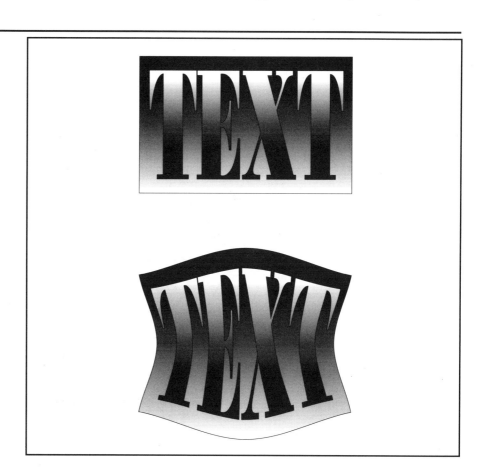

always get your original object back, no matter how much you've twisted and contorted it.

Let's go through the process of adjusting the envelope of an object. For this exercise, you'll need a CD-ROM drive so that you can use the clip art on the CorelDRAW CD-ROM. To begin with, we'll take one of the flags that comes with CorelDRAW's clip art library and make it fly. The flag in question is called PIRATEFL.CDR, and can be found on the CD-ROM in \CLIPART\FLAG\OTHERS.

You might want to choose a flag more in keeping with wherever you live for this exercise—this one is non-partisan unless you spend most of your time on the Spanish Main.

To transform the static flag in Figure 7.2 into one that's flapping in the breeze, do the following:

1. Load PIRATEFL.CDR into CorelDRAW. It comes as a group of objects, which is good enough for this example.

2. Select the group and then select the Edit Envelope item from the Effects menu. A secondary menu with four options will appear beside the Effects menu, as shown in Figure 7.3.

FIGURE 7.2:

A flag about to flutter

FIGURE 7.3:

*The envelope edit
options*

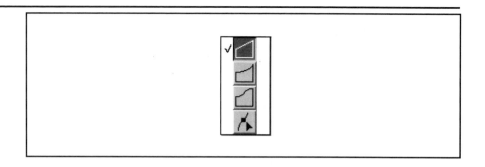

3. The purposes of the first three tools are fairly obvious. The last one looks suspiciously like the CorelDRAW shape tool. If you select it, you'll be able to manipulate the edges of the envelope as you would any other Bézier curves.

4. After you have selected the envelope shape tool, the envelope of the flag will appear as broken red lines with node marks. If you click on the node marks, curve handles will appear. You can grab the marks and drag them, and you can bend the envelope's sides with the curve handles.

5. You might want to use the first of the four envelope edit tools—the straight line—to work with the left vertical edge of the flag.

As with the basic CorelDRAW shape tool, learning to edit an envelope so it comes out looking more or less like what you have in mind takes a bit of practice.

COPYING ENVELOPES

Having created an envelope for one object, you can easily apply it to any number of others. For example, Figure 7.4 was created with a single drawing operation.

1. Import FLAGS5.CDR into the CorelDRAW work space along with the Jolly Roger.

2. Select the Union Jack with the pick tool.

3. Select Copy Envelope From from the Effects menu. An arrow cursor with From? will appear.

4. Click on the Jolly Roger. The Union Jack will take on the same envelope.

OTHER ENVELOPE TOOLS

There are two other items in the Effects menu which pertain to envelopes. The easiest one to understand is Clear Envelope, which will simply undo everything you've done to the envelope of an object and return it to its original rectangular state. This can be pretty dramatic if you've previously twisted an object into an unrecognizable state.

The other one, Add New Envelope, might be a bit harder to understand at first. CorelDRAW gives every object one envelope by default. However, you can add as many additional envelopes as you like. It's often the case in applications which call for involved contortions of an object's envelope that you can't get everything to work out with the effects available. In these cases, you can add one or more additional envelopes to an object to further bend it.

Note that when you use Clear Envelope on an object with multiple envelopes, you will only clear the most recently added envelope. If an object has three envelopes, you must select Clear Envelope three times to clear them all.

The Clear Envelope function is useful if you want to step back through a number of envelopes. If you want to clear them all, you can use the Clear Transformations item of the Transform menu. This assumes, of course, that the object in question does not embody any other sorts of transformations—stretching, rotation, and so on—which you might want to retain.

Constraining Envelopes

There are two keyboard constraints you can use if you're editing an envelope using one of the first three envelope tools. If you grab a side or a corner of an envelope and drag it while holding down the Ctrl key, the opposite side or corner will move in the same direction. Holding down the Shift key will cause it to move in the opposite direction. Holding both Ctrl and Shift will cause all four corners or sides—depending on what you've grabbed—to move in accordance with the movement of your mouse.

Figure 7.5 illustrates the effects of these constraints.

ADDING PERSPECTIVE

The perspective tools in the Effects menu are useful in making objects look three-dimensional. As the name suggests, they allow you to manipulate the

FIGURE 7.5:

Using the envelope constrain keys

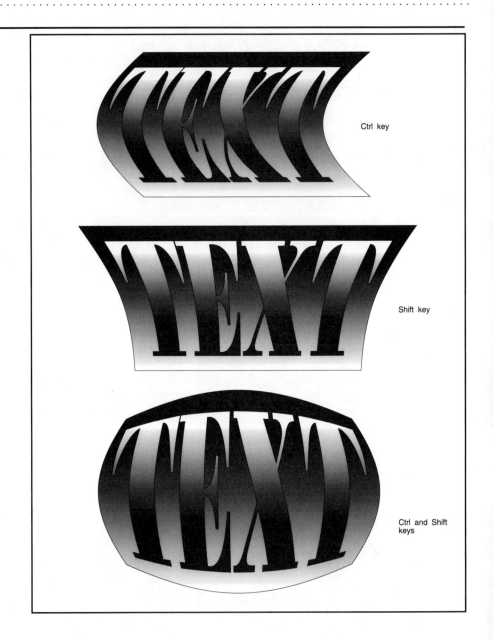

Ctrl key

Shift key

Ctrl and Shift keys

perspective of an object such that it appears to be viewed from an angle other than straight on.

As discussed briefly in Chapter 1, a great deal of our perception of things as being solid is based on the lies our eyes like to tell us. For example, if you look at a large, rectangular physical object—such as an office building—from its base, it will appear to taper upward even if it is in fact a perfect rectangular solid. Our perception translates this apparent flaw in reality into a sense of the distance the building towers above the street.

Obviously, it's not all that hard to represent such perceptions on paper, and the results can be very effective. You might consider the two bits of text in Figure 7.6. The lower one suggests a sense of size, even though both objects are of the same average dimensions.

Most physical objects which exist in the space beyond your eyes can be thought of as having *vanishing points*. There are some obvious examples of this. In the case of the office building as seen from the street, if you were to draw imaginary lines up the walls until they met in the atmosphere above the building, the point where they met would be a vanishing point. A more classic example is that of a railroad track stretching into the distance. While the rails are in fact parallel, they appear to meet in the distance. The point where they appear to meet is the vanishing point.

In fact, an object can have two vanishing points—one vertical and one horizontal—depending upon your point of view. Figure 7.7 illustrates this.

FIGURE 7.6:

A simple example of perspective drawing

A drawing exhibiting both horizontal and vertical perspective

CorelDRAW helps you establish and maintain the vanishing points of an object. This allows you to effortlessly add realistic-looking perspective to any ostensibly flat object by reproducing the effect caused by a single view-point. Figure 7.8 illustrates an example of using the perspective and vanishing-point features of CorelDRAW. As with the envelope functions, you can edit, add, copy, and clear a perspective. To create the right view of the wall in Figure 7.8, I duplicated the top wall and used the Edit Perspective item of the Effects menu to add perspective to it, using the following procedure:

1. Select the object and then select the Edit Perspective item from the Effects menu.

FIGURE 7.8:

Adding perspective

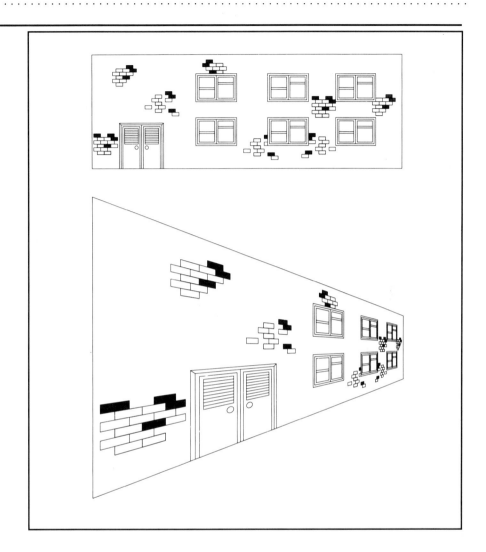

2. Grab each of the right-hand corner nodes and drag them closer to the horizontal axis of the wall. Note that a cross will appear at the extreme right of your work space as you adjust these nodes. This represents the vanishing point.

3. Grab each of the left-hand corner nodes and drag them away from the horizontal axis of the wall. The vanishing point will move still closer to the right edge of the wall.

USING GUIDES TO FIX A VANISHING POINT

The CorelDRAW *guides* are adjustable horizontal and vertical blue lines that you can place in your work space to give you something with which to align objects. To bring a guide into your work space, do the following:

1. Use the Show Rulers item of the Display menu to enable the rules if they are not currently visible.

2. Place your mouse cursor on one of the rules, then click and drag it into the work space. A broken blue line will follow it.

You can have multiple guides in your work space. They will not appear in your final drawing.

If you bring one horizontal and one vertical guide into your work space, the place where they intersect can serve as a common vanishing point for multiple objects adjusted with the perspective tools. Simply manipulate them so their individual vanishing points coincide with the intersection of the guides, and your drawing should look right.

When you no longer need the guides, you can delete them.

USING BLENDS

Blends are arguably the most interesting of the tools in the CorelDRAW Effects menu. Blending will allow you to select two dissimilar objects in your work space and have CorelDRAW generate any number of intermediate objects between them in which the characteristics of the first object gradually blend into the second. Blending will produce intermediate shapes. If the fill characteristics of the two initial objects are different, CorelDRAW will attempt to fill the intermediate objects with intermediate fills as well—although there are some catches to this. It will also blend line weights.

You can blend all sorts of things, including text, simple objects, open paths, and even complex objects. In the latter case, however, you should bear in mind that blending two fairly complex objects will create a number of complex intermediate objects which might result in a drawing sufficiently complex to overload a PostScript printer.

Let's try a simple blend. Figure 7.9 illustrates a blend between two type faces and two gray levels. To create this drawing, do the following:

1. Set the letter H in 400-point Helvetica and the letter T in 400-point Times Roman.

2. Give both characters fine outlines. Fill the H with white and the T with black.

3. Select both characters.

FIGURE 7.9:

Blending an H and T from two typefaces

4. Select the Blend Roll-Up... item from the Effects menu.

5. When the Blend box appears, click on Apply.

After a brief pause, a number of intermediate objects will appear between the H and the T. If you check the preview screen, you'll observe that they have intermediate gray levels, too.

Note that whenever you blend two objects, all the intermediate objects will initially be drawn grouped. The group does not include the two objects you started with. If you don't like the results, you can banish them and try again by simply hitting the Del key to delete the new group of objects.

If you like the appearance of a blend but you want to have it blended in the opposite direction—that is, with the current last object foremost instead—you can ungroup the intermediate objects, select all the objects in the blend including the originals, and select the Reverse Order item of the Arrange menu to change the order in which the objects are drawn in the Corel-DRAW work space.

There are more applications for the blend tool than you might initially imagine. One of them is to create highlights and other airbrush effects. Figure 7.10 illustrates an example of this technique.

In this example, the highlights on the leaves and petals of the flower were created by drawing the outline of each object and then an inner object which represents the brightest area of each. The two objects were then blended.

You can create synthetic fountains by blending between two rectangular objects from a linear fill and two concentric objects for a radial fill. This will allow you to do things that conventional fountain fills can't. Experiment with it.

Blend Options

The Blend dialog box has several options. The blend Steps option sets the number of intermediate objects which will be created when you blend two initial objects. This defaults to 20. You should experiment with this value, not only to see what happens on your screen but also to see what the result looks like on your printer. Increasing it will produce more complex drawings which will take longer to print. They may look better—the blends so created may appear smoother—but after a certain point you'll find that more intermediate objects don't necessarily improve the appearance of your drawings. You will probably want to change the blend Steps setting in relation to the size and spacing of your initial objects. If the area between them spans most of a page, for example, you might want to increase this value.

The Rotation field allows you to specify how much each intermediate object will be rotated. In many applications of the Blend function, this can be left at zero. Figure 7.11 illustrates a blend which uses rotation.

By default, the Blend roll-up menu will appear with its step mode enabled. If you click on the color-wheel icon, it will change to provide you with a control to set the blend between colors. This will only be of use if the two objects to be blended are actually filled with different colors.

By default, color blends run directly between the two colors involved. Using the color-wheel analogy of the Blend roll-up menu, the colors of the intermediate objects are drawn from a straight line between the two extreme colors of the source. The Rainbow option will cause the intermediate objects

FIGURE 7.11:

Using rotation with blending

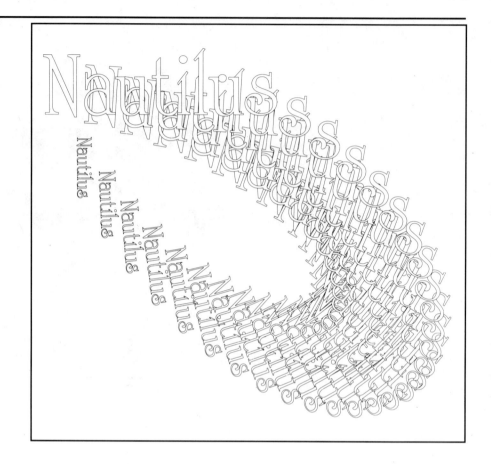

to have their colors selected from a line running around the color wheel. When this option is enabled, buttons will appear to allow you to set the direction for the trip around the wheel.

The last blending option—and perhaps the most difficult to understand—is Map Nodes. When CorelDRAW blends two objects, it looks for the first node in each object and maps its transformations to these. The first node corresponds to the point where you began drawing each object, and can be quite arbitrary. In some cases, this has no effect on the blending process and in some cases—such as in blending text—the nodes in question will be in consistent places all the time.

There are instances in which you might not want CorelDRAW to choose the nodes it uses for blending. You can specify them yourself if you select the Map Nodes option. If this box is clicked, CorelDRAW will provide you with a bent arrow cursor to select a node on each of your initial objects before it begins blending.

The Map Nodes feature is useful in overcoming the effects of blending two objects in which the default matching nodes are on alternate sides of the objects. In such cases, the blend will tend to cross over itself, with the result that the center objects will usually be very small. Figure 7.12 illustrates an example in which the Map Nodes option has been used.

FIGURE 7.12:

*Using the Map
Nodes option*

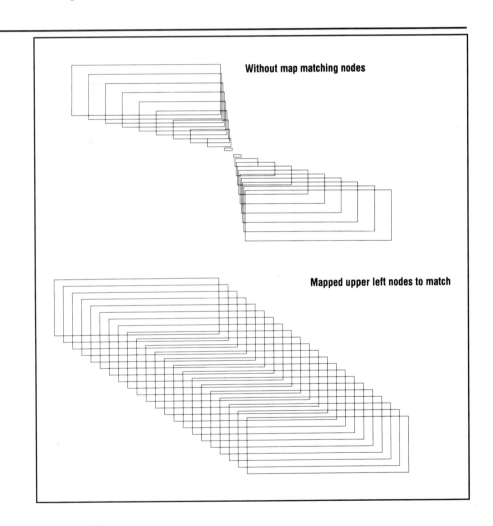

Without map matching nodes

Mapped upper left nodes to match

Blend Limitations

A blend between two different spot colors cannot be printed as a spot color on a commercial printing press.

There are a few limitations you might want to bear in mind when you're using the blend tool. They all involve fill patterns.

If you attempt to blend between objects having spot-color fills, Corel-DRAW will use process colors to create the intermediate fills. There is an exception to this—if you attempt to blend between two tints of the same spot color, all the intermediate objects will still be filled with the spot color in question, but at intermediate tint values.

EXTRUDING OBJECTS

The last item in the CorelDRAW Effects menus is the Extrude function. Extrusion is a dedicated special effect for adding the illusion of depth and three dimensions to two-dimensional objects. It works by drawing in the additional objects necessary to give a flat piece of art some solidity.

Figure 7.13 illustrates the results of extrusion. While you can extrude anything you like, this effect is most often used on text.

The massive text effect in Figure 7.13 was actually created using a variety of CorelDRAW tools, though extrusion is the most obvious one. Here's how it was done:

1. Set the word MASSIVE in 400-point Univers Black type.

FIGURE 7.13:

A massive text effect using the Extrude function

2. You might want to turn the Snap To Grid feature on, set to four grid points per inch.

3. Edit the envelope of the text using the second envelope edit function—the single arc—to bend the top of the text envelope upwards by half an inch and the bottom up by a quarter of an inch.

4. Fill the text with 60 percent black and give it a thin black outline.

5. Select Extrude Roll-Up from the Effects menu. Leave the H offset at zero and set the V offset to −1.33 inches, or −8,00 picas and points. Enable the Perspective option if it's not currently enabled, then set the Depth to 50.

6. When the extrusion is complete, all the new objects will be grouped together, excluding the original text. Select the text and give it a radial fountain fill with the center set to white and the outer edges set to black. This is the opposite of the default radial fill setting.

7. If you want to complete the example, you can set the words TEXT EFFECT in Times Roman, place them in a round-cornered box, and position the object appropriately.

Extrusion is usually done based on a vanishing point, as discussed earlier in this chapter. The vanishing point is set using the H and V offset fields of the Extrude dialog box. If both of these values are positive, the extrusion will appear to originate above and to the right of the original object. If they're both negative, it will appear to originate below and to the left. In the case of the massive text effect, the extension was below, but centered.

The Perspective option of the Extrude dialog box causes extrusion to take place using an imaginary vanishing point. If you turn this option off, extrusion will take place parallel to the original object. The Depth will be disabled—the imaginary second object will be the same size as the original one, displaced by the offset values.

There are four modes of the extrusion roll-up menu. The default mode that we've just been discussing is selected by the uppermost of the four icons along the left side of the menu box. The next icon down selects the perspective and rotation control, which will allow you to set the view point for an extruded object either graphically or numerically. The third icon down selects the location for the illumination source. The last one allows you to define how color will be used in the new objects to form the extrusion.

USING MASKS

Masks are extremely useful tools, though they might seem a bit obscure at first. Masks allow you to generate holes in things. Figure 7.14 illustrates an example of using a mask.

As with most of the more interesting special effects under CorelDRAW, the chrome plated letters in Figure 7.14 are a combination of the work of several tools. The use of a mask, however, is what makes the whole effort work. Figure 7.15 illustrates another use of masks, that of having text within text.

This is how the drawing in Figure 7.15 was created:

1. Set the words Baroque Dogwhistle Concerto repeatedly using the CorelDRAW text tool in paragraph mode. You can make entering this text a lot easier if you type it in once, select it with the mouse cursor, copy it with Ctrl-Ins, place the cursor at the end of the text, and repeatedly hit Shift-Ins to paste it back into the text-entry window. Select 9-point Gatineau as the font.

2. Give this text a black fill and no outline.

3. Set the words Baroque Dogwhistle Concerto in 72-point Gatineau bold, with Concerto on the second line. Use the shape tool to

FIGURE 7.14:

Chromium through a mask

FIGURE 7.15:

A hole in some text

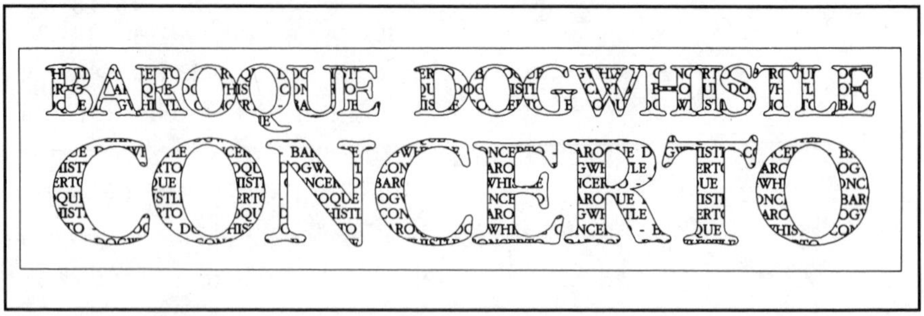

adjust its size and position until it looks roughly like the text in Figure 7.15. You may have to resize the whole text object with the select tool.

4. Draw a rectangle about the size of the first text frame.

5. Center the big text in the rectangle.

6. Select the rectangle and the big text and then select Combine from the CorelDRAW Arrange menu.

7. Give the newly combined object a white fill and a fine black outline. This will be the mask.

8. Position the mask over the small text.

You can see the result of using a mask by bringing up the preview with the F9 key.

Whenever you combine two closed paths in this way, the inner one will become a hole in the outer one. If the combined object is filled, rather than left with no fill, the object will serve as a mask, obscuring everything beneath it except whatever is visible through the hole.

USING ARROWHEADS

Figure 7.16 illustrates one of two things, either an airplane capable of flying in two directions at once or a somewhat extreme use of CorelDRAW's arrowhead facility.

By default, CorelDRAW terminates lines with flat ends. You can see this if you specify a really heavy line—the ends will be rectangular. There are some simple alternate line terminators available in the outline tool's precise-adjustment box.

You can also have arrowheads. Figure 7.17 illustrates a few of the default arrowheads available through the outline pen tool's precise-adjustment box.

Because arrowheads are considered integral parts of a line, the size of the arrowheads changes relative to the thickness of the lines they're associated with. If you increase the thickness of a line, its arrowheads will get larger.

If you have a path comprising several line segments, the arrowheads will appear only at the ends of the path, not at the ends of each segment. In addition, the arrowheads will only appear if you select them for an open path.

FIGURE 7.16:

A bidirectional 747 line terminator

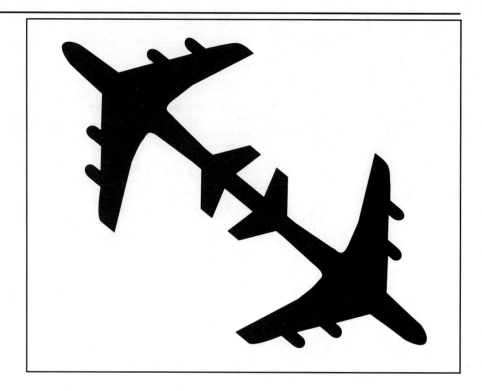

To select an arrowhead, do the following:

1. Select the line you want to apply arrowheads to.

2. Select the outline pen box from the outline pen tool flyout menu.

3. Click on the left or right arrow button. These correspond to the ends of your lines.

4. Choose an arrow from the resulting menu.

The Options buttons below the arrowhead selector buttons will allow you to use several additional functions with arrowheads, namely:

◆ Swap—Exchanges the start and end arrowheads.

◆ Edit—Invokes the Arrowhead Editor.

◆ Delete from List—Removes the currently selected arrowhead from the arrowhead list.

An assortment of arrowheads

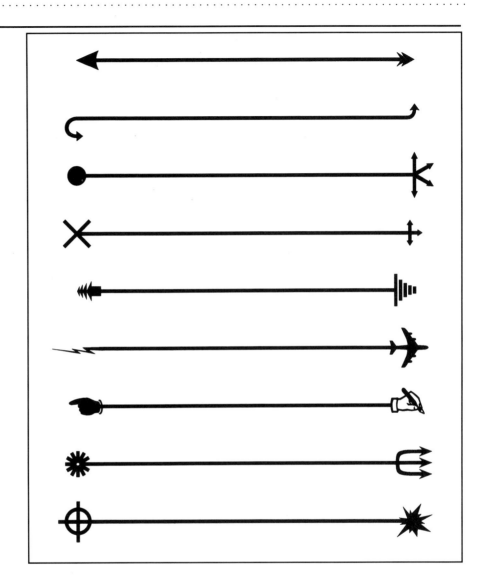

You can also create your own arrowheads. You can have CorelDRAW make an arrowhead from any selected object in your CorelDRAW work space. Simply select the object and then select Create Arrow from the Special menu. CorelDRAW will ask you if you want to create an arrow from the selected object and, if you do, will add it to the list of arrowheads, to appear in the Arrows selector of the outline pen tool's Outline Pen dialog box.

There are a few restrictions on what you can make into an arrowhead. For one thing, it must be a single closed path—it can't consist of several grouped objects.

Once you've created an arrowhead, you cannot actually change its appearance. You can, however, change an arrowhead's size relative to the line it will be drawn on, as well as its position and the extension of the line. To do this, get to the Arrows selector in the outline tool's Outline Pen dialog box, select your new arrowhead, choose Options, and click on Edit to get to the arrowhead editor.

Figure 7.18 illustrates the Arrowhead Editor.

You can move an arrowhead by grabbing one of the hollow node markers and dragging it around. You can resize and position it using the highlighting box and solid corner markers around it. Finally, there's a node mark at the end of the line on which the arrowhead will be drawn. This allows you to adjust the end of the line relative to the arrowhead. In this case, I moved the line further left to make it end in the horse's tail, rather than in the middle of its back, where it defaulted. The arrowhead creation tool has relatively little sense of equestrian anatomy.

FIGURE 7.18:

Fine-tuning an arrowhead

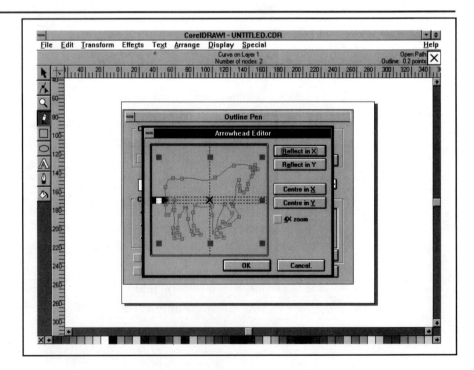

USING LAYERS

One of the things that the users of drafting packages have long enjoyed has been the ability to draw on layers. This is something that CorelDRAW can manage as well. If you have been imagining CorelDRAW's workspace as being a sheet of paper thus far, the layering facilities of the package can be thought of as turning it into a stack of clear acetate sheets.

The layering mode of CorelDRAW is dead easy to work with. By default, you'll always draw on the uppermost layer, or Layer 1. This is initially the "active" layer. To create a drawing with additional layers, open the Layers roll-up menu from the Arrange menu. Click on the right arrow button. Select New from the resulting menu.

You can create as many layers as you want. You can also edit the characteristics of layers after you have created them by selecting a layer from the Layers roll-up menu layer selector and then selecting Edit. The Layer Options dialog box will appear.

You can define the following characteristics for a layer:

You can enable the Layers roll-up menu by hitting Ctrl-1.

You can also get to the Layer Options dialog box by double clicking on a layer name.

◆ Visible—If you disable this option, objects on the layer will not appear in the CorelDRAW workspace.

◆ Printable—If you disable this option, objects on the layer will not print.

◆ Locked—If you enable this option, objects on the layer will not be editable in any way.

◆ Color Override—If you enable this option and choose a color, all the objects on the layer will be displayed in wireframe mode with their outlines drawn in the selected color. This will not affect how they print, only how they're displayed.

◆ Name—By default, each layer is called Layer, followed by its number. You can change this to any text string you like.

When you add objects to the CorelDRAW workspace, they'll be added to whichever layer you have currently selected with the Layers roll-up menu, the active layer. You can, however, select objects on any visible layer, and manipulate any object that isn't on a locked layer. Note that if you duplicate an object, its duplicate will appear on the same layer as the source object, even if this differs from your current layer.

If you cut or copy an object from a different layer and then paste it back into the CorelDRAW workspace, it will be pasted into the current layer. The layer an object occupies is always displayed in the status bar at the top of the CorelDRAW workspace.

There are two additional layers which are always created by CorelDRAW, and which are accessible through the Layers roll-up menu. The Guides layer contains—perhaps predictably—the guides. The Grid layer will display the grid pattern in the CorelDRAW workspace if you have made it visible.

 *You cannot make the Grid the active layer.*

Note that if you double click on one of these extra layers in the Layers roll-up menu to call up its Layer Options dialog box, you can change the colors used for the grid and guides. You can also make them printable, should you have a reason to do so.

You can copy or move objects between layers in two ways. The simplest approach involves cutting or copying the objects in question from wherever they are and then pasting them to the currently active layer. You can achieve the same result much more rapidly, however, by selecting the objects you want to copy or move and then selecting the CopyTo or MoveTo item of the Layers roll-up menu. Click on the layer you want the objects copied or moved to.

You should get into the habit of thinking of CorelDRAW's facilities in terms of layers. You can use layers to separate elements of complex mechanical drawings—architectural plans, for example—but they're also handy for organizing complex graphics which would traditionally be handled as single-layer works. For example, as you work through a complex drawing, change layers and lock the layers which contain elements of the drawing you're satisfied with. You might also consider using the Color Override options on these completed layers to increase the screen-update speed, or make them entirely invisible. Once locked, a layer's contents can't be accidentally moved or deleted.

WRAPPING UP

Special effects are only special until everyone else starts using them. The best ones come not from a book but from your own head and, indirectly, from a firm understanding of how to make CorelDRAW do what you want it to do. Six months from now there may be 747s and quarter horses ending lines everywhere you look.

As with everything else under CorelDRAW, the special-effects tools it offers have tremendous potential for overuse. You might want to consider how much more attractive one effect is than one on every page.

FAST
TRACK

CHAPTER

8

route for end-users to get professional quality at a reasonable
cost. The emergence of service bureaus lets you send in your
PostScript art and pick up the color output in the same day.
The average user of CorelDRAW can get quality output
without needing to purchase the equipment capable of
producing it.

8

Using

Color

orelDRAW handles color in a particularly elegant way. It allows you to work with color in whichever of several color "models" best suits your requirements. It has drawing and object manipulation tools that will let you manipulate color in ways that conventional artists can only imagine.

If there is a drawback to CorelDRAW's color facilities, it's arguably that color printers, unlike color monitors, are not all that commonplace. Being able to draw something you can't reproduce is of questionable worth. However, there are a number of output options available for color artwork—we'll discuss them later in this chapter.

Color art from CorelDRAW can look superb. Because of the inherently simple approach to color specification which Corel provides—essentially an extension of the gray-level tools you're already familiar with—you will probably find that it will not take you very long to learn the mechanics of color using CorelDRAW.

In addition to giving you the tools to draw in color, CorelDRAW can also generate color separations, the special film which print houses require to do color printing. This can save you a lot of money in applications which require commercial color printing—color separations are costly when they're created by traditional methods.

The program can even separate bitmapped images, and CorelDRAW's bitmapped separations are surprisingly good. We'll have a look at these in a moment as well.

If all this sounds a bit Martian at the moment, you might want to ignore it until we get into the details of using separations.

A PRINT HOUSE PRIMER

Later in this chapter, we'll discuss stand-alone color printers, those glorious little boxes which actually generate color art. However, even the best of these machines doesn't really do justice to what CorelDRAW can output. Its best work is handled by print houses.

The mechanics of printing in color are a bit involved, and will be dealt with as they crop up. However, there are a few terms with which you should probably familiarize yourself before you begin. These have to do with the way printing presses actually reproduce color art.

A printing press is a mechanical system which deposits ink on paper—analogous to a laser printer, which does this electronically. Modern printing presses, of the sort you're likely to encounter if you go somewhere to print your CorelDRAW art, print with *photoresistive plates.* These are metal plates coated with a photographic emulsion which, when processed, will cause the black areas of the plate to accept ink and the white areas not to. Ink spread across the plate will stick to the black areas, and from there will be transferred to paper.

While they look quite different, printing plates work in the same way as 35-millimeter film. One notable difference is that it doesn't take two pressmen to lift a roll of 35-millimeter film into most cameras.

In most cases, printing is done in *signatures.* A signature is a single sheet of paper which holds a number of pages. The number of pages is usually an even power of two, as the signature will get folded some number of times before it's trimmed to produce the final pages. Signatures of eight and 16 pages are common. Bearing in mind that a signature of 16 pages requires that all 16 pages get printed at once, you can imagine the size of the printing plates involved.

Printing plates are made by contact-printing them from immense negatives. The negatives for each page are stripped together, so that they're positioned in the right order for printing. The order for a publication having multiple signatures can get quite intricate, since the page order has to come out correct after each signature has been folded, trimmed, and added to other signatures of the completed print job.

If your publication will be folded in half and stapled, or *saddle-stitched*, half of each signature will appear at the back of the book and half at the front. Publications which are bound with square spines—such as this book—are referred to as being *perfect bound*. In this case, each signature is folded in half and all the signatures follow one after the other. It's worth noting that figuring out the order of the pages is the responsibility of the print house. You need never concern yourself with it—although there is one particular situation in which you may want to, which we'll discuss shortly.

In order to print color, each sheet of paper must run through one printing press, or station, for each color. As we'll discuss shortly, a full-color photograph or piece of CorelDRAW art usually requires four actual colors of ink.

In order to print color art, the color image has to be reduced to a number of monochrome negatives to produce monochrome plates. If you want to print a drawing which has black and red in it, there will ultimately be a black plate and a red plate. The black station of the press will have—predictably—black ink in it. The red one will have red ink. Even though your pages will come out with two colors of ink on them, no one station will have to lay down more than one color of ink.

The process of creating these individual monochrome negatives from a color original—whether the original is a sheet of paper or a drawing file—is called *color separation*. Traditional color separation, in which an optical scanner or separator filters the image into its component colors, has several drawbacks. Being an optical process, it's inexact—you always lose something in the separation process, so there's no assurance that your original art will be separated in such a way as to print exactly as the original did. Secondly, separations are among the most expensive parts of pre-press negative preparation. Finally, they're time-consuming, and the sooner you need them, the more they cost.

CorelDRAW allows you to generate color separations from drawn art without the intermediate step of using an optical scanner or separator. It bypasses all three of the above problems, and the results are superb. It can also handle bitmapped separations.

COLOR PROCESSES

You can work with color by assigning arbitrary colors to the objects in your CorelDRAW art while hoping for the best. If you can restrict your use of color to a few basic and predictable colors, simply knowing what to click and when will get you through basic color applications.

This isn't very adventurous, however. It denies you most of the power of CorelDRAW's color facilities, and it also denies you the opportunity to understand the theory behind what you're doing.

Unlike monochrome art, which is just black ink—or black laser printer toner—on white paper, color is a process. In drawing with color, a lot of what you can do and much of the way you do it will be determined by the medium which ultimately will create the colors you use. Just as monochrome art is limited by the mechanical qualities of the printer it will be output on—the screen limitations of a 300 dot-per-inch laser, for example—so too are color processes at least partially a function of the device that will be rendering your drawings as hard copy.

It's important to keep the color process you'll be using in mind, especially if your color art is ultimately to be reproduced at a print house. Poorly thought-out color implementations can look bad and get really expensive.

Let's start with some of the theory of color.

There are two ways of creating color. They're called *subtractive* color and *additive* color. Each one relates to a particular medium. CorelDRAW allows you to specify color both ways, as we'll see.

A computer monitor uses additive color. In its quiescent state, a computer monitor is black and emits no light. In order to make color appear on the screen of a monitor, colored light must be added to its blackness.

 *You can see the primary additive and subtractive colors on Plate 2 of the color insert in this book.*

The three primary colors of additive color are *red, green,* and *blue.* The picture tube of a monitor contains three electron guns which excite spots of red, green, and blue phosphor on the inside face of your monitor, creating light. The relative intensities of the three colors for any given pixel on your screen determine the color you see for the pixel in question.

Printing on paper involves the use of subtractive color. A sheet of paper is initially white, that is, it is reflecting all colors of light equally. If you put some blue ink in one area of the page, that area will become a good reflector of blue light but a poor reflector of other colors of light. The blue ink serves as a filter, keeping non-blue colors from reflecting.

The three primary colors of subtractive printing are *cyan, magenta,* and *yellow.* Cyan is a medium blue, and magenta is an electric purple-red that is rarely used by itself. You can see these colors on the cover of the CorelDRAW CD-ROM that's included with the CorelDRAW package. The three horizontal lines are magenta, the square to the left of the balloon is cyan, and the triangle to the right is process yellow.

In theory, if you mix equal amounts of cyan, magenta, and yellow ink, you'll wind up with black. In fact, it's impossible to produce absolutely pure inks, so mixing equal amounts of them doesn't result in pure black, but usually in a muddy brown color. For this reason, areas of a color graphic which are supposed to have equal amounts of cyan, magenta, and yellow are instead printed with percentages of black.

Color printing thus actually involves four colors of ink, these being cyan, magenta, yellow, and black, and you will frequently hear full-color printing referred to as four-color printing. The four colors are often designated by the letters C, M, Y, and K, where K stands for black.

You might be able to see the difference between three- and four-color printing if you're interested. Many newspapers use only three-color printing, as the color definition on newsprint frequently does not justify using a black plate. Most other commercial printing is done with four colors. If you can find the same color advertisement in a newspaper and in a glossy magazine, you will probably be able to observe the difference produced by using a black plate.

It's possible to create any color you like with percentages of these four colors of ink. Creating color in this way is called using *process colors*.

There are a number of potential pitfalls in using process color. For example, if you specify a color which is composed of 90 percent of each of the cyan, magenta, and yellow inks, the fill in question will have a 270-percent ink density. Printing presses can certainly handle more than 100 percent ink density—the exact amount varies from press to press—but this is certainly excessive. As a rule, 240 percent is the upper limit.

Optical separations deal with high ink densities through a process called *black removal*. If you specify a particular color as being 50-percent cyan, 60-percent magenta, and 40-percent yellow, some or all of the shared percentages of each of these three ink colors can be removed and transferred to black. This serves to reduce the overall amount of ink deposited on the page.

CorelDRAW does not do black removal automatically if you specify a color as numerical percentages of ink. In using process colors created this way, you must be careful not to create fills which will use an excessive amount of ink if the final destination of your art will be a printing press. You can coerce CorelDRAW into working out black removal values for you—this will be discussed later in this chapter. Alternately, you can easily work them out for yourself.

In the preceding example, you could reduce the color

50 cyan
60 magenta
40 yellow

to the color

20 cyan
30 magenta
10 yellow
30 black

by removing 30 percent from each color and substituting a 30-percent black. The two colors would print the same, but the total amount of ink on your page would be 40 percent less in the second example. In practice, neither of

PLATE 1

CorelDRAW's bitmap color-separation facilities. The top image is a scanned bitmap that has been separated digitally by CorelDRAW from a TIFF file. The bottom image is the same scan separated optically from a 35-millimeter slide.

PLATE 2

The primary subtractive and additive colors, and the results of combining them

Cyan

Magenta

Yellow

Black

Red 100% M 100% Y

Green 100% C 100% Y

Blue 100% C 100% M

PLATE 3

Rex, *by Bill Frymire of Vancouver, British Columbia. This drawing is so complex that it is impossible to image all of it at once. The "hard copy" of the drawing was created by exposing each square tile, one at a time, onto a single piece of film.*

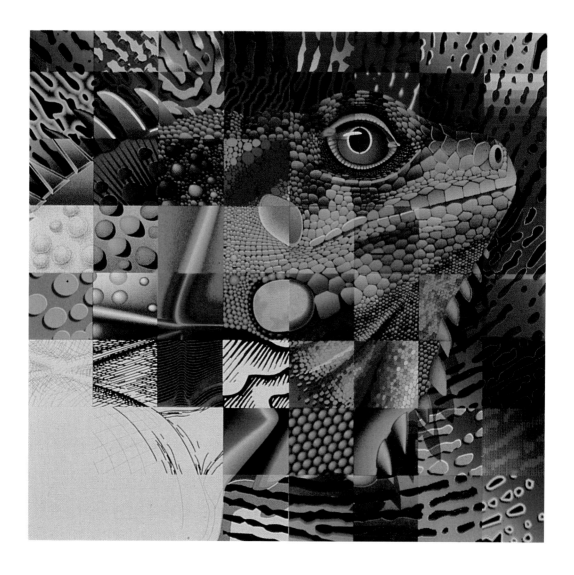

PLATE 4

Laiva, *by Matti Kaarala of Helsinki, Finland*

PLATE 5

Lifetime, *by Ceri Lines of Hsinchu, Taiwan*

PLATE 6

Venice, *by Peter McCormick of Sun City West, Arizona*

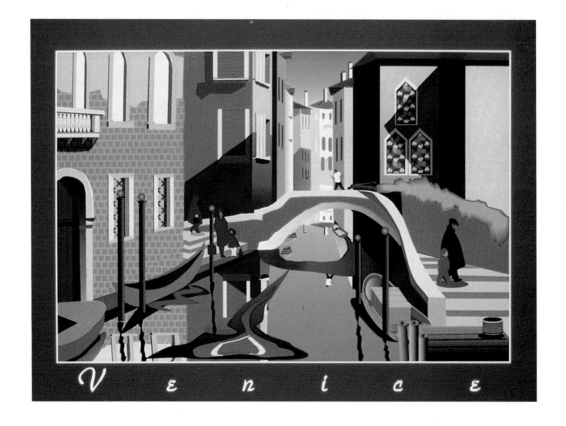

Magic, *by Lea Tjeng Kian of West Java, Indonesia*

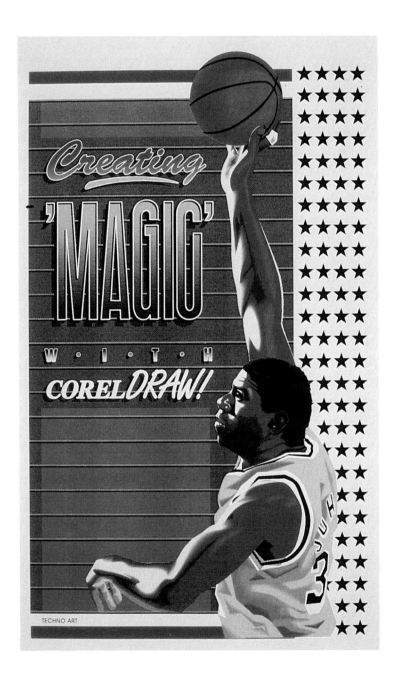

PLATE 8

Techdraw, *by Guy Terrier of Herblay, France*

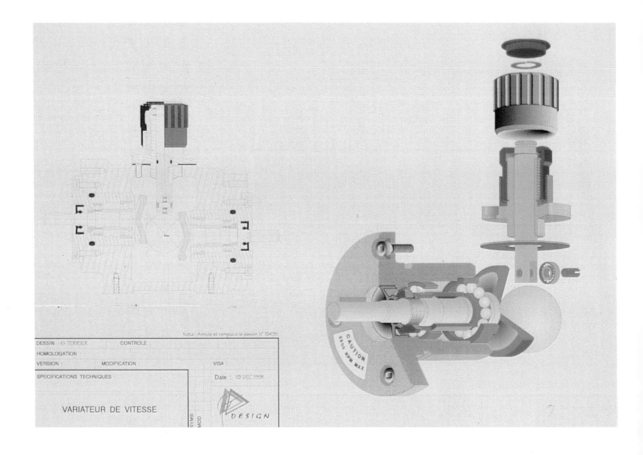

these ink combinations would be really excessive for most printing presses, although as a rule the second one would look nicer, especially if it were being used to print a screened fill. High ink densities are more likely to bleed and run, especially on high-speed web presses, and this can be quite noticeable in a screened area.

PANTONE COLORS

Process color has its limitations. Because of the potential impurities in color inks, it's impossible to specify a process color and know you'll get precisely that color in your final output, especially if you're planning to have your output mechanically printed. When exact colors are required, the printing industry uses a second way of specifying colors. This is called *spot color*. The most frequently used method of specifying spot color is through the use of the Pantone color-matching system.

 A good example of the use of a Pantone color as a spot color is the purple border around the picture named Venice *in the color insert of this book. This is an effective use of a single spot color.*

The Pantone system is incorporated into CorelDRAW, something which you'll probably learn to love if you deal with color a lot.

The Pantone system simply assigns numbers—and in a few cases, names—to specific mixed ink colors. The Pantone company creates books with color swatches for each of its numbered colors, so that if you specify a particular Pantone color, your printer will be able to look at his or her Pantone book and see exactly that color.

For reasons which will become apparent in the next section, "Color Separations," it's not practical to specify a different Pantone color for each object in a complex drawing and plan to have them printed this way. Spot color is used mainly when you want to have an additional color in a drawing and you want that color to match a known color exactly.

One frequently finds, for example, that corporations or particular products are associated with certain colors which are defined by Pantone numbers—consider the blue in the IBM logo or the yellow which borders *National Geographic* magazine every month. If you wanted to create a drawing which contained an IBM logo using IBM's particular blue color, you might well use process colors for your drawing, but you would need a Pantone color for the logo. The Pantone color would become the fifth color in your drawing if there were four-color art in there as well.

COLOR SEPARATIONS

As discussed briefly earlier in this chapter, four-color printing is handled by four separate single-color printing presses, one for each color of ink. In order to print a colored object, four separate plates must be created, one for each press. These are created from four film negatives.

If you wanted to print a color photograph, the photograph would first have to be made into color separations. Separations are actually four black-and-white negatives which represent the four color components of an original image. In creating separations—or seps—the photograph would be scanned first for its cyan component, then for its magenta component, and finally for its yellow component. The fourth piece of film would be created by finding any components the first three have in common and using black removal. Color separation is both expensive and time-consuming.

CorelDRAW's artwork starts out in a digital form, and the software is capable of manipulating it in a lot of ways. One of these is to create color separations.

If you have a drawing which uses color, you can have CorelDRAW output four sheets of paper for each page, one each for the four process colors. It can also output negatives. If you load your laser up with clear film rather than paper, the result will be usable separations—sort of.

We'll get to that "sort of" in a moment.

Color separations are usually accompanied by what is called a *color key* or *chroma key.* Because a separation is very hard to read—it consists of four pretty inscrutable negatives—a chroma key is pretty well indispensable. It is, simply, four sheets of film printed in the four process colors from the four negatives of the separation and then taped together. The result is a *proof* or test image of the picture in the separations. If you have a color printer available you can create instant color proofs, of course, but a chroma key will show not only the colors, but the potential separation effects as well. You can remove one or more of the sheets of film from them to see what your picture would look like without some of its color components.

Printers can usually arrange to get chroma keys made for you from any separations you happen to generate. While modestly expensive—expect to spend twenty or thirty dollars to get a set of chroma keys made—this gives you the best indication of what your separated images will look like without going to the expense of actually printing them.

In the drawing titled Laiva *in the color insert of this book, the registration of each of the color separations is critical. If the black layer is at all out of register, the figure loses its impact. That is why a registration mark (a cross within a circle) is always included when making a separation.*

There is special laser-printer film for applications which involve printing on film. If you use normal clear acetate, there's a good chance that the fuser of your laser printer will melt it, necessitating a trip to the shop for your printer.

You can use Corel-PHOTO-PAINT to adjust the colors and other elements of bit-mapped graphics before CorelDRAW separates them.

This gets back to the "sort of" from a few paragraphs ago. Color separation is a very exacting process. If you specify an area in your drawing as being filled with a color composed of specific percentages of inks, the inks will be printed as screens—assuming that they aren't all 100 percent. As we discussed earlier in Chapter 4, printing screens one on top of another can cause them to interfere, producing aberrations in the final drawing. In order to get around this, separations must be created with their screens at different angles and with spot shapes designed not to interact with each other.

In order for all this to work, the screens of the four layers of a color separation must be printed very accurately—in most cases, with more accuracy than can be managed by a 300 dot-per-inch laser printer. As a result, if you load your own laser with clear film and print separations on it, you will get something to print with, but it may not produce particularly attractive results.

If your seps are going to be run through a web press onto newsprint for the local shopping center throwaway, you might well be prepared to live with this lack of quality. If you're planning to print to glossy paper on a sheet-fed press—a combination which is capable of doing better things—you should consider using higher quality output.

If you print your CorelDRAW files as separation negatives to disk files, you can have them output on a PostScript typesetter. The results of doing color separations this way rival anything that can be done through optical separations.

If your CorelDRAW graphics include color bitmaps, these too will be separated. You might well wonder if you could use CorelDRAW as a separation engine to separate scanned photographs. In fact, you can. Plate 1 of the color insert in this book illustrates a color image which has been optically separated and then handled by CorelDRAW.

While CorelDRAW's separations are not the equal of really good optical separations, they're pretty respectable. They're also a great deal less expensive and a lot quicker to create.

To get the best separation quality, use Graphic Workshop for Windows (on the companion Disk 2 of this book) to convert your scanned images into the TIFF format and import them into CorelDRAW in this form. Use the Stretch & Mirror function of the Transform menu to adjust the size of an imported bitmap, preferably by integral expansion values.

SIGNATURES AND COLOR IMPOSITION

The next section of this book will deal with a very arcane subject, one which you might want to avoid. You can, too. It might not even have any bearing on your applications of CorelDRAW and color. If you choose to plow through it, however, you will understand a lot more about how print houses deal with color print jobs; and if you use a lot of color in multiple-page publications, you'll probably be able to prune your print bills substantially.

When you have a multiple-page document printed, it's handled in signatures, as we discussed earlier. For the sake of this discussion we will deal with a single 16-page signature, although these principles apply to any signature size.

A 16-page signature will result in eight actual pages, each page having two sides. If this signature will be part of a publication to be saddle-stitched—folded in half and stapled in the middle—there will be four actual sheets of paper.

The press that prints your signature will do so with two massive plates, one for each side of the page. This is assuming that this signature will only be printed in black. If you want full color on both sides, there will be eight plates.

Print houses charge for color printing based on the number of plates they use. The efficient use of color will reduce the number of plates involved and, hence, the cost to get your printing done.

It's a lot more efficient to print color on one side of a signature than to do so on both. This reduces the number of plates from eight to five. In this case, if you can position your color art on some pages and not on others, you will require less color and less in your budget.

Figuring out where the color will appear is a bit tricky at first. Figure 8.1 illustrates how the pages work out in a single signature of a saddle-stitched publication. If you have color on page 1, color will also be available on pages 8, 9, and 16. Depending on how your printer actually handles this signature, it might also appear on 4, 5, 12, and 13. Note that the numbering system your print house uses may also differ from what is shown in Figure 8.1, which simply numbers the *signature* pages.

FIGURE 8.1:

The color imposition for a 16-page signature

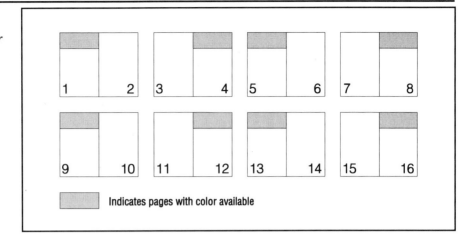

Indicates pages with color available

The position of the color in a signature is called the *color imposition.* Most print houses have diagrams or tables of one sort or another to help you work out the color imposition for various signatures as it relates to their presses. While it's important to consult with your print house before you start trying to figure out how best to use color, don't be dismayed if you can't make any sense of the charts they provide for you. These things are invariably drawn up by people who work with color impositions every day.

To further confuse the color imposition issue, consider that if you add the above signature to a completed publication, the page numbers will change. Figure 8.2 illustrates the above signature as the second signature of a 64-page saddle-stitched book.

Note that half the color has found its way—inconveniently—to the back of the book. One of the attractions of perfect binding is that if you open a color section, all the color stays in the same place.

Grappling with color imposition is tedious at first. If you ignore it and just put your color art where it looks like it should go, your print house will love you. They'll just open up color wherever it's needed, probably to the detriment of your final bill. By understanding how to juggle the positions of your color pictures, however, you can make a severe dent in that bill—if you use color with an eye as to how it will be printed.

FIGURE 8.2:

A multiple-signature publication

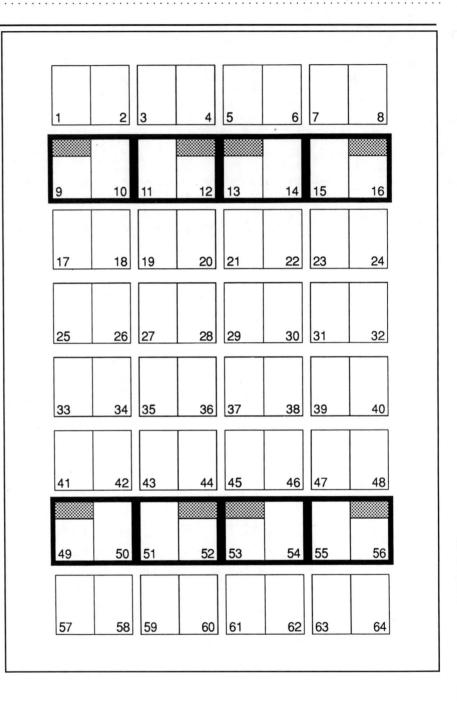

USING COLOR SEPARATIONS

 If you're using Ventura 4.0 for Windows and you have the optional Color-Pro and Separator package, you'll be able to handle color graphics as poured-in art. This is beyond the scope of this book—consult the Ventura documentation for more details.

If you wanted to incorporate CorelDRAW artwork into another document—a Ventura Publisher chapter or a PageMaker page, for example—you would normally just export it into a suitable file and import it into your final document. This is not quite as easy if your artwork is in color.

In most cases, if you plan to have your final document reproduced by a print house, you will have to provide the printer with the artwork for your document and the color separations separately. The place where your color art is to go should have a black-and-white version of it to mark its place. It is traditional to scrawl "Pos" or "Position Only" over the picture so the printer knows it's not to be reproduced in black and white. To be completely traditional, you should use a light blue chinagraph pencil to mark your position-only pictures. This is done for more than just traditional reasons—the final printing film which a printer assembles is usually made up in a darkroom under red lights. Blue chinagraph pencil marks are fairly easy to read under these conditions.

FILM STRIPPING

Print houses do not necessarily expect you to have all your separation art assembled perfectly aligned in a full-page negative sandwich when you give it to them. If your pages consist of some type, a spot-color overlay, and a few four-color separations, it's usually the case that you will provide all the elements separately—clearly labeled—along with a mockup to illustrate how everything is to be assembled. The film will then be taped, or "stripped" together.

 If you do use Ventura Publisher with its color extensions, or if you use Corel-DRAW itself to create complex four-color pages, so that no stripping is involved, your print bill will be further reduced.

Film work is not done for free—like everything else they do, printers will charge you for it, based in part or totally on the amount of time it takes them. If you can create a separation in which all the graphic elements are positioned properly and won't require cutting apart and repositioning, you'll save a bit on film stripping.

As most of the places that produce high-resolution PostScript output on film charge by the page, grouping or "ganging" multiple images onto a single set of color separations will save you a bit on output charges, too. However, make sure you don't group so much CorelDRAW art onto a single page as to overload the PostScript interpreter in the typesetter. PostScript phototypesetters have the same sorts of limitations as PostScript printers do, and in some cases they're less accommodating.

USING SPOT COLORS WITH SEPARATIONS

The most common use of spot colors is to add a second color to an otherwise black and white page. You might also want to add a fifth color to a four-color page to ensure a specific Pantone color in artwork which requires it. However, in doing so, make sure that the print house you'll be dealing with actually has a five-station press to handle your work.

If you specify five different spot colors in addition to black, you will get six sheets of output for your drawing if you ask for separations when you print. Unless you happen to be dealing with a printer with a six-station press—they exist, but they're anything but common—this will be of no real use to you.

In situations in which you need lots of different colors, specify the colors as process colors and use four-color printing.

You can usually have any Pantone color you want as a spot color. However, you should know that many print houses will charge you less if you choose one of the three primary process colors as your spot color. The next most favorable colors are usually *warm red* and *reflex blue*—Pantone colors 2 and 6, respectively—as these are commonly used colors of mixed ink which print houses tend to have on hand.

Many spot colors can yield several additional colors if you mix them with black. For example, if you print a 50 percent black screen over the usual warm red spot color—100 percent magenta and 100 percent yellow—the result will be a warm brown, the exact color being determined by the percentage of red.

PHOTOTYPESETTER OUTPUT CONSIDERATIONS

PostScript photo-typesetters are also referred to as "imagesetters."

A PostScript phototypesetter which is capable of outputting CorelDRAW PostScript files actually consists of two distinct elements. The typesetter itself is merely an engine which can put dots on photographic film. This is referred to as the back end. The other half, the front end, is the PostScript interpreter and a big box of technology called a raster image processor, or RIP. These same functions exist in a PostScript laser printer, but the division between them is rarely meaningful.

In theory, a phototypesetter with a PostScript interpreter is just a laser printer with better resolution, and anything which you would normally output to a laser printer can be sent to a typesetter as well. This is almost true—it only really starts to fall apart when phototypesetters find themselves confronted with complex color plates to produce.

Phototypesetter output can range in resolution up to 2540 dots per inch, which is the natural resolution of the phototypesetter engine. The same PostScript file which will produce 300-dot output on a laser printer should produce 2540-dot output on a typesetter. However, to begin the discussion of the limitations of a phototypesetter, you might consider that a four-inch line output to a 300 dot-per-inch laser printer will have 1200 dots in it. The same line output on a phototypesetter will have 10,160 dots in it. In both cases, the processor in the printer will have to calculate the position of every dot. All other things being equal, it will take the typesetter eight times as long to draw the line.

Despite its impressive size and price tag, the PostScript interpreter of a phototypesetter usually doesn't have all that much memory to use for actually interpreting PostScript. It's not uncommon to find one with only two or three megabytes, which is less than many PostScript lasers. Therefore, complex CorelDRAW art which will output successfully to a PostScript laser may not always output to a phototypesetter.

Many output services charge by the minute for output time. Understanding a bit about PostScript and PostScript interpreters may help you to make the best use of this time. There are two characteristics of PostScript output which CorelDRAW allows you to fine-tune with an eye to controlling the time it takes a phototypesetter to print your drawings—namely, the number of stripes in a fountain and the degree of flatness in curved lines.

Figure 8.3 illustrates the CorelDRAW Print Options dialog box with these two parameters.

Traditionally, a PostScript fountain is actually made up of 256 levels of gray. In practice, having CorelDRAW output complex shapes filled with such a fountain would result in drawings which take ages to print. Because of this, CorelDRAW's PostScript output has always had a smaller number of stripes. However, the number of fountain stripes is very much a trade-off. If you use too many, your output will take a long time to emerge—not a

FIGURE 8.3:

The fountain stripe and flatness adjustments of the CorelDRAW Post-Script Print Options dialog box

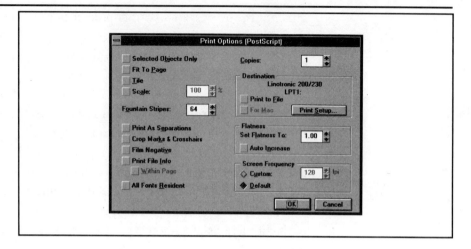

desirable characteristic if you're paying for it by the minute—or it may prove so complex as to be unprintable. If you use too few stripes, the individual stripes will become visible and your fountains will not appear as smooth transitions.

The optimum stripe value varies between output devices and there is no universally ideal setting. However, most output services will be able to tell you what the value for their particular equipment is. It happens to be 92 for the output service I use.

The other parameter, flatness, really tells the PostScript interpreter how careful it has to be when it draws curved lines. This includes the curved lines in type, by the way. As the flatness value is set higher, the PostScript interpreter is given more freedom to replace complex curves with straight line segments, which are much easier to calculate. This will cut down the output time considerably for a drawing with many curved lines, but if you increase the flatness value too much, the individual straight line segments will become visible and your drawing will look dreadful.

Figure 8.4 illustrates the result of too much flatness.

The normal flatness value is 1.00. You will probably find that for fairly uninvolved output you can leave it at this. For pages with a lot of curves on them, you should consult your output service for the highest flatness value you can get away with before your curves start getting visibly chunky.

Some CorelDRAW art output with a normal flatness value on the top and with the flatness set far too high on the bottom

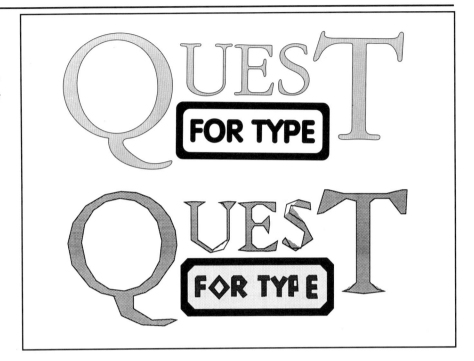

While you're clicking about in the CorelDRAW Print Options (Post-Script) dialog box, you should consider the Film Negative item. A photo-typesetter outputs to photographic film rather than to bond paper. You have your choice of clear film, for use by a printing house, or photographic paper such as conventional phototypesetters use, for sticking down to art boards. Note that both are usually referred to as film. You also have a choice of having the typesetter generate a negative or a positive image.

If you select Film Negative from the Print Options dialog box, the typesetter will generate film which is a negative image and which is mirrored right to left. This is how a print house will want it, for use in making plates. If you do this, make sure you explain what you've done and what you want your output service to do. If you simply hand them a disk and tell them to output the files on it as negatives, they may well tell their typesetter to invert the image a second time, resulting in positives.

WORKING WITH COLOR PRINTERS

The alternative to color print shops is color printers. Having your Corel-DRAW artwork printed on a printing press is great if you need 10,000 copies and can wait a week, but if you want fast results or a small print run, having a color-output device in-house might be more attractive.

A color printer is also almost essential as a proofing device if you'll be doing a lot of color art with CorelDRAW.

The most flexible color output available at the moment is afforded by the QMS ColorScript 100 using the Mitsubishi G650 color print engine, which manages to print with quality almost comparable to that of a laser printer. Versions are available to handle up to 11-by-17-inch paper. The ColorScript is an expensive machine, however, starting at just under $10,000 as of this writing. It's also expensive to use, although it's still a lot cheaper to output a color proof from a ColorScript printer than it is to go down to your local print shop and get a chroma key made. Texas Instruments also makes several excellent color PostScript printers.

If you want to step down in price quite a bit, the Hewlett Packard PaintJet and DeskJet 500C printers start at under $1,000. Their color facilities are not equal to those of a ColorScript, but they're pretty impressive. They don't support PostScript, of course, but you can drive one directly from CorelDRAW. At the moment, a PaintJet would be my choice for a color proofing device.

The Hewlett Packard PaintJet XL300 is a 300 dot-per-inch PostScript color inkjet printer—a pretty reasonable middle ground between the lower resolution PaintJets and the much more expensive wax-transfer color Post-Script devices.

NOTE NOTE *Some color graphics reproduce on certain color printers better than on other printers. The drawing titled* Venice *in the color insert prints quite well on one of the thermal-transfer printers, such as the QMS ColorScript 100, while the colors in the drawing* Lifetime *could appear saturated. This distinction is an important consideration when determining where to print your color art.*

LOW-COST COLOR PROOFS

There is actually another alternative to color proofing. It's cheap and reliable, although it's none too fast.

With the advent of drawing programs such as CorelDRAW and of dedicated business graphics programs such as Harvard Graphics, yet another cottage industry has appeared—executive slide houses. Because business presentations frequently call for 35-millimeter slides with charts and graphs on them, quite a few companies have begun to offer output services which will render CorelDRAW files on film. The usual cost per slide is between five and ten dollars. You can frequently find a slide house that will allow you to upload your CDR files by modem, and you can usually have your slides back the next day.

Most slide houses use high-end film recorders which have 24-bit color. This means that the colors in your CorelDRAW art will be selected from a palette of over 16 million possible colors to appear on your slides. This rivals what any print house can do.

The only drawback to using slides as color proofs is that they're small—a slide projector is all but essential. On the other hand, you'll be hard pressed to find any other color proofing technique which gives you a more accurate representation of the colors you've selected.

SPECIFYING COLOR IN CORELDRAW

Process color consists of only three or four actual ink plates, but the process of defining the color you want can be a little complex. CorelDRAW offers you a variety of options in selecting colors. Each has its place, and you'll probably want to experiment with them all until you get a feel for the one which best suits your applications.

Figure 8.5 illustrates all the ways you might select a fill color. While one of them is, in fact, selecting a spot color—something you'd be unlikely to do in a drawing with so many different colors—the others all represent equally valid ways of specifying the same color.

The color selection dialog boxes are extensions of the line and fill specification dialog boxes discussed in Chapter 4. You can select the method by which you specify color (the color model) by clicking on one of the four options on the Model drop-down menu in the upper-right corner of a color specification dialog box.

Note that no matter how you specify a process color, CorelDRAW stores the internal representation of the color in the same notation. You're free to use whatever color model you find most comfortable, or to use multiple models in the same drawing if you like.

FIGURE 8.5:

How to paint a parrot

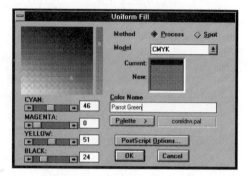

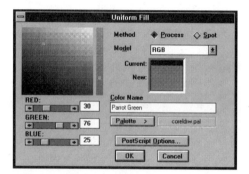

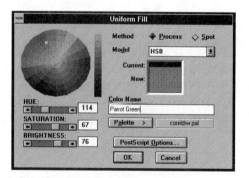

FIGURE 8.5:

*How to paint a parrot
(continued)*

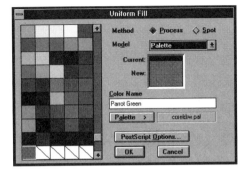

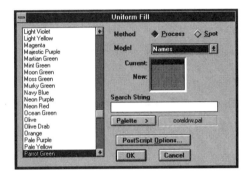

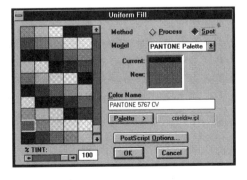

THE CMYK MODEL

The most obvious way to define a color, based on what we've discussed in this chapter, is to specify the amount of cyan, magenta, yellow, and, optionally, black ink required to produce it. CorelDRAW calls this the CMYK model. You can define a color by adding the appropriate amounts of cyan, magenta, yellow, and black ink together.

The advantage of using the CMYK model is that most art-supply stores and some color-separation houses can provide you with color-swatch books based on it. The CorelDRAW reference card, which comes with the package, has a basic process-color chart as well. While the colors you'll see on your screen will be approximations, you can look up the exact color you want in a color book and set the corresponding percentages of cyan, magenta, yellow, and black in CorelDRAW.

Earlier in this chapter, we discussed black removal in four-color printing. There's a bit of a peculiarity in the way CorelDRAW specifies colors under the CMYK model and what it can do to help you out with black-removal problems. At the left side of the color dialog box there's a large color fountain which is, in fact, a visual color selector. If you imagine a huge three-dimensional color fountain which runs from white to black and includes all the possible colors in between, this box will always illustrate a fragment of the fountain which contains the currently defined color, as set by the cyan, magenta, yellow, and black ink percentage controls in the lower-left corner of the box.

The small vertical stripe to the right of the visual selector illustrates the currently selected color's black level. The bottom of the fountain represents the color with no black added. The top is the color with fifty percent black added.

In both of these visual selector boxes, the current color is indicated by a small square area.

If you select a color by clicking in one of the visual selectors, the sliders and the percentage numbers in the lower-left corner of the dialog box will also change their settings accordingly. However, CorelDRAW will also automatically calculate the black removal for the selected color, and you'll observe that at least one of the cyan, magenta, or yellow percentages will always be zero in this case.

If you prefer to specify color by numerical percentages, you can do so and then click in one of the visual selectors above the current color—essentially selecting for a second time the color you've just specified—to make CorelDRAW do the black removal.

THE RGB MODEL

The second approach to defining colors is with the RGB (the additive red, green, blue) model. This model really offers you exactly the same range of colors as did the CMYK model; it merely provides a different way to define them. If you have CorelDRAW output your art as color separations—which are always handled in the CMYK model—all your RGB values will be converted to CMYK values behind your back.

The RGB model does not, however, provide a way to do black removal.

Under the RGB model, you specify a color as percentages of red, green, and blue. If you prefer, you can use the visual selectors, as with the CMYK model.

The RGB model may prove to be more comfortable if you've worked with color primarily in a computer-based environment, as this is how computers tend to define it.

THE HSB MODEL

The HSB color selector dialog box looks a bit different from the previous two dialog boxes in that the primary visual selector is round. The HSB model defines colors as hue, saturation, and brightness values.

The round color selector serves to illustrate the relationship of these three factors. Unlike the previous two visual selectors, the HSB wheel always represents all the available colors.

The outer rim of the HSB wheel represents all the colors. Under CorelDRAW, there are 360 possible choices, one for each degree around the wheel. Color zero, at the right side of the wheel, is red. Color 90 is light green. Color 180, at the left side of the wheel opposite red, is almost cyan. Color 270, at the bottom, is purple. The middle of the wheel is the combination of all colors, and is white.

At the outer edge of the wheel, all the colors are fully saturated. As you move toward the center, the percentage of saturation diminishes.

The small vertical fountain to the right of the wheel is the brightness value.

The HSB model suffers from considerably coarser resolution than do the previous two models—you cannot use it to specify color as accurately as you can under the CMYK or RGB models. However, it will probably prove more comfortable to people with a fine-arts background, as this is often how color is discussed in books on painting and color illustration.

USING THE COLOR PALETTE

Clicking in the X box at the left end of the palette strip with your left mouse button will assign a transparent fill to the objects you have selected. Clicking in it with the right button of your mouse will assign a line of zero width, and hence no color, to the outlines of your selected objects.

There's a quick way to assign palette colors as fills under CorelDRAW. Running along the bottom of the CorelDRAW workspace is a strip of colored boxes. These correspond to the colors in the Palette dialog box. If you select an object and then click in one of these boxes with the left button of your mouse, the object will be assigned the appropriate fill value. If you click in a box with the right button, the object will be assigned the corresponding line color. The preview swatch in the upper-right corner of the CorelDRAW workspace will indicate the line and fill colors you've selected.

There isn't enough room to show the entire range of palette colors in the CorelDRAW workspace at once, so you can pan through them using the right and left arrows at the ends of the palette display. Clicking on one of the arrows with the left button of your mouse will move the display by one box. Clicking with the right button will move it by one set of boxes.

Palette-color changes which you make while working on a drawing under CorelDRAW are saved to a file called CORELDRW.PAL in the same subdirectory where CorelDRAW itself resides. Once you've defined colors you like once, they'll be available for all subsequent drawings. This file is actually just a text file, and you'll probably find that editing it by hand is a simple way to make changes to the palette entries—especially for deleting lots of unwanted colors. The Windows Notepad application is ideal for editing files like this one.

Here are a few lines of CORELDRW.PAL:

"Black"	0	0	0	100
"White"	0	0	0	0
"Blue"	100	100	0	0

"Cyan"	100	0	0	0
"Green"	100	0	100	0
"Yellow"	0	0	100	0
"Red"	0	100	100	0
"Magenta"	0	100	0	0
"Electric Blue"	60	60	0	0
"Twilight Blue"	40	40	0	20
"Grass Green"	60	0	40	40
"Banana Yellow"	0	0	60	20
"Flamingo Pink"	10	68	26	0
"Majestic Purple"	20	60	0	20
"100C100M100Y100K"	100	100	100	100
"Parrot Green"	100	0	80	0
"Spent Uranium"	0	0	70	36

Each line represents a palette entry. The leftmost field is, of course, the name. Most of the ones shown here are the default names which come with CorelDRAW. A few, such as Parrot Green, Flamingo Pink, and Spent Uranium, are custom colors which I've defined. The color 100C100M100Y100K is one of CorelDRAW's default palette entries—it's what you'd get if you slapped on all the ink you could, and represents the theoretically blackest black one could generate without actually contracting for the delivery of a black hole. It's unclear what one might do with such a color.

The four numbers to the right of each name are the cyan, magenta, yellow, and black percentages which represent the colors in question.

NAMED PROCESS COLORS

The fourth color-specification model offered by CorelDRAW is the use of named colors. In this version of the color specification dialog box, the color selector will be replaced with a list of predefined color names. You can assign one of them to the object whose color you're defining by clicking on it.

If you defined a new color in one of the previous three models, you can also assign it a name. If you do so, your new color name will be added to the named color list, and you can subsequently assign it to other objects.

The advantage of using named colors is that you can quickly fill or outline multiple objects with the same colors without having to remember a list of color percentages. While not as flexible as actually specifying each color value individually, using named colors is considerably faster when defining a color as Neon Red or Forest Green is close enough.

PANTONE COLORS

You can reach the spot-color, or Pantone-color, selector from one of the process-color selectors by selecting the Spot button in a fill dialog box. The resulting dialog box will look a little like the palette selector, but with a different range of colors and controls.

You can select any of the Pantone colors by clicking on the appropriate color swatch. You can also select them by name, which will probably be of more use to you if you're actually referring to a Pantone color book. To pop up the list of named Pantone colors, select Names from the Model control.

You can't edit the actual percentages of inks which make up Pantone colors, as these are defined by Pantone, Inc., and there's not much use in a standard which isn't Standard. However, you can select the percentage of a particular color you choose for a fill. The percentage defaults to 100—it can be adjusted using the control in the upper-right corner of the spot color selector.

One problem which crops up quite often in using Pantone colors is in converting them to process colors. You may find that a project which started out as two-color art has suddenly acquired a more liberal budget and can now expand out to full four-color printing. More often, you'll be confronted with someone who has specified a fifth color as a Pantone shade while you have only four actual colors—four press stations—to work with.

While Pantone, Inc. itself provides no easy way to convert between Pantone and process colors, save for matching them by eye, CorelDRAW can do almost perfect translations very easily. If you have a Pantone color selected as the fill for an object and you want to use a process color instead, simply select the object, bring up the appropriate fill dialog box in spot-color mode, and switch to process-color mode using the CMYK model. A process color matching the previously selected Pantone color will appear in the selector.

If you're generating art for high-quality reproduction for a very exacting application—a glossy corporate image pamphlet for which money is no object, for example—substituting process colors for Pantone colors will probably get you stood up against a wall and shot. If you're working up a bit of clip art for the local weekly newspaper, you can safely look anyone you like in the eye and defy them to tell the difference. For such projects, CorelDRAW's Pantone-to-process-color translation is just about flawless.

Windows Colors and Real Colors

Even after you've used Windows for a while, you might not fully understand just how it really works with color. Usually this doesn't matter. However, when you're working in color under CorelDRAW, a bit of insight into just what happens behind the scenes may make CorelDRAW's color previews a bit more meaningful.

In the 16-color modes of VGA cards, there can be only 16 unique colors on the screen at once, chosen from 64 possible colors. If you consider this for a moment, you can see that Windows would have a bit of a problem if two applications running in two windows each wanted its own color scheme. While each may be constrained to 16 unique colors, having both of them visible at once could require that there actually be 32 unique colors on the screen at once, which the display hardware cannot do.

Windows avoids this by forbidding applications to change the screen colors. There are 16 colors defined by Windows, and all Windows applications must use them and only them. You can redefine which of the available colors will be used for specific areas of the screen using the Colors item of the Control Panel, but you can't change the actual colors themselves.

When you fill an object with a color defined as 60-percent black, 100-percent cyan, and 100-percent yellow—I called this color Jungle Green—CorelDRAW cannot simply change one of the screen colors to Jungle Green to use when you ask for a preview of your drawing. Instead, what it does is *dither* a shade which most closely approximates Jungle Green.

Dithering is a very complicated mathematical process for representing colors which aren't really available. To simplify the above color definition, you can think of Jungle Green as being 60 percent black and 100 percent green. Allowing that pure green and pure black *are* available in the Windows color scheme, CorelDRAW can cook up a pretty good approximation of Jungle Green by filling an area with pure green and then seeing that six out of every ten green pixels in that area are replaced with black.

By the same token, when you look at a palette swatch or a filled color object in the CorelDRAW preview, CorelDRAW will approximate the colors it doesn't have by dithering. Again, this will give you an idea of what the colors in question look like, but these dithered colors are frequently only very crude approximations of the real thing. When you're selecting colors for fills, you should use a process color book or a Pantone book to arrive at the actual colors you want. When you're looking at a preview, keep in mind that the colors are probably dithers.

This situation can be improved upon by running Windows on a SVGA card with a 256-color driver. This is discussed in greater detail in Appendix A.

DESIGNING WITH COLOR

Having the facility for using color can be a double-edged sword. You can produce some very nice-looking graphics and excellent pages. You can also produce pictures which look as if they were left out in the rain.

Designing effectively with color is an exercise in restraint. It's also a very good opportunity to consider what you're actually trying to achieve with your pages. It's all too easy to be blown away by the color tools in Corel-DRAW, slapping color onto anything that doesn't move or salute, but the results of the unbridled use of color rarely look attractive.

In many cases, the sparse use of color can do a lot more than having it all over a page.

APPLYING COLOR
TO BLACK AND WHITE PAGES

The simplest use of color is to ornament or otherwise enhance an intrinsically black and white graphic or page. This applies whether the design in question is for a stand-alone graphic or for a complete page. A small amount of color on an otherwise monochrome page will serve to focus the eye to the colored area, even if the color is not what you might expect.

If the purpose of adding color to a page is to make it more eye-catching, to serve as an additional method of focusing your readers' attention, there is a good argument for exercising restraint in the way you apply color. A colored headline, a single colored graphic, or a few spot-color rules or ornaments are all things which stand out from a page. Having sprung for a color signature in your publications, you might well question the economy of using your color facilities only now and again, but a page which is littered with colored graphics and other regalia might as well have been left black and white. The focus of such a page will have been lost in the myriads of colored images.

Color drop caps—capital display letters used to begin a text passage—can be exceedingly effective. Just as a large or ornate drop cap serves to focus the attention of someone looking at a black-and-white page, a colored one can be even more eye-catching, especially if it's the only object with color on the page.

If your publication lends itself to having icons, symbols, or logos in it, these also make ideal applications for color.

COLOR GRADIENTS AND FOUNTAINS

One of the things which plagues magazines and other multiple-page publications is that white paper is, well, so white. You can make a particular page stand out by changing this. One way to do so is simply to instruct your print house to lay a screen of some fairly muted color behind whatever's on your page. However, a still more interesting way to do so is to have CorelDRAW produce a large fountain in such a color. This will not only make the background of your page something other than white, but it will also make it more visually interesting, as it won't simply be a constant tone.

You can also fill specific areas of the page or individual elements with color fountains and other effects in which you blend colors or change their density.

Color fountains are no more difficult to do than black and white ones. They were discussed earlier, in Chapter 4. However, there are a few things worth noting about fountains and color:

◆ CorelDRAW's fountains take a moderately long time to output. This is true whether you're sending them to a 300 dot-per-inch laser printer or a PostScript phototypesetter.

◆ Keep in mind how your color will be printed. A fountain which blends between two Pantone colors, for example, is well within the capabilities of CorelDRAW but will be of no use when you actually take your artwork to a printer. If there were 128 actual levels of gradation in such a fountain, you'd need a 128-station printing press to reproduce it.

◆ If you're using spot colors, make sure your fountains work with single colors. They can blend between varying densities of a single color. In order to blend between two colors, you must work with process colors and be planning on full-color printing.

◆ Remember that the colors generated when you preview a fountain are dithers, as discussed previously, and are hence frequently approximations of the true colors that will be printed.

COLOR TEXT EFFECTS

Adding color to text—especially for use as eye-catching exported headlines—is an ideal application for CorelDRAW. There are all sorts of things you can do in this area.

Simply setting type in color isn't all that exciting and you can usually manage this without CorelDRAW's help at all. Setting text with a color fountain running through it is a lot more interesting, and is effective because it isn't seen all that often.

Colored text often looks a lot more interesting against black or some other dark color than it does against white, largely because people are used to seeing white pages. If your document will be handled by a print shop, you can have your desktop-publishing type reversed out of a black background.

In this case, a colored headline graphic against a black background can be stripped into your black page and look really striking. If you do try this effect, bear in mind that large black areas will tend to bleed into small white ones when your work finally gets printed. If you have small type on your page, consider setting it in a bold face rather than a medium one to give it a better chance of surviving the printing process.

COLORING CLIP ART

Adding color to some of the monochrome clip art which accompanies CorelDRAW can be a quick, painless way to generate color graphics. Be warned, however—it's not as easy as it looks. Many of the pictures in the CorelDRAW clip art sampler are really designed to be reproduced in black-and-white, and will take a bit of cunning to colorize effectively.

Human subjects are the most difficult ones to color. The contours of a human face are hard to represent in objects, and a solid color fill seems to emphasize the lack of details far more than a white one does.

WRAPPING UP

Most experienced graphic artists are a bit nervous about experimenting with color, because their experience has been with print houses, and the results can be embarrassingly costly if they don't work out. Print houses generally print what you give them—whether or not it's actually what you wanted.

CorelDRAW, especially when it's coupled with a color proofing device like a PaintJet printer, provides a much friendlier way to learn about color. You can try out color effects and just get some experience with the nuances of color applications, all without incurring any excessive print bills or nasty surprises.

When you weigh it against the cost of a couple of print jobs which don't work out, you might find that you can justify the cost of a PaintJet pretty easily.

FAST
TRACK
CHAPTER
9

To create air brush effects, ... 409

select the air brush tool from the toolbox. Open the Soft Brush
Settings item in the Options menu to set the air brush characteristics. Select a color to paint with from the Palette workbox
and set the brush characteristics using the Width workbox.
Hold down the left mouse button and drag the air brush cursor
in the image area to paint.

To clone one image into another, ... 409

select the clone tool from the toolbox. Click on the center of
the source image with the right mouse button. Paint with the
left mouse button in the center of the area of the destination
image where the cloned image fragment is to go.

Using

CorelPHOTO-PAINT

n the first chapter of this book, we discussed the distinction between traditional painting applications, such as PC Paintbrush or Windows Paintbrush, and true drawing applications like CorelDRAW. Each type of software has its own distinct use. By now, you will be familiar with what CorelDRAW can accomplish. Paint programs will not allow you to deal with graphic elements as objects, but they will allow you to deal with photo-realistic subjects in such a way that they still look realistic.

A paint program is the digital equivalent of an artist's canvas, combined with a really good camera and a well equipped darkroom. If you have a scanner or a source of scanned images, a paint program will let you retouch images in ways that conventional photographic methods can only dream about. In addition, of course, you can actually create original images from scratch using the tools of a paint program.

You will probably be familiar with at least one simple paint application, this being the Windows Paintbrush program that accompanies Windows itself. While unremarkable in comparison to higher end painting software—such as the CorelPHOTO-PAINT application to be discussed in this chapter—Windows Paintbrush offers all the essential elements of painting. It provides you with a digital canvas, to which you can apply the equivalent of paint.

The CorelPHOTO-PAINT application is Windows freehand brush after a massive growth spurt. It has been refined and vastly enhanced to make it a powerful tool for retouching and adjusting scanned photographs. It's less ideally suited to painting original images—although you certainly can use it for this if you want to—probably on the assumption that you'll be using CorelDRAW to actually create drawings.

Here are some of the salient characteristics of CorelPHOTO-PAINT:

◆ It handles bitmapped images with any number of colors, in a variety of popular file formats.

◆ It allows you to edit images with more colors than your screen can display.

◆ It allows you to retouch individual pixels or to work with larger areas of an image.

◆ It allows you to selectively or globally "filter" your images. Filtering provides such features as sharpening, softening, removing spots, and so on.

◆ It allows you to smudge and blend details of an image.

◆ It allows you to draw new elements into an existing image.

◆ It allows you to merge multiple image fragments into a single image.

In fact, this is an abbreviated list. The capabilities of CorelPHOTO-PAINT are considerable.

NOTE
NOTE

While it has been licensed by Corel Systems for inclusion in the CorelDRAW package, Corel-PHOTO-PAINT was actually written by the ZSoft company, the authors of PC Paintbrush. If you're already familiar with ZSoft's PC Paintbrush for Windows application, you'll find CorelPHOTO-PAINT similar.

BITMAPPED GRAPHICS

Bitmapped graphic files of the type CorelPHOTO-PAINT works with have characteristics which are markedly different from those of an object-oriented drawing, such as a CorelDRAW CDR file. The easiest way to think of a bitmapped graphic is as a two-dimensional matrix of colored dots. If the matrix is fine enough, the individual dots will not be visible as such, and the matrix will look like a coherent picture. Your monitor is such a matrix. The dots in a bitmapped graphic are called "pixels."

As far as CorelPHOTO-PAINT is concerned, bitmapped graphics come in four flavors. Monochrome pictures have two colors—black and white—and all the dots in a monochrome image must be one of these colors. Note that in a discussion of bitmapped graphics, the phrase "black and white" does not mean quite the same thing as it does in its more conventional use in a discussion of photography. A black and white photograph also includes innumerable intermediate shades of gray.

There are image files in the formats that CorelPHOTO-PAINT supports which will have something other than the number of bits of color discussed here. You can still work with these files. For example, if you open a 4-bit file—one with 16 colors—CorelPHOTO-PAINT will promote it internally to 8 bits and work with it as such. True color files having 16 or 32 bits of color will be adjusted to 24 bits.

In dealing with bitmaps, a photograph with gray levels is called a "gray-scale" image. In effect, gray-scale bitmaps are really color bitmaps in which all the colors are levels of gray.

Color bitmaps come in two types for CorelPHOTO-PAINT—256-color, or "8-bit" images; and true-color, or "24-bit" images. In the former case, all the colors in the image must be derived from a "palette" of no more than 256 distinct colors. Each color can be defined to suit the image, so different 256-color images will have differing palettes. In fact, a picture with 256 distinct colors can look essentially photographic.

Bitmaps with 24 bits of color information can have an unlimited number of colors—every pixel can be a different color. There are actually 16,777,216 possible colors evenly distributed across the visible spectrum available to a 24-bit image. Such images can provide you with absolutely faithful color for scanned bitmaps.

There are a number of other considerations you might want to keep in mind about these latter two types of bitmaps. To begin with, scanned images which are stored as 8-bit images can usually be compressed to some extent, so that they need occupy less space on your disk. This is not true of 24-bit images. All other things being equal, a 24-bit image requires three times the memory or disk space of an 8-bit image. In practice, because 8-bit images can be compressed and 24-bit images cannot, the ratio will usually be considerably higher.

Most of the really interesting things CorelPHOTO-PAINT can do with images requires that they be in the 24-bit format. It can quickly "promote" 8-bit images to 24 bits internally. You should keep in mind that in reducing a 24-bit image to 8 bits of color, a certain amount of cheating will transpire behind your back. The resulting 8-bit file will not have quite as accurate color definition as the 24-bit image it was derived from. The extent to which this cheating visibly affects your pictures will depend to a large extent on the nature of the images you work with.

It's worth noting that image scanners which produce color scans generate them as some species of 24-bit image, even if their driving software offers the option of subsequently reducing them to 8-bit files. If you can afford the disk space, it's highly desirable to work with color bitmaps as 24-bit files.

In addition to working with color images, CorelPHOTO-PAINT also has facilities to handle gray-scale pictures, and it will convert its internal color graphics to gray scale if you like. Gray scale images are always stored with 8 bits of color information—or more properly, gray information. There is no 24-bit gray format, as neither your eye nor any output device currently available could really make use of 16,777,216 distinct levels of gray. An 8-bit gray-scale file allows for 256 distinct gray levels, which is sufficient to create the appearance of continuous tones.

Gray-scale images typically compress better than color images and are generally easier to work with. If the ultimate destination of the files you'll be working with under CorelPHOTO-PAINT will be a monochrome output device, you should create gray-scale versions of your graphics.

Bitmapped graphic files in the following formats can be loaded and saved by CorelPHOTO-PAINT:

◆ PCX—This is the native format of PC Paintbrush.

◆ GIF—This is the format most often used to exchange scanned color graphics over bulletin boards. It was created by CompuServe.

> **NOTE** *A 300 dot-per-inch PostScript laser printer can really only reproduce about 32 distinct gray levels, and if you print a 256-level gray-scale file to such a printer, the extra gray information will be absorbed and adjusted to create the 32 most appropriate gray levels.*

◆ BMP—The is the native format of Microsoft Windows Paintbrush, and is used to provide Windows with wallpaper, among other things.

◆ TGA—This is the TARGA format, originally created by the Truevision company. Among other things, it's the most common output format for image scanners.

◆ TIF—This is the TIFF format, and is a common import format for many desktop publishing packages, such as Ventura Publisher and PageMaker.

◆ MSP—This is the old format supported by Microsoft Windows prior to the introduction of Windows 3.0. It's not widely used any more.

All of the foregoing formats can save files having up to 24 bits of color, with two exceptions. The GIF format can only support up to 8 bits of color. The MSP format can only support black and white images.

Each of these following formats has particular compression characteristics—that is, the format you choose will have some bearing on how big a disk file is required to store your images.

◆ PCX—Provides some compression, but PCX uses a compression method which is much better suited to drawings than scanned images. In some cases—especially when it's confronted with 24-bit files—PCX compression will result in files that are bigger than they would have been uncompressed. The PCX format does not allow you to turn the compression off in these cases.

◆ GIF—Provides the most effective possible compression, but only for images with up to eight bits of color. The catch to this is that GIF files take somewhat longer to read and write than other formats do.

◆ BMP—Provides no compression at all. Files with 8 or fewer bits of color will occupy more disk space than necessary if they're stored as BMP files. In most cases, scanned 24-bit images should be stored with no compression, so BMP files are a good choice for such pictures.

- ◆ TGA—Provides optional compression, which is similar in effective-ness to that of the PCX format. You will certainly want to choose to create uncompressed TGA files if you're working with scanned 24-bit images.

- ◆ TIF—Provides optional compression similar to that of the GIF for-mat. The catch is that many applications which read TIFF files will not read TIFF files which use this particular type of compression.

- ◆ MSP—Provides modest compression for monochrome images. Unfortunately, applications which will use MSP files are exceed-ingly rare.

If you want to use image files in formats other than these—or if you want to use CorelPHOTO-PAINT's output in applications which require alternate image file formats—the Graphic Workshop for Windows package provided on the companion disk for this book can be used to translate your files.

There's an important catch in using bitmapped graphic files. Many graphic file formats, including the ones that CorelPHOTO-PAINT works with, are poorly standardized. Chief among these are the TIFF format, which comes in more variations than could be counted on the fingers of a healthy centipede. You may encounter files you want to work with that CorelPHOTO-PAINT won't read, and you may also encounter applications that won't read files that CorelPHOTO-PAINT creates. In some cases, run-ning the offending files through Graphic Workshop for Windows will sneak around this problem—assuming that Graphic Workshop for Windows will read them.

RUNNING CORELPHOTO-PAINT

Figure 9.1 illustrates the basic geography of CorelPHOTO-PAINT. There are four principal elements displayed here. The large window with a picture in it is the actual work space, corresponding to the drawing area under CorelDRAW. The Palette window at the bottom is used to select the colors you will be drawing with, if you want to actually add elements to a picture.

FIGURE 9.1:

CorelPHOTO-PAINT in action, illustrating the layout of its windows

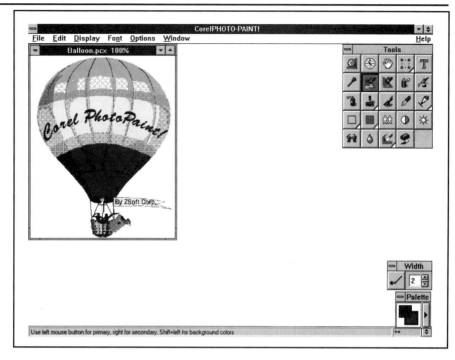

 *Corel-PHOTO-PAINT's speed will be affected to some extent by the size of the image you're working on. If you plan to work on large 24-bit color images, a 486 system with 8 or 16 megabytes of memory is probably essential.*

The Width window allows you to select the width and shape of the brush used for drawing—unlike conventional liquid paint, CorelPHOTO-PAINT allows you to draw with any shape brush you like. The large window full of icons entitled Tools and located to the right of the picture window is the CorelPHOTO-PAINT toolbox. This corresponds in function to the CorelDRAW toolbox, although as you'll note there are many more tools in this one.

Note that you can move any of the windows to keep them out of your way. You can also hide them if you don't need them at the moment. The picture window can be resized—if you make it smaller than the picture you're working on, scroll bars will appear to let you move around the image. Unlike CorelDRAW, CorelPHOTO-PAINT allows you to have multiple images loaded at once. The topmost one will be the one where drawing takes place, but you can bring whichever one you like to the top.

A TEN MINUTE TOUR OF CORELPHOTO-PAINT'S MENUS

One of the laudable aspects of CorelPHOTO-PAINT is its organization. Even before you really understand its capabilities, you can work out where to start looking for them by observing one simple rule. Everything that affects whole images is handled by a menu item. Everything that affects part of an image is handled by a tool, at least initially. In the latter case, you may use a menu choice to modify the effects of a tool.

As there are fewer menu items than there are tools, we'll discuss them first. They correspond well to the basic functions of the software as you're likely to need them.

LOADING AND SAVING FILES

The File menu of CorelPHOTO-PAINT looks a lot like the File menu of other Windows applications, and its items invoke predictable functions. To load a file, select Open. A dialog box like the one in Figure 9.2 will appear.

If you have been using the Open Drawing dialog box of CorelDRAW, you'll find that this one behaves similarly. The large selector to the left of the box will present you with file names of the type you have currently selected, or with file names of all the types CorelPHOTO-PAINT can recognize if

FIGURE 9.2:

The CorelPHOTO-PAINT Load a Picture from Disk dialog box

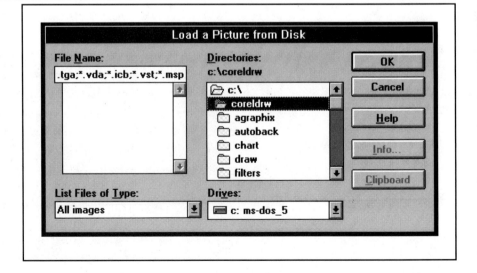

that's how you have set the box up. The choice of which files to display can be made using the file type selector control directly below the file name selector.

The directory selector in the center of the box and the drive selector below it work exactly like the corresponding elements of the CorelDRAW Open Drawing dialog box. You can select a subdirectory to move into or the previous directory—the one with a backslash after it—from the larger selector, and you can change drives using the drive selector below it.

The Info button at the right side of the box can be exceedingly useful. Highlight a file name by clicking on it once and then click on Info. If you enable the Show Thumbnail checkbox of the Image Info box that appears, a reduced version of the selected file will appear, as in Figure 9.3.

There are two things to keep in mind about the Image Info window. First of all, if there is not enough memory to load the image you want to see a thumbnail of, no picture will appear. Secondly, if an image is loaded, the colors of any images previously loaded into the work space of Corel-PHOTO-PAINT may change. This isn't permanent, and things will return to normal as soon as you close the Image Info window.

Saving a file under CorelPHOTO-PAINT is no more complex than loading one. The Save item of the File menu will allow you to update the file from which you have loaded an image with whatever changes you make while in CorelPHOTO-PAINT. The Save As item will allow you to save an image to a new file, leaving the previous file untouched. Selecting Save As

FIGURE 9.3:

The Image Info box
with a thumbnail image

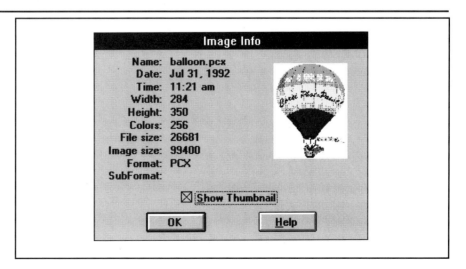

will prompt you for a file name and type, using a dialog box like the one in Figure 9.4.

You can select a format from the List Files of Type control below the principal file name selector. Note that this list will not present you with inappropriate file types. For example, it knows that GIF files don't support 24-bit color images, and if the file you're attempting to save is a 24-bit color image, you'll find that the GIF format will not be in the list.

As noted earlier, two of the image file formats supported by CorelPHOTO-PAINT can be stored with or without compression. If you choose one of these, the File Sub-Format control will allow you to choose whether you want to have your file compressed or not.

In addition to the file formats discussed earlier in this chapter, CorelPHOTO-PAINT will save files to the EPS, or encapsulated PostScript format. Files saved from CorelPHOTO-PAINT in this format cannot be loaded back into CorelPHOTO-PAINT or CorelDRAW. They're only useful for inclusion in desktop publishing documents and by other applications which will import EPS graphics. Having said this, I should note that in almost all such applications you can get better results from other, dedicated image file formats, and with significantly smaller disk files in the process.

FIGURE 9.4:

The Save a Picture to Disk dialog box

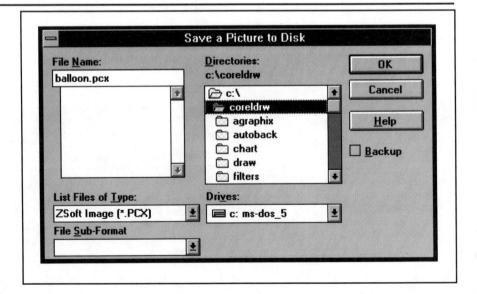

PRINTING FILES

While CorelPHOTO-PAINT has its greatest use as a "front end," sending images to other applications, you might want to print pictures directly from it to see what they'll look like as hard copy. To do so, select Print from the File menu. A dialog box like the one in Figure 9.5 will appear, showing the name of your particular printer.

There are a number of options you can use to fine-tune CorelPHOTO-PAINT's printing facilities.

Print Size

The Print Size group of options will allow you to select the size of your printed image, as well as to deal with the potential for moiré patterns and other aberrations which printing may cause. The effects of multiple screens, as discussed in Chapter 4, are equally applicable to printing the matrix of pixels of a bitmapped graphic using the matrix of dots of a laser printer.

Selecting the 1 to 1 option will totally eliminate any possible moiré effects. It will probably leave you with a postage-stamp size printed image,

FIGURE 9.5:

The dialog box for printing

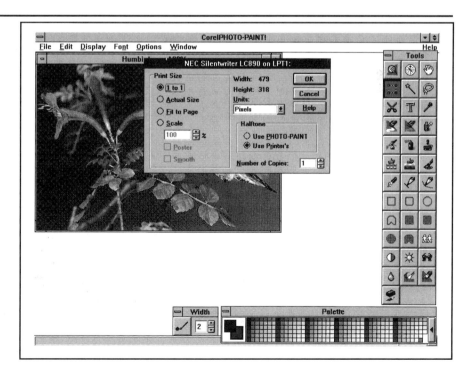

however. A 640 by 480 pixel picture printed on a 300 dot-per-inch printer using this option will occupy 2.13 by 1.60 inches.

In most cases, the Actual Size option will have the same effect. The exception is in printing some types of TIFF files, which can include information that defines a different size for printed pixels.

The Fit to Page option will scale your picture up or down to more or less fill the page. This is likely to cause printing aberrations, especially if you are printing fairly small images.

Finally, the Scale option allows you to scale an image up or down when it's being printed. If you choose a scale size which represents an integral multiple or submultiple of the image's natural size—100 percent, 200 percent, 50 percent, and so on—you'll reduce the likelihood of visible printing aberrations.

The Scale option offers two suboptions. Select the Poster control to tile your picture over multiple pages if it won't all fit on one sheet of paper. Choose the Smooth control to have CorelPHOTO-PAINT attempt to smooth out the chunkiness which may appear if you scale a picture up by several hundred percent.

Halftone

Undo has a short memory. It lasts precisely as long as it takes you to do something else. It only remembers your most recent action. If you draw something and then change one pixel of your drawing, selecting Undo will reverse that one-pixel change, not the drawing action that preceded it.

The halftone control allows you to select either CorelPHOTO-PAINT's internal halftoning procedure or the halftoning provided by your printer. The latter case will only be available if your printer does, in fact, support halftoning. While you should experiment with this option to get a feel for how it works, in most cases you'll find, if you have a choice, that your printer's internal halftoning function produces the best results.

UNDOING MISTAKES

The Undo item of the Edit menu is perhaps CorelPHOTO-PAINT's most beloved feature. Select it, and the most recent action you performed will be undone. The menu item will, in fact, change to tell you exactly what it proposes to undo. You can also hit Alt-Backspace to invoke the Undo function.

Cut, Copy, Paste, Delete

The four block functions work under CorelPHOTO-PAINT just as they do under CorelDRAW and other Windows applications. They involve the use of one of the selection tools, which has not been discussed yet. This tool works just like the pick tool under CorelDRAW.

You can select any area of an image under CorelPHOTO-PAINT. If you subsequently select the Cut item from the Edit menu, it will be copied to the Windows Clipboard and deleted from your image. It can be pasted into another image, another area of your current image, or into another application entirely through the Windows Clipboard. The Copy item performs the same function, save that it does not delete the original selected area from your image.

The Paste function will allow you to paste the current Clipboard contents into an image. There's a major catch to this—whatever you attempt to paste must have come from a bitmap, or the Paste item will be disabled. You can't paste CorelDRAW objects or Windows Write text into CorelPHOTO-PAINT's work space.

The deleted area will be filled with the current background color.

Actually, there's a second catch, which will be explained in greater detail in just a moment when we deal with the Paste From item.

The Delete item works like the the Cut item, save that it doesn't copy anything to the Clipboard. It simply removes the selected portion of your drawing.

Copying to and Pasting from Files

The Copy To item of the Edit menu will allow you to select an area of an image and write it out to a new image file. In effect, you can crop smaller sections from a larger picture.

The Paste From item of the Edit menu will allow you to import an image from another file and merge it with the image you're presently working on.

There's a catch in using the Paste From item with 256-color files. If you open a 256-color file and then attempt to use Paste From to merge in a second 256-color image—which presumably will use 256 different colors—the total number of colors in use will be 512, or 256 more than can actually be supported. CorelPHOTO-PAINT gets around this by "remapping" the

As will be discussed later in this chapter, the Corel-PHOTO-PAINT tool will allow you to select irregular areas, as well as rectangular ones. If you attempt to write such a selected area to a new file using Copy To, CorelPHOTO-PAINT will actually write a rectangular area just big enough to enclose the selected portion of your image. All image files are, after all, rectangular.

colors of the imported image to those of the image it's about to become part of. This means that it replaces every color in the imported image with its closest match in the existing image.

If both pictures have similar palettes, this can work very well. If they don't, it can result in a noticeable color shift in the imported picture. For example, if you attempt to paste a red parrot into a picture of a green jungle, there will be few if any available red shades in the source palette, and the parrot will be remapped to green.

This doesn't happen if you're working with 24-bit images, as such images can have as many different colors as they need. If you want to merge two 256-color images together and sneak around this problem, do the following:

1. Convert the main image to 24 bits. The procedure for doing this will be discussed in a moment.

2. Import the picture you want to merge with the main image.

3. Convert the resulting picture back to 256 colors. This will also be discussed in a moment.

In fact, this procedure doesn't generate any more than 256 colors—it simply helps CorelPHOTO-PAINT to create a new palette that reflects the best 256 colors for the combination of the two images.

You should not encounter any problems with merging multiple gray-scale images using the Paste From item. By definition, all 256-level gray-scale images have the same 256 grays.

CONVERTING AMONG FORMATS

The Convert To item of the Edit menu will allow you to convert among monochrome, 256-color, 256-gray-level, and 24-bit color images. If you select it, a secondary menu will appear. The selection which matches your current image type will be disabled.

In all cases, the Convert To options will open a new window with a new image in it. Your original image will not be altered.

Converting a color image to black and white will involve a significant loss of detail. There are three ways to do this in CorelPHOTO-PAINT. The Line Art option will create a high-contrast image—any pixel which is fairly bright will become white and any pixel which is fairly dark

Over half of the interesting things that CorelPHOTO-PAINT can do only work with 24-bit and gray-scale images. Despite the memory penalties, you should convert 256-color images to 24 bits if you will be manipulating them extensively and optionally convert them back to 256 colors when you're done.

will become black. The Printer Halftone will produce a very coarse mechanical halftone. The Screen Halftone will produce what's called an error-diffused halftone. Examples of all three effects can be seen in Figure 9.6.

Converting a 24-bit image to 256 colors involves some juggling, as the destination image will have a substantially restricted range of colors. The process used, called "error-diffused dithering," attempts to deal with colors that are no longer in the destination picture by alternating pixels of the available colors. This usually works very well, although it will occasionally produce some unexpected aberrations.

Converting other images to 24-bit color will not diminish their color resolution at all.

Converting other images to gray-scale pictures will, of course, make all their colors into gray levels. A 24-bit image thus converted will require a lot less memory.

USING FILTERS

The CorelPHOTO-PAINT filters are among its most interesting facilities. They can be used to make subtle alterations in an image, or to radically alter what your pictures look like. While they are easy to use, you'll find that it will take you a while to really get a feel for how best to apply them.

The filters can work alone or in conjunction with the CorelPHOTO-PAINT selection tools, to be discussed presently. If there's nothing selected in an image when you invoke a filter, the entire image will be filtered. If you have selected an area, only the selected portion of your image will be filtered.

Most of the filters will only work with 24-bit and gray-scale images. If you want to filter a 256-color picture, you will have to convert it to 24 bits first.

Figure 9.7 illustrates the effects of the filters available in Corel-PHOTO-PAINT. It's worth noting that in each case this represents the default effects of these filters—prior to actually filtering anything, each filter will call up a dialog box to allow you to adjust the parameters of its operation.

Each of the filter control dialog boxes has a button called Screen Preview. Click on this to have the effects of the filter as you've set it up applied temporarily to your image. If you like what you see, click on OK to make the changes permanent. If you don't, adjust the controls and click on Screen Preview again to fine-tune the filter, or click on Cancel to give up

The first image is an
original 24-bit picture.
The next three images
are the same picture
sent through the
Convert To Line Art,
Printer Halftone, and
Screen Halftone func-
tions, in that order.

FIGURE 9.6:

The first image is an original 24-bit picture. The next three images are the same picture sent through the Convert To Line Art, Printer Halftone, and Screen Halftone functions, in that order. (continued)

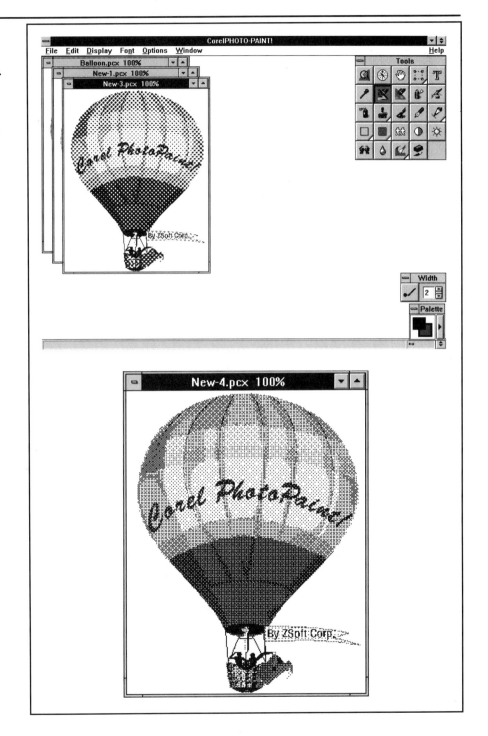

FIGURE 9.7:

An unfiltered image and the results of each of the CorelPHOTO-PAINT filters on it.

Add Noise

Blend

FIGURE 9.7:

An unfiltered image and the results of each of the CorelPHOTO-PAINT filters on it. (continued)

Brightness and Contrast

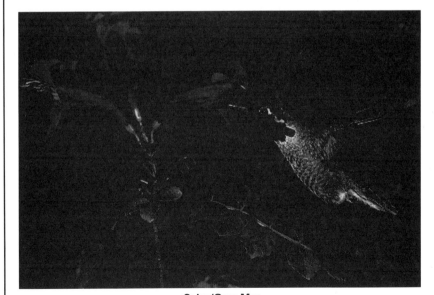

Color/Gray Map

FIGURE 9.7:

An unfiltered image and the results of each of the CorelPHOTO-PAINT filters on it. (continued)

Diffuse

Edge Detect

FIGURE 9.7:

An unfiltered image and the results of each of the CorelPHOTO-PAINT filters on it. (continued)

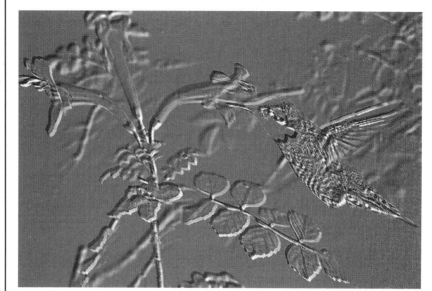

Emboss

Equalize

An unfiltered image and the results of each of the CorelPHOTO-PAINT filters on it. (continued)

Motion Blur

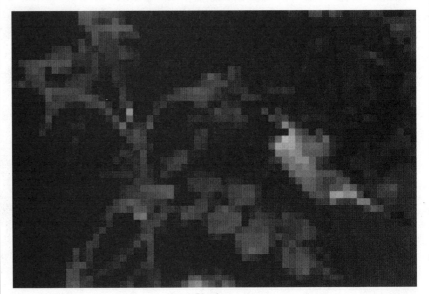

Pixelate

FIGURE 9.7:

An unfiltered image and the results of each of the CorelPHOTO-PAINT filters on it. (continued)

Remove Spots

Sharpen

on the filter entirely. In the latter case, your image will revert to the way it was before you selected the filter.

Add Noise

The concept of noise in images is a bit obscure—it dates back to the early days of radio. Random interference with radio signal does actually manifest itself as noise. When television came along, the same interference appeared as visual aberrations. The most common example of this is the random dots ("snow") that appear on a television screen after a station has signed off for the evening, or when you stop paying the cable bill. This "visual noise" has also appeared in computer imaging. Image processing, such as that performed to computer-enhance photographs, deals with such things as visual noise.

In fact, the computer algorithms that attempt to minimize the effects of noise in images use approaches similar to those of the audio equipment which undertakes similar tasks for sound.

The Add Noise filter of CorelPHOTO-PAINT does just the opposite, of course. It will apply an even screen of random noise to an image. This will make pictures look textured and less precise. It can help make drawn or computer-generated images look more photographic.

The Add Noise filter control offers the following adjustments:

◆ Variance—this controls the amount of noise to be added to your picture. A higher number will make it noisier.

◆ Distribution—this applies a curve to the distribution of the noise added to your picture. Using bell curve distribution will make the effect of the noise more subtle.

◆ Channel—this allows you to define which primary colors in your image will receive the noise.

Blend

The Blend filter will smooth out the details of your image by blending adjacent pixels. This will have result of diffusing details, making the image look like it's being viewed through frosted glass.

The Blend filter control offers the following adjustments:

◆ Blending—this control adjusts the degree to which pixels will be blended.

◆ Wide Aperture—this option will cause each blended pixel to represent a larger area of the original image.

Brightness and Contrast

The Brightness and Contrast filter will allow you to interactively adjust the brightness and contrast of an image. It's fairly self-explanatory, and the two slider controls in its adjustment box can be thought of as behaving just like the brightness and contrast controls on a television set or computer monitor.

Color/Gray Map

The Color/Gray Map filter allows you to graphically define how the colors or gray levels in an image should be adjusted. This is fairly easy to understand in working with gray-scale images, in that the graph presented by the filter simply maps the current gray levels of your image to new gray levels. It will take a bit of experimenting to really understand what this means to a color image.

The Color/Gray Map filter control offers the following adjustments:

Having defined a remap curve, you can save it to disk and subsequently load it back into the Color/Gray Remap filter dialog box.

◆ Preset—this selector offers you a number of predefined remap curves to perform particular tasks, such as enhancing the shadows in an image.

◆ Channel—this selector defines which primary colors are to be remapped.

◆ Style—this selector defines how you can adjust the curve in the graph display of the Color/Gray Map filter dialog box.

The manipulation of remap curves can provide you with tremendous control over an image's appearance. Plan to experiment with this filter for a while.

Diffuse

The Diffuse filter will make an image appear as if it's being viewed through pebbled glass or a window covered with raindrops.

The Diffuse filter control offers the following adjustments:

◆ Width and Height—these controls adjust the size of the area being diffused for each pixel. If you like the analogy of viewing an image through pebbled glass, these controls can be thought of as adjusting the size of the pebbles.

◆ Identical Values—if this option is enabled, changing one of the Width or Height controls will automatically change the other as well.

◆ Color Shift—if this option is selected, the diffusion process will introduce new colors into your image.

Edge Detect

The Edge Detect filter will usually make your images look unspeakably bizarre. What it actually does is scan through your image and look for sudden transitions in color or brightness that would indicate the edges of objects in the picture. It will outline all the edges it finds in the selected edge color and fill in the rest of the picture with the selected fill color.

The Edge Detect filter control offers the following adjustments:

◆ Sensitivity—increasing this value will make the filter more likely to decide that a change in color or brightness is an edge. It will usually add more details to the filtered image.

◆ Color—this control chooses the color to be used to fill the non-outlined parts of your drawing.

◆ Edge—this control chooses the color to be used to trace edges.

NOTE
NOTE

The Primary, Secondary, and Background items in the Color and Edge controls refer to the currently selected palette colors. The CorelPHOTO-PAINT palette will be discussed later in this chapter.

Emboss

The Emboss filter will make an image look as if it has been made into a paper sculpture, a bas-relief stone carving, or a brass rubbing, depending on your point of view. The effect is usually more effective when it's applied to gray-scale images—to be sure, when it's complete, your image will be a gray-scale image, or an image based on a progression of brightness of some other single color.

The Emboss filter control offers the following adjustments:

◆ Direction—paper sculptures only look three dimensional if they're illuminated from some direction other than straight on. This control allows you to choose the direction of the effective illumination for the embossing process.

◆ Color—this control will allow you to select the color for embossing. If you like the analogy of a paper sculpture, this control selects the color of the paper.

Equalize

The Equalize filter is probably the most sophisticated tool CorelPHOTO-PAINT offers you for retouching the appearance of images. It's also the most difficult to use well, and the one worthy of the most experimentation. It adjusts the distribution of colors or gray levels in an image. Used correctly, it will allow you to enhance the detail and contrast of an image.

When you select the Equalize filter, a dialog box will appear with a "histogram" in it, that is, a graph with a series of vertical lines in it. The horizontal axis of the graph represents the increasing brightness of the colors or gray shades in your image. Each line represents one distinct color or gray level. The vertical axis represents the number of times each color is used in the image.

The three movable pointers below the histogram readout represent the low, medium, and high values of the histogram. They correspond to the three numerical controls in the box—you can set these quantities either by dragging the pointers or by using the numerical controls.

While you will want to experiment with this filter to really understand what it can accomplish, here are a few guidelines:

◆ Moving the high value up will tend to place more of an image in shadow, that is, it will tend to make the darker areas darker still.

◆ Moving the high value down will tend to remove more details of an image from shadow, that is, it will make the darker areas lighter.

◆ Moving the low value down will tend to extract darker areas of an image from shadow. This will usually make the image look lighter and more exposed.

◆ Moving the low value up will tend to push details into shadow. This usually has the effect of making the image look as if it has a higher contrast, as if the lighting of the picture was more directional.

◆ Moving the middle value down will tend to lighten an image, merging the contrast levels of middle-tone details. In extreme applications, the results often look like a photograph that has been left in the sun too long.

◆ Moving the middle value up will tend to enhance the differences between middle-range details. This will usually make an image look darker, but with formerly bright details brighter still.

Motion Blur

The Motion Blur filter simulates the effect of a photograph of a moving subject taken with a slow shutter speed. It's most convincing when it's applied to subjects that look as if they were actually moving when the picture in question was taken. In this case, you should select a blur direction which corresponds to the apparent direction of the subject of your picture.

The Motion Blur filter control offers the following adjustments:

◆ Direction—selects the direction in which the subject will appear to be moving when the filter has processed your image.

◆ Speed—controls the amount of blur, corresponding to the apparent speed of the subject.

Pixelate

The Pixelate filter will create the effect of merging pixels in a rectangular area together. This is commonly seen in television news videos in which the identity of someone is concealed.

The Pixelate filter control offers the following adjustments:

◆ Width and Height—these controls adjust the size of the area being posterized for each pixel.

◆ Identical Values—if this option is enabled, changing one of the Width or Height controls will automatically change the other as well.

The effect of the CorelPHOTO-PAINT Pixelate filter is also referred to as "spatial posterization" by other applications.

Remove Spots

The Remove Spots filter will scan an image and look for small details which are markedly out of keeping with their surroundings. When it finds such details, it will attempt to fill them in with colors or gray levels interpolated from the surrounding area.

The Spot Size selector of the Remove Spots dialog box will allow you to specify how big a detail can be before the filter no longer considers it a spot, and hence will leave it alone. If you select the Large spots option for an image with a lot of fine details, some of the details you want to keep may up and vanish along with the spots you've called up the filter to dispense with.

Sharpen

The Sharpen filter will increase the contrast of an image by increasing the differences between adjacent pixels. Depending on the nature of your image, this may make it look sharper or just grainier—the latter effect often occurs on images which have been converted from 24-bit files down to 256-color pictures and back again.

The Sharpen filter control offers the following adjustments:

◆ Sharpen Amount—controls the degree to which your image will be sharpened.

◆ Wide Aperture—if you select this option, the Sharpen filter will tend to enhance the details of an image to a greater degree.

USING TRANSFORMS

The Transform item of the Edit menu offers the bitmapped equivalents of some of the tools in the CorelDRAW Transform menu. These functions will perform simple transformations on the spatial characteristics of all or part of an image. Unlike most of the filters discussed in the foregoing section, these features can be used with 256-color images.

The Flip Horizontal and Flip Vertical options of the Transform item will flip a picture into a mirror image of itself along the horizontal and vertical axes respectively. The Invert option will make an image into a negative of itself. This has the predictable effect for monochrome and gray-scale images—negative color images look very strange indeed.

The Outline option will trace the edges of details in your picture. This can look quite interesting in monochrome and gray-scale images. While this option will work when it's applied to color images, the results rarely look meaningful. If you've ever played with MacPaint on a Macintosh, you'll find that this option behaves like the MacPaint Trace Edges feature.

The Rotate 90° option does pretty much what you'd expect of it.

The Area option of the Transform item will allow you to perform a number of tasks, combining several in one action if you like. Specifically, you can:

The Undo function of Corel-PHOTO-PAINT will not undo the Rotate 90 Degrees function if it's applied to an entire image. The only way to undo this is to select Rotate 90 Degrees three more times.

◆ Flip horizontally and vertically.

◆ Resize an image by any percentage you like.

◆ Rotate by 90, 180, or 270 degrees.

◆ Deskew an image. This means rotating it by between one and three degrees, usually to compensate for a slight misalignment when it was scanned.

CHANGING THE DISPLAY

Unlike Corel-DRAW's images, bitmapped graphics have very finite limits to their detail. Zooming in on a bit-mapped graphic will make its individual pixels larger, but you won't see any detail that wasn't there in the normal view. Don't expect the zoom mode of Corel-PHOTO-PAINT to offer you the same flexibility as that of CorelDRAW.

The Display menu offers you functions to change the way Corel-PHOTO-PAINT displays an image while you're working on it. Depending on what you're doing at the moment, you might want to see your entire image or zoom in on part of it. CorelPHOTO-PAINT offers a variety of options to let you quickly arrive at the zoom and view you need.

To zoom in or out on a picture, select the Zoom item from the Display menu. A secondary menu will appear with a list of zoom factors. Select one that's appropriate.

The 100% (No Zoom) item of the Display menu will return your image to its default state. You can also invoke this function by hitting Ctrl-1.

Keep in mind that if you use the zoom facilities to make a picture twice as large on your screen, it will only affect what you see, not what's in the picture itself. The contents of your image will not be affected by anything you do with the Zoom menu.

The Zoom to Fit item of the Display menu will automatically choose one of the zoom factors available in the Zoom secondary menu so that your image will fill the entire CorelPHOTO-PAINT window. In fact, this will usually be an approximation—what this function really does is choose a zoom factor that will fill the available space as closely as possible without cropping any portion of your image.

Zooming in and out can also be handled with the zoom tool. This will be discussed in greater detail later in this chapter.

One important difference to keep in mind between the zooming facilities of CorelPHOTO-PAINT and that of CorelDRAW is that Corel-PHOTO-PAINT only allows you to zoom in and out by a number of predetermined factors. This is in keeping with the nature of bitmaps— zooming in by an arbitrary factor, as you can do under CorelDRAW, would usually leave you with a very ugly screen display.

There are two other useful functions of the Display menu that pertain to the way your image looks in the CorelPHOTO-PAINT workspace. The Full Screen item will make the most of your monitor by automatically maximizing CorelPHOTO-PAINT and hiding the menu bar and window title. You can still use the menus in this mode, but you might find them a little hard to locate. They can be called up from the keyboard using Alt key combinations, as follows:

- Alt-F—File menu
- Alt-E—Edit menu
- Alt-D—Display menu
- Alt-F—Font menu
- Alt-O—Options menu
- Alt-W—Windows menu
- Alt-H—Help menu

You can disable the Full Screen mode either though the Display menu or by hitting Ctrl-F, either one of which will reinstate the menu bar and window title of CorelPHOTO-PAINT.

Down in the lower-right corner of the CorelPHOTO-PAINT window, you'll find a button with two arrowheads in it if you have the help bar enabled. Clicking on this will toggle the Full Screen mode. See the section on Preferences later in this section for a discussion of enabling the help bar.

The Full Screen mode will prove useful if you're working with a large, complex graphic on a monitor with relatively small dimensions—640 by 480 pixels, for example. If you use a higher resolution monitor and a

With the Show Screen mode active, none of the menu or editing functions of Corel-PHOTO-PAINT will work until you hit Esc.

Windows driver, you'll probably find that the extra real estate the Full Screen mode provides you isn't worth the effort.

The Show Screen item of the Display menu will hide absolutely everything but the image you're working on under CorelPHOTO-PAINT. It exists so that you can use a screen-capture program to take a snapshot of just the image you're working on. This is a function you're unlikely to use all that often. Hitting the Esc key will return you to the normal CorelPHOTO-PAINT interface.

Managing Workboxes

CorelPHOTO-PAINT will maintain up to three small "workboxes," or floating windows. These contain the toolbox, the palette selector, and the brush width and shape selector. While it's usually possible to have them visible and just drag them out of your way, there will be times when you don't need them and would like them removed entirely. The Workboxes item of the Display menu will allow you to show or hide all or some of the workboxes.

When you select the Workboxes item, a secondary menu will appear to let you toggle the state of all the workboxes or of each individual one. You can also access these features with Ctrl key combinations, as follows:

The quickest way to hide a workbox is simply to double click in its system menu icon, the small box in the upper-left corner of each workbox window.

- ◆ Ctrl-A—Show or hide all the workboxes.
- ◆ Ctrl-W—Show or hide the brush width and shape workbox.
- ◆ Ctrl-P—Show or hide the palette workbox.
- ◆ Ctrl-T—Show or hide the toolbox.

Optimizing the Display

You might find the Optimize Display option of the Display menu useful, depending on the type of images you work with and the maximum number of colors your monitor can display. Specifically, if you attempt to display an image with more colors than your monitor can handle—a 24-bit image on a 256-color monitor, for example—this menu item will allow you to tell CorelPHOTO-PAINT how best to show you the image. Enabling this feature will cause it to use a higher quality display algorithm to approximate the extra colors. Disabling it will allow it to use a much simpler, but usually less attractive, approach to managing the display.

Predictably, the optimized display option may look better, but it will also cause CorelPHOTO-PAINT to slow down considerably. You might want to leave the display un-optimized if you find the speed reduction it entails noticeable, enabling the Optimize Display option only when you want to deal with fine color adjustments or details of the image you're working on.

SELECTING FONTS

The Font menu of CorelPHOTO-PAINT will allow you to select fonts in which to draw text with the text tool of the toolbox. While considerably more will be said about this facility when we come to discuss the text tool, you might want to familiarize yourself with the font resources of Corel-PHOTO-PAINT now.

Like CorelDRAW, CorelPHOTO-PAINT draws its fonts from the Windows TrueType font manager. Therefore, all the TrueType fonts that CorelDRAW installed in Windows will be available under Corel-PHOTO-PAINT.

The font selection process under CorelPHOTO-PAINT does not work quite as it does under CorelDRAW. You can select a font with the Select item of the Font menu. Each time you do, the name and point size of the font will be added to the Font menu, for a maximum of four selections at any one time. Adding a fifth selection will displace the first selection added to the list.

Figure 9.8 illustrates the Font dialog box.

You can choose a previously selected font by selecting it from the Font menu. You might also want to use the keyboard shortcuts for this function. Hitting Alt-F followed by the four numbers 1 through 4 will select the corresponding font from the Font menu.

Note that in choosing a font and point size with the Select item of the Font menu, you can also enable several effects, including italics and boldface, if the font in question supports them, as well as underlining and strikeout.

The relationship between the point size of type under CorelPHOTO-PAINT and the amount of space it occupies in an image may not be quite as apparent as it is under CorelDRAW. Keep in mind that a CorelDRAW image has absolute measurements, and type is drawn relative to these. A point can really be $1/72$ of an inch. A bitmap has no absolute dimensions—only dimensions

The Font dialog box

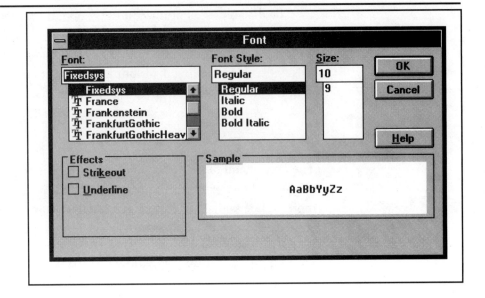

relative to whatever will print it. By default, CorelPHOTO-PAINT treats one point of type as two pixels of a bitmap. As such, if you set 100-point type in a 320 by 200 pixel bitmap, each uppercase letter should be about as tall as your image.

Font selection will become more relevant when we discuss the text tool later in this chapter.

DEFINING CORELPHOTO-PAINT'S OPTIONS

The Options menu of CorelPHOTO-PAINT offers you a number of ways to fine-tune the features of the software, and to change the artistic characteristics of its tools. In some cases, you'll find that it controls things which can also be dealt with in other ways. You can choose the one that works best for you.

Note that the Soft Brush Settings and Tile Pattern options will not be discussed herein. They relate to specific tools, and will be handled in the discussions of the tools in question.

Brush Style

The Brush Style item will allow you to control the size and shape of the brush you'll use for drawing and performing other graphic operations under CorelPHOTO-PAINT. These characteristics can also be controlled using the Width workbox, which also offers you access to the related dialog box.

Figure 9.9 illustrates the Select a Brush Style dialog box.

In drawing lines or applying effects to areas of an image under CorelPHOTO-PAINT, the shape of the brush you use will affect the appearance of your work. A round brush will behave as a pen would. A linear brush will make what you draw look sculptured and perhaps calligraphic, as the width of your lines will change with their angle.

The Set Size button on the Select a Brush Style dialog box will provide you with controls to adjust the size of a brush. Brushes can be up to 40 pixels across.

It's worth keeping in mind that the Cancel button of the Select a Brush Style dialog box will not cancel any changes you have made to the current brush size.

Color Tolerance

There are a number of operations in which CorelPHOTO-PAINT will look for one color and replace it with another. They'll be discussed in detail when we deal with the tools that invoke them. In practice, these functions don't work quite the way you might expect them to—or, at least, they shouldn't. In a 24-bit image you can have as many different colors as there are pixels in the picture. If you tell CorelPHOTO-PAINT to look for all the yellow pixels for a particular operation, what you really mean is all the pixels which are more or less yellow.

FIGURE 9.9:

The Select a Brush Style dialog box

The Color Comparison dialog box will allow you to specify the meaning of "more or less" in numerical terms, so that when CorelPHOTO-PAINT is looking for colors, it will know how far removed a color can be from the specified color. The fill and replace operations are affected by the settings in this dialog box.

The controls in this dialog box will allow you to set the range of the red, green and blue primary colors that define the spread of colors that CorelPHOTO-PAINT will accept when it's comparing colors. In practice, you will probably find that you have to experiment with this function a bit to fully understand it.

Gradient Type

The Gradient Type function will allow you to define how CorelPHOTO-PAINT draws gradients. A gradient is equivalent to a fountain fill under CorelDRAW. As we'll discuss when we come to the CorelPHOTO-PAINT tool section, you can apply gradient fills to any closed area of an image under CorelPHOTO-PAINT.

The Select a Gradient Effect dialog will allow you to select whether a gradient will be drawn horizontally, vertically, or radially. Under CorelPHOTO-PAINT, a radial gradient will be a series of concentric rectangles, rather than the ellipses generated in CorelDRAW.

The Brightness control will adjust the overall brightness of your gradient. If you increase its value, your gradient fills will become lighter.

Palette

The Palette item of the Options menu opens something of a can of worms under CorelPHOTO-PAINT, as it deals with one of the unkind realities of 24-bit color. In essence, a 24-bit image offers you more color choices than you'd probably like. The Palette function offers you some controls to help you manage them.

To begin with, there are 16,777,216 distinct colors available under CorelPHOTO-PAINT when you're working on a 24-bit color image. In order to set up a palette selector to allow you to use all these colors at once, you'd need a monitor about 159 feet high, and no doubt your own nuclear generating station to run it. Consequently, CorelPHOTO-PAINT's Palette workbox only shows you a limited selection of colors at any one time.

This can be likened to the palette selector at the bottom of the CorelDRAW window.

The Palette function of the Options menu offers you controls to help you better manage the Palette workbox. Specifically, it will let you define one color or a range of them to be displayed, so you can subsequently use them for drawing.

The All Colors option of the Palette item allows you to affect the overall color distribution of the colors in the Palette workbox. You can change the overall brightness and contrast, as well as the general color distribution. The example Palette workbox display in this dialog box will show you the effect of your choice.

The Color Picker function will allow you to select one color from your current palette and adjust its color. Color is defined as the percentage of red, green, and blue light involved in the color in question. If you have the Channel control set to Red—which is how it defaults—the slider in the center of the box will define the amount of red being used. The box to the left of it will define the amount of blue and green. Move the cross hair selector up to increase the amount of blue and right to increase the amount of green.

Changing the Channel control will change the functions of the two color-selection controls.

The Range of Colors option allows you to define the group of colors available in the Palette workbox. Chances are you'll want to adjust this fairly often if you're creating original art with CorelPHOTO-PAINT. This dialog box, in conjunction with the Load and Save features of the Palette function, will allow you to create and retrieve particular color palettes you find useful. For example, if you were painting an area of sky, you might want a palette that was predominantly light blue.

To use the Adjust Palette Color Range dialog box, do the following:

1. Select the start color of the range you want using the left mouse button.

2. Select the end color of the range with the right mouse button.

3. Click on the Build Range button.

Note that the number of colors involved in the range will be determined by the physical number of intervening tiles in the palette, not by the difference

> **NOTE** *When you make changes to a color using one of the palette options, your screen may look a bit peculiar for a few seconds as CorelPHOTO-PAINT recalculates its internal color palette for display. This is harmless, and things will return to normal as soon as it has worked out how to display your new colors.*

in the two colors you have selected. Thus, if you wanted to create a palette that was entirely shades of green, you would do the following:

There's a selection of well designed palettes provided with CorelPHOTO-PAINT. You'll find them in the \CORELDRW \PHOTOPNT \PALETTES directory.

1. Select the first color in the palette with the left mouse button.

2. Use the controls in the Start group to adjust this color to a suitable shade of green.

3. Select the last color with the right mouse button.

4. Use the controls in the End group to adjust this to a different shade of green.

5. Click on the Build Range button.

The huge scope of colors available when you're editing 24-bit images makes it desirable to have lots of dedicated palettes on tap.

You can load a palette previously saved to disk using the Open Palette option of the Palette function and save the current palette to a new palette file using the Save As Palette option. This will allow you to create palette files you can call for when you need a specific range of colors.

Setting Your Preferences

There are a few things about CorelPHOTO-PAINT which you can fine-tune to suit your taste. These are adjustable through the Preferences item of the Options menu. However, you'll probably find that most of the application defaults have been pretty well chosen.

The At Startup control allows you to define what will appear when CorelPHOTO-PAINT first boots up. The default is to have the File Open dialog box appear, on the assumption that you'll probably want to get busy and work on an image. If you will normally be starting with a blank image, you might want to select New instead. If you're not sure, select Nothing, and then use the appropriate item of the File menu once CorelPHOTO-PAINT gets going. You can also select the About box—you probably won't want to do this, as most users get tired of the exploding camera graphic fairly quickly.

The Units item will allow you to choose the units in which you want CorelPHOTO-PAINT to display measurements. The default is pixels, which is arguably the most practical choice for an application that measures everything this way internally. Choosing a finite unit of measure, such as inches, is a bit artificial, as there is no fixed number of pixels in an inch. Doing so will probably complicate your use of CorelPHOTO-PAINT later on.

If you enable the Keep Thumbnail Files option, every time Corel-PHOTO-PAINT saves a file, it will write a second file with the extension THB to hold a very small version of the real image. These files serve the same function as the thumbnail previews in CorelDRAW's CDR files. They allow the CorelPHOTO-PAINT functions that open image files to more rapidly show you a small version of the contents of the file you're interested in, prior to actually opening it.

There are a few catches to the THB files. They take up space, especially if you have a lot of them around, and you might have to take some care not to confuse them. For example, if you have two files in the same subdirectory called PICTURE.PCX and PICTURE.TIF, both of which are worked on by CorelPHOTO-PAINT, the resulting PICTURE.THB will reflect the contents of the most recently saved file. It will thus be incorrect half the time.

The Monitor Gamma option will allow you to change how bright images in CorelPHOTO-PAINT will be displayed. This will compensate for the inherent brightness of your monitor. Note that this control will not affect the images you edit under CorelPHOTO-PAINT—it only controls how they're displayed.

The correct gamma value for your monitor can be set by loading the file GAMMA.PCX from \CORELDRW\PHOTOPNT\SAMPLES and adjusting the Monitor Gamma control. This image consists of twelve large boxes with twelve smaller boxes within them. The optimum gamma setting is when the twelve smaller boxes vanish, or as many of them vanish as possible. After you have changed the gamma value, click on Screen Preview to see the effect of the change.

You might want to enable the VGA Palette option if you have a 16-color Windows screen driver installed—such as the standard 16-color VGA driver that Windows defaults to when you first install it for a VGA system—and you will be using CorelPHOTO-PAINT to edit gray-scale images. Not all 16-color drivers will get along with this mode—if the compatibility test fails or misbehaves, click on Cancel.

The VGA Palette option can crash Windows in some cases—make sure there's nothing running with an unsaved document when you try this feature.

The Memory Options dialog box will allow you to tell CorelPHOTO-PAINT how to deal with situations in which it needs more memory than Windows is prepared to give it. In such circumstances, it can resort to using "virtual" memory if you enable this option. Virtual memory means using a big disk file and pretending it's memory. This is very slow compared to real memory, but it's arguably better than CorelPHOTO-PAINT simply refusing to work altogether.

You should limit the amount of virtual memory CorelPHOTO-PAINT can allocate—it's not advisable to let it shanghai every free byte on your hard drive, for example, lest you find yourself in a situation where there's no room to save the file that CorelPHOTO-PAINT has stored in virtual memory.

If you have a RAM disk set up in your system, consider using this as your virtual memory drive.

Note that you can define up to four drives for virtual memory, with each one separated by a semicolon. For example, here's how I have this string set up:

D:\;C:\;E:\;I:\

Some forethought will help you make the best use of your available drive space as virtual memory. On my system, Drive D is a RAM drive. It's the fastest place to store things, so it will be used first. If there isn't enough room on the RAM drive, CorelPHOTO-PAINT will try the hard drive on Drive C. The next choice is Drive E, which is a removable hard drive cartridge. This is large, but pretty slow—it's a drive of almost last resort. Drive I is actually another system on the network. It has lots of free space, but network access is fairly slow and tying up drive space on someone else's computer, however temporarily, has been known to start medium-size guerrilla wars.

If you're contemplating using a networked drive as virtual memory—especially if it's the server of a large network—make sure the network's administrator knows about your plans.

The Min KB and Max KB fields of the Memory Options dialog box will allow you to tell CorelPHOTO-PAINT how much of Windows' memory it can allocate for itself. These values are in kilobytes—in each case,

Allowing Corel-PHOTO-PAINT to allocate huge tracts of memory for itself may slow down other Windows applications that are running concurrently.

the minimum value is 64. If you use a large Max KB value, CorelPHOTO-PAINT will have less cause to resort to virtual memory, and will thus run quicker. This assumes that you actually have enough memory in your system to allow CorelPHOTO-PAINT to allocate as much of it as you've assigned.

ARRANGING WINDOWS

The Window menu of CorelPHOTO-PAINT will allow you to arrange the placement of multiple-image windows in the main CorelPHOTO-PAINT window if you have more than one picture open at a time. The Cascade item will attempt to arrange your pictures such that each one is slightly below and to the right of the underlying one. The Tile item will attempt to arrange them so that none of them overlap—or so that each one overlaps by the same amount, if space is tight.

The Cascade item is useful of you have several large image windows open, as it will make sure that there's always part of each one visible to click in, should you want to bring it forward. The Tile item is preferable if you'll be working on several small images—bringing a window forward under CorelPHOTO-PAINT can be fairly time-consuming, and having all the windows visible at once will reduce the time it takes to move from image to image.

Every image you have open will live in a window with a Minimize and Maximize button. As with Windows applications under the Program Manager, clicking the Minimize button will compact the window down to an icon in the lower-left corner of the CorelPHOTO-PAINT window. There's a complete discussion of Minimize and Maximize buttons in Appendix A of this book.

The Arrange Icons item of the Window menu will tidy up all the currently minimized icons in CorelPHOTO-PAINT's main window, much as the Arrange Icons item of the Windows Program Manager will clean up the icons in a window.

The Duplicate item of the Window menu will create a new window with a copy of the current foremost image. Duplicated images are not new pictures, but additional windows on the same drawing. This allows you to have multiple views of the same picture available at once. You can, therefore, move from window to window, working on different parts of the same picture, or have a normal and a zoomed-in view. The remaining items in the

Clicking on a minimized image icon under CorelPHOTO-PAINT will cause it to "assert" its color palette in the CorelPHOTO-PAINT window. Nothing terribly bad will happen, save that if you have an image window visible when you do it, its colors may become very peculiar until you click in it again. Mostly, it's just time-consuming. Use the Arrange Icons function to tidy up your CorelPHOTO-PAINT workspace and avoid this.

Window menu of CorelPHOTO-PAINT will be the names of whatever files you have open at the moment. Selecting one will bring the corresponding image forward just as if you'd clicked in it.

THE PALETTE WORKBOX

Most of what you can do with the palette has been discussed previously, in dealing with the Palette item of the Options menu. In drawing, the Palette workbox is useful for selecting the three current drawing colors—the primary, secondary, and background colors. The currently selected colors can be seen in the corresponding areas of the Palette workbox, as shown in Figure 9.10.

To select the primary color, click on a colored tile in the Palette workbox with the left button of your mouse. To select the secondary color, click on a colored tile with the right button of your mouse. To select the background color, hold down the Shift key and click on a colored tile with the left button of your mouse. You can change these selections as often as you like.

The uses of these colors will be discussed as they come up in the next section of this chapter.

If you're working on a 256-color image, the colors in the Palette workbox represent all the available colors. In a 24-bit picture, they represent 256 out of about sixteen-million—the Palette item of the Options menu can be used to change the colors.

The large button at the right of the Palette workbox can be used to "fold" the Palette workbox. Clicking it once will hide the color tiles of the Palette workbox, leaving only the current color selection indicator. Clicking it again will return the Palette workbox to its normal state.

Changing one of the colors this way for a 256- color image will cause all instances of the affected color in the image to change as well. This cannot be undone.

FIGURE 9.10:

The selected colors in the Palette workbox

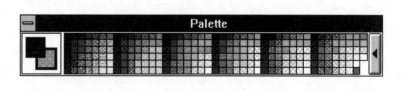

If you double click on one of the colored tiles in the Palette workbox, a dialog box will appear to allow you to change the color you've selected.

THE WIDTH WORKBOX

The Width workbox only does two things, and so is very easy to understand. It sets the line width and the brush shape. The line width, as handled by the rightmost control, can range from zero pixels though 40 pixels. The line width will determine the thickness of lines created by the CorelPHOTO-PAINT drawing tools.

You might wonder about the usefulness of a zero-pixel line. There are some tools which draw filled shapes, such as a round corner rectangle drawn in the primary color and filled with the secondary color. If you don't want such a shape outlined at all, set the Width control to zero.

The brush shape is set by clicking on the brush shape icon at the left side of the Width workbox. A dialog box will appear, allowing you to choose among the seven available brush shapes.

The round brush draws normal lines. The remaining brush shapes will draw calligraphic lines to some extent, just as oblong pen shapes do under CorelDRAW. Consider that a tall, skinny vertical brush drawing a 10-pixel line will be 10 pixels wide when it's moving horizontally but only one pixel wide when it's moving vertically.

The currently selected brush shape will be indicated by the Width workbox's brush icon.

THE TOOLBOX

Double clicking on any tool icon with the right mouse button will call up Windows help for that tool.

While it's important to be familiar with CorelPHOTO-PAINT menus, you'll probably find that the toolbox gets used a great deal more. It selects the drawing modes of CorelPHOTO-PAINT, as well as provides you with quick access to a number of commonly used features, such as zooming in and out.

If the toolbox is not visible, you can make it visible by using the Workboxes item of the Display menu, or hitting Ctrl-T.

Figure 9.11 illustrates the tools available under CorelPHOTO-PAINT and what they do.

Your CorelPHOTO-PAINT toolbox may not look quite like the ones in Figure 9.11. If you click on the system menu icon in the upper-left corner of the toolbox window, you'll find that it includes an item called Layout. Select Layout and a dialog box will appear, offering you a variety of options to define the way the toolbox will look.

The CorelPHOTO-PAINT toolbox may be grouped or ungrouped. The ungrouped mode will allow you to see all the available tools, at the expense of a somewhat larger toolbox. The grouped mode will reduce the number of tool icons, but some of the remaining ones will have sprouted triangular sections in their respective lower-right corners. Clicking on one of these sections will call up a flyout menu similar to the ones used in CorelDRAW. These flyout menus will let you change the current function of the tool in question.

The tools with flyout menus—the grouped tools—are set up so that several similar functions are grouped together. For example, CorelPHOTO-PAINT allows you to draw four basic types of filled objects—rectangles, round corner rectangles, ellipses, and polygons. In grouped mode, only one of these will appear in the toolbox. The one that is currently visible can be selected by using the flyout menu for this tool group.

Many of the tools can be constrained to move or draw things horizontally or vertically by holding down the Shift key. By default, this will

If you're using an 800 by 600 pixel screen driver, try setting up the toolbox in its ungrouped mode with three columns. This will allow you to position it along the right side of your screen. If it's positioned in the upper-right corner, the palette workbox fits neatly below it, leaving lots of room to place pictures.

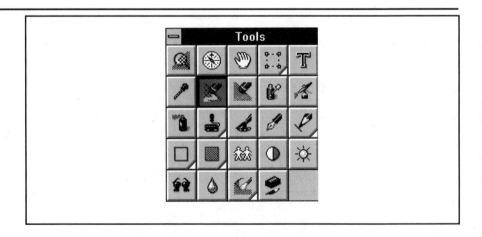

FIGURE 9.11:
The CorelPHOTO-PAINT tools

constrain movement horizontally. Hit the Shift key to toggle between horizontal and vertical constraint.

The toolbox Layout menu also allows you to define the number of rows and columns of the toolbox window.

As a rule, the toolbox is a bit daunting in its ungrouped mode, but a lot easier to work with. If you're using a 640 by 480 pixel screen driver, you'll probably find that it's a bit unwieldy in this form—it occupies too much of the screen, and you'll probably want to use it grouped.

TOOLS THAT CHANGE THE DISPLAY

One of the most useful tools in moving around a picture under CorelPHOTO-PAINT is the zoom tool. It allows you to magnify portions of your image to deal with them in greater detail. Once you've selected the zoom tool, clicking in your image with the left button of your mouse will zoom in and clicking with the right button will zoom out. Each zoom will be by a factor of two.

If you zoom in to 1600 percent—maximum zoom—a grid will be displayed over your image to help you distinguish the individual pixels. At this zoom factor, your picture will be unrecognizable.

The CorelPHOTO-PAINT zoom tool works very differently from the one in CorelDRAW. You can't select an area under CorelPHOTO-PAINT and zoom in on it, as that's not really the way bitmaps work. This may take some getting used to.

You can zoom in pretty tightly on an image under CorelPHOTO-PAINT—so much so that its individual pixels will become exceedingly noticeable.

If you zoom out past the default one-to-one zoom, CorelPHOTO-PAINT will actually shrink the window your image resides in to correspond to the size of the image. There's a minor inconvenience in this, as the window will not automatically regrow if you zoom in again. You'll have to resize it by hand.

If you'll be working zoomed-in on an image, duplicate it and zoom in on the duplicate. Use the original image for navigation, clicking on the area you want to work in with the locator tool.

Having zoomed in or out, you can quickly return to the standard one-to-one view by double clicking on the zoom tool icon in the toolbox or by hitting Ctrl-1.

If you use the Duplicate item of the Window menu to create multiple views of an image—possibly with different zooms as well—the locator tool will help you find portions of a picture. Select the locator tool and click on any image window with one or more duplicates. All the duplicated images will adjust themselves to show you the same area.

The hand tool will let you move around quickly in an image that's too big to fit in its window. Select the hand tool and click and drag in the image window you want to adjust. The scroll bars will move accordingly, and your image will be redrawn when you release your mouse button.

The hand tool is an alternative to using the scroll bars to position an image in its window.

TOOLS THAT SELECT AREAS

Selecting areas under CorelPHOTO-PAINT is analogous to selecting objects or groups of objects under CorelDRAW, save that everything in a selected area will be selected under CorelPHOTO-PAINT, even if part of it seems to extend past the selection box. Likewise, nothing outside a selection box will be selected, even if this means that part of it is selected and part of it isn't. Keep in mind that there are no objects in CorelPHOTO-PAINT—just a matrix of pixels, none of which knows anything much about the others.

You can select areas to move them, copy them, cut and paste them, and to modify their contents.

If you have your toolbox grouped, all the selection tools will be in one group, and only one will be visible at a time.

The simplest selection tool is the *selection box,* which behaves just like the CorelDRAW pick tool. It can be used to select rectangular areas. Click on this tool and drag a selection box over the area of your drawing that you want to select.

The lasso tool allows you to select irregular areas. If you click on this tool, you'll be able to draw an outline around any portion of your image to select it. The part of the lasso cursor that draws is the end of the rope. The Lasso takes a considerable degree of mouse coordination to use well.

The scissors tool allows you select a polygon-shaped area. This means that you can define the selection area as any number of straight lines. Click on the Scissors tool and click on points between which you want selector lines to appear. Double click on the final point to close the polygon and select the image section within. A scissors tool polygon can include up to 200 lines.

The magic wand tool—like all good magic—is the most mysterious and unpredictable selection tool. You can use it to select an area in which all the adjacent pixels are of a similar color. For example, if you had a picture of a red parrot against a green jungle, clicking anywhere on the parrot with the magic wand tool would select the entire parrot, more or less as if you had laboriously traced around it with the lasso tool.

The Color Tolerance item of the Options menu can be used to define how similar colors must be to be included in a magic-wand selection.

Selection Functions

In selecting an area with the selection box tool, if you hold down the Shift key, the selection box will be constrained to be a perfect square. If you hold down the Shift key while using the scissors tool, the lines of the polygon it creates will be constrained to be horizontal, vertical, or diagonal.

Once you have selected an area, a marquee or "gadget box" will appear around it, similar to the selection box of CorelDRAW. If you grab and drag one of the small rectangles at the corners of a gadget box, the selected area within it will be resized. Holding down the Shift key will keep the resizing proportional.

Once you have selected a portion of an image using one of the selection tools, you can move it around the image window you're working with. When your mouse cursor is within the gadget box, it will turn into a hand. Click and drag the fragment to its new location.

Dragging a selected fragment will normally cause the area formerly occupied by it to be filled with the current background color—white, by default. If you hold down the Shift key while dragging a fragment, the original fragment will stay in place and a copy will move. Note that the Shift key also constrains the movement of a selected fragment. As soon as your fragment has moved slightly, release the Shift key to regain full control of it.

If you hold down the Ctrl key while you're moving a fragment, a trail of images will remain behind it. This can produce some startling effects.

You can also "nudge" a selected fragment one pixel at a time using the cursor movement arrow keys.

Selected fragments can be manipulated using any of the functions of the Edit menu which would otherwise manipulate an entire image. You can flip and rotate fragments and apply filters to them. This will allow you, for example, to sharpen or add noise to selected areas of an image.

 *Resizing a bitmap fragment arbitrarily may introduce abberations into the picture.*

 Double click on the selection box or lasso tool icons to select your entire image. Double click on the magic wand tool icon to call up the Color Tolerance box.

ADDING TEXT TO AN IMAGE

The text functions of CorelPHOTO-PAINT have been discussed in conjunction with the Font menu earlier in this chapter. Adding text to an image is relatively simple. Select the text tool from the CorelPHOTO-PAINT toolbox. A dialog box will appear to allow you to enter text. When you click on OK, the text you've entered will be drawn in your image. The font characteristics will be whatever you have defined using the Font menu. Text is always drawn using the secondary palette color.

Once text has been drawn on your screen, you can move it around by grabbing the gadget box it lives in. If you resize the gadget box, the text will remain the same size, but it will repour to suit the new dimensions of the box it lives in. CorelPHOTO-PAINT will always pour your text to automatically wrap its lines.

DRAWING LINES

NOTE NOTE *Soft brushes are only available in the 24-bit and gray-scale modes under CorelPHOTO-PAINT.*

There are four tools to deal with simple line drawing—the freehand brush tool, the pen tool, the line tool, and the curve tool. The freehand brush tool will allow you to draw freehand lines with a soft brush—we'll discuss soft brushes in a moment. The pen tool will allow you to draw lines using a solid color. The two line tools handle drawing straight lines and Bézier curves, just like the two modes of the pencil tool under CorelDRAW.

If your toolbox is grouped, the two line tools will be grouped together, and only one will be visible at a time.

The Paintbrush tool is very useful if you want to draw photo-realistic objects, in that its lines are not hard objects of a single color. Depending on how you set up the Paintbrush tool, it will draw lines with edges that blend into the surrounding image.

To adjust the characteristics of the Paintbrush tool, either select the Soft Brush Settings item of the Option menu or double click on the Paintbrush tool icon. A dialog box will appear with the following controls:

◆ The Edge control will determine whether the Paintbrush tool will draw soft or hard lines.

◆ The setting of the Density control will determine the thickness of each stroke of the Paintbrush tool. It can range from −100 for very fine strokes to 100 for very bold strokes.

◆ The Transparency control will allow you to adjust how much the object over which you paint will show through your brush strokes. If this control is set to zero, your brush strokes will be completely opaque—like oil paint. If it's set to 100, they'll be completely transparent, which is a lot like painting with clear water. At intermediate values, they'll be partially transparent.

◆ The Fade Out control will cause the density of a brush stroke to diminish as it proceeds. If this control is set to something other than zero, your brush strokes will disappear as you drag the Paintbrush cursor. This is very much like what happens when you use a real Paintbrush and the paint on it is gradually exhausted.

◆ The Spacing control adjusts the space between brush strokes. A value of zero will give you reasonable brush control. A value of one will give you superb brush control, but the brush will be very, very slow. Values above one will increase the space between strokes. This is an interesting effect for some sorts of drawings, but it will make it impossible to draw continuous lines.

The freehand brush tool will draw in the primary color if you draw with the left mouse button and in the secondary color if you draw with the right mouse button. It will draw using the line width and brush shape defined by the Width workbox. Using something other than a round brush combined with a fairly high width value will allow you to draw calligraphic lines of varying width, depending on their angle. This effect can be reminiscent of the effect of ink brushes, as used in Japanese calligraphy.

Holding down the Shift key while using the freehand brush tool will constrain the cursor.

The pen tool behaves like the freehand brush tool in many respects, except that it always draws hard lines, with no transparency or softness. It's the tool to use if you want to change a few pixels. In the latter case, you would zoom in on the pixels you want to change and click on each one using the pen tool.

The pen tool always draws in the primary color using the current brush shape and size. Holding down the Shift key will constrain its movement either horizontally or vertically.

The line tool will allow you to draw straight lines using the current primary color. Note that it doesn't behave quite like the pen tool under CorelDRAW. Having selected the line tool, you should click and hold where

The freehand brush tool performs numerous internal calculations for each brush stroke it applies to an image. If you move your mouse cursor quickly, the brush strokes will be placed erratically, as there will be a pause between them as the tool does its internal figuring. Move the freehand brush cursor slowly to achieve the most attractive lines.

Clicking in your image area with the right mouse button when you have the pen tool selected will cause the primary color to change to whatever color is under the pen cursor at the time.

you want your line to start and drag the mouse cursor to where you want it to end.

The line tool will draw lines at the width set by the Width workbox, and using the current brush shape.

Holding down the Shift key while you draw lines will constrain them to be either horizontal, vertical, or diagonal.

You can hit the Esc key while you are part way through drawing a line to make the line vanish, should you want to start again.

After you've drawn one line, if you click and hold at another location in your image area with the right mouse button, a new line will appear from the end of the first line to the line tool cursor. You can drag the cursor to position the line. In this way, you can add as many joined lines as you like.

If you hold down the Ctrl key when you use this feature, the additional lines will start at the beginning point of the first line, rather than the end. This is useful, for example, to draw multiple radial lines emerging from a central point.

The curve tool allows you to place smooth Bézier curves in an image. It works like a combination of the CorelPHOTO-PAINT line tool and the CorelDRAW pencil tool in its Bézier curve mode. To use it, click where you'd like the curve to start and drag a line to where you want it to end. A line with a box at each end and two circles along its length will appear. The circles are Bézier curve handles, and behave just as these handles would under Corel-DRAW. Grab the handles to manipulate the line.

Note that the line shape is determined by the relative position of the handles to the end points. If you drag the square line-end markers, the line will also bend.

Click anywhere else to complete the line—it will be redrawn in the current primary color at the current line width. The curve tool does not use the current brush shape—all its lines are drawn using a round brush.

To draw multiple connected curves:

1. Draw the first curve and then click and hold the right mouse button to complete it. This will cause the first curve to be drawn and a new curve to appear from the end of the first one to the location of your mouse cursor.

2. Manipulate this curve as before.

3. Click and hold using the right mouse button to add a third curve, and so on.

As with the line tool, holding down the Ctrl key when you click the right mouse button will cause the subsequent curves to begin at the start point of the initial line, rather than the end point.

DRAWING SIMPLE SHAPES

The hollow and filled shape tools can draw rectangles, round corner rectangles, ellipses, and polygons. If your toolbox is grouped, only one hollow tool and one filled tool will be visible.

Shapes are always drawn in the current primary color and filled shapes are filled with the current secondary color.

To draw a rectangle, round-cornered rectangle, or ellipse, select the appropriate tool from the CorelPHOTO-PAINT toolbox and drag the mouse cursor over the area where you want the shape to appear. Note that ellipses behave a bit differently under CorelPHOTO-PAINT than they do in Corel-DRAW. The point where you first click your mouse will become the center of the ellipse; dragging your mouse out from this point will cause the ellipse to expand.

If you hold down the Shift key while dragging to form a rectangle, round-corner rectangle, or ellipse, your shape will be constrained to be a perfect square or circle.

The polygon tools behave like the scissors tool discussed earlier, except they draw shapes, rather than select areas. To draw a polygon, click where you want the first line to start and then click repeatedly to place additional line segments in your image area. Double click to close the polygon. If you hold down the Shift key while drawing a polygon, its lines will be constrained to be horizontal, vertical, or diagonal. A polygon can have up to 200 sides.

Shapes are drawn using the current line width, as set by the Width control workbox.

If you draw an ellipse with the left mouse button, it will behave normally. Afterward, drawing subsequent ellipses with the right mouse button will cause the ellipses to be drawn using the center point of the first ellipse. This makes it easy to draw concentric ellipses.

While you're free to choose for yourself, many designers regard round-corner rectangles used to frame images or hold text as being unprofessional.

If you're using a display card with an odd aspect ratio—EGA cards and some full screen desktop publishing monitors may do this, as will some VGA monitors if you adjust them incorrectly—ostensibly "perfect" squares and circles may not look right. They are being drawn correctly, however.

ERASING

 One common use of the eraser tool is to erase around part of an image. Selecting the vertical brush shape and zooming in makes doing this pretty easy.

The eraser tool allows you to erase areas of an image to the current background color. In fact, what the eraser tool really does is serve as a species of pen tool that can only draw in the background color. It will erase using the currently selected brush shape.

If you double click on the eraser tool, your entire image will be erased to the current background color. You should send your mouse scurrying to the Undo option of the Edit menu if this happens accidentally.

CHANGING COLORS

The color replacer tool has an icon which looks a lot like the eraser tool. It provides you with a brush that will replace any pixels of the current primary color with the secondary color. In a 24-bit or gray-scale image, it will in fact replace colors which are more or less like the primary color, with the exact degree of "more or less" being set using the Color Tolerance item of the Options menu.

To use the color replacer:

1. Set the primary color to the one you want to replace.

2. Set the secondary color to the one you want to replace it with.

3. Set the brush width and shape.

4. Select the color replacer tool.

5. Click and drag over the area you want to replace.

The color replacer can be constrained by holding down the Shift key.

Double clicking on the color replacer tool will replace all the instances of the primary color in your entire image with the secondary color.

The eyedropper tool can be very handy in conjunction with the color replacer tool, as well as for several other functions. If you select it and click in your image with the left mouse button, the current primary color will be set to the color of the pixel under the eyedropper tool. Clicking with right button will change the secondary color. Clicking with the left button while the Shift key is held down will set the current background color. If you think of your image as being liquid, the eyedropper can be thought of as sucking up a bit of paint and squirting it out in the appropriate Palette workbox color selector.

If you're working on a 24-bit image, using the eyedropper tool to select a new color will cause the new color to replace the nearest color in the current palette.

FILLING AREAS

The fill tools of a bitmapped paint package like CorelPHOTO-PAINT behave in a fundamentally different way from fills under CorelDRAW. Filling in CorelPHOTO-PAINT is analogous to pouring liquid paint into a container. If the container is closed, the paint will remain contained within it. If it has any leaks, you'll spend the next few hours cleaning up paint.

Things happen more rapidly under CorelPHOTO-PAINT, but the results can look similar to a paint spill.

There are three fill tools, all with similar paint-roller icons. The basic paint roller tool will fill using the current primary color. The pattern paint roller tool will fill using the current tile fill. The gradient flood fill paint roller will fill using a gradient, similar to a CorelDRAW fountain fill. If your toolbox is grouped, these three tools will be grouped together and only one will be visible at a time.

Figure 9.12 illustrates examples of these types of fills.

The first and perhaps the most important thing to know about using the fill tools is that it only takes one pixel to form a leak. If you attempt to fill an area with even one pixel missing from its enclosure, the fill will escape. In this case, use the Undo function of the Edit menu, plug the leak, and try again.

The paint roller tools each have a drop of paint dangling from their cursors. This is where the fill originates—when you click to begin filling, it's this point that must reside within the enclosed area where the fill is to appear.

FIGURE 9.12:

Examples of solid (left), tiled (middle), and gradient (right) fills

A flood fill is a "recursive" function, which means that each pixel it encounters before returning to the initial pixel requires a bit of memory to be tied up temporarily. It's possible that running CorelPHOTO-PAINT on a system with very little memory and attempting to fill a very complex area may exhaust the available memory, preventing the fill tool from completely filling the area. In this case, you'll have to click in the unfilled part to carry on.

The fill functions perform what's called a "bucket" or "flood" fill—alluding to the idea of paint being poured from a bucket and flooding a closed area. What really happens within CorelPHOTO-PAINT is as follows:

1. CorelPHOTO-PAINT looks at the pixel under the dangling paint drop of the flood fill paint roller cursor.

2. It looks at the pixel beside it. If it's the same color as the original pixel, it replaces this pixel with the fill color.

3. It looks at the pixel beside the second pixel, and performs the same function.

4. It keeps doing this until it encounters a pixel that's not the same color as the original pixel, at which point it stops, returns to the original pixel and tries again in a different direction.

5. When it can no longer find a direction to try, the fill is complete.

In the case of 24-bit images, CorelPHOTO-PAINT's definition of a pixel color which is different from the initial pixel will be determined by the settings in the Color Pattern Tolerance dialog box. Setting the color tolerance higher will make it less likely for the fill function to decide that a pixel is unlike the source pixel, and hence to stop filling.

The tile pattern paint roller tool will fill an area with tiles. The current tile can be selected using the Tile Pattern item of the Options menu.

In fact, tiles are simply PCX files. You can create your own tiles by selecting a reasonably small area of an image and then using the Copy To item of the Edit menu to save the selected fragment to a new PCX file. You might want to keep any new tiles you create in the \CORELDRW\ PHOTOPNT\ directory, along with the tiles that come with Corel-PHOTO-PAINT.

Using fragments of scanned images as tiles can create startling images, as in Figure 9.13.

Note that when the tile pattern paint roller tool is selected, the usual selected color tiles of the Palette workbox will be replaced by the currently selected tile.

Double clicking on any of the flood fill paint roller tools will call up the Color Tolerance dialog box.

The gradient paint roller tool will fill an area with a fountain that ranges from the current secondary color to the background color. This can be used to make formerly flat objects look like they have natural shading.

A scanned image which has been filled using a tile fragment cut from a different scanned image

The direction of the gradient can be set using the Gradient Type item on the Options menu.

The gradient paint roller tool can be used—in theory—on 256-color images, but the results will almost always be dreadful. It's at its best working with 24-bit images and gray-scale pictures. It can produce the most convincing gradients if the secondary and background colors are both of the same hue but of different intensities. A gradient of light blue to dark blue would look better than a gradient of light blue to dark green. Actually, almost anything would look better than a gradient involving blue and green, except perhaps one involving black and neon purple.

When the gradient paint roller is selected, the usual selected color tiles of the Palette workbox will be replaced by an example of what the current gradient would look like. This will have far fewer bands and, hence, look a lot coarser than the gradient would look in reality.

There's a trick to using gradients to make drawn objects look real. Always keep in mind where the imaginary light source is for your drawing, and use gradient fills so that the light parts of the fills are in those areas which would be most brightly illuminated.

FIXING MISTAKES

The Undo function of the Edit menu has been discussed previously—selecting it will reverse the most recent operation you've performed. The local undo tool allows you to apply this feature selectively.

The Undo function actually works by keeping two copies of your current image in memory—the one you're working on and one which reflects the one you're working on prior to your most recent change. Selecting Undo from the Edit menu will copy the latter image over the former image, effectively wiping out your most recent change.

Note that when you change tools, the current image is automatically copied to the backup image, making it impossible to undo your previous action. Many of the CorelPHOTO-PAINT tools allow you to call up dialog boxes by double clicking on them. While this is handy, it will make your most recent operation permanent. Each of these dialogs is also available through the CorelPHOTO-PAINT menus—accessing them as menu items will not disable the Undo function.

The local undo tool is a brush with peculiar properties. It does not draw in a color; rather, any place it draws will have the current image replaced with the backup image. In effect, then, any place it draws will be undone.

The local undo tool will undo using the current line width and brush shape, as set by the Width workbox. Zooming in a few steps prior to using the local undo tool can make it a bit easier to control.

Double clicking on the local undo tool will invoke the global Undo feature—that is, it's equivalent to selecting the Undo item from the Edit menu. Once you've done this, local undo will no longer be active until you change something else in your image.

Aside from fixing mistakes, the local undo tool will allow you to selectively undo parts of a larger effect. For example, you could apply a filter to all or a large area of an image and then use the local undo tool to restore selected areas back to their previous appearance.

Holding down the Shift key will constrain the local undo tool to move either horizontally or vertically.

As an aside, most of the icons used by CorelPHOTO-PAINT's toolbox are fairly intuitive. The little bottle in the local undo icon may not be, especially if you haven't used a typewriter since you got your computer. It's a bottle of correction fluid, the white fluid that typists use to correct mistakes.

SPRAYING PAINT

Not using an air brush is one of the few things that's truly unfortunate about handling graphics in software. Air brushes are unspeakably fun, even if using one involves a noisy compressor, a hose that lives to get in your way and the fairly real possibility for spraying parts of yourself with ink. CorelPHOTO-PAINT includes two tools which will allow you to spray virtual paint—the spraycan tool and the air brush tool.

Double clicking on the spraycan icon will call up the brush Shape dialog box.

The spraycan tool is the simpler of the two. Not surprisingly, it simulates the artistic effect of running down to Sears, buying a can of spray paint, and decorating a wall. Specifically, the spraycan tool will paint a random pattern of dots, such that the dots will all fall within an area defined by the currently selected brush and line width. In other words, it departs from a traditional spray can in that it does not necessarily have a round spray. If you're artistic about graffiti, you can set up the spraycan tool to have a calligraphic brush.

The minimum spray width is three pixels.

The spraycan tool will spray in the current primary color if you spray with the left mouse button held down and with the current secondary color if you spray with the right mouse button held down.

Double clicking on the airbrush icon will call up the Soft Brush Settings dialog box.

The spraycan tool is useful when you want to create a fairly crude-looking spray. The airbrush tool is a better choice if you want a more refined spray. It can be a soft brush, depending on the Change Airbrush Settings dialog box of the Options menu.

The airbrush tool will paint in the current primary color if you hold down the left mouse button and in the current secondary color if you hold down the right mouse button. Holding down the Shift key will constrain it to move horizontally or vertically. As with a real airbrush, the paint will get deeper the longer the brush remains in one place or the more times you pass over the same area.

As with the soft-brush functions of the Paintbrush tool, you'll get the best results from the air brush if you move it fairly slowly.

CLONING IMAGES

The last of the painting tools is also the most remarkable. While the clone tool will take some practice to use well, it has the potential to create images which could never be duplicated using conventional optical photographic techniques. It allows you to paint using another image as a soft brush.

The clone tool has two modes—capture and paint. The capture mode is invoked by the right mouse button. Having set the capture of an image with the clone tool, you can paint it somewhere else with the left mouse button. "Somewhere else" can be in another image.

Figure 9.14 illustrates the workings of the clone tool.

To clone an image, click at the center point of the image area you want to clone using the right mouse button. Using the left mouse button, begin painting where you want the cloned image to be replicated. The place where you initially click with the left mouse button will correspond to the center of the source image, as defined by the right mouse button. As you move the clone cursor, the source image will be copied into the destination image like a sort of exceedingly intelligent paint.

The clone cursor brush will be defined by the current brush as set in the Width workbox. The clone tool uses a soft brush—you can think of it as an air brush. If you have the Change Soft Brush Settings dialog box set up for a soft brush, it will tend to feather your source image into the destination area.

FIGURE 9.14:

The clone tool in action. The capture mode picked up the first image and the paint mode applied it to the second image.

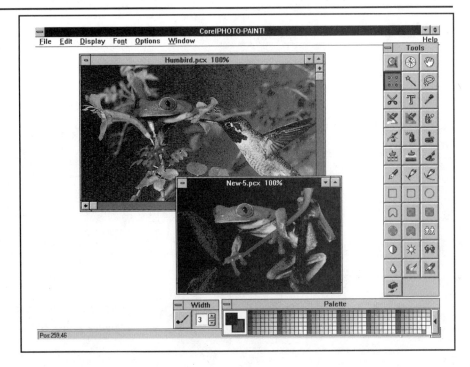

You can constrain the clone cursor brush to move horizontally or vertically by holding down the Shift key.

The clone tool has some amazing potential—plan to experiment with it to get a good feel for what it's capable of.

RETOUCHING SCANNED PHOTOGRAPHS

One of the really handy things about CorelPHOTO-PAINT is that it allows you to effectively retouch scanned images—both to overcome the effects of scanning and to improve on your original images. You can do some pretty drastic things using the retouching facilities of CorelPHOTO-PAINT if you want to—adding or removing people from pictures, replacing one background with another, and so on.

As an aside, the potential for radical photographic retouching has commercial applications. If you've ever stood in a check-out line at the supermarket and regarded the front page of a sensational tabloid, wondering idly how they come by those absolutely authentic pictures of living 3000-year-old accountants, Elvis buying sneakers at a mall in Oregon, or aliens who all look remarkably like Abraham Lincoln, rumor has it that you've been looking at the work of a package like CorelPHOTO-PAINT. Because each of the several available photographic-retouching applications goes about its work slightly differently, people who use this sort of software a lot claim to be able to tell which one has been used to generate a particular image.

The secret to good photographic retouching is in the observation that nature abhors straight lines, and rarely uses them. You can usually arrive at convincing retouching by looking at the areas around whatever you'll be changing and finding a way to make the change look like part of them. The CorelPHOTO-PAINT retouching tools are designed to help you do things gently, making changes to images without upsetting them.

Each of these tools is a brush—its shape and thickness will be that of the current drawing brush, as defined by the Width workbox. They can be constrained to be horizontal or vertical by holding down the Shift key.

For the most part, these tools are only useful in the 24-bit color and gray-scale modes of CorelPHOTO-PAINT. Some, like the freehand contrast tool, will ostensibly work on 256-color images, but the results are rarely attractive.

Double clicking on any tool but the smear tool will call up the Brush Shape dialog box. Because the Smear tool is a soft brush, double clicking on it will call up the Change Soft Brush Settings dialog box.

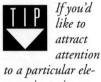

If you'd like to attract attention to a particular element in a picture without being obvious about it, increase its contrast.

The contrast tool allows you to adjust the contrast of areas of an image. When you select it, the Palette workbox will change to provide you with a contrast adjustment control. The numerical value of the contrast adjustment can range from −100 to +100. Increasing the contrast of part of your image by using values greater than zero will make the dark colors darker and the light colors lighter. Decreasing it by using values less than zero will have the opposite effect.

The brighten tool will actually brighten or darken an area in your image. When you select it, the Palette workbox will change to show you a control to set the amount of brightening or darkening this tool will perform. Selecting values less than zero will result in the brighten tool darkening those areas of your image that you use it on.

Note the distinction between the contrast and brighten tools. Set up with positive values, the freehand contrast tool will make dark areas darker and light areas lighter. The brighten tool will make all areas lighter under these conditions.

The tint tool will apply a tint of the current primary color to selected areas of your image. Its icon suggests the idea of looking at things through colored sunglasses. The degree of tinting can be effectively adjusted by choosing a suitably saturated primary color prior to selecting the tint tool.

The blend tool can be thought of as a brush dipped in water and applied to a watercolor painting. When you select it, a control will appear in the Palette workbox to allow you to set the degree of blending. Increasing the value of this control will make the blend tool more effective, and cause it to blend pixels to a greater degree.

One particularly handy effect of the blend tool is in dealing with the effects of scanning. Scanners frequently add details to an image that weren't there to begin with, or which were unnoticeable before the scanner got hold of them. The blend tool is a useful function to dispense with these.

The smear tool is similar to the blend tool, in that it will blur the distinction between pixels. The smear tool, however, is considerably more radical. It's also a soft brush—its characteristics can be set through the Change Soft Brush Settings dialog box of the Options menu.

Whereas the blend tool tends to average adjacent pixels, the smear tool actually remembers the colors of the pixels it passes over, and drags them into adjacent pixels. The effect is, as the smear tool icon suggests, like dragging a cotton swab over an area of a wet oil painting.

Figure 9.15 illustrates the effects of the blend and smear tools.

Among other things, the blend tool is handy for applying motion streaks to objects in an image.

The smudge tool will randomly interchange the pixels under its brush. This has the result of making selected areas of your picture look indistinct, much as if they were being viewed through pebbled glass.

Finally, the sharpen tool will allow you to selectively sharpen areas of your picture. It attempts to enhance the differences between selected areas of an image. When you select it, the Palette workbox will display a control to let you manage the degree of sharpening.

Setting the sharpening factor too high will cause the colors in the areas you sharpen to gravitate towards fully saturated primary colors, making your image look like a serious printer's error.

WRAPPING UP

As with CorelDRAW, there's a decided limit to what you can learn about CorelPHOTO-PAINT from a book. The best way to really make it into a useful tool is to spend an afternoon experimenting with it. Its facilities will stagger you.

It's worth keeping in mind that while CorelPHOTO-PAINT was included with the CorelDRAW package as a "front end," to provide images for import into CorelDRAW, the PHOTO-PAINT package was originally written as a stand-alone drawing and retouching application. Especially if some of your work involves using scanned images, you might well find that CorelPHOTO-PAINT has numerous applications for pictures that will never get near a CDR file.

FIGURE 9.15:

The blend (top) and smear (bottom) effects

AST
RACK

HAPTER

10

can be considered the powerhouse of CorelCHART. The Chart option is used to customize the specific characteristics of the current chart type. Use the Chart and Arrange options to control the placement of elements in the chart and put the finishing touches on your presentation.

can give you the chance to make your presentation even more dynamic. The charts which you have created can be exported in 17 different file formats for use with a range of DOS, Windows, and Macintosh applications, including CorelSHOW.

10

Using

CorelCHART

I f you are really a number-cruncher at heart, CorelDRAW has added a module that will make your heart jump for joy— CorelCHART. Now it is possible to take the skills which have been presented in earlier chapters and use them with your spreadsheet or database information to create graphs and charts which are clear and explanatory.

You can't fully understand what it meant to try to create graphs with a flair in the past if you have not been there. First, the numbers were crunched in a spreadsheet. Then, you could go to the graphing program bundled with the spreadsheet and produce a graph which could be one of six types of graphs with maybe four colors for emphasis. After you prepared the graph, it was necessary to open your word processor, and hope that the graph was compatible with the word processor.

Or you could go directly into another graphics program such as Harvard Graphics, and import the spreadsheet data. In this way, there may have been a dozen or so types of charts, and 16 colors to enhance the presentation. After that, the graph could be saved in one of several file types for use in your word processor.

The new CorelCHART module now puts all of these features into one package. The resulting graphs and charts can even be used in the Corel-SHOW module for a presentation slide show—but we will discuss CorelSHOW in the next chapter.

THE STUFF OF CORELCHART

This new module included with CorelDRAW makes it possible to enhance your presentations and graphs with informative graphics, color enhancements previously undreamed of, and the ability to incorporate your Corel-DRAW drawings and enhanced text.

You may feel intimidated by the wealth of features in CorelCHART, but it all works in the same manner as CorelDRAW features. This means that you are not really learning a new program, simply adding new features to your knowledge.

The charts can be customized with titles, headers, footnotes, and axis headings. The text can be sized, and the font or typeface can be changed for just one text area or for all. You can emphasize your message with boldface, italics, underlining, or any combination you want.

Did you just design the corporate logo with CorelDRAW and then decide to use it in your charts and presentation slides? Well, just place the graphic in the chart and make your presentation!

There are now 18 basic chart types. These include bar graphs, area graphs, histogram, scatter charts, and 3D charts. Each chart has from a single graph type to seven different variations.

If you are preparing several types of data in the same chart, one can be displayed as a line chart over another shown as a bar chart. The possibilities will be difficult to discuss in their entirety in just this chapter.

GALLERY OF CHART TYPES

The different chart types have anticipated most of the needs of even the sophisticated spreadsheet addict. The charts can even be altered using the Chart drop-down menu to be three-dimensional as if they were part of a video game. After you select a chart type or style, the data specified in the data range of the data sheet is applied, and a graph or chart is displayed.

The 18 chart types are organized in the Gallery drop-down menu by the orientation of the chart:

◆ Vertical Bar is suggested for use with limited time-series data and multiple series. This can be combined with a Line chart.

◆ Vertical Line is best used with a few groups of data for clarity. This can be combined with a Bar chart.

◆ Vertical Area can display small groups of data with continuous series.

◆ Horizontal Bar suggested for use with limited time-series data and multiple series. This can be combined with a Line chart.

◆ Horizontal Line is best used with a few groups of data for clarity. This can be combined with a Bar chart.

◆ Horizontal Area can display small groups of data with continuous series.

◆ Pie shows each of the data series in relationship to the whole.

◆ 3D Riser displays independent elements as objects rising from the surface of a 3D plane.

◆ 3D Floating displays independent elements as objects over a 3D plane.

◆ 3D Connect Series displays the relationship of series data, possibly in comparison to other series.

◆ 3D Connect Group displays the relationship of group data, possibly in comparison to other groups.

◆ 3D Surface is best for displaying continuous data across a 3D plane.

◆ 3D Scatter gives a three-dimensional view of the intersecting points of two sets of data.

◆ Scatter shows the intersecting points of two sets of data.

◆ High-Low-Open-Close is typically used to plot stock quotes during a given period of time.

◆ Spectral Mapped can be used to show demographic distribution.

◆ Histogram is best used to plot the frequency of data within value sets. It is suggested as a means to plot bell curves.

◆ Table Charts are displayed as row and column tables for clarification of data in a second presentation.

After selecting a chart type and the specific variation of that chart, the Chart View is updated. (It is automatically updated if you set that as the default mode under the Window drop-down on the menu bar.) If the Auto Update has been set off, Redraw Window is used to manually update the chart to reflect a change in the chart type, or in the data.

If you select a chart type, tweak it a little to your liking, and then decide to look at the data in a different chart type, don't worry about having to reselect the original chart type and its enhancement. CorelCHART keeps track of how you set a specific chart type and returns you to that same setting if you decide to change back to the previous chart style.

Vertical and Horizontal Charts

Within the groups of vertical and horizontal charts, there are three basic chart types: Bar, Line, and Area graphs. When you are working from the Gallery drop-down menu and are trying to decide which style suits your needs, a model of each type is displayed as you move the cursor through the list of variations of the basic chart type. Figure 10.1 shows a Vertical Side-by-Side Bar chart.

Each of the Bar, Line, and Area graphs supports seven variations. The Vertical and Horizontal Bar graph variations are

 *The alternative to using the cursor keys to preview the models is to use the mouse to click and **hold** as you move through the options on the submenu.*

◆ Side-by-Side

◆ Stacked

◆ Dual Axis Side-by-Side

◆ Dual Axis Stacked

◆ Bipolar Side-by-Side

◆ Bipolar Stacked

◆ Percent

Vertical and Horizontal Line and Area graphs support the same variations since the two chart types are essentially the same:

◆ Absolute

◆ Stacked

◆ Bipolar Absolute

◆ Bipolar Stacked

◆ Dual Axis Absolute

◆ Dual Axis Stacked

◆ Percent

Vertical Side-by-Side Bar chart

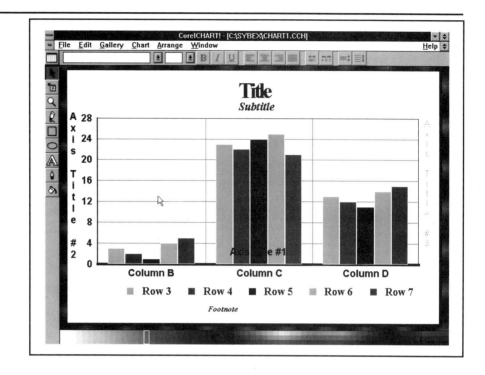

TIP *When you have set the basic chart type, select one of the data groups and use the Chart drop-down to select Draw as Bar (or as Line depending upon the initial chart type). The data group will then assume the second chart type. This is only possible with Bar and Line type graphs.*

Possibly, the selection of a Bar chart is just not what you want and a Line chart is not just it either. Well, data elements of either chart style can be set to display as the other type. If you are showing what the changes from 1991 figures look like against the figures from 1992, you might show 1991 as a Bar chart, and 1992 as a Line chart.

Pie Charts

For those of you who want to have your chart and a pie too, you have three basic types of Pie charts: a simple Pie chart, a Ring Pie, or Multiple Pies. These charts are detailed in the Gallery drop-down as:

◆ Pie

◆ Ring Pie

◆ Multiple Pies

◆ Multiple Ring Pies

◆ Multiple Proportional Pies

◆ Multiple Proportional Ring Pies

These Pies can be tilted, rotated, and sized. The Pie can also be sliced and exploded, slightly or well detached from the Pie for emphasis. See Figure 10.2 for an example of a Multiple Pie chart.

The Ring Pie and the variations of the Ring Pie are more like a bundt or angel food cake form with the center missing.

The Multiple Pies chart types display more than one pie at a time for use with more than one group of data. The Multiple Proportional Pies in turn display individual pies in a size which better shows an individual data group's size in relationship to the size of other data groups.

3D Charts

And now to look at charts from a new dimension—3D charts. Within the group of 3D charts are six basic chart types and the variations which can be selected:

3D Riser	Bars
	Pyramids
	Octagons
	Cut-Corner Bars
3D Floating	Cubes
	Spheres
3D Connect Series	Area
	Ribbons
	Steps
3D Connect Group	Area
	Ribbons
	Steps
3D Surface	Surface
	Surface with Sides
	Honeycomb Surface
3D Scatter	XYZ Scatter
	XYZ Scatter with Labels

FIGURE 10.2:

Multiple Pies chart

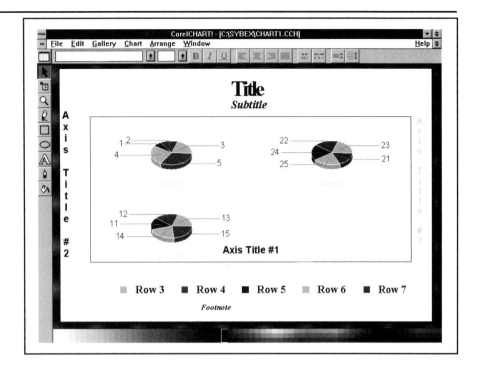

As the names imply, these charts, or graphs, have three dimensions and can display multiple sets of data more clearly than a simple Bar or Line chart can. Even stacked graphs have a difficulty in keeping the elemental data groups clear in relation to each other.

Once you have selected your basic 3D chart type, sit down for a moment. If you really want to tune the perspective, the Show 3D View tool can be selected from the Chart drop-down on the menu bar to turn the table or chart in a more meaningful direction (see Figure 10.3).

The reason I said to sit down for a moment is that the 3D View tool can give you vertigo if you are not ready for the movements it can do with your 3D chart. It can turn it on its top, bottom up, or pivoted on any axis.

Special Chart Types

The final five chart types are grouped together because they have special uses and do not fit the mold of the other groupings. Because they have more specialized uses, they are listed at the bottom of the drop-down for faster access to the more commonly used chart types.

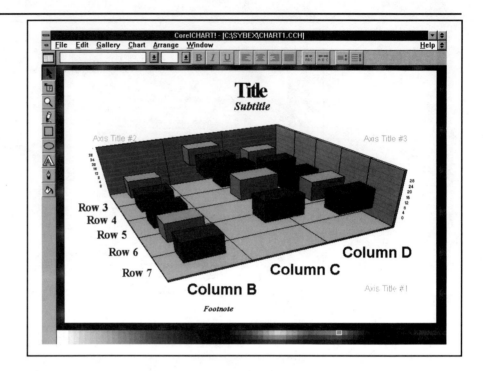

The Scatter, or XY, chart is used to plot the relationship between data groups or series on a single XY coordinate base. The variations on the Scatter type are:

◆ X-Y Scatter

◆ X-Y Dual Axes

◆ X-Y with Labels

◆ X-Y Dual Axes with Labels

The High-Low-Open-Close chart type displays the data or information as a series of vertical lines showing a High and Low point, or an Open and Close point. See Figure 10.4 for a High-Low chart. This is commonly used in the stock market and the variations on the basic High-Low type are:

◆ HiLo

◆ HiLo Dual Axes

◆ HiLo Open

◆ HiLo Open Dual Axes

◆ HiLo Open Close

◆ HiLo Open Close Dual Axes

If you need to plot data distribution, the Histogram chart type is appropriate, and offers both a vertical and horizontal orientation.

The final chart type in the Gallery drop-down is Table Charts, which despite the pluralization of its name has no variations. The data is displayed in a basic row and column layout.

Once a chart type has been selected, you are limited only by your imagination for enhancing the look of your presentation. The existing text can be manipulated in shape, typeface, look, placement, and order, while the individual elements of the graph can also be changed to increase impact.

FIGURE 10.4:

High-Low chart

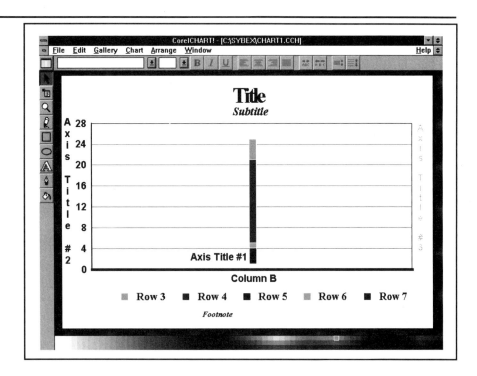

Before we go any further discussing the ways that the charts can be handled using the toolbars and the Chart drop-down, we need to take a look at the Data side of the equation, or rather of the graph.

THE DATA MANAGER, OR SETTING THE DATA RANGE

To chart a graph, it is necessary to provide CorelCHART with some numeric data. This data is formatted like a spreadsheet or a ledger book, in rows and columns. In the Data Manager, the columns are headed with letters, and the rows are numbered consecutively.

A worksheet in CorelCHART does not have the calculating functions and features of a spreadsheet. It uses the layout because it is commonly seen and understood, and lends itself to formatting the data for the charts.

CELLS AND THE WORKSHEET

If your data is off the screen to one side or the other, you can close down the column width to two characters and then see more columns on the screen. Move the mouse pointer to the vertical line separating the column headers. A bar will appear with an arrow pointing to the left and the right. Click and drag with the bar to open or close the column width.

The worksheet is made up of rows and columns in cells which each contain a single piece of data or text (see the Data Manager window in Figure 10.5). A cell is addressed by the row number and column letter, i.e., A1 is the first column to the left and the first row from the top of the worksheet.

When you are marking the data as the Data Range to graph, you paint the cells with the mouse. Let's say that you go to the cell at the top-left corner of the block of data, click on the first cell, and drag the mouse over any adjacent cell to be included. As you paint the cells, you will see the cells displayed in reverse video; instead of black characters on a white background, the selected data displays as white on black.

The other *tags* which are set in the Data Manager window are Title, Subtitle, Footnote, Row Headers, Column Headers, Axis Title #1, etc. As you select one of these tags, you will notice that the Set and Show buttons now say, for example, Set Title and Show Title.

If some of the cells are not adjacent to each other, start by marking the first cells as just described. Then move to the next cell(s) and click and drag

FIGURE 10.5:

Data Manager window

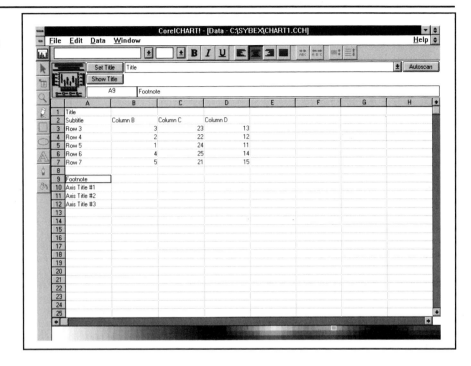

FIGURE 10.5:

Data Manager window

the mouse across the new cell(s), but this time hold down the Ctrl key while doing the click-and-drag operation. Follow this step for any non-adjacent cells. (This is the standard method for Windows spreadsheets.)

ENTERING DATA IN THE WORKSHEET

Now that we know what the worksheet is, let's get some data on it so that we can create a chart. There are three different methods for getting the data on the worksheet.

If you have a small amount of data, you could just enter it manually. This is very simple. Use your mouse or the cursor arrow keys to select the cell you want to use as the starting point.

To enter the data, simply start typing. If the Number Format has been set to General, the numbers will be right justified and the text will be displayed as left justified. When you have finished with the contents of the first cell, you could just press Enter.

If you press Enter while entering data, the cell pointer moves to the next cell down from where you are working. This is fine if all of the data is to be in just one column. But if you want the data to go across the columns, you would enter the data, press ↵, and then use the cursor or mouse to back up one cell and move over one cell. These are what are known as extra key strokes.

You can speed up the data entry by pressing the cursor arrow that indicates the direction you would move to instead of pressing Enter after each cell. This is the same as pressing Enter and then using the cursor keys to move, just fewer keystrokes.

The second way that you can get your data on the worksheet is to import it. This is done by selecting Import Data from the File drop-down on the Main menu bar (or pressing Ctrl-I). When the Import File with File Type dialog box appears, you can select from eight different types of data files:

CSV (*.CSV)	Comma Separated Value, ASCII text
SSV (*.TXT)	Space Separated Value, ASCII text
TSV (*.TXT)	Tab Separated Value, ASCII text
dBase (*.DBF)	Database files created with dBASE III Plus, dBASE IV, FoxBASE+, FoxPro 2, FoxBASE+/*Mac*, Clipper 5, and other xBase applications
DIF (*.DIF)	Established as a common means of interchanging data
Excel (*.XLS)	Microsoft Excel for DOS, Windows, and Macintosh
Harvard (*.CH?)	Harvard Graphics data
Lotus (*.WK?)	Lotus 1-2-3, versions 2.01 and 3

With these predefined data file formats, CorelCHART can read your spreadsheet or database file directly onto the worksheet. This is just the raw data and does not import the formulas (in the case of spreadsheets) or memo fields (in the case of dBASE files). While the dialog is open, you can protect your data by checking the Read Only check box on the right side of the dialog box.

Alternately, there is a third method to bring in your data: Dynamic Data Exchange, or DDE. First, you have to have your Windows spreadsheet open and the worksheet active in the spreadsheet window. Then, mark and copy the data range using the standard Windows Edit/Copy. Change back to the CorelCHART window and the Data Manager. From the Edit drop-down, select Paste Link. This creates a dynamic link to the original source of the data.

When the origin of the data is opened, the link checks to see if there are any DDE links. If so, the data on the CorelCHART worksheet is updated with the data from the source file.

Once the data is in the Data Manager, moving around the worksheet can be done with either the cursor keys or the mouse. The arrow keys move you one cell at a time in the direction of the arrow. The PgUp and PgDn keys move the worksheet up and down one screen page at a time. If you press the Ctrl key at the same time as you use PgUp or PgDn, you will move one screen page to the left or right.

When using the mouse, the scroll bars to the right and bottom give fast access to general areas of the worksheet.

If you know the cell address where you want to go, you can use the Data drop-down from the main menu bar to select Go To Cell. This brings up the Go To Cell dialog where you can enter the cell address.

With imported data, as well as manually entered data, you still need to select your data range, titles, headers, and such. Data ranges set in a spreadsheet do not follow when imported.

If you want to add or remove rows or columns on the worksheet, you must first click on the row or column header. If Insert is selected from the Edit drop-down, a row will be inserted before the current row (if a row header is selected; otherwise, a column is inserted). A selected row or column is deleted from the current position if Delete is selected from the Edit drop-down.

CHART STYLE SETTINGS

The CorelCHART worksheet is used to format the data for the charts. You select blocks for cells, either consecutive or in different locations on the worksheet, and define them as the data range.

The top border of the worksheet displays the Chart View button (which looks like a miniature graph); two buttons arranged vertically, Set and Show; a drop-down of the data format tags; and a button at the far right of the border labeled AutoScan.

The Set and Show buttons actually change their dialog as you select a different data format tag from the drop-down list—Title displays the buttons as Set Title and Show Title, Data Range displays Set Data Range and Show Data Range.

The AutoScan button is used to scan the data entered and set what it perceives as the logical data and data format tags. It prefers the Title in the top-left corner, followed below by the Subtitle. The Data Range should start at cell B3 and progress down and to the right from that point. The rest of the tags must be set manually.

The Chart View button in the upper-left corner of the worksheet shows the relative positioning of each of the data format tags. This is used in conjunction with the tags drop-down menu and the Show pushbutton.

Using the Data Manager Toolbar and Text Ribbon

When a format tag is selected and the Show… button is pressed, the appropriate part of the graph is highlighted and the matching cell(s) defined as holding the data are also highlighted.

In the same manner, select a range of cells, select Data Range (or another tag) from the format drop-down and then click on the Set… button. This procedure is used to define a cell or series of cells for each of the data format tags. The format elements start with the highest level of title or header and end with the Data Range:

- Title is the top title or description on the chart.
- Subtitle typically is a description following the Title.
- Footnote appears at the bottom of the chart.
- Row Headers appear as row, or series, headers on the chart.
- Column Headers appear as column, or group, headers on the chart.
- Axis Title #1 displays a title for the first, or X, axis.
- Axis Title #2 displays a title for the second, or Y, axis.

◆ Axis Title #3 displays a title for a third, or Z, axis in a 3D chart.

◆ Data Range defines the data in rows and columns for conversion to the selected chart.

The toolbar across the top of the CorelCHART window is used to control the text formatting of the data while viewing it in the Data Manager. The Chart View button, in the upper-left corner of the desktop, is used to switch back and forth between the chart window and the Data Manager window.

Across the rest of the desktop is the Text Ribbon with two drop-down lists, seven text-formatting buttons, and four spacing control buttons.

The two drop-down lists are used for selecting a typeface and a point size, respectively, for the worksheet. The font typeface list is made up of all active Windows fonts and fonts generated by add-ins such as Adobe Type Manager.

The next three buttons are used to set font styles. Bold, italic, and underline attributes are applied to the currently selected cells simply by clicking on the buttons. These font styles can be used separately or in combination with each other.

To control the justification of data or text on the worksheet, the next four buttons define left justified, centered, right justified, and full justified, respectively.

The final four buttons control elements of spacing. The first button tightens the spacing between characters, while the second button loosens the spacing between characters, also known as *kerning*. The last two buttons control the tightening and loosening of spacing between the lines (known in printing as *leading*).

The Main Menu Bar in the Data Manager

The main menu bar also is used to format and define the data used by the chart. The options are selected from the Data drop-down.

Select Data Orientation from the Data menu bar to define the nature of the data on the worksheet. You can define the rows or the columns as the data series. And, you can specify that the Data Values will go across cells or down cells.

If you select Alignment from the Data drop-down, you can specify the manner in which the text is justified in the worksheet columns. The selections—General, Left, Right, and Center—are the same as using the alignment buttons on the Text Ribbon.

The display of numbers, dates, and time can be formatted by selecting Number Format from Data. In the dialog box which appears (see Figure 10.6), you can select from a scroll list of 55 different numeric, date, or time formats. These include exponential abbreviations, currency, percentage, AM/PM designations, and other format definitions.

The Exchange option on the Data drop-down is used to literally exchange the values in an entire row or column with those of another row or column. You first select whether the exchange is row-with-row or column-with-column. Enter the first series in First Row/Column, and the second series in Second Row/Column.

To reorder the data in a single row or column, use Sort on the Data drop-down menu. First, select a range down a column or across a row. Then select Sort to bring up the Sort dialog. If the data you want to sort is in column form, check By Rows for Sort method; otherwise, if the data is across columns (or in a row form), select By Columns.

You can then check whether you want the data sorted in Ascending or Descending order. To control the Sort further, enter a number in Sort Key. This indicates the first character of the data to start the sort on. Just the highlighted data will be reordered.

Now that we are familiar with the Data Manager and how to set the Data Range, let's go back to the Chart View and discover the power of CorelCHART through its graphics toolbox.

FIGURE 10.6:

Number Format dialog box

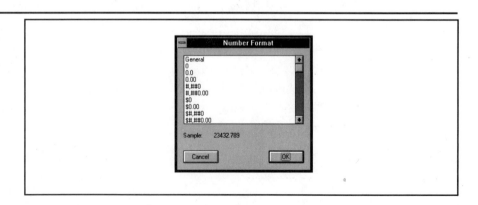

THE GRAPHICS TOOLBOX, OR TOOLS

The graphics toolbox (as I like to call it) is actually three specific areas of the Chart View window—the text ribbon, the toolbar, and the Chart and Arrange selections on the main menu bar.

CUSTOMIZING TEXT IN THE CHART

The chart is made up of a set of text entries provided from the Data Manager tag definition list (see Figure 10.7) and custom text, or notations, provided by the user.

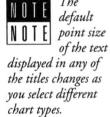

The default point size of the text displayed in any of the titles changes as you select different chart types.

A main Title is defined in the Data Manager and displayed by Corel-CHART as bold text centered across the top of the chart. The default typeface is a sans-serif font.

A Subtitle is placed directly below the Title as bold, italicized text centered in a text box extending across the chart. The default for Subtitle is a serif typeface. The text for the Subtitle can be defined in the Data Manager.

FIGURE 10.7:

Data Manager tag definition list

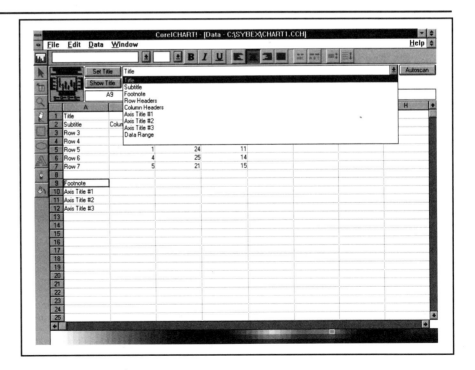

A Footnote can be defined in the Data Manager as well. It displays right justified in a text box across the bottom of the chart. The default text setting is with a serif typeface.

The four different Axis Titles are displayed as sans-serif text centered in a small box above the axis point.

The Row and Column Headers are displayed as sans-serif text. Because the headers are more than one item and are displayed as a group, there is no text box which can be sized or stretched like all the rest of the text elements.

An implicit text element, which is automatically generated by Corel-CHART, is the scale text. This is the numeric values shown along the different axes to show scale. This is typically set as 9-point sans-serif text, right justified. Scale text is treated as a group just as the Row and Column Headers are.

The last set of text which is entered and displayed in the chart is the user-entered notations. This defaults to 16-point sans-serif text, left justified in individual text boxes.

All of the text elements can be changed by one of four different methods. If you click on a text element with the secondary, or right, mouse button, a flyout menu appears, giving you access to functions available from the Chart drop-down on the main menu bar. Or, you could go to Chart and select the option you want.

Or, you could highlight the text with the Text tool from the toolbar, and go to the text ribbon or the color palette to make changes to the element attributes. Or, finally, you could simply select the entire element with the pick tool, and then make the text changes or other changes.

The Text Ribbon in Action

Across the rest of the desktop is the text ribbon with two drop-down lists, seven text-formatting buttons, and four spacing-control buttons.

The two drop-down lists are used for selecting a typeface and a point size, respectively, for the text used in the chart. Changes to Titles, Subtitles, Footnotes, annotations, and such can be changed individually. If you make a change to a Row or Column Header, the change affects all of the elements in the header.

The font typeface list is made up of all active Windows fonts and fonts generated by add-ins such as Adobe Type Manager. The sizes in the second drop-down are those available for the typeface selected in the first drop-down.

The next three buttons are used to set font styles. Bold, italic, and underline attributes are given to selected text in the chart simply by clicking on the buttons. These font styles can be used separately or in combination with each other.

To control the justification of text selected in the chart, the next set of four buttons define left justified, centered, right justified, and full justified, respectively.

Because the notations which you add can be more than one line in length, the final four buttons control elements of spacing. The first button tightens the spacing between the letters, while the second button loosens the spacing between characters, also known as *kerning*. The last two buttons control the tightening and loosening of spacing between the lines (known in printing as *leading*).

USING THE TOOLBAR FOR GRAPHICS EMPHASIS

CorelCHART uses the same graphics toolbar that you are probably already familiar with from CorelDRAW (see Figure 10.8). If you know the Toolbar and are ready to go to work, why not skip ahead to "Chart and Arrange—the Powerhouse of CorelCHART"?

FIGURE 10.8:
The toolbar

Corel provides a toolbar which gives you the ability to "pick" items for enhancements, draw freehand or in shapes on the chart, add texture or figures to elements of your chart, etc. The toolbar is the vertical bar on the left side of the window.

When you are using the Data Manager, the Toolbar is "grayed-out," or inactive, but when you are in the Chart View, the tools are available for action. The first button at the top of the toolbar is not so much a tool as a switch. It looks sort of like a miniature spreadsheet and is used to switch to the Data Manager window. That button is then followed by the pick tool, the context-sensitive pop-up menu tool, the zoom tool, the pencil tool, the rectangle tool, the ellipse tool, the text tool, the outline tool, and the fill tool.

The Pick Tool

When you want to make a change to an element of the chart, you must first select the element. This is accomplished by selecting the pick tool, shaped like an arrow, and clicking on the element.

If the element selected is a title, the element is surrounded by a box with eight handles, or nodes, at the four corners and in the middle of each side. If you click and hold the mouse on one of these handles, a two-headed arrow appears. This arrow can then be dragged to expand or contract the dimensions of the bounding box around the title. If you click and hold in the center of the box, a four-headed cursor appears and you can move the entire box in any direction.

More than one element of the chart can be selected at one time by selecting the first element, and then, while holding down either Shift key, clicking on any additional elements. Subsequently, a change to one object affects all selected objects.

When you use the Ctrl and Shift keys with a mouse action, certain constraint actions occur, making control of the actions easier.

◆ Ctrl-Move limits the Move direction to either left and right, or up and down.

◆ Ctrl-Stretch stretches in one direction in increments equal to the size of the bounding box.

◆ Ctrl-Shift-Stretch stretches in two opposite directions in increments equal to the size of the bounding box.

◆ Shift-Stretch stretches in two opposite directions.

◆ Shift-Select allows you to select more than one element at a time.

The Pop-up Menu Tool

The context-sensitive pop-up menu tool is a quick-access tool which duplicates the actions of the drop-downs on the main menu bar. Its actions can also be duplicated by clicking the second or right button on your mouse. In all cases, when you want to change the features of an element in the chart, the pop-ups will differ according to what the element is and what type of chart you currently have displayed.

The pop-up menu tool displays a miniature sheet of paper with an arrow projecting from the upper-left corner when selected. Point the arrow at the element you need to change and click the left mouse button. At this point, a pop-up menu is displayed with the actions which are relevant for the element selected.

Typically, the options on the pop-ups are either switches (indicated by an arrow to the left if they are on), or lead to dialog boxes. These pop-ups will be discussed in detail in the final section of this chapter.

The Zoom Tool

The zoom tool looks like a magnifying glass and is used to give a closer look at a section of the Chart View window. When you select the zoom tool from the toolbar, a flyout menu is displayed with six buttons. These buttons select the size you want to change the window to—Fit-in-Window, 25%, 50%, 100%, 200%, and 400%.

Once the window has been resized, you can move around in it using the mouse and the scroll bars to the right and at the bottom to see hidden areas (in the larger magnifications).

The Pencil Tool

To draw freehand on the chart, you select the pencil tool from the toolbar. When you have clicked on the button, a flyout appears with four additional buttons. These options control the manner in which you can draw on the screen. A simple cross hair is displayed on the screen when you have selected the appropriate drawing tool.

The first option constrains your drawing efforts to straight lines only. These lines can be drawn at any angle, but if you want to draw a line as a perfect vertical or horizontal line, hold down the Ctrl key while you draw the line. Drawing with the straight line tool is done by clicking at a starting point and dragging to the ending point. Releasing the mouse button means that you are finished with that line.

If you want to draw polygons, select the triangle, or second, tool. Unlike the other three options, this drawing tool is used differently. You click at a starting point and release the mouse button. Then you move to a second point and click, move to another point and click, and so on. When the figure has been completed, double-click the mouse at the ending point. The shape will then be filled with the current background color.

The third option of the pencil flyout is the freehand drawing tool. This tool works with the click-and-drag method. The line drawn follows the exact path you draw.

If you want to point something out on the chart, the last option on the pencil flyout is used to draw arrows. After you select the tool, simply click at the starting point and drag to the element you want to point at. A double wide line is drawn from the starting point to the last point with an arrowhead pointing to the last point.

The Rectangle Tool

The rectangle tool is used in the same manner as the rectangle tool in CorelDRAW. After selecting the tool, a cross-hair is displayed on the screen. Click at a starting point and drag to the ending point on the screen. You will see the rectangle appear and follow the cross hair as you draw. If you want the rectangle to be a perfect square, hold down the Ctrl key while you drag the mouse.

The Ellipse Tool

The ellipse tool is used in the same manner as the ellipse tool in CorelDRAW. After you select the tool, a cross hair is displayed on the screen. Click at a starting point and drag to the ending point on the screen. You will see the ellipse appear and follow the cross hair as you draw. If you want the ellipse to be a perfect circle, hold down the Ctrl key while you drag the mouse.

The Text Tool

The item on the toolbar that looks like the letter A is the text tool. With this tool, you can highlight some or all of an existing title or header and change its typeface, boldface it, or whatever. Or, you can add your own special notations that could not be included in the basic titling of the Data Manager. If you are adding your own notations, the tool icon is a cross hair until you click on a starting point for the text insertion, at which time it becomes the standard I-beam icon.

With the I-beam and existing text, simply highlight to indicate which text is to be changed. This text can have its typeface changed or be reentered as a different text string.

The Outline Tool

 Remember that colors that you select may not appear exactly as you expect on the screen. The display of colors is controlled by the quality of your video hardware.

The outline tool is used to control the width and color of the outlines around the graphical elements of the chart. You must first select the outline with the pick tool. Then, when you click on the outline tool icon in the toolbar, a flyout will appear.

The top row of the flyout is used to set the width of the line(s). The first option brings up a dialog box to set the width (in points) manually. The second option sets the outline with no line. The other options on the first row are preset line widths.

The second row controls the colors of the outline element. The wheel icon of the first option brings up the Color dialog box, where you can select from the entire color palette. The second option sets the outline with pure white, while the third option is for pure black. The remaining options on the color row are preset values of gray.

The Fill Tool

The fill tool is one of the more powerful tools in CorelCHART. With fill, you can assign any color from the palette, use color fountains (either preset or custom), and maybe even get carried away with the full potential (there are more than 100 preset effects which can be used).

If you just want to assign straight color that is on the palette at the bottom of the window, it is simpler to click on the element and then select the color from the palette. When you click on a color with the left mouse button, the color is assigned to the background; when you click with the right button you assign the color to the outline or edge of the element.

Clicking on the fill tool displays a flyout with 12 options. With these options, you select solid colors, fountain fills, bit-mapped pictures (BMP files), Windows Metafile images (WMF files), and so on.

The first option is used to bring up the Color dialog where you can select from 40 preset colors, or you can custom mix your own colors. Approximately 150 colors are also available in the palette at the bottom of the window.

The second option, which looks like a miniature window, is the doorway to the quick pick tool. The quick pick tool duplicates the last three options on the first row of the fill flyout and the last four options on the second row. Quick pick gives you quick access to 13 different background patterns, more than 20 fountain fill effects, 20 BMP pictures, and more than 60 packaged WMF images ranging from office equipment to world globes.

With the Quick Pick dialog box open, you can use the drop-down menu to select images or the browse buttons directly underneath the image to move through the available images. If you click on the Edit button, you will be taken to the appropriate editing screen where you can change an existing image, or create your own. When you are ready to use an image, click on Apply.

The third option of the fill flyout indicates that there is to be no fill used in the selected element.

The fourth tool option brings up the Open File dialog where you can choose a WMF file to use as the fill of the selected element in the chart. This dialog does give you the option to look at files in drives and directories other than the default \CORELDRW\CHART\VECTORS directory.

To get to the Bit map Editing dialog box, select the fifth option on the fill flyout. This will let you choose from existing BMP images and edit them, or even create your own images. The use of bitmapped pictures can greatly clarify or clutter a chart, so be judicious. Also, if a bitmapped picture is applied to one face of a 3D graph element, all visible faces will be filled with the picture. The picture will be sized to fit in each of the different faces of the element.

The bit-mapped pictures (BMP) included with Corel products can also be used with Windows for the desktop pattern (and the Windows BMP files can also be used with Corel). If you want to use the Corel BMP files on your desktop, copy the files to your Windows directory. If you want to use the Windows BMP files in your Corel creations, copy the Windows files to the \CORELDRW\CHART \BITMAPS directory. Unfortunately, neither program is set up to let you select where the files are found.

Corel stores the Windows Metafile files (WMF) in the \CORELDRW\ CHART\VECTORS directory.

Using vector graphics, or WMF images, and bit-mapped pictures slows down the repainting of the chart every time you change it, or change Windows windows.

The last option on the first row of the fill flyout will bring up the Fountain Fill Effect dialog. In this area, you can select from the fountains supplied by Corel, or create your own. You can control the starting and ending colors and the type of dissolve; flip the image around; and other sorts of tricks. It is sort of like being in a television studio with all the toys, or tools, that the professionals get to work with.

The first and second options on the second row set the background of the selected element as pure white or pure black, respectively. The remaining four options on the flyout are preset hatch patterns that can be applied to the chart. A more extensive selection of these is available in the quick pic tool.

FILLING THE COLUMNS WITH GRAPHICS

You can also enhance the graphical elements of your charts by placing figures in them rather than just assigning colors to them. These graphics are accessed by selecting File/Place and then choosing a file type (or application) that the figure has been saved in. The 16 different file types which CorelCHART currently can place are:

- ◆ CorelTRACE (EPS)
- ◆ CorelPHOTO-PAINT (PCC, PCX)
- ◆ Windows Metafile (WMF)
- ◆ Windows Bitmap (BMP)
- ◆ AutoCAD DXF (DXF)
- ◆ CompuServe Bitmap (GIF)
- ◆ Computer Graphics Metafile (CGM)
- ◆ GEM File (GEM)
- ◆ HP Plotter HPGL (PLT)
- ◆ IBM PIF (PIF)
- ◆ Illustrator 88, 3.0 (AI, EPS)
- ◆ Lotus PIC (PIC)
- ◆ Macintosh PICT (PCT)

◆ Paintbrush Bitmap (PCX)

◆ TARGA Bitmap (TGA)

◆ TIFF 5.0 Bitmap (TIF)

If you are placing one of these graphics on one of the planes of a 3D chart, the graphic will be scaled to fill the plane, *and* each of the other planes as well.

THE PALETTE

The color palette displayed across the bottom of the screen is used in the Chart View to set the fill and outline color of elements in the chart. The color palette displays pure white, 29 shades (or patterns) of gray, pure black, and 120 other colors in VGA color mode.

When a color is selected from the palette by clicking with the left mouse button, the color is assigned as the fill color. Clicking on a color with the right button sets the color as the frame, or outline, color.

If you select a color combination and then start entering text on the chart with the text tool, the text will use that color setting until it is changed again. If you decide to change the colors of text after it has been displayed, or of a graphical element in the chart, simply highlight the text, or select the element, and select the new color.

CHART AND ARRANGE —
THE POWERHOUSE OF CORELCHART

Now that we have looked at the basics of chart types in the Chart View and their relationship to the data in the Data Manager window, we can look at how CorelCHART lets you fine-tune that chart you are presenting today.

The Chart drop-down on the main menu bar is the front door to controlling the visual attributes for any chart type created in the Chart View. However, this section is being presented in the order of relationship to the type of chart you currently have selected. This is because the options and dialog boxes offered to you in the drop-down menu change from chart type to chart type.

The drop-down options comprise toggle options (switching on and off with each click of the mouse), flyouts for quick selections, and access to dialog boxes where you select from a list of additional items of detail.

The simple toggle options are shown as a prompt that either has a check mark in front of it (indicating that the feature is on), or no check mark. A flyout is indicated by a ➤ symbol in the right margin of the drop-down. When you click on one of the options with a ➤ symbol, another drop-down appears for you to select from. A dialog box option is shown with the prompt text followed by ellipses.

All of the different chart types use the same Legend dialog box and Display Status dialog box.

Legend

Clicking on Legend leads to the Legend dialog box where you can control the Legend Display and Legend Layout. If you set Display Legend to on, you have the further control options of:

◆ Autofit Legend Text

◆ Text to left of marker

◆ Text to right of marker

◆ Text below marker

◆ Text above marker

◆ Text on marker

In the Legend Layout, you can check any of the options—Automatic Legend Orientation, Vertical Legend, or Horizontal Legend. If you select Vertical Legend or Horizontal Legend you are asked to set the number of markers per column or row, respectively.

Display Status

With the Display Status dialog, shown in Figure 10.9, you can check the following options to toggle their display if you wish:

◆ ALL Text

◆ NO Text

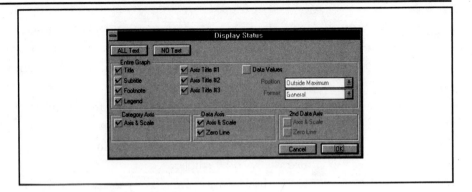

- ◆ Title
- ◆ Subtitle
- ◆ Footnote
- ◆ Legend
- ◆ Axis Title #1
- ◆ Axis Title #2
- ◆ Axis Title #3
- ◆ Axis Title #4 (if available in the dialog)
- ◆ Data Values
- ◆ Axis & Scale for Category Axis
- ◆ Axis & Scale for Data Axis
- ◆ Zero Line for Data Axis
- ◆ Axis & Scale for 2nd Data Axis (if available in the dialog)
- ◆ Zero Line for 2nd Data Axis (if available in the dialog)

If you check Data Values in the Entire Graph section, you can further set the position and number format (which we have discussed earlier).

With that in mind, we will start looking at the further options of each chart type in the same basic order that they are offered to you in the Gallery drop-down.

Vertical and Horizontal Bar Charts

The Chart drop-down for bar charts has 15 different options to use in customizing your presentation. The descriptions that follow are stated in reference to Vertical Bar charts. For Horizontal Bar charts, Top is Left, Bottom is Right, Left is Top, and Right is Bottom.

Figure 10.10 shows the drop-down menu for Bar charts with the flyout for Category Axis open.

Category Axis The Category Axis options are as follows:

◆ Display on Top places the Axis titles across the top of each column. This can be used at the same time as Display on Bottom.

◆ Display on Bottom places the Axis titles across the bottom of each column. This can be used at the same time as Display on Top.

◆ Show Grid Lines toggles the display of the vertical lines separating the columns of data.

FIGURE 10.10:

The Chart drop-down for Vertical and Horizontal Bar charts

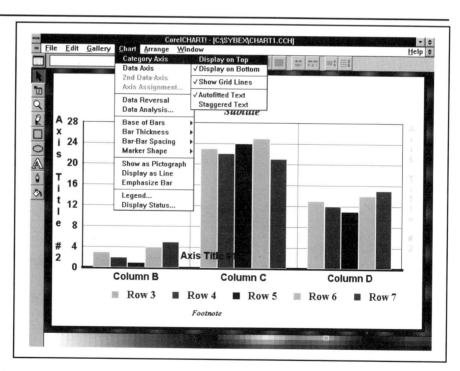

◆ Autofitted Text sizes the text of the Axis titles according to the amount of space available. This disregards any size settings made through the text ribbon.

◆ Staggered Text places the Axis titles displayed on the top or bottom of the chart on separate line levels for clarity.

Data Axis The Data Axis options are as follows:

◆ Display on Left places the axis scale along the left vertical edge of the chart. This can be used at the same time as Display on Right.

◆ Display on Right places the axis scale along the right vertical edge of the chart. This can be used at the same time as Display on Left.

◆ Linear Scale displays the values of the data as a linear scale. You set the scale as either Linear Scale or Log Scale.

◆ Log Scale displays the log values of the data as the scale. You set the scale as either Log Scale or Linear Scale.

◆ Scale Range brings up the Scale Range dialog box where you can set the display to Exclude Minimum and/or Exclude Maximum scale values along the axis. The Range Method can be set to Automatic or Manual Scale. If you select Manual Scale, you must enter a starting and ending value for the scale.

◆ Number Format displays the Number Format dialog which we covered in "The Main Menu Bar in the Data Manager" section of this chapter.

◆ Grid Lines brings up the Grid Lines dialog for controlling the display of the horizontal and vertical grid lines, and other marks associated with the grid lines.

◆ Ascending Scale is toggled on to display the graph with the baseline at the bottom or the left side, and the data values graphed upward or to the right.

◆ Autofitted Scale adjusts the size attribute for the Axis scale value according to the space available.

◆ Staggered Scale displays the Axis scale on the sides in a staggered pattern.

2nd Data Axis The 2nd Data Axis brings up a flyout identical to the Data Axis flyout and is available only if the Gallery chart type is one of the Dual Axis types.

NOTE *You must leave at least one series on each of the axis assignments. Otherwise, go to the Gallery and select a chart type other than Dual Axis.*

Axis Assignment If your chart is one of the Dual Axis types, you can click on Axis Assignment to bring up the Axis Assignment dialog box. The dialog lets you select and *move* the data series from one axis to another. If you want to move more than one at a time, hold down the Shift key as you click on your selections with the mouse. Then click on the Move button to change the axis for the selected series.

Data Reversal Clicking on Data Reversal displays a flyout with two options—Reverse Series and Reverse Groups. This reverses either the order of the data series within a group, or data groups across the chart's primary axis. This is the same for Pie charts.

Data Analysis If you have selected a series riser or legend marker, this option on the Chart drop-down leads to the Data Analysis dialog box where you can configure a Line chart overlay based upon the selections from the following list of options:

- Mean
- Standard Deviation
- Connected Line
- Smooth
- Moving Average
- Linear Regression—$y = a0 + a1x$
- Common Log Regression—$y = a(\log 10\ x) + b$
- Natural Log Regression—$y = a(1n\ x) + b$
- Exponential Regression—$y = a(xb)$
- Polynomial Fit—$y = a0 + a1x + a2x2 = 0 + anxn$
- Show Formula
- Show Correlation Coefficient

Setting Moving Average on opens the optional attributes for Order and Scientific or Financial analysis of the data.

Base of Bars   A flyout appears when you click on Base of Bars. This flyout gives you the option to set the baseline to From Zero Line or From Minimum Value. Setting From Zero Line is best used when you have negative values in your data set.

Bar Thickness   To change the substance of the bars displayed in the chart, click on Bar Thickness, wait for the flyout to appear, and select the thickness from the values—Minimum, Minor, Default, Major, and Maximum. If you use the cursor keys to move through the options, a miniature chart at the top of the flyout will indicate the size relationship of the different bar thicknesses. The settings used here are also affected by the settings in the next option, Bar-Bar Spacing.

Bar-Bar Spacing   The amount of space can be controlled by selecting the Bar-Bar Spacing options and indicating your setting from the choices—Minimum, Minor, Default, Major, and Maximum. If you use the cursor keys to move through the options, a miniature chart at the top of the flyout will indicate the size relationship of the different bar spacing. This setting affects the settings of the Bar Thickness.

If you do not select a data series before using the Marker Shape option, the first data series will be the series assigned the marker attribute.

Marker Shape   A setting from the flyout which appears when you select Marker Shape changes the graphical representation of the bar to one of the 15 shapes listed in the flyout. The shapes are named:

- Rectangle
- Rotated Star
- Plain Plus
- Circle
- Diamond
- Pirate X
- Plain X
- Triangle
- Skewed Star
- Fat Plus
- Star

◆ Soft X

◆ Pirate Plus

◆ Fat X

◆ Castle Block

If you use the cursor keys to move through the options, a miniature chart at the top of the flyout will indicate the different shapes of the markers. The markers will scale to fit the two dimensions of the bar in relationship to its data value and the settings of Bar Thickness.

Show as Pictograph This option toggles on and off to control the use of vector graphics in the display of the chart. The grid lines are displayed on top of the bars, and the bars are segmented at each grid intersection into a series of stacked bars (not to be confused with Stacked charts).

Display as Line Selecting this option toggles the display of one of the data series as a Line chart over the rest of the data series being displayed as Bar charts. One of the data series must have first been selected by clicking anywhere in one of the series bars, or on one of the series titles. This is the opposite of Display as Bar in the Chart drop-down for Line charts.

Emphasize Bar If you want to change the coloring of a single bar in a data series, use the toggle option Emphasize Bar. This only affects the selected bar. As long as you have Emphasize Bar checked, any display attributes you change will only affect the selected bar.

Vertical and Horizontal Line Charts

The first six options—Category Axis, Data Axis, 2nd Data Axis, Axis Assignment, Data Reversal, Data Analysis—and the last two options—Legend and Display Status—on the Chart drop-down for Vertical and Horizontal Line charts are identical in function to the first six and last two options for Vertical and Horizontal Bar charts. This can be seen by comparing Figure 10.11, below, with Figure 10.10.

Show Markers After selecting a data series, click on Show Markers in the Chart drop-down to toggle the display of the markers for the series. No

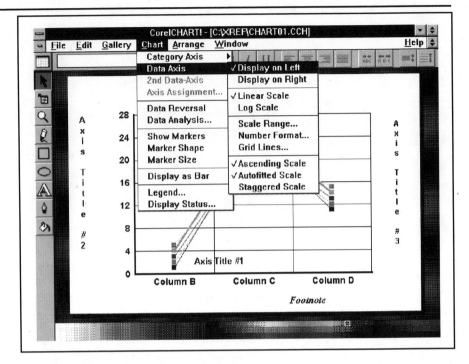

check mark is displayed alongside the option in the drop-down because it toggles for individual series, not all series.

Marker Shape   Clicking on the Marker Shape option brings up the flyout with the 15 marker shapes that were discussed above in Bar charts.

Marker Size   You can control the size of all markers displayed through the flyout that appears when you use the Marker Size option. The sizes to select from are Small, Medium Small, Medium, Medium Large, and Large. If you use the cursor keys to move through the options, a miniature chart at the top of the flyout will indicate the different sizes of the markers.

Display as Bar   The Display as Bar option is available when your chart is a Line chart. You first select a data series, and then click on Display as Bar. The selected series will then be displayed as a Bar chart behind the lines of the other data series being displayed as Line charts. This is the opposite of Display as Line in the Chart drop-down for Bar charts.

Vertical and Horizontal Area Charts

The first six options—Category Axis, Data Axis, 2nd Data Axis, Axis Assignment, Data Reversal, Data Analysis—and the last two options—Legend and Display Status—on the Chart drop-down for Vertical and Horizontal Area charts are identical in function to the first six and last two options for Vertical and Horizontal Bar charts. This can be seen by comparing Figure 10.12, below, with Figure 10.10.

The only different option used in Vertical and Horizontal Area charts is Base of Area, and that corresponds to Base of Bars for Bar charts.

A flyout appears when you click on Base of Area. This flyout gives you the option to set the baseline to From Zero Line or From Minimum value. From Zero Line is best used when you have negative values in your data set.

FIGURE 10.12:

Chart drop-down for Vertical and Horizontal Area charts

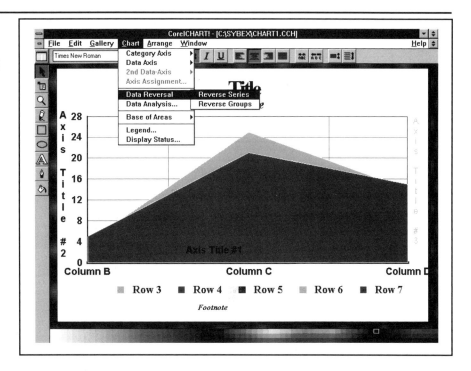

Pie Charts

Pie charts offer 15 different options to control the appearance of your charts, including the common Legend and Display Status options. Figure 10.13 shows the Chart drop-down for Pie charts with the Pie Tilt flyout open for selection.

Pie Tilt The flyout displayed when you choose to change the Pie Tilt gives you five angles of tilt—No Tilt, Minor, Default, Major, and Maximum. These angles range roughly from five degrees from vertical for No Tilt to five degrees from horizontal for Maximum. If you use the cursor keys to move through the options, a miniature chart at the top of the flyout will indicate the different angles of tilt.

Pie Thickness If you want to change how thick your Pie chart appears, you can select from No Thickness, Minor, Default, Major, and Maximum on the Pie Thickness flyout. If you use the cursor keys to move through the options, a miniature chart at the top of the flyout will indicate the different thicknesses.

FIGURE 10.13:

Chart drop-down for Pie charts with flyout for Pie Tilt open

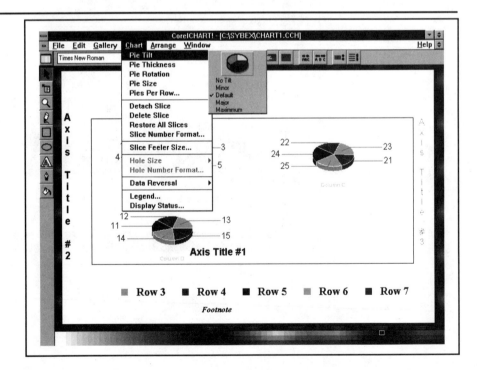

Pie Rotation You can control the position of the first "wedge" of the Pie chart by using the Pie Rotation flyout. Here, you can select the rotation from No Rotation, 45 Degrees, 90 Degrees, 180 Degrees, and 270 Degrees. The direction of the rotation is counter-clockwise. If you use the cursor keys to move through the options, a miniature chart at the top of the flyout will indicate the different positions of the segments when rotated.

Pie Size The flyout displayed when you choose to change the Pie Size gives you five sizes to choose from—Minimum, Minor, Default, Major, and Maximum. If you use the cursor keys to move through the options, a miniature chart at the top of the flyout will show you the relative sizes.

Pies Per Row Clicking on Pies Per Row brings up a dialog box where you can change the number of pies which are displayed on a single row when you have selected a Multiple Pie chart type from the Gallery. This can also affect the size of the pies according to how crowded you make things vertically.

Detach Slice To emphasize one of your data groups in all of the data series, you could display a detached slice of the pie. To do this, you must first select the slice, or wedge, that represents the data group you wish to emphasize. Then click on Detach Slice from the Chart drop-down.

You can then choose from five levels of detachment—No Detachment, Minor, Default, Major, and Maximum. If you use the cursor keys to move through the options, a miniature chart at the top of the flyout will show you the relative position of the slice in relationship to the rest of the pie.

Delete Slice The Delete Slice option on the Chart drop-down is an action option, meaning that it deletes the slice as soon as you click on it. The data group represented by the slice must first be selected. Then, just click on Delete Slice, and the slices for each data series will disappear, leaving a wedge missing in the pie. The slices can be restored by using Restore All Slices.

Restore All Slices If you decide that you want to restore slices which you have deleted, simply click on Restore All Slices from the Chart drop-down. This will restore all slices removed.

Slice Number Format Selecting the Slice Number Format option brings up the Number Format dialog which we have seen used in so many other places in CorelCHART.

Slice Feeler Size What Corel is referring to when they speak of the "slice feeler" is sort of like the curb feeler we had on our cars back in the 1950s and '60s. Specifically, they are referring to the two-segmented line leading from a pie slice to the call-out for that slice.

When you click on Slice Feeler Size, you are then presented with a graphic dialog box (see Figure 10.14) where you can change the length of the two-segmented line at any of the three connecting points, or nodes. As you move these nodes back and forth, you will see the percentage values in Horizontal, Feeler Length, and Center Dist. (distance) change.

When you return to the Chart View window, you will see the change in the length of the feelers. A change to the feeler for one slice affects all slices in the series if the chart is a Multiple Pie type. Remember, the default setting for each of the lengths is 50%.

Hole Size If you are using one of the Ring Pie charts, you can select the Hole Size options to get at the flyout that controls the size of the center hole in your ring pies. The sizes that you can choose from are Minimum, Minor, Default, Major, and Maximum. If you want No Hole, just use a Pie chart, rather than a Ring Pie chart.

FIGURE 10.14:

The Slice Feeler Size dialog box

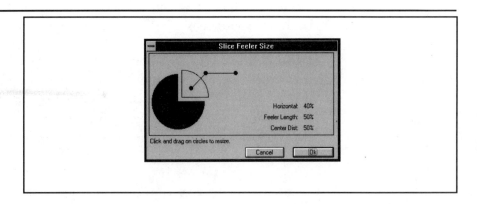

Hole Number Format The Number Format dialog box is displayed with the standard number formats that you can choose from. This is identical to all other uses of the Number Format dialog.

Data Reversal Clicking on Data Reversal displays a flyout with two options, Reverse Series and Reverse Groups. This reverses either the order of the data series within a group, or the data groups themselves. This is the same as for Bar charts.

3D Riser, Floating, Connect Series, Connect Group, and 3D Surface Charts

The 3D Riser, 3D Floating, 3D Connect Series, 3D Connect Groups, and 3D Surface chart types all share a common set of options accessible from the Chart drop-down, as can be seen in Figure 10.15. The Connect Series and Connect Group charts have one additional option in the fourth set of options—Riser Types—which will be discussed following the common Riser Colors options.

FIGURE 10.15:

Chart drop-down for 3D Riser, Floating, Connect Series, Connect Groups, and Surface charts, with flyout for Preset Viewing Angles

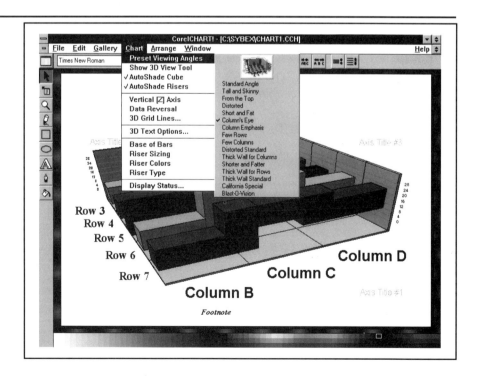

Preset Viewing Angles There are two different ways that you can start the fine-tuning of your presentation charts—the Preset Viewing Angles option and Show 3D View Tool. First, we will address the preset angles.

When you select this option, a flyout appears to the right with 16 preset angles to use:

◆ Standard Angle
◆ Tall and Skinny
◆ From the Top
◆ Distorted
◆ Short and Fat
◆ Column's Eye
◆ Column Emphasis
◆ Few Rows
◆ Few Columns
◆ Distorted Standard
◆ Thick Wall for Columns
◆ Shorter and Fatter
◆ Thick Wall for Rows
◆ Thick Wall Standard
◆ California Special
◆ Blast-O-Vision

With these, you can change the plane of view.

Show 3D View Tool A short ways back in this chapter, I warned you to sit down because you were going to be doing things to your chart that could cause vertigo; well, we have arrived at that moment. You can select the Show 3D View Tool option from the Chart drop-down to see and change *any* dimensional aspect of your 3D chart.

When you have selected this option, a box appears on your screen with four small graphics across the top, one larger graphic, a check box, and two pushbuttons at the bottom.

The four figures at the top of the window in Figure 10.16 are actually buttons which you click on to use a particular 3D tool. These tools control 3D Movement, 3D Perspective, 3D Box Proportions, and 3D Rotation. When you have selected one of these, it appears as the larger figure in the center of the screen.

By clicking and using click-and-hold techniques on any of the arrows, you will change that aspect of the chart. If you have checked the Show Graph check box below the figure, you will see an outline showing the actions on your chart.

When you are satisfied and want to see the full effect, press the Redraw button at the bottom of the box. If you do not like the effect, you can change back to the original chart by pressing the Undo button. To return to the Chart View, click on the Close button in the upper-left corner of the 3D View box.

AutoShade Risers The option to AutoShade Risers is a toggle used to control the color effect on the Riser elements of the chart. When this option is checked, the risers are shaded on appropriate planes.

FIGURE 10.16:
The 3D View tool

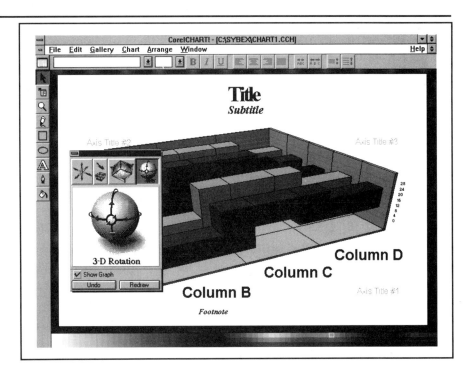

AutoShade Cubes The option to AutoShade Cubes is a toggle which turns the use of shading on the walls and floor on and off.

Vertical [Z] Axis If you need control of the Z-axis scale, select the Vertical [Z] Axis option. This brings up a flyout with these options:

◆ Linear Scale toggles on and off

◆ Log Scale toggles on and off

◆ Scale Range brings up the Scale Range dialog box where you can set the display to Exclude Minimum and/or Exclude Maximum scale values along the axis. The Range Method can be set to Automatic or Manual Scale. If you select Manual Scale, you must enter a starting or ending value for the scale.

◆ Number Format displays the Number Format dialog which we covered in "The Main Menu Bar in the Data Manager" section of this chapter.

Data Reversal This option displays the Data Reversal flyout where you can toggle the Reverse Series and Reverse Groups options to on or off. These two options can be used together or separately.

3D Grid Lines The 3D Grid Lines option brings up the 3D Grid Lines dialog box where you can control exactly which grids are needed in your chart.

3D Text Options To use the 3D Text Options, you must first select one of the text elements of the chart. When you have selected an element and clicked on the 3D Text Options in the Chart drop-down, a dialog box appears offering you these choices:

◆ Autofitted text

◆ All headers same size

◆ Headers change size with perspective

These are made by checking the appropriate check boxes in the dialog box.

Base of Bars As we have seen earlier in this section, setting the Base of Bars controls the placement of the starting base for your chart. This is best used with negative values where the negative values are displayed below the Zero Line and positive values are displayed above. Otherwise, the negative values could be used as the starting baseline, or Floor, and confuse matters.

Riser Sizing The Riser Sizing option displays a flyout with 16 different percentage combinations for controlling two dimensions of the riser size in the chart. If you use the cursor keys to move through the options, a miniature chart at the top of the flyout will show you the relative sizes.

Riser Colors Selecting Riser Colors pops up a flyout where you can toggle the first five settings on or off, and select the sixth to do some custom blending:

◆ Color Risers by Face

◆ Color Risers by Series

◆ Color Risers by Group

◆ Color Risers by Height

◆ Color Risers by Angle

◆ Color Range—leads to the Color Range dialog where you can custom select the color blend you want to apply to the checked elements.

Riser Type To add more control on your risers in either the Connect Series or Connect Groups chart types, you can display the following flyout of choices:

◆ Connected Area

◆ Connected Ribbons

◆ Connected Steps

◆ Bars

◆ Pyramids

◆ Octagons

◆ Cut-Corner Bars

◆ Floating Cubes

◆ Floating Spheres

◆ Floating Areas

If you use the cursor keys to move through the options, a miniature chart at the top of the flyout will show you the riser types.

3D Scatter Charts

The first six and the last two options for 3D Scatter Charts are identical to the rest of the 3D chart type options that we have already discussed (see Figure 10.17). These options are Preset Viewing Angles, Show 3D View Tool, AutoShade Cube, Data Reversal, 3D Grid Lines, 3D Text Options, Legend, and Display Status. The remaining four options which we will now cover are Data Point Size, Data Point Shape, Tie Lines, and Data Point Colors.

Data Point Size To control the size of the Data Points used in the chart, select Data Point Size, and then select a size from the flyout that appears. If you use the cursor keys to move through the options, a miniature chart at the top of the flyout will show you the Data Point sizes.

FIGURE 10.17:

Chart drop-down for 3D Scatter Chart with Data Point Size flyout open

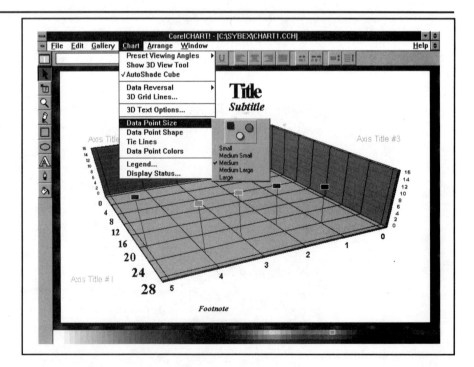

Data Point Shape A setting from the flyout which appears when you select Data Point Shape changes the graphical representation to one of the 15 shapes listed in the flyout:

◆ Rectangle

◆ Rotated Star

◆ Plain Plus

◆ Circle

◆ Diamond

◆ Pirate X

◆ Plain X

◆ Triangle

◆ Skewed Star

◆ Fat Plus

◆ Star

◆ Soft X

◆ Pirate Plus

◆ Fat X

◆ Castle Block

If you use the cursor keys to move through the options, a miniature chart at the top of the flyout will indicate the different shapes of the markers.

Tie Lines Tie lines are used to tie the data points of the Scatter charts to the scales displayed around the chart. A flyout is displayed when you click on Tie Lines with four options that are toggles:

◆ Tie Line to Floor

◆ Tie Line to Lt. Wall (Left Wall)

◆ Tie Line to Rt. Wall (Right Wall)

◆ Tie Line to Neighbor

Data Point Colors You can also control the color options of the data in the Scatter chart from the flyout that appears when you select Data Point

Colors from the Chart drop-down. The six toggle options are:

- ◆ Color by Face
- ◆ Color by Series
- ◆ Color by Group
- ◆ Color by Dist. from Lt. Wall (Distance from Left Wall)
- ◆ Color by Dist. from Rt. Wall (Distance from Right Wall)
- ◆ Color by Dist. from Floor (Distance from Floor)

Scatter Charts

Figure 10.18 shows the Chart drop-down for Scatter charts.

X-Axis   X-Axis is used to select the point of display for data on the x-axis.

- ◆ Display on Top places the Axis titles across the top of the chart area. This can be used at the same time as Display on Bottom.
- ◆ Display on Bottom places the Axis titles across the bottom of the chart area. This can be used at the same time as Display on Top.

FIGURE 10.18:

Chart drop-down for Scatter charts with X-Axis flyout open

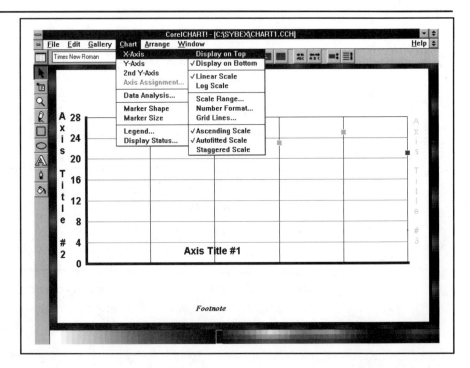

◆ Scale Range brings up the Scale Range dialog box where you can set the display to Exclude Minimum and/or Exclude Maximum scale values along the axis. The Range Method can be set to Automatic or Manual Scale. If you select Manual Scale, you must enter a starting and ending value for the scale.

◆ Number Format displays the Number Format dialog which we covered in "The Main Menu Bar in the Data Manager" section of this chapter.

◆ Grid Lines brings up the Grid Lines dialog for controlling the display of the horizontal and vertical grid lines, and other marks associated with the grid lines.

◆ Ascending Scale is toggled on to display the graph with the baseline at the bottom or left side, and the data values graphed upward or to the right.

◆ Autofitted Scale adjusts the size attribute for the Axis scale value according to the space available.

◆ Staggered Scale displays the Axis scale on the sides in a staggered pattern.

Y-Axis Y-axis presents you with a flyout menu where you toggle the following options:

◆ Display on Left places the Axis titles along the left vertical edge of the chart. This can be used at the same time as Display on Right.

◆ Display on Right places the Axis titles along the right vertical edge of the chart. This can be used at the same time as Display on Left.

◆ Linear Scale displays the values of the data as a linear scale. You set the scale as either Linear Scale or Log Scale.

◆ Log Scale displays the log values of the data as the scale. You set the scale as either Log Scale or Linear Scale.

◆ Scale Range brings up the Scale Range dialog box where you can set the display to Exclude Minimum and/or Exclude Maximum scale values along the axis. The Range Method can be set to Automatic or Manual Scale. If you select Manual Scale, you must enter a starting and ending value for the scale.

- ◆ Number Format displays the Number Format dialog which we covered in "The Main Menu Bar in the Data Manager" section of this chapter.

- ◆ Grid Lines brings up the Grid Lines dialog for controlling the display of the horizontal and vertical grid lines, and other marks associated with the grid lines.

- ◆ Ascending Scale is toggled on to display the graph with the baseline at the bottom or left side, and the data values graphed upward or to the right.

- ◆ Autofitted Scale adjusts the size attribute for the Axis scale value according to the space available.

- ◆ Staggered Scale displays the Axis scale on the sides in a staggered pattern.

2nd Y-Axis The 2nd Y-Axis brings up an identical flyout to the Y-Axis flyout and is available only if the Gallery chart type is one of the Dual Axis types.

Axis Assignment If your chart is one of the Dual Axis types, you can click on Axis Assignment to bring up the Axis Assignment dialog box. The dialog lets you select and *move* the data series from one axis to another. If you want to move more than one at a time, hold down the Shift key as you click on your selections with the mouse. Then click on the Move button to change the axis for the selected series.

Data Analysis This option on the Chart drop-down leads to the Data Analysis dialog box where you can configure a Line chart overlay based upon selections from the following list of options:

- ◆ Mean
- ◆ Standard Deviation
- ◆ Linear Regression—$a0 + a1x$
- ◆ Common Log Regression—$y = a(\log 10\ x) + b$
- ◆ Natural Log Regression—$y = a(1n\ x) + b$
- ◆ Exponential Regression—$y = a(xb)$
- ◆ Polynomial Fit—$y = a0 + a1x + a2x2 = 0 + anxn$

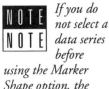 *If you do not select a data series before using the Marker Shape option, the first data series will be the series assigned the marker attribute.*

Marker Shape A setting from the flyout which appears when you select Marker Shape changes the graphical representation of the bar to one of the 15 shapes listed in the flyout. The shapes are named:

◆ Rectangle

◆ Rotated Star

◆ Plain Plus

◆ Circle

◆ Diamond

◆ Pirate X

◆ Plain X

◆ Triangle

◆ Skewed Star

◆ Fat Plus

◆ Star

◆ Soft X

◆ Pirate Plus

◆ Fat X

◆ Castle Block

If you use the cursor keys to move through the options, a miniature chart at the top of the flyout will indicate the different shapes of the markers. The markers will scale to fit the two dimensions of the bar in relationship to its data value and the settings of Bar thickness.

Marker Size You can control the size of all markers displayed through the flyout shown when you use the Marker Size option. The sizes to select from are Small, Medium Small, Medium, Medium Large, and Large. If you use the cursor keys to move through the options, a miniature chart at the top of the flyout will indicate the different sizes of the markers.

High-Low-Open-Close Charts

High-Low Charts, as used in stock analysis and such, have a smaller set of options which can be used to customize charts, as can be seen from Figure 10.19.

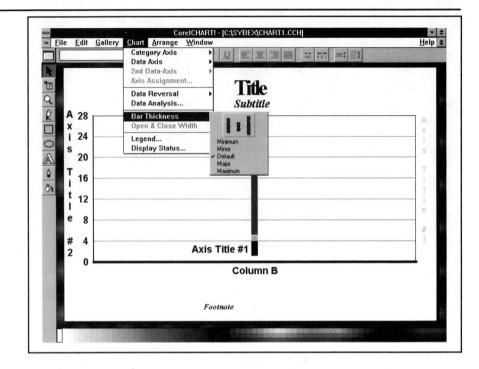

Category Axis Category Axis is used to control the locations and specifications of text and grid lines.

◆ Display on Top places the Axis titles across the top of the chart. This can be used at the same time as Display on Bottom.

◆ Display on Bottom places the Axis titles across the bottom of the chart. This can be used at the same time as Display on Top.

◆ Show Grid Lines toggles the display of the horizontal and vertical grid lines, and other marks associated with the grid lines.

◆ Autofitted Text adjusts the size attribute for the Axis text according to the space available.

◆ Staggered Text displays the Axis text on the sides in a staggered pattern.

Data Axis Data Axis is used to access the flyout menu for controlling the display of prompts and the scale.

◆ Display on Left places the axis text along the left vertical edge of the chart. This can be used at the same time as Display on Right.

◆ Display on Right places the axis text along the right vertical edge of the chart. This can be used at the same time as Display on Left.

◆ Linear Scale displays the values of the data as a linear scale. You set the scale as either Linear Scale or Log Scale.

◆ Log Scale displays the log values of the data as the scale. You set the scale as either Log Scale or Linear Scale.

◆ Scale Range brings up the Scale Range dialog box where you can set the display to Exclude Minimum and/or Exclude Maximum scale values along the axis. The Range Method can be set to Automatic or Manual Scale. If you select Manual Scale, you must enter a starting and ending value for the scale.

◆ Number Format displays the Number Format dialog which we covered in "The Main Menu Bar in the Data Manager" section of this chapter.

◆ Grid Lines brings up the Grid Lines dialog for controlling the display of the horizontal and vertical grid lines, and other marks associated with the grid lines.

◆ Ascending Scale is toggled on to display the graph with the baseline at the bottom or left side, and the data values graphed upward or to the right.

◆ Autofitted Scale adjusts the size attribute for the Axis scale value according to the space available.

◆ Staggered Scale displays the Axis scale on the sides in a staggered pattern.

2nd Data Axis The 2nd Data Axis brings up a flyout identical to the Data Axis flyout and is available only if the Gallery chart type is one of the Dual Axis types.

Axis Assignment If your chart is one of the Dual Axis types, you can click on Axis Assignment to bring up the Axis Assignment dialog box. The dialog lets you select and *move* the data series from one axis to another. If you want to move more than one at a time, hold down the Shift key as you click on your selections with the mouse. Then click on the Move button to change the axis for the selected series.

Bar Thickness To change the substance of the bars displayed in the chart, click on Bar Thickness, wait for the flyout to appear and select the thickness from the values—Minimum, Minor, Default, Major, and Maximum. If you use the cursor keys to move through the options, a miniature chart at the top of the flyout will indicate the size relationship of the different bar thicknesses.

Open & Close Width To change the width of the open and close bars displayed in the chart, click on Open & Close Width, wait for the flyout to appear and select the thickness from the values—Minimum, Minor, Default, Major, and Maximum. If you use the cursor keys to move through the options, a miniature chart at the top of the flyout will indicate the size relationship of the different bar widths.

Spectral-Mapped Charts

Spectral-Mapped charts indicate changes over a broad spectrum of data.

X-Axis X-axis is used to select the point of display for data on the x-axis.

- Display on Top places the Axis titles across the top of the chart area. This can be used at the same time as Display on Bottom.
- Display on Bottom places the Axis titles across the bottom of the chart area. This can be used at the same time as Display on Top.
- Show Grid Lines displays grid lines for this axis.
- Autofitted Text adjusts the size attribute for the Axis text according to the amount of space available. This disregards any size settings made through the text ribbon.
- Staggered Text displays the Axis text on the sides in a staggered pattern.

Y-Axis Y-axis presents you with a flyout menu where you toggle the following options:

- Display on Left places the axis scale along the left vertical edge of the chart. This can be used at the same time as Display on Right.

- ◆ Display on Right places the axis scale along the right vertical edge of the chart. This can be used at the same time as Display on Left.

- ◆ Show Grid Lines brings up the Grid Lines dialog for controlling the display of the horizontal and vertical grid lines, and other marks associated with the grid lines.

- ◆ Autofitted Text adjusts the size attribute for the Axis text according to the space available.

- ◆ Staggered Text displays the Axis text on the sides in a staggered pattern.

Data Reversal This option displays the Data Reversal flyout where you can toggle the Reverse Series and Reverse Groups options to on or off. These two options can be used together or separately.

Spectrum The Spectrum option (see Figure 10.20) leads to a flyout with three toggle options—Linear Scale, Log Scale, and Ascending Scale—and three options which lead to dialog boxes. The first two dialog options—Scale Range and Number Format—have already been covered earlier in the section. The last option, Spectrum, displays a dialog box where you can set a color blend to be used in the Spectral Mapped chart.

Marker Shape A setting from the flyout which appears when you select Marker Shape changes the graphical representation of the data point to one of the 15 shapes listed in the flyout. The shapes are named:

- ◆ Rectangle
- ◆ Rotated Star
- ◆ Plain Plus
- ◆ Circle
- ◆ Diamond
- ◆ Pirate X
- ◆ Plain X
- ◆ Triangle
- ◆ Skewed Star

FIGURE 10.20:

Chart drop-down for Spectral-Mapped charts with Spectrum flyout open

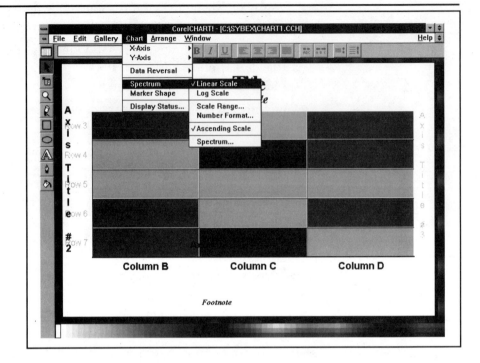

- ◆ Fat Plus
- ◆ Star
- ◆ Soft X
- ◆ Pirate Plus
- ◆ Fat X
- ◆ Castle Block

If you use the cursor keys to move through the options, a miniature chart at the top of the flyout will indicate the different shapes of the markers.

Histogram

Histograms are a special chart type used to display differences between largest and smallest data values. This chart type is typified by the bell curve. Figure 10.21 shows the menu options for a Horizontal Histogram.

Chart drop-down for Horizontal Histogram with Interval Axis flyout open

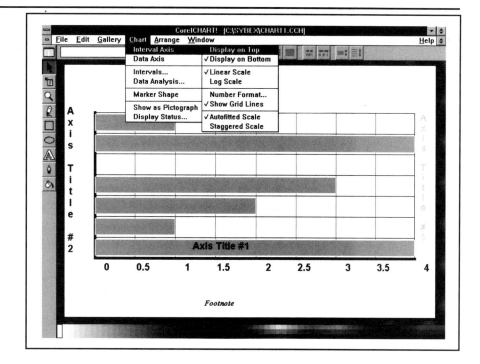

Interval Axis This option allows you to specify scale and gridlines along the *horizontal* axis, and to select number format.

◆ Display on Top places the Axis titles across the top of the chart area. This can be used at the same time as Display on Bottom.

◆ Display on Bottom places the Axis titles across the bottom of the chart area. This can be used at the same time as Display on Top.

◆ Linear Scale displays the values of the data as a linear scale. You set the scale as either Linear Scale or Log Scale.

◆ Log Scale displays the log values of the data as the scale. You set the scale as either Log Scale or Linear Scale.

◆ Number Format displays the Number Format dialog which we covered in "The Main Menu Bar in the Data Manager" section of this chapter.

◆ Show Grid Lines displays grid lines for this axis.

◆ Autofitted Scale adjusts the size attribute for the Axis scale value according to the space available.

◆ Staggered Scale displays the Axis scale on the sides in a staggered pattern.

Data Axis   This option allows you to specify Scale and gridlines along the *vertical* axis, and to select number format.

◆ Display on Left places the axis scale along the left vertical edge of the chart. This can be used at the same time as Display on Right.

◆ Display on Right places the axis scale along the right vertical edge of the chart. This can be used at the same time as Display on Left.

◆ Linear Scale displays the values of the data as a linear scale. You set the scale as either Linear Scale or Log Scale.

◆ Log Scale displays the log values of the data as the scale. You set the scale as either Log Scale or Linear Scale.

◆ Number Format displays the Number Format dialog which we covered in "The Main Menu Bar in the Data Manager" section of this chapter.

◆ Grid Lines brings up the Grid Lines dialog for controlling the display of the horizontal and vertical grid lines, and other marks associated with the grid lines.

◆ Ascending Scale is toggled on to display the graph with the baseline at the bottom or left side, and the data values graphed upward or to the right.

◆ Autofitted Scale adjusts the size attribute for the Axis scale value according to the space available.

◆ Staggered Scale displays the Axis scale on the sides in a staggered pattern.

Intervals   The Intervals option brings up a dialog box where you set either Automatic or Manual. If you select Manual, you can then set the number of intervals.

Data Analysis This option on the Chart drop-down leads to the Data Analysis dialog box where you can configure a Line chart overlay based upon selections from the following list of options:

◆ Mean

◆ Standard Deviation

◆ Connected Line

◆ Smooth

◆ Moving Average

◆ Linear Regression—a0 + a1x

◆ Common Log Regression—y = a(log10 x) + b

◆ Natural Log Regression—y = a(1n x) + b

◆ Exponential Regression—y = a(xb)

◆ Polynomial Fit—y = a0 + a1x + a2x2 = 0 + anxn

◆ Show Formula

◆ Show Correlation Coefficient

Setting Moving Average on opens the optional attributes for Order and Scientific or Financial analysis of the data.

Marker Shape A setting from the flyout which appears when you select Marker Shape changes the graphical representation of the data point to one of the 15 shapes listed in the flyout. The shapes are named:

◆ Rectangle

◆ Rotated Star

◆ Plain Plus

◆ Circle

◆ Diamond

◆ Pirate X

◆ Plain X

◆ Triangle

◆ Skewed Star

◆ Fat Plus

◆ Star

◆ Soft X

◆ Pirate Plus

◆ Fat X

◆ Castle Block

If you use the cursor keys to move through the options, a miniature chart at the top of the flyout will indicate the different shapes of the markers.

Show as Pictograph   This option toggles on and off to control the use of vector graphics in the display of the chart. The grid lines are displayed on top of the bars, and the bars are segmented at each grid intersection into a series of stacked bars (not to be confused with Stacked charts).

Table Charts

The Table Charts are a simple row and column table, as seen in Figure 10.22. The options offered for controlling the appearance of the tables in your presentation are fairly basic in their functions.

FIGURE 10.22:

Table chart with Chart drop-down options

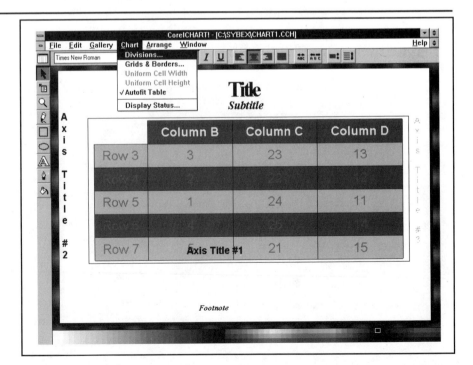

Divisions When you select Divisions, a dialog box is used to make the changes to the table. In the category of Rows/Columns Color Selection, you make your selection from three radio buttons (only one can be active at any one time),

◆ No Color Division

◆ Color by Rows

◆ Color by Columns

and a single check box—Include Headers.

A second category, Rows/Columns Color Setting, is used to enter values for:

◆ Number of rows/columns between grids

◆ Number of rows/columns per color

◆ Number of rows/colors to cycle through

Grids & Borders The Grids & Borders dialog box shows you a graphical representation of the placement of the lines displayed in the chart. You can set the lines on or off simply by clicking on the desired lines, or by using the Select All or Deselect All buttons to control all lines at once.

Uniform Cell Width This is a toggle for controlling the width of the cells in the table if Autofit Table is toggled off.

Uniform Cell Height This is a toggle for controlling the height of the cells in the table if Autofit Table is toggled off.

Autofit Table The Autofit Table option is a toggle which sizes the text of the table according to the amount of space available. This disregards any size settings made through the text ribbon.

ARRANGE—TO LAYER OR NOT

The Arrange drop-down found on the main menu bar works in the same manner as the Arrange item in CorelDRAW. However, the use of Arrange is limited to changing the order, or layering, of the annotation items which you add to your chart through the toolbar and its various tools. The Chart View and the chart displayed on it are always the back or bottommost layer.

EXPORTING YOUR CHARTS FOR USE IN OTHER APPLICATIONS

Corel does not provide a Corel PostScript filter. They suggest that you use the standard Encapsulated PostScript filter, even if you just intend to import the chart into another Corel application.

The filter for Macintosh file types only prepares the data for use in a Macintosh application. You might use a device such as the Deluxe Option Board from Central Point Software to transfer your file from the IBM to a Mac disk, or use Apple's Apple File Exchange software on a Mac equipped with a FDHD floppy drive to read the IBM 3 1/2" disk on the Mac.

Once you have created an analysis of the project and the chart that will show the whole picture, do you just want to print it out and stuff it into your brief, or do you want to make it an integral part of your presentation? Corel has provided export filters for 17 of the most commonly used file formats in order to make it easier for you to include exactly what you want, where you want it. These 17 formats give you the latitude to use your charts in applications on both IBM and Macintosh systems.

◆ Windows Bitmap (BMP)

◆ CorelPHOTO-PAINT (PCC, PCX)

◆ AutoCAD DXF (DXF)

◆ CompuServe Bitmap (GIF)

◆ Computer Graphics Metafile (CGM)

◆ GEM File (GEM)

◆ HP Plotter HPGL (PLT)

◆ IBM PIF (PIF)

◆ Illustrator 88, 3.0 (AI, EPS)

◆ Macintosh PICT (PCT)

◆ Matrix/Imapro SCODL (SCD)

◆ Paintbrush Bitmap (PCX)

◆ TARGA Bitmap (TGA)

◆ TIFF 5.0 Bitmap (TIF)

◆ Windows Metafile (WMF)

◆ WordPerfect Graphic (WPG)

◆ Encapsulated PostScript (EPS)

Simply select your desired format from the List Files of Type drop-down and Corel will do the rest for you. Then open your application, whether it be on DOS, Windows, or a Macintosh and import (or place) your chart.

WRAPPING UP

In closing, the use of CorelCHART in presentation graphics and charts is one of the best tools to come from Corel. It allows you to control the data and text aspects of your chart through the Data Manager. The data used can be manually entered, or imported from the major spreadsheets and database programs available today.

You can pick from 79 different types of charts in which to present your data. You can rotate your chart, spin it on an axis, and much more. You can even use your CorelDRAW graphics or graphics from any of 16 different file types to give emphasis to the different elements of the charts.

Once you are satisfied, you can save your chart in any of 17 industry-standard graphics formats, or take it a step further and use CorelSHOW to make a slide show with your graphics and charts as the essential elements. Good luck, and we will see each other again in the next chapter on CorelSHOW.

FAST
TRACK

CHAPTER

11

A presentation in CorelSHOW is made primarily of two things, ... **484**

the elements or graphics you place in the pages of each show, and the special effects (F/X) you use when they are displayed as a slide show on-screen. "The Two Es of CorelSHOW— Elements and Effects" shows you how to paste the graphics on a page (or screen) and then discusses the effects that you can set for each frame (if used in a slide show).

To place graphics on the individual pages **488**

of a presentation, you use the Insert item from the Main menu bar. The pages are made up of two distinct sections—the background and the foreground. A background is exactly the same for all of the *pages* in a presentation, while the foreground is the part where you can place different elements in a page order that best conveys your presentation to the intended audience. You can insert objects and files from Corel applications and other Windows programs (including sound objects if you are set up for sound) using Object Linking and Embedding (OLE).

A slide show allows you to add special effects **493**

to your presentation which are not possible in a paper show. When you are developing a PC slide show, you have the additional ability to add special effects to control the manner in which each slide is displayed on the screen, how long it remains, and the order in which it appears.

when you are using CorelSHOW and importing figures and animation files. These points and hardware quirks that Corel wants you to know about are discussed in the section "Special Notes from Corel." It is also important to read any READ.ME files which are added to the original disks just before shipping. These files cover last minute changes and discoveries which could not be included in the printed manuals because of timing issues.

Using

CorelSHOW

 mong the excellent tools in the CorelDRAW package is CorelSHOW, which gives you the chance to put all of your work together and show it off. Whether you want to simply print out a sequence of drawings, charts, and other elements for a prospectus, or you need to prepare a slide show to present to a prospective client, Corel-SHOW gives you the means to put all of the elements together. If you have a sound card in your computer system and are using Windows 3.1 or Windows 3.0 with multimedia extensions, you can even insert sound objects into the individual slides.

THE TWO ES OF CORELSHOW— ELEMENTS AND EFFECTS

CorelSHOW is very simple in its function—it acts simply as a poster board, light table, or slide tray to organize the elements of a project. You can create a background for the pasteboards; paste in the different elements (combining more than one element in a single page or slide); and, if you intend to show the sequence on-screen, add transition effects which a few years ago were limited to high-powered (and high-priced) video studios.

There is even a CorelSHOW Run-time Player provided so that you can distribute your slide show to viewers who may not have a copy of the CorelSHOW software intalled on their computers. This is provided by Corel and there is no additional distribution cost associated with it.

CorelSHOW does not provide any means to change the elements which are placed on the pages. That is left up to CorelDRAW, CorelCHART, etc. You simply put the elements together, organize them, reorganize them, set the display time for each element, and maybe get carried away with the video special effects (or F/X as they are called, after the custom in the video and film industries).

Putting Elements on the Pages

When you first open CorelSHOW, you are presented with the Welcome to CorelSHOW dialog box shown in Figure 11.1. You can choose to open an existing presentation or a new one at this point.

If you click on the Start a New Presentation box, you are given a default page count of five pages (or slides). You can increase this value now or at any time during the development of your project. For matters of consistency, I will refer to the individual pages of the presentations as slides, since that is my favorite use of a show program.

There are two elements to the slides—the graphics that you place in them and a background that you can optionally include. Each of these elements is selected individually, while the F/X you assign affect the slide as a whole.

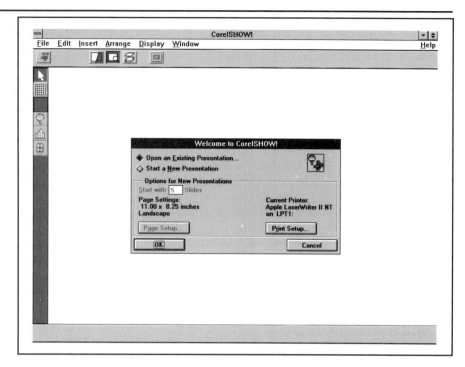

The Background View The background element has the characteristic
that only one background can be used with any one slide show. So you want to
be careful when you select your background.

Background elements can be set by using the CorelSHOW toolbar (see
Figure 11.2) along the left side of the slide window. You can set or change the
background either from the background window or from the slide view. The top
button is the ever-familiar pick tool for selecting elements of a figure.

The second button on the toolbar brings up a Display dialog box which
shows you the backgrounds which have been saved in a .SHB file. Corel-
SHOW starts with a background file named SAMPLES.SHB which is located in the \CORELDRW\SHOW\BACKGRDS\SAMPLES directory (see
Figure 11.3). In this background library, there are 25 great designs to choose
from.

If you do not find the background you want, click on the Change
Library button, and Corel will take you into the Select Background dialog
box where you can select another background library.

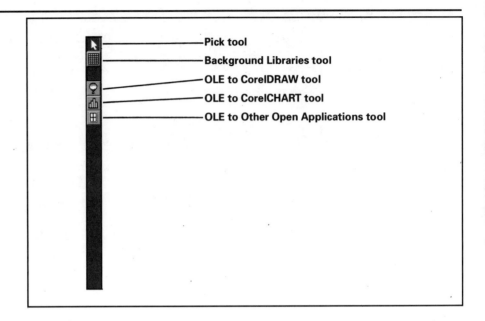

Pick tool
Background Libraries tool
OLE to CorelDRAW tool
OLE to CorelCHART tool
OLE to Other Open Applications tool

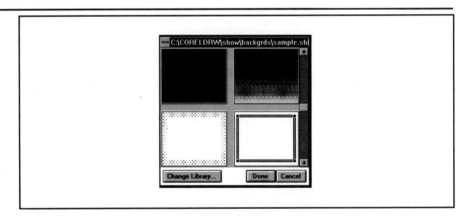

If you want to create your own background, you will use the Object Linking and Embedding (OLE) process for bringing in a figure from CorelDRAW and placing it in the slide. You must first go to the button bar displayed across the top (see Figure 11.4) and press the Background View button.

Once you are in the Background View, you can press the Backgrounds Libraries tool or one of the OLE applications tools on the toolbar. If you select

FIGURE 11.4:

Button bar at the top of the window

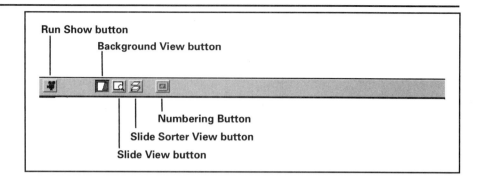

one of the OLE applications tools, go back to your slide and create a box (with the crosshair cursor) where the object is to be placed. In the OLE application, select your figure, go to the Main menu bar and select Edit/Copy.

Now you can go back to CorelSHOW by either pressing Alt-Tab or closing the application. When you are back in the Background View window, go to the Main menu bar and select Edit/Paste or Edit/Paste Special. Your graphic will now be placed in the slide as the background.

If you want to save the background for later use, you have two ways to go. You go up to File/Save Background in both cases. In the Save Background dialog box, you can save the background as a file by itself simply by entering the file name (the extension of .SHB is automatically assigned) and pressing Enter.

However, if you want, you can also build a background library. In the Save Background dialog, you can see a check box labeled Insert in Library. By clicking on the check box and selecting an existing file name (or entering a new one), you can add the background which you have created to the library file, rather than create a library of one figure.

Because of the speed delays caused by over-active graphics, it is recommended that you use Edit/Omit Background to suppress the background and speed the redrawing of the screen. When you are ready for the final pages, or slides, simply go back to Edit/Omit Background and check it again to remove the check mark which indicates that the background is not shown.

A background can be made up of more than one graphical element, but remember that the whole background is displayed through the slide show. Once you have your background, you are ready to create the rest of your slides.

NOTE *AutoDesk Animator files can be used only by themselves. You cannot place more than one Animator figure as the background, or as an element in the foreground, of a slide.*

The Slide View When you have finished with the background, you return to the front, or Slide View, by clicking on the Slide View button in the button bar at the top of the window. Now you can put the rest of the slides together.

When you open a CorelSHOW file with more than one slide to it, you will see a series of page icons starting at the bottom-left corner of the window. These are used for moving from one slide to another. Just click on the page icon that you wish to work on and it will become the current window.

Now that you are ready to add your graphics to the slide, you can access the applications where they were created using the same technique that we just discussed for backgrounds. However, with foreground figures, you can use either the three OLE applications tools in the toolbar or use the Insert drop-down menu from the Main menu bar.

Working with the Insert Drop-down Menu When working with the Insert drop-down menu, you can selectively insert either an Object, a File, or an Animation file from AutoDesk Animator. If you have a graphic in mind, but you want to use just part of the figure, select Object from the drop-down menu. You will then be presented with a scroll list of programs and files from which CorelSHOW can link objects. These are also indicated below:

◆ CorelCHART 3.0 —.CCH

◆ CorelDRAW Graphic —.CDR

◆ CorelPHOTO-PAINT Picture —.PCX

◆ Package —*.*

◆ Paintbrush Picture —.BMP, .MSP, .PCX

◆ Sound —.WAV

(Applications with OLE capabilities may also appear in the Insert-Object list.) Once the graphic is displayed in a window in the application, select the object(s) of the figure that you wish to use in your CorelSHOW slide. Then select Edit/Copy from the application Main menu bar. Once you have copied the object(s) to the Windows Clipboard, return to CorelSHOW, and select Edit/Paste to insert the object(s) into the slide.

In the sixth slide (shown in Figure 11.10), I selected CorelDRAW Graphic and opened *Corel3* (a drawing by Chris Purcell, one of the winners in the CorelDRAW World Design Contest). While in CorelDRAW, I selected Edit/Select All and then used Edit/Copy to place all of the objects in the picture on the Windows Clipboard. Then I switched to CorelSHOW by pressing Alt-Tab and selected Edit/Paste to place the figure in the slide.

Figures 11.5 through 11.10 represent a slide show demonstrating the development of *Corel3* with the objects, or elements, of the figure gradually incremented.

I find that the File option from the Insert drop-down menu is more complete in the selection of file types. When you select this option from the menu, you are then taken to the Insert File dialog box. You can select from the following application file types in the List Files of Type scroll box:

◆ CorelCHART 3.0 (.CCH)

◆ CorelDRAW Gra (.CDR)

◆ Paintbrush Pic (.BMP)

◆ Paintbrush Pic (.MSP)

◆ Paintbrush Pic (.PCX)

◆ Sound (.WAV)

The Sound icon need not be placed directly in the slide frame. It need only be in the window indicated by the page icon(s) at the bottom of the window.

(Applications with OLE capabilities may also appear in the Insert-File list.) When inserting sounds, you must load the .WAV file into the Sound Recorder and then use Edit/Copy to place the sound on the Clipboard prior to returning to CorelSHOW and using Edit/Paste to place the sound in the slide. Sounds are indicated in a slide with the Microphone icon. However, this icon does not display on-screen or print out.

If you press the last tool in the toolbar, the OLE to Other Open Applications tool, you will see a flyout menu with icons for any applications which are currently open or for which objects are already placed in the current slide. (This flyout menu is similar to the menu you see when you click on the magnifying glass in CorelDRAW to pick the view you want). Objects which you select in an application accessed through this button can be pasted into CorelSHOW using either Edit/Paste or Edit/Paste Special. Paste Special just asks you which application the object is coming from.

FIGURE 11.5:

Slide One with five CorelDRAW graphic objects

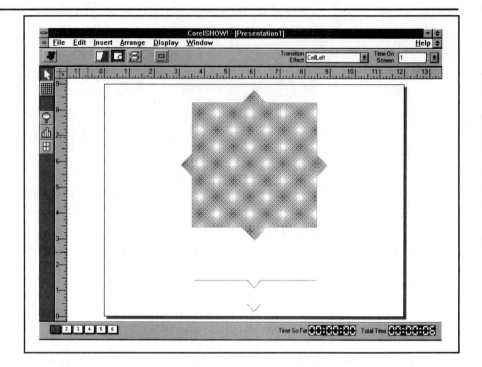

FIGURE 11.6:

Slide Two with 13 CorelDRAW graphic objects

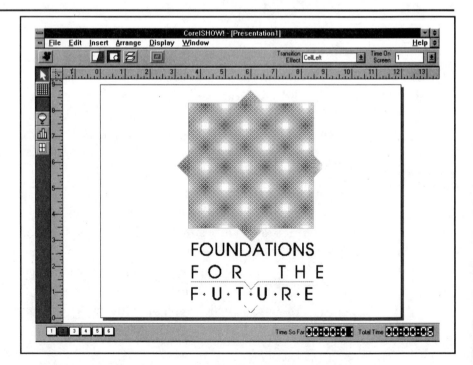

FIGURE 11.7:
Slide Three with 38 CorelDRAW graphic objects

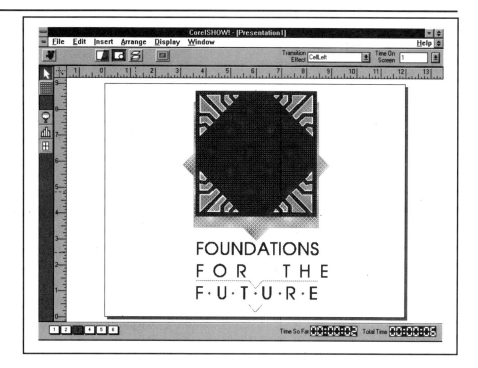

FIGURE 11.8:
Slide Four with 39 CorelDRAW graphic objects

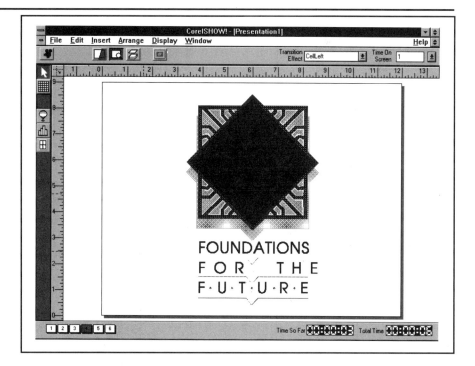

Slide Five with 73 CorelDRAW graphic objects

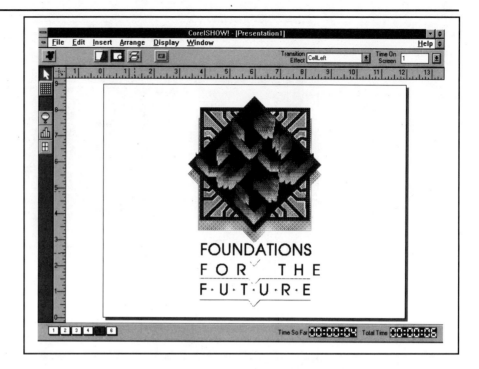

Slide Six with 90 CorelDRAW graphic objects

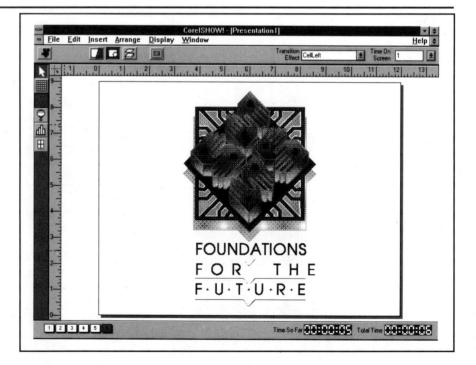

Adding Slides Adding pages, or slides, is simply a matter of selecting Insert/New Page (or pressing Ctrl-N). You will then be prompted by a dialog box asking how many pages you want and whether you want them inserted before or after the current page. When you have clicked on OK, you are returned to the Slide View on the last page inserted.

The Slide Sorter View, or Organizing the Slide Show

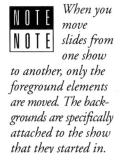

If you happen to use Edit/Select All before you use Edit/Cut to remove a slide, all of the slides will be selected and removed.

Now that you have a series of slides with all the elements pasted up, let's make sure that they are in an order that shows them off to the best advantage. Possibly the best way to do this this is to spread them out on the light table, or Slide Sorter.

This can be accomplished by clicking on the Slide Sorter View button in the button bar at the top. Then all of the slides will be laid out in front of you.

You can change the order of the slides by using the click-and-drag process. Select a slide and drag it to the approximate position where you want it. As you drag the slide around, you will see that the space between slides turns black as the slide moves over it. This is the position that the slide would move into if you released it at this point.

If you find yourself with extra or unwanted slides, you can delete the slides individually by clicking on each one and then using Edit/Cut to remove them from the order. You can recover a deleted slide by immediately selecting Edit/Undo.

While you are in the Slide Sorter, you have access to the slide Numbering button. You use this button to set the order of the slides, rather than dragging them around the light table. The first slide you select after pressing the Numbering button becomes the first slide in the order. The second slide selected becomes the second, and so on.

When you move slides from one show to another, only the foreground elements are moved. The backgrounds are specifically attached to the show that they started in.

Another use of the Slide Sorter View is to add slides from another slide show. Open both shows in the window, using Arrange All to place them in an accessible position. Then use Edit/Cut or Edit/Copy to move slides from one show to another.

F/X—The Special Effects

As promised, you can use CorelSHOW to produce some very exciting effects for your slide shows. There are two drop-down menus on the button bar which are accessed by clicking on the down arrow next to either the Transition Effect or Time On Screen boxes.

The Transition Effect list is made up of 22 different ways that you can make the slide appear on the screen.

◆ CellLeft

◆ CellLeftDissolve

◆ CurtainClose

◆ CurtainOpen

◆ Dissolve

◆ HorizBlind

◆ HorizBlindDissolve

◆ VertBlind

◆ VertBlindDissolve

◆ WipeDown

◆ WipeLeft

◆ WipeRight

◆ WipeUp

◆ ZoomIn

◆ ZoomInSlow

◆ ZoomInFast

◆ ZoomInDissolve

◆ ZoomOut

◆ ZoomOutSlow

◆ ZoomOutFast

◆ ZoomOutDissolve

◆ Animation—Only used with AutoDesk Animator Pro figures

The Time On Screen list is used to set the amount of time in seconds an individual slide is displayed during the show. This amount is set by selecting a slide and then clicking the down arrow and selecting a time interval.

◆ 1

◆ 2

◆ 3

- ◆ 5
- ◆ 10
- ◆ 20
- ◆ 30
- ◆ 45
- ◆ 60

As you set the time for each slide, you will notice that the two timers in the bottom-right corner of the window are changing. The first timer indicates the amount of time the show has taken up to, but not including, the current slide. The second timer shows the total time for all the slides when shown.

The time a slide stays on during a show is accurate when run with the CorelSHOW Run-time Player module. When the movie-camera icon, to the far left of the button bar, is pressed, the show pauses for each slide so that you can examine the effect demonstrated.

The Rest of the Tools of CorelSHOW

The Main menu bar has additional tools which are used to further customize the presentation or show which you are preparing.

File and Edit

From the File menu, you can access the Page Setup dialog box where you determine, either before you start or during the preparations, what type of presentation you want and how it will be interpreted as a page. You can choose from:

- ◆ Letter
- ◆ Legal
- ◆ Tabloid
- ◆ Slide
- ◆ Screen
- ◆ Custom
- ◆ Overhead
- ◆ A3

◆ A4

◆ A5

◆ B5

As you click on each one of these, you will see a predefined dimension listed in the Horizontal and Vertical dimension boxes. You can change these settings only if you have selected the Custom page definition. If you have selected Custom, you can also determine whether the measurements you use are in inches, millimeters, picas/points, or points.

You also have control over the orientation of the page by checking either the Portrait or the Landscape check boxes at the top of the dialog box.

You can click on File/Run Screen Show to run the slide show instead of clicking the Run Show button on the button bar.

On the Edit menu, you will also see Edit CorelDRAW Graphic as a selection. This is dimmed if you do not have a CorelDRAW object selected on the page, but if you have selected one, pressing this menu item will open CorelDRAW and the original figure.

After working with the figure, you use File/Exit & Return to Corel-SHOW to go back to CorelSHOW. You will also be prompted to update the linked figure that you have just edited.

The Edit/Links menu item is used to open the Link Properties dialog box (see Figure 11.11). Any objects which you have placed in the slide show with OLE or Paste Special will be listed here with their applications.

You can select from these buttons at the bottom of the dialog box:

◆ Open Source—opens the application which the object was created in.

◆ Update Now—updates an object which has been changed since it was embedded in the slide.

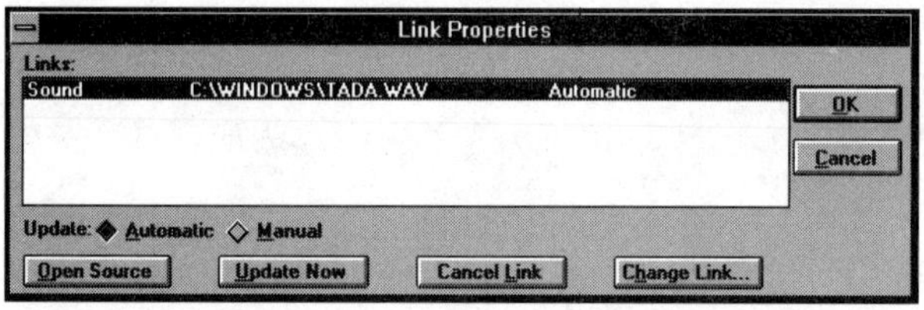

FIGURE 11.11:

The Link Properties dialog box

Link Properties

Links:
Sound   C:\WINDOWS\TADA.WAV   Automatic   OK
Cancel

Update: ◆ Automatic ◇ Manual
Open Source   Update Now   Cancel Link   Change Link...

◆ Cancel Link—removes the object and its link from the presentation.

◆ Change Link—gives you a fast means of selecting a different file in place of the current one.

You can also select whether an object is automatically updated when it is changed, or manually updated; you select an object from the list and click on the update method you want. If you select Manual, you use the Update Now button to make any updates to the object once it has changed.

Arrange

The Arrange menu is used to organize the elements of the individual slides in relationship to each other. The slide is essentially made up of layers of elements. You can arrange the elements by selecting from To Front, To Back, Forward One, and Backward One. To Front and To Back place the selected element at the extreme front or the extreme back of the slide, respectively.

Fit Object To Page should be used with care. This item stretches the selected object to fill the page, regardless of the object's original orientation.

Display

NOTE *The display of the rulers can be set either in the Ruler Setup by checking the Display Rulers box, or from the Display menu.*

You can control the zero line of the rulers by selecting the Rulers Setup item. This will take you into a dialog box where you can set a starting value on the ruler such that the top and left corners on the page are in relationship to the ruler. You can also control whether they are displayed in inches, millimeters, picas/points, or points.

You can turn the display of the rulers on and off by checking the Display/Display Rulers menu item.

Guidelines can also be set up to aid you when placing objects in a slide. When you click on Guideline Setup in the Display drop-down menu, you can set both the Horizontal and Vertical placement from the Guidelines dialog box which appears. You can also select Add, Delete, Move, or Next (to change the Next guideline) to control a series of these guidelines. Guidelines are like the background you placed in the presentation, in that one set of guidelines remains for the entire show.

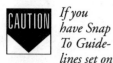

If you have Snap To Guidelines set on and are sizing an object while holding down the Shift key (which makes sizing changes from both or all directions identically), the object will jump to guidelines and not size evenly. Try turning Snap To off, and remember the Edit/Undo menu item.

You can also select Snap To Guides from the dialog box or directly from the Display menu. When you set Snap To Guides on, as you move the objects (or elements) around on the slide (or page), they will naturally gravitate to the guidelines as they get close. This can be very helpful for placing related objects on progressive slides.

The Save Settings item on the Display menu is used to keep the new settings as the *permanent* settings whenever you open CorelSHOW.

SPECIAL NOTES FROM COREL

Corel places README files in the CORELDRW directory, which have installation tips, video card notifications, and other news that could not be included in the manuals. Use the Windows Notepad to read these files.

The current version of CorelSHOW has several minor limitations which you should be aware of. These affect the colors you can import, the use of special effects in CorelCHART, AutoDesk Animator Pro animation files, and Microsoft Excel files.

CorelSHOW will not import graphics with 256 colors. While the figures can be copied to the Windows Clipboard, and then inserted into your page, they will only be 16 colors. It is recommended that you use CorelPHOTO-PAINT as an intermediate step in the importing process from applications other than Corel products.

If you have placed fountain fills (multicolor effects) or bitmap or vector graphics in your charts prepared with CorelCHART, it will not be possible to link them through the Windows Clipboard. Corel is always working to solve reported problems such as this, and you should remember to send in your registration card in order to be notified of any updates.

AutoDesk animations will show full-screen only on VGA graphics systems with the Windows VGA driver installed. Even with the appropriate driver installed, there are several VGA cards which are experiencing problems when Animator Pro files (FLI or FLC) are shown with CorelSHOW. Check the README files for the most current list of video cards with questionable results.

Files created with Microsoft Excel 4.X must be saved as Excel 3.0 format files in order to place them in the presentations.

WRAPPING UP

The joys that you experienced when you first started using CorelDRAW can now be completed by combining your creations with some imaginative titling, some music you capture with your SoundBlaster Pro board, and maybe some packaging (again created with CorelDRAW) to distribute your latest innovations. Consider sending PC slide shows run with the CorelSHOW Run-time Player instead of greeting cards the next time you want to send best wishes to your nephew or niece, brother or sister, etc.

TWO

Guide

to

Design

his section of *Mastering CorelDRAW 3* will help you apply your skills at operating the package to real-world design issues. It will provide you with a resource of ideas and a wealth of tips and guidelines to help you transform your knowledge of the operation of CorelDRAW as software into an understanding of the application of CorelDRAW to art and commercial graphics.

FAST TRACK

CHAPTER

12

you'll often be confronted with fairly commonplace images. It's rare that you'll be able to draw genuinely new, unusual subjects. You can make people look at them, however, by the treatment you give them. Illustrating a subject in an unusual context, from a perspective not normally seen, in juxtaposition with another image—these are all ways to take an image out of the ordinary. Consider "Rex," the creature that graces the cover of this book. Clearly, when you've seen one iguana, you've not seen them all.

remember that there are exceedingly few truly universal images. Try to determine who your audience is, what they're predisposed to be told, and what exactly you're trying to say to them. Keep in mind that most audiences have a conception of themselves which is probably different from your own. Try to understand how members of your audience see themselves.

by making your graphic images pointedly out of context. For example, the Lifetime graphic in the color insert of this book does this very effectively—the image of sand dunes and that of gears are very much out of keeping with each other, and finding them both in the same graphic attracts your attention to the entire image. One of the powerful aspects of graphic arts is that it enables you to create images that could never exist in "real life."

To find visually effective characteristics, ... **512**

keep in mind that a drawing need not literally depict its subject. Not all qualities can be conveyed effectively in a visual medium. This is especially true of things that are normally experienced through nonvisual attributes—feel, taste, aroma, sound—and of intangible things, such as value, tradition, danger, and so on. In many cases, when confronted with the challenge of creating effective graphics to express these sorts of objects or ideas, you'll have to cheat and find related characteristics that can be handled visually. For example, since you can't very well draw a loud amplifier, you might want to consider drawing a big one, suggesting that it's powerful.

CHAPTER 12

Designing

for

Good

Effect

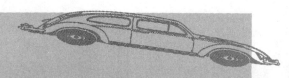

The letter A developed from the Phoenician aleph and the Greek alpha. It is first found in Latin. The capital letter A is found in Etruscan and Latin. The northern Semitic and was retained in...

You've probably realized by now that CorelDRAW is not as difficult to use as it first appears when you peel the shrink wrap off its box. At this point, you have mastered the mechanics of making the package work, thanks in large part to its combination of a well designed user interface and simple tools.

The next section of this book will deal with the real function of Corel-DRAW—that of design. Most likely, the reason you bought CorelDRAW was not to create complex Bézier curves, set optimum screen densities, or be able to create type in a hundred fonts. It was to create finished art.

It may well be argued that any book which purports to make you into an artist is lying to you. Design—whether it's done with pencils or with paths and nodes—is very much an art, and one which cannot be learned over the space of a couple of chapters. The real task in mastering CorelDRAW is in learning to use your mechanical skills in an artistic way.

In this chapter, we'll look at some of the fundamental elements of design, and some approaches to using CorelDRAW in ways that will make your graphics visually interesting and eye-catching—which is, to an extent, the whole objective of commercial art. With an eye for design and Corel-DRAW, you will be able to produce quick and effective commercial art without going to the expense of using a graphics house.

Some of the examples in this chapter are actually complete pages, incorporating both CorelDRAW's output and some text, in this case from Ventura Publisher. We'll discuss the finer points of importing CorelDRAW into desktop publishing documents in Chapter 10.

CREATING INTEREST

It's difficult to look at a visually exciting image and define precisely why that particular picture appeals to you or attracts your attention when other, similar ones do not. However, by developing an intuitive sense of these intangible characteristics, you'll make the transition from a CorelDRAW operator to a CorelDRAW artist.

Creating interest can involve taking an object which we are already familiar with, such as the image of an iguana, and making us take a second look at the figure. Take, for instance, the drawing named *rex* in the color insert of this book. What is it that catches your eye? Is it the eye of the iguana? Is it the textures and colors applied to the image?

Rex offers a multitude of perspectives on an iguana, ranging from a black and white sketch in the lower-left corner to a more life-like depiction in the upper-right corner. In between is a tiled collage of different colors and textures. Each single tile presents a color and texture combination that could be used alone as an eye-catching effect for the entire iguana. But the artist has chosen to combine all of the tiles into a rich mosaic, for an even more compelling and visually exciting drawing.

You probably have seen photographs of the most mundane things—computer circuit boards, jet engine turbines, sunglasses—which have been rendered striking and exciting because of the way in which they were photographed. People get paid a lot for making computer circuit boards look interesting and, considering how many of them there are and how much they all look alike, perhaps rightly so.

A computer circuit board is a thin green slab of epoxy resin with some black chips soldered to it, and there's nothing in the least bit sensuous or exciting about one as you hold it in front of your face. However, the interesting images of these things which turn up in magazine ads are never photographed as they would appear in front of your face. The camera is often positioned at an impossibly oblique angle, such that you see the board as if you were very small and standing amongst its circuitry. Sometimes the board will be lighted in an unusual way, or placed in unlikely surroundings.

The reason that high-priced photographers can make you look at a photograph of a computer circuit board when you thought you had no real interest in doing so is that they can show you the thing in a way that you'd not normally see it. While they cannot make the board itself any less dull, they can apply a unique *treatment* to the subject, and it is this treatment that makes you look at the photograph.

A good example of an ordinary drafting assignment made into an eye-catching drawing is *Techdraw*, also found in the color insert of this book. By adding color to the figure on the right, the draftsperson has become an artist.

If you were to place a sheet of paper over the right half of the figure, all you would see is a pen-and-ink figure of a mechanical device. The use of shading and color in the right-hand figure accents the cutaway portion and draws your interest more into the layout of the piece of equipment being shown. (Certainly, many drafting programs have the ability to add color to the project; but how many of them allow you to export the results in the manner that CorelDRAW does?)

Human beings are sensuality junkies. If you create visual art which looks like visual art they've already seen, you will not provide them with any new experiences, and you will not attract their attention as a result. If there were a set of numbered rules for designers, this would be the first: Make your graphics innovative and different from the backdrop of everything around them. This is one of the keys to making graphics effective.

 Effective graphic designers are method actors at heart. It helps to pretend to be a member of your intended audience to get a feel for what will appeal to its real constituents.

DEFINING YOUR AUDIENCE

Before you can create effective graphics, you have to define your audience (or your vidience, as it were). More specifically, you have to ask yourself two important questions concerning your potential viewers, namely,

◆ What are you trying to say to them with the graphic you're attempting to create?

◆ What are they predisposed to be told?

A good graphic—that, is, an effective graphic—is by no means a universal thing. Visual messages are meaningful only if they're created with the framework of their intended audience in mind. Unfortunately, it's often very difficult for an artist to separate his or her own framework from that of a prospective audience.

Simple graphics invariably work better than complex ones. Avoid the temptation to use CorelDRAW's facilities for filling a page with unwarranted detail. Long before your printer refuses to print it, your audience will refuse to look at it.

Before you can create effective graphics, it's often necessary to do a bit of long-distance psychoanalysis of the attitudes and predispositions of the people you expect to see your work. There are a number of other things you might want to think about in defining your audience. For example, if you perceive your audience as being characteristically busy, then complex graphics which take a lot of time to appreciate would be inappropriate. If your audience can be expected to be cultured and refined, you can use classical allusions and sophisticated images effectively. If your audience has some special characteristic—they're all jet-engine turbine designers, for example, or all teachers—you can create images which involve their inside knowledge. Such images can be both visually interesting and effective because they involve your audience directly.

None of this sort of analysis is particularly easy, and it's usually complicated by the problem of trying not to color your observations about your audience with your own predispositions.

RULES AND HOW TO BREAK THEM

Use the CorelDRAW Perspective and Extrude functions to make objects appear to be viewed from odd angles—a quick way to make things visually unusual.

One of the best general approaches to design is to create images which obviously have a set of rules associated with them and then to break those rules strategically. Figure 12.1 illustrates two magazine pages. They both have essentially the same contents, but the right-hand one is arguably more eye-catching because it deliberately violates an obvious rule, that of keeping graphics within boxes.

Most graphics are ultimately constrained to some sort of fixed boundaries, and these frequently represent the most appealing targets for breaking rules. Consider, to begin with, that every piece of art which emerges from your laser printer does so with a frame around it, this being the periphery of the paper it's printed on.

Figure 12.2 presents two illustrations of the same graphic. They're both the same size, but the right one has violated the boundary of the box it resides

FIGURE 12.1:

Breaking an obvious visual rule

FIGURE 12.2:

An approaching ship

in, and thus implies greater proximity or greater size. By failing to be successfully constrained by the box it's printed in, it suggests that it's big.

One of the most effective boxes to do this with is the periphery of a sheet of paper. Having a picture which is printed partially off the paper implies that its subject is big or strong—or has some superlative characteristic—without having to say so.

One of the longstanding rules of typography is that the characters in text shouldn't touch. However, consider the two headlines in Figure 12.3. The second one might be said to be bad typography, but it's visually striking. It seems to imply that the message in the text is so potent and full of meaning that the width of the text is barely able to contain it.

As with all design elements, this sort of headline has its place. If you use this effect constantly, it will soon cease to be an effect at all. Secondly, if you use it in the wrong place it will be counter-effective. Fat, bulging titles might be very badly out of place on a menu, for example.

One of the more effective design effects is that of juxtaposition, of combining images which would not normally be seen together. CorelDRAW is, of course, a superb tool for this, as it will allow you not only to combine disparate graphics, but to manipulate them so that they fuse together seamlessly. The picture in Figure 12.4 is an example of using two unrelated images.

If a flock of pigs flew over your town you'd probably notice them. Just about everyone would notice them. There's a perfectly obvious reason for this. It violates another rule: Pigs don't fly. Showing a squadron of them in a V formation would be an example of creating a graphic to show something that has never been seen.

When you're breaking rules in a graphic, strive to make the rules and the fact that they're being deliberately broken obvious.

A few years ago, most designers would have felt that you could use any color you like in a design—with three notable exceptions, these being cyan, magenta, and yellow. These primary colors were only for the eyes of printers and pressmen. However, in attempting to create eye-catching designs, someone must have observed that there were three colors which, as if by mutual conspiracy, had never been seen. They've become quite common by now.

Another important rule of typography is that type should be easily readable. There are more reasons for violating this rule than can readily be

FIGURE 12.3:

Two approaches for doing titles

FIGURE 12.4:

The popular prefaded blue-denim personal computer

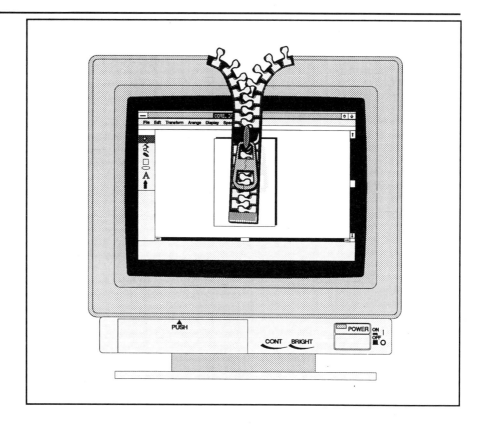

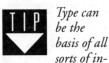

Type can be the basis of all sorts of interesting graphic effects. But make sure you differentiate between type that should merely look like words and type which is actually intended to be read.

counted with small numbers. One example of this rule-breaking which has been cropping up a lot in magazine design of late is the apparent thyroid problem which drop caps seem to be having. Consider Figure 12.5.

This is another example of violating a rule to express something through the impression of size. The statement which the immense drop cap in the last example makes is that the page it is part of is extremely important. It would be nice if it could be printed on a billboard so that *all* of its important words could be set in enormous type, but, the constraints of publishing being what they are, the first thing you read will have to set the tone.

CREATING EFFECTIVE GRAPHICS FOR INTANGIBLE THINGS

Perhaps more often than designers would prefer to admit, the visual message in a graphic is to convey the characteristic of something being superlative— or, at least, of having more of something than it used to have, or more than its competitors have. We have become a somewhat graph-oriented culture, and designers are often asked to represent nonvisual things as visual. Consider the graphics in Figure 12.6, which represent some nonvisual phenomena in perfectly understandable visual forms.

In the figure entitled *Lifetime* in the color insert, we can see a clear example of the artist's use of tangible objects to express intangible concepts. If we are to infer from the title that the artist is making a statement concerning time, we can further expect that the juxtaposition of the clocks, the hourglass, and the sands refers to the measurement and passage of time.

This just goes to show you that the extent of CorelDRAW's ability to produce these elements frees you to explore your artistic creativity.

One of the tasks one can avoid is the redrawing and scaling of each of the clock faces. If CorelDRAW's tools were less able to accomplish the mechanical tasks, you would find yourself having to work more on the technical chores than on the expression of your ideas.

Expressing that a nonvisual quality is *greater* has generally involved presenting it occupying more *area,* or an area which is further removed from the bottom of the page. Even people who are not by nature analytical have a certain predisposition to graphs and analogous structures.

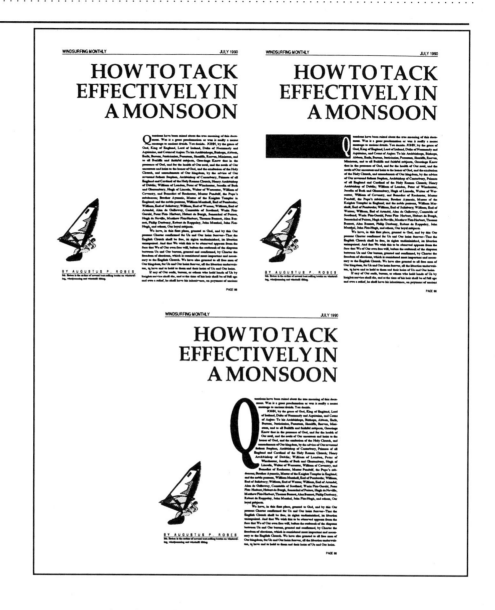

Consider the problem of depicting an amplifier with the intent of creating an effective amplifier advertisement. Most people buy amplifiers because they want to hear music. Allowing that even mediocre amplifiers have pretty good specifications these days, the deciding factor will probably be how loud the amplifier in question can make your music sound. Unfortunately, loudness is a characteristic which is difficult to convey in visual

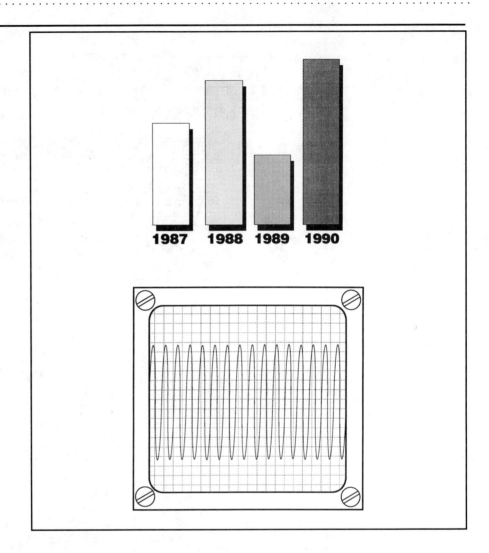

terms. However, consider that most people will regard an amplifier which is capable of rocking the foundation of a building and setting off seismographs as being strong. Although it might turn into an ambitious project, these are occurrences which can be illustrated with drawings. On a simpler level, big amplifiers will be regarded as being stronger than little amplifiers. Thus, while you probably can't depict a loud amplifier all that well visually, you can certainly depict a big one.

TIP

CorelDRAW is not a camera, and if the sponsor of your work had wanted a photographer, he or she could probably have hired one. Remember, the power of CorelDRAW is often in its ability to create images that are beyond the abilities of photorealistic techniques.

Another of the obvious rules of design is that graphics should depict their subjects accurately. You can often break this rule very effectively. In Figure 12.7, the picture on the left is a more accurate drawing of a Porsche than the picture on the right. However, the picture on the right implies that it's a drawing of a much faster Porsche: The visual implication is that the car was so fast that it was half off the page before the picture could be printed.

If your graphic is intended to sell Porsches, you might consider that anyone who's likely to buy a Porsche will probably already know what one looks like, and will not require the advertisement merely to be able to recognize one. One of the things which really recommend Porsches is their ability to go fast. Depicting a fast Porsche is therefore a lot more important than depicting a whole Porsche.

There are, to be sure, all sorts of qualities which cannot be expressed with graphics that imply bigger, stronger, or otherwise more potent. Creating effective graphics in these situations requires a bit more of the aforementioned long-distance psychoanalysis.

FIGURE 12.7:

Two views of a fast car

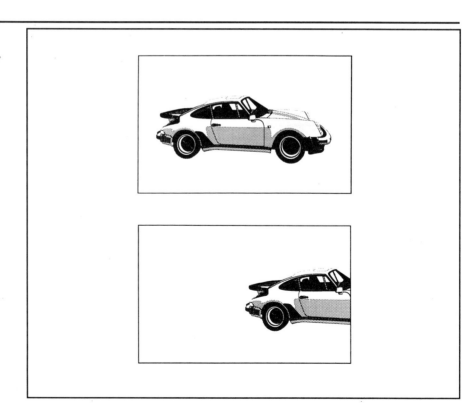

Let's start with a fairly obvious example. Consider how you would create an effective graphic which depicts a really appetizing hamburger. You could draw a picture of a burger, but this has a lot of potential pitfalls. If you draw a burger with pickles on it, it will not be appetizing to people who don't like pickles. Of course, you could leave off all the things which *might* be unappetizing, but then you'll be left with a pretty bare burger. If your graphic is viewed by someone who's just eaten, it won't be effective no matter how you draw it.

This particular example is useful because it has been solved countless times. In effect, this allows you countless opportunities to cheat, (see how other people have solved the problem). Consider the advertisements for McDonalds. McDonalds is very effective at selling hamburgers. They do so often without implying that their burgers are good to eat, and they run many of their advertisements during the evening, when they might well assume that most of the people watching them have already eaten.

McDonalds doesn't actually sell hamburgers in their advertisements. They sell characteristics of McDonalds which are more readily depicted in a universal way through the essentially visual medium of television—things like fast, friendly service and clean restaurants; and still more subtle things, like happy families or an exciting lifestyle, depending on which ad you happen to catch.

There's an important rule to be learned by studying McDonalds' advertising: In attempting to create effective graphics, you must determine which qualities of the thing you want to depict can be conveyed to your audience visually.

Here's a slightly less commercial problem. Draw a picture of perfume. In this problem, let's assume that budgetary constraints preclude the use of a scratch 'n' sniff sample of the perfume in your drawing.

It's wholly impossible to convey the aroma of perfume visually. However, smells are evocative, perfumes especially so. Since you can't draw a picture of the smell, you should probably give some thought to drawing a picture of what the smell evokes. This is another, fairly major violation of the rule that a drawing must accurately depict its subject.

DESIGNING PAGES

If you leaf through the Symbol and Clip Art Libraries book which accompanies CorelDRAW, you'll find a lot of great *images.* You won't find any good *pages,* though. It is, after all, a catalog.

 *Never forget that everything you draw will be framed by the edges of the paper it's printed on. Always try to make your graphics work within the context of this frame.*

As we discussed earlier in this chapter, just about every application of graphics involves some sort of a boundary. Most often it is the edge of your page, but if you're designing graphics for packaging, for example, it might be the edges of a box. Whatever your boundaries consist of, you should regard them as being part of your complete design. A graphic stuck on a page is a picture; a graphic which becomes part of the page is a design.

With the exception of the sorts of conceptual art which are no longer considered fashionable—paintings of polar bears in snow storms or black cats in tar pits, for example—every page will have a *focus,* either intentionally or not. A focus is that which first draws your eye to the page and leads you into whatever else is there.

You might consider that absolutely everything you look at contains a focus of this sort, this being the thing which draws your eye out of the background of visual images. At the moment, you can probably see not only this book but also the room around you. However, the book is the focus of your attention.

An important distinction between this book and most of the graphics and subsequent pages you'll create is that you bought this book, and you are presumably motivated to read it because you *want* to know what it has to say. In many cases, the audience of your graphics will not be so motivated, and the first task of your work will be to keep them from simply turning the page or focusing on something else.

In creating complete pages, strive to design graphics that have a single focus to catch one's eye and then to lead it into the rest of the page.

If you merely create images without regard to the final design of the pages they'll rest on, the ultimate focus will be left to chance. However, if you take into account the way people look at things, you can focus their attention to great advantage. You can attract them into your page and direct their attention where you want it when they first start considering the contents of the page in general. This is true with both wholly visual pages and with pages which combine graphics and text.

In creating an effective page design with an unequivocal focus, you must once again think about both your audience and what you're trying to convey. This second point bears some discussion, because it's often unclear to designers what they're really supposed to focus the attention of their audiences on.

For an example of this, try to read a coffee-table book. It's very nearly impossible. Coffee-table books consist of pages which are mostly pictures, drawn together with a thread of text that runs from page to page and fills up the left-over spaces. The text is hardly the focus of the pages. Each time you turn a page, your eye will be drawn to the photographs, which typically occupy a lot more space than the text does. When you do try to read, you will find that your reading is constantly distracted.

Coffee-table books aren't meant to be read. The text is usually little more than an ornament, or a condescension to people who feel that there's something less than refined in looking at books which have nothing but pictures in them. The focus of the pages is the pictures.

Coffee-table books also have the advantage of a captive audience, something which few applications for graphics can assume.

Consider the things which catch your eye, that is, things which focus your attention to a particular part of a page. These things fall into two broad classes. The first is simply that which is visually different from its surroundings—a picture in a page otherwise filled with text, a dark area in an otherwise light image, a brightly colored object against a background of otherwise muted colors. The second is an image which you find interesting or remarkable for its content.

The first class of focus elements is universal. These things will work for everyone who sees them. The second tends to be more audience-specific.

A page which lacks a clear focus is much less appealing than one which implicitly directs the attention of someone looking at it. People are lazy in this respect, especially if they're in a hurry. They want their eye to be told where to go and how best to appreciate the page with the least amount of effort on their part. This may be kind of slothful and un-zenlike, but it's the way things are.

The elements of a well-designed page are often said to *lock together*. There is a clear path for the eye, from the initial focus through the material on the rest of the page. The arrangement of objects on the page is visually pleasing. The page conveys an amount of information which is in keeping with the viewer's ability to absorb it.

Figure 12.8 illustrates two examples of the same page. They both have the same information, but the one on the left doesn't really lock together. The

FIGURE 12.8:

*Two pages with the
same content but dif-
ferent degrees of focus*

picture is obviously the focus of the page, but it doesn't lead one's eye anywhere in particular. There's type all over creation, and if you want to read the type you have to wander around trying to find it. There's no obvious order to it, either—your eye will have to pause frequently to decide where to look next. By contrast, the page on the right pulls you into its center to look at the picture and then up to the copy fairly effectively.

USING WHITE SPACE

One of the principal pitfalls of CorelDRAW is actually its ability to create complex pages. Someone once remarked that music consists of both the notes and the pauses between them; the same can be said of page design. In creating a page, you should try to find the balance between a page which is too sparse to have any sort of direction to it at all and one which is too cluttered and busy to have an obvious direction amidst the tangled underbrush. Pages which consist primarily of white space—unless it's done deliberately for effect—suggest that there's nothing to look at on the page, or at least not enough to make it worth pausing to consider what might be there. Pages which consist of a wall of type or a barrage of images, on the other hand, are intimidating. They convince someone considering the page that it will take a lot of mental effort to figure out what's happening.

There is very little point in conveying a lot of information which no one reads. It's arguably better to create pages which say less, but which do so in a way that makes them hard to skip over.

You can open out a dense page—let it breathe, in designers' terms—by introducing some white space into it. If you're working with color, of course, this may translate into colored space. The important thing is that the space in question not have anything distracting in it.

There are all sorts of ways to introduce some white space into a page. If you have a large graphic on the page, consider reducing it or positioning it so that only part of it is visible. Inasmuch as CorelDRAW lets you change the density of the fills in your drawings, you might want to try lightening the graphics you've used. A fainter picture can often be a lot less dominating. If the page contains text, set some of the text in a large spindly font with lots of leading. We'll discuss the uses of text in this regard in greater detail in Chapters 13 and 14.

Most publications—books, magazines, quarterly reports, and so on—have a lot of text and graphics in them. Designing one of the pages with a larger amount of white space can be an effective way to call attention to it. Multiple-page publications, furthermore, offer superb design opportunities for setting up rules and then breaking them deliberately.

An interesting use of white space is shown in the color insert in the drawing entitled *Venice*. Here, the white space is actually colored *burgundy* to set the graphic off from the rest of the page. However, if you were to frame the figure with a white border, the figure would lose a good deal of its emphasis. The burgundy ties into the burgundy shading of the wall at the left side of the frame.

However, using the colored framing alone is not enough. By adding the word Venice, the artist has given the frame enough of an additional detail so that the frame is not plain. And at the same time, the text does not distract from the picture as a whole; rather, it gives it the final element of dimension, just as the small amounts of text in coffee-table books keeps the white space from overpowering the pictures.

DESIGNING WITH TWO PAGES

The possibility of having more than one page is something many designers overlook. If you're creating pages for a magazine, pamphlet, or anything which is bound—like a book—consider that although you may work on one page at a time, your audience will regard your work as two facing pages. When someone opens a magazine, the initial focus of what's before them will be a pair of pages.

By ignoring the fact that there are two pages in front of someone looking at your graphics, you could easily create a *page spread* that doesn't work very well. On the other hand, if you bear in mind that most of your pages must work with at least one other page, you can often do some clever things with the spread.

Most double-page spreads are intended to focus initial attention somewhere in the upper left corner of the left page. If this area is occupied by an interesting graphic, it will lead the eye of a reader naturally into the page. If it starts with some unremarkable-looking type, the reader will tend to wander around the two pages, looking for an obvious focus.

Spanning the *gutter* between two pages is a singularly effective way of tying the two pages together. However, you can't actually print a picture which prints right to the edge of a page on a conventional laser printer. If you want to be able to do this, you'll probably have to have your final pages handled by an output service or a typesetting house with a PostScript typesetter.

DESIGNING LOGOS AND SYMBOLS

No other area of design speaks to the reality of contemporary Western civilization better than that of designing symbols. A well designed symbol conveys at a glance a lot about whatever it symbolizes, and a glance is the most that some people can spare. In a world where you can seldom hope for more than a moment of someone's attention, an art form which only requires a moment to fully appreciate seems destined to ascend in importance.

The most obvious use of icons outside of user-friendly computer interfaces is in corporate logos. Logo design has been refined to a high art, and with good reason. Logos are commissioned by the most rushed members of society, upper-management executives. It's not surprising that they regard them as being important.

Designing functional logos requires the application of many of the design criteria which have come up in this book, and it entails ignoring a few others. A good logo will catch the eye, say what it has to say, and be gone. Logos which seek to provoke curiosity, appreciation, subtlety, contemplation, or the enjoyment of good commercial art creatively executed have failed before they even start. People don't stare at logos that long.

In this chapter we'll have a look at the rudiments of designing logos and symbols with CorelDRAW. By definition, a good logo is one which has not been seen before, so you won't be able just to modify the examples in this chapter. Hopefully, though, you'll be able to use the approaches explained herein and apply them to your own logos.

APPROACHING LOGOS

The intensity of your design effort for a logo or symbol will probably vary. If the project in question is to design a set of symbols for an annual report or a dinner menu, for example, you will probably not want to spend a full week brainstorming what they should look like. Logos which look like they'll be around for a while, however, usually call for at least this much involved research. The final result of your work may well be a pretty simple graphic, but designing a logo that says everything it's supposed to is by no means a simple task. You'll find this to be exceedingly evident if there are several people involved in the process of ultimately accepting the logo you're designing. Everyone seems to think that a logo should say something different.

A logo is a unique sort of symbol. Consider the requirements for a company logo:

◆ It must express what the company it represents *is.*

◆ It must express what the company it represents *aspires to be,* or thinks it is or will be.

◆ It must please the eye, and express positive visual associations for the company it represents.

◆ It must communicate across great distances of culture, background, and personal predisposition.

◆ It must work very, very fast.

There are secondary, mechanical considerations, too. For example, logos which incorporate color should usually be reproducible in black-and-white as well.

There are few perfect logos, and few occasions in which everyone involved in the design and acceptance of a logo will agree that one is perfect, even if it actually is.

Let's have a quick walk through the above criteria. The first one is representative of the sorts of problems you'll encounter in working out a good logo design. Expressing what a company is involves finding out a lot about it and the people behind it. This is tied in with the second point, that is, finding out what it thinks it is and what it aspires to. A logo for a metal-plating company might properly depict an organization whose by-products get into the local water table and kill fish, but you would probably find that a logo with dead fish on it would not be very well received.

Consider further that corporations, like individual people, will rarely tell you what they really want. One doubts that IBM told the creator of its logo that it wanted a design to convey its character as being monolithic, omnipresent, and immense. One of the skills of whoever it was who designed the IBM logo was the ability to read between the lines of what was said to find the true character of IBM—as seen by IBM, of course.

The most difficult element of logo design exists not in your Corel-DRAW workspace, but in the heads of the people who will look at it after it becomes reality. A symbol is a sort of substitution code. Consider the one in Figure 12.9.

Printed out, this symbol weighs almost nothing. It doesn't smell, doesn't make basso honking noises at five in the morning, never needs feeding, and isn't good to eat. However, I trust it still conveys all the attributes of a cow.

The reason I believe this logo may work is that this conception of a cow and that of pretty well anyone else likely to see the logo should be about the same. I believe I can safely use the symbol without worrying about its being misinterpreted.

Logos are typically seen by a wide range of audiences— it's not very practical to "target" a particular group of people. Avoid images that may confuse or displease some groups.

FIGURE 12.9:

An idea for a logo for Cow, Inc.

In marked contrast to the cow circumstances is the Sanskrit symbol for good fortune. (Sanskrit is an old pictographic language which originated around what is now Tibet.) Upon consideration I have decided not to illustrate the symbol. Although it would be a positive symbol for anyone familiar with Sanskrit, its meaning has been changed perhaps irrevocably because of more recent events. It is a swastika. Today, this would probably not be a good logo for any company, even if it were run by someone well versed in Sanskrit.

These sorts of cultural predispositions are rarely as obvious or as easily understood as most people's reactions in this particular case.

The final criterion on the list of logo requirements is that a logo must work fast, for reasons we discussed above. This doesn't really put any immediate strictures on your designs, but it might provide you with some guidelines. Pictures convey ideas a lot more readily than words. Pictures are also a lot more universal. The word "America" would probably be meaningless to a Bedouin who spoke no English. On the other hand, there probably aren't many people on earth who wouldn't recognize an American flag.

Some things, however, can't be represented well as pictures. Returning to a previous example, it's hard to draw a picture of IBM. It's often difficult to convince the owners of a company that the name of their enterprise should be reduced to a few squiggles and a bit of abstract art. In these cases, a logo which uses type and applies some graphic elements to it might well be more appropriate.

USING TYPE LOGOS

The easiest way to create a symbol is to stylize some type. This will usually *not* result in the most effective logo—as mentioned above, if you *could* represent what you want with a picture, the result would be a more universal logo which communicated its ideas a lot more readily. However, this is not always practical, and, more to the point, there isn't always the time available to do it.

We'll get into the design of pictographic logos later in this chapter.

Anyone can typeset a name, and even if after weeks of head scratching you ascertain that the company you're designing a logo for really would work best with just its name set in Helvetica with a box around it, you're not likely to get away with it. A logo has to look like a graphic—a piece of commercial art—rather than words.

One of the most effective ways to turn type into a graphic is to run the characters together. Using the shape tool in CorelDRAW, select each character in the name which is to become your logo and move them until they touch. Experiment with different typefaces and varying amounts of overlap between characters to produce different degrees of logo-ness. Some typefaces work better than others for this effect. Garamond is my favorite victim in this case. Very lineal faces, such as Helvetica, don't work as well.

Figure 12.10 illustrates various degrees of success using this approach.

If the name of the company in question has some nonalphabetic punctuation in it, consider doing something with it. For example, ampersands are fertile ground for manipulation, especially if you choose a typeface with an interesting one. Figure 12.11 has some examples of the creative use of punctuation.

It would be a fair complaint to suggest that none of the preceding examples says anything about the companies they represent. This is very often the case when one is confronted with creating a logo out of text. There is almost nothing a logo can express visually about a law firm, for example, beyond vague ideas of honesty, stability, and so on.

In many cases, a text-based logo can aspire only to being eye-catching. If the logo will exist in an environment where the qualities of the company it represents are well known, this may be enough. For example, the Kraft Foods logo is nothing more than the word Kraft set in a pretty pedestrian-looking sans-serif type. However, since almost everyone knows that Kraft makes food, one could argue that little more needs to be said.

FIGURE 12.10:

Running characters together

FIGURE 12.11:
Using nonalphabetic characters in logos

There are a lot of things which CorelDRAW can do to text to simply make it visually interesting. More to the point, some of the effects that are no trouble for CorelDRAW would be very difficult to achieve through mechanical means and as such will not have been seen before. Figure 12.12 illustrates a number of hypothetical logos which are really nothing more than special effects.

While perhaps interesting, these logos are conceptually shallow. They say nothing, and like most other special effects they lose their magic and appeal quickly. The logo for a one-time-only trade show, a publication which will be produced once and never again, or an advertisement that's to run for only a short time can probably be treated in this way with acceptable results. Something which is to endure—a logo which will adorn a corporation that plans on being around for a while, for example—should have more substance to it.

Designing Graphic Logos

The problem with designing graphic logos is that you very often have to actually draw the things. While people who call themselves artists probably wouldn't shy away from such an experience, drawing does take time.

Logos designed solely to be eye-catching

The alternative to this is to work up a logo from clip art or a scanned image. This is cheap, odious, and not at all artistic, but it can be an effective way to produce quick results. One of the questions which people rarely ask about a successful logo design is, How did you do this?

Coming up with visual icons to represent the intangible values and aspirations of a company can be a difficult undertaking. Some companies, such as Apple Computer, have obvious visual connections. However, one might well argue that Apple's logo doesn't really fulfill very many of the criteria of good logo design. It says nothing at all about the company it represents, save that Apple is successful enough to be able to afford four-color printing on virtually every document which bears its corporate symbol.

Figure 12.13 is a corporate logo. It's an interesting study in logo design. As an exercise in design, you'll probably appreciate it better if you've not seen it previously, and don't know what it stands for.

This is a much beleaguered symbol. It has been given all sorts of disparaging names, including the happy donut, the exploding cabbage, the self-destructing pizza, and the nuclear basketball. It may or may not deserve them, but it's hard to differentiate between what people feel about the symbol and what they feel about the corporation. Canadians will unquestionably recognize this as being the symbol of the Canadian Broadcasting Corporation. When it first came out, a lot of people thought it was a new logo for the Continental Can Company.

The CBC logo might actually be quite clever. If you regard the big C as being a broadcast antenna and the curves emanating from it as being stylized radio waves, it's a very interesting depiction of the rather abstract process of broadcasting. I have never met anyone else who interpreted it this way,

FIGURE 12.13:

A genuine corporate logo

however, and most of the people to whom I've suggested this analysis had to scratch their heads for a while to regard it as such.

This logo is moderately eye-catching. It's usually printed in orange ink against a blue background, which certainly makes it more eye-catching still. It provokes a certain amount of curiosity, but its actual meaning—if the analogy of an antenna is actually what was in the mind of its designer—is so obscure as to make its message unlikely to be seen by most people.

It might well be argued that a logo whose meaning is subject to this degree of interpretation and uncertainty probably should go back to the drawing board—or be loaded back into CorelDRAW—for one more set of revisions.

In general, a company which makes things should be a lot easier to design for than one which provides intangible services. The CBC logo, above, is a good example of someone trying to represent something intangible in a visual way.

Designing a graphic logo for a lawyer, a stockbroker, or an investment counselor would be a lot more difficult. You'll probably find yourself pressed into using some pretty well-worn symbols if you're confronted with such a task. Consider how many of the logos used to represent medical products or services contain a caduceus—a staff with two entwined serpents and two wings at the top. The caduceus is a dreadful symbol—the actual connection it has to medicine is lost to most people—and it appears to be used only because of a kind of unwritten agreement that it might be appropriate, given the lack of anything better.

Using Abstract Graphics

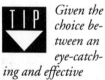

Given the choice between an eye-catching and effective logo and one that is merely faithful to the organization or concept it represents, go for the one that's eye-catching. If no one notices it, it has failed before it starts.

An awful lot of logos use graphics which are simply abstract and eye-catching, but say nothing. Consider the Compaq computer logo, which has a color fountain running through it. The message in this logo, as with most good logos designed this way, is in the general design and typography. The fountain is simply an attention-getting device.

Confronted with a design problem in which there are no obvious symbols available—or one in which the good symbols have already been used—this is not a bad way to approach your design. It implies that the company in question has a sense of originality and abstract thinking, which is better than saying nothing at all. An abstract graphic that looks abstract doesn't take a lot of time to appreciate.

One really elegant source of abstract graphics in CorelDRAW is the PostScript Textures library. Figure 12.14 illustrates some potential uses for these.

At the other end of the spectrum, the Dover books of public-domain clip art may provide you with a limitless supply of potential symbols and adornments if your designs are destined for more traditional clients.

If you apply abstract thinking to your logo designs, you might well find that you can do some particularly clever things with them. Figure 12.15 is another well-known Canadian logo, that of the Canadian National railway. Many people who think consciously about these things regard this as being the most brilliant logo one could ever come up with for a railroad. They say you can almost hear the rattle of wheels on steel rails and the sound of a train's horn echoing in the mountains as you look at it.

FIGURE 12.15:

The CN logo

WRAPPING UP

The best drawing package in the world is useless without someone who can use it, and using it involves a lot more than knowing which menu items to click. Creating graphics with CorelDRAW is a mechanical process, but creating good, effective graphics takes a sense of design.

One of the best ways to develop a sense of design is to analyze designs which are effective for you. Try to make a point of noticing advertisements, magazine page designs, and other examples of commercial art which catch your eye. Having done so, figure out why they caught your eye. It's neither ethical nor particularly productive to lift ideas from existing graphics, but the exercise of figuring out why particular graphics have worked can teach you a lot about design.

As touched on briefly in the chapter on exporting graphics from CorelDRAW, you can apply symbols—icons—to all sorts of designs. A well-chosen symbol can tie the pages of a publication together, reinforce the feeling of unity at a large trade show or seminar, or relate disparate products together.

In designing logos and other symbols with CorelDRAW, you'll have the advantage of being able to try out new designs and variations quickly. One school of symbol design recommends that you create a logo by drawing what you think it should have in it and then removing everything you can take out without it becoming meaningless. CorelDRAW allows you to undertake exercises like this easily and without a lot of redrawing and mechanical work.

**To export a vector graphic to Ventura or
PageMaker,** **541**

you must use CorelDRAW's export filters to create suitable
files from your CDR graphics. If you'll be printing your
desktop publishing documents to a PostScript printer, EPS files
will usually be the best choice. Alternatively, use GEM files for
the GEM version of Ventura Publisher, or Windows Metafiles
for the Windows version of Ventura or for PageMaker.

In exporting a graphic with a fountain, ... **546**

be aware that not all the file formats used by popular desktop
publishing software will deal with fountain fills. You cannot export fountains to the GEM format used by Ventura Publisher
and hope to get workable results. The EPS format is the best
choice, but only if you'll be using a PostScript printer. If none
of the vector formats accepted by your desktop publishing package handles fountains well, consider exporting your drawing to
a bitmapped format.

To export through the Clipboard, ... **548**

select any graphic in a CorelDRAW drawing and then select
Copy from the Edit menu. This will copy the graphic to the
Clipboard. Having done this, switch to your desktop publishing package, select the frame you want to import your graphic
into, and select Paste from the Edit menu of the desktop
publishing package. Note that Ventura Publisher will prompt
you for a file name under which to save the pasted graphic so
that the program will be able to find it when you open your
chapter next time.

you can export lines of text as graphics from CorelDRAW. To create headlines using some of CorelDRAW's many text effects, create the headlines as graphics and export them to a file format that's suitable for use with your desktop publishing software. Once again, the EPS format is the best choice if you'll be outputting your pages to a PostScript printer. If you use a format which supports exporting as text or curves, choose curves.

13

Integrating with Desktop Publishing

The letter A developed from the aleph and the Greek alpha. It was relatively semitic and northern Latin. The capital letter A is first found in Latin. The Etruscan and in the required in Latin.

While it's a great tool all by itself, CorelDRAW really shows its versatility when it's used in conjunction with desktop publishing packages. The strengths of something like Aldus PageMaker or Ventura Publisher—primarily in text formatting—ideally complement the graphic strengths of CorelDRAW. In addition, CorelDRAW's rather generous contingent of typefaces makes it a first-class source of headlines and other small bits of display type.

If your applications involve creating complete documents, as opposed to just discrete pictures, you'll probably find that CorelDRAW and Ventura or PageMaker will form an ideal working environment.

There are two fairly disparate areas to concern yourself with when you load up CorelDRAW with the intention of creating art for export to another application. The first concerns the actual mechanics of handling the exporting of your picture. Much of this was dealt with in Chapter 5, but we will discuss a few more considerations here. The second and perhaps even more intangible aspect of this task is creating graphics which work in the design of the pages they'll ultimately become part of.

In the first part of this chapter, we'll deal with exporting CorelDRAW's graphic files, to Ventura Publisher documents for the most part. Ventura is a good example of desktop publishing software, as it embodies most of the facilities—as well as most of the gremlins—found in other packages of this type. If you use a different desktop publishing package, you'll find that most of the exporting issues are about the same from the point of view of CorelDRAW.

Note that while the examples in this chapter are illustrated by screens from the GEM version of Ventura, users of the Windows implementation will find that almost everything works the same way.

The second main part of the chapter, the design discussion, will be essentially independent of the software you use to create your pages.

BASIC EXPORTING CONSIDERATIONS

Read Chapter 5 carefully before you start exporting graphics. There are numerous options in many of Corel-DRAW's export filters which can affect the quality of your exported graphics.

The CDR files which are native to CorelDRAW are, at the moment, unique to it as well. No non-Corel application will read them. However, by now you know that there are all sorts of ways to represent a drawing in a disk file.

Each of the drawing-file formats which CorelDRAW will import and export has its own way of representing the basic paths and other elements which make up a drawing. Each format also has certain limitations.

As a simple example of this, the GEM drawing-file format—which Ventura Publisher likes to use for most of its drawings—doesn't handle text in the same way that CorelDRAW's CDR files do, with the result that a CorelDRAW drawing exported to a GEM file invariably has all its text reduced to paths. If you import a GEM file with text in it back into CorelDRAW, the text will not be editable as text for this reason.

The WMF import filter in the GEM version of Ventura will not read the WMF files exported by CorelDRAW correctly. Don't try this import path.

This sort of basic problem often makes exporting CorelDRAW files for use with other applications something other than painless.

VERY SIMPLE EXPORTING USING THE CLIPBOARD

The Windows version of Ventura Publisher will read WMF files directly. If you'll be using Windows Ventura, WMF is a better export choice than GEM.

Let's start with a very simple example of exporting, one in which most of the catches have been ironed out beforehand. All Microsoft Windows-based applications which can exchange graphics through the Windows Clipboard do so using a common file format. This is called a Windows Metafile. In fact, the data exchanged between Windows applications in this way never actually winds up as a disk file. As far as the programs which use the Clipboard are concerned, the data is simply handed transparently between applications.

The Clipboard has cropped up occasionally before in using Corel-DRAW. Let's use it once again to investigate the operation of a Windows Metafile.

For this exercise, boot up Windows and then load CorelDRAW.

1. Load or create a small to medium-size drawing. Note that the amount of object data you can store in the Windows Clipboard is somewhat limited, and if you attempt to export a really big picture from CorelDRAW using the Clipboard, Windows will refuse to handle the operation. If this happens, you'll see a dialog box which tells you so.

2. Having created your drawing, select it and copy it to the Clipboard using the Copy item of the Edit menu. Although nothing will appear to have changed, your drawing will now be living in the Windows Clipboard.

3. Load up Write, the word processor which comes with Windows. You can leave CorelDRAW running while you do so. (Running applications concurrently under Windows is discussed in Appendix A.) Write will open with a blank document.

4. Select the Paste item from Write's Edit menu. Your original CorelDRAW drawing will appear at the top of the page which Write is creating.

Figure 13.1 illustrates a Write document with some imported CorelDRAW art.

FIGURE 13.1:

Using CorelDRAW art in Windows Write

Wombdecker, Fizzbatt, Mezzleharp, Zorpfmonger,
Dreedle, Dreedle, Dreedle, Claymore & Leech
C O R P O R A T E   L A W Y E R S

```
Mr. Augustus R. Robes
Crabapple Computers Inc.
1304 San Silicon Way,
Coppertown, CA 94607

February 12, 1990

Dear Mr. Robes,

     I am writing in regards to the legal matter which you requested we
pursue on your behalf. I and my collegue Mr. Leech have done an
extensive investigation of the matter and we have come to the following
conclusions.

     i)    You cannot copyright the little noise that a computer
           mouse makes when it clicks and expect people to pay
           you a licence fee for clicking their mice.

     ii)   A drawing of a box with knobs on it on the back of a
           cocktail napkin dated 1952 will not hold up in court
           as evidence that you invented color television.

     iii)  You cannot patent letters of the alphabet.

     iv)   We can envision no potential for financial gain on
           your part if you do go ahead and sue yourself,
           although we will be happy to take the case if you like.

     In short, while it is our understanding that working in the
microcomputer industry does involve a considerable degree of litigation,
we urge you to consider well what or who you plan to take to court
before contacting us. We have a general rule of thumb that if it barks,
rusts or sheds its leaves in the fall, you would be better off not
attempting to sue it.


     Sincerely,


     M. X. Wombdecker Sr.

     cc: G. Leech
     MXW/acc
```

 Exporting large graphics through the Windows Clipboard can be very time-consuming, and the process can't be interrupted if you run out of patience.

Because both Write and CorelDRAW can use this common export format—the Clipboard—there is little possibility for something to go wrong in the transition between applications. Admittedly, this was a fairly trivial example: The Clipboard does not allow for very large or complex drawings to be exported in this way, and, further, Windows Write is hardly a desktop publishing program. Bear in mind, though, that you can use this process quickly and easily with any suitable Windows-based application, and this includes PageMaker and the Windows version of Ventura. We'll look at the latter case in more detail shortly.

EXPORTING BITMAPPED IMAGES

 Most of Corel-DRAW's export filters will not export bitmapped elements in your CDR files correctly. Only the EPS format will allow you to have line art with bitmapped elements.

As we discussed earlier in this book, CorelDRAW allows you to export drawings in a host of formats in order to make your CorelDRAW artwork suitable for use with as many import applications as possible. In the case of desktop publishing software—which typically import a large number of file formats for much the same reason—you will usually find yourself confronted with several format possibilities.

The simplest and most foolproof way of exporting drawing files is to export your file as a bitmap. Although on the one hand this method has serious drawbacks, on the other hand it overcomes a large number of potential file format inconsistencies by simply ignoring them.

As you know, CorelDRAW exports bitmaps in several formats, the most useful of these being PCX and TIFF. Of these, TIFF is most often the least desirable, as it's poorly defined and likely to cause trouble. Therefore, for simple monochrome graphics, you should consider always using PCX files for bitmap files (as far as CorelDRAW is concerned). The following discussions, in fact, will assume that you are using the PCX format for bitmaps.

If you export a CorelDRAW drawing to a PCX file, the resulting bitmapped image will be unscalable and quite inflexible as graphics go. If you want it to appear at its best upon importing it into a desktop publishing document, you will be forced to use it at the size you exported it. Furthermore, if your final output is bound for a Linotronic typesetter, you will find that bitmapped images don't improve in appearance with higher resolution printers.

The advantage to exporting a bitmapped image, on the other hand, is that there will be virtually no possibility that anything nasty will happen to your drawing in the trackless wastes between CorelDRAW and a desktop publishing program. A bitmap file—especially a monochrome one—is a pretty immutable object, and what you see on your monitor is really what you'll get in printed output. Very few things in desktop publishing can get away with making this claim.

Exporting a CorelDRAW drawing as a bitmap file requires lots of forethought. Because a bitmap file cannot be scaled once it has been exported without losing some quality, you must make sure that your image is properly sized before you export it. Furthermore, you must export it at the 300 dots per inch it was created with if you want it to look as good as it would simply as CorelDRAW output. This also requires some forethought, in that you'll have to allow for a lot of disk space to hold really big 300-dpi bitmap files. Finally, bitmapped files take a long time to print. The larger they are, the longer they take.

In summary, exporting CorelDRAW art to bitmapped files is fool-proof, but, because of the work and planning necessitated by this format, it's best left as a last resort, for use if every other option has failed.

Using PCX Files with Ventura

In Ventura, imported graphics are always poured into *frames* on your document pages. In order to load a graphic into a document, you would select the Load Text/Picture item of the Ventura Files menu, choose the appropriate file format, and select your file.

Having poured a PCX file into a frame in Ventura, you will have to use the Sizing & Scaling dialog box from Ventura's Frame menu to ensure that it gets treated properly. Ventura defaults to scaling imported bitmap files to fit the frames they're poured into—much to the dismay of the graphics themselves, which often look dreadful as a result.

In order to force Ventura to let your imported PCX file find its natural scale, select the By Scale Factors option in the Sizing & Scaling dialog box, as shown in Figure 13.2. The Pict. Width field on the lower left will be enabled, and will be filled in with the natural scale of the image at the resolution you selected with CorelDRAW. If you don't alter this value, you'll get essentially the same picture that you would have gotten had your exported graphic been printed directly from CorelDRAW to a 300-dpi laser printer.

You can crop PCX images with Ventura with no loss of quality.

There are a few potential bugs in even this simple example of exporting. First of all, you should know that when you import a PCX file into Ventura,

FIGURE 13.2:

The Sizing & Scaling dialog box in Ventura Publisher for Windows

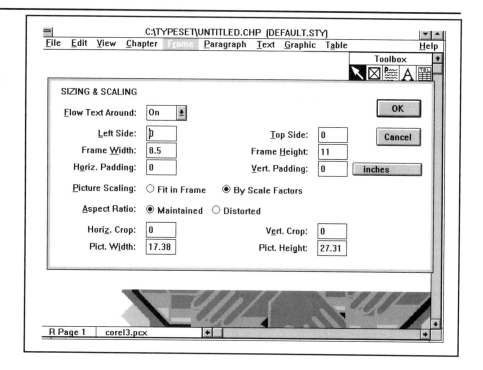

it creates a second file called an IMG file. This is just another image-file format—it happens to be the one which Ventura likes to use. It's a bit better at compressing bitmapped data than a PCX file, but not much. If you start out with a 120-kilobyte PCX file exported from CorelDRAW, plan on there being at least that much more space occupied by the resulting IMG file when Ventura gets through with it.

It would be convenient if CorelDRAW could export directly to IMG files, but it doesn't do this at the moment. You can, however, use an external file-conversion utility such as Graphic Workshop to convert PCX files to IMG files before Ventura gets to them, allowing you to delete the PCX files and have only one copy of your exported image on hand, rather than two.

The use of IMG files by Ventura can create a second, rather weird problem, but this will be discussed a bit later in the chapter, in the "Exporting EPS Files" section.

The other difficulty you might encounter is a genuine bug in Ventura. It's visible in Figure 13.3. This is a PCX file which was exported from CorelDRAW and subsequently imported into Ventura Publisher.

If the horizontal dimension of a PCX file is not evenly divisible by eight—which can happen quite easily under CorelDRAW—the exported file may have up to seven unused pixels at the end of each line. The PCX file instructs Ventura to ignore them, but Ventura chooses to ignore the instruction instead, and rounds the image width up to the next highest eight-pixel boundary. CorelDRAW, for its part, should clear the unused pixels at the ends of the lines, but it doesn't. They usually contain random black or white dots. The result is frequently the accretion of fur at the right edges of CorelDRAW files exported as PCX bitmaps.

Fortunately, this is an easy thing to get around in Ventura. Simply reduce the horizontal dimension of the frame which contains the image, cropping the fur in the process.

FIGURE 13.3:

The attack of the hairy right margin

EXPORTING LINE ART FILES

The best way to export line art—such as a CorelDRAW drawing—is as line art. CorelDRAW can produce readable line art files in all sorts of specialized formats and in three fairly general ones: Windows Metafile, CGM, and GEM. Virtually all applications which can import line art files will read at least one of these. PageMaker, for example, uses Metafiles. Ventura will read all three.

In theory, when CorelDRAW exports a drawing into a GEM file, for example, it simply translates its own notation for each object in the drawing into GEM notation. In practice, things don't always work out that well. There are some things which a CDR file can do which a GEM file cannot, as discussed in Chapter 5. In addition, the GEM format has a size restriction. It can only hold drawings of a finite level of complexity. (The specific numbers and factors for this and related limitations are listed in the CorelDRAW Technical Reference that comes with the package.) This level is none too great, and you will find that it's pretty easy to create a CorelDRAW drawing which cannot be exported to a GEM file because it exceeds the format's limits.

The principal catch in this for GEM Ventura users is that while GEM Ventura will import many types of line art files, it actually converts them all to GEM files before it goes to use them (with one exception, which we'll discuss in a moment). Therefore, even though it's frequently possible to export CorelDRAW art to a Windows Metafile when it cannot be successfully exported to a GEM file, you will not really have sneaked around the problem if your ultimate destination is a Ventura document. Ventura will be unable to translate all of your Windows Metafile into its GEM work file, and you won't be any further ahead.

The Windows version of Ventura is a bit more reasonable about this—in addition to GEM files, it will read Metafiles directly, that is, without translating them into GEM files. Instead, it insists on translating them into Placeable Metafiles. The only drawback to this is a brief pause while it performs the translation, a trivial penalty to be sure. As a rule, you will encounter far fewer importing problems using Metafiles imported into Windows Ventura than you will using GEM files imported into GEM Ventura.

PageMaker will also read Metafiles directly.

The original CDR file from which the drawing in Figure 10.3 was created was too complex to export to a GEM file. If you encounter such a drawing, CorelDRAW will warn you that some of the objects in your original drawing will not be present in your exported file.

You should also note that there is not a one-to-one correspondence between the drawing objects in a GEM file and those in a Windows Metafile. This occasionally results in extraneous lines cropping up in Metafiles imported into Ventura chapters. For this reason, it's preferable to export your CorelDRAW art to GEM files if it's to be imported into Ventura chapters rather than having an extra stage in the translation process.

Exported GEM files are typically pretty compact as line art goes. GEM can support most of the basic attributes that you're likely to use in drawings under CorelDRAW. This includes color, and if you have installed Ventura with one of its color screen drivers, you will see your imported GEM files in the same colors in which CorelDRAW shows them if you use the preview window. If you're using Ventura under Windows, the color capabilities of Ventura will be the same as those of your Windows driver.

This is more than just a light show. Ventura allows you to output separate black and spot-color plates, just like CorelDRAW does. With a bit of coordination, you can export CorelDRAW art with spot-color into a GEM file and have Ventura produce two-color pages for you, handling both its own spot-color text and CorelDRAW's spot-color art.

GEM files have problems with some of CorelDRAW's more sophisticated effects. Fountains, for example, frequently bewilder them. Figure 13.4 shows a fountain which was created under CorelDRAW, exported as a GEM file, and imported into Ventura Publisher. Likewise, PostScript effects and PostScript-related parameters, such as screen frequency and dot shape, are ignored by GEM files. The CorelDRAW PostScript textures cannot be exported to GEM files.

The major advantage to using GEM files in Ventura or Metafiles in PageMaker is that what you see on your screen is really what you'll get when you print your output. Your desktop publishing software will actually interpret the GEM file or Metafile you import and draw what it finds right on your screen. The position of a line-art graphic on your screen will match up perfectly with its final position on your printed pages, making it possible to

If you export graphics with color fills or fountains as gray-level TIFF files, they'll import into Ventura Publisher or PageMaker and print as halftones on a PostScript output device.

FIGURE 13.4:

A CorelDRAW fountain exported to a GEM file, with unsatisfactory results

wrap text around a GEM graphic without having to worry about the picture overlapping it.

GEM and Metafile graphics are true line art. If you output a Ventura or PageMaker chapter containing some GEM or Metafile art exported from CorelDRAW to a high-resolution PostScript typesetter, you'll get to see the advantages of having a high-resolution printer in your art as well as in your text. Further, because they are line art, you can stretch both Metafiles and GEM files with no loss of quality once they're imported into PageMaker or Ventura.

The algorithm which translates the paths of a GEM file into laser-printer data in Ventura is not quite as clever as the one in CorelDRAW. The lines it forms are often not as neat as you might like them. For example, when it is confronted with a path which is formed with half dots (a problem we discussed in Chapter 3), Ventura usually manages to guess wrong. Therefore, CorelDRAW graphics which have lots of small, delicate paths often don't look as good as you might like them to when you handle them as GEM files and output them to a 300-dot-per-inch laser printer. This affects text, among other things, and small text a lot more noticeably than large text. The text problem often manifests itself as type in which the lines forming the characters are noticeably thicker or thinner than they should be in some places.

In instances where you want to export small or precise graphics and you want to ensure that they make the trip with as little distortion as possible, the final solution is usually to use EPS files. However, this approach is not without its drawbacks.

VENTURA AND THE WINDOWS CLIPBOARD

If you're using Ventura Publisher for Windows, there's an additional way to export moderate-size graphics from CorelDRAW to Ventura chapters. You can pass them though the Clipboard in much the same way as discussed earlier in this chapter when the destination application was Windows Write.

When you import a graphic into Ventura through the Clipboard, Ventura will prompt you for a file name to store the graphic in, as illustrated in Figure 13.5. If you bear in mind that all the elements of a Ventura chapter are stored as individual files, this makes sense. Clearly, Ventura can't rely on the graphic remaining in the Clipboard the next time it goes to open the chapter in question.

To use this importing path, do the following:

1. Select the objects you want to export from CorelDRAW using the selector tool.

2. Select the Copy function from the CorelDRAW Edit menu. Copying your graphic to the Clipboard may take a few seconds if it's moderately big.

3. Switch to Ventura Publisher.

4. Add a frame to your chapter to put the graphic in and select it.

5. Select Paste from the Ventura Edit menu. As there's a Metafile on the Clipboard, this item should actually say Paste Metafile.

6. Select a file name to store the Metafile data in.

Note that there is no way to paste a graphic from the Windows Clipboard into the GEM version of Ventura even if you're running it under Windows.

FIGURE 13.5:

*Importing a graphic
from the Clipboard into
a Ventura chapter*

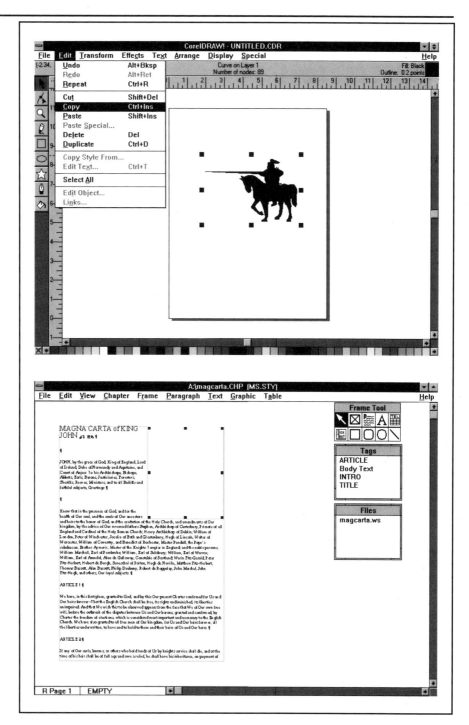

FIGURE 13.5:

Importing a graphic from the Clipboard into a Ventura chapter (continued)

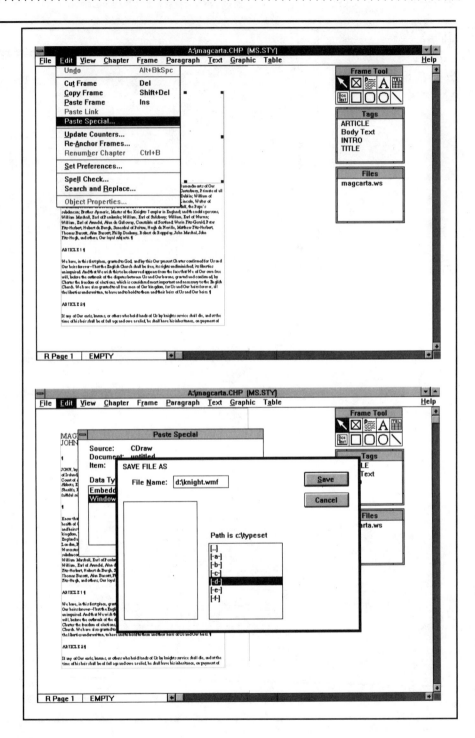

*Importing a graphic
from the Clipboard
into a Ventura chapter
(continued)*

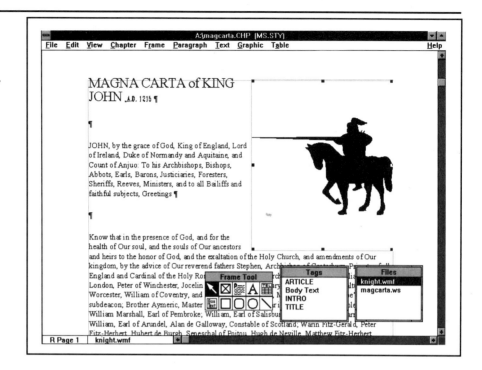

EXPORTING EPS FILES

We have discussed EPS (encapsulated PostScript) files to some extent in Chapter 5. To understand how best to export graphics from CorelDRAW using EPS, however, you'll have to immerse yourself in their lore for a few more pages.

*Including
very complex EPS
files on an
already complex page
may create a combined PostScript
graphic that has too
many paths to print.*

To begin with, encapsulated PostScript files can only be used with a PostScript printer. If you plan to use a LaserJet Plus to print the documents you'll ultimately be importing your files into, PostScript files will be of little use, except perhaps in the area of printing preview images, which we'll discuss shortly.

PostScript is actually a programming language, rather than a line-art graphic format. It has been specifically fine-tuned to write programs which deal with printed pages. In its simplest sense, when an application wants to print a page to a PostScript printer, it writes a program which defines the page and sends the program to the printer. Ideally, the printer interprets the program and does what it says, generating the page the program had in mind.

In order to import a PostScript file and show it to you on your screen, as CorelDRAW does, the software which does the importing must have the equivalent of the PostScript language which is resident in a PostScript printer. CorelDRAW is one of the few PC applications which have this facility. On the other hand, Ventura Publisher is one of the many which do not, even though it is capable of importing PostScript files.

Adobe, the creator of PostScript, recognized that not every program which would be importing PostScript files could be expected to contain the considerable complexity of a PostScript interpreter. To alleviate this situation, Adobe dreamt up something called PostScript encapsulation. The principle of encapsulated PostScript is simple. Allowing that the body of a PostScript program is a great black mystery for most applications, files which are intended for use by programs like Ventura are fitted with headers that tell Ventura in capsule form everything it needs to know about the drawing that the rest of the file will produce when it finally hits a PostScript printer. This includes things like the size of the drawing, called the bounding box. The bounding box is a rectangle which just encloses the final drawing. Knowing this, Ventura can fit the drawing into a frame even though it doesn't really know what the drawing is.

Not being able to interpret a PostScript file directly, Ventura would be unable to show you what one looked like before sending it on its way to a PostScript printer. To address this deficiency, Adobe added another element to the PostScript encapsulation process, involving the creation of a preview image. This is simply a bitmapped picture which looks roughly like the drawing which should ultimately emerge from a PostScript printer. The encapsulation header tells programs like Ventura how to find the preview image, and the preview is tacked onto the end of the PostScript program.

In Ventura, if you import an encapsulated PostScript file which has a preview, the preview image will appear in the frame you've put the graphic in. If there is no preview, Ventura will draw an X through the frame. The graphic will still print, but you will not be able to see it on your screen. Note that versions of Ventura prior to 2.0 did not deal with previews, and always drew an X through a frame containing an encapsulated PostScript file whether it had a preview or not.

If you use EPS files in Ventura Publisher or PageMaker and attempt to print the documents which contain them to a non-PostScript printer, such as a LaserJet, the preview image will be printed instead.

You should note that if you print a Ventura document containing an encapsulated PostScript file to a LaserJet Plus printer, the preview image itself will appear in place of the graphic. This is invariably not as good as real PostScript output would be, but it's better than nothing.

CorelDRAW allows you to specify the resolution of the preview image when you are creating an encapsulated PostScript file. If you anticipate outputting Ventura documents with CorelDRAW EPS files to a LaserJet, select the highest resolution previews.

POSTSCRIPT LIMITATIONS

In theory, exporting CorelDRAW art to an encapsulated PostScript file is the best way to import it into another application—assuming that the ultimate destination of the art in question will be a PostScript printer, of course. PostScript files never get translated; thus they never lose anything in the process. They take full advantage of the superb graphics-rendering facilities resident in PostScript printers. They allow you to have PostScript-dependent entities like font hinting preserved in your exported files. Exported PostScript files can employ the whole range of CorelDRAW's substantial talents, including PostScript textures, fountains, and the like.

There are a few catches to all of this in practice.

The system of preview images in PostScript files has one obvious weakness: You don't see your actual exported drawing when it has been poured into a Ventura document. Instead, you see the preview. While CorelDRAW's EPS previews invariably look more or less like its EPS files, the position of the preview in a Ventura frame is frequently quite different from that of the actual art.

Figure 13.6 illustrates an example of this problem. The frame on the left is the PCX file from Figure 13.3, above. The frame on the right is the printed output of the same graphic imported as an EPS file. The two frames appear to have the same pictures in the same positions in Ventura, but the right picture has actually been output slightly lower in the frame.

Unfortunately, this phenomenon is not at all consistent. The disparity between what you see in Ventura when you import an EPS file from CorelDRAW and what actually gets printed can be quite pronounced. If you require that your EPS graphics be very accurately positioned, plan on having to undertake some trial and error.

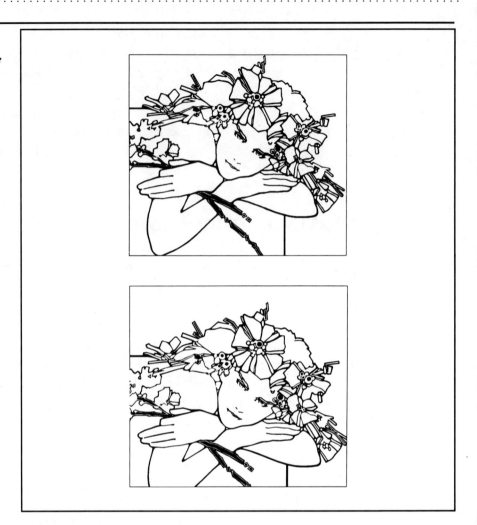

This is an irritating problem, but it's often worth putting up with in order to get the best possible results from graphics exported by CorelDRAW.

Part of the aesthetic of drawing for export, to be discussed in the next section of this chapter, involves creating simple graphics which do not detract from the page they're to be imported into. More fundamental than this, however, is the practical requirement that imported graphics not be so busy that they overwhelm your printer.

A document output by Ventura to a PostScript printer faces the same limitations that a graphic printed by CorelDRAW does. Every PostScript printer has a finite number of paths which it can deal with on a single page, and if you attempt to exceed this value, the results will not be as expected. Usually the page won't print at all, as we've seen previously.

If you import an EPS file from CorelDRAW into a Ventura document, the number of paths in the CorelDRAW drawing will be added to the number of paths in the Ventura page it has become part of. A Ventura page with lots of type, rules, and other elements may have a pretty good helping of paths on its own.

Complex documents with complex graphics imported into them often attempt to print things which are beyond the scope of your printer, even though the page and the graphics were printable before they were combined. It's very difficult to tell when you've exceeded the available number of paths for your printer just by looking at a page.

As a rule, if you're using CorelDRAW to create graphics for export, make sparing use of fountain fills and PostScript textures. When you do use them, try to do so in small, fairly simple objects. Along the same lines, avoid using lots of complex line graphics on the same page. For example, the girl in Figure 13.6 will print if she finds herself on a Ventura page. You can usually get away with two drawings of her if the page doesn't have an inordinate amount of type on it. When I tried having one drawing at each of the four corners of a page, I found that it was certainly more than the printer was able to deal with.

Ventura and IMG Files

Ventura has an unusual quirk which might sneak up on you if you aren't aware of it, should you attempt to create pages having certain combinations of imported graphics. It can cause things you weren't anticipating to print or appear on your screen.

When you first import an EPS file from CorelDRAW into a Ventura document, Ventura looks for a preview image. The preview image actually lives at the very end of the PostScript file, which can be quite a way in for a complex graphic. To avoid having to find its way to the end of the PostScript file every time it wants to update its screen with the preview image, Ventura makes a copy of the preview and stores it in an IMG file. If your EPS file is called PICTURE.EPS, Ventura will create PICTURE.IMG to store the preview in.

As you may recall from earlier in the chapter, Ventura will also translate your file into an IMG file if you attempt to import a PCX or TIFF file into a Ventura document. As it happens, this sort of IMG file and the sort of file in which Ventura stores previews aren't structured quite the same inside, but this doesn't actually matter. The important thing is that both sorts of files are named the same. If you import a file called PICTURE.PCX, Ventura will create a new file called PICTURE.IMG.

This is where the quirk comes in. If you create a Ventura document and attempt to import two files called PICTURE.PCX and PICTURE.EPS, they will each be translated to PICTURE.IMG, and one of them will overwrite the other. Depending on which file gets loaded first, you may find that the preview of your EPS file suddenly looks a lot like the contents of your PCX file, or that your PCX file prints like a very crunchy-looking version of your PostScript graphic.

You can avoid this problem very easily. Make sure you never have two graphics in the same directory which share the same file names and different extensions if you plan to import them into Ventura Publisher.

It's important to bear in mind that Ventura doesn't treat its imported files in the way that CorelDRAW does. If you import a file into a Corel-DRAW document, the contents of the file become part of the document. Importing a file into a Ventura document, on the other hand, simply tells Ventura about the existence of the file. Each time you open a Ventura document containing imported graphics, Ventura must retrieve each graphic from its original file. Because every graphic is a separate file residing on your disk, its contents can be modified without Ventura knowing it—even if it is Ventura which is inadvertently responsible. Thus, if a graphic gets modified or trashed after it has been imported into a Ventura chapter, it will stay trashed, and it will print trashed.

This is true whether you trash it yourself or Ventura does it for you.

GEM Ventura's Cropping Problem

If you import a large graphic into a chapter under the GEM version of Ventura and subsequently attempt to alter its position in its frame interactively —that is, by holding down the Alt key and dragging the graphic with the mouse—you will quite likely find that all or part of the contents of the frame will suddenly become littered with scraps of the Ventura side bar. The results can sometimes look like a bitmapped Dali painting, and they are the sort of thing which usually precedes a major system crash. In this case, this is a harmless bug, and as soon as you release your mouse it will vanish. It has to do with the way Ventura allocates memory for large graphic files while it's working with them.

Figure 13.7 illustrates a lesser degree of this problem. The side bar in the middle of the frame, the one with the hand pointer, is not supposed to be there.

FIGURE 13.7:
Ventura's cropping bug

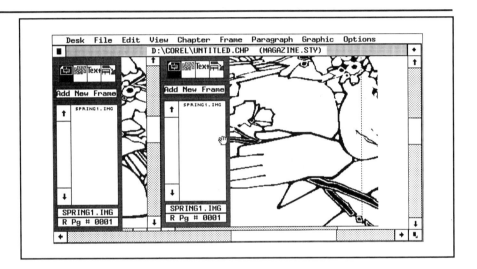

WORKING WITH PAGEMAKER 4.0 FOR WINDOWS

Importing graphics files into PageMaker for Windows is a straightforward operation using the File/Place command. When you click on this option in the File menu (or press Ctrl-D), you are taken into the Place File dialog box.

From the Place File dialog box, you can move to the directory where your graphics files are located. Once you're in the right directory, the names of all graphics which you can import into PageMaker for Windows will be visible in the Files/Directories scroll list. PageMaker 4.0 includes filters for:

◆ Corel PHOTO-PAINT PCX

◆ Windows Bitmap BMP

◆ Windows Metafile WMF

◆ Encapsulated PostScript EPS

◆ TIFF 5.0 TIF

NOTE *If you have a graphic in your Page-Maker publication currently on-screen and you have selected it, when you use File/Place and select a graphics file, you will see one additional radio button (Replace entire graphic) which you can select. If you click on this button and accept the rest by clicking on OK, the new graphic image will replace the graphic image you had selected on-screen.*

When you click on a graphics file with a valid extension, PageMaker changes the radio button option Place to read An Independent Graphic. If you click on OK or double-click on a file name, the graphic will then be imported into the PageMaker publication.

If the file is of substantial size, you may be presented with a warning in a dialog box. If you click the Yes button in the dialog box, the graphic will be placed in the publication as an integral part of it. Clicking on the No button places a *link* to the graphics file in the PageMaker publication. If you intend to send the publication on to a service bureau, you *must* include the graphic file on the disk (or with the publication when you transfer it via modem), or it will be missing when the whole publication is printed out.

All of the images imported into PageMaker 4.0 print out on a PostScript laser printer with equal quality. However, you must remember that a Windows metafile (WMF) is placed in the Windows Clipboard exactly as it appears in CorelDRAW, and therefore will be in color (if used), even if you wanted to indicate gray scales for quality control. If this creates a problem in your printout, simply export the image to CorelDRAW as a Windows bitmap (BMP), and you will be able to select gray scale from the dialog box.

For transferring your graphics to PageMaker on the Macintosh, remember to export the CorelDRAW graphics as either encapsulated PostScript (EPS) or Illustrator 88 (AI, EPS) files. Then use Apple File Exchange, the Deluxe Option Board from Central Point Software, or another means to transfer your graphics file to a Macintosh disk for use in the Macintosh version of PageMaker.

DESIGN ELEMENTS AND EXPORTING

Creating graphics which export successfully from CorelDRAW is largely a mechanical problem. Having read the first part of this chapter, you should be fairly conversant with the options you have available for getting your CorelDRAW art into the documents of other programs.

Creating graphics which really work when they're imported into complete pages is quite a different problem, one of design rather than of software. Unfortunately, the features which make CorelDRAW really powerful also make it capable of producing wildly inappropriate art if you don't think about the final destination of your pictures.

It might well be argued that some of the PostScript limitations we discussed a while ago aren't limitations so much as they are features. If you create an imported graphic which is so complex as to keep your page from printing, consider that PostScript may be telling you that you are creating a page which is far too busy to be attractive.

This would probably be argued most stridently by the customer-support people at the company that made your printer should you call to complain about this limitation in their hardware.

Graphics which look good all by themselves don't necessarily look good when you import them into a desktop publishing page. The addition of a few columns of type and some potentially distracting headlines can often destroy the effect of an otherwise attractive piece of art.

FINDING A FOCUS

As we discussed in the last chapter, a page which really works is a page with a focus. The design must lead one's eye into the page and then to wherever the contents of the page actually start. In a publication having a lot of similar pages, a well designed page will be eye-catching enough to be noticed amidst all the others. Page design can often do more to make a page readable than the content itself, especially when you're dragging yourself along to the last page of a long, dry article.

You should also consider that pages of type suffer from an inherent flatness—they're two-dimensional by nature. Graphics which stand out from the pages they've been poured into will give the entire page a sense of depth, and make it more interesting.

There are lots of ways to do this. One of the effects which magazine publishers use a lot is to pour fountains into otherwise flat graphics, such as bar charts. Depending on the complexity of the overall page, you might be able to use them too. Consider the two pages in Figure 13.8.

FIGURE 13.8:

*Giving a chart
some depth*

JOHN, by the grace of God, King of England, Lord of Ireland, Duke of Normandy and Aquitaine, and Count of Anjou: To his Archbishops, Bishops, Abbots, Earls, Barons, Justiciaries, Foresters, Sheriffs, Reeves, Ministers, and to all Bailiffs and faithful subjects, Greetings Know that in the presence of God, and for the health of Our soul, and the souls of Our ancestors and heirs to the

Hugh de Neville, Matthew Fitz-Herbert, Thomas Bassett, Alan Bassett, Philip Daubeny, Robert de Roppelay, John Marshal, John Fitz-Hugh, and others, Our loyal subjects.

We have, in this first place, granted to God, and by this Our present Charter confirmed for Us and Our heirs forever- -That the English Church shall be free, its rights undiminished, its liberties unim-

If any such heir shall be under age and a ward, he shall, when he comes of age, have his inheritance without relief or fine.

The guardian of the land of any such heir shall take therefrom only reasonable revenues, customs, and services, without destruction and waste of men or property; and if We shall have committed the wardship of any such to a sheriff, and he commits destruction, We will take amends from him, and the land shall be committed to two lawful and discreet men of that fee, who shall be answerable for the issues to Us.

The guardian, so long as he shall have the wardship of the land, shall keep up and maintain the houses, parks, fishpondspools, mills, everything pertaining thereto, out of the issues of the same, and shall restore the whole to the heir when he comes of age; stocked with ploughs and grain as the season requires and the issues of the land can reasonably bear.

Heirs shall be married without loss of station, and the marriage shall be made known to the heirs next of kin before it be contracted.

A widow, on the death of her husband, shall immediately and without difficulty have her marriage portion and inheritance. She may remain in her husband's house for forty days after her husband's death, within which time her dower shall be assigned to her.

No widow shall be compelled to marry so long as she wishes to live without a husband, provided, however, that she give security that she will not marry without Our assent.

Neither We or Our bailiffs shall seize any land or rent for payment of debt so long as the debtor's chattels are sufficient to discharge the same; nor shall the debtor's sureties be distrained so long as the debtor is able to pay the debt. If the debtor fails to pay, then his sureties shall answer the debt.

If anyone who has borrowed from the Jews any sum, great or small, dies before the debt has been paid, the heir shall pay no interest on the debt so long

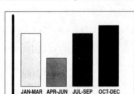

honor of God, and the exaltation of the Holy Church, and amendments of Our kingdom, by the advice of Our reverend fathers Stephen, Archbishop of Canterbury, Primate of all England and Cardinal of the Holy Roman Church; Henry Archbishop of Dublin; William of London, Peter of Winchester, Jocelin of Bath and Glostonbury, Hugh of Lincoln, Walter of Worcester, William of Coventry, and Benedict of Rochester, Master Pandulf, the Pope's subdeacon; Brother Aymeric, Master of the Knights Templar in England; and the noble persons, William Marshall, Earl of Pembroke; William, Earl of Salisbury; William, Earl of Warren; William, Earl of Arundel, Alan de Galloway, Constable of Scotland; Warin Fitz-Gerald, Peter Fitz- Herbert, Hubert de Burgh, Seneschal of Poitou,

paired. And that We wish this to be observed appears from the face that We of Our own free will, before the outbreak of the disputes between Us and Our barons, granted and confirmed, by Charter the freedom of elections, which is considered most important and necessary to the English Church. We have also granted to all free men of Our kingdom, for Us and Our heirs forever, all the liberties underwritten, to have and to hold to them and their heirs of Us and Our heirs.

If any of Our earls, barons, or others who hold lands of Us by knights service shall die, and at the time of his heir shall be of full age and owe a relief, he shall have his inheritance, on payment of ancient relief.

JOHN, by the grace of God, King of England, Lord of Ireland, Duke of Normandy and Aquitaine, and Count of Anjou: To his Archbishops, Bishops, Abbots, Earls, Barons, Justiciaries, Foresters, Sheriffs, Reeves, Ministers, and to all Bailiffs and faithful subjects, Greetings Know that in the presence of God, and for the health of Our soul, and the souls of Our ancestors and heirs to the

Hugh de Neville, Matthew Fitz-Herbert, Thomas Bassett, Alan Bassett, Philip Daubeny, Robert de Roppelay, John Marshal, John Fitz-Hugh, and others, Our loyal subjects.

We have, in this first place, granted to God, and by this Our present Charter confirmed for Us and Our heirs forever- -That the English Church shall be free, its rights undiminished, its liberties unim-

If any such heir shall be under age and a ward, he shall, when he comes of age, have his inheritance without relief or fine.

The guardian of the land of any such heir shall take therefrom only reasonable revenues, customs, and services, without destruction and waste of men or property; and if We shall have committed the wardship of any such to a sheriff, and he commits destruction, We will take amends from him, and the land shall be committed to two lawful and discreet men of that fee, who shall be answerable for the issues to Us.

The guardian, so long as he shall have the wardship of the land, shall keep up and maintain the houses, parks, fishpondspools, mills, everything pertaining thereto, out of the issues of the same, and shall restore the whole to the heir when he comes of age; stocked with ploughs and grain as the season requires and the issues of the land can reasonably bear.

Heirs shall be married without loss of station, and the marriage shall be made known to the heirs next of kin before it be contracted.

A widow, on the death of her husband, shall immediately and without difficulty have her marriage portion and inheritance. She may remain in her husband's house for forty days after her husband's death, within which time her dower shall be assigned to her.

No widow shall be compelled to marry so long as she wishes to live without a husband, provided, however, that she give security that she will not marry, without Our assent.

Neither We or Our bailiffs shall seize any land or rent for payment of debt so long as the debtor's chattels are sufficient to discharge the same; nor shall the debtor's sureties be distrained so long as the debtor is able to pay the debt. If the debtor fails to pay, then his sureties shall answer the debt.

If anyone who has borrowed from the Jews any sum, great or small, dies before the debt has been paid, the heir shall pay no interest on the debt so long

honor of God, and the exaltation of the Holy Church, and amendments of Our kingdom, by the advice of Our reverend fathers Stephen, Archbishop of Canterbury, Primate of all England and Cardinal of the Holy Roman Church; Henry Archbishop of Dublin; William of London, Peter of Winchester, Jocelin of Bath and Glostonbury, Hugh of Lincoln, Walter of Worcester, and Benedict of Rochester, Master Pandulf, the Pope's subdeacon; Brother Aymeric, Master of the Knights Templar in England; and the noble persons, William Marshall, Earl of Pembroke; William, Earl of Salisbury; William, Earl of Warren; William, Earl of Arundel, Alan de Galloway, Constable of Scotland; Warin Fitz-Gerald, Peter Fitz- Herbert, Hubert de Burgh, Seneschal of Poitou,

paired. And that We wish this to be observed appears from the face that We of Our own free will, before the outbreak of the disputes between Us and Our barons, granted and confirmed, by Charter the freedom of elections, which is considered most important and necessary to the English Church. We have also granted to all free men of Our kingdom, for Us and Our heirs forever, all the liberties underwritten, to have and to hold to them and their heirs of Us and Our heirs.

If any of Our earls, barons, or others who hold lands of Us by knights service shall die, and at the time of his heir shall be of full age and owe a relief, he shall have his inheritance, on payment of ancient relief.

It's also advisable to plan your graphics with a bit of rule-breaking in mind. If you deliberately create art which doesn't fit easily in regular rectangular frames, you'll have a good opportunity to do something interesting with it when it has been imported into pages. Figure 13.9 illustrates a couple of somewhat uncommon shapes for graphics.

CLIP ART AND ORNAMENTS

In some cases, the graphics you export from CorelDRAW will have been created for specific reasons. For instance, charts, graphs, and technical illustrations are specifically created to augment the information in the text they'll ultimately be surrounded by. It's probably not a good idea to get too creative with these sorts of graphics. A design which diminishes the informational value of graphics that have been created primarily to be informative has allowed art to get in the way of the publication's purpose.

To a large extent, however, graphics are meant to serve as ornaments. A page which has nothing but type on it can be intimidating, and perhaps uninteresting and difficult to read. The inclusion of a few pictures, even if they're only tangential to the nature of the text, will make your desktop publishing chapters more approachable. Further, if you are creating a document with multiple pages, graphic ornaments can serve to tie the pages together. Publications with multiple pages frequently tie them together by using a large graphic on the first page and then smaller versions of it or fragments of it on subsequent pages. Figure 13.10 illustrates an example of this technique used over a multipage spread.

In Ventura, you can pour graphics into frames and then make the frames appear on every page using the Repeating Frames item of Ventura's Frames menu. This is a handy way to use graphics of the ornamental sort, as new graphics will automatically appear as you add more pages to your document.

ICONS

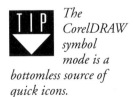

The CorelDRAW symbol mode is a bottomless source of quick icons.

One of the more functional applications of ornamental graphics in desktop publishing is icons. While they are probably something of a by-product of the growing use of graphic user interfaces like Windows, icons are nonetheless an elegant way to highlight important areas of text or to allow your readers to locate pertinent parts of a document quickly.

FIGURE 13.9:

Using nonrectangular graphics

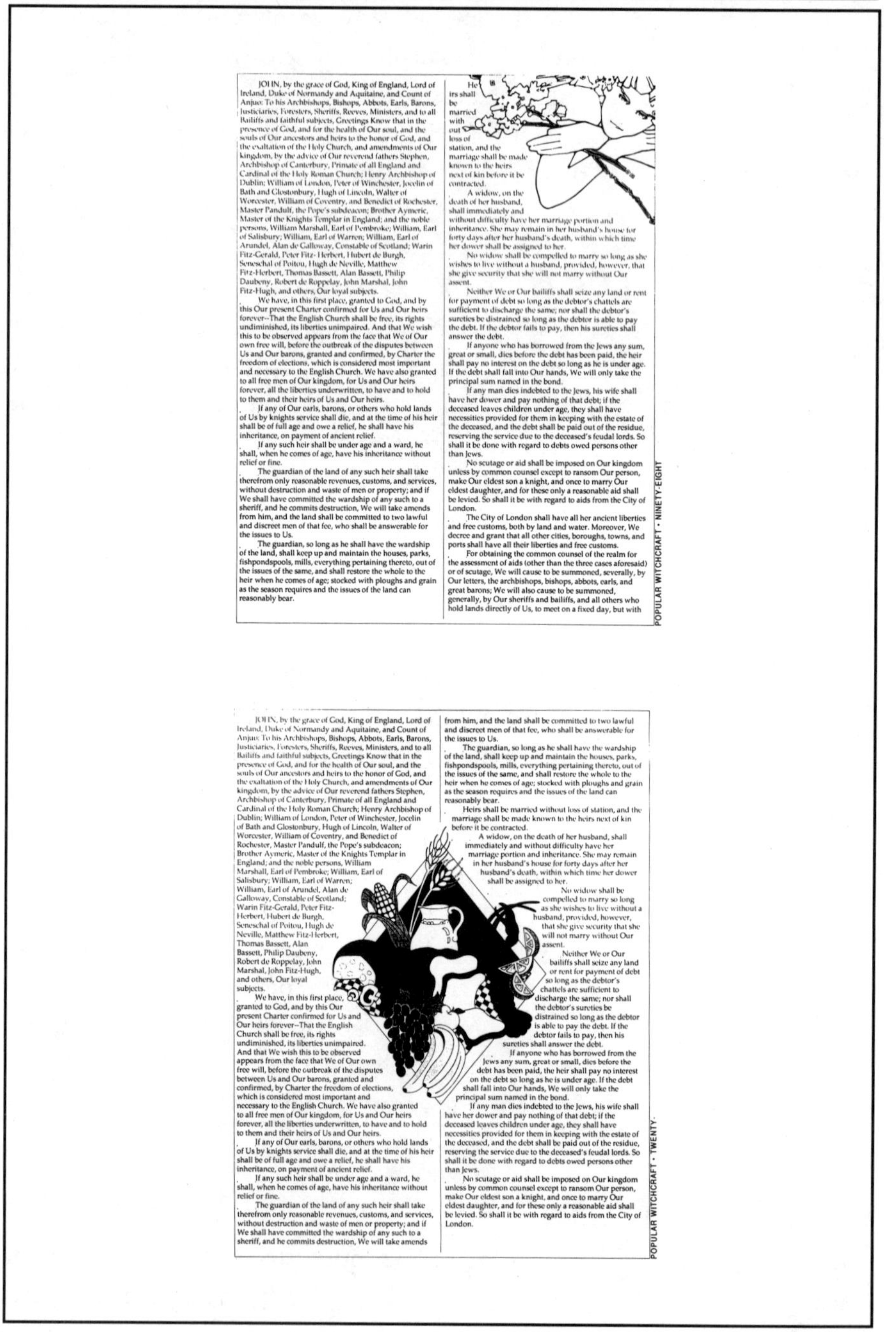

FIGURE 13.10:

*Using graphic fragments
to tie pages together*

LIVING WITH TROPICAL BIRDS

HAVING YOUR PET
SHRIEKING IN YOUR EAR
AT TWO IN THE MORNING
ABOUT ITS BURNING NEED
FOR CRACKERS MIGHT
DRIVE YOU TO KEEPING IT
IN THE MICROWAVE. THIS
ARTICLE DISCUSSES WAYS
TO REASON WITH PETS
THAT TALK BACK

Figure 13.11 illustrates the use of icons.

You can use just about any graphics you like as icons, but they work best when the icon images are fairly simple and easy to spot. This is handy, as the sorts of images which make good icons are also the easiest ones to cook up in CorelDRAW.

In Ventura, the frames containing your icons can be tied to the text they're associated with, so that if you do something to cause the text to move, even to change pages, the icons will reposition themselves. After creating an icon and pouring it into a frame, give it a name using the Anchors & Captions dialog box of Ventura's Frames menu. Then, you can place an anchor for the named frame in the text next to which you want it placed by hitting Ctrl-C and then F5. If you later change anything in the text or layout such that the icons are no longer positioned where you'd like them, you can reposition them by selecting Re-Anchor Frames from the Edit menu.

If you plan to create large documents with lots of pages and lots of icons—a book, for example—you'll probably find that setting up all the individual instances of the icons is a bit tedious. There's a shortcut of sorts which you can use with Ventura if you plan ahead:

1. Use CorelDRAW to create all your icons and export them to GEM files.

2. Create a dummy chapter for your book in Ventura.

3. On the first page of the dummy chapter, create the frames for your icons and pour in the GEM files from CorelDRAW.

4. Duplicate the frames enough times to allow for the greatest possible number of icons in your longest chapter. Give each new frame a unique and easily predictable name, such as Warning 1, Warning 2, Warning 3, and so on.

5. Place the frames such that they're all at a constant distance from the left side of the page. Their vertical position doesn't matter, and they can overlap if necessary.

6. Go through the text files for your chapters and install the anchors. The syntax for an anchor under Ventura is as follows:

    <&Warning 2[^]>

    The text after the ampersand (here, *Warning*) is the name you gave the icon in question with the Anchors & Captions dialog box. You

*Adding some graphic
icons to a document*

Installing PageMaker   **5**

layouts. You will be given the opportunity to select the
individual templates you want installed.

- **PCL Templates**. If you have a printer in the Hewlett-Packard LaserJet family or some other printer that can use that
  company's Printer Command Language (PCL), select this
  option to install the PCL equivalents of the PostScript
  templates described in the preceding paragraph.

To select or deselect individual Setup options, press the **Ctrl** key
as you click the left mouse button. To select a *range* of options,
click the first option, and then hold down the **Shift** key as you
click the last option in the range.

When you're finished, click the **Setup** button. Now you'll see a
Select directory dialog box again.

Later, when you're asked to make specific filter and template selections in the **Aldus Setup** window, the installation program will
keep track of the amount of space you'll need for each option. At
the bottom of the screen you'll see a changing display indicating
how much room remains on your hard disk. You'll be warned if a
selection will require more disk space than is available.

If you need more disk storage than is available, a number will be
displayed at the bottom of the screen preceded by a minus sign.
This figure represents how much more space you need.

You can free that extra disk space without leaving **Aldus Setup.**
Remember, Windows 3.0 lets you run more than one application
at a time. Simply call up the **Windows File Manager** and delete
files you don't need from your disk. Then return to the **Aldus
Setup** window and continue with the installation.

Here are the detailed instructions:

1. Double-click the **Program Manager** icon to open the
    Program Manager window.

2. From the **Program Manager** window, double-click the
    Main icon to open the **Main** window.

can use a named icon only once in each chapter, which is why you had to make lots of duplicates. The caret in the square brackets tells Ventura that this frame is to be relative to and above the anchor.

7. Pour your text into the dummy chapter and save the chapter under a new name.

8. Select Re-Anchor Frames from the Edit menu. Ventura will position all your icons for you.

9. Delete the unused icons from the first page.

As a final note, a few icons on a page are effective. Having an icon for every other paragraph is distracting, and the effectiveness of your icons will quickly diminish. Icons can be a superb use of exported graphics, but, as usual, only if you apply them sparingly.

HEADLINES

In creating headlines for export from CorelDRAW, try to select a typeface which matches or at least complements the type in the documents to which the headlines will be imported.

The type facilities of CorelDRAW have been expounded upon at length earlier in this book, and if you've played with them a bit you could probably expound on them yourself as well. The range of typefaces and type effects which CorelDRAW offers far exceeds anything you could manage with desktop publishing software all by itself.

While it requires a bit of forethought to achieve, you can easily create your headlines in CorelDRAW and export them to Ventura. Because the PostScript typefaces available under Ventura are also available under CorelDRAW, you can easily match the fonts in your headlines to work with the type for your body copy. Helvetica under CorelDRAW looks like Helvetica under Ventura, for example.

There is a multitude of effects you can add to headlines with CorelDRAW. Figure 13.12 illustrates a variety of them, but these are only a small fraction of what you can get together.

When you go to export your headlines, you will probably have to give a bit of thought to the format you should use. The positioning problems inherent in EPS files make them less than ideal for headlines which will have to be placed accurately relative to the other elements on your page. Moreover, the path constraints of GEM files make some complex heads impossible in this format. If your headlines include fountains, intricate

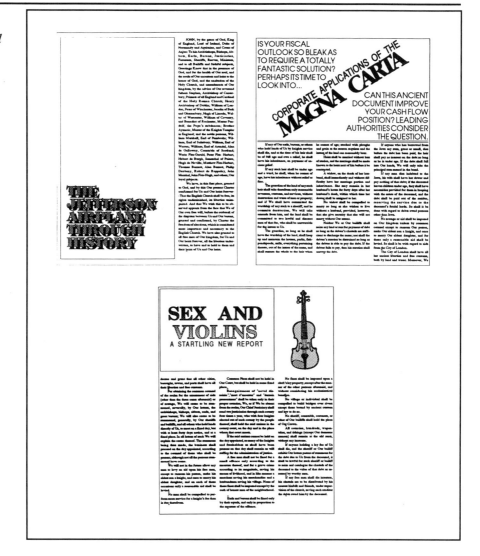

FIGURE 13.12:

Some headlines created in CorelDRAW and exported to Ventura

drawings or PostScript textures, you'll be stuck with EPS files and a bit of fine-tuning once you get to Ventura.

From a design perspective, you should consider that a large headline will invariably serve as the focus of your page. As such, the nature of your headlines should set the tone of whatever your publication actually deals with. Headlines set in antique Germanic type, however interesting or eye-catching they may be, would probably not be appropriate for the stockholders' report of a computer manufacturer.

Consider using smaller versions of an interesting-looking headline, instead of graphics, as ornaments or as a way to tie the pages of an article together. Some documents don't lend themselves to text used in this way, but varieties of headlines can often work where graphics can't.

It's a good rule to insist that all the type effects on a page look as if they have a reason for being there. It's another good rule to limit yourself in the variety of typefaces and effects you use. A corollary to this rule suggests that most pages should have no more than one serif face and one sans-serif face on them.

If you use a particular font for your headlines, consider using it as well for subheadings, captions, and other nonbody text to make the headline face relate to the rest of the document. Try to avoid creating a dominant, bold headline graphic if the rest of your page design uses fairly light type and thin rules. It's important to observe the difference between a headline which serves as a focus for your page and one which dominates it, distracting one's eye long after a focus is no longer needed.

It's said of type that nobody reads it if it's bigger than 14 points. In fact, people do not, as a rule, read headlines. They look at them, but they don't analyze them for meaning in the way that they do body text. There are a number of things you should bear in mind about your headlines in this light.

To begin with, avoid creating ornate heads which are hard to read, or people will be even less likely to bother trying. Secondly, avoid headlines with lots of words in them.

The really important thing to consider about large type is that, as most people are conditioned to ignore it, it's notoriously hard to proofread effectively unless you really think about what you're doing. There's a legendary example of this which took place quite a few years ago. Time magazine ran on its back cover an advertisement which contained the word *America* in enormous type across the page. Only as it was being printed did one of the press operators notice that the word had been spelled incorrectly. He stopped the press and the error was fixed, fortunately before any copies hit the streets. However, in the aftermath of this it was discovered that over sixty people had proofed the ad without ever noticing the mistake.

DROP CAPITALS

Ventura allows you to create drop capitals as a special effect in the formation of a paragraph tag, but its facilities are limited to the fonts it has and the effects it can manage with them. You can create far more interesting drop caps in CorelDRAW and import them into Ventura chapters as graphics.

There isn't a lot you *can't* do in creating a drop cap. Some of them get pretty strange. If the opening headline of a document is fairly plain, you can focus someone's attention on the start of the text most effectively by using a noticeable drop cap. Some page designs extend the idea of a drop cap to the entire first word of the text.

Figure 13.13 illustrates some drop capitals and other similar effects created in CorelDRAW and exported to Ventura. Note that we can get away with using fountains and PostScript textures in these examples because they are elements of pages which aren't very complex.

Some magazine and book page designs use drop capitals rather than subheads. Occasionally, you'll find one which manages to combine both, as shown in Figure 13.14.

EXPORTING TEXT BOXES

One of the reasons page designers like graphics so much isn't really artistic at all—it's wholly pragmatic. If you pour a text file into a Ventura chapter, you'll probably find that it doesn't fill the chapter perfectly. Depending on the luck of the draw, you'll either wind up a few paragraphs shy of a full final page or a few paragraphs over.

A good page design allows you to compensate for text files of inconsiderate lengths by having some flexibility built into the nontext elements. For instance, if you have lots of graphics on a page you can resize some of them a bit to force the text to fit. However, if this isn't practical, the next best thing is to use text boxes.

A text box, or quote box, is nothing more than a box surrounding a bit of pertinent-sounding text set large and stuck in the body of your document. Figure 13.15 illustrates some examples of text boxes. Ventura can create these, but CorelDRAW can do a lot more with them in terms of using text effects. Also, if you export text boxes from CorelDRAW as graphics, you can

A long, long time ago in a kingdom far away where nobody goes anymore, there lived a fair young princess named Vanilla. All around her there were brave princes, valiant knights, noble squires and happy, downtrodden peasants who lived lives of exciting, medieval brutality. However, Vanilla knew none of this. She spent her days locked in a tower reading trashy novels and tie-dying the palace cats.

One bright summer day when the hyacinth was in bloom and the crack of shattered bones rich on the air from the jousting fields, a strange knight came to the kingdom in search of the fair maiden Vanilla. He bore a letter from an unknown prince, requesting the hand of this fabled princess in marriage.

The king was amazed when first he read the letter.

''A bit desperate, lad.'' he muttered through his beer. ''Princesses gettin' hard t' find?''

A long, long time ago in a kingdom far away where nobody goes anymore, there lived a fair young princess named Vanilla. All around her there were brave princes, valiant knights, noble squires and happy, downtrodden peasants who lived lives of exciting, medieval brutality. However, Vanilla knew none of this. She spent her days locked in a tower reading trashy novels and tie-dying the palace cats.

One bright summer day when the hyacinth was in bloom and the crack of shattered bones rich on the air from the jousting fields, a strange knight came to the kingdom in search of the fair maiden Vanilla. He bore a letter from an unknown prince, requesting the hand of this fabled princess in marriage.

The king was amazed when first he read the letter.

''A bit desperate, lad.'' he muttered through his beer. ''Princesses gettin' hard t' find?''

A long, long time ago in a kingdom far away where nobody goes anymore, there lived a fair young princess named Vanilla. All around her there were brave princes, valiant knights, noble squires and happy, downtrodden peasants who lived lives of exciting, medieval brutality. However, Vanilla knew none of this. She spent her days locked in a tower reading trashy novels and tie-dying the palace cats.

One bright summer day when the hyacinth was in bloom and the crack of shattered bones rich on the air from the jousting fields, a strange knight came to the kingdom in search of the fair maiden Vanilla. He bore a letter from an unknown prince, requesting the hand of this fabled princess in marriage.

The king was amazed when first he read the letter.

''A bit desperate, lad.'' he muttered through his beer. ''Princesses gettin' hard t' find?''

easily resize them in Ventura if you have to adjust the length of your document a bit.

One particularly elegant way to create text boxes is to use CorelDRAW in conjunction with Windows Write, the word processor which comes with Windows. As discussed earlier in this book, you can copy small chunks of text from Write to CorelDRAW through the Clipboard. While these chunks are limited to 250 characters, this is usually more than enough for a text box.

Replacing and augment-ing subheads with drop capitals

To create some text boxes, do the following:

1. Run Windows, then run Write and CorelDRAW at the same time.

2. Load the text of your document into Write. Chances are your docu-ment will not have been written in Write format, in which case you can just load it as an ASCII file. You will not be modifying the document itself, nor will you be saving it back to disk when you're done.

3. Find a suitable line or two of text in Write. Highlight it and copy it to the Clipboard using the Copy item of the Edit menu in Write.

4. Bring CorelDRAW forward. Use the text tool to open the Text dialog box.

5. Paste the text in the Clipboard into the Text dialog box by holding down the Shift key and hitting Ins.

6. Set the text into a suitable text box. If the text you've used is a frag-ment of a sentence, it's appropriate to indicate this with an ellipsis.

Once you've created a text box, it's usually practical to export it as a line-art file, that is, as a GEM file for Ventura. If you're using the Windows version of Ventura, you can export it directly through the Clipboard. If your applica-tion for CorelDRAW and Ventura involves laying out a lot of chapters

FIGURE 13.15:

*Text boxes exported
from CorelDRAW*

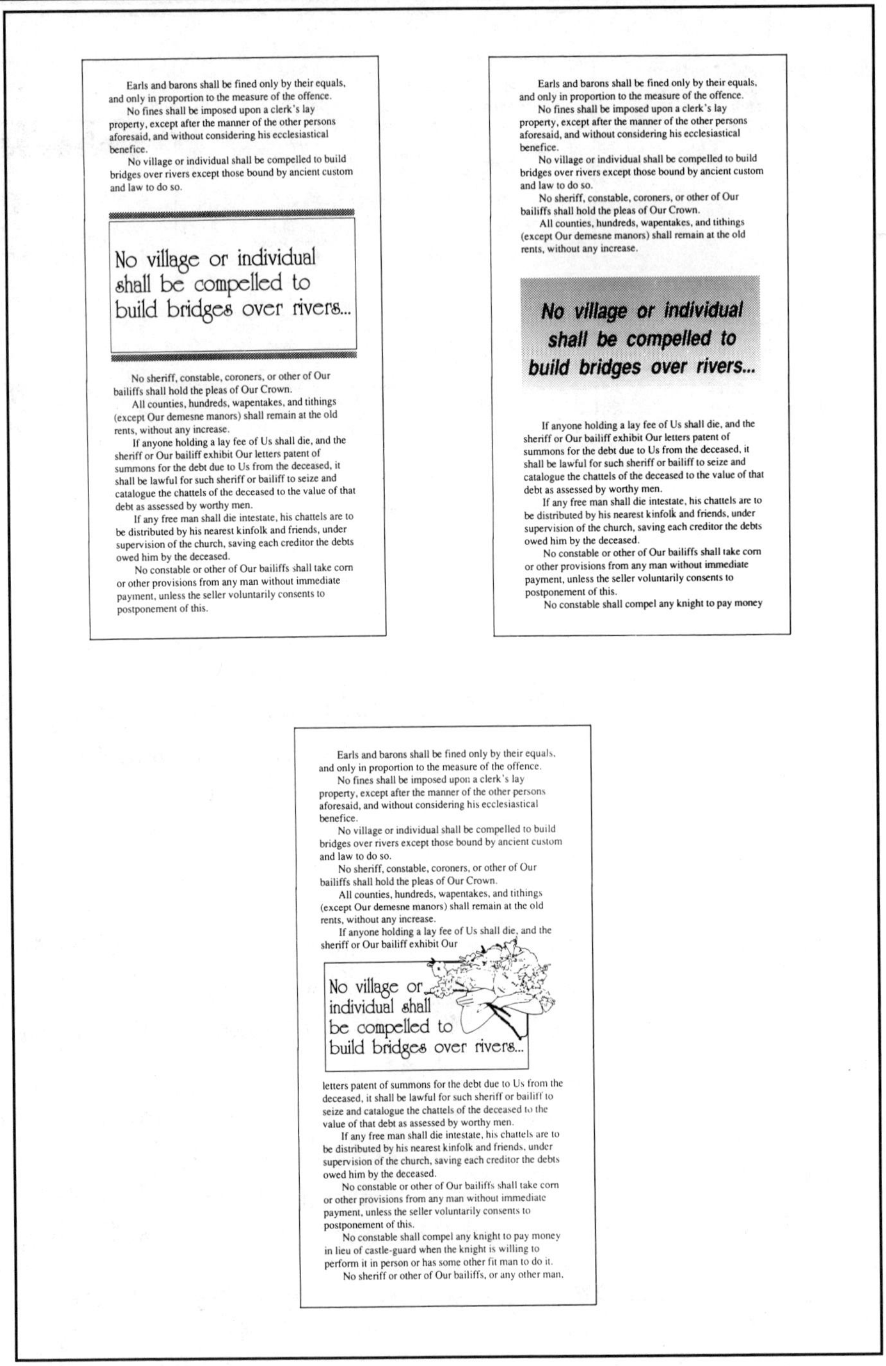

Earls and barons shall be fined only by their equals, and only in proportion to the measure of the offence.

No fines shall be imposed upon a clerk's lay property, except after the manner of the other persons aforesaid, and without considering his ecclesiastical benefice.

No village or individual shall be compelled to build bridges over rivers except those bound by ancient custom and law to do so.

No village or individual shall be compelled to build bridges over rivers...

No sheriff, constable, coroners, or other of Our bailiffs shall hold the pleas of Our Crown.

All counties, hundreds, wapentakes, and tithings (except Our demesne manors) shall remain at the old rents, without any increase.

If anyone holding a lay fee of Us shall die, and the sheriff or Our bailiff exhibit Our letters patent of summons for the debt due to Us from the deceased, it shall be lawful for such sheriff or bailiff to seize and catalogue the chattels of the deceased to the value of that debt as assessed by worthy men.

If any free man shall die intestate, his chattels are to be distributed by his nearest kinfolk and friends, under supervision of the church, saving each creditor the debts owed him by the deceased.

No constable or other of Our bailiffs shall take corn or other provisions from any man without immediate payment, unless the seller voluntarily consents to postponement of this.

Earls and barons shall be fined only by their equals, and only in proportion to the measure of the offence.

No fines shall be imposed upon a clerk's lay property, except after the manner of the other persons aforesaid, and without considering his ecclesiastical benefice.

No village or individual shall be compelled to build bridges over rivers except those bound by ancient custom and law to do so.

No sheriff, constable, coroners, or other of Our bailiffs shall hold the pleas of Our Crown.

All counties, hundreds, wapentakes, and tithings (except Our demesne manors) shall remain at the old rents, without any increase.

*No village or individual
shall be compelled to
build bridges over rivers...*

If anyone holding a lay fee of Us shall die, and the sheriff or Our bailiff exhibit Our letters patent of summons for the debt due to Us from the deceased, it shall be lawful for such sheriff or bailiff to seize and catalogue the chattels of the deceased to the value of that debt as assessed by worthy men.

If any free man shall die intestate, his chattels are to be distributed by his nearest kinfolk and friends, under supervision of the church, saving each creditor the debts owed him by the deceased.

No constable or other of Our bailiffs shall take corn or other provisions from any man without immediate payment, unless the seller voluntarily consents to postponement of this.

No constable shall compel any knight to pay money

Earls and barons shall be fined only by their equals, and only in proportion to the measure of the offence.

No fines shall be imposed upon a clerk's lay property, except after the manner of the other persons aforesaid, and without considering his ecclesiastical benefice.

No village or individual shall be compelled to build bridges over rivers except those bound by ancient custom and law to do so.

No sheriff, constable, coroners, or other of Our bailiffs shall hold the pleas of Our Crown.

All counties, hundreds, wapentakes, and tithings (except Our demesne manors) shall remain at the old rents, without any increase.

If anyone holding a lay fee of Us shall die, and the sheriff or Our bailiff exhibit Our

No village or
individual shall
be compelled to
build bridges over rivers...

letters patent of summons for the debt due to Us from the deceased, it shall be lawful for such sheriff or bailiff to seize and catalogue the chattels of the deceased to the value of that debt as assessed by worthy men.

If any free man shall die intestate, his chattels are to be distributed by his nearest kinfolk and friends, under supervision of the church, saving each creditor the debts owed him by the deceased.

No constable or other of Our bailiffs shall take corn or other provisions from any man without immediate payment, unless the seller voluntarily consents to postponement of this.

No constable shall compel any knight to pay money in lieu of castle-guard when the knight is willing to perform it in person or has some other fit man to do it.

No sheriff or other of Our bailiffs, or any other man.

which might use text boxes in this way, you might want to create four or five of them for each chapter before you start, pulling interesting quotes from various parts of the chapter, and using them as needed when you start working through your pages.

Text boxes do help to break up pages which are otherwise nothing but type, and therefore their use isn't wholly a layout convenience. However, you'll probably find that their major attraction is for getting you out of awkward situations when there's just not enough text to fill in the spaces.

Page designers are often accused of regarding body copy as fill or gravel, that stuff that occupies the white space around their design elements. Editors are often accused of regarding graphics in the same light. You might want to consider where your sympathies lie, and attempt to strike a balance, keeping an open mind concerning possible conflicts.

WRAPPING UP

Using CorelDRAW in conjunction with a desktop publishing package allows you to marry two powerful applications and get the best of both. However, more than this, it allows you to be editor, page designer, and artist all at the same time. While this might leave you busier than you would have been otherwise, it will also allow you to bring a more unified perspective to the chapters you create. Having control over all the elements of a page gives you the potential for creating designs in which the graphics really suit the text, and the overall page design accurately reflects the mindset of its intended audience.

FAST
TRACK

CHAPTER

14

**If you wish to add to CorelDRAW's diversity
of type,** **577**

the package allows you to create your own fonts, a procedure
that's discussed in detail in Appendix B. It will not teach you
how to actually design typefaces, however. Type design is an
extremely complex art form, and one which is not easily
mastered. Avoid creating text typefaces until you really understand what you're doing.

To mix several different type families, ... **588**

creating a graphic or a page, try to choose families which are
distinct from one another. For example, choosing two nearly
identical serif typefaces will make your type look peculiar, for
no obvious reason. It's a good rule to limit yourself to no more
than one serif and one san-serif face per page.

To add emphasis in body copy, ... **591**

avoid using typewriter text effects in typeset body copy—
specifically boldface and underlining. These elements tend to
distract your readers, making it less likely that they'll actually
read what you've written. Italics are a much better choice.

Designing

with

Type

Type can be among the most powerful of design elements. It can communicate far more than just the meanings of the words you set. Used correctly, it can evoke deeper levels of meaning, suggesting culture, setting, and style. If your applications for CorelDRAW include using it to set type, you should give some thought to the basics of type as an art form.

The richness of type as an art form is evidenced by its diversity. You may already have a feel for this if you've played with the wide variety of typefaces which accompany CorelDRAW. However, this is actually a very tiny fraction of the typefaces which have been created in the long and rather twisted history of type. If you find the diversity of type available in CorelDRAW inadequate as it stands, you might want to consult Appendix B of this book: It tells you how you can create your own fonts.

NOTE *The earliest recorded instance of a typesetting machine was as the work of William Church. It was run through an organ keyboard.*

UNDERSTANDING TYPEFACES

One of the distinctions which will turn up in this chapter is that between body copy and headlines, a distinction reflected in the fact that typefaces are designed specifically for use as either body faces or display faces. (This was touched on in Chapter 3, but it's worth clarifying here. You're reading body copy now, in the Garamond typeface. In a moment, you'll notice a line which reads "The History of Helvetica," which is headline copy, in Garamond Small Caps Bold.)

Many type families—we'll discuss these shortly—have both body- and display-face variations. However, it's important to distinguish between these two applications of type and not to interchange them. Body faces are designed to be set small and used in words that are to be read, as in the body copy of an advertisement or the paragraphs of text on a book page. They tend to be light and simple. Display faces are designed to be set large and have visual impact, as in headlines, titles, banners, and posters.

Body faces don't make for interesting headlines. They lack the intensity to stand out from a page. Display faces, on the other hand, don't produce body copy which is easy to read—the type has too much detail, and is too busy to allow one's eye to get on with reading the words.

Most of the faces which come with CorelDRAW are display faces. Some, such as Times or Helvetica, are really intended for use as body faces— these are useful if you actually want to use CorelDRAW to set body type in its paragraph mode or for use as display faces when you want to match a body copy face. In general, though, CorelDRAW's typeface assortment is heavily weighted in favor of display faces because much of what it does with type is a display-face application.

THE HISTORY OF HELVETICA

The first automatic typesetting machine, the Linotype, was invented in 1886. The company that made it still exists—its descendent is the Linotronic PostScript phototypesetter.

You certainly do not need to understand anything about the history of typography in order to use the type facilities of CorelDRAW. However, much of the rationale behind applying type to design problems may be seen in the way type has evolved into its present form. The forces which drove it were at least partly a result of the demands of designers for specific typographic features. (The other part was the requirement of type foundries, the companies which design and manufacture type, to dominate their respective markets and sell lots of faces.)

The Helvetica typeface has a long, fairly convoluted history which will probably help you to understand why type is the way it is.

Helvetica is a *sans-serif* (meaning without serifs) typeface, and though it has a long history, it is a comparatively recent development as movable type goes. The first typefaces were considerably more ornate. Helvetica is called a lineal typeface, that is, one in which all the stalks and elements of the typeface design are essentially lines of the same width.

The earliest precursor to Helvetica is thought to be a face called Egyptian, released by William Caslon IV in 1816. Caslon was a noted type designer, among other things—you may have noticed that the Casablanca typeface which comes with CorelDRAW is in fact Caslon, named after him.

Egyptian was not particularly "Egyptian" in appearance; nor was it much like the faces which Caslon and other type founders of the period were used to. It was exceedingly plain and lacked all vestiges of the then common ornamentation of type. Most notable was the absence of serifs, which made it look rather sparse and did not endear it to the typesetters of the period. In those days, type was set entirely by hand and the serifs on the characters helped to keep the edges of the type from wearing down prematurely.

The Egyptian face created only a mild stir in typographic circles. Several similar faces appeared for a short while, but it was a long time before sans-serif type gained any significant acceptance.

 On a Linotype machine, type was stored in two drawers, or cases. Capital letters were stored in the upper one, hence the terms uppercase and lowercase text.

Mechanical typesetting was born in the latter part of the nineteenth century with the invention of hot lead type. While one may regard this as being simply a convenience, a quicker and perhaps more economical way to arrive at the results previously managed by hand, it was really as much of a revolution in its day as laser printers and desktop publishing are now. The advent of typesetting machines made books and newspapers of the sort we're used to a practical reality, and it also made the use of sans-serif type less problematic.

Much of the early design of type and typesetting originated in Germany—Gutenberg seems to have founded a tradition of typesetting there which long survived him. When mechanical typesetting had grown to be widely accepted, Berthold AG, one of the great German type foundries, released a face called Akzidenz-Grotesk. It looked a lot like Helvetica does now. It was also one of the earliest instances of the appellation Grotesk, or grotesque, applied to sans-serif type.

Figure 14.1 illustrates Helvetica and Akzidenz-Grotesk. It's worth mentioning that this type was not set from the original hot metal dies for

FIGURE 14.1:

*Helvetica and
Akzidenz-Grotesk*

Helvetica	Akzidenz-Grotesk
Helvetica Bold	**Akzidenz-Grotesk Bold**
	Akzidenz-Grotesk Light
	Akzidenz-Grotesk Light Bold

Akzidenz-Grotesk. This face was recently reintroduced by Adobe as a Post-Script font.

Despite what you might think, the appellation *grotesk* does not imply that its designers thought the face was particularly ugly. The etymology of grotesk is a bit complex; the term has been applied in typography mainly as a synonym for *gothic*. Gothic is a somewhat vague term in typography, and it would be very hard to define concisely—you'll probably get a feel for it as you become more familiar with various typefaces. It is usually used to imply that the face in question is somehow evocative of traditional or conservative type design.

Akzidenz-Grotesk was originally intended for use as a display face. In a world rich with ornate faces, the simple, decisive lines of a sans-serif face stood out, and made for a good display face. It was released in medium condensed and bold condensed faces.

Early in the history of commercial printing, typeface designers realized that type naturally lent itself to being designed in families, that is, in a number of weights which were visually distinct from one another but which had similar enough characteristics to appear to have sprung from the same root.

The initial weights of Akzidenz-Grotesk were eventually supplemented until there was a moderately full family around it. This included a medium-weight face, which no one particularly liked. It also included several more varieties of display faces. There was a light face, an expanded face, and an extremely light version called Akzidenz-Grotesk Skelett, that is, skeletal.

There are quite a few important things to note in the evolution of Akzidenz-Grotesk. First of all, it was well received because it was distinct from the faces which were in common use at the time. Secondly, it was well received as a display face, that is, as a face intended for use in headlines, titles, and so on. The normal weight, added to the family fairly late in its development, was intended for use in body copy, but it was something of a failure. This may be attributed to the general apprehension of designers, then as now, that one body face looked pretty much like another, and that there was little cause for embracing a new one. It also might be attributed to the rather unfriendly appearance of sans-serif faces used to set body copy.

Akzidenz-Grotesk became quite popular, but its name, among other things (it didn't sound any less weird back then), precluded its successful marketing in the English-speaking world. The name eventually faded away in German typesetting circles, too, although it returned briefly in the late 1950s as Akzidenz-Grotesk 57. Very recently, it has again been reborn as AG Old Face, a phototypesetting face faithfully copied from the original metal type of 1896.

It's worth noting that Akzidenz-Grotesk found its greatest popularity in Switzerland. Helvetica, in fact, was commissioned by a Swiss type foundry. It was designed in the 1950s by Max Meidinger, and it is clearly based on Akzidenz-Grotesk. At about the same time, a French type designer, Adrian Frutiger, was creating Univers. Helvetica and Univers look exceedingly similar, although you will notice a few design differences. If you become very conscious of type, you may come to feel that Univers, with its slightly more flowing style and more sensuous feel, expresses something subtly different from Helvetica. Both Helvetica and Univers are included with Corel-DRAW—you can see them both in Figure 14.2.

One of the important distinctions between Akzidenz-Grotesk and both Helvetica and Univers is that the latter two faces were designed as complete, unified families of type. We will discuss the significance of this in greater detail later in this chapter. However, Helvetica suffered from a lot of name troubles early in its life, as its various weights got called different things in different circumstances. Hence, at various times Helvetica Light and Helvetica Extralight were in fact the same face, and it became difficult to specify something in a particular weight of Helvetica and know what one was going to get. The Helvetica family as it appears today in CorelDRAW (under the name Switzerland) is shown in Figure 14.3.

Univers, by comparison, was always named consistently with numerical values for its various weights; Univers 45 is the name for the light weight, for example. While perhaps not as descriptive as the names applied to Helvetica, the numbering system was consistent. There are designers who favor Univers over Helvetica for this reason.

Helvetica
Univers

Note the different shapes of the S.

Helvetica   Univers

There are countless variations on the original Akzidenz-Grotesk face extant today. This includes buckets of authorized Helvetica derivations designed by the descendants of the type foundry which created Helvetica itself. You'll encounter extended Helvetica, rounded Helvetica, Helvetica designed expressly for body copy (book-weight Helvetica), and so on. There are also countless knock-offs of these fonts under other names.

The evolution of Helvetica was unquestionably commercially driven to some extent, but in it you can also see the demands of designers for particular sorts of type, or for type to perform certain functions. These functions will probably crop up in your applications of type under CorelDRAW. You might consider the problems in type evolution when you're thinking about the problems of suiting type to your graphics.

FIGURE 14.3:

The Helvetica family

Helvetica
Helvetica Italic
Helvetica Bold
Helvetica Bold Italic
Helvetica Black
Helvetica Black Italic
Helvetica Light
Helvetica Light Italic
Helvetica Narrow
Helvetica Narrow Italic
Helvetica Narrow Bold
Helvetica Narrow Bold Italic

TYPES OF TYPE

 Our present alphabet was in use by the Romans by about 400 BC. Lowercase letters, however, didn't appear until about 789 AD, when Charlemagne required that the books of the Christian church be made more readable.

Type design is a rather esoteric art. The plethora of software packages which ostensibly allow one to design custom typefaces will attest to this. They make designing bad type exceedingly easy. Actually, if you have a background in typeface design (or if you're presently employed by one of the type foundries), you *can* design good type with some of them.

Figure 14.4 shows a character under construction. This is the sort of thing which goes on for each character of a typeface being designed.

In considering type, it's important to realize that every typeface was designed with a lot of reasoning behind it, and that all that reasoning was expended to design it for a specific function. Before people read your type, they'll see it as a graphic element. Its visual appearance, and whatever it evokes or fails to evoke as a graphic, will color their perception of your words.

FIGURE 14.4:

*How a character
is designed*

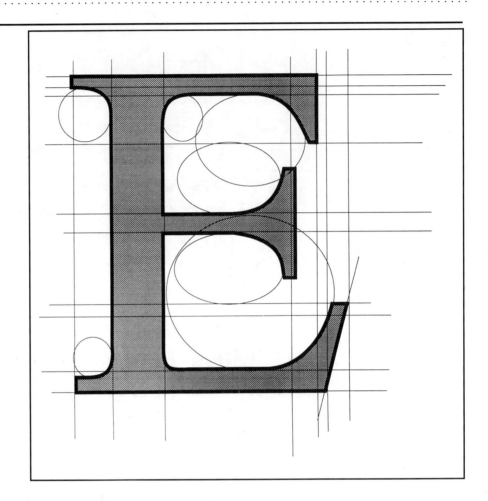

Consider the type samples in Figure 14.5. All four of these paragraphs have the same words in them, but they read differently. If you came upon each of them in isolation, your approach to what they had to say would probably be modified by their appearances. Before you read it, the visual style of the type speaks.

The type samples in Figure 14.5 are a bit extreme. The ornate details of the second sample, for instance, are extremely evocative but hardly ever used, except as an effect. The message in the typeface is too broad, too evidently a message to be appealingly evocative. Rather than a subtle suggestion, it's something of a pie in one's face.

Let's consider four more type samples, as seen in Figure 14.6.

FIGURE 14.5:

Different body faces

> *As soon as peace is restored, We will banish from Our kingdom all foreign knights, crossbowmen, attendants, and mercenaries who have come with horses and arms to the harm of the kingdom.*
>
> As soon as peace is restored, We will banish from Our kingdom all foreign knights, crossbowmen, attendants, and mercenaries who have come with horses and arms to the harm of the kingdom.
>
> *As soon as peace is restored. We will banish from Our kingdom all foreign knights. crossbowmen. attendants. and mercenaries who have come with horses and arms to the harm of the kingdom.*
>
> As soon as peace is restored, We will banish from Our kingdom all foreign knights, crossbowmen, attendants, and mercenaries who have come with horses and arms to the harm of the kingdom.

These four faces are a bit less extreme, but each has a particular style and a particular message. The paragraph set in Helvetica looks crisp and sterile, and suggests something of a technical or businesslike nature. The passage in Caslon looks gothic—in the typographic use of that word—and suggests age and stability. The sample of Optima seems sparse and ascetic, suggesting that its words will be to the point, with no ornamentation. The text in Times Roman has a sense of neutrality about it, perhaps because Times is such a commonly used font.

It may well be argued that only type gurus and perhaps owners of CorelDRAW will analyze type to this extent. However, the subtleties of type affect people who see it, whether they think about it or not, and you can make this visual aspect of type work for you by choosing type which suits the tone of whatever you're designing. There are a lot of useful guidelines for choosing type, but the first one is always to make sure that the message of your type-face agrees with the message of the rest of your drawing (or poster or page).

As soon as peace is restored, We will banish from Our kingdom all foreign knights, crossbowmen, attendants, and mercenaries who have come with horses and arms to the harm of the kingdom.
Helvetica

As soon as peace is restored, We will banish from Our kingdom all foreign knights, crossbowmen, attendants, and mercenaries who have come with horses and arms to the harm of the kingdom.
Caslon

As soon as peace is restored, We will banish from Our kingdom all foreign knights, crossbowmen, attendants, and mercenaries who have come with horses and arms to the harm of the kingdom.
Optima

As soon as peace is restored, We will banish from Our kingdom all foreign knights, crossbowmen, attendants, and mercenaries who have come with horses and arms to the harm of the kingdom.
Times Roman

Consider the two graphics in Figure 14.7. The images are the same, as are the words which have been appended to them. However, the two typefaces involved alter the overall effect of the two graphics considerably. The upper version, set in Helvetica, lacks any cohesiveness between the text and the graphic. The elegant, flowing lines of the picture clash with the hard, sharp edges of the type. One has the feeling that the type and the picture exist as separate entities, with little in common except that they've been placed on the same page.

The second image works a great deal better. The lines of the type—in the Benguiat face this time—work well with the drawing, and the picture complements the words. The whole graphic locks together, and one is not confronted with two contradictory visual messages upon considering it.

FIGURE 14.7:

Two examples of type and a drawing. One works, one doesn't.

There are certainly reasons to break the rules, although, as we discussed in Chapter 12, you should only do so consciously and creatively. One fairly obvious example is in setting small type. Text which is smaller than about nine points begins to get difficult or impossible to read if it's handled in an ornate font. A simple, sans-serif font like Helvetica will survive at small point sizes far better than a serif one.

One is often confronted with similar mechanical constraints. I once produced a chart using Caslon, which looked fine until I had to add more information to it, at which point the width spread out far too much. The solution was to set all the type in a horizontally condensed face. CorelDRAW comes with a few such faces, one of which is Helvetica Narrow. I could also have used Futura Light—a font which is almost as condensed—without a significantly different visual effect.

It might be argued that the chart could have been done using a serif face simply by transforming it into a compressed face, squeezing the type horizontally until it fit. This approach seems elegant in theory, but isn't all that workable in practice. Condensing an ornate font in this way usually leaves you with rather ugly type. Genuine condensed versions of typefaces are designed as such, from scratch.

You also might decide simply for effect that you want to break the rule of having your typefaces match your graphics. The results of doing so can be eye-catching and effective simply because they *don't* work as unified graphics; rather, they contrast. Consider Figure 14.8.

As with all elements of design, try to do this sort of thing with a reasonable measure of subtlety and with some thought as to whose eye you're trying to catch. A graphic which is eye-catching because it's simply bad or loud and obnoxious isn't necessarily effective.

TYPE FAMILIES

The typefaces which come with CorelDRAW are, for the most part, supplied in families. If you use a font like Garamond, for example, you can introduce variations in your text using the italic, bold, and bold italic versions of the face.

If you've used a Macintosh, you might have noticed that the Mac algorithmically produces italics from medium type by simply skewing the font slightly, and bold by laterally expanding each character a bit. This works for

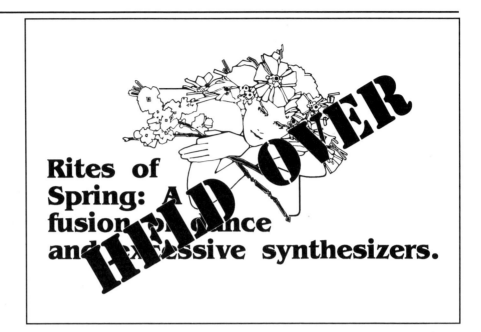

crude dot-matrix printing, but it isn't nearly good enough for true typesetting. For instance, each of the faces of Garamond is a separate font—someone originally designed Garamond four ways.

One important rule in creating graphics of any sort—and especially
when using type—is that human beings subconsciously attach meaning to
everything they see, or, perhaps more precisely, look for meaning in everything they see. For this reason, everything you do in creating a design should
appear to have been done for a deliberate reason.

The subtle differences between fairly similar typefaces can be make an
excellent illustration of this rule. Consider the type in Figure 14.9.

In reading the paragraph in Figure 14.9, you may be struck with the
sense of something being wrong with it. It seems peculiar without an obvious reason for it. If you look closely, however, you might be able to pick
out the reason: some of the words have been set in Times Roman and some
in Garamond. These two faces are very similar, but they're different enough
that they look different side by side.

Figure 14.10 illustrates the same text with very different fonts. This
may be a good example of bad typography, but it isn't as disturbing as the

As soon as peace is restored, We will banish from Our kingdom all foreign knights, crossbowmen, attendants, and mercenaries who have come with horses and arms to the harm of the kingdom.

As soon as peace is restored, We will banish from Our kingdom all foreign knights, crossbowmen, attendants, and mercenaries who have come with horses and arms to the harm of the kingdom.

first one. In this case it's obvious that something has been done, and it might be the case that the designer did it for some conscious reason.

Typefaces should be selected and used with some conscious reasoning in mind. If you have a good reason for choosing Garamond, say, over Times Roman at some place in your graphic, chances are that you will not have an equally good reason for using Times Roman rather than Garamond somewhere else in the same graphic.

As a rule, you should not have type from more than two families in a single graphic or on a single page. Furthermore, the two families should be visually distinct. The best application of this rule is to make one of the families a serif font, and the other a sans-serif font. The functions the different families are put to should also be distinct—the serif face for body copy and the sans-serif face for heads, for example, if you're designing complete pages.

Once again, you can break this rule if you have a good reason, but think about it carefully before you do. A design which incorporates a welter of different typefaces can be eye-catching if it's done for the right reasons, but it's far more likely simply to be confusing.

The faces which have condensed, extrabold, and other variations offer a powerful facility for introducing variations on your type without violating the two-family rule. For example, Helvetica and Helvetica Narrow look pretty good together—they're different faces, but they still appear to be from the same family.

USING BOLD AND ITALIC

 Italic type was first designed in 1501 by Aldus Manutius, after whom the company that created the PageMaker desktop publishing package is named.

CorelDRAW allows you to employ the usual additional type fonts of italic and boldface. In some cases, you can use the condensed or extrabold versions of standard faces for additional effect. But these facilities offer a world of opportunity for bad design if you don't apply them with restraint.

The expressive potential of typography has probably been expounded upon at sufficient length. Aside from being able to evoke, through your choice of typefaces, a particular state of mind in someone looking at your design, you can also add emphasis and direction to the words you set through the use of related faces. However, just as you can visually misdirect or confuse someone by choosing the wrong typeface, so too can you render your words ineffective by misapplying the family members of a good typeface.

If you look through a few pages of this book, you'll probably notice all the section heads. They're very obvious and eye-catching, in that they're in boldface. Because this book is intended to serve at least partially as a reference work, the effect of having heads snagging your attention is appropriate. It allows you to skim through the book and easily identify the subjects of the various sections.

Boldface text within a paragraph will also catch your eye. In most cases, though, you should probably not try this technique. Reading body text with boldface words scattered through it is uncomfortable. Your eye will be constantly distracted by the nearest bold word or passage. Boldface should never be used in body text for emphasis unless you particularly want your readers to pick out key words at the expense of the flow of the copy in general.

If you want emphasis in body text, use italics. Because they are the same weight as the rest of the type, italics will not immediately stand out from the page (unless, of course, they are overused). They *will* be noticeable as the text is read, which is when you want them to be noticeable.

As with other attention-getting devices, changes in type fonts are at their best if you use them sparingly. Text which is mostly italicized with bold heads between every paragraph quickly loses the effectiveness of all the emphasis these differences usually convey.

When you apply text to a CorelDRAW graphic, you can do a lot toward integrating the text and your picture by considering how best to apply certain types of text. For example, consider that boldface type might integrate nicely into a drawing which has a lot of dominant black areas. Likewise, a simple but elegant application is the use of italicized text if your drawing has any slanted elements. If the slant of your drawing doesn't happen to match the slant of your italics, you might have to skew the text mechanically.

Type purists will probably react with horror at this idea—italics are not merely slanted type. However, it's often necessary to take a few liberties with the typefaces to make them do what you want. This is what makes CorelDRAW so useful.

GUIDELINES FOR USING CORELDRAW'S FACES

There are all sorts of reasons to recommend one typeface over another. For example, a graphic with many curved objects lends itself to a serif typeface, preferably one with lots of curves of its own, such as Garamond or Caslon. A graphic which looks sparse and mechanical might work well with a similarly designed face. Friz Quadrata is a particularly useful typeface in this regard, in that although it is a serif face, it still maintains the appearance of being rather chiseled and lean, without flowery ornamentation.

The rest of this chapter consists of discussion about many of the specific typefaces included with CorelDRAW and how you might want to apply them. These ideas are by no means rigid—you can ignore them whenever you feel it's appropriate—but they might help you to find the most effective faces for your applications.

Bear in mind that this discussion incorporates a lot of personal bias as well. You'll quickly develop your own attitudes about type as you work with it, quite possibly disagreeing passionately with mine. Art will do that to you.

The following discussion is arranged alphabetically by the proper commercial names of the fonts. The corresponding CorelDRAW pseudonym is shown alongside in parentheses. For an illustration of these typefaces, refer to Figure 14.11.

FIGURE 14.11:

Typefaces which come with CorelDRAW, and their special CorelDRAW names (small print)

Avant Garde (Avalon)	(Switzerland Cond Light) Helvetica Cond Light
Aachen (Aardvark)	(Switzerland Inserat) **Helvetica Inserat**
American Typewriter (Memorandum)	(Homeward Bound) Hobo
Arnold Böcklin (Arabia)	(Ireland) IRONWOOD
Bauhaus (Bahamas)	(Jupiter) JUNIPER
Bauhaus Heavy (Bahamas Heavy)	(Koala) *Kaufman*
Bauhaus Light (Bahamas Light)	(Monospaced) Letter Gothic
Brush Script (Banff)	(Lincoln) **Linotext**
Benguiat (Bangkok)	(Linus) *Linoscript*
Bodoni Poster (Bodnoff)	(Motor) **MACHINE**
Bookman (Brooklyn)	(Mystical) *Mistral*
Caslon (Casablanca)	(Nebraska) New Baskerville
Caslon Open Face (Casper OpenFace)	(New Brunswick) New Century Schoolbook
Century Oldstyle (Centurion Old)	(Ottawa) Optima
COTTONWOOD (Cottage)	(Palm Springs) Palatino
Cooper Black (Cupertino)	(Paradise) *Park Avenue*
Dom Casual (Dawn Castle)	(Paragon) *Parisian*
Eras (Erie)	(Penguin) PEIGNOT
Eras Black (Erie Black)	(Penguin Light) PEIGNOT LIGHT
Eras Light (Erie Light)	(Posse) ▪
Friz Quadrata (France)	(President) *Present Script*
Fette Fraktur (Frankenstein)	(Prose Antique) Post Antiqua
Franklin Gothic (Frankfurt Gothic)	(Renfrew) **Revue**
Franklin Gothic Heavy (Frankfurt Gothic Heavy)	(Southern) Souvenir
Freestyle Script (Freeport)	(Stamp) **STENCIL**
Futura (Fujiyama)	(Technical) Tekton
Futura ExtraBold (Fujiyama ExtraBold)	(Timpani) Tiffany
Futura Light (Fujiyama Light)	(Timpany Heavy) **Tiffany Heavy**
Garamond (Gatineau)	(Toronto) Times Roman
Helvetica (Switzerland)	(Umbrella) UMBRA
Helvetica-Black (Switzerland Black)	(Unicorn) University Roman
Helvetica-Light (Switzerland Light)	(USA Black) **Univers Black**
Helvetica-Narrow (Switzerland Narrow)	(USA Light) Univers Light
Helvetica Cond (Switzerland Cond)	(Vogue) VAG Rounded
Helvetica CondBlk (Switzerland Cond Black)	(Zurich Calligraphic) *Zapf Chancery*

AACHEN BOLD (AARDVARK BOLD)

Aachen is a massive and rather eye-catching display face. It doesn't actually look all that attractive, but it's hard to miss. It's also hard to read if you set it small. Aachen doesn't purport to be subtle.

This would be a good face for applications in which you want a headline or title to be noticed but you don't really care what people think of it. Ugly type may not be very pleasing, but it's difficult to ignore. If you're printing in color, set the Aachen type in purple against a black background and it will have its maximum effect.

If you can get more than a dozen words on a page in Aachen, you've set them too small.

AMERICAN TYPEWRITER (MEMORANDUM)

American Typewriter is obviously a gadget face, a special effect. It doesn't really look like it has come from a typewriter—for one thing, it's proportionately spaced. It is evocative of typewriters, however, and is useful for this reason. It's also useful in all sorts of type-based graphics, as it's a serif face with a lineal design—there are no points, picks, or other sharp edges. It worked well as the basis for the giant A graphic at the beginning of this book for just this reason.

Despite appearances to the contrary, American Typewriter does not make a good body face. It's great for heads in which you want to suggest a connection with an office, with writing, with archaic machinery, or with individuals as opposed to machines or corporations. Typewriters are evocative of individual typists or authors; type is evocative of companies and organizations big enough to afford typesetters. This distinction may vanish as laser printers become common household appliances.

ARNOLD BÖCKLIN (ARABIA)

Arnold Böcklin is one of the nicest ornate faces to come with CorelDRAW. It's not overused too much yet, although it's becoming more common. It looks a bit pseudo-medieval, invoking perhaps more of a T.E. White version of the Middle Ages than a historical one. It comes off looking rich and intricate without looking too much like a cliché.

Having said all this, I want to add that Arnold Böcklin is among the easiest of faces to overuse or use inappropriately. Because it's quite specific in what it evokes, it clashes with just about anything that isn't in keeping with its nature.

Arnold Böcklin probably has the distinction of being the most unreadable typeface ever created if you mistakenly use it as a body face.

AVANTE GARDE (AVALON)

Avante Garde is certainly one of my favorite sans-serif faces. It has the clean, distinct lines of Helvetica but, as its name implies, it's a bit more daring and adventurous. It's a good choice when your application calls for a sans-serif face and you consider Helvetica or Univers too overused or too conservative. Some of the capital letters of Avante Garde, such as the Q, are particularly attractive, and it's tempting to work in text with Qs in it just to be able to see them.

Much of the appeal of Avante Garde is its clean, breezy appearance. This tends to vanish when you use the bold weight of this font. Bold Avante Garde isn't ugly—it's just not quite as appealing as the medium face is.

Avante Garde makes a good face for doing headlines and other bits of display type, especially if the other font in your design is something fairly pedestrian, like Times Roman.

BAUHAUS (BAHAMAS)

Bauhaus is Avant Garde with an attitude. It has the clean lines of a sans-serif face, but it also has a distinct personality. It looks elegantly European, precise, but not sterile. It's a good face to use when you don't want your type to look too ornate but you still want it to be distinct and eye-catching.

The light version of Bauhaus is so light as to be easily missed. This makes it of questionable use for complex pages, but it can be tremendously effective in graphics which have a lot of white space. It can come off as being very understated and subtle.

The heavy face of Bauhaus is bold enough to be noticed from across a warehouse of used neon signs, but it still possesses many of the attributes of the medium weight of this face.

BENGUIAT (BANGKOK)

Benguiat is a particularly ornate serif face, evocative of turn-of-the-century poster art, among other things. It looks a bit bohemian, and suggests that the design it's part of is sensual and perhaps somewhat debauched. Benguiat is a rather specialized typeface, and one which you probably won't have call to use all that often. However, it's very effective in the right context, because it's so rich in images.

Obviously, the aforementioned richness is audience-dependent. It may conjure up allusions to the heyday of turn-of-the-century Europe, but only for people who are familiar with these ideas. It will just look flowery and overdone if you apply it to the headlines for a book on chartered accountancy, for example.

Perhaps the biggest drawback to Benguiat is that it's attractive enough to lead one to use it in places where it doesn't belong. I've yet to find anything practical to do with it, although I'd like to.

BODONI POSTER (BODNOFF)

Bodoni is another special-purpose typeface. It's not quite art deco, but it's reminiscent of the period. As such, it doesn't give the too-obvious, campy appearance of simply using art deco type, but it still manages to evoke the period and culture.

Ignoring this aspect of its design, Bodoni is also a rather attractive display font in its own right. It's as bold and noticeable as Aachen, but it's nowhere near as unpleasant to look at. It looks sophisticated and dignified even though it's kind of enormous. Like Aachen, however, Bodoni should not be used to set small type—it gets very nearly unreadable.

Bodoni, like so many other specialized faces, makes a good effect when it happens to match the direction of the rest of your design. It's not suited for general use, however. You wouldn't want to use it as the display face in book design, for example. Its distinctiveness would work against you in this case—one's eye would become so interested in the visual appeal of this interesting font as to be distracted from the principal intent of your design.

BOOKMAN (BROOKLYN)

Bookman, as its name suggests, is a very well crafted body face for setting books. It's included with most PostScript printers, and it is used quite frequently for body copy in desktop publishing applications. Having it available in CorelDRAW therefore allows you to create graphics which perfectly match or complement the type in a desktop-published document.

As a body face, Bookman is a bit less horizontally condensed than Times Roman. It takes up more space, which is both handy if you want to fill a lot of paper with relatively few words and functional if you want those words to be more easily read.

If you apply Bookman to a stand-alone graphic in CorelDRAW, you'll probably notice that it's unusually easy to read. While visually unremarkable, it's useful for this purpose.

BRUSH SCRIPT (BANFF)

Brush Script is one of the more severely abused special-effect typefaces. This is at least partially because it makes good press-on lettering, having fat stalks that are less likely to break off, and it has worked its way into letterhead, business cards, and other sorts of quick printing.

While not unattractive in isolation, Brush Script suffers from overexposure. It has become something of a cliché, and it's probably worth avoiding for this reason. It seems to cry out, "Look here—special effect in progress—film at eleven!"

Besides all that, there's a certain perversity in using a four-thousand-dollar laser printer to simulate handwriting, the very thing it was created to do away with.

CASLON (CASABLANCA)

I'm never sure if I like Caslon better for its appearance or for the typographic traditions it evokes. If it's the latter case, it'll be effective only for other people interested in type. Visually, though, Caslon manages to be eye-catching yet restrained and distinguished at the same time. Its disproportionately large caps and ascenders make type set in it look large without seeming massive.

Caslon doesn't make a bad body face, although its real strength is in doing heads and titles. It's well suited to designs in which you want to suggest age, stability, conservative values, and so on.

CASLON OPENFACE (CASPER OPENFACE)

Just as italics are more than just slanted type, open-face type is more than just type with an outline. Caslon Openface is rarely used because it's not all that dominant. If anything, though, it enhances the gothic qualities of basic Caslon. If your design isn't too busy, Caslon Openface can look elegant and understated without getting lost.

CENTURY OLD STYLE (CENTURION OLD)

Century is a somewhat gothic—grotesk—serif face. It's a bit more ornate than Times Roman, but also more horizontally condensed than Bookman. It doesn't work badly for heads, although it appears to be a body face. It's enough like Times to get away with using Times for a body face and Century for large, bold heads.

Gothic faces are another of those subtle applications of type that only other type gurus will consciously recognize. Century suggests the gothic qualities of stability and permanence without being really obvious about it.

COOPER BLACK (CUPERTINO)

It's said that Cooper was designed by a farsighted printer with nearsighted clients. It's a nice-looking typeface for titles, although it might be alleged to suffer a bit from looking like the sort of face a press-on lettering company would embrace. Cooper has the advantage of standing out from an otherwise busy page by virtue of its boldness, while at the same time not detracting from its surroundings by looking ugly or weird. It evokes hand-set type and an age of simpler things.

Because Cooper covers a lot of area, it's a great face to use for extreme type-based CorelDRAW graphics. Like American Typewriter, it's a good base for fitting text to.

COTTONWOOD (COTTAGE)

If you ever get caught in a time warp and have occasion to design the signboard for an 1880's saloon, this is the typeface to have on hand. Because

Cottonwood is type that seems to resound with every Western movie cliché ever uttered, it's pretty hard to miss what this typeface evokes. For most applications, it's pretty hard to find a use for it, too.

DOM CASUAL (DAWN CASTLE)

Brush script faces are an acquired taste. Dom Casual is perhaps less overtly laid back than most of them, but it still looks like press-on lettering. It seems to evoke a sort of amateurishness, or perhaps a lack of refinement. There are unquestionably times when you might want this effect in a typeface. However, Dom Casual looks a bit too casual—it has much the same attitude about it as a salesman wearing very unbusinesslike clothes so as to mask his intentions until it's too late to escape him. Few of us are fooled by salesmen like that anymore, and likewise few readers will really respond to the feel of Dom Casual.

ERAS (ERIE)

The Eras font—also available in light and heavy versions—is a sans-serif face which has the crisp, uncluttered lines of Helvetica but quite a lot more distinction about it. It seems to sprawl out across a page, suggesting that it's not quite as restrained as Helvetica, but perhaps not quite as extreme as Bauhaus. Eras is a good choice when you need a sans-serif face with just a bit of personality.

FETTE FRAKTUR (FRANKENSTEIN)

The CorelDRAW pseudonym for this face describes it pretty well. Type set in Fette Fraktur is, for the most part, decorative and very Germanic looking. It's also wholly unreadable. Many of the characters, such as the uppercase A, are unrecognizable. The lowercase ones fare a bit better. This is a great font for using with the CorelDRAW blend function when you never really wanted the resulting image to be recognizable as words to begin with.

FRANKLIN GOTHIC (FRANKFURT GOTHIC)

The subtleties of sans-serif faces are often hard to appreciate. In isolation, one Helvetica clone looks pretty much like another.

Franklin Gothic is different from Helvetica in that its caps and ascenders are quite a bit smaller in relation to its normal lowercase letters. Type set in Franklin has a rather dominant look to it. It suggests that whatever it says is so important as to fill up every square inch of the paper it covers.

If your design calls for a sans-serif font and you've done Helvetica to death, Franklin is a particularly attractive alternative. It's provided in an extrabold face, too, which adds to its usefulness.

FREESTYLE SCRIPT (FREEPORT)

Given the choice between Freestyle Script and Brush Script—assuming that you must use a script face at all—the former is probably a better choice. For one thing, it looks more like handwriting. It's also a great deal less common. If you use it very sparingly, so that its precision as a font doesn't become apparent, it might even be mistaken for handwriting.

A script face such as this one can be effective if you apply it cleverly. The juxtaposition of a precise graphic and what seems to be a bit of handwriting can be very eye-catching. Consider using it to add your signature to a graphic in the way that a painter might sign a painting.

If you have more than a couple dozen characters set in Freestyle Script on the same page, you're probably overdoing it.

FRIZ QUADRATA (FRANCE)

Friz Quadrata manages to combine the hard, crisp lines of a sans-serif font with the attractiveness of a serif face. It looks businesslike and technical, and, as its real name suggests, somewhat contemporarily German. Friz is a font which is rarely used, and as such is a good face to use for doing something different with type.

Friz Quadrata works well in heads for things like corporate reports and technical publications, and in graphics where the subject is mechanical, technical, scientific, or perhaps financial. It suggests that its demeanor is serious, but that there is an element of humanity in this otherwise serious subject.

FUTURA (FUJIYAMA)

Futura is a sans-serif font which is both more condensed and bolder than Helvetica. It's better suited to heads in which you want to get a lot of type into a small space, and the generally punchier appearance of Futura is more likely to get noticed.

Futura is arguably a bit less interesting and appealing than Helvetica— what it gains in visibility it lacks in appearance. It's good for applications in which its contribution to your design is secondary to its usefulness in other areas, specifically that of being a good, unmistakable headline face. Its extrabold version is extremely hard to ignore.

GARAMOND (GATINEAU)

Garamond is one of the most attractive serif faces, and its appeal grows the bigger you make it. It's particularly ornate, but its ornamental elements, predominantly its serifs and large, flowing capitals, seem to have been designed with precisely the right amount of subtlety to go unnoticed most of the time. You're reading a version of it right now. Garamond is one of the few serif faces which looks just as good in bold as it does in medium.

Garamond is a good face for use in headlines and titles if you want to convey a sense of culture and style without adding elements of other, specific design criteria; that is, it doesn't look too gothic or too antique or too modern, and so forth.

One unique quality of Garamond is that it looks good tightly kerned. If you use the CorelDRAW shape tool to squeeze all the space out from between its characters, Garamond flows naturally into a sort of quasi-graphic font. Headlines created in this way don't lose too much readability, and they do make really attractive design elements.

Helvetica (Switzerland)

Helvetica Narrow (or Switzerland Narrow to Corel-DRAW) is a dedicated version of Helvetica designed to be narrow. Helvetica Condensed is really just Helvetica that has been squeezed horizontally. The former usually looks better.

Helvetica is often accused by designers of being unadventurous, dull, over-used, lacking in dynamics, devoid of distinction, and the opiate of typesetters everywhere. All of this may well be true. If for no other reason than its almost daily appearance in everything from newspapers to macaroni labels, Helvetica is so common as to be a noneffect. It evokes nothing. It is the safest sans-serif font you can use.

There are certainly instances in which you will want to set type that says nothing other than the actual words you set. Helvetica has its place for this reason. It doesn't presuppose anything on the part of its ultimate readers, either. Someone who dislikes anything old may take unkindly to type set in Caslon; the Luddites among us will be bothered by Friz Quadrata. While your readers will never get excited about Helvetica, they'll never object to it, either.

In addition, Helvetica as it appears in CorelDRAW is available in an enviable family of faces ranging from condensed and light versions up to an extrabold weight. This makes it extremely versatile.

You should consider using Helvetica when you want your graphics to speak and your words merely to convey information. It's also applicable if you anticipate the words you'll be setting to be read by a large and varied group of people. Finally, if you can't decide on what you want your typeface to evoke, it may be better to have it say nothing than to have it say something inappropriate.

Hobo (Homeward Bound)

Hobo is another special-effect face. It's not unattractive in small doses, but its rather obvious statement of being laid back and funky starts to pall after a while. It's good for effects, but you wouldn't want to see it every day.

There are some designs, especially for publications, in which the use of one-of-a-kind typefaces like Hobo works. Some magazines, for example, will have markedly different designs for the head of each feature. In these cases, you can justify one head in Hobo, one in Chancery, and another in ExtraGalactica Condensed Gothic, if you like, without any one of them getting stale.

You might think of typefaces such as Hobo as being a joke. A lot of designers do. In this case, consider it in the following context, taken from Robert Heinlein: The first time you tell the joke you're a wit. The next time you tell it, you're a halfwit, and so on, in a geometrical progression.

IRONWOOD (IRELAND)

Not in the slightest bit Irish in appearance, Ironwood is another extreme special-effect face in the tradition of the Cottonwood face mentioned earlier. It's sort of prickly and unfriendly in appearance, and looks like it might have been used to set business cards for William the Conqueror. It's hard to imagine a contemporary use for it.

JUNIPER (JUPITER)

The Juniper face is another period font in the tradition of Ironwood, above. It seems to be designed to look like the hand-set poster type of the latter half of the 1800s, and might be used to evoke this period. Unlike Ironwood, it's not impossible to read, which is probably an asset in a typeface. Juniper is an interesting face, but as typography goes, pretty poorly designed. Your eyes can get tired of it very quickly.

KAUFMANN (KOALA)

Of all the script faces which come with CorelDRAW, this one is the least frequently used in general, and as such perhaps the least objectionable. Unlike the more ornate brush script fonts, Kaufmann looks like it might have been handwriting once. It suggests simplicity and the existence of a human being behind all the technology responsible for a printed page.

LETTER GOTHIC (MONOSPACED)

Letter Gothic is a monospaced lineal font which is frequently found on typewriters and especially in computer printers. While it's quite plain and uninspiring, it has a number of useful features. The first of these is that it is monospaced, and as such, multiple lines of dissimilar characters will be aligned vertically. It's very handy for setting things like columns of numbers, computer program listings, and so on.

As a typeface, Letter Gothic implies a sense of simplicity, adding even less color to text set in it than do faces like Times Roman and Helvetica. However, because it's monospaced you'll find that text set in this font occupies a lot more space, all things being equal.

LINOSCRIPT (LINUS)

While still technically a script face, Linoscript doesn't attempt to be an imitation of handwriting. It's just a very ornate, fairly light font. It manages to evoke the idea of script without the fairly obvious visual cliché of machine-set handwriting.

While there are not all that many applications in which any script font is really applicable, Linoscript is probably more suited for them than most.

LINOTEXT (LINCOLN)

Linotext is the most commonly found Germanic font, and has appeared in all sorts of contexts for years. It was frequently used for newspaper mastheads until recently, and is still used for things like titles on diplomas and other display applications. It's not all that easy to read, but it tends to be used in places where it's not really meant to be read.

If you want to evoke the sorts of things people traditionally associate with formal Germanic type, this is the font to do it.

MACHINE (MOTOR)

Machine is clearly a special-effect typeface which has been created with the sole object of looking massive. It's very successful at this. However, lacking lowercase letters and being pretty ponderous in appearance, it has relatively few applications.

MISTRAL (MYSTICAL)

Mistral is probably one of the most attractive script faces but, sadly, also one of the most overused. It manages to look exceedingly non-technical by virtue of its erratic structure, but is still fairly readable. It's so unlike something which would come from a typesetter as to circumvent the issue of typeset handwriting, as discussed earlier.

The only drawback to Mistral is that it's widely used, and it's not as eye-catching as it used to be for this reason.

NEW BASKERVILLE (NEBRASKA)

The New Baskerville typeface (what CorelDRAW calls Nebraska) was designed by John Baskerville in 1757. It has absolutely nothing to do with the fictional occupants of 221b Baker Street, as is occasionally suggested, as it predates Conan Doyle by over a century.

New Baskerville is a nice, somewhat gothic serif face which is usually found in body copy. It's not bad for heads, either, if you're trying to create a design in which the heads fit comfortably into the rest of a page—assuming that the rest of the page is a bit gothic too.

One way of regarding New Baskerville is that it's the ideal choice when you would have used Times Roman if it weren't so badly overused already. Baskerville is just a bit more interesting visually, but it stops short of really coloring your text with any real visual character to overshadow the intent of your words. An article concerning the great courtesans of seventeenth-century Moldavia and a pamphlet on the nutritional characteristics of baby food can both be set in New Baskerville with equal effect, although I'd much rather read the article about great courtesans.

NEW CENTURY SCHOOLBOOK (NEW BRUNSWICK)

New Century Schoolbook is, rather obviously, another book face. It's actually a bit heavy for use as a body face unless you'll be setting it moderately large—say twelve points or better. It's a bit austere as a headline face unless you're deliberately trying to create very dry-looking designs. Like Bookman, it's a bit more elongated than body faces tend to be. It fills up more space as a result, but it's a bit easier to read than something set in Times, for example.

Much of the rationale for using Baskerville is applicable to Schoolbook if you have the space. I think that Schoolbook crosses the boundary between gothic and dull; Baskerville has just enough of a gothic flavor to make it interesting, while Schoolbook is just bland enough to make it lifeless. This is a really subjective point, of course, and one which you should consider carefully for yourself if you have applications for this sort of type.

OPTIMA (OTTAWA)

Optima is a rather unique typeface, and one which you will probably grow to appreciate as you work with CorelDRAW. It's not really a serif face, but it's not a sans-serif face in the way that Helvetica is, either. It bulges and curves a lot, and keeps one's attention in situations where Helvetica would long since have lost it. Optima has the advantage of looking clean and modern without looking sterile and mechanical.

You'll probably find that Optima doesn't make a really good headline face. Set large, its starts to show its delicate curves and fairly thin lines far too much. It looks underfed, and one's eyes start looking for a valve on it to pump a bit more air into it. However, in less demanding applications where its lack of muscle isn't a problem, Optima can convey the impression of being refined, sophisticated, and elegantly understated.

PALATINO (PALM SPRINGS)

Palatino has applications in much the same areas as Baskerville. It makes a good body face, and as it turns up in the PostScript font list of Ventura Publisher as such, you might find that having it available in CorelDRAW is extremely helpful when you're creating graphics for export. Compared to Baskerville, Palatino is a bit less artsy, but it still manages to be visually interesting. Once again, it's a good choice for when you're weary of Times.

PARISIAN (PARAGON)

One wonders if Parisians really ever liked this sort of typography. Parisian is a fairly evocative face—it suggests overtones of art deco. As with all specialized faces, it's useful if you need this effect but probably counterproductive for anything else. If the content of the graphics you attach to Parisian type doesn't match the direction of the type, you'll probably just confuse your readers.

PARK AVENUE (PARADISE)

Park Avenue is another special-effect typeface. It's a particularly troublesome one at times, as it's a bit inconsistent. Some of its characters, such as the upper case A, for example, are kind of attractive, if rather overdone. Others, such as the lower case e, seem out of place. The lower case n always looked to me as if it had been lifted from one of those old Irish typefaces.

Used sparingly and in the right context, Park Avenue can be effective. However, it's a typeface that's really easy to overuse.

PEIGNOT (PENGUIN)

Peignot is a splendid display face for several reasons. It has a particularly crisp, business-like look to it without being sterile in the way that Helvetica is. It seems to imply that beneath its serious exterior it has something just a bit amusing to say—its hard lines frequently connect with slight curves.

In addition, Peignot is not all that frequently used. It's probably worth mentioning—should anyone ask you what face you've used—that the name is pronounced pin-yo, rather than pig-not, which is what many designers tend to call it.

PONDEROSA (POSSE)

Evocative of spaghetti Westerns, breakfast cereals with no natural ingredients at all, and mid-sixties television, Ponderosa is unreadable at sizes less than 48 points and intolerable at sizes above it. If you're confronted with setting a saloon sign, choosing between Cottonwood and Ponderosa would be pretty difficult.

POST ANTIQUA (PROSE ANTIQUE)

Post Antiqua is neither a script face nor a serif display face. It has no serifs, but it's not lineal like Helvetica, either. It has some of the attributes of Optima, but it's far less technical looking. Post Antiqua succeeds in suggesting an earlier time without offering any suggestion as to which time it's interested in. It evokes a sense of age and permanence without being particularly overt about it.

PRESENT SCRIPT (PRESIDENT)

Present Script has much of the appeal of Mistral but isn't nearly as common. It's also not nearly as bold, which might have something to do with its relative obscurity. Present Script seems to speak of a time when words were drawn rather than written. It intrigues the eye with its lines. If its origin seems obscure—different people will see it as anything from cuneiform to Celtic graffiti—it's useful for its ambiguity. It suggests something displaced from the familiar without imposing a specific place or culture on the text set in it.

REVIEW (RENFREW)

Review is a special-effect typeface with much the same problems as Hobo or Cooper Black. It's not unattractive, and it's certainly bold enough to get noticed almost anywhere. However, it seems to call attention to itself not so much because it has a particular style about it, but rather because it's obviously strange looking.

SOUVENIR (SOUTHERN)

Souvenir seems to dangle just this side of being a special effect. It's a very attractive face, and manages to be sort of bold, to have a sort of serif design about it, and to evoke a sort of gothic flavor—but not quite. Not a face which is frequently employed, Souvenir is useful for this fact alone.

Faces like Souvenir are a good choice when you just want something different and you aren't sure what it should be. It doesn't have any particular feel to it, and it's unlikely to be inappropriate. At its worst it's still noticeable, and even moderately dignified looking.

STENCIL (STAMP)

There's little opportunity to mistake what Stencil evokes. If your graphic has something to do with packing crates, military vehicles, or civil servants, this font was made for you.

TIFFANY (TIMPANI)

Tiffany is a particularly ornate serif face, but a fairly well designed one. You might even be able to get away with using it on a regular basis for heads and titles if your application allows for a bit of character. Even in its medium weight, Tiffany is eye-catching, and it gets very hard to miss in its extrabold version, Tiffany Heavy. This latter face is probably a bit too nouveau something-or-other to suit serious designs.

You might want to regard Tiffany as being New Baskerville taken several steps further. It's a serif face which might be used in place of Times when you're not only tired of Times but want people to know that you've denounced it and everything that looks like it.

TIMES ROMAN (TORONTO)

Most of what could be said about Times has already been discussed indirectly in discussing the faces that can be compared to it. By virtue of its extensive use, it shares with Helvetica a neutrality and lack of extreme character. Type set in it will not really be colored by the typeface. It also won't be particularly interesting visually, but there are times when you want this quality in your type.

Times is the model of a well-designed typeface. It's moderately condensed, but it still reads well. The boldface version looks bold and substantial without looking heavy. While Times was designed as a body face, the bold version is an acceptable headline face.

UMBRA (UMBRELLA)

It might be worth noting that Umbra comes from the Latin for shadow (as, in fact, does umbrella). If you look at it carefully, you'll observe that it consists of the shadows which would have been left by a lineal face such as Helvetica—but without the typeface itself. Umbra is a pleasing special effect if it's not used too often.

UNIVERS (USA)

As we discussed earlier in this chapter, Univers was created for much the same reason as Helvetica, and the two fonts can be applied in similar contexts. However, Univers looks a bit different from Helvetica. Its light face flows a bit more, and doesn't look as constrained. Its extrabold weight, Univers Black in CorelDRAW, is a bit more condensed than Helvetica Black.

UNIVERSITY ROMAN (UNICORN)

University Roman is unquestionably a special effect, although it's a particularly pleasing one. It looks like Times Roman the morning after. While it would not do to apply it too frequently, the odd use of University Roman can be very eye-catching. In the right context, it might be regarded as an eccentric relation—entertaining for its peculiarities, but harmless and inoffensive.

One of the positive features of University Roman is its fairly condensed design. One of its negative features is that it's pretty hard to read. Don't set anything that really should be read and understood in this face.

VAG ROUNDED (VOGUE)

VAG Rounded is among the most useful of sans-serif faces—or, at least, it's one of my favorites. It has all the attributes of Helvetica but its rounded stalks make it much more distinctive. It looks decidedly European, and is a good choice when you want type that looks clean and uncluttered but are tired of the usual sans-serif fonts.

ZAPF CHANCERY (ZURICH)

In recent years, Chancery has come to be the forerunner in grossly overused display faces, by virtue of its appearance as one of the staple fonts in Post-Script printers. While not a particularly bad face as ornate fonts go, Chancery is very easy to overuse. It looks like someone has deliberately attempted to be artistic. Looking at type set in Chancery often makes one think that a simple day-glo sticker saying, "The designer is in" would have sufficed.

The hard lines and calligraphic appearance of Chancery make it ideally suited for specific design applications. However, keep in mind that Chancery is unfortunately easy to apply, so it turns up everywhere. Even with the most well-thought-out design criteria in mind, you might wind up creating a rather hackneyed bit of type inadvertently.

WRAPPING UP

Until very recently, graphics and page-creation software were pretty crude stuff, and required little concern for art. In many areas of microcomputer applications this is still true, and most computer users seem to feel that whatever comes out of a computer is either right or wrong, with no room for interpretation or creative argument.

CorelDRAW, which is just dripping with nuance and subtlety, seems to fly in the face of attitudes such as these—and doubly so when it's dealing with typography.

If you're new to the nuances of typography, you might want to deliberately try to notice type. See if you can judge the effect that different typefaces and their applications have on your appreciation of the words you read. This is something which slips by the conscious perception of most people, but if you are to make full use of the expressive potential of type, you'll need to have a conscious understanding of it.

Hardware,

Software, and

Using Microsoft

Windows

You can get away with knowing very little about Microsoft Windows if all you're interested in is running CorelDRAW. If CorelDRAW is already set up on your system and you just need to make it go, all you really need to know is contained in the second part of this appendix, the section entitled "Using Microsoft Windows." However, there are a number of things about Windows you might have to know in order to optimize its operation, and the operation of CorelDRAW, for your specific system. This is the main topic of this appendix. If you know how to work with Windows, you can make CorelDRAW a much more useful tool.

In addition, Windows is a very useful package in its own right. It incorporates a powerful, consistent user interface, and if you learn its basic set of dialogs, menus, and other phenomena, you'll be most of the way towards knowing how to run any Windows-based application.

This appendix will discuss Windows and the hardware it needs to operate. It will be especially useful if you're still shopping for a computer to run CorelDRAW on, as it includes information about the various levels of performance you can expect from Windows and CorelDRAW with various sorts of computers.

This appendix deals exclusively with Windows 3.1. As you might imagine, there were earlier versions of Windows—the version of CorelDRAW that this book deals with will not have its full functionality under them, and therefore they won't be mentioned herein. Figure A.1 illustrates Windows 3.1.

FIGURE A.1:

A view of Windows

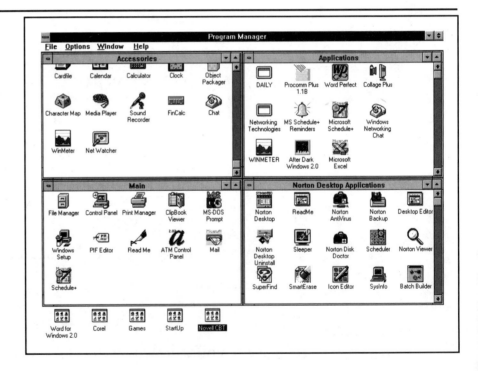

HARDWARE AND SOFTWARE REQUIREMENTS OF CORELDRAW

Defining the hardware you'll need to make CorelDRAW work for you might be a difficult task. Much of the question is somewhat subjective, predicated on such things as the likely complexity of the drawings you plan to create, the time you'll have to create them, the quality of the results you expect and, most important, whom you can lean on to foot the bill for equipment.

With the exception of the last point, all of this is intimately tied to one of the catch 22s of computers. You won't really know what level of hardware you need until you're well into learning about CorelDRAW, and by then it will be too late to take any of the equipment back if it turns out not to be what you need.

We can look at a few guidelines for hardware, but ultimately you'll be forced to take your best shot. In all cases—especially if someone else is paying the bills—it's a lot better to buy computer hardware which is more powerful than your application requires than hardware which can't really do the job.

The minimum hardware upon which CorelDRAW will run at an acceptable clip is an 80386-based machine. Technically, it can squeak by on an 80286-based system if the system has at least two megabytes of memory, but the results will be glacially slow for most of the things that make CorelDRAW worth having.

The 80386 processor actually comes in multiple flavors. The basic 80386 chip—referred to as the 80386DX in some circles—can be run at speeds up to 33 megahertz as of this writing. Faster chip speeds will run your applications in less time.

For users who want the performance of an 80386 but don't have the budget for a high-end machine, there's a slightly less powerful version of the 80386 called the 80386SX. There are two things that make it distinct from the 80386—its top speed is 25 megahertz and it can address substantially less memory. However, on this latter point, both versions of this chip can address more memory than most users will ever need or be able to afford.

If you can't afford a high-end 80386 system, one of the many 80386SX-based systems may prove an ideal compromise.

The current generation of systems as of this writing is based on the 80486 processors. The top speed for these is 66 megahertz. These, too, come in two flavors—the 80486DX and 80486SX. The DX version includes an on-chip floating-point math coprocessor—a useful feature for some applications, but of no use to CorelDRAW—and several other enhancements that make it somewhat faster. The SX version is, predictably, less expensive. It also has a lower top speed.

If you intend to use CorelDRAW to produce serious, fairly complex graphics, you should give serious thought to an 80486 based system, with a DX processor running at 33 megahertz minimum. The edit-in-preview mode, one of the really worthwhile features of the 3.0 release of CorelDRAW, all but insists on this level of hardware.

MEMORY CONSIDERATIONS

For historical reasons, the memory situation on 80386- and 80486-class machines is a bit fragmented. There are several sorts of memory, each of which does something just a little different.

The basic memory that programs run in is usually called system, conventional, or DOS memory. There can be as much as 640 kilobytes of it. This used to be a lot of memory—now it's an extremely tight fit for many applications, CorelDRAW among them. A no-frills 80386 machine will probably come with this memory and little more.

There are two forms of memory which exist beyond the limits of DOS memory, called *expanded* and *extended* memory. These two words are enough alike that it's often hard to remember which is which.

An 80386 or 80486 machine can actually address memory beyond one megabyte, the official end of the road for the earlier PC-XT compatible computers. This extra memory is called extended memory. Unfortunately, a computer running DOS can't just make this extra memory appear on the end of the basic 640 kilobytes of DOS memory. Extended memory is useful for storing data under software which knows how to access it, but it does not expand the basic memory of a computer which has some extended memory installed.

Windows—which is considerably smarter than DOS in its use of memory—can do exceedingly clever things with extended memory, allowing it to look like lots of conventional memory as Windows switches between tasks, and so on. A complete overview of the memory management facilities of Windows could occupy a book all by itself. However, unlike DOS, Windows can make conventional memory and extended memory both look like just plain memory to your applications.

You must have some extended memory in the machine on which you run CorelDRAW. Windows will run if there is no extended memory, but it compensates for the lack of it by writing a lot of scratch files to your disk, saving things there which would usually be placed in extended memory. This will slow Windows down enormously.

The second sort of extra memory is expanded memory, also called LIM memory. LIM stands for Lotus, Intel, and Microsoft, the three companies which pioneered the standard of expanded memory. Unlike extended memory, expanded memory does not require any additional addressing capability of the machine it's installed in. It is applicable to old-style PC-XT compatible machines, which is really what it was designed for.

Expanded memory is slower to work with than extended memory. However, because it has been around longer and is applicable to a larger range of PCs, it's supported and used by a variety of programs.

The current generation of 80386 and 80486 machines don't come with expanded memory *per se,* although you can make some of their extended memory look like expanded memory for DOS applications that use it. For the purposes of running CorelDRAW, you can just ignore the whole issue of expanded memory. Windows' memory management facilities will make all of the available system memory look like the kind of memory CorelDRAW needs.

How Much Memory Is Enough?

Microsoft Windows' display box maintains that it will run on a system with a mere 640 kilobytes of DOS memory and 256 kilobytes of extended memory. This is technically true, in much the same way that you can drive from Alaska to Texas in an open Jeep. It's possible, but no one would actually want to do it.

For practical purposes, Windows requires a minimum of two megabytes of extended memory, including the basic 640 kilobytes of DOS memory which Windows must have just to boot up in a useful frame of mind. With this configuration, you'll be able to run CorelDRAW, although you'll find that it gets very tedious when confronted with large, complex

The amount of memory you have in your system represents a straight trade-off between time and money, all other things being equal. The more memory you buy, the less time CorelDRAW will take to perform complex tasks. Memory is relatively cheap.

drawings. You'll also find that even though CorelDRAW itself can run on a system with two megabytes of memory, the other modules produce unpredictable results and can cause system failures.

Four megabytes of memory is workable—eight is decidedly better. I run CorelDRAW on a 33-megahertz, 80486 system with 16 megabytes of memory. It runs very quickly under these conditions, and there is virtually no waiting for Windows to juggle its memory.

Fortunately, memory expansion is one of those things you can change your mind about after the fact. You can always add more memory to your system if you find yourself dissatisfied with the performance of Windows.

Having said this, you might want to think about memory expansion when you go shopping for hardware. Most new systems have room for some additional memory on the motherboard; that is, you can just buy additional memory and plug it in. If you want to add memory beyond what is allowed for on-board expansion, you will have to buy additional memory cards—you must pay not only for the memory, but also for the circuit board which holds it.

One of the questions to ask about a potential computer, then, is how much on-board memory expansion space there is. Consider that if you will be using CorelDRAW in a serious application you will probably eventually want 16 megabytes of memory, even if you can't afford it right away. It's worth finding a system which allows for at least this much on-board memory.

Cache Memory

When you go computer shopping—especially if you'll be buying an 80486-based system—you'll probably also hear about something called "cache" memory. This is well worth listening to, as cache memory has the potential for dramatically enhancing the performance of your system.

When a processor executes software, it does so by "fetching" the basic instructions of the software from the memory they reside in. This fetching process is time consuming, as time goes on a computer. It's the nature of software that some sequences of instructions get executed, and hence fetched, over and over again.

The memory that software lives in when it's working, called "dynamic" memory, is fairly slow. A processor cache is a smaller chunk of much faster "static" memory that's at the sole disposal of the processor. Whenever the processor fetches an instruction, it puts it in the cache as well as executes it. If it needs that instruction again, it can fetch it from the much faster memory of the cache.

Because a processor cache is finite—and relatively small in comparison to the system memory in a computer—it will eventually get full of instructions. When this happens, the oldest instructions in the cache will fall out the bottom to make room for newer ones. If the processor subsequently needs the deleted instructions, it will have to fetch them once again from memory.

A cache becomes increasingly effective as it gets larger. It also becomes more expensive, of course, although the price of cache memory isn't what it used to be. There is no optimum size for a processor cache—get all the cache memory you can afford. A 256-kilobyte cache will not go to waste on an 80486 system running Windows.

There's a second sort of cache involved in running Windows. It will be discussed in a moment.

Windows Memory Tips

As mentioned before, Windows has a finite amount of memory to work with. Large applications, such as CorelDRAW, run more efficiently if they have lots of memory. You will improve the performance of Windows and of CorelDRAW if you give them all the memory you can.

Here are several caveats concerning Windows and available memory:

◆ Avoid Terminate-and-Stay-Resident (TSR) programs. Programs which provide pop-up utilities, such as SideKick, tie up memory when they're loaded. Most of them can't be used under Windows in any case, so make sure they aren't running before you run Windows.

◆ Avoid Windows gadgets. There is an increasing library of interesting programs which you can run under Windows concurrently with CorelDRAW. These provide things like a screen clock, a free-memory display, a fancy screen saver, and so on. All of these programs occupy memory.

◆ Simplify your CONFIG.SYS file. If you really want to free up the last bit of available memory for use with Windows, have a quick look at your CONFIG.SYS file. The DOS manual which came with your system will aid you in interpreting its contents. Some users may have extravagant numbers of files and buffers allocated, which tie up memory. You might also have device drivers in there which are not needed under Windows. If you have a network driver in your CONFIG.SYS file, for example, you'll probably find that removing it frees a lot of memory. Note that Windows does not even need ANSI.SYS.

◆ Create a permanent swap file, as discussed in the Windows documentation.

Obviously, some of the above suggestions may interfere with other operations of your computer—those which do not involve Windows.

DOS 5.0 Drivers

When you install Windows 3.1 under DOS 5.0, there are a number of the included device drivers that Windows can install for you. It's worth understanding these. They will appear in the CONFIG.SYS file in the root directory of your boot drive, usually drive C.

The most fundamental driver is HIMEM.SYS, which tells Windows how to access the extended memory in your system. If this driver is not installed, Windows will assume that there are only 640 kilobytes of memory in your computer, no matter what's actually there. The HIMEM.SYS driver will be loaded with a line that looks like this:

```
DEVICE=HIMEM.SYS
```

The EMM386.EXE driver will make some of the extended memory in your system look like expanded memory for DOS applications that require it. This driver will be loaded by a line that looks like this:

```
DEVICE=EMM386.EXE 2048
```

The number at the end of the line refers to the number of kilobytes of extended memory that EMM386.EXE will convert to expanded memory. Since this expanded memory will no longer be available to Windows, you should restrict the amount of memory—if any at all—that you'll be using in this way. If you install EMM386.EXE in the following way, no expanded memory will be reserved:

```
DEVICE=EMM386.EXE NOEMS
```

Note that EMM386.EXE should be installed, even if you have no need for expanded memory under DOS; it's used by Windows if you want to allow expanded memory for a non-Windows application running in a DOS session from Windows.

The RAMDRIVE.SYS driver will create an artificial disk drive in extended memory if it's used. If your system has two floppies and a hard drive, installing RAMDRIVE.SYS will make a drive D appear. This will behave like a normal hard drive, except that as soon as you turn your computer off, all its contents will vanish.

A memory disk, or RAM drive, can be very useful to hold temporary files if your work generates a lot of them, as this scratch space will clean itself up every time you turn off your computer. However, it will tie up extended memory that could otherwise be useful under Windows. If you'll be using your system primarily to run Windows and Windows applications, you should probably not install a RAM drive.

Finally, the SMARTDRV.SYS driver will create a disk cache. This behaves somewhat like a processor cache, as described earlier. Each time an application attempts to read a file, the computer must get the contents of the file from your hard drive, a relatively slow operation. Some kinds of software—Windows applications being among them—are noted for accessing the same parts of files over and over again. In a system with a disk cache, the first time an area of the disk is read it's stored in a block of extended memory set aside for the purpose. On subsequent reads, the block can be read from memory, rather than from the disk, memory being a good deal faster.

There are slightly different SMART-DRV.SYS files included with DOS 5.0 and with Windows 3.1. You should use the one that's in your Windows directory—among other things, it allows for a larger maximum cache size.

As with a processor cache, when the disk cache gets full the oldest entries in it will be discarded, and will have to be read from the disk again the next time they're called for. Accordingly, a disk cache will increase in effectiveness as you increase its size. The SMARTDRV.SYS driver can be loaded like this:

```
DEVICE=SMARTDRV.SYS 2048 256
```

The first number on this line tells SMARTDRV.SYS how many kilobytes of memory to set aside for the disk cache. The second number tells it how small to make the cache under Windows—the cache will get smaller under Windows so that more extended memory will be freed up.

There will invariably be a lot of additional lines in your CONFIG.SYS file. You might want to consult your DOS and Windows manuals for a more complete explanation of their functions. There may also be drivers installed to support other hardware, for example, a network, a removable hard drive or CD-ROM player, a FAX card, a sound card, and so on.

DISPLAY CARDS

Part of the issue of speed in a computer running CorelDRAW is tied up in how fast the screen updates. Part of the usefulness of CorelDRAW in the long term will therefore be governed by your choice of display cards and monitors.

Some of the considerations affecting your choice of a display card will be governed by characteristics of Microsoft Windows. If you're not too clear about where Windows fits into the picture yet, you might want to skip ahead to the section which explains it ("Using Microsoft Windows") and return to this page once you understand what Windows is all about.

There are many specialized monitors and display cards which can run Windows and, hence, CorelDRAW. However, for practical purposes the most useful type of displays are ones which have VGA cards or cards which offer VGA graphics as well as other options.

A standard VGA card only offers one display mode that's useful for running Windows—the 16-color business-graphics mode. It allows for a screen that's 640 by 480 pixels. When you first install Windows for a VGA display, this is how it will be set up.

Most "super" VGA cards allow for at least two options in addition to this. You can usually have 640 by 480 pixels at 256 colors or 800 by 600 pixels at 16 colors. In many higher end cards you can have 800 by 600 pixels at 256 colors, or even 1024 by 768 pixels.

Having a display with more pixels on it will make most applications, CorelDRAW included, a good deal easier to use. Higher resolution displays mean that things like roll-up menus won't get in your way, and that the CorelDRAW display will be better able to draw things so you can see what you're working on. For most serious work under CorelDRAW, an 800 by 600 pixel display is all but essential.

Seeing things in 256 colors will be of considerable advantage if you'll be using color under CorelDRAW. If you're using a 16-color display, and

CorelDRAW wants to show you a color that isn't available in the 16 colors defined by Windows, it must approximate or "dither" the color. While better than nothing, dithered colors require a bit of imagination to interpret correctly. CorelDRAW can get a lot closer to accurate color representations if it has 256 colors to work with.

Actually, there's a third broad class of display modes available in some high-end super VGA cards. Cards which have one megabyte of video memory and a special chip called a DAC can provide you with "high color" graphics. With these cards, up to 32,767 different colors can be displayed at once. This will allow CorelDRAW to display its colors as they'll be printed.

The catch to all these extra modes is that, all other things being equal, a screen with more pixels or more colors, or both, takes longer to update and will tie up more memory, which in turn will further slow down Windows. A low-end 80386 system can seem pretty snappy with a standard VGA 640-by-480 pixel, 16-color driver and infuriatingly slow when driving an 800-by-600 pixel, 256-color super VGA card.

If you buy a super VGA card, it will list the modes it supports on its box. It should also specifically state that the card comes with Windows 3.1 screen drivers to support these modes. Because all Super VGA cards are different, Windows itself does not include drivers to support them in anything other than the standard VGA display mode.

Here are some of the better Super VGA cards available at the moment:

 Appendix B includes a discussion of using multiple screen drivers under Windows. With a bit of juggling, this will allow you to have drivers for various color depths and resolutions on tap, and to use whichever mode is appropriate to the work you'll be doing.

◆ Paradise—These are among the fastest conventional Super VGA cards, and are available with up to a megabyte of memory as of this writing. The high-end Paradise cards include a DAC for high-color support up to 800 by 600 pixels.

◆ Tseng Labs 4000—These cards are fairly fast. The 4000X cards support a DAC for high-color displays up to 800 by 600 pixels.

◆ Trident 8900—These cards are fairly fast and very inexpensive. As of this writing, they do not support high color.

◆ Oak Technologies—These cards are fairly fast and moderately inexpensive. As of this writing, they do not support high color.

◆ ATI—These cards are fairly fast and moderately expensive. The ATI XL card includes support for high color up to 640 by 480 pixels as of this writing.

Note that there are numerous other Super VGA card manufacturers, many of whom make cards which are just as suitable for use with Windows. Also, note that there are a lot of Super VGA cards which use the same chips as the foregoing cards, but which are given other brand names. You can tell which chip set is in use on a Super VGA card by looking at the large, black, square chip in the center of the card. It will have the following markings if it corresponds to one of these manufacturers:

♦ Paradise—The letters "WD," for Western Digital, the manufacturer of Paradise cards.

♦ Tseng Labs—The number 4000.

♦ Trident—A stylized trident and the number 8900.

♦ Oak Technologies—The word "Oak."

♦ ATI—the abbreviation "ATI."

ACCELERATED VGA CARDS— A WONDERFUL CHEAT

Much of the apparent speed of your computer running Windows will be determined by the time it takes to update your screen. In some aspects of using Windows software, managing the screen can take more time than whatever the software is actually supposed to be doing.

The latest generation of Super VGA cards have been designed specifically to address this. Called "accelerated" cards, they contain dedicated computers of their own. Rather than forcing Windows to actually draw dialog boxes, menus, and such, an accelerated VGA card allows Windows to simply specify what it wants drawn and then get on with its own tasks, leaving the drawing up to the card itself. As the computer on an accelerated display card is dedicated to the task of managing graphics, it can do so much more rapidly than the general purpose computer that runs Windows.

For practical purposes, there is little that happens under Windows which an accelerated display card can't make instantaneous.

There are a number of accelerated cards available—as of this writing, they are somewhat more expensive than conventional Super VGA cards. The

While the S3-based accelerated display cards may not be the fastest, they can still perform most graphic operations in no discernible time. They are also among the least expensive boards of this type.

most popular and the most cost-effective cards at the moment are those based on a chip called an 86C911, made by a company called S3. Among these cards are the Orchid Fahrenheit 1280 and the Diamond Speedstar.

An Orchid Fahrenheit 1280 card with one megabyte of memory and the DAC option supports high color at 640 by 480 pixels as well as 256 colors at up to 1024 by 768 pixels and 16 colors at up to 1280 by 960 pixels. The current Orchid driver set includes a Windows Control Panel function that allows you to switch between modes.

If you'll be using CorelDRAW extensively to produce complex graphics, an accelerated VGA card is arguably the single most useful hardware choice you can make.

MICE

Windows and CorelDRAW are both virtually useless without a mouse. Mice are the unthought-of extra element in any computer which uses Windows.

Mice long ago replaced modems as the cheapest peripheral device available for microcomputers. They come in all sorts of permutations and levels of compatibility. A good mouse is a joy to use. A bad one is a first-class nuisance.

In order to work well with CorelDRAW, a mouse must be able to track movement accurately and it must be compatible with Windows. Both of these things are relative qualities.

The basic mechanism of a mouse is so simple that anyone with an injection-molding machine and a few transistors can knock off working mice without having to undergo lengthy and unpleasant night-school engineering courses. For this reason, a lot of questionable mice exist. The difference between these mice and good mice will become apparent once you've used a cheap mouse for a while.

Cheap mice often track badly; that is, they don't translate movements of your hand to movements of the cursor very accurately. Still more annoying, most cheap mice have fairly coarse resolution. This means that you must move the mouse over a large distance relative to the movement of the cursor on your screen. On a normal-size desk with a normal amount of desk clutter, this usually means picking up the mouse frequently when you come to the peripheries of the clear space you've set aside for a rodent run.

Get a mouse pad. Most desktops don't provide very good traction for a mouse, with the result that your mouse will prove hard to position accurately. A cloth-surfaced mouse pad is an inexpensive way around this.

Good mice feature accurate tracking, tight resolution, reliable buttons, and case designs that don't require you to contort your hand into a Vulcan salute every time you want to grasp the mouse.

A second consideration is the *driver* with which the mouse and Windows interface. Every mouse works differently, and the common element that makes it possible for all these diverse mice to communicate with Windows is a memory-resident program called a driver. As with VGA cards, the driver for one brand of mice probably won't work—or won't work very well—with another brand.

A driver that refuses to communicate with Windows will transform an otherwise great mouse into something that is useful only as a cat toy.

Mice such as the ones by Microsoft and Logitech are good, reliable choices for use with CorelDRAW. There are many other very good mice as well, but if you are unable to try out a potential mouse with CorelDRAW before you whip out your charge card, make sure you know you're buying one that will work.

The difference in price between a good mouse and a bad one is minimal, especially in comparison to the cost of the rest of your system hardware. There is little sense in having anything less than the best.

Hard Drive Space

After you've installed Windows, you can pare its hard-drive requirements down a bit, but the resulting Windows package will be somewhat short of features.

The amount of hard drive space needed to run CorelDRAW without its getting cramped will be determined by how you expect to use it. Windows 3.1 needs a minimum of eight megabytes of disk space in which to sprawl out and get comfortable, and will refuse to even install itself if there's less than this available. Even with this much, you'll have to forego a number of useful accessories—the package requires 10 megabytes if you want all its features enabled.

Aside from serving as a platform from which to launch CorelDRAW, Windows is a nice place to work. It's handy to be able to step out of CorelDRAW and write a letter or edit a bitmap file and then step right back to where you left off. This sort of convenience doesn't cost extra—Windows comes with a very well engineered word processor and a Windows-based paint package—but it ties up disk space. The word processor alone needs about 200 kilobytes.

CorelDRAW requires between 11 and 34 megabytes of hard drive space, depending on how much of it you choose to install. The 34 megabyte figure assumes that you'll be installing it from a CD-ROM—installing it from floppies will make substantially fewer TrueType fonts more available, which will shave a few megabytes from this number. Note that this number includes lots of fonts and other accessories, but no drawing files as yet. You'll need more room still to store files.

In addition to all this, Windows frequently likes to write temporary files in the course of managing its memory and spooling print jobs. These files never stick around after a Windows session is over, but you will require enough free disk space to accommodate them for what little time they do exist. Plan on at least a couple of megabytes.

You can make Windows work a lot faster by allocating a permanent swap file. The procedure for doing this can be found in the Windows documentation. A permanent swap file of about two megabytes or better is a worthwhile size.

Obviously, you can get away with an 80-megabyte hard drive if CorelDRAW will be the only thing running on your machine. However, most users run several applications at various times. In most cases, you'll need a much larger hard drive to accommodate CorelDRAW and everything else you'll be doing with your computer.

Having Windows on hand makes it easy to add additional Windows-based applications. You might want to add the Graphic Workshop for Windows package from the companion disk for this book—a decidedly small Windows application as these things go. Consider also Word for Windows as a replacement for Windows Write, Microsoft Excel to link into Corel-DRAW through OLE if your applications call for a spreadsheet, and so on.

Hard drives are available in sizes of up to a gigabyte as of this writing—that's 1000 megabytes. People often buy drives this big, and, in most cases with good reason.

PRINTERS AND CORELDRAW

This section will present a quick overview of printers for use with CorelDRAW. For a much more complete discussion of printing, consult Chapter 6 of this book.

The ultimate destination of everything CorelDRAW handles will be a printer of some sort. CorelDRAW pictures can pass through a few hands along the way—you might import a CorelDRAW picture into a desktop-publishing document before it finally finds its way to hard copy, for example—but printers are a primary concern in using CorelDRAW.

As with any well-behaved Windows application, CorelDRAW prints through Windows. In other words, it actually tells Windows where the picture is and lets Windows handle the printing. In this way, CorelDRAW can be somewhat printer-independent.

This starts to unravel a bit because different printers have different capabilities, and CorelDRAW has been written to take advantage of everything that high-end printers can muster. Once you've gotten into using CorelDRAW you'll see that some of its more innovative tricks and features rely on special characteristics of specific printers. This is dealt with in Chapter 6.

Windows deals with printers through the use of printer drivers, which contain the specialized code to handle the details of individual printer protocols. With the appropriate drivers, CorelDRAW can print the same picture through Windows to a dot-matrix printer or to a quarter-million-dollar PostScript RIP typesetter, and in most cases, will get the best output each of these devices can provide.

Windows comes with a rich selection of printer drivers. Most of the popular dot-matrix printers are supported, as well as a host of plotters. Both LaserJet-compatible and PostScript laser printers are also supported by Windows. It's this latter group of devices which CorelDRAW really likes to deal with.

Quite a few third-party Windows printer drivers also exist to support specialized printers for which Windows itself does not provide drivers.

Adding a printer driver is covered in the Windows documentation. As with most Windows features, it's all handled with a couple of mouse clicks and a brief pause.

It's worth mentioning that people frequently choose printers for some of the wrong reasons—or at least, for reasons which aren't as valid as they used to be. Laser printers produce much better work than dot-matrix printers do. They're faster and much quieter too. It used to be that this came with a price—low-end lasers used to cost many times what a high-end dot-matrix printer did, and lasers used to be beasts to maintain. Both these things have changed. A "personal" four-page-per-minute laser printer now costs

There are some rather exotic devices which masquerade as Windows printers. For example, the FaxIt package from Alien Software will make a FAX board behave like a printer under Windows. You can FAX documents directly from CorelDRAW by printing to the FAX device.

only a bit more than a 24-pin dot-matrix printer does, and even these ostensibly slow lasers can bury dot-matrix printers in the dust. Based on user-interchangeable parts, lasers are no longer difficult to maintain.

LaserJet Printers

The most commonly found type of laser printers suitable for use with CorelDRAW are LaserJet Plus-compatible printers. The LaserJet Plus itself is a product of Hewlett-Packard. In fact, it has been superseded by the LaserJet Series II which itself has been superseded by the LaserJet III; but this fact doesn't essentially change the following discussion. It incorporates a fairly simple page description language, a protocol by which software can describe the text and images it wants the printer to output. This language is usually referred to as PCL, for *printer control language.* CorelDRAW speaks PCL when you tell it to print to a LaserJet.

Being a very simple language, PCL has been rewritten for quite a few other laser printers. These printers are said to emulate the LaserJet Plus, and, because PCL is quite uncomplicated to write, most PCL emulations are flawless.

A LaserJet-compatible printer is a very simple machine as laser printers go. It represents relatively little research and development on the part of the company which makes the printer, and as a result these printers are usually pretty inexpensive. Some of the personal lasers are available for well under a thousand dollars as of this writing.

LaserJet-compatible printers can turn out first-class work when they're driven by CorelDRAW. In fact, a LaserJet Plus can do a few things that a PostScript printer—the expensive sort of laser—cannot.

LaserJet Plus-compatible printers are limited to a resolution of 300 dots per inch, which is not quite reproduction quality, but it is extremely close. In order to handle the graphics which CorelDRAW sends to a LaserJet Plus, such a printer requires a minimum of one and a half megabytes of memory. This latter feature is important to keep in mind. Some low-end lasers come with half a megabyte of memory installed. These printers look pretty competitive in price until you go to add the cost of the extra memory required to make them do anything more than basic text.

The actual Hewlett-Packard LaserJet III is a very clever superset of the original LaserJet, and it will do things LaserJet compatibles cannot. For example, it will accept a PostScript cartridge, discussed below, making itself bilingual. It will also print what are called modulated dots.

If you look closely at a diagonal line printed by a 300-dot-per-inch laser printer, you'll notice that the edges of the line are a bit irregular. This affliction is usually called "jaggies." The LaserJet III makes jaggies a lot less noticeable by changing the size of the black dots it prints to more accurately fit them into the edges of lines. The result is that the 300-dot-per-inch output of a LaserJet III usually looks almost as good as the 600-dot-per-inch output of, for example, a Varityper PostScript plain-paper typesetter. The LaserJet III is a surprisingly inexpensive printer, starting at just over thirteen hundred dollars.

PostScript Printers

PostScript is a page-description language which performs the same function PCL does on a LaserJet-compatible printer. PostScript, however, does it with a lot more class and rather better facilities. The PostScript language makes it possible for CorelDRAW to do a number of things which aren't possible on a LaserJet.

In order to print a simple CorelDRAW drawing to a LaserJet Plus printer, CorelDRAW would have to create an enormous bitmapped picture on the PC which created the drawing—enormous meaning about one megabyte of data for a full page—and then port this information to the printer. This requires a lot of time to make up the picture and a lot more to send it out through the printer port. It also requires a lot of free memory and disk space.

In printing the same drawing to a PostScript device, CorelDRAW would wind up doing a great deal less work. PostScript printers define pictures as objects, just as CorelDRAW does, and PostScript printers can use all of the path types and so on which are fundamental to the workings of CorelDRAW. Printing an image to a PostScript printer simply involves CorelDRAW translating the internal notation it uses to represent objects into the PostScript language, and sending the resulting PostScript code to the printer.

With a few exceptions—which have been discussed in this book—the same PostScript program which is sent to a 300-dot-per-inch LaserWriter can also be sent to a 2500-dot-per-inch Linotronic PostScript phototypesetter for typeset-quality output. Thus, you can create drawings under CorelDRAW with the help of a PostScript laser and then take your files to a typesetting shop with a PostScript typesetter for final output.

A PostScript printer has a very sophisticated graphics library inside it, along with a fast computer to drive it. PostScript printers are usually based on the 68000 series processors which are found in Apple Macintosh machines. For this reason, a PostScript printer is able to handle graphics operations which CorelDRAW itself cannot. One example of these is filling an object with a complex pattern. Figure A.2 illustrates some examples of this. These patterns are referred to in CorelDRAW as *PostScript textures*. They're defined in the PostScript language and can be printed only on a PostScript printer.

As noted in the section on LaserJet Plus printers, there are a few things that LaserJets can do which PostScript printers cannot. In PostScript there is a fixed upper limit to the number of paths an object can contain. The actual value varies from printer to printer and with the particular revision level of PostScript your printer uses. If you exceed this limit, the extra objects—or your whole drawing—will not print.

The maximum number of paths PostScript will accept is extremely high, and you'd have to create a fairly complex drawing to exceed it. CorelDRAW, however, is more than capable of doing this. In fact, it does so now and again without half trying. Figure A.3 is an example of a Corel-DRAW document which will not print on a PostScript printer. The problem is in the fountain in the word *Violin*. CorelDRAW creates fountains like this as myriads of individual paths, and the myriads have proven too complex for the printer.

Because a LaserJet Plus is just sent a bitmap when it prints, it has no limitations of this sort. This should explain how the unprintable violin was printed.

PostScript Clones The biggest drawback to PostScript has long been that it costs so much. A large part of the price of a PostScript printer is the licensing fee the printer manufacturer must pay to Adobe, the creator of PostScript, for the use of the language.

The high cost of PostScript has prompted a number of printer manufacturers to do with PostScript what was done earlier with PCL, and a number of laser printers are now available with PostScript-compatible

FIGURE A.2:

PostScript textures used in a drawing

*A CorelDRAW drawing
which will not print on
a PostScript device*

languages, or PostScript "clones." However, cloning PostScript is not anywhere near as simple as cloning PCL was.

As of this writing, none of the PostScript clone printers emulate Post-
Script perfectly. In addition, none of them are all that much less expensive
than comparable printers which support real PostScript. Moreover, if you don't
know laser printers extremely well, a PostScript clone can cause you some
problems if you run into one of the imperfect areas of its emulation. Should
you not get the output you expected, you will be confronted with the question of whether the fault is in your drawing, in CorelDRAW, or in the printer.

All things considered, CorelDRAW makes sufficiently exacting demands on its output devices as to make a PostScript-clone printer inadvisable.

PostScript clones are unquestionably improving, to be sure. Some time ago, Microsoft and Apple announced a joint effort to develop a PostScript-like page-creation language, largely in response to Adobe's refusal to provide detailed descriptions of the inner workings of PostScript. Further, the existence of the clones has driven the prices of real PostScript printers down, and probably will continue to do so as the competition gets hotter.

Multiple-Mode Laser Printers

PostScript is a programming language. It's quite possible to write an emulation of PCL in PostScript. If you downloaded such a program to a PostScript printer, the printer would turn into a LaserJet Plus temporarily, accepting LaserJet graphics and page description commands rather than those of PostScript.

In fact, pretty much all of the latest generation of PostScript printers incorporates a feature which handles this automatically. At the touch of a switch or with a couple of stabs at a front panel menu, you can choose between LaserJet Plus emulation or PostScript. This allows you to have things both ways—you can use PostScript to get the most of what CorelDRAW offers in the way of features, and PCL when you encounter a drawing with too many drawing paths.

This facility is available on such printers as the Apple LaserWriter IINTX and the NEC LC800 series, among others. It's not a particularly expensive feature to implement and is one well worth having. You can also have it on a LaserJet II or LaserJet III by buying a PostScript cartridge.

A PRINTER PATCH

Under some—apparently mysterious—circumstances, Windows will refuse to print to its standard printer devices, such as LPT1. If you attempt to print in the normal way, nothing much will happen and eventually Windows' print spooler will take time out and show you an error dialog box.

There is a way around this that works for some setups and not for others. The only way to know is to try it out. You will have to modify

WIN.INI, as discussed in Appendix B, adding a line which contains a dummy device. This is the section of WIN.INI that's involved:

```
[ports]
LPT1:=
LPT2:=
LPT3:=
COM1:=9600,n,8,1
COM2:=9600,n,8,1
COM3:=9600,n,8,1
COM4:=9600,n,8,1
EPT:=
FILE:=
LPT1.DOS=
LPT2.DOS=
LPT1.PRN=
```

The last line is the dummy device you'll have to add. Technically, this should cause anything printed to it to wind up in a file. However, since the file's name is LPT1, a reserved DOS device, it sneaks its way to the printer, apparently (when it works) circumventing whatever stops things from getting there directly.

As an aside, this technique comes straight from Microsoft's technical support people, who couldn't really explain why it happens either.

USING MICROSOFT WINDOWS

When you first start your computer, DOS loads into memory from your hard disk and starts to run.

The basic functions of DOS—and of any other operating system—are as follows:

◆ To provide you with a way to run programs

◆ To provide your programs with basic services, such as reading the keyboard, writing text to the screen, opening disk files, and so on

◆ To handle the computer's housekeeping functions, such as coping with disk errors or managing the printer ports

◆ To provide some fundamental file functions, such as displaying a disk directory or typing a file

Purists will note that not all of these things are done by DOS *per se*—some are handled by the BIOS in your computer. For the sake of this discussion, let's allow that all of these things are handled by the operating system, of which DOS is the visible component.

A PC is a text-based computer. This means that it defaults to working with characters rather than pictures as does, for example, a Macintosh or an Amiga. This is not to say that a PC can't do first-class graphics for use with programs like CorelDRAW. However, its native language is text. DOS, insofar as it deals with the outside world, likes to think of things in terms of text. If a program asks DOS to go fetch a character from the keyboard, DOS will be able to cope with the request handsomely. Asked to draw a picture on the screen, however, DOS will be confused at best. It provides no real graphics facilities.

You can think of Windows as being a sort of DOS-extension environment. It bolts onto DOS and makes it into a graphic operating system. With Windows running, commands can be entered by clicking on pull-down menu items, applications can run in dedicated areas of the screen (not surprisingly, these areas are referred to as *windows*), and so on.

In addition, DOS is designed to run a single program at a time. Windows gives it the ability to have several programs going at once, allowing you to jump between them as your work demands.

Applications such as CorelDRAW are written with the assumption that Windows will be in place before you run the application. When Corel-DRAW wants to refresh a drawing on your screen, for example, it does so by calling a part of Windows. Windows handles all the graphic functions of CorelDRAW, among other things.

The power of Windows is that it does all the hard parts involved in maintaining a user-friendly interface, leaving CorelDRAW to handle the actual tasks of manipulating paths and objects and such.

There are a number of drawbacks to Windows. For one thing, it's somewhat memory-hungry. Applications like CorelDRAW, which do a lot, are also memory-hungry. Running several big applications often requires more memory than Windows currently knows how to address.

Windows gets around this memory problem in various ways. When an application starts to run short of memory, Windows will spill part of the application which is not being used, part of itself, or some of the application's data, to a disk file. It's very clever in this respect, and is constantly juggling its memory so applications running under it will have enough memory to work, even when it isn't actually available by most accounts.

As a rule, starving Windows for memory doesn't make it crash and, much to its credit, rarely keeps it from ultimately performing a task. It just slows it down a great deal as it investigates alternatives to stashing things in memory that it doesn't have.

THE ART OF THE MOUSE

In moving around Windows and using the functions of CorelDRAW, you will need to know a bit of the terminology of mice. Being a very simple device, there aren't too many ways to do the things you can do with a mouse, so this section will be pretty short.

When you move your mouse around on your desk, a *mouse cursor* will move on the screen. This defaults to looking like an arrow pointing to the upper-left corner of your screen, but it may change its shape under Corel-DRAW and other applications when the program wants to indicate that something out of the ordinary is happening. For example, when an action is taking place which does not permit your computer to do anything else until it's done—such as saving a file—the mouse cursor will turn into an hourglass, the *wait cursor*. It will turn back into whatever it was previously when the wait's over.

Most mice for the PC come with two or three buttons. For most operations, CorelDRAW recognizes only the leftmost button of the mouse—when you're instructed to click the mouse button, you should always use the left button.

You can, in fact, assign one of several tasks to the right button on a multiple-button mouse under CorelDRAW—consult the Preferences box of CorelDRAW for a list of them.

Clicking on something under Windows involves moving the mouse cursor to the thing you're to click on and then pushing and releasing the mouse button very quickly. *Double-clicking* involves doing the same thing but clicking twice in rapid succession. You may find that this doesn't work very well when Windows first comes out of the box. The Windows Control Panel allows you to adjust the double-click time to suit your mouse and your fingers.

Dragging or *grabbing* something involves placing the mouse cursor on the thing to be dragged, holding down the mouse button, and pulling the thing to someplace else on the screen. When it gets there, release the mouse button.

Selecting an area of the screen—something which is done frequently under CorelDRAW—involves dragging the mouse cursor over an area such that a selector box is drawn. A selector box, or rubber-band box, is just a rectangle drawn with broken lines which indicates the area traversed by the mouse.

You should make sure you understand these ideas, as they're pivotal to the operation of Windows and, therefore, of CorelDRAW.

WALKING THROUGH WINDOWS

It's beyond the scope of this book to provide a detailed explanation of Windows and its operation. Chances are you wouldn't need one, anyway. Windows is a very intuitive system and you'll probably find that you're able to pick it up without much study.

We will not get into the installation of Windows or of CorelDRAW, as both of these procedures are explained quite adequately in the documentation for these two packages. As a matter of fact, in both cases all you need do is run the installation programs provided with Windows and CorelDRAW, respectively, and answer the questions.

This section will explain those aspects of Windows which are relevant to the operation of CorelDRAW. In these examples, we'll assume that you have installed the two packages according to their respective defaults so that Windows lives in the C:\WINDOWS subdirectory and CorelDRAW lives in a subdirectory called C:\CORELDRW.

In order to run Windows, you must issue the command WIN, which runs WIN.COM. This will display the Microsoft logo and, a while later, the Main screen of Windows. If you have a less-than-stellar computer, the Windows logo will become annoying after a while—consult the documentation for Graphic Workshop for Windows on Disk 2 of the companion disks of this book for instructions on changing it to a graphic of your own choice.

Figure A.4 illustrates the Windows Main screen.

If you move your mouse cursor to the icon of an application file and double-click on it, Windows will run it. If the application was written for Windows—the WRITE.EXE program which comes with Windows is such an application, as of course is CorelDRAW—it will come up in a window on the screen. Virtually all non-Windows applications can also be run reliably from within Windows, although by default they'll occupy the entire screen while they're active.

Here's something important to remember when you're using Windows: If you have multiple tasks going at once, you can flip quickly between them by holding down the Alt key and hitting the Esc key. You can easily have, for example, CorelDRAW and CorelPHOTO-PAINT running at the same time and flip between them using Alt-Esc.

If you hit Ctrl-Esc, a box with a list of all the currently running tasks will appear, allowing you to select the one you want to switch to.

FIGURE A.4:

The Main screen of Windows

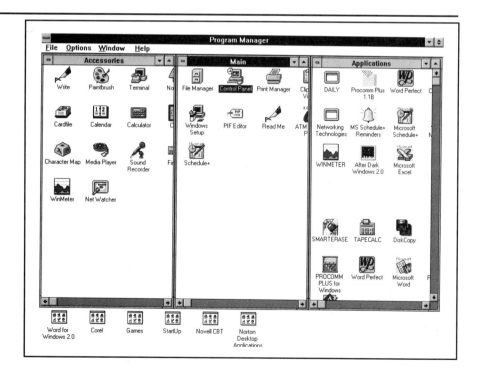

Windows itself is a Windows application—it's referred to as Program Manager in the Ctrl-Esc box. The Main screen which comes up when you first run Windows behaves just like any other Windows application in the way it uses its menus, controls, dialogs, and so forth. Once you understand how to use it—it will be presented in the following section—CorelDRAW will be a great deal easier to master.

Working with Controls

One of the really powerful aspects of Windows is its consistency. All Windows applications are constrained to behave themselves according to certain guidelines. Thus, if you know how to work the controls and menus and whatnot of one Windows application, you're well on your way to knowing how to run any other one.

Once an application has opened a window for itself, you can change the size and position of the window with the mouse. If you grab the top bar of the window you can drag the window to a new location. Grab the lower-right corner of the window and you'll be able to make it larger or smaller.

There are two boxes in the upper-right corner of most Windows applications. One has a downward-facing arrow and the other an upward-facing arrow. The downward-facing arrow is the *minimize button* and the upward-facing arrow is the *maximize button*. These are examples of Windows *controls*.

If you click on the minimize button, the window for the application will vanish. A small icon representing the application will appear somewhere along the bottom of your screen.

A minimized application is still running, and if you minimized it in the middle of a task, it may continue executing the task even though you can no longer see it. When you go to print a picture from within CorelDRAW, for example, CorelDRAW basically hands the picture to another Windows application called Print Manager, which does all the work. Print Manager comes pre-minimized—when it's running all you'll see is its icon.

You can return a minimized window to its former state by double-clicking on its icon.

The maximize control causes the window of an application to grow from whatever its current size is to the maximum size the screen allows.

You can have lots of open windows on the screen at once, and you needn't minimize the ones you aren't using just to get at the one you want to use. You can bring any window to the front of the screen by clicking in some part of it. Having done this, anything you type will be received by the application in this window. This is referred to as the *active window*. Figure A.5 illustrates a stack of windows and the result of clicking in a window that is behind others.

Working with Menus

The minimize and maximize controls are really shortcuts. Windows provides a lot of shortcuts like this. The long way to minimize and maximize an application's window is to use the appropriate *menu items*.

Most Windows applications have some menus. CorelDRAW has quite a few. The names of the menus are displayed along the top of the application's window in what is called the *menu bar*. If you click on a menu name and hold the mouse button, a menu will drop down. Drag the mouse down the screen and the various menu items will be highlighted as the mouse cursor passes over them. If you release the mouse button when an item is highlighted, that item will be selected.

Inside the front cover of this book you'll find the principal Corel-DRAW menus and their corresponding dialog boxes. Dialog boxes will be discussed shortly.

Some items in a menu may appear dim relative to the rest of the items in the menu. These are inactive items, and cannot be selected. There is usually some logical reason for an item to be inactive. For example, the Close item might be inactive when there's nothing to close. Once a file has been opened, this item will become active.

To a large extent, becoming proficient in the use of any Windows application is a matter of learning what's in each of its menus and what each item actually does.

Every Windows application has one menu in addition to those appearing in its menu bar. This is called the *system menu,* and it is available by clicking in the box in the extreme upper left of an application's window. The location of this box and the appearance of a typical system menu are illustrated in Figure A.6.

Should you be curious, Windows highlights its menu items with a black bar if you're using a 16-color driver and with a blue bar if you're using a 256-color driver. If you're not certain what sort of driver you have installed, pull down a menu.

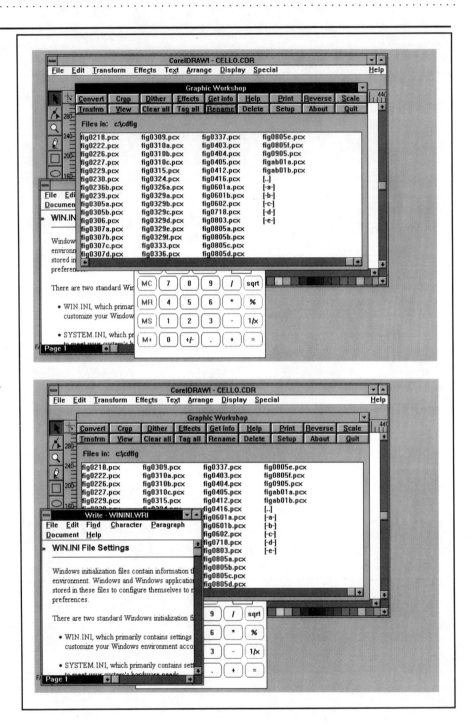

FIGURE A.6:

The system menu of a Windows application

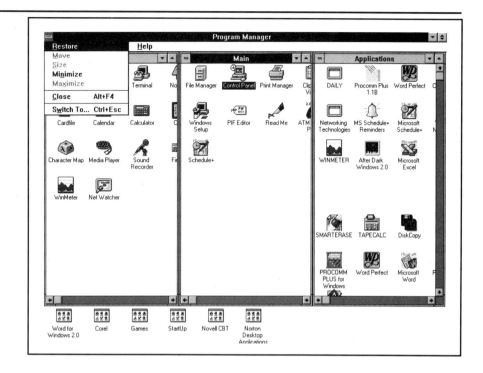

The system menu has items which, among other things, will minimize and maximize an application's window just as the two controls we discussed a few minutes ago did. It also has a Close item, which is used to terminate the application.

Most system menus feature an About item. If you click on the About item of an application you should see a box which tells you the name of the company that wrote the program, possibly the names of the programmers involved in its creation, and usually a version number. The version number will be important if you have to contact the application's manufacturer for help. Figure A.7 illustrates the About box of CorelDRAW.

There's a very important shortcut involved in the system menu. If you double click on the control that brings up the system menu, you'll terminate the application. This is a handy way to exit in a hurry. If you double click on this box in the Program Manager screen of Windows, you'll be asked if you want to quit Windows. A click on OK ends your session and returns you to DOS.

FIGURE A.7:

*The About CorelDRAW
info box*

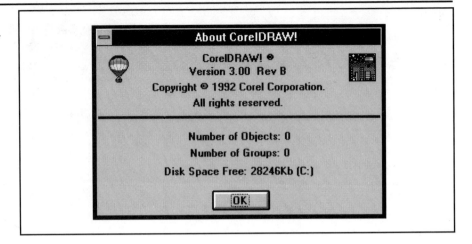

If you ever find yourself lost while you're working with Windows, you might want to consult the menu entitled Help. Selecting any item in this menu will bring up a box with information about the general area you've selected, along with directions to find more specific help.

Figure A.8 illustrates some help.

Working with Dialog Boxes

Windows applications usually communicate with you through *dialog boxes,* or *dialogs* for short. A dialog is any box which pops up to tell you something, to wait for a reply, or to ask a question.

There's a lot of rather involved terminology relating to dialog boxes under Windows, much of it only of interest to Windows gurus and Windows programmers. You don't really need to know any of it: Dialogs are designed to be self-explanatory, and the ones under CorelDRAW are even better than usual in this respect.

Any dialog which wants a reply will contain one or more *controls.* The most common sort of control is a *button.* A button contains some text— usually a word or two—which defines what clicking on that control will do. Many dialogs will have one default button, indicated by the extra thickness of its outline. If you hit the ⏎ key on your keyboard while such a dialog is active, the default action will be selected and whatever would have happened had you explicitly clicked on the default button will transpire.

FIGURE A.8:

Various Windows
Help boxes

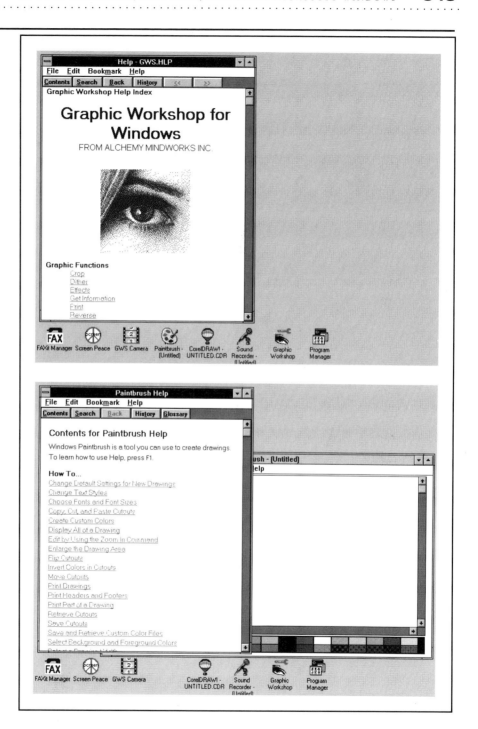

FIGURE A.8:

Various Windows Help boxes (continued)

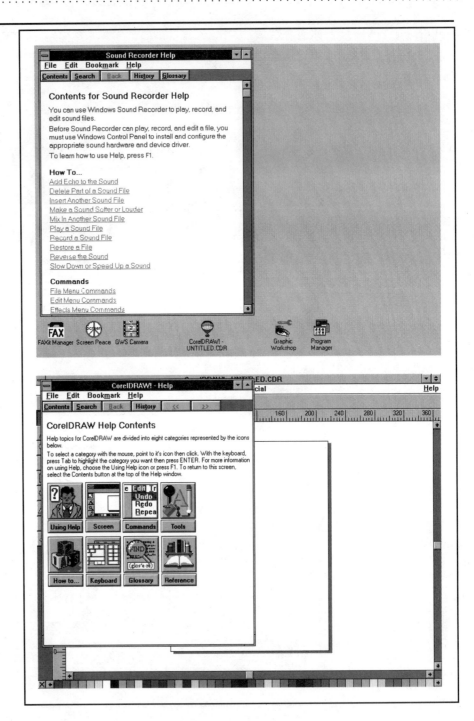

Of late, many Windows applications—CorelDRAW included—have changed the appearances of some standard Windows controls, check boxes among them. While a standard Windows check box consists of a square with a cross through it, you'll find the check boxes under CorelDRAW to be diamonds with smaller colored diamonds within them to signify that they've been checked. They work the same way as the original check boxes, however.

Many dialogs contain *radio buttons*. These are analogous to the buttons on a car radio's station selector. If you click on one from a set of radio buttons, that button will be selected and all the others will be deselected. Radio buttons are used to select one action from a list of several in cases where only one of them can be performed at a time. In Figure A.9, there are two sets of radio buttons, each with one button selected. When you may select more than one action (or set more than one condition) at a time, you will be presented with another group of controls known as *check boxes*.

Figure A.9 also contains a couple of *scroll bar* controls. These allow you to scroll a list of text or other material which is too long to fit in the available space all at once. Clicking on the arrows at the top or bottom of a vertical scroll bar will bring additional lines of text into the list box, one line at a time. Clicking in the gray area of the scroll bar will scroll larger increments. The small box within the gray area, called the "thumb," shows your relative position within the list. When the thumb is close to the top of the scroll bar, the contents you see are close to the top of the list; when the thumb is closer to the bottom, the contents you see are closer to the end of the list. If you drag the thumb down the scroll bar, the contents of the list will change in relation to the box's location. Horizontal scroll bars work in a similar fashion.

File Dialogs The File dialog box is a special dialog for opening and saving files. Figure A.10 illustrates what one looks like in CorelDRAW. Other Windows applications may use variations on this dialog, although all the important elements of it will be present in some form no matter where

FIGURE A.9:

A dialog showing various buttons, bars, and boxes

Print Setup
Printer
◆ Default Printer
(currently Apple LaserWriter on LPT1:)
◇ Specific Printer:
Apple LaserWriter on LPT1:
Orientation ◆ Portrait ◇ Landscape
Paper Size: Letter 8 1/2 x 11 in Source: Upper Tray
OK   Cancel   Options...   Network...

FIGURE A.10:

A File dialog as it appears in CorelDRAW

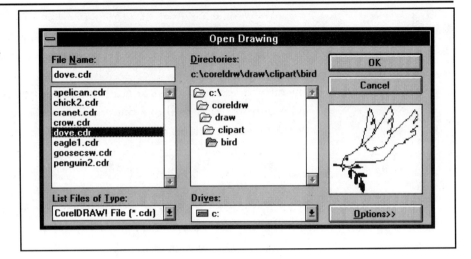

Double clicking on an existing file name will select it and then effectively click on the OK button, all without having to move your mouse. It's a quick way to select and open a file.

You might well wonder how folders got into all this. Folders contain files on a conventional desktop. Note also that the File Manager application of Windows is represented by an icon that looks like a file cabinet. Microsoft is clearly very fond of this metaphor.

it turns up. In this case, the dialog is being used to open a file, but the same box would be used if you try to save one.

The File Name control of the File dialog box is a "combo box"—it allows you to enter a file name or to select an existing file name. To enter a file name—for example, to save a file to a new name—click in the single line field at the top of the box, type in the file name and then click on the OK button. To select an existing file name—as you would do when opening a file to work on it—click on one of the names in the file list. You may have to use the scroll bar in this list to see all the file names in a fairly full directory.

The List Files of Type box lets you set a file server controlling which file names to display according to the file name extension of the filter. This list changes from application to application, and may be different for opening and saving files.

The Directories control will show you the current directory path and provide you with a list of the available directories relative to the current path. The little yellow symbols are folders—your current path will be indicated by an open folder. Double click on a different entry in this list to change directories.

The control below the list of directories will allow you to change drives. If you click on it, a list of the available drives in your system will appear. Note that the symbols beside the drive letters will tell you what sort of drive each entry represents.

The large window to the right side of the File Open dialog box is the preview window. If you select a CDR file to open by clicking on it once, a thumbnail version of its contents will appear in this window. You can see what's in a file before you actually open it by using this facility.

If you have any really old CDR files created by a version of Corel-DRAW older than 2.0, the preview function will not work. In this case, the preview window will have a line through it.

Keyboard Shortcuts

CorelDRAW offers keyboard equivalents for just about everything. Virtually all of the menu items, the choices in dialog boxes, and so on can be selected using the keyboard.

Keyboard shortcuts are handy because, once you get used to Corel-DRAW, you'll find that in many cases the keyboard is a much more convenient way to perform some operations than mousing around is. For example, an action which might take several drags and clicks can often be repeated in CorelDRAW simply by hitting Ctrl-R, the shortcut for the Edit menu's Repeat option.

All menu options can be handled by using two keyboard commands. The first activates the menu, and the second selects a specific option from the menu. The menu command is always an Alt combination, which means it's entered by holding down the Alt key on your keyboard and hitting a letter key before letting go of Alt. The option command is a normal letter, by itself.

One commonly used keyboard equivalent is Alt-F to activate the File menu and then O to select the Open option. This will open a file; that is, it will bring up the File dialog to allow you to load a drawing file into CorelDRAW.

The keyboard equivalents for every menu item are listed in the menus themselves. Figure A.11 illustrates the File menu of CorelDRAW. You will notice that in the menu bar, the F in File is underlined. This indicates that the key to access the File menu is Alt-F. If you hit Alt-F when CorelDRAW is running, the File menu will drop down and stay visible until you hit a second key to select an option or do something to dismiss the menu. The screen in Figure A.11 was captured immediately after hitting Alt-F.

FIGURE A.11:

The CorelDRAW File menu, illustrating keyboard equivalents for some of its items

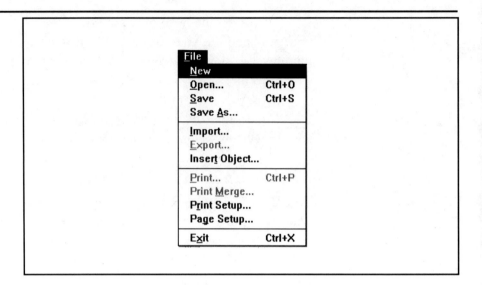

You will also note that there is something on the same line as the Open menu item, this being ^O (a caret character and the letter O). The caret represents the Control, or Ctrl, key. In this case, there are actually two keyboard equivalents for opening a file. You can use Alt-F O or you can use Ctrl-O. Obviously, the latter requires one less keystroke.

There is no printed list of keyboard equivalents in CorelDRAW, nor is one needed. The menus themselves will tell you what they are. You will find that over time you'll learn the ones that help you out most.

Note that keyboard shortcut commands are always sent to the application whose window is foremost on your screen, that is, to the active window. If the application in your active window doesn't recognize a particular keyboard shortcut, it will beep and ignore it.

B

Fine-Tuning

CorelDRAW

he CorelDRAW options that you'll most likely want to change are handled through dialog boxes within the application itself. There are, however, numerous lesser known options and adjustments available to help make CorelDRAW still more useful. While a bit arcane and not quite as user-friendly as clicking a few buttons in the Preferences dialog box, these features are well worth knowing about.

This appendix will deal with some low-level adjustments for Corel-DRAW. If you're new to Windows, you might want to leave these things alone for a while—they are not essential to the basic operation of CorelDRAW.

MODIFYING CORELDRW.INI

If you mangle COREL-DRW.INI, CorelDRAW will not work, or will behave unpredictably. Before you try anything in this section, make a copy of CORELDRW.INI on a floppy disk. If CorelDRAW misbehaves later on, restore your backed-up CORELDRW-.INI file.

The CORELDRW.INI file, located in the \CORELDRW\DRAW subdirectory of your hard drive, is a catch-all for options used by CorelDRAW. It's a pure text file—you can modify it by opening it with the Windows Notepad application.

Each line in the CORELDRAW.INI file tells CorelDRAW something. The CORELDRAW.INI file is separated into sections. Each section begins with a title in square brackets.

Note that some lines in the file begin with semicolons. The semicolon is called a comment symbol—CorelDRAW ignores everything on a line after a semicolon. You can use semicolons to precede comments in the CORELDRW.INI file. You can also use them to make lines invisible—this is called "commenting out" a line. If you want to try a change to CORELDRW.INI but you aren't sure you'll want to keep it, do this:

1. Make a copy of the line you want to change.

2. Put a semicolon at the beginning of the first copy.

3. Change the second copy.

If you subsequently want to undo the change to CORELDRW.INI, delete the changed line and remove the semicolon from the commented-out line.

CorelDRAW reads its relevant option settings from CORELDRW.INI when it boots up. Other parts of it, such as some of its import and export filters, will read things from CORELDRW.INI throughout your Corel-DRAW session. Note that if you make changes to CORELDRW.INI part way through a CorelDRAW session, in most cases they will not take effect until the next time you run CorelDRAW.

Each line in CORELDRW.INI that actually specifies an option is of the form:

ThisIsAnOption=Something

In this hypothetical example, the string *ThisIsAnOption* is called a "key." When CorelDRAW wants to know the default value for *ThisIsAnOption*, it will read this line from CORELDRW.INI and take whatever is to the right of the equal sign as its value.

It's important to know what you're doing when editing COREL-DRW.INI. CorelDRAW doesn't do a lot of error-checking when it reads lines from CORELDRW.INI. If the line to the right of the equal sign is not what CorelDRAW is expecting, it may behave unpredictably.

Note also that there are some things in CORELDRW.INI that just shouldn't be changed.

In some entries, options are set as either yes or no. These entries expect to have a number to the right of the equal sign. Zero represents no and one represents yes.

The following are the user-adjustable sections you'll encounter in CORELDRW.INI and the options they allow you to change.

[CDRAWCONFIG]

This is arguably the most useful section of CORELDRW.INI. It allows you to fine-tune a number of things that will make CorelDRAW a lot easier to use. A few of these lines will allow you to deal with some fundamental peculiarities in the way CorelDRAW behaves.

Application Paths

There are several lines in this section which define where CorelDRAW and its various ancillary applications are located on your hard drive. These are as follows:

```
Applic=C:\CORELDRW\DRAW
ConfigDir=C:\CORELDRW\DRAW
FontsDir=C:\CORELDRW\FONTS
CorelFiltersDir=C:\CORELDRW\FILTERS
AutoBackupDir=C:\CORELDRW\AUTOBAK
```

Most of these options are really only useful if you're running over a network, or if you're typing to spread CorelDRAW over several hard drives or hard drive partitions. For example, the *AutoBackupDir* line defines where CorelDRAW will put its backup files—these will be discussed in the next section. By default, they will appear in your \CORELDRW\AUTOBAK directory. You could, however, send them elsewhere—to a RAM drive, for example, if you only want them to stick around for a while, or over a network to another system if you want to protect them from the possibility of a local hard drive crash.

Here's what each of the foregoing entries does:

◆ *Applic* is the path where CorelDRAW itself and all its ancillary files live. Among these files are CORELDRW.EXE, CORELDRW.INI, USERPROC.TXT, PROLOG.CMP and the HLP and PAN files for CorelDRAW.

◆ *ConfigDir* tells CorelDRAW where to find its configuration files. This allows, for example, the bulk of CorelDRAW to live on a server for a network but your personal configuration to reside on your system. These files include CDCONFIG.SYS, COREL-DRW.BPT, CORELDRW.DOT, CORELDRW.END, CORELDRW.INK, CORELDRW.IPL, CORELDRW.PAL and any PAT files.

◆ *FontsDir* specifies where CorelDRAW should look for any WFN fonts it will be using. We'll discuss these in greater detail later on in this chapter. In most cases this entry won't matter, as you'll be using TrueType fonts, which are supplied directly through Windows.

◆ *CorelFiltersDir* tells CorelDRAW where to find the files that handle its import and export filters. These will have the extension DLL and will start with the letters IMP and EXP, respectively.

◆ *AutoBackupDir* defines where CorelDRAW will put its automatic backup files.

File Backups

One of CorelDRAW's most thoughtful or most annoying features, depending on your disposition, is its automatic backup facility. Left to its own devices, it will periodically put itself on hold and write the file you're working on to a CDR file in whatever directory the *AutoBackupDir* line specifies. Though this file is a genuine CDR file, it will have the extension ABK. If something were subsequently to happen to the file you were working on, you could rename the ABK file to a CDR file, move it to wherever you normally keep your CDR files, and work with this saved version.

The problem with automatically backing up is that it occurs unexpectedly—CorelDRAW cannot know that it's interrupting a moment of blinding inspiration; and on slower equipment especially, it can be infuriatingly time-consuming.

You might well feel that you can be relied upon to manually back up your work without CorelDRAW's assistance. While you can't actually switch off the automatic backup feature, you can render it harmless. The line

AutoBackupMins=10

tells CorelDRAW how many minutes it should allow between backups. In my CORELDRW.INI file, I have this changed to:

AutoBackupMins=10000

This will restrict it to making automatic backups only after it has been working on the same drawing for about seven days without interruption, an interval most of us can live with. Assuming that you don't usually work on the same drawing for seven days, the automatic backup function will never trouble you.

The *MakeBackupWhenSave* option tells CorelDRAW whether to create BAK files. If this option is enabled, CorelDRAW will rename your existing CDR file to a BAK file prior to saving a new version of a drawing. Thus, there will always be a recent version of your work available, should you damage your primary CDR file.

Having this feature enabled does mean that a lot of BAK files will appear in the subdirectory where you keep your CDR files. As CDR files tend toward obesity, this can tie up quite a lot of drive space if you aren't fairly scrupulous about killing your BAK files when you no longer need them. Especially if you're working with somewhat restricted hard drive space, consider disabling this feature.

Display Controls

As of this writing, Windows screen drivers are available for some high-end super VGA cards to manage resolutions of up to 1280 by 960, and for specialized desktop publishing full-page monitors with higher resolutions still. When you increase the resolution of a display, everything on it gets smaller.

This allows you to fit more things on your screen at a time, and in the case of CorelDRAW will also mean that you'll see drawn objects with greater clarity.

Unfortunately, things of fixed size—such as the toolbox icons of CorelDRAW—can get pretty hard to see at these high resolutions. If you use one of these drivers, you might want to locate the following two lines in CORELDRW.INI:

```
BigPalette=0
BigToolbox=0
```

If these items are set to 1 rather than 0, the toolbox icons and the palette tiles at the bottom of the CorelDRAW window will both double in size. Figure B.1 illustrates the result of using these switches on a 1280-by-960 driver.

As an aside, many Windows users initially use the highest resolution modes their display hardware will allow. There are several caveats to keep in mind about this. The first is that not all VGA monitors will synch properly at high screen resolutions. If your monitor starts to emit a high-pitched shriek and the image on it goes into paroxysms, shut everything down very quickly. A monitor can damage itself and the display card it's connected to under these conditions.

Secondly, many monitors will sync at higher resolutions in their 16-color modes than they can when driven with 256 colors.

Finally, while a 1024-by-768 or 1280-by-960 pixel screen driver will let you have lots of windows open on your screen at once, these modes are hard to work with for most people. You'll probably find that you have to sit with your nose pressed to the glass to read small text, and that after about half an hour your eyes will start to feel like golf balls. If you believe that the electromagnetic radiation that monitors emit isn't all that healthy, a display that forces you to cuddle up with its picture tube to get any work done is probably to be avoided.

Good monitors are a lot easier to read under these conditions than are inexpensive ones. One of the computers I work on has a Sony HG monitor which is quite readable at 1024 by 768 pixels for most Windows applications. There's another one with a low-cost, no-name monitor which is equally capable of synching at this resolution, but is all but impossible to work with.

Enabling the *MaximizeCDraw* option will cause CorelDRAW to maximize itself when it starts up. It will behave as if you had explicitly clicked the maximize button. Most users will want to enable this option—it's disabled

FIGURE B.1:

CorelDRAW on a 1280-by-960 Windows driver with normal palette and toolbox settings (top) and with big palette and toolbox settings (bottom)

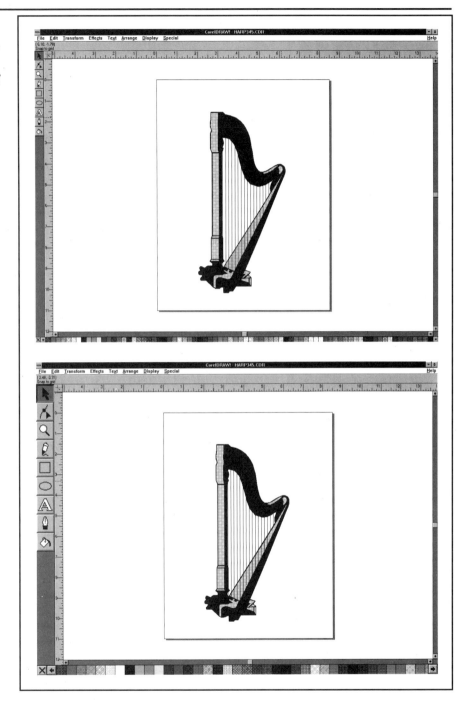

by default. The *3DLook* option tells CorelDRAW whether to display its controls, buttons, rulers, and such as three-dimensional sculpted objects or as old-style two-dimensional objects. Disabling this option will improve Corel-DRAW's screen-update speed marginally for extremely slow hardware.

Clipboard and Export Options

The *CalligraphicClipboard* line defines whether CorelDRAW will transfer calligraphic lines to the Clipboard as such, or as simple fixed-width lines. This will also determine whether some of CorelDRAW's vector-export filters will export calligraphic lines with their calligraphic attributes intact. If this option is disabled, things will copy to the Clipboard more quickly, and they'll export into smaller files for those formats supported by export filters that check this option.

Setting this line to 1 will enable the export of calligraphic lines. Setting it to 0 will disable this function, replacing any formerly calligraphic lines with normal lines.

The *ClipboardFountains* line determines whether objects with radial fountain fills will be sent to the Clipboard with their fills intact. This can take a long time to perform.

The *ExportTextAsCurves* option tells CorelDRAW whether to represent text in some exported vector-file formats as editable text or as curves. The formats in question are discussed in Chapter 5. Enabling this option will make sure that exported graphics with text objects always look right, even if the eventual destination of your exported files has radically different font facilities. Disabling this option will mean that exported vector files with text in them will have that text editable, but it probably won't look as it did under CorelDRAW.

You should leave this option enabled if you'll be exporting vector files to be used in a desktop publishing package, word processor, or any other application that will not actually be modifying the files.

The *TextOnClpMetafile* option tells CorelDRAW whether to export text which has been copied or cut to the Windows Clipboard as text or curves. If this option is enabled, text will be handled as text when it's sent to the Clipboard. This may mean that subsequently pasting CorelDRAW graphics with text in them to other Windows applications will result in noticeable changes to the text objects. This will unquestionably happen if you have any WFN

One way to cheat past this is to create synthetic fountain fills using the Blend function under CorelDRAW. For example, blending between two concentric ellipses with different densities of blue will produce the effect of a radial fill, but with fewer actual drawing objects involved.

fonts in your drawings. Unless you can think of a good reason to do otherwise, you should leave this option disabled, so that text will be passed to the Clipboard as curves.

Process-Color Palette

The *CMYKPalette* line specifies the most recently selected CMYK palette. This is updated whenever you exit CorelDRAW. There's little need to change it manually.

Default Font

The *DefaultFont* line specifies the default font that CorelDRAW will use if you start adding text to a drawing prior to making a font selection. As CorelDRAW is shipped, this will be 24-point Avalon medium. (Avalon is CorelDRAW's name for Avant Garde.)

This is how this line will usually be set:

DefaultFont=Avalon,1,24

The first item after the equal sign is the font name. The second is its weight and effects, interpreted as follows:

1 represents normal

2 represents bold

4 represents italic

8 represents bold italic

The third item on the line is the size of the font in points. It can range from 0.7 to 1440 points—something intermediate to these extremes is recommended.

Drawing Controls

The *DelayToDrawWhileMoving* value defines how long you have to pause while dragging an object around the screen before CorelDRAW will begin to regenerate it. This setting will be ignored if the *ShowObjectsWhenMoving* option is not enabled or (with text) if *MaxCharsToDrawDuringKern* is less than 10.

The *ShowObjectsWhenMoving* option tells CorelDRAW whether to display a wire-frame image of objects which are being dragged around in the Corel-DRAW workspace. This can usually be left at its default value of one, that is, enabled. You might want to disable it if you have a particularly slow system.

The *INKPalette* line defines the most recently used spot color. It's updated when you exit CorelDRAW and need not be adjusted by hand.

The *MaxCharsToDrawDuringKern* option defines the number of characters which you can select for kerning with the pick tool and still have CorelDRAW redraw each character as you work. If this number is set fairly high, the redrawing time of the characters will make your mouse movement a bit erratic as you try to manually kern text. Note that you can increase this value from its default somewhat if you're using a fairly high-end system. You might want to decrease it on slower systems.

Printing Controls

The *FontRasterizer* option tells CorelDRAW whether to print text at small sizes using its internal font rasterizer. When it's enabled, the option allows CorelDRAW to improve on the hinting of small fonts, as discussed in Chapter 6. You will usually want this option enabled—this is how CorelDRAW is configured by default. Some Windows printer drivers won't deal with text printed with the rasterizer option correctly, in which case you should disable this option.

The *PSBitmapFontLimit* sets the number of characters in a drawing which can be converted to bitmaps by the font rasterizer when CorelDRAW is driving a PostScript printer. Bitmapped characters may look better when small text is printed, but they tie up a lot of PostScript printer memory, which is why CorelDRAW likes to use them sparingly. Only text which will result in fairly small characters is considered for conversion to bitmaps—at 300 dots per inch, fonts must be under 18 points. Only some fonts are suitable for use in this way—CorelDRAW will apply rasterization where it's applicable.

You might want to reduce the value of this field if you encounter Post-Script printer errors on drawings with a lot of small text, indicating that the rasterizer is getting a bit overambitious. You can reduce it to zero if you'll be outputting your drawings to a high-resolution PostScript phototypesetter.

The *PSComplexityThreshold* option specifies the maximum number of nodes in a filled path for printing. If an object has more nodes than this,

CorelDRAW will split it into multiple smaller objects to print it. This won't affect its appearance, but it will increase the print time a bit.

If you encounter errors when you're attempting to print complex objects—especially those with fountain fills—reduce this value. Values as low as 200 or 300 may be required for PostScript printers with relatively little memory.

The *WarnBadOrientation* option tells CorelDRAW whether to warn you if your printer's page orientation differs from that of the drawing you're about to print—for example, trying to print a landscape-oriented drawing to a portrait-mode page. Note that if you print through CorelMOSAIC, the orientation will be adjusted automatically.

Text Controls

The *SpellLanguage* setting allows you to define the language dictionary that CorelDRAW will use for its internal spelling checker. The available choices as of this writing are English, French, German, Swedish, Spanish, Italian, Danish, Dutch, Portuguese, Norwegian, and Finnish.

The *SpellDict, HyphenationDict,* and *ThesaurusDict* lines specify the dictionary files that CorelDRAW's text functions will use. They should not be manually changed.

[CORELDRIVERS]

Lying to CorelDRAW about Post-Script printers—telling it that a particular driver is a PostScript printer when it really isn't—can cause an awful lot of meaningless PostScript code to rumble unexpectedly into the output tray of your printer.

The *CorelDrivers* section tells CorelDRAW which of the available Windows printer drivers can be treated as PostScript drivers. CorelDRAW can do things with PostScript printers that it can't manage with non-PostScript devices, such as printing PostScript texture fills.

You might have to manually add a line to this section if you add a new PostScript driver to Windows. This would happen if you were to buy an unusual PostScript printer which came with a special Windows printer driver.

This is a typical line in this section:

```
PSCRIPT=1
```

The key is the name of the printer driver—it would be PSCRIPT.DRV in this case. The value after the equal sign will be 1 if the device can be treated as a PostScript device and 0 otherwise.

[MOSAIC]

The *Mosaic* section tells CorelDRAW where to find the CorelMOSAIC program, should this program be needed to open files. You might have to modify this if you change the location of CorelMOSAIC on your hard drive. There's only one line in this section—it looks like this:

```
Applic=C:\CORELDRW\DRAW\CORELMOS.EXE
```

[CDRAWIMPORTFILTERS] AND [CDRAWEXPORTFILTERS]

The *CDrawImportFilters* section tells CorelDRAW how to associate imported file formats with its specific import filters. The import filters are stored as Windows "dynamic link libraries," or files with the extension DLL.

There are few occasions to change things in this section. You might wish to do so if you find yourself working with files having nonstandard extensions. For example, HPGL files usually have the extension PLT, for "plot," but there are some applications which export them using other extensions, HGL being the next favorite. Rather than having to manually change the file specification each time you go to import a file, you can change the appropriate line in CORELDRW.INI.

The last item in a line in the CDrawImportFilters is the file specification for the import filter. Specifically, in this case you would change

```
HPGL=IMPHPGL.DLL,"HP Plotter HPGL",*.PLT
```

to

```
HPGL=IMPHPGL.DLL,"HP Plotter HPGL",*.HGL
```

Note that you can also change the name of the import filter, the text that appears in quote marks. This will change the name as it appears in the File Type control of the Import file selector under CorelDRAW.

The *CDrawExportFilters* section does the same thing for the CorelDRAW export filters. You might want to change the file extension field for a filter if the application to which you'll be exporting files prefers a different extension.

It's probably fair to say that a few years ago, when CorelDRAW was younger, the naming conventions for some file formats were a good deal more chaotic than they are now. It's quite likely that you won't have to meddle with these sections at all.

[CorelDrwFonts]

The *CorelDrwFonts* section is a holdover from earlier versions of Corel-DRAW, which used their own proprietary WFN fonts rather than Windows' TrueType fonts, as the package does now. In most cases, you won't need anything in this section. However, it is exceedingly handy for including old WFN fonts in CorelDRAW's font list.

The section which discusses TrueType fonts later in this appendix will offer a few reasons why you might actually prefer to use CorelDRAW's older font standard.

You can add a WFN font to CorelDRAW by placing a line like this one in the *CorelDrwFonts* section of CORELDRW.INI:

```
Meath=0 MEATH.WFN
```

In this case, I have added one of my favorite third-party fonts, Meath, from Cassady and Greene. It was actually released as a PostScript font, and was converted to a WFN font by WFNBOSS, a font-conversion package which accompanied earlier versions of CorelDRAW. The WFNBOSS package has largely been rendered obsolete by the introduction of TrueType fonts.

In the line above, the key is the name of the font. The number after the equal sign tells CorelDRAW not to assume that Meath is resident in Post-Script printers—which it isn't, of course. The second item after the equal sign is the actual file name for the Meath font. This file must be located in the fonts directory, as specified by the FontsDir entry discussed earlier in this appendix.

A lot more will be said about this section of CORELDRW.INI.

In adding a CorelDRAW WFN font to the *CorelDrwFonts* section of CORELDRW.INI, you should also add a line to the *CorelDrw20FontMap* section to tell CorelDRAW a few things about the new font. Here's the appropriate line for Meath:

```
MEATH.WFN=Meath 420,0,0,0
```

This tells CorelDRAW the average width of the characters in the font being added. Fortunately, this is very easy to work out, as CorelDRAW comes with a program to do it for you. It's called WFNSPACE. To use it, get to a DOS prompt by double clicking on the MS-DOS icon in the Windows Program Manager. Change directories to \CORELDRW\DRAW. By default, your WFN fonts should go in \CORELDRW\FONTS. To find out the settings for Meath, then, I typed:

WFNSPACE \CORELDRW\FONTS\MEATH.WFN

{CorelDrwSymbols}

The *CorelDrwSymbols* section assigns English names to the WFN files that are used to provide symbols to the symbol mode function of CorelDRAW. Here are a few lines from this section:

Animals=animals.wfn
Architecture=arch.wfn
Arrows-Filled=arfilled.wfn
Arrows-Outlined=arrowsot.wfn
Balloons=balloons.wfn
Banners+Awards=banward.wfn

There are several reasons for modifying entries in this section. You might not like the descriptions chosen by CorelDRAW for some of its symbol libraries, in which case you're free to change them. The key for each line—the text to the left of the equal sign—is the name that will appear in the CorelDRAW Symbols dialog box.

Note that CorelDRAW sorts the lines in this section alphabetically when it loads them.

If you wanted the Animals library to be called Beasts instead, you would change the line

Animals=animals.wfn

to this:

Beasts=animals.wfn

{PSResidentFonts}

The *PSResidentFonts* section specifies the fonts CorelDRAW can assume are resident in your PostScript printer, and the corresponding fonts available to CorelDRAW. Note that while CorelDRAW uses its own synthetic font names by default, a PostScript printer expects to have its font specifications defined by commercial font names. For example, if you want to print something with the CorelDRAW Avalon font, a PostScript printer would expect to be told to use Avant Garde.

Here are some lines from this section:

```
Aardvark-Bold=Aachen-Bold 0
Arabia-Normal=ArnoldBoecklin 0
Avalon-Normal=AvantGarde-Book 3
Avalon-Bold=AvantGarde-Demi 3
Avalon-Italic=AvantGarde-BookOblique 3
Avalon-BoldItalic=AvantGarde-DemiOblique 3
Bahamas-Normal=Bauhaus-Medium 0
```

The number at the end of each line tells CorelDRAW whether to assume that the font is resident in a PostScript printer. If it's 0, the font won't be resident in any PostScript printers. If it's 1, the font is resident in all PostScript printers—the Times Roman font falls into this group, for example. If it's 3, the font is resident in newer PostScript printers having at least the standard 35 resident typefaces.

If you specify a font as being resident when it's not— or if you forget to download fonts you've told Corel-DRAW you would— the text in question will print in Courier, and usually none too attractively.

If you have a printer which has an external hard drive to store additional fonts, or if you will be manually downloading fonts to your printer prior to printing with CorelDRAW, you can assign the appropriate fonts the number 1. This will prevent CorelDRAW from sending their font definitions to the printer, reducing the time required to print drawings that use them.

Changing the font type number of CORELDRW.INI is a good way to handle downloadable fonts which you will always download. If you'll just do this now and then, use the All Fonts Resident option of the CorelDRAW Print dialog box.

{CorelHPGLPens}

The *CorelHPGLPens* section tells the CorelDRAW HPGL import and export filters how many pens they should pretend to have and what colors the pens correspond to. By default, it defines eight pens—you can make Corel-DRAW behave like a Hewlett Packard plotter with up to 256 pens. That such a plotter would have a pen carousel about the size of a truck tire is, of course, no concern of CorelDRAW.

Note that this section will not appear in CORELDRW.INI until you have used one of the HPGL filters at least once.

These are the default pen definitions:

```
P1 = Black
P2 = Blue
P3 = Red
P4 = Green
P5 = Magenta
P6 = Yellow
P7 = Cyan
P8 = Brown
```

The key of each line is the pen number—it should be the letter P followed by the number of the pen to be defined. The color names are defined by the entries in the *CorelHPGLColors* section, to be discussed next. The color names must match exactly, or the pens in question will be black.

If you export a PLT file from CorelDRAW with pens that don't really exist in the plotter that will ultimately reproduce it, the undefined colors will be drawn using the first pen in the plotter.

{CORELHPGLCOLORS}

The *CorelHPGLColors* section assigns a color definition to the color names set up in the *CorelHPGLPens* section. The colors are defined as percentages of cyan, magenta, yellow, and black. These are the default lines for this section:

```
Black= 0 0 0 100
Blue= 100 100 0 0
Red= 0 100 100 0
Green= 100 0 100 0
Magenta= 0 100 0 0
Yellow= 0 0 100 0
Cyan= 100 0 0 0
Brown= 0 50 100 25
```

The four numbers to the right of the equal sign on each line define the percentages of cyan, magenta, yellow, and black ink, respectively. Keep in mind that CorelDRAW knows that pen 2 is blue and that blue is 100 percent cyan and 100 magenta based on the appropriate entries of these two sections. If you change the P2 definition in the *CorelHPGLPens* section to

P2 = Elephant

and the corresponding line in *CorelHPGLColors* to something like:

Elephant = 0 0 0 50

CorelDRAW will think that elephant is a color and that pen 2 draws it. In this case, I've defined elephant as being middle gray—if you're seeing elephants of other colors you might have been staring at your computer for too long.

Note that this section will not appear in CORELDRW.INI until you have used one of the HPGL filters at least once.

Up to 256 colors can be defined.

When CorelDRAW exports drawings to HPGL files, it bases its color selections on the color definitions in the *CorelHPGLColors* section of COREL-DRW.INI. For the best results, these should match the true colors of the actual pens in your plotter. CorelDRAW will trust that pen 2 in this example will in fact be blue—rather than elephant.

CORELDRAW AND FONTS

As discussed earlier in this book, CorelDRAW originally managed its own fonts in a proprietary font format. These fonts were stored in files with the extension WFN—apparently standing for "Waldo's fonts" (early in its development, CorelDRAW was called Waldo).

The WFN format is still used to provide symbol libraries for the CorelDRAW symbol mode.

CorelDRAW remains capable of using WFN fonts. The TrueType fonts which Windows supplies it with are arguably better, however, as they provide hinting. (Hinting was discussed in Chapter 4.)

When you install CorelDRAW, up to 256 new TrueType fonts will be added to Windows. This makes them available not only for use with CorelDRAW, but with all your other Windows applications as well. There are, however, several catches to this:

1. Every time you run Windows, it must look through all its True-Type fonts and make a note of their existence. This takes no time at all if you're using the handful of fonts that comes with Windows. It will take a significant amount of time if these have been augmented with 256 new fonts, however attractive these fonts may be.

2. Not all Windows applications like having 256 new fonts to use. Ventura Publisher for Windows, for example, locks up every time you run it if all these extra fonts are available.

3. There is no mechanism built into the TrueType font system for renaming the fonts.

4. All these fonts take up a lot of room. If you allow CorelDRAW to load its full complement of 256 fonts from its CD-ROM onto your hard drive, your \WINDOWS\SYSTEM directory will contain about 10 megabytes worth of TrueType fonts.

Some of these catches have sub-catches. A few also have solutions.

To begin with, there is no way to reduce the amount of time Windows takes to set up its TrueType fonts—all other things being equal, it's proportional to the number of fonts you have installed in your system. You can, however, cheat on this a bit if you need only some of these fonts under CorelDRAW. This will also address the issue of the disk space that a full complement of CorelDRAW's TrueType fonts can occupy.

When it's first installed, CorelDRAW provides WFN fonts as well as TrueType fonts for quite a few typefaces. The fonts in question are listed in the *CorelDrwFonts* section of CORELDRW.INI, discussed earlier, with their lines commented out. If you remove the corresponding TrueType fonts from Windows and uncomment these lines in CORELDRW.INI, you'll have the same fonts online, but only in CorelDRAW. Windows won't have to deal with them when it first boots up.

Keep in mind, however, that WFN fonts don't print quite as well as TrueType fonts—they lack hinting, and may look a bit crunchy if they're printed at small point sizes on a 300 dot-per-inch printer.

Deleting TrueType fonts under Windows is pretty effortless. Open the Windows Control Panel and select the Fonts section. Click on the fonts you want to delete and then click on the Remove button. When a prompt box appears asking if you really want to delete the fonts in question, make sure you enable the Delete Font File From Disk option.

In contemplating the deletion of some of CorelDRAW's TrueType fonts, you might also think about removing some of the similar faces. For example, from Chapter 14 you will recall that the Helvetica and Univers typefaces—Switzerland and USA under CorelDRAW's naming convention—are essentially similar unless you're a bit of a type guru. You might well decide that one lineal san-serif typeface is quite enough, in which case Univers can probably go. The Franklin Gothic and Futura typefaces—Frankfurt and Fujiyama to CorelDRAW—might be dispensed with as well using this ideology.

Weeding your fonts extensively will also help get around the second of the foregoing catches, that of some Windows applications crashing when confronted with too wide a selection of TrueType fonts.

The problem of renaming TrueType fonts may or may not mean much to you. If you're used to the commercial font names that the printing industry and many desktop publishing packages use to define fonts, the synthetic font names in CorelDRAW may prove bothersome. The principal font reference in CorelDRAW is a huge poster. Unless you actually pin this to your wall, it's a bit awkward to deal with.

Disk 2 of the companion disks for this book includes a tool which will automatically rename all the CorelDRAW TrueType fonts to their proper commercial names. It requires about 10 megabytes of free disk space to operate—and it will take a while. Note, however, that this procedure involves modifying the WIN.INI file in the \WINDOWS directory of your hard drive. It is *essential* that you back this file up before you start. Here's how to rename your fonts.

1. Place Disk 2 of the companion disks in the A drive of your system.

2. Go to the \WINDOWS\SYSTEM directory of your hard drive.

3. Enter:

    A:ZIPPER A:FIXFONT

4. The command to rename the fonts is FIXFONT. You must give it the letter of a drive where it can create a temporary directory to store about 10 megabytes of fonts. In this example, we'll assume that this will be drive C. Enter:

FIXFONT C:

5. The FIXFONT command will take some time to complete, and will print a lot of fairly meaningless text on your screen. Ignore it until the DOS prompt returns. When it's done, all your renamed fonts will be in a subdirectory called \FIXFONT on the drive you specified.

6. Run Windows.

7. Use the Notepad application to open the WIN.INI file in the \WINDOWS directory of your hard drive. Delete the lines in the *fonts* section from:

Aardvark Bold (True Type)=C:\WINDOWS\SYSTEM\AARDVKB.FOT

through to:

ZurichCalligraphic (True Type)=C:\WINDOWS\SYSTEM \ZURICHE.FOT

8. Open the Fonts section of the Control Panel.

9. Click on the Add button.

10. Change to the \FIXFONT directory. All your newly renamed fonts should appear.

11. Click on Select All.

12. Make sure that the Copy Fonts to Windows Directory option has been enabled.

13. Click on OK.

14. When the font installation is complete, you can get out to a DOS prompt and delete the contents of the \FIXFONT directory, followed by the directory itself.

The font-renaming procedure uses a shareware utility called RENAMETT. You will be able to find it in the \WINDOWS\SYSTEM directory of your hard drive. You might want to look at its accompanying documentation, RENAMETT.DOC, should you want to rename a few fonts of your own later on.

CREATING FONTS WITH CORELDRAW

One of the more exotic facilities of CorelDRAW is its rather painless approach to allowing you to create your own custom fonts and symbol sets. A symbol set is actually a font with nonalphabetic characters. While the symbol libraries that accompany CorelDRAW are WFN fonts, held over from earlier editions of the package, TrueType fonts can also appear in the symbol entry dialog. The WingDings font, for example, is treated as a symbol library under this mode.

Creating a worthwhile text typeface from scratch is a serious undertaking—typeface design is an art which only *appears* easy. In this example, we'll look at using the font creation functions of CorelDRAW to create a small custom symbol library. The principles are the same for creating actual fonts, however, should you feel ambitious. This section will deal with the process of creating a font of guitar-chord frames.

Creating a new TrueType font with CorelDRAW involves exporting each character in the font as a separate object to the TrueType export filter. The TrueType export filter has some unique characteristics, as compared to the more conventional filters which have appeared elsewhere in this book. You can export multiple objects to the same TrueType file name. Rather than overwrite each other, as they would do if you were exporting drawings to EPS or PCX files, they'll each form one character in the font being created.

Font symbols created by CorelDRAW must adhere to a fairly strict set of guidelines. Each character must be a combined set of objects, but it may contain no previously combined objects or groups. It should also contain no overlapping objects, as combined objects which overlap tend to knock out areas of each other, which looks odd.

Figure B.2 illustrates the symbol set we'll be creating in this example. These are only the major chords—if you actually have an interest in using CorelDRAW to typeset guitar music, you'll no doubt wish to add quite a few additional chords.

FIGURE B.2:

The guitar chord symbol set

NOTE *You can find the CDR file (CHORD. CDR) that I used to create these symbols on Disk 2 of the companion disks for this book, should you want to create some chords of your own. The resulting TrueType font is also there, as CHORD.TTF.*

The obvious way to draw these symbols would be to create a master chord frame and then to stick dots on copies of it for each of the chords. This is so obvious and easy to do that one would assume instinctively that it couldn't possibly work, and one would be right. The dots would overlap the lines, with the result that the overlapping parts would print as white rectangles, as shown in Figure B.3.

The way to actually create these symbols involves a bit of cunning. It's illustrated in Figure B.4. In this approach, the four master tiles on the right side of the illustration are duplicated to form the illusion of dots in the chord frame. This runs into a bit of trouble in chords such as D or G, where there's a dot on an outer string. In these cases, you'll actually have to insert a couple of nodes in the outer edge of the chord frame, convert the intervening area of the line to a curve, and bend it outward.

FIGURE B.3:

How not to create a symbol

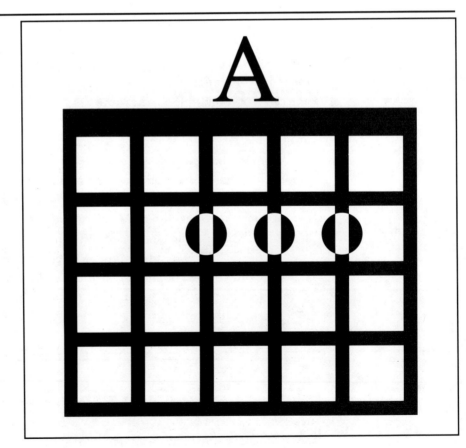

*The right way to build
a chord*

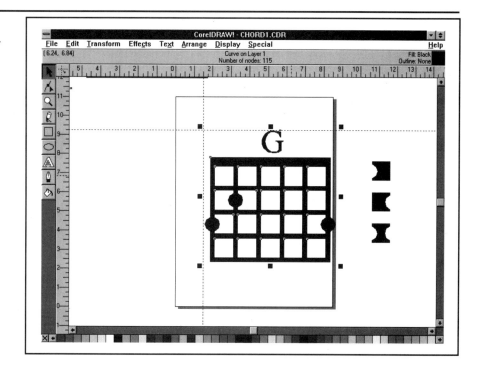

Note that both the chord frame and the little square tiles within it are
drawn as four lines, not as rectangles.

These symbols are much easier to create if you set up the CorelDRAW
grid at eight points to the inch. Each tile is 1.25 inches across. There's no
harm in drawing each frame quite large—each one nearly fills the Corel-
DRAW workspace in the example file I've used here—because the drawing
will never be printed.

Having assembled a chord frame, put the letter designation for the
chord in the drawing as follows:

1. Set the letter in 124-point Times Roman and place it above
the frame.

2. Convert the letter to curves.

3. Break the letter's curves apart.

When your chord frame is complete, combine the whole thing, including
the letter. If you're drawing in wire-frame mode, you might wish to check the
preview to make sure that it has come out looking as it should.

Save the CorelDRAW file with your chord frames as CHORD.CDR. This will establish the default name for the TrueType font file which will contain your font.

A TrueType font's characters are numbered, the numbers corresponding to the ASCII character codes for an alphabetic font. A font can have characters running from number 33 through 255. Unless you will ultimately be creating a font in which every character will be used, you should also create a dummy character along with the characters you plan to export, and make this the first character in the font. In most fonts, this is a rectangle with a diagonal line through it; in this example, I used a guitar drawn from yet another CorelDRAW symbol library. The dummy font character will be used to fill in any unused character positions in the CorelDRAW Symbol dialog box.

Don't make your dummy symbol too complicated, or it will slow down the display of the Symbol dialog box.

You must now export your characters to a TTF typeface file. The position of the characters being exported through the TTF export filter will affect their ultimate positioning relative to where you click your mouse when you finally go to use this font as a symbol set. Therefore, it's a good idea to make sure that all the characters in the font will be consistently positioned in the CorelDRAW workspace. You can do this easily with the CorelDRAW guides.

Zoom out until you can see all the symbols you have created. This should leave the actual printable part of the CorelDRAW workspace as a small rectangle in the center of your screen. Drag one horizontal guideline and one vertical guideline from the rulers surrounding the work space and place them so that they intersect near the upper-left corner of the printable rectangle. Your workspace should look something like the one in Figure B.5.

Turn on the Snap To Guidelines option in the Display menu if this has not been done previously. When you drag your first symbol into the printable part of the workspace, it will snap to the guides, as will all the subsequent ones.

Position the first symbol in your font—the dummy symbol if you'll be using one—and select it. Open the Export dialog box from the File menu and select the TrueType Font, TTF export filter. Click on the Selected Only option and then click on OK.

The TrueType Export dialog box is shown in Figure B.6. When you export the first symbol or character in a font, there are a number of elements in this box you must deal with. Specifically, you will have to give your font a name, entered into the TTF Family Name field. Select one of the Styles

FIGURE B.5:

Guides arranged to position the font characters

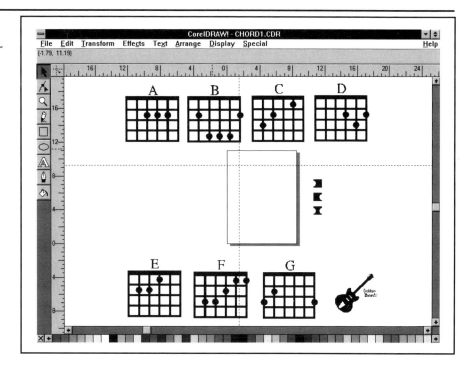

FIGURE B.6:

The CorelDRAW True-Type Export dialog box

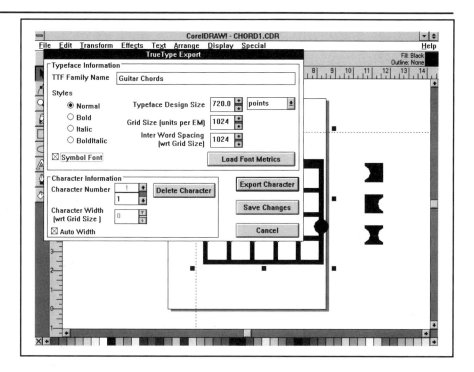

options—the default Normal style will suffice for a symbol font. If you will be creating a symbol font, that is, one which is to appear in the Symbols dialog box under CorelDRAW, make sure you enable the Symbol Font option below the Styles list. Leave everything else in this box as it defaults.

Click on the Export Character button when you've set up the box correctly.

Repeat this procedure for each character in your font—drag it into the printable area of your workspace so it snaps to the guides and then export it to the font file you've created. Note that on subsequent characters there will be no need to set up the font name or any of the other options—in fact, most will have been dimmed by CorelDRAW—and the Character Number control in the lower-left corner of the dialog box will automatically increment itself.

When you're done, exit from CorelDRAW—it must be restarted when you add TrueType fonts to Windows.

To add your new font to Windows, do this:

1. Open the Control Panel from the Windows Program Manager.
2. Select the Fonts item.
3. Click on the Add button.
4. Select your new font.
5. Click on OK.
6. Close the Control Panel.

When you next boot up CorelDRAW, you should find your new font available in the Symbol dialog box.

Using

CorelMOSAIC

CorelDRAW is designed to work with one file at a time. In most cases this is appropriate for the applications it's put to, but now and again you'll find that things would be considerably easier if you could work with multiple drawings for certain operations. The CorelMOSAIC program is an appendix to CorelDRAW which takes over in these situations.

CorelMOSAIC can be thought of as a file manager that deals specifically with picture files—a more specialized version of Norton Commander or the Windows File Manager application. Because it deals with pictures, it allows you to see them as visual images, rather than just as file names.

CorelMOSAIC will actually work with both CorelDRAW's native CDR files and with several other types of files as well. Specifically, you can run CorelMOSAIC to manage CDR files, bitmapped files in the formats supported by CorelPHOTO-PAINT, CorelSHOW files, Adobe Illustrator AI files, EPS files, and CorelCHART files.

In displaying a CorelSHOW file, only the first screen in the file will appear in a thumbnail frame.

CorelMOSAIC comes with CorelDRAW, and was installed when you installed the CorelDRAW package.

You might want to boot up CorelMOSAIC now to work through its operation as we go. The opening screen will look something like the window in Figure C.1.

The little images in a CorelMOSAIC window, called "thumbnails," are representations of the files being managed. In the case of CorelDRAW's CDR files, these will be the thumbnail preview images in the files themselves. In working with bitmapped images, CorelMOSAIC will have to unpack each file and create a scaled-down representation of it to display.

 Once Corel- MOSAIC starts reading a directory, it can't be interrupted. Setting it loose on a directory with lots of files in it, such as a CD-ROM, can entail a protracted wait.

LOCATING FILES

Before CorelMOSAIC can do anything else, you'll have to point it to the location of the files you want to work with. Select the Open Directory item of the File menu. A typical CorelDRAW Open Directory dialog box will appear. Select the file type you want CorelMOSAIC to work with using the List Files of Type selector in the lower-left corner of the dialog box. Use the other controls to move to the directory you want to work with. Click on OK. CorelMOSAIC will assemble its collection of thumbnails based on what it finds in the directory you've selected.

If you select All Files as the file type in the Open Directory dialog box, Corel-MOSAIC might encounter files of a type it doesn't recognize. It will represent these files with an exclamation point icon, rather than a thumbnail.

EDITING FILES

Each of the file types that CorelMOSAIC recognizes corresponds to one of the applications in the CorelDRAW package. CorelMOSAIC is aware of this. If you double click on one of its thumbnails, it will immediately launch the application the file in question corresponds to and tell it to load the file you've selected. Double clicking on a CDR file, for example, will run CorelDRAW and load the file you clicked on as if it had been selected with the Open item of the CorelDRAW file menu. Bitmapped image files will be handled by CorelPHOTO-PAINT.

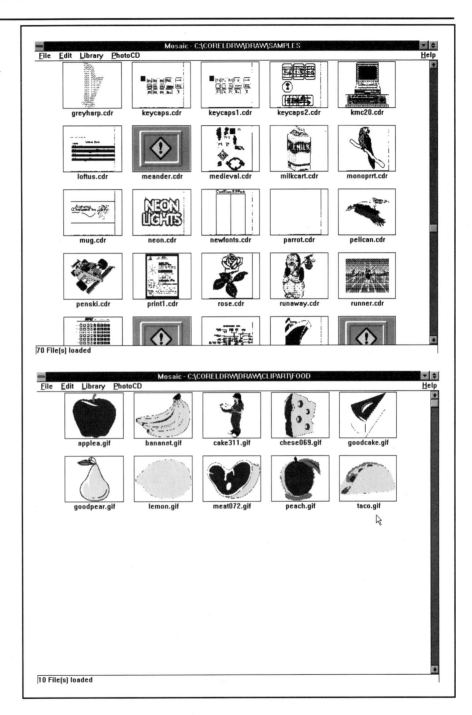

FIGURE C.1:

The opening screen of CorelMOSAIC, looking at a directory of CDR files (top) and looking at a directory of GIF files (bottom)

CorelMOSAIC will instigate only one copy of an application at a time. If CorelDRAW is running when you double click on a CDR file's thumbnail in CorelMOSAIC, the current contents of CorelDRAW will be discarded and your selected file will be loaded.

As an application launcher, CorelMOSAIC can't do anything you can't manage equally well with the individual applications involved. It just makes selecting a file and getting its application going a little easier.

MANAGING LIBRARIES

One of the most useful applications of CorelMOSAIC for users with finite amounts of hard drive space is in working with libraries. Libraries are archives of picture files in which each picture has been compressed. CorelDRAW CDR files can typically be compressed down to about a quarter of their usual size when you store them in a library.

CorelMOSAIC will allow you to add files to a library, delete files from a library, and extract files. Libraries under CorelMOSAIC are treated in much the same way as subdirectories with picture files in them. You'll see all the pictures in a library as thumbnails, and double clicking on one will start up the appropriate application and load the file.

At least, this is almost true. There are two catches to it. The first is that opening a library is relatively slow, as each picture must be read from the library to create a thumbnail for it. As a rule, opening a library on a hard drive with CorelMOSAIC is about as time-consuming as reading a directory worth of individual pictures from a CD-ROM.

The second catch is that none of the CorelDRAW applications—save for CorelMOSAIC itself—has any idea of what to do with a library. When CorelMOSAIC runs CorelDRAW and hands it a file from a library to work with, what it really does is unpack the file from the library behind your back, restoring it to a normal CDR file. It will prompt you for a drive and directory to unpack the file into.

When you save a file which originally came from a library, the saved version will not be replaced in the library. You will have to explicitly replace it in a library with CorelMOSAIC.

Libraries are a good way to store pictures you might want to get at from time to time, but which you're unlikely to want to change. They're a handy place to put clip art, for example, and you might want to consider moving the clip art that CorelDRAW installs on your hard drive to libraries if you won't be needing it too often and you'd like to save some space.

CREATING A NEW LIBRARY

To create a new library, do the following:

1. Open a directory which contains files you want to archive using the Open Directory item of the File menu. Thumbnails of the relevant files will appear in the CorelMOSAIC window.

2. Select whichever of the thumbnails you want to archive by holding down the Shift key and clicking on the individual pictures; or select the Select All item of the Edit menu to select all the pictures in your current directory.

3. Select the Add Images To Library item of the Library menu. A File Open dialog box will appear.

4. Enter a name for your new library. Click on OK.

5. A dialog box will ask if you want to create a new library. Click on Yes.

The Corel-MOSAIC application uses essentially the same file compression algorithm as does the GIF file format. If you attempt to store GIF files in Corel-MOSAIC libraries, you'll find that the libraries take up more space than the GIF files did on their own. Most scanned 24-bit images won't compress well either.

The amount of space a library saves for you will be determined by the type and complexity of the files you store. The CDR files that CorelDRAW uses often compress quite effectively. I stored CDR files from the BIRD subdirectory of the CorelDRAW sample clip art in a library. The original 91,442 bytes of CDR files resulted in 68,994 bytes of library files.

When CorelMOSAIC creates a library, it actually writes two files to the disk. The one with the extension CLH is actually the library. The one with the extension CLB is a file of image headers which allows CorelMOSAIC to quickly display thumbnails of the images in the library.

It's important to note that when CorelMOSAIC opens a library, it actually works with the CLB file but extracts your individual image files from the CLH file. If the CLB file is damaged or accidentally erased, the images will still be available in the CLH file, but they'll be inaccessible by CorelMOSAIC.

There's a useful secret to keep in mind about CorelMOSAIC. In earlier versions of CorelDRAW, CorelMOSAIC actually managed its CLH files using an external archiving program called LHARC. Every time it wanted to extract a file from a library, for example, it would call LHARC behind your back to do the work. In this release of CorelDRAW, the code from LHARC has been built into CorelMOSAIC itself, making it unnecessary to have LHARC around. This keeps it from getting lost, which was a common occurrence under earlier versions of the software.

In incorporating the functions of LHARC into CorelMOSAIC, the authors of the CorelDRAW package didn't change the LHARC file format appreciably. Thus, you can still unpack a CLH file using LHARC. While LHARC is no longer provided with the CorelDRAW package, you'll find it on Disk 2 of the companion disks for this book, should you encounter the problem of a CLH file with no corresponding CLB file.

Here's how to use LHARC under these circumstances.

> **NOTE** **NOTE** *The LHARC program is shareware. If you use it, you should pay its author. Complete details can be found in the documentation for LHARC.*

1. Get to a DOS prompt by double clicking on the MS-DOS icon in the Windows Program Manager.

2. Change to the directory where your CLH files are located.

3. Copy LHARC.EXE from the companion Disk 2 for this book.

4. To extract all the files from the library BIRDS.CLH, you would type **LHARC BIRDS.CLH.**

There is one minor catch to all this. Every file that LHARC extracts from a CorelMOSAIC library will report a "CRC error." This is not a problem, and can be ignored.

Note that aside from its role in disaster recovery, you could use LHARC to add and remove files in a CLH archive. This is not a good idea, as doing so will cause the CLH file and its corresponding CLB file to disagree.

EXPANDING FILES FROM A LIBRARY

Pictures previously stored in a library can be expanded out to normal files again. To expand pictures from a library, do the following:

1. Open the library which contains the pictures you want to expand using the Open Library item of the Library menu.

2. Select whichever of the thumbnails you want to expand by holding down the Shift key and clicking on the individual pictures; or select the Select All item of the Edit menu to select all the pictures in your library.

3. Select the Expand Images From Library option from the Library menu. CorelMOSAIC will prompt you for a directory in which to store the expanded files.

Keep in mind that the files you expand from a library will probably be somewhat bigger than the library itself. Make sure that the drive you expand them to has sufficient room.

USING KEYWORDS

One of the less-than-obvious facilities of the CorelDRAW CDR file format is its facility for maintaining a list of search keywords in each file. If you select one or more CDR files in the CorelMOSAIC window and then select the Keywords item of the Edit menu, a dialog box will appear that will display the current keywords for the first selected file. If you have multiple files selected, the Next and Previous buttons in this dialog box will let you step through them.

Each key word—or perhaps more correctly, key phrase—should say something about the picture it accompanies. Keyword entries can be longer than a single word.

Having established keywords for a group of drawings, you can search a directory of CDR files with CorelMOSAIC for drawings of specific characteristics. For example, if you had a directory with hundreds of CDR files of animals, you could find all the birds by looking for the keyword "bird" with CorelMOSAIC.

Figure C.2 illustrates the Keyword Search dialog box. It can be called up by selecting the Select by Keyword item of the Edit menu.

In fact, the search facility of CorelMOSAIC is a bit more sophisticated than it would first appear. Note the controls to the left of the latter search fields in Figure C.2. These can be set to AND or OR. If you want to find all the birds in a group of CDR files that were also predators, you might set up the search box to look for the keywords "bird" and "predator," with the control for the "predator" field set to AND. If you wanted to find all the files which contained birds or predators, you would set the control for predators to OR. In the second case, the search would turn up both predatory and non-predatory birds and other predatory species—tigers, wolves, and so on.

Having selected a group of files by keyword, you can add them to a library or print them. Printing from CorelMOSAIC will be discussed next.

FIGURE C.2:

*The CorelMOSAIC
Keyword Search
dialog box*

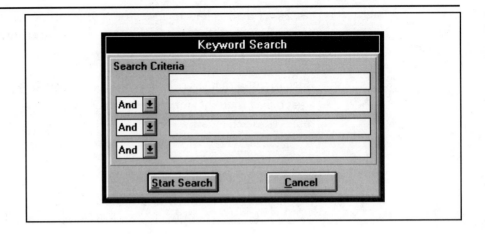

PRINTING FROM CORELMOSAIC

There are two ways to print from CorelMOSAIC—you can either print each selected image on its own sheet of paper, or you can print many small thumbnail images on the same sheet.

If you select some thumbnails (using your mouse, the Select All item of the Edit menu, or keywords), selecting the Print Selected Files item of the File menu will cause CorelMOSAIC to work through each file on your list, calling CorelDRAW, CorelPHOTO-PAINT, CorelSHOW, or CorelCHART to print them. In each case, the appropriate application will be run and loaded with the file in question. The application will then behave as if you'd selected the Print item from its File menu, followed by the Exit item.

You will see the appropriate Print dialog box for the first file that's printed.

Selecting the Print Thumbnails item of the File menu will generate a page like the one in Figure C.3.

CORELMOSAIC AS A FILE DIALOG

When you open a file under CorelDRAW and click on the Options button, you'll find a button which says *Mosaic.* Click on it instead of opening files in the usual way, and you'll be able to see your files as thumbnails under CorelMOSAIC. Double click on the picture you want to work with.

FIGURE C.3:

A page of thumbnails printed from CorelMOSAIC

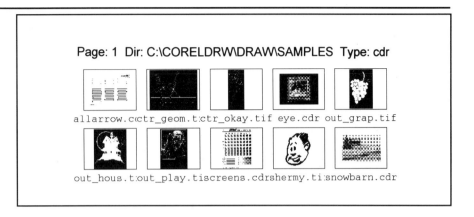

There is no inherent advantage to using CorelMOSAIC in this way, except that it's a bit easier to spot one picture among many in a crowded directory using CorelMOSAIC, especially if you've forgotten what each of them is.

PHOTO CDS

The Photo CD process is a new technology developed by Eastman Kodak. It will provide you with a CD-ROM that holds digitized images of your photographs.

The Photo CD menu allows you to open a Photo CD and convert its images to other bitmapped formats, such as PCX, TIFF, and BMP. The Photo CD images are stored as 24-bit files. If you double click on a Photo CD thumbnail, it will automatically be exported to a 768-by-512 pixel, 24-bit BMP file.

You can also export Photo CD pictures to EPS files. Note that these are not suitable for importing into CorelDRAW. They also do not include preview headers—while you can import those into desktop publishing applications, such as Ventura Publisher or PageMaker, they will not be visible on your screen.

APPENDIX D

Using

CorelTRACE

and CorelDRAW

Autotrace

Tracing bitmapped images is one of the rather magical facilities of CorelDRAW. Although not without limitations, the tracing features let you import a scanned image as a PCX, BMP, or TIFF file, and more or less automatically draw an object-based version of it. The results are often far better than the original.

While you could trace images by hand with most drawing packages, CorelDRAW will actually do the whole thing for you. All you need do is point to the things you want to trace and turn it loose. It will draw curves around the shapes in your original bitmapped picture.

In addition to this, CorelDRAW comes with an off-board tracing program, CorelTRACE. The CorelTRACE package allows you to automatically trace whole images without any human intervention. You can fine-tune the tracing procedures it uses to get the best possible results for diverse types of source files. We'll discuss CorelTRACE in detail in the second half of this appendix.

Nothing this useful could really be as easy as it seems, and this is certainly true of tracing bitmaps. It takes very little time to explain how the process works, but you will need to practice to get a feel for how to make it work well.

HOW TRACING WORKS

CorelDRAW does not come with PCX files for you to trace. You will only need this facility if you have PCX files of your own.

It's important to understand what CorelDRAW does when it goes to trace a bitmapped object. First of all, it treats each pixel in question as either black or white—if you attempt to trace a gray-scale or color image file, Corel-DRAW will treat it as a high-contrast black and white picture for the process.

When you click the tracing cursor—what the pencil cursor turns into when you've selected a bitmapped object—CorelDRAW ascertains whether the cursor is resting on a black pixel or a white pixel. It then begins to work its way outward from this point until it encounters a pixel of the opposite color. When it finds one, it decides that it has located the edge of the object you want to trace, and it constructs a path around the periphery of it.

When it's looking for the edge of an area, CorelDRAW always works to the right, that is, in the direction indicated by the long arm of the tracing cursor. Figure D.1 illustrates an area being traced.

It's generally the case in tracing complex drawings that you can start in either a white area or a black area. The resulting paths, however, will be

FIGURE D.1:

The tracing cursor at work, positioned to trace the model's left eye

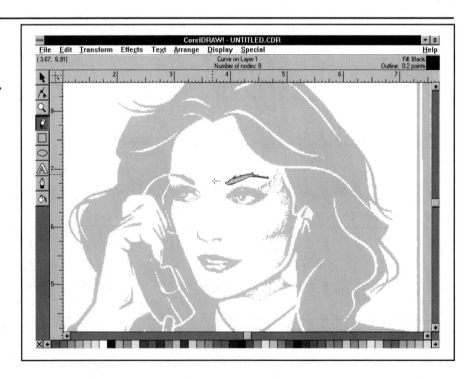

slightly different. Note that if you start in a white area far away from any black areas, the program may fail to find the object to trace.

Although it may look like CorelDRAW traces by working its way around the actual image on your screen, the fact is that it works with the bitmapped image in memory. Thus, if the area you're tracing extends beyond the edges of the CorelDRAW work space, the whole thing will still be traced. This also explains why the program is able to continue tracing even when you've hidden the bitmap from view.

In tracing an area, CorelDRAW always creates closed paths and fills them. By default, it fills them with black. This can produce some unexpected results if you're working in the edit wire frame mode and you don't check the stroke and fill characteristics in the preview window.

CHOOSING ORIGINALS

The most important step in successfully tracing a bitmapped image is in choosing the bitmap you want to trace. Good originals can produce excellent tracings. Poorly chosen ones—however interesting their subjects may be—will probably just frustrate you.

Figure D.2 shows a bitmapped image and the CorelDRAW trace of it. The picture on the left illustrates a type of drawing that makes for a good tracing original. It has few details, and lots of clean, sharp lines. There is no

FIGURE D.2:

A good bitmap for tracing (left), and the traced results (right)

cross-hatching, and there are no occurrences of single pixels. There are a lot of round surfaces, none of which will suffer if they lose a bit of accuracy in the tracing process.

TRACING THE ORIGINAL

The picture on the right in Figure D.2 illustrates a tracing of the bitmap. This picture started life as a PCX file called ARTDECO.PCX. The process of tracing it is pretty easy to follow.

1. Start with an empty work space. Import ARTDECO.PCX from wherever you keep your clip art. Make sure you select the For Tracing option in the Import dialog box.

2. Select the resulting bitmap by clicking with the pick tool on the bitmap's perimeter.

3. Zoom in on a section of the picture—the man's head is a good place to start.

4. Select the pencil tool. If you have selected the bitmap properly, the cursor turns into an oblong cross. If it turns into the regular pencil icon, you need to start again from step 2.

5. Place the cursor on one of the black areas and click. You might have a bit of a wait, depending on the complexity of the detail you've selected, as CorelDRAW constructs a path around the detail.

6. Repeat step 5 for the rest of the black areas you want traced.

The Show Bitmaps option of the Display menu can be used as a toggle to hide the bitmapped image temporarily, leaving the trace by itself so you can see what you've actually drawn.

You may find that some objects in the picture will appear to have vanished in the preview. The hat-check girl's face, for example, will probably be missing. This is because CorelDRAW fills each traced object with black, and her face is an object. After tracing a picture, it's usually necessary to go through it and pick out the objects in which this has happened, bringing them forward if necessary and filling them with white.

Note that bitmaps imported for tracing will not print, so if you elect to leave the bitmap in place it will not affect your final output. However, when you're completely finished using a bitmap, you can reduce the size of your CDR file considerably by selecting the original bitmap object and deleting it.

FINE-TUNING TRACED OBJECTS

There are two adjustments in the Preferences dialog box of the Special menu which affect the way CorelDRAW handles tracing. They can be found in the box which pops up if you click on the Curves button. By setting these appropriately, you can make CorelDRAW do a lot of the work in creating a well-traced bitmap.

When CorelDRAW attempts to trace an area of your bitmapped image, it has to decide how accurately to follow the contours of the surfaces it encounters. On the one hand, if it tracks everything perfectly, the result could be a very complex outline with countless individual paths. On the other hand, if it ignores all small details, it might well ignore some important ones. Obviously, the amount of detail CorelDRAW should preserve will vary with the nature of each image you trace.

The Autotrace Tracking item of the Preferences-Curves dialog box allows you to set the number of pixels below which CorelDRAW will ignore details. If you set this value low—below 4—CorelDRAW will create fairly intricate traced lines which will represent every detail and hiccup in the surfaces of your original, possibly including some you didn't really want. If you set it high (above 6), CorelDRAW will trace your bitmaps with smooth, flowing lines.

It's often helpful to change this value repeatedly throughout a tracing session.

The Straight Line Threshold value in the Preferences-Curves dialog box is the other important control in handling tracing. It tells CorelDRAW how close a curve can come to being straight before CorelDRAW can just go ahead and use a straight line to trace it. Using straight line segments will keep the straight lines of the original from taking on slight curves due to tracing errors. It will also speed up the final printing of your drawing. If you're tracing a bitmap which is all straight lines to begin with—an architectural drawing, for example—set this value high. High would be 8 to 10. In this case, only surfaces which are obviously curved will be traced as curves. Everything else will be handled with straight line segments.

Having traced a bitmap, you will very likely have to do a bit of path manipulation by hand. The tracing algorithm in CorelDRAW is not flawless, and its work usually needs some polishing up. The shape tool is very useful for moving paths around, removing unwanted nodes, and so on.

Figure D.3 illustrates one quarter of the rose of a lute—in fact, the rose that was missing from the lute we drew back in Chapter 2. This is a good example of the sort of drawing which needs some fine-tuning. The original in this figure was scanned from the designer's blueprint for the lute. The individual elements of the center of the rose traced well enough, but the rings surrounding it did not. The tracing algorithm couldn't get them to come out round. I replaced them with actual circles.

In tracing the rose, what CorelDRAW really did was draw objects which represented the spaces between the wooden parts of the rose—the cutouts rather than the lines. It was occasionally necessary to clean these up by dragging their nodes around.

FIGURE D.3:

The lute rose: original (left) and trace (right)

USING TRACED OBJECTS

The objects you create by tracing can be treated just like anything else you draw in CorelDRAW. Having traced an image and set the line stroke and object fills to your liking, group the objects together. You can now duplicate them, transform them, and position them easily.

You can fill traced objects with any of CorelDRAW's fills—you aren't restricted to black or even to solid fills, although you should keep in mind the potential complexity problems if you elect to use fountains. Figure D.4 illustrates a traced image with some interesting fill patterns.

The chief problem with tracing *per se* is that tracing bitmaps can result in a picture with an excessive number of paths. The cutout cat in Figure D.5

FIGURE D.4:

Using fills with a traced pattern

—shown in both its bitmapped and object-oriented forms—is a classic example of this.

This picture looks as if it would be an ideal subject for bitmap tracing. It is, too, except that all the little white areas resulted in a picture with so many objects that CorelDRAW bogged down enormously toward the end of the tracing session. In addition, the resulting picture took an extremely long time to trace and was too complex to print to a PostScript printer. This output was done with a LaserJet.

This might give you an idea of the practical upper limit of detail for tracing bitmaps.

FIGURE D.5:

Killer cat

USING CORELTRACE

The interactive tracing mode built into CorelDRAW has both advantages and drawbacks. It's quick and easy to use, and it allows you to adjust the paths created by tracing as you go. However, it can be very time-consuming to use if you have a lot of art to trace. It's also very restricted in the controls it can bring to bear on the tracing process. Different sorts of art must be traced in fundamentally different ways to come up with acceptable results.

As an obvious example, consider the difference between tracing the bitmap in Figure D.1 and mechanically drawing the house in Chapter 2.

The CorelTRACE application which comes with CorelDRAW is a batch-image tracer. You can give it a whole list of bitmap files to trace, set it to work, and go for a Coke. It will trace each one, writing corresponding drawing files to disk. In addition, CorelTRACE offers you a wide range of controls to fine-tune its tracing abilities to the art to be traced. You could, for example, set up a tracing procedure which was fine-tuned for tracing mechanical drawings.

Like CorelDRAW itself, CorelTRACE is easy to use in its default configurations, and flexible once you start to work with it. As you get a better feel for its capabilities, you'll be able to manipulate its various parameters and get more exacting results from it.

The images which CorelTRACE uses as source art can come from a number of places. Obviously, a scanner is one of the most useful of these, as it will allow you to create bitmaps from all sorts of existing hard-copy art. Because CorelTRACE can compensate for all sorts of deficiencies in a scanned image, you needn't have a particularly good scanner to create usable originals. A hand scanner is often adequate. Some of the art which I've used with CorelTRACE has been scanned using a FAX machine.

Given this, you will get better results with less fine-tuning and experimentation if you begin with a high-resolution scanned image.

You can also use public-domain image files as source art for CorelTRACE. If you convert a full-color image file—such as one of the countless public-domain GIF files you can find—into a gray-scale TIFF file, you can frequently trace the picture with some very interesting results.

CorelTRACE will import images in the PCX and TIFF file formats for tracing. It exports EPS files, which must then be imported into CorelDRAW if you wish to manipulate them. This is a slight inconvenience, as it takes longer for CorelDRAW to import an EPS file than simply to open a corresponding CDR file. However, EPS files can be used immediately in many other applications—you can import one directly into most desktop-publishing software if you'll be outputting your document to a PostScript printer.

Basic Tracing

While CorelTRACE can deal with a wider variety of source images than can CorelDRAW's internal tracing function, many of the limitations discussed earlier in this chapter still apply to it. You will want to keep the following things in mind when you're considering a bitmapped image for possible tracing:

◆ Monochrome art with simple, well-defined lines will always produce the best traced line art.

◆ CorelTRACE cannot see areas of a bitmap which have been filled with a pattern, such as a gray or textured fill. It will try to make lots of little objects out of such areas, usually not what you had in mind.

◆ While CorelTRACE can often deal with complex art, it may produce so many objects as to make the art unprintable if you're using a PostScript printer.

◆ Bitmapped art which uses gray effects may not produce terribly faithful traced line art, although you can often produce some interesting drawings with it.

◆ High-resolution scans generally produce better traced line art than coarse scans. However, you can often fine-tune CorelTRACE to compensate to some extent for low-resolution scans.

◆ You can often get workable results from less-than-ideal source art, but you should plan to have to work with it for a while.

You should probably start with simple original images when you're first getting used to CorelTRACE.

Outline and Centerline Tracing

While you can fine-tune a number of the tracing parameters of Corel-TRACE—we'll discuss these shortly—there is one fundamental choice you'll have to make before you begin tracing anything. CorelTRACE can handle its tracing using either outline or centerline tracing. It's important to have a clear understanding of what these features do.

If you have played with any of the CorelDRAW clip art which looks like it has been traced, you may have noticed that it's rather oddly put together. Drawings which have white areas within black areas are usually created by drawing the black area as a solid filled object and then drawing the white area on top of it, also as a solid filled object. In complex drawings, you might encounter multiple alternating black and white areas.

Figure D.6 illustrates how a traced drawing is usually structured.

In tracing an image, an automatic tracing program will typically start with the outermost black area and work around it. It will then find the next innermost white areas and work around them, repeating this procedure until everything has been traced. It's easy to see how a traced image gets built up as alternating black and white objects using this approach.

This procedure is called outline tracing. It's the approach you would use to trace most types of bitmapped art.

The alternate approach to tracing, centerline tracing, is intended for use with drawings having many fine lines but no fills. Schematics, architectural plans, and other line art would trace well using the centerline option of CorelTRACE. In this mode, the tracing algorithm simply traces over all the lines, making no attempt to form them into closed paths.

Figure D.7 illustrates the difference between outline and centerline tracing.

A SIMPLE TRACING SESSION

It's extremely handy, when you're tracing something, to have CorelTRACE and CorelDRAW running at the same time. Because in many cases you will have to experiment with the settings of CorelTRACE to produce the line art you want, you'll find it's useful to be able to pop in and out of CorelDRAW to check your results or to print them. We'll discuss an alternate approach to printing your traced drawing files at the end of this chapter.

When you first boot up CorelTRACE you should see its main window, as in Figure D.8. The Open button will call up an Open One or More Files to Trace dialog box to allow you to select files. Each time you select a file, it will be added to the file list, the initial blank white box to the right of the Open button. Once you have selected all the files you want to trace, clicking on the Trace All button will put CorelTRACE to work.

*How traced art is
usually created*

Outline versus center-line tracing

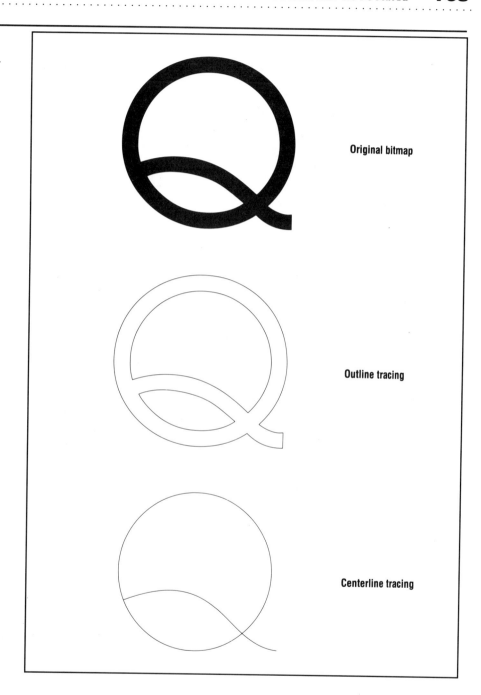

Original bitmap

Outline tracing

Centerline tracing

FIGURE D.8:

The main window of CorelTRACE

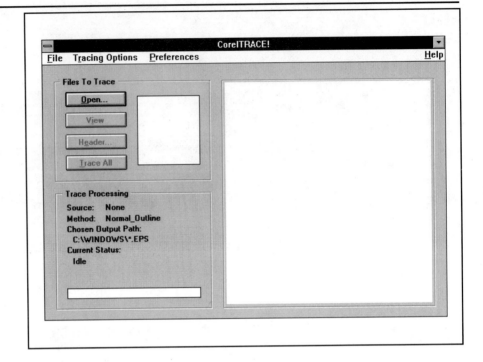

If you select a single file from the file list and click on the View button, a representation of the file's contents will appear in the large white area on the right side of the CorelTRACE window. The Header option will provide you with numeric information about a selected file, such as its dimensions and the number of colors it supports.

Once you give it one or more files to work with and tell it to get started, CorelTRACE needs no further human assistance.

In this example, we'll trace the picture shown in Figure D.9. This started life as a PCX file called TRAVEL.PCX. This file is a pretty good subject for tracing. The results will automatically be saved as TRAVEL.EPS.

You might want to open the Output Options item of the File menu to define where you want your traced EPS files to reside. Note that this box will also allow you to instruct CorelTRACE as to how to handle situations where the file it's saving would overwrite an existing file.

If you were to import TRAVEL.EPS into CorelDRAW and print it, the results would look a lot like TRAVEL.PCX. Figure D.9 illustrates the two files. The source picture has well over 600 objects. It's difficult to specify the

A bitmapped source file on the top and a traced version of it on the bottom

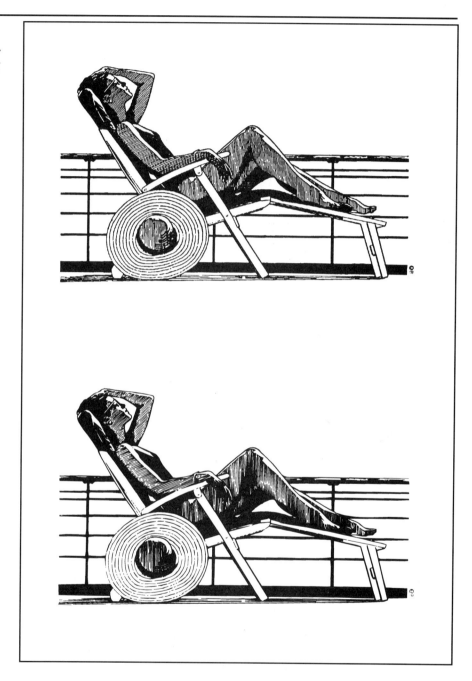

exact upper limit of objects a particular PostScript printer will handle. Among other things, the nature of the objects will affect the calculation—all other things being equal, a printer can deal with many more straight lines than curved ones, for example. It's probably fair to say, however, that this picture is starting to stretch the limits of what you can reliably print.

CENTERLINE TRACING

Unless your work brings you into contact with a lot of mechanical drawings, you may never use centerline tracing, except perhaps for special effects. Using the centerline trace feature on a source image which normally would be handled with outline tracing can produce an interesting drawing, if technically a badly traced one.

The drawing in Figure D.10 is a Sierpinski curve, a mathematical object which, if made complex enough, will have an internal area approaching half the area it occupies. Mathematicians love these sorts of things. For our purposes, though, it's useful to note that this curve is a line drawing and that it, in fact, contains no curves at all. It's made up entirely of straight line segments.

The bitmapped Sierpinski curve was, in fact, not scanned into a PCX file at all. I wrote a small program to generate it mathematically. As a result, this example has no potential for scanner misalignment and other aberrations.

If you use the default centerline trace option on this image, the results would probably upset Mr. Sierpinski to no small degree. Using this set of options, CorelTRACE attempts to balance its centerline tracing for source images which contain curves. Therefore, it tends to make corners that are not right angles into curves, as seen in Figure D.11.

In order to properly trace the Sierpinski curve, you'd have to create a new set of tracing parameters. This is pretty easy to do—simply select one of the unused items, labeled simply as three dots, from the Tracing Options menu, and then select Edit Option. The ideal settings for an image like the Sierpinski curve would allow for no curved segments at all. These settings are shown in Figure D.12. Don't worry if some of these things aren't all that meaningful as yet.

The Sierpinski curve as a bitmapped image (top) and a traced image (bottom)

*Using the default center-
line tracing options on a
Sierpinski curve*

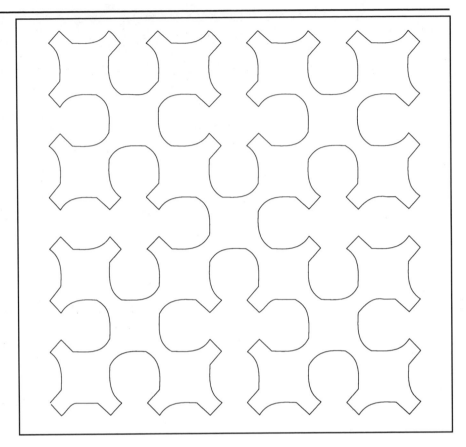

FIGURE D.12:

*Centerline tracing op-
tions for images such as
the Sierpinski curve*

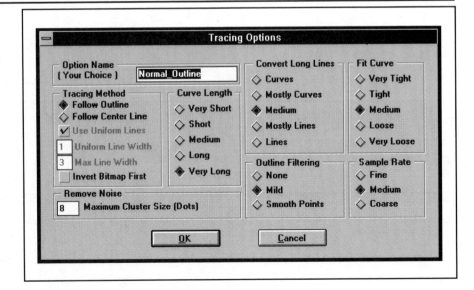

ADVANCED TRACING OPTIONS

The tracing options CorelTRACE allows for in its Tracing Options box let you cope with less-than-ideal bitmapped source files. You can create a number of special-case tracing parameters for use with the sorts of files you may typically encounter.

Here's a quick look at what the various options do.

Tracing Method

As we've discussed previously, the Tracing Method options determine whether CorelTRACE will treat a source bitmapped image as a centerline or outline drawing. If you select Follow Center Line, you can specify a number of things about the lines CorelTRACE draws. The Max Line Width setting determines how thick the lines that CorelTRACE creates can get. The Use Uniform Lines option will force the program to create lines of a constant width for all the lines it creates in tracing a bitmap. If this is not selected, it will attempt to judge the line width to use from the source image. If you do select Use Uniform Lines, you can specify the line width to use by typing it into the Uniform Line Width field.

The Invert Bitmap First option will simply flip the source bitmap black for white. The resulting trace will also be flipped black for white, often a useful effect.

Note that once an image is traced you can assign different line widths to whichever lines you like when you get your drawing into CorelDRAW.

Remove Noise

The concept of noise in an image might be a bit hard to grasp at first. It refers to instances of one or more isolated dots in a bitmap—dots which probably shouldn't be there, or at least shouldn't be traced.

Historically, interference with radio signals was referred to as noise because you could hear it. When television came along and buried radio, the same interference manifested itself as visual problems, but the engineers who'd come up from the radio plants were used to calling it noise, and so the name stuck. With the advent of computers, aberrational visual data acquired the name because the same engineers, now a bit gray around the edges, were too set in their ways to want to think up something new to call it.

The Remove Noise item tells CorelTRACE to ignore isolated dots in clumps smaller than the threshold value you set in this field. You can set this value to anywhere between 2 and 999 pixels. Setting it too low may cause CorelTRACE to generate objects you don't want in the drawing. Setting it too high may cause it to leave out details you do want.

Curve Length

The Curve Length options tell CorelTRACE how long a single curved line can be before it has to stop and begin a new line. Since there is a finite number of perturbations CorelTRACE can handle in a single curved line, this affects the amount of detail it can render in whatever drawing it's creating. Choosing Very Short will preserve the greatest amount of detail, but it will probably create a large and complex EPS file. Such a file will take up lots of disk space, will take longer to import into CorelDRAW, and may present you with printing problems if it's sufficiently involved.

Convert Long Lines

The Convert Long Lines options tell CorelTRACE how much to favor generating curves over straight lines. If your source image has nothing but straight lines in it, such as the Sierpinski curve, you would choose Lines. Once again, this setting presents you with something of a trade-off between the faithfulness of the tracing that CorelTRACE performs and the size and complexity of the eventual drawing. Having it convert all lines to curves, even if they appear as nearly straight lines, may produce the best picture, but it will also produce the most complex drawing file.

Outline Filtering

The Outline Filtering options let you tell CorelTRACE what to do when it comes to a sharp corner in an object it's tracing. The most obvious thing for it to do is create a line which bends as the image bends. However, especially if the image has been scanned at a fairly low resolution, you might find that corners which should in fact be round are being squared off. In such cases, setting the Outline Filtering option to Mild or Smooth Points will cause CorelTRACE to round off the corners a bit.

Fit Curve

A bitmapped image will, of necessity, be an approximation of an original photographic image. The degree to which it approximates the original is determined by how many dots per inch it was scanned at. Unfortunately, it's often the case that one must work with low-resolution scans.

If you draw your source images from public-domain monochrome graphics, you'll probably find that the majority of these have the dimensions 576 by 720 pixels, or roughly the size of a sheet of letter-size paper printed at 75 dots per inch. This is the fixed dimension of a MacPaint file—these images have been ported over from Macintosh systems. Among the first popular low-cost microcomputer image scanners was something called Thunderscan, a system which turned the Macintosh ImageWriter dot-matrix printer into a rudimentary scanner. The availability of the Thunderscan and MacPaint on the Mac saw a huge library of images (albeit of rather low resolution) grow up around this system.

The Fit Curve setting allows you to tell CorelTRACE how closely it should follow the contours of the bitmap it's tracing. There are trade-offs involved here. The obvious one is that having CorelTRACE follow every bump and hiccup of a bitmap may well result in a very large and complex file. However, the other thing to consider is that such a file may not actually look as good as one generated with much looser curve-fitting.

By allowing CorelTRACE to use looser curve-fitting, you will give it the option of extrapolating in areas where the coarse resolution of a scanned image has left out details. It can actually smooth out rough lines in these cases, producing a traced image which looks better than the original bitmap image did.

Sample Rate

The Sample Rate setting tells CorelTRACE how often it should look at the bitmap it's tracing as it decides where to put the nodes of the lines it generates. This has much the same effect as curve-fitting does. Setting the sample rate to Fine will cause CorelTRACE to more accurately follow the contours of the source bitmap, although if the bitmap is a bit coarse to begin with, you might not want it to do so.

CorelTRACE Preferences

There are a few additional options which you might find useful in the Preferences menu of CorelTRACE.

If you enable the Trace Partial Area command, CorelTRACE will pause before tracing an image and place a CorelDRAW selection marquee over the picture to be traced. You can move and resize the selector to indicate what portion of the source image you want to trace. Click OK when you're done.

Disabling the View Dithered Colors option will change the way CorelTRACE displays color images on your screen while it's working. If you have a 256-color screen driver and you turn this option off, you'll probably find that the images in the CorelTRACE window prior to tracing look better. This has no effect on what your final traced EPS files will look like.

The Color Reduction options tell CorelTRACE how to deal with color source files. Images with lots of colors will tend to produce more traced objects. Reducing the number of colors or gray levels will allow CorelTRACE to create fewer spurious objects based on minor variations in color. Reducing it too much will cause CorelTRACE to oversimplify your images, leaving out important details.

Using CorelTRACE Files

You can import the EPS files that CorelTRACE produces into most applications which will use encapsulated PostScript files. However, because they do not contain EPS preview images, you will not be able to see them if your software normally displays the contents of EPS art. For example, Ventura Publisher, when confronted with an EPS file directly from CorelDRAW, will draw a cross through the frame which contains the drawing.

In order to add a preview image to an EPS file, you must import it into CorelDRAW and then export it again with the Image Header option set to a resolution other than None.

In the meantime, if you're tracing images and you want a quick way to print what you've done to see what it looks like, you might want to do the following. This procedure assumes that you have a PostScript printer connected to LPT1.

The EPS files which CorelTRACE exports are complete PostScript programs which, when sent to your printer, will cause it to print the drawings they contain. To print one without having to import it into CorelDRAW, have a copy of DOS running in memory along with CorelTRACE. When you have finished tracing an image, do the following:

1. Hit Alt-Tab or Alt-Esc to pop over to the DOS prompt.

2. If your file is called TRAVEL.EPS, you can print it by typing the command **COPY TRAVEL.EPS LPT1**.

If you have a 386 or 486 system you can make this even easier. There's an infrequently mentioned feature in Windows which allows you to have text-based applications, such as DOS, running in windows rather than in full-screen mode. Once you have opened the DOS prompt, hit Alt-↵ and the familiar Windows screen will return with DOS trapped in a window. You can keep this in an otherwise unused corner of your screen and just click in it when you want to print something, as shown in Figure D.13.

A HISTORICAL NOTE

Earlier versions of CorelDRAW came with generous samplers of clip art, just as the current one does. However, much of the clip art was provided either in drawing files other than the CDR format—EPS and CGM files, for example—or as high-resolution PCX bitmap files, which had to be traced.

In these earlier versions of the software, both the importing and tracing facilities of CorelDRAW got a lot of exercise.

The current version of CorelDRAW comes with all its clip art in CDR files—there's nothing to trace or import before using it. As with the import facilities discussed in Chapter 5, you might actually find that you never have need of CorelDRAW's tracing tools, sophisticated as they are.

FIGURE D.13:

Printing EPS files from a DOS window

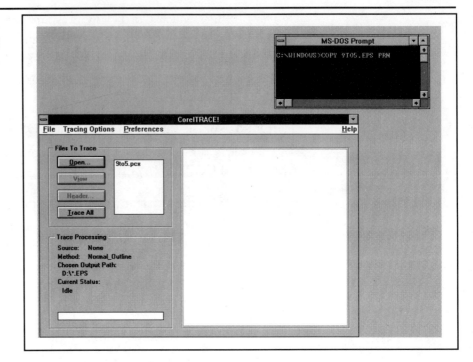

INDEX

Selections from The SYBEX Library

DESKTOP PUBLISHING

The ABC's of the New Print Shop
Vivian Dubrovin
340pp. Ref. 640-4
This beginner's guide stresses fun, practicality and original ideas. Hands-on tutorials show how to create greeting cards, invitations, signs, flyers, letterheads, banners, and calendars.

The ABC's of Ventura
Robert Cowart
Steve Cummings
390pp. Ref. 537-9
Created especially for new desktop publishers, this is an easy introduction to a complex program. Cowart provides details on using the mouse, the Ventura side bar, and page layout, with careful explanations of publishing terminology. The new Ventura menus are all carefully explained. For Version 2.

Desktop Publishing with WordPerfect 5.1
Rita Belserene
418pp. Ref. 481-X
A practical guide to using the desktop publishing capabilities of versions 5.0 and 5.1. Topics include graphic design concepts, hardware necessities, installing and using fonts, columns, lines, and boxes, illustrations, multi-page layouts, Style Sheets, and integrating with other software.

Mastering CorelDRAW 2
Steve Rimmer
500pp. Ref. 814-9
This comprehensive tutorial and design guide features complete instruction in creating spectacular graphic effects with CorelDRAW 2. The book also offers a primer on commercial image and page design, including how to use printers and print-house facilities for optimum results.

Mastering Micrografx Designer
Peter Kent
400pp. Ref. 694-4
A complete guide to using this sophisticated illustration package. Readers begin by importing and modifying clip art, and progress to creating original drawings, working with text, printing and plotting, creating slide shows, producing color separations, and exporting art.

Mastering PageMaker 4 on the IBM PC
Rebecca Bridges Altman, with Rick Altman
509pp. Ref. 773-8
A step-by-step guide to the essentials of desktop publishing and graphic design. Tutorials and hands-on examples explore every aspect of working with text, graphics, styles, templates, and more, to design and produce a wide range of publications. Includes a publication "cookbook" and notes on using Windows 3.0.

Mastering Ventura for Windows *(For Version 3.0)*
Rick Altman
600pp, Ref. 758-4
This engaging, hands-on treatment is for the desktop publisher learning and using the Windows edition of Ventura. It covers everything from working with the Windows interface, to designing and printing sophisticated publications using Ventura's most advanced features. Understand and work with frames, graphics, fonts, tables and columns, and much more.

SYBEX

FREE BROCHURE!

Complete this form today, and we'll send you a full-color brochure of Sybex bestsellers.

Please supply the name of the Sybex book purchased.

_____

How would you rate it?

_____ Excellent   _____ Very Good   _____ Average   _____ Poor

Why did you select this particular book?

_____ Recommended to me by a friend

_____ Recommended to me by store personnel

_____ Saw an advertisement in _____

_____ Author's reputation

_____ Saw in Sybex catalog

_____ Required textbook

_____ Sybex reputation

_____ Read book review in _____

_____ In-store display

_____ Other _____

Where did you buy it?

_____ Bookstore

_____ Computer Store or Software Store

_____ Catalog (name: _____)

_____ Direct from Sybex

_____ Other: _____

Did you buy this book with your personal funds?

_____ Yes   _____ No

About how many computer books do you buy each year?

_____ 1-3   _____ 3-5   _____ 5-7   _____ 7-9   _____ 10+

About how many Sybex books do you own?

_____ 1-3   _____ 3-5   _____ 5-7   _____ 7-9   _____ 10+

Please indicate your level of experience with the software covered in this book:

_____ Beginner   _____ Intermediate   _____ Advanced

Which types of software packages do you use regularly?

_____ Accounting   _____ Databases   _____ Networks

_____ Amiga   _____ Desktop Publishing   _____ Operating Systems

_____ Apple/Mac   _____ File Utilities   _____ Spreadsheets

_____ CAD   _____ Money Management   _____ Word Processing

_____ Communications   _____ Languages   _____ Other _____

(please specify)

Which of the following best describes your job title?

_____ Administrative/Secretarial   _____ President/CEO

_____ Director   _____ Manager/Supervisor

_____ Engineer/Technician   _____ Other _____
(please specify)

Comments on the weaknesses/strengths of this book: _____

_____

_____

_____

_____

Name _____

Street _____

City/State/Zip _____

Phone _____

PLEASE FOLD, SEAL, AND MAIL TO SYBEX

-- -- -- -- -- -- -- -- -- -- -- -- -- -- -- -- -- --

SYBEX, INC.
Department M
2021 CHALLENGER DR.
ALAMEDA, CALIFORNIA USA
94501

SYBEX

SEAL

Companion Disk Instructions

The set of two companion disks for *Mastering CorelDRAW 3* includes the following resources:

◆ A selection of CDR files. These are some of the winners of the CorelDRAW World Design Contest—you'll find them reproduced in the color insert of this book as well, on plates 3–8. You'll find them useful in machine-readable form, as you can actually see how the artists created these superb images.

◆ Graphic Workshop for Windows. This is a flexible shareware package for manipulating bitmapped graphic files. It will help you specifically in getting files into CorelPHOTO-PAINT and into CorelDRAW as imported bitmapped elements.

◆ FixFont. This package will quickly and effortlessly rename all the installed CorelDRAW TrueType fonts so that they appear under their standard commercial names. Complete instructions for its use can be found in Appendix B.

◆ Chord. This is the sample guitar chord font discussed in Appendix B, stored as both a CDR file and a TrueType font.

◆ LHARC. Mentioned in Appendix C, this is a handy tool to have around for reclaiming files in damaged CorelMOSAIC libraries.

◆ PBREAK. This is a program for resetting a PostScript printer and is discussed in Chapter 6.

Most of the files on these two disks are stored in ZIP archives to make them smaller. You must uncompress them prior to using them. You can do this with PKUNZIP if you have it, or with the ZIPPER.COM program that's included on each of the disks. ZIPPER.COM must be run from a DOS prompt. If you are presently in Windows, double click on the MS-DOS icon to get to the DOS prompt.

To decompress the REX.ZIP file (assuming that Disk 1 is in drive A of your computer), type **A:ZIPPER A:REX**. Prior to issuing this command, you should be logged into the drive and directory where you want the contents of REX.ZIP to appear.

In all cases, the contents of the ZIP files on these disks will be files much larger than the ZIP files themselves were. Make sure you have a lot of free hard drive space. Finally, note that ZIPPER can take a fair bit of time to unpack large ZIP files—be patient.

The following are the ZIP files on the companion disks:

DISK 1:   REX.ZIP—*Rex* (the iguana) by Bill Frymire

LAIVA.ZIP—*Laiva* (the tall ship) by Matti Kaarala

VENICE.ZIP—*Venice* (the canal scene) by Peter McCormick

MAGIC.ZIP—*Magic* (Magic Johnson) by Lea Tjeng Kian

DISK 2:   LIFETIME.ZIP—*Lifetime* (the desert with timepieces) by Ceri Lines

TECHDRAW.ZIP—*Techdraw* (the mechanical drawing) by Guy Terrier

GWSWIN10.ZIP—Graphic Workshop for Windows

FIXFONT.ZIP—The font-renaming package

This version of Graphic Workshop does not include a Windows installation program. You must install it in Windows yourself to use it (a simple operation). See GWS.WRI for information about using Graphic Workshop—it will be unpacked from GWSWIN10.ZIP.